HARVARD STUDIES IN BUSINESS HISTORY

I

Edited by N. S. B. GRAS

STRAUS PROFESSOR OF BUSINESS HISTORY
GRADUATE SCHOOL OF BUSINESS ADMINISTRATION
GEORGE F. BAKER FOUNDATION
HARVARD UNIVERSITY

LONDON : HUMPHREY MILFORD

OXFORD UNIVERSITY PRESS

John Jacob Astor, Aged about Seventy-five

JOHN JACOB ASTOR
Business Man

BY

KENNETH WIGGINS PORTER

RESEARCH ASSISTANT IN BUSINESS HISTORY
GRADUATE SCHOOL OF BUSINESS ADMINISTRATION
GEORGE F. BAKER FOUNDATION
HARVARD UNIVERSITY

VOLUME II

Cambridge, Massachusetts
HARVARD UNIVERSITY PRESS
1931

PRINTED AT THE HARVARD UNIVERSITY PRESS

CAMBRIDGE, MASS., U. S. A.

CONTENTS

VOLUME II

LIST OF ILLUSTRATIONS

LIST OF DOCUMENTS

JOHN JACOB ASTOR

CHAPTER XII

THE CHINA TRADE AND EUROPE, FROM THE WAR
TO WITHDRAWAL FROM BUSINESS,
1815–1834

UP TO the outbreak of the War of 1812, Astor's trade with China had not been very complicated. Usually he had sent only one vessel a year to Canton, once or twice, two. His cargoes had consisted chiefly of furs, ginseng, and specie, sometimes including camlets, a few piculs of cochineal and quicksilver, occasionally a few hundred piculs of cotton, iron, and blackwood. In return Astor had received black and green teas, usually more green than black, nankeens, silk piece-goods, sewing silk, chinaware, sugar, cassia, and a miscellaneous assortment of minor articles.[1] Some of these goods were disposed of at private sale over the counter of Astor's own shop in New York, some were sold at public auction, other portions were shipped to agents in such ports as Baltimore, and others were exported as freight to correspondents in Bordeaux, Hamburg, and the Madeiras.

Just before the outbreak of war two changes in policy had appeared. Astor began to send ships to the North West Coast to collect furs for sale in China; he also purchased two small vessels, a brig and a schooner, in which he might export his Chinese goods to Europe, especially to the Mediterranean, receiving European products in return.

Although, as we have seen, the war entirely cut off Astor's trade with China for its duration, he had, during its early days, enjoyed the good fortune of receiving two vessels from China, and the large profits received through the sale of their cargoes at war-time prices caused him to look with a favorable eye upon the prospects for the China trade when hostilities should cease. Soon after word of peace had reached New York, he wrote to one of his London correspondents, Thomas Wilson, stating: "I have partly resolved not to engage in any european business unless something would occasionally be done in Exchange, my object will be to the Canton trade & perhaps something in Furs on that I have not yet fix'd."[2]

In one way the war had proved advantageous to Astor. The British blockade had caused the prices of vessels to drop considerably, and Astor had taken advantage of that fact to acquire quite a little fleet at a low price. At the end of the war he probably owned more vessels than at any time before or after. Lying at New York were the ship *Enterprise*, his first North West Coast vessel, the ship *Hannibal*, which had taken General Moreau to Europe in 1813, and the brig *Seneca*, even then being fitted out for a China voyage. At Le Havre was the ship *Fingal*, which had sailed the previous fall as a flag of truce, and at Nantes the schooner *Boxer*, which had run the blockade early in the year. The brig *Macedonian*, which, like the *Boxer*, had slipped through the British blockade in January, was well started on a voyage to China. The ship *Beaver* was laid up in Canton harbor, where she had been blockaded since early in 1813. The brig *Pedler* (which had been bought in the Hawaiian Islands late in 1813 by Astor's agent, Wilson Price Hunt, and which Astor did not as yet know he owned) was somewhere between the Islands and the Columbia River. The brig *Forester*, which had sailed from England in the spring of 1813 to relieve Astoria, was wintering on the coast of California. Besides these vessels, Astor also owned a one-eighth share in a schooner called the *Flirt*, which had sailed for Bordeaux from New Orleans in the early fall of 1814, but it is hardly worth while to investigate this vessel's whereabouts. Suffice it to say that at the end of the War of 1812 Astor was the owner of nine vessels: four ships, four brigs, and a schooner, at that time lying at New York,

Nantes, Le Havre, Canton, and on the coast of California, or proceeding to their respective destinations, Canton and the Columbia River. Of these vessels, he had owned before the war only the *Enterprise* and the *Beaver*. The greatest number of vessels he had ever previously possessed in the course of one year had been five, which he had accumulated during the maritime depression caused by the embargo, with the intention of pressing the trade with renewed vigor when these restrictions should be removed. Unfortunately, the coming of war had forced him to dispose of most of them again. Had ships been the only requisite, Astor would have been marvelously well prepared to carry on a trade with China or with any other part of the world.

Astor's first care, after the arrival of peace, was to send a vessel to Canton with a cargo including "bread and salt provisions" for the *Beaver's* return voyage.[3] This vessel was also to bring back a cargo of China goods to the eager market offered by the United States, but teas were not to be stressed in the return cargo, for, according to Astor, "the consumption has very much decreased so that for some years to come will [*sic*] not want half the quantity we used to do."[4] The return cargo of this vessel was to be furnished from the proceeds of its outward cargo and from bills on London.[5] As early as January 7, 1815, Astor was in correspondence with William Waln about getting ginseng for the outward cargo. On that date he said that he would join Waln in buying 25,000 or 30,000 lbs. at 50 cents per lb. or less, and three days after the arrival of peace he suggested that Waln might purchase from 20,000 to 40,000 lbs. on joint account for 50 cents or 65 cents per lb. or 20,000 lbs. for Astor alone. Alternatively, Astor would take Waln's ginseng as freight, for $7\frac{1}{2}$ per cent of the proceeds should Astor's vessel be the first or nearly the first at Canton after the war, otherwise for 5 per cent. Waln thereupon made a proposition for sending ginseng by Astor's vessel which was accepted.

Astor wanted to be quite sure that his first vessel to China after the arrival of peace should make a speedy, safe, and successful voyage. To that end, by February 17 he had "partly engaged the most pushing man as commander." A few days later he declared, "this vessel . . . has without exception the first & most active *Master in the World* I pay him $5000 extra."[6] The captain who won this encomium from the usually noncommittal Astor was F. A. De Peyster, who had been a boy before the mast on the *Beaver's* maiden voyage in 1805, and four years later had become second officer of Astor's brig *Fox*. The vessel he was to command on this voyage was the brig *Seneca*, of about 300 tons.

But so short a time had passed since the end of hostilities that a good captain and a good vessel were not the sole requisites for a safe voyage to the Pacific. There was a strong possibility that some British war vessel, ignorant of the coming of peace, might capture the *Seneca* and hold her so long that the object of her voyage would be ruined. Consequently, Astor wrote to James Monroe, suggesting the advisability of sending a vessel to the Pacific with the news of peace, both to notify the American ships lying at Canton of that event and to advise the U. S. sloops-of-war *Peacock* and *Hornet* to refrain from the destruction of British property for which the United States might later have to pay. Astor offered to send his brig, then ready to sail, for that purpose, if she could be protected by dispatches which he would take free of charge, as well as by a protection from the State Department and from Mr. Baker, British chargé d'affaires. The vessel would go by way of the Cape of Good Hope and leave dispatches there for Mr. Baker. In support of these suggestions Astor sent his friend C. C. Cambreleng to see both Monroe and Baker,[7] and also wrote to the Russian minister, Andrew Daschkoff, requesting him to assist in obtaining "some dispatches . . . from Mr Baker conveying the news of peace to the British commanders in those seas with a letter from him requesting all british ships not to molest said vessel." It seems, however, that Daschkoff's intercession was of little avail, for in a letter to him dated March 11 Astor said, "M^r. Cambreleng wrote to me that he had delivered your letter to M^r. Baker himself, what M^r. Baker gave me is nothing, first it amounts to nothing & second it came too late to answer any purpose, I am still the same obliged to you."[8]

The inadequacy of Mr. Baker's papers did not deter Astor from the projected voyage, and on March 13 the *Seneca* cleared for China with a cargo composed of 5,405 otter skins, 8,495 fox skins, and $39,000 in specie.[9] Captain Cowman, Astor's "king of captains" (apparently recently deposed from his royal estate by De Peyster), acted as supercargo. John Whetten also seems to have been concerned in the voyage, for the vessel, on clearing, was actually described as belonging to him, though it seems evident that Astor was the principal owner. She had reached the Cape of Good Hope by May 10, passed the Straits of Sunda by June 16, and had encountered the *Peacock*, one of the U. S. war vessels which Astor had suggested the *Seneca* might warn of peace.[10] She reached Canton by July 5, and sailed on November 18 with the usual cargo of teas, silks, nankeens, chinaware, and cassia[11] for John Jacob Astor, and arrived at New York on the last day of April, 1816, thus completing the first China voyage of an Astor ship after the war.

In the meantime the brig *Macedonian*, which had sailed from New York in January, 1815, before the news of peace had reached America, had arrived at Canton on July 2 and there had taken on the usual cargo for Astor and the captain, Curtiss Blakeman. With this cargo she sailed for New York on September 15,[12] arriving on January 18, 1816.[13] On the 29th of May, Astor fulfilled his promises to his Canton correspondents by sending to China[14] the ship *Fingal*, which had returned from France early in the month. This vessel was of 389 tons, and was commanded by a Mr. Vibberts.[15] She arrived at Canton on

November 2 with a cargo consisting of ginseng, furs, dollars, and small iron spikes.[16]

At Canton the *Fingal's* captain discovered, like other Astor captains, a difficult commercial and financial situation. An agent of Stephen Girard at Canton, writing on September 23, 1815, thus described the condition of affairs at that port: "we found [h]ere ten or eleven American vessels. Eight of them having arrived here since the ratification of the Treaty was known'd, with ginseng, Cochineal, opium &c &c & have hurried their Goods in the Market, fearing a depression & have actually caused what they were in fear of by their improper conduct, the Chinese finding them so pressing have naturally retired & it is difficult at present to procure even an offer for Goods, as for the State of Bills you may judge, of them Sir from the circumstance of Mr John Jacob Astor's having been disposed of yesterday for Six Shillings the Dollar or $33\frac{1}{3}$ pct below par, such a discount is what no one had ever anticipated." Three weeks later the same agent wrote that two ships belonging to Astor had been forced to load "with Bills at 6% & also an additional charge of $2\frac{1}{2}$ pr Ct for endorsement."[17] These two Astor ships were probably the *Fingal* and the *Beaver*, both of which were at Canton on November 15; the *Seneca* was also there, but was due to sail very shortly, on November 18.

The *Beaver* sailed on November 26, and the *Fingal* on the 29th.[18] The *Beaver*, with a cargo which consisted principally of black teas, intended for Amsterdam, arrived at New York on March 22, 1816, nearly four and one-half years after she had left that port on the last previous occasion. The *Fingal*, however, was wrecked on February 17 in the Straits of Gaspar. News of the disaster reached New York on June 8, and on August 2 the survivors arrived in the *Ontario* from Batavia, which they had reached in the *Fingal's* boat. Among them were Captain Vibberts, N. G. Ogden, the *Beaver's* supercargo, and George Ehninger, Astor's nephew.[19] So, a little over a year after the news of peace had reached the United States, three Astor vessels, the *Macedonian*, the *Seneca*, and the *Beaver*, which had returned that year from Canton, were lying at New York.

It will be recalled that shortly before the outbreak of war two new factors had entered into Astor's China trade. A ship had been sent to the North West Coast with a cargo of goods to be bartered with the natives for furs, which in turn were to be sold in Canton. Moreover, small vessels owned by Astor himself had begun to make voyages to Europe with cargoes of China goods, returning to New York with various products, some of which could be sold in that city, while others were to be re-exported to China.

As far as we have described it, Astor's commerce with China since the war has appeared to be of a very simple character, just as it had been during the few years after he first entered the China trade. But now the relations between his interest in the China trade and his activities as a fur trader and general merchant, relations which had always been very close, were about to become even more complex than they had been immediately before the outbreak of the war. Canton and New York were no longer to be the only two ports concerned in the China trade. Various cities and localities in Europe and in countries bordering on the Pacific Ocean were to be no less closely associated with the trade of the Orient. Sometimes, indeed, three fleets of vessels belonging to Astor would be operating simultaneously, one between New York and Europe, another between New York and China, and a third in the Pacific Ocean. The trade carried on in the Pacific Ocean, in connection with the North West Coast, California, the west coast of South America, and the Hawaiian Islands is of sufficient importance to be considered separately. The trade in which European ports play a rôle of major importance can best be studied side by side with the China trade in its older and simpler aspects. When the ship *Enterprise*, commanded by John Ebbets, cleared for the Columbia River on June 28, 1815, and the brig *Boxer*, which had arrived from Nantes early in June, 1815, cleared for Gibraltar on July 10 under the command of James Clark, Astor's post-war foreign trade entered a new period.[20]

Astor was now in the prime of life, not much over fifty years old. Nevertheless, he had come to realize that the exceedingly complicated character which his trade with China was now to assume, together with the greatly increased attention which he meant to give to the fur trade, would necessitate expert and interested assistance. He consequently looked about him for a suitable partner. The man on whom he fixed was Albert Gallatin, who was a couple of years older than Astor and had come to America from Switzerland about four years before Astor's arrival. He had attained nearly as great distinction in the political life of the nation as Astor had reached in commercial pursuits. Gallatin had just returned from Europe, where he had been engaged as peace commissioner, and on October 9, 1815, Astor wrote him "a long letter proposing that he should become a partner in Mr. Astor's commercial house. He had, he [Astor] said, at that time a capital of about $800,000 engaged in trade. He estimated his probable profits at from $50,000 to $100,000 per annum, interest and all expenses deducted. 'I propose to give you an interest of one-fifth, on which I mean to charge you the legal interest; if you put any funds to the stock, interest will be allowed to you of course.'"[21]

It seems, however, that Gallatin was never particularly attracted by this "most generous offer." "His reasons for refusing," as given *in camera* to his eighteen-year-old son, James Gallatin, "were" that "although he respected Mr. Astor, he never could place himself on the same level with him." The frivolous and rather snobbish James believed that he understood his father's feelings perfectly. "I am not surprised," he

commented superciliously, "as Astor was a butcher's son at
Waldorf — came as an emigrant to this country with a pack
on his back. He peddled furs, was very clever, and is, I believe, one of the kings of the fur trade. He dined here," James
concluded casually, "and ate his ice-cream and peas with a
knife."

It is probable, however, that neither Astor's lowly origin nor
his plebeian table-manners were the primary cause of the elder
Gallatin's rejection of the offer of a partnership. A far more
likely explanation is that, knowing Astor of old, Gallatin's
Calvinistic conscience shrank from some of the commercial
tricks which he feared he would have to endure should he become Astor's partner. It will be remembered that Gallatin
had played a leading, though an unwilling, rôle in the profitable Chinese mandarin comedy of the year 1808, which had
been staged by Astor with the assistance of the amiable
Thomas Jefferson. Consequently, he looked upon Astor with
a wary if friendly eye. But probably he gave Astor the same
reason for his refusal as he did when the offer was repeated in
1821, that "he must not die rich after holding the posts he
has."[22] At any rate Gallatin had an excellent pretext for refusing without giving offence, since he had been offered in November, 1815, an appointment as minister to Paris, and though
at the time he had positively declined the offer, he finally accepted it early in January, 1816.[23]

Astor was now forced to look around him for some other
partner, and the thought of training up a young man to act as
his assistant came to his mind, as it had in times past. Since
his eldest son, John Jacob, had been mentally incompetent
from birth, or at least from a very early age, it was inevitable
that he should think of his second son, William Backhouse
Astor. William B. Astor had been born in 1792, and as early
as 1800 was sent to the private school of the Rev. Mr. Smith at
Stamford, Connecticut.[24] At the age of sixteen he had been

sent to Heidelberg, near his father's old home, where he had remained two years. He had then probably returned home for a visit,[25] and had been sent to Göttingen in 1810.[26] While there he selected as his tutor a youth only a year older than himself, later to be famous as the Baron von Bunsen. Till late in 1814 young Astor continued his studies at Göttingen, where Schopenhauer was his friend and fellow student,[27] and also spent some time in travelling about the war-ridden countries of Europe, much to the uneasiness of his father, who on several occasions expressed the fear that "William . . . is no more." He returned to America in November, 1814, on his father's ship the *Hannibal*, but did not expect to remain there any length of time, as he was planning to return to Europe by the early summer of 1815.[28] Young Astor's tastes, indeed, seem to have been entirely literary and scholarly at this time. Within William B. Astor's own lifetime, and even while his father was still alive, evidences of artistic ability were not lacking among the kin of the Astors and Todds.

In pursuit of his plan, William B. Astor returned to Europe in 1815 and settled down at Paris, where he devoted himself to the study of French literature. We learn from a letter of March 19, 1816, that he was at that time intending to leave for Italy on the first of the next month. But a peremptory order from his father changed his plans and two days later he was in Liverpool on the point of sailing for New York,[29] where he was to prepare himself to become his father's assistant and successor in business. Great as his disappointment must have been, we have no record that he ever made any demur. The scholar was discarded for the business man, the French classics for the ledgers and letter books of his father's New York office, and William B. Astor entered upon the business career which was to end only with his death more than three-score years later.[30] From 1818 until the Astors in 1827 withdrew from foreign trade conducted in their own ships, William B. Astor

Astor, probably in his Fifties

was the junior member of the firm of John Jacob Astor & Son. We have already mentioned that on July 10, 1815, Astor's brig the *Boxer* (formerly rigged as a schooner) cleared for Gibraltar, under the command of James Clark. This was the first vessel owned by Astor to sail for Europe since the arrival of peace. The *Boxer* returned on January 24, 1816, "62 days from Smyrna, and 27 from Gibraltar, with fruit, drugs, wool, &c. to John Jacob Astor." The connection of this voyage with the China trade will later be made evident. On March 29, 1816, the brig *Macedonian*, still commanded by Curtiss Blakeman, sailed from New York, for "Columbia River and Canton,"[31] according to the marine news, but as a matter of fact for Canton only, where she arrived on July 15, having "performed a remarkably quick voyage" of "290 days for the round trip" from Canton to Canton.[32] On May 30, 1816, a new Astor ship, commanded by F. A. De Peyster, had likewise cleared for Canton. This was the *William and John*,[33] which had evidently been so christened to commemorate the entrance of William B. Astor into his father's business. The *William and John* was a ship of 371 tons which had been built for Astor in 1815 by Christian Bergh.[34]

One would think, on recalling the list of nine vessels owned by Astor at the end of the war, that no more would be needed for some time. But two of these vessels, the *Forester* and the *Pedler*, were still in the Pacific, and, indeed, the first was destined never to come to New York. Moreover, the Pacific trade in the otter furs and seal skins of the North West Coast and in sandalwood from the Hawaiian Islands, which was henceforth to be an important feature of Astor's China trade, had already diverted the *Enterprise* from the direct traffic between New York and Canton. The *Hannibal*, described as a "first rate New York built ship, which sails very fast of 525 tons," had cleared from Charleston on March 19, 1815, under the command of Joseph Ridgway, to take freight of rice and cotton to

Europe. Later in the year she was sold at Le Havre.[35] It does not appear why Astor decided to get rid of this ship, but, at any rate, its sale reduced the number of vessels at his disposal early in 1816 to five. Indeed, the launching of the *William and John* really operated almost providentially to fill the gap in the Astor fleet left by the wreck of the *Fingal*, since the new vessel sailed on her maiden voyage only a few days before word of the other vessel's loss reached New York. The *Seneca*, commanded by James Clark, cleared for the East Indies on the last day of September,[36] and was the third and last Astor vessel clearing for Canton during 1816. Clark had taken the *Beaver* to Europe during the summer, presumably with the cargo of black teas for Amsterdam which she had brought from China.[37]

Before the *Seneca* had cleared for Canton, Astor had been concerned in several voyages to the Mediterranean. The brig *Boxer*, commanded by Captain Mix, had cleared for Gibraltar on February 9, 1816, and had returned to New York from Smyrna and Gibraltar on September 15 "with an assorted cargo, to John Jacob Astor, owner, and C. C. Cambreling." In the meantime the brig *Alexander*, which Astor seems to have purchased for the Mediterranean trade, commanded by Captain Summers, had arrived at New York on June 19, 1816, "34 days from Gibraltar, with quicksilver, to John Jacob Astor." Astor had also received goods on August 5 from Leghorn and Gibraltar on a schooner not owned by him.[38]

As a result of these Mediterranean voyages, some of the cargoes of Astor ships at Canton for the season 1816–17 presented new elements. The brig *Macedonian*, which arrived at Canton on July 15, 1816, brought not only such familiar commodities as $110,000 in specie, 180 piculs of ginseng, 500 pieces of camlets, and 450 piculs of ebony, but also such unfamiliar wares for an Astor ship as 40 piculs of opium and 133 piculs of quicksilver, a commodity which had only once before appeared in the cargo of an Astor ship, when the *Beaver* carried a small consignment of 27 piculs in 1805. The omission of furs from this cargo is another unusual feature. The *William and John*, which arrived at Canton on October 1, had a cargo of $150,000 in specie, 70 piculs ginseng, 360 land-otter skins, 2,000 fox skins, 610 pieces of camlets, and a very large quantity of lead and steel, 2,800 piculs and 933 piculs, respectively. She also had on board 30 piculs of quicksilver, but no opium. The *Seneca*, which arrived at Canton on February 26, 1817, brought specie to the amount of $54,000, and 9 piculs of ginseng, 832 piculs of lead and 505 of iron, 160 piculs of quicksilver and 95 of opium.[39] So we see that quicksilver and lead from Gibraltar and opium from Smyrna, as well as some iron and steel from the north of Europe, began in 1816 to take a conspicuous place in the list of Astor's imports into China. Since, according to Dr. Kenneth Scott Latourette, quicksilver and opium did not become regular articles of import into China by Americans till about 1816,[40] Astor must have been one of the pioneers in their introduction.

The articles of export on Astor's vessels in the season 1816–17 presented no new features. The *Macedonian*, which had left Canton on October 2, 1816,[41] arrived at New York on the 26th of January, 1817, with the usual cargo,[42] part of which was re-exported on April 12 to Havana on the *Macedonian*, commanded by De Lamater;[43] and two months later the *William and John*, which had sailed from China on December 4, 1816,[44] reached New York. The *Seneca*, with a cargo for "John J. Astor, and John Whetten, owners," did not arrive at New York till December 2, 1817, and was, in consequence, too late to sail again for China in that year. Her place had been taken by the brig *Boxer*, which had been employed since the war in the Mediterranean trade. The *Boxer*, under the command of William Brevoort, cleared for Canton on March 14, 1817, and was followed late in the next month by the ship *William and John*, Curtiss Blakeman in command. Here another innova-

tion appeared: up to this time Astor vessels clearing from New
York for China had usually proceeded directly either about
Cape Horn or the Cape of Good Hope, stopping only for wood,
water, or provisions, until they reached Canton, unless they
belonged to the category of North West Coast vessels. The
William and John, however, was to go by way of Gibraltar,
where she would probably complete her cargo with quicksilver
and lead. This was another example of the importance which
Mediterranean products were assuming in Astor's trade with
Canton. The brig *Alexander*, Captain Summers, had cleared
for Gibraltar on July 16, 1816, and returned to New York on
January 14, 1817, from Smyrna and Gibraltar "with fruit,
opium, goat's wool, box-wood, &c. to John Jacob Astor,
owner." Part of this cargo, together with some camel's hair
and oil-stones, was advertised for sale in New York, while
some of the opium probably made up part of the *Boxer's* cargo.
Another brig, not owned by Astor but bringing part of her
cargo of quicksilver, fruit, and port wine to his order, had arrived at New York from Gibraltar on November 5, 1816, and
doubtless also contributed to the *Boxer's* invoice of exports.[45]

The *Boxer* reached Canton on July 21, 1817, sailed for New
York on September 30,[46] and arrived at that port on January
27, 1818. The *William and John* had arrived at Canton on November 12, sailed December 19, and arrived at New York on
April 27, 1818.[47] The *Boxer*, soon after her arrival, sailed for
St. Petersburg under Captain Copland, returning to New York
on August 25, 1818, with a cargo of hemp and duck. Immediately after her arrival she was successfully offered for sale.[48]
Early in 1818 the brig *Pedler*, which had returned from trading
in the Pacific on October 16, 1816,[49] had gone to Gibraltar and
Smyrna, under Jonathan Eldridge, arriving at the latter port
on February 7 and leaving a week later for Canton.[50] This
voyage strengthened the precedent set by the *William and John*
in making a voyage to Canton by Gibraltar. The brig *Seneca*,

under James Clark, cleared for Canton on March 10, 1818,[51] and the *William and John*, commanded by William Brevoort, did likewise in June.[52] As in the previous year, the *William and John* went by way of Gibraltar, where she unloaded part of the *Seneca's* China cargo and doubtless took on quicksilver, specie, lead, or some similar consignment of commodities for the Canton market.[53] As usual, three Astor vessels had cleared for Canton in 1818.

Before all of these vessels could return and be unloaded, John Jacob Astor had sailed for Europe [54] for the benefit of his health, and matters at the New York office were placed entirely in the hands of his son and partner, William B. Astor, assisted by his confidential clerk, William Roberts.[55] But though Astor would not be present in the flesh in that office at 8 Vesey Street [56] to which he had moved from his earlier quarters at 69 Pine Street in March, 1817,[57] still there would be no departure from that policy in foreign trade which he had been developing since the war. It will be proper, then, for us to cast a glance back over the years which have elapsed since the war and examine the condition of Astor's China trade at that time. During the past four years he had followed the policy of sending three vessels annually to Canton, and in the earlier portion of this period brigs plying between New York and the ports of Gibraltar and Smyrna had been employed to bring quicksilver, lead, and opium to be used as part of the cargoes of Astor's China vessels. Later this policy had been modified somewhat so that vessels proceeded from New York to Canton by way of Gibraltar or of Gibraltar and Smyrna, loading products of these ports directly, without the intervention of an intermediary brig. Other vessels were being employed in scouring the Pacific for goods to be sold in China. These operations were to be continued as long as Astor carried on the China trade in his own bottoms, but this side of his foreign trade deserves separate treatment.

During this same period Astor's China trade had undergone a process of contraction. When the war ended, he was the owner of nine vessels, all but two purchased during the war. After the war, he became the owner of two additional vessels, the brig *Alexander* for the Mediterranean trade and a newly built ship to ply between New York and Canton. But early in 1819 his fleet had been so reduced by sale and shipwreck that he was the owner of only the brigs *Pedler* and *Seneca* and the ship *William and John,* then engaged in China voyages, and the ships *Beaver* and *Enterprise,* employed in the Pacific trade. Both his Mediterranean brigs, the *Boxer* and the *Alexander,* had disappeared from his roll of vessels, as had his China brig, the *Macedonian.*[58]

Another feature of Astor's China trade since the war was his vigorous but apparently only temporary attention to the smuggling of Smyrna opium into China. Inasmuch as the introduction of the "foreign mud," as the Chinese graphically and contemptuously described the narcotic, was rigorously forbidden, Astor's participation in the trade was utterly illegal, excusable only upon the flimsy but commonplace grounds that "everyone else does it." It is said that the only Canton firm which did not trade in opium was Olyphant & Co., of New York, who won on account of this commercial squeamishness the nickname of "Zion's Corner" from their rivals.[59]

The intensity of Astor's interest in trade with Smyrna, already noted, would in itself create a strong presumption of participation in opium smuggling in the case of any merchant who was also engaged in the China trade, but we need by no means depend entirely upon circumstantial evidence. Seven cases of opium, valued at $3,539.75, which had been imported on March 18, 1816, by J. Moses & Sons for Henry Sergeant from Gibraltar and Malaga, were ten days later shipped to Canton on the *Macedonian* by John Jacob Astor,[60] and doubtless formed part of the 40 piculs (more than 5,000 lbs.) of that drug imported into China on that vessel in the same year. The *Seneca*, which arrived early in 1817, brought 95 piculs.[61] Evidence of Astor's position in opium-smuggling is presented in a letter from the firm of J. & T. H. Perkins, of Boston, to their agent in Leghorn, March 24, 1818. "From the intention of the Chinese to be very strict about Opium, the competition you fear we think will not exist. *We know of no one but Astor we fear*. It is our intention to push it as far as we can. . . . Situated as we are we do not attach much consequence to the introduction of Opium in China, as it may be kept on board untill an opportunity offers to sell it deliverable alongside. Persons with a limited time for their vessels to stay, will not adventure, we think. . . . There was a parcel of Opium from the Gulf of Persia last year & purchased by Astor, for about $3 & sent to China where it was pronounced to be without value, & returned."[62]

The Turkey opium, being much inferior to that of Bengal, and employed, it is said, largely in adulterating the latter, could not be sold in very large quantities, and consequently formed only a comparatively insignificant part of American imports into China.[63] It seems likely that Astor soon concluded that the importation of opium was more troublesome than profitable; possibly his unfortunate experience with the parcel from the Persian Gulf played some part in this decision. At any rate, we have no record, after 1818, that he sent any of his own vessels to Smyrna, and there is only scattered mention of his receiving goods from that port as freight, whereas in the three previous years he had annually sent one or two of his vessels to Smyrna. In all probability Astor's trade in opium practically ceased after 1818,[64] never having been an essential feature of his commerce with China.

There remains to be considered another factor of Astor's China trade after the war. During the dozen years in which he had been engaged in commerce with Canton prior to the outbreak of war, he had never possessed a resident agent, but had depended on his captains and supercargoes, assisted occasionally by one of the merchants located at Canton, for any necessary services in buying or selling goods in that port. One of these merchants whose assistance he had occasionally engaged was Daniel Stansbury, and to him he wrote early in March, 1815: "I have as yet no permanent agent at Canton. Should you not come home next season please to enform me how long you will remain in Canton & whether you will do my business in case I do not send an agent. I have long wished to have a person there who should do Business for me only and as now I contemplate not to engage in any other Business but that to Canton I can make it any object to you or any other gentleman."[65]

Stansbury, however, did not become Astor's Canton agent. That place was taken by Nicholas Gouverneur Ogden, brother of the prominent New York merchant Samuel G. Ogden. It will be remembered that Nicholas Ogden had gone out from New York in 1813 as supercargo of the Astoria relief ship, the *Lark*. When this vessel had been wrecked off the Hawaiian Islands, he had made his way to Canton on one of the fur-trading vessels which made Honolulu their headquarters and had there acted as supercargo to Cornelius Sowle of the *Beaver*, in the place of Wilson P. Hunt, who had returned to Astoria. Ogden had remained at Canton probably for about two years, from early in 1814 to early in February, 1816. He had left Canton for New York in the ship *Fingal*, had been wrecked in the Straits of Gaspar eleven days after sailing,[66] and, after reaching Batavia in the ship's boat with other survivors, had arrived at New York early in August, 1816, having gone through the unusual experience of being shipwrecked twice on the same voyage, once on the outward and once on the homeward passage. It would not have been surprising had he developed a reputation as a Jonah. Astor, however, was not superstitious, and some time after his arrival at New York offered him a one-fifth share in his China trade if he would act as the firm's Canton agent. We do not know exactly when this arrangement went into effect or at what time Ogden returned to China to take up his new duties. It seems, however, that the partnership must have begun some time in 1817, since such documents as we possess indicate that the sales from the *Seneca's* second Canton voyage were the first from which Ogden received a share of the profits.[67] This vessel reached New York in December, 1817, and it may be that Ogden had purchased part of her return cargo before leaving Canton on the *Fingal*, early in the previous year.

At Canton it was Ogden's duty to dispose of merchandise brought there by Astor vessels and to purchase goods for their return cargoes. On March 2, 1819, an agreement had been made between Ogden and John Jacob Astor & Son whereby the firm "assume to take their own separate account, at the market value in New York, all such goods as they shall ship abroad after that date, either to foreign or domestic ports."[68] This made Ogden's profits entirely dependent on the New York price of the goods purchased through his agency, and threw on John Jacob Astor & Son the gain or loss of sales outside of New York, including the sale of many shipments in ports in the United States, in France, in the West Indies, and in most of the ports in Europe outside the British Isles, where the East India Company had a monopoly. Thus Astor on departing for Europe in 1819 had left both the New York and the Canton offices of his firm under capable oversight.

From June, 1819, to the spring of 1826, Astor spent much more time in Europe than in America; he was in Europe until the fall of 1821, divided the next year or two between the two continents, and spent in Europe the period of nearly three years between June, 1823, and the spring of 1826. But the foreign trade of John Jacob Astor & Son during this period probably owed almost as much to John Jacob's experience and ability as if he had been personally present in the New York office. Two vessels of the three which had sailed for Canton in the previous year arrived at New York before Astor's departure in June, 1819. The *Seneca*, which had sailed from Canton on October 1, 1818,[69] arrived at New York on February 11, 1819.[70] The *Pedler*, which had left Canton on October 29,[71] having made her outward voyage by way of Smyrna, doubtless to secure a consignment of opium, developed a bad leak, and did not reach New York till March 29. Immediately after her arrival, probably without unloading, she made a voyage to Le Havre, under Captain Vermilye, returning by way of Plymouth.[72] The *William and John*, which cleared from Canton late in 1818 or early in 1819, set another precedent by sailing to Amsterdam,[73] where she arrived in the summer of 1819.[74] There the captain, William Brevoort, disposed of 5,112 chests of tea, a total of 370,000 lbs.[75] Brevoort had returned to New York by April 16, 1820,[76] but the *William and John* herself remained in Europe, for some time in the season of 1819–20 she again arrived at Amsterdam with 5,000 chests of tea, weighing 269,804 lbs. (of which 1,354 chests, or 100,196 lbs., still remained unsold at the end of the season).[77] The *William and John* was back in China by February, 1820, and the period between the summer of 1819 and that month was not long enough to allow the vessel to go from Amsterdam to Canton, from Canton to Amsterdam, and again to Canton. Therefore, this second consignment of tea must have been landed at Amsterdam during the latter part of 1819 and must have been part of the same cargo of which a portion was sold at that port in the season 1818–19. It seems probable that part of the *William and John's* cargo was disposed of in various ports of Europe other than Amsterdam and the vessel turned over to the command of one of the mates or the supercargo, who secured in Europe a cargo suitable to the China market and left Europe for Canton late in 1819 without first returning to New York.[78]

Since the *William and John* had not returned to New York in 1819 (and also for other reasons, among which it is barely possible was John Jacob Astor's departure for Europe), no Astor vessel left New York for Canton in that year. This was the first year of which this could have been said since 1814, when commerce with China was crippled by the war. The brig *Seneca* was no longer available for the use of the firm, as she had been sold on May 19, 1819, to John Whetten,[79] who had previously been concerned in her. It is true that the *Pedler*, which had made a China voyage in 1818 and 1819, did sail again in the fall of the latter year, but it was to the North West Coast and not directly to China that she sailed. Her voyage was similar to that which had just been completed by the *Enterprise*, which had arrived at New York from Canton early in September, 1819, after an absence of more than four years, during which she had touched at many other Pacific ports besides Canton.

However, though no China voyages were made in 1819, the firm of John Jacob Astor & Son was not without a fresh supply of China goods for the year 1820. Though no longer holding any interest in the *Seneca*, the firm had chartered some space in the vessel for the return passage of her voyage of 1819 and 1820, which was completed on March 14, 1820; this vessel consequently brought John Jacob Astor & Son a large consignment of teas, nankeens, silks, and chinaware. Some China goods were also brought as freight by the ship *Clothier*, which arrived on May 7.[80] Moreover, the *William and John*, commanded by Captain Bunker, which had arrived at Canton on February 3, 1820,[81] from Europe, had returned to New York on September 17, 1820.[82]

Although 1819 had seen no Astor vessel clearing from New York for Canton, in the following year John Jacob Astor & Son returned to a more normal interest in the China trade. The first ship to clear for Canton in 1820 was the *Enterprise*, commanded by one of Astor's most faithful captains, William Brevoort. The *Enterprise* sailed on April 16,[83] and arrived on August 24, with a cargo consisting of $50,000 in specie, 2,190 land-otter skins, 2,630 fox skins, 126 seal skins, 71 piculs of copper, and 1,932 piculs of quicksilver.[84] The unusually large quantity of quicksilver in the cargo — a hundred piculs or so had been the largest amount previously recorded — is accounted for by the fact that no Astor ships had sailed from New York to China for nearly two years prior to the *Enterprise's* departure. During this period at least half a dozen vessels, principally brigs and schooners, had arrived at New York from Smyrna, Madeira, Cadiz, and Gibraltar, bringing to New York firms, among which was John Jacob Astor & Son, cargoes consisting of wine, raisins, salt, brandy, nuts, furs, and quicksilver. It is probable that the portions of these cargoes intended for the Astor firm consisted largely or entirely of quicksilver, for they advertised 5,000 or 6,000 lbs. of the metal for sale in New York during the fall of 1818.[85]

On November 28, 1820, a new Astor vessel cleared for Canton.[86] This was the *Henry Astor*, a ship of 377 tons, which had been built by Henry Eckford.[87] She was named after John Jacob Astor's elder brother, the prosperous butcher who had helped John Jacob during his early years in New York City. James Clark, a captain who had been long in Astor's service, commanded the ship on her maiden voyage. Part of the cargo probably consisted of quicksilver from Gibraltar.[88] Astor now owned two ships engaged in the direct trade between New York and Canton, and a ship and a brig collecting commodities in various Pacific ports for final sale in Canton. The policy of making the outward or the return voyage, or both, by way of Europe seems to have been speedily discontinued. His firm had also invested in a schooner of 188 tons, called the *Ariadne*, which had been put under the command of Summers, formerly the commander of a Mediterranean brig belonging to Astor, and which made at least one voyage to Hamburg; but this was another experiment speedily discontinued, and the schooner was sold in 1821.[89] The *Beaver*, which had gone to South America in 1817, had returned in 1820, but, having been given up for lost, had been in the meantime surrendered to the underwriters. This episode will be considered separately.

The *Enterprise* left Canton on January 19, 1821, arrived at New York on May 27, and under command of William Brevoort returned almost immediately to Canton, where she arrived on December 7, 1821,[90] part of her cargo probably consisting of quicksilver, lead, and specie, which had come to John Jacob Astor & Son on four or five different vessels from Cadiz and Gibraltar during the first half of 1821;[91] she sailed from Canton on March 18, 1822,[92] arriving at New York on August 12, 1822. The *Henry Astor* had reached New York on December 4, 1821, too late to allow a return voyage to be inaugurated in the same year. She cleared for Canton under the command of James Clark on January 6, 1822,[93] arrived at Canton on May 25, 1822, sailed for the United States on September 18,[94] after an unusually long stay at Canton, and arrived at New York on February 3, 1823.[95] On August 19, 1822, just a week after the *Enterprise*'s arrival, the ship *William and John*, which, under the command of Astor's veteran captain, John Ebbets, had been engaged in the Pacific trade, reached New York, and was sent two months later to Canton under command of William Brevoort, probably including in her cargo specie and quicksilver from Gibraltar, Trieste, and Cadiz.[96] Apparently the *Enterprise* and the *William and John* were being employed alternately in the Pacific trade and in the direct trade between New York and Canton, while the *Henry Astor* was used only for the latter purpose. It is also worth while as a sidelight upon Astor's relations with his subordinates to note the regularity with which James Clark, William Brevoort, and John Ebbets appear as commanders of Astor vessels. These men had all commanded Astor vessels since the time of the war, and Brevoort and Ebbets even longer.

Astor's presence in New York from the fall of 1821 to the spring of 1822 does not seem to have affected the China trade of his firm in the slightest, as, indeed, there was no reason why it should. However, it is at least possible that Astor, during his next stay in New York from the fall of 1822 until the spring of 1823, may have suggested a revival of the policy which had been applied in 1817 and 1818, namely, the sending of vessels to China from New York by way of Gibraltar. At any rate, late in March, 1823, the Astor firm advertised for freight or passengers to Gibraltar on the *Henry Astor*, which cleared on April 6 under the command of Captain Rossiter, and was the only Astor vessel to sail for China during 1823. However, more than one vessel arrived at New York from China during that year. On August 17 the brig *Pedler*, commanded by Captain John Meek, which had been cruising in the Pacific for nearly four years, reached New York. On December 7 arrived the ship *William and John*,[97] which had reached Canton on April 8 and sailed therefrom on July 6. The *Henry Astor*, which arrived at Canton on September 12, 1823,[98] found the situation there considerably changed, so far as the firm of John Jacob Astor & Son was concerned. Nicholas G. Ogden, who had been John Jacob Astor & Son's Canton agent for about six years, had died on August 15, 1823,[99] and consequently the *Henry Astor* had to be loaded without his valuable assistance. Nevertheless this unfortunate event did not prevent the ship from sailing on November 25,[100] with the usual cargo, arriving at New York on March 23, 1824. She sailed again for Canton a month later, still under the command of Rossiter. Part of her cargo doubtless consisted of quicksilver and specie which half a dozen brigs had brought to John Jacob Astor & Son and other New

York firms during the previous year from Cadiz and Gibraltar.[101] Another part consisted of a few thousand dollars' worth of the American Fur Company's furs.[102]

The *Henry Astor*, however, was the only Astor vessel to clear for Canton during 1824. The *Enterprise* had made a Hamburg voyage in 1823, under the command of Captain Black,[103] with an outward cargo consisting partly of China goods from her own last voyage and from that of the *Henry Astor*,[104] and partly of some $10,000 worth of peltries belonging to the American Fur Company,[105] and a return cargo made up of "lead, iron, hollow glass and linens," partly as freight. She had then gone on a Pacific voyage under command of John Ebbets. The *Pedler*, which had returned from such a voyage in the late summer of 1823, had been successfully offered for sale early in September. The *William and John* was similarly advertised and sold early in January, 1824.[106] This left Astor, at the time of the *Henry Astor's* clearing for Canton, in possession of only three vessels, the *Henry Astor*, the *Enterprise*, and a new brig, the *Tamaahmaah*, which had left New York for the Pacific in the spring of 1824 to act as the *Enterprise's* consort. It was evident that by the beginning of 1824 the firm of John Jacob Astor & Son were not only definitely contracting their foreign trade, but even giving strong evidence of withdrawing altogether.

The *Henry Astor*, which had reached Canton on August 11, 1824, and sailed for New York on October 21,[107] arrived at her home port on March 10, 1825. Late in the next month she was offered for sale, and in July seems to have been either owned or chartered by E. Stevens & Sons. Late in December the *Enterprise* arrived from Canton after a brief trading voyage in the Pacific,[108] and thereafter drops out of sight, doubtless having been sold. Astor was left with but one vessel, the brig *Tamaahmaah* trading in the Pacific. His withdrawal from the China trade conducted in his own vessels, which had definitely begun late in 1823, was by the end of 1825 practically complete. The decision to withdraw was probably due to the increasing scope of the American Fur Company's activities, which, added to Astor's interest in real estate on Manhattan Island, probably occupied so much of the firm's time that none could be spared for the intricacies of the China trade.

A story told by Joseph A. Scoville, the always interesting and frequently unreliable chronicler of New York commercial life in the first half of the nineteenth century, may throw some light on Astor's withdrawal from the East India trade.

It [the China trade] was a great business. A house that could raise money enough thirty years ago [this was written in 1862], to send $260,000 in specie could soon have an uncommon capital, and this was the working of the old system. . . . They started her [the ship] from here in the month of May, with a cargo of perhaps $30,000 worth of ginseng, spelter, lead, iron, &c., and $170,000 in Spanish dollars. The ship goes on the voyage, reaches Whampoa in safety, (a few miles below Canton). Her supercargo in two months has her loaded with tea, some china ware, a great deal of cassia or false cinnamon, and a few other articles. Suppose the cargo, mainly tea, costing about 37 cents (at that time) per pound on the average.

The duty was enormous in those days. It was twice the cost of the tea at least: so that a tea cargo of $200,000, when it had paid duty of 75 cents per lb. (which would be $400,000) amounted to $600,000. The profit was at least 50 per cent. on the original cost, or $100,000, and would make the cargo worth $700,000.

The cargo of teas would be sold almost on arrival (say eleven or twelve months after the ship left New York in May), to wholesale grocers, for their notes at 4 and 6 months — say for $700,000. In those days there was *credit given by the United States* of 9, 12, and 18 months! So that the East India or Canton merchant, after his ship had made one voyage, had the use of government capital to the extent of $400,000, on the ordinary cargo of a China ship as stated above.

No sooner had the ship . . . arrived . . . than her cargo would be exchanged for grocers' notes for $700,000. These notes could be turned into specie very easily, and the owner had only to pay his bond for $400,000 duty, at 9, 12, and 18 months, giving him time actually to send two more ships with $200,000 each to Canton, and have them back again in New York before the bonds on the first cargo were due.

John Jacob Astor at one time of his life had several vessels operating in this way. They would go to the Pacific (Oregon) and carry from thence furs to Canton. These would be sold at large profits. Then the cargoes of tea to New York would pay enormous duties, which Astor did not have to pay to the United States for a year and a half. His tea cargoes would be sold for good four and six months paper, or perhaps cash; so that for eighteen or twenty years John Jacob Astor had what was actually a free of interest loan from government of over *five millions* of dollars. Astor was prudent and lucky in his operations, and such an enormous government loan did not ruin him as it did many others.

Scoville then went on to describe others whom it did ruin, and the effect their misfortunes had on the tea market. At that time, he said, among the great tea houses of America were

Thompson, of Philadelphia; Perkins, of Boston, and Thomas H. Smith, of New York. In 1826, the market became overstocked, the tea cargoes had come in so fast that the government got scared about the duties. At that time the credit given to tea importers was twelve, eighteen and twenty-four months — one third at each period before they were made to pay the heavy duties. . . . The Collector of Philadelphia . . . got frightened in respect to Thompson, and refused to take his bonds any longer. . . . Finally, it was agreed that Thompson should place his tea importations under the Custom House lock, as security, and when he wanted teas he should enter only the quantity needed, pay the duty, and take it out of the government charge. . . . But Thompson had a plan to carry out . . . and for a while it succeeded. He would enter and pay duty on (say) one hundred chests, and then forge a *permit* for one thousand chests or five thousand packages and at once ship them on to his New York agents, Smith & Nicoll. There was no sale in Philadelphia for such a quantity of teas, and there was great danger of Mr Thompson being detected, if he had sold it in that city.

These teas as fast as they arrived here were offered at auction by John Hone & Sons, the great auctioneers of their day. Thompson sent on seven cargoes.

John Jacob Astor at that time held a large quantity of teas. So did Thomas H. Smith. To keep the market from being entirely broken down by the terrific quantity of tea Philadelphia Thompson was forcing upon it, both Astor and Smith became buyers, and bought nearly all that was offered, with the intention of re-exporting the tea so purchased to the Mediterranean, thus relieving the New York tea market, and enhancing greatly the value of their own tea cargoes. The teas so sold by Thompson were bought by Astor & Smith, for the duty without debenture, when it was discovered that Thompson was a defaulter. The duty was more than the cost of the tea in China. When the Government seized in Philadelphia and New York all the teas imported by Thompson, they sold them *en-*

titled to debenture, and Astor & Smith purchased teas at such a low price that when they were exported, and they received from Government the face of the *dedenture* [*sic*], the teas had really *cost* nothing shipped.

Strange as it may seem, even under these favourable circumstances, the teas shipped to Europe were a loss, for they did not sell in the Mediterranean ports for a sum sufficient to pay freight, duties, and other charges.

The only way the purchasers were benefitted was by the relief of the New York tea market.[109]

If Astor had not, as we have seen, completed the process his firm had already begun and withdrawn from the trade between Canton and New York, as carried on in his own vessels, in 1825, the experience described by Scoville might well have been enough to make him sever his connection with that commerce. Possibly he had seen from afar what the tea market had in store for it because of this overexpansion and in consequence had decided that his withdrawal from the China trade should be the result of wise forethought rather than of sorry afterthought. If Scoville's account of his actions in connection with Thompson's attempt to swindle the government is correct, Astor was endeavoring merely to keep up the price of his last two cargoes, or possibly only his last cargo, of tea, which had arrived in New York in 1825.

Late in 1825, as we have seen, Astor's decision to withdraw from the China trade, as conducted by him for a quarter of a century, had been carried out with such completeness that only one vessel remained in his possession, namely, the brig *Tamaahmaah*. In the previous year Astor and others had sent this vessel to the Pacific with the object of selling her to the natives of the Hawaiian Islands, a plan which had not yet succeeded. In intention, therefore, Astor by the end of 1825 had quite definitely withdrawn from foreign trade of every kind as conducted in his own vessels. Nevertheless it seems that Astor found it difficult to break away completely from a trade in which he had been engaged for over a quarter of a century. Perhaps, indeed, his son had been the most responsible party in forming this policy of retirement. Moreover, Astor's connection with the fur trade, so long as it continued, would always give him a powerful impulse toward the Canton fur market. It was there that his choicer furs would meet the best sale, and it was hard to begin paying freight on peltries which had formerly been shipped in his own vessels. Apparently, too, the market for China goods had soon recovered from the effects of Thompson's attempt to cheat the United States Customs. At any rate a letter from the Perkinses of Boston, written on February 15, 1827, revealed that Astor had reconsidered his well-weighed cessation of attention to foreign trade in his own bottoms. "The fair profits from the China trade this year," we read, "will, we apprehend, induce considerable undertakings. Mr. Astor having entered it anew was unexpected to us."[110]

It seems that, early in 1827, Astor had chartered the ship *Splendid* and put his old captain, F. A. De Peyster, in command. There is no mention that any furs belonging to the American Fur Company were put on board, though some $21,000 worth had been sent on this vessel in 1825.[111] It is quite possible, however, that furs from the Company which had been to Astor's own account formed part of her cargo. It also seems likely that goods from the Mediterranean took up, as usual, a good deal of space in the vessel's hold. Since the last Astor vessel to China, the *Henry Astor*, had sailed in the late spring of 1824, about half a dozen vessels from Cadiz, Gibraltar, and Marseilles had come to New York, bringing "salt, wine, quicksilver, wood, etc.," "steel, brimstone, &c," and "merchandise" to various merchants, among whom were the members of the firm of John Jacob Astor & Son. Portions of these cargoes — 2,000 flasks of quicksilver, 3 cases of Turkey opium — had been offered for sale at various times during this period,[112] but probably some remained to be utilized in making up the *Splendid's* cargo. Whatever the character of the merchandise on board, we know that her property was insured for

$20,000 to Canton and back, at a premium of 3 per cent.[113]
The vessel sailed about the middle of April, and was at Whampoa late in October. She returned to New York, "with teas,
silks, nankeens, &c. to J. J. Astor & Son, C. H. Hall, and P. S.
Crary & Co.," after the unusually short passage of 107 days
from Canton.[114] This was the last ship to be sent to Canton by
the Astor firm, whether owned or chartered by them.

With the *Splendid's* return, one period in Astor's China trade
was definitely ended, and there began another phase in which
this trade was comparatively unimportant. It was thenceforth
carried in the bottoms of other ship-owners instead of, as formerly, in vessels owned or chartered by the Astor firm, since the
last Astor-owned vessel, the *Tamaahmaah*, had been sold in the
Hawaiian Islands in February, 1828. On January 24, 1829, the
Boston firm of Bryant & Sturgis, prominent in the China trade,
wrote Astor in these words: "It has been intimated to us that
you have a quantity of Goods intended for Canton, which you
may be disposed to send out on freight — We have it in contemplation to Send a ship Soon, & intend to let her touch at an
intermediate Port for a Cargo. but if a considerable quantity
of fright at a fair rate should be offerd we would let her go
direct — Will you do us the favor to say if you are desirous of
shipping, & if So about what quantity you would send if terms
could be agreed —"[115] We do not know whether Astor accepted this particular offer, but we can be certain that he accepted similar propositions from this and other firms.

Astor's relations with the China trade during these later
years were principally inspired by his position at the head of
the American Fur Company. He had returned to America in
the spring of 1826; the six years which followed were his last
as an active merchant, and in 1832 the condition of his health
caused his return to France. His shipments to Canton during
this period consequently consisted very largely of furs, sometimes shipped on the account of the American Fur Company,

occasionally on his own. In the fall of 1827, expressing his disappointment in having failed to purchase a lot of beaver, he said, "Had I gotten it I would have sent it out of the country to China," with the intention of bolstering up the New York market.[116] His furs he sent to Charles N. Talbot, J. P. Sturgis & Co. (Canton agents of Bryant & Sturgis), and Olyphant & Co. (of "Zion's Corner"). He also sometimes shipped lead and quicksilver, or purchased goods in Canton by means of a letter of credit. The returns he took in teas, silks, and nankeens. He often specified that, whenever he engaged space in a ship from Canton to New York, he should be allowed all or a part of that space on the outward voyage free of charge. Sometimes he made shipments on joint account with such men as D. W. C. Olyphant and Charles N. Talbot.[117]

The China goods which Astor received seem to have been disposed of principally in the United States, and usually in New York City, by such firms as Haggerty, Austen & Co., L. M. Hoffman & Co., Hoffman & Sons, Bulaid & Caswell, Josiah Dow & Co., and Joshua Moses. Some were shipped to a Mr. Ellmaker and to A. & G. Ralston, in Philadelphia, and to Benjamin French, of Boston. Bryant & Sturgis, of Boston, once contracted for practically a whole consignment of Astor's young hyson tea. The little sent abroad seems to have all gone to Welles & Greene, of Le Havre. The poverty of material on the China trade in Astor's letter book for 1831-38, compared with the enormous amount in that for 1813-15, reveals the minor position to which his commerce with China had descended.[118] He continued to receive and dispose of consignments of China goods until the summer of 1834, by which time he had also withdrawn from the American Fur Company. The business of the New York office had been conducted since 1832 by William B. Astor, John Jacob being in Paris, though he kept closely in touch with the various transactions in which his capital was employed. His retirement both from the fur trade and from the commerce with China had doubtless been inspired by the same reasons, advanced age (he was now over seventy), increasingly poor health, and a consequent desire to withdraw from troublesome and intricate commercial enterprises and devote so much time and strength as still remained to money-lending, Manhattan Island real estate, and investments in various promising stocks. Thus ended a commercial connection of more than a third of a century with the East Indies, during more than a quarter of a century of which Astor had conducted the trade in a substantial fleet of his own vessels.

Perhaps the best idea of Astor's position in the China trade during the first quarter of the nineteenth century can be found in Philip Hone's obituary remarks on the day of Astor's death.

> The fur trade was the philosopher's stone of this modern Croesus; beaver-skins and musk-rats furnished the oil for the supply of Aladdin's lamp. His traffic was the shipment of furs to China, where they brought immense prices, for he monopolized the business; and the return cargoes of teas, silks, and rich productions of China brought further large profits; for here, too, he had very little competition at the time of which I am speaking. My brother and I found Mr. Astor a valuable customer. We sold many of his cargoes, and had no reason to complain of a want of liberality or confidence. All he touched turned to gold and it seemed as if fortune delighted in erecting him a monument of her unerring potency.

This description is not literally true; it was written twenty-seven years after Philip Hone had withdrawn from the auction business in which, from 1800 to 1821, he had been brought into close contact with Astor, and the latter's importance in Hone's mind had greatly increased with the passage of the years.[119] It can be stated with some justice that Astor "monopolized the business" of shipping furs to China during this period. Some years after the time of which Hone was speaking, Astor held such a position in the Canton fur market that only his death or withdrawal from the business was regarded as offering an opportunity for anyone else to send a cargo of furs to that port.[120] But to anyone who has glanced over the list of New

York ships trading with China during the period of Hone's activity, or who has even casually inspected the notices of arrivals and departures of China vessels in the New York newspapers of that day, the statement that Astor "had very little competition" in the commerce with Canton will sound rather strange. The value of Hone's statement lies rather in its revelation of his own attitude to Astor. It is not without significance that during the height of Astor's activity in the China trade, say for the first five years after the War of 1812, his position was so commanding that it was possible for one at that time actively engaged in auctioning off China cargoes to believe, more than a quarter of a century later, that Astor had enjoyed a virtual monopoly of that commerce during those years.

NOTES

1. Ms. book, Whitehall, London, East India Office, East India Company Records, China Factory Records, Diaries, vol. 135, pp. 44, 108, 109; vol. 143, pp. 112, 122, 124; vol. 146, pp. 113, 125–128; vol. 149, pp. 151–152, 155–156; vol. 151, pp. 24, 126–129; vol. 158, pp. 116–119, 130; vol. 165, pp. 115, 122–123; vol. 169, pp. 132–133, 140, 142, 148; vol. 173, pp. 128, 129, 134.

2. Ms. book, Baker Library, Astor Papers, Letter Book i, 1813–15, pp. 480–481, John Jacob Astor, N. Y., February 21, 1815, to Thomas H. Wilson, London.

3. *Ibid.*, p. 495, John Jacob Astor, N. Y., March 5, 1815, to Cornelius Sowle, Canton.

4. *Ibid.*, pp. 498–501, John Jacob Astor, N. Y., March 4, 1815, to Nicholas G. Ogden, Canton.

5. *Ibid.*, pp. 496–498, John Jacob Astor, N. Y., March 4, 1815, to Baring & Co., Canton.

6. *Ibid.*, pp. 425, 428, 473, 474, 483, John Jacob Astor, N. Y., January 7, 10, February 14, 17, 22, 1815, to William Waln.

7. Ms., Department of State, Washington, D. C., Miscellaneous Letters, January–March, 1815, John Jacob Astor, N. Y., February 20, 21, 1815, to James Monroe, Acting Secretary of State.

8. Ms. book, Baker Library, Astor Papers, Letter Book i, 1813–15, pp. 478, 508–509, John Jacob Astor, N. Y., February 20, March 11, 1815, to Andrew Daschkoff.

9. Ms. book, Whitehall, London, East India Office, East India Company Records, China Factory Records, Diaries, vol. 199, 1815–16, pp. 128–129, 130, 134.

10. *New-York Gazette and General Advertiser*, March 14, 1815, p. 2, col. 2; March 1, 1816, p. 2, col. 1; October 27, 1815, p. 2, col. 3.

11. Ms. book, Whitehall, London, East India Office, East India Company Records, China Factory Records, Diaries, vol. 199, 1815–16, pp. 128–129, 130, 134.

12. *Ibid.*

13. *New-York Gazette and General Advertiser*, January 19, 1816, p. 2, col. 2.

14. Ms. book, Baker Library, Astor Papers, Letter Book i, 1813–15, pp. 496–498, John Jacob Astor, N. Y., March 4, 1815, to Baring & Co., Canton; pp. 498–501, John Jacob Astor, N. Y., March 4, 1815, to Nicholas G. Ogden, Canton; p. 502, John Jacob Astor, N. Y., March 6, 1815, to George Ehninger, Canton.

15. *New-York Gazette and General Advertiser*, May 30, 1815, p. 2, col. 1.

16. Ms. book, Whitehall, London, East India Office, East India Company Records, China Factory Records, Diaries, vol. 199, 1815–16, pp. 129, 131, 134.

17. Ms., Girard College, Philadelphia, Girard Papers, 1815, nos. 591, 723, Arthur Garland, Canton, September 23, November 15, 1815, to Stephen Girard.

18. Ms. book, Whitehall, London, East India Office, East India Company Records, China Factory Records, Diaries, vol. 199, 1815–16, pp. 128–129, 130, 134.

19. *New-York Gazette and General Advertiser*, March 23, 1816, p. 2, col. 2; June 8, 1816, p. 2, col. 1; August 3, 1816, p. 2, col. 1.

20. *Ibid.*, June 29, 1815, p. 2, col. 4; July 11, 1815, p. 2, col. 3.

21. Adams, Henry, *The Life of Albert Gallatin* (1880), p. 555.

22. Gallatin, Count, ed., *A Great Peace Maker: The Diary of James Gallatin, Secretary to Albert Gallatin* (1914), pp. 80, 174, November 27, 1815, January 1, 1821. All sorts of stories were going about concerning the relations of Astor and Gallatin, probably largely inspired by Astor's offer of a partnership. George W. Erving, whom Astor's daughter and son-in-law had ousted from his bed on the *John Adams* in 1811, wrote to James Monroe on February 24, 1816, saying: "I suspect upon no light grounds that his [Gallatin's] connection with Mr Astor is about to be strengthened by a marriage of his son James with the youngest daughter of Astor." On March 18 Erving added: "it has been proposed to leave the son [James Gallatin] here in a counting house, I perceive that he does not like this; — & I doubt also whether he will easily be brought into the plan of marriage." (Ms., Library of Congress, Monroe Papers, vol. xv, Writings to Monroe, March 19, 1815–October 21, 1816, George W. Erving, N. Y., February 24, March 18, 1816, to James Monroe.) From what we know of James Gallatin, Erving judged his probable reactions to a clerkship in a counting-house or a marriage to Astor's fifteen-year-old daughter, Eliza, with almost inspired accuracy. Astor's wealth never seems to have made nearly so strong an impression upon James Gallatin as his Johnsonian conduct at meal-time. In November, 1820, while at Paris, James Gallatin set down these observations in his diary: "Really Mr. Astor is dreadful. Father has to be civil to him, as in 1812–13 he rendered great service to the Treasury. He came to *dejeuner* today; we were simply *en famille*, he sitting next to Frances [James Gallatin's sister]. He actually wiped his fingers on the sleeves of her fresh white spencer. Mamma in discreet tones said, 'Oh, Mr. Astor, I must apologize; they have forgotten to give you a serviette.' I think he felt foolish." (Gallatin, *op. cit.*, pp. 167–168.) It must be admitted that in this instance Astor seems to have suffered a relapse to the manners of days when he and Peter Smith sat about the camp fires of the Mohawks. It is rather hard to account for it otherwise, unless the incident has been incorrectly re-

ported, as Astor was no stranger to such company as that represented by the Montreal fur magnates.

23. Stevens, John Austin, *Albert Gallatin* (1911), p. 341. As late as March 19, 1816, Gallatin was forced, in a letter to a Mr. T. R. Gold, to state: "The information you have received that I was concerned with Mr. Astor in the importing business is altogether erroneous. I never have been, nor am I at present, either directly or indirectly, connected with that gentleman in any business whatever. I am not engaged and do not intend to engage in any commercial pursuits." (*Gallatin, Albert, The Writings of*, Henry Adams, ed., 3 vols. (1879), vol. i, p. 689.) This statement would seem to have been of a sufficiently sweeping character to put at rest all rumors of a partnership, present, past, or prospective, between Astor and Gallatin.

24. *New York Genealogical and Historical Record*, vol. vii (April, 1876), p. 93.

25. The arrival of a W. G. Astor at New York from Liverpool is mentioned as having taken place late in November, 1810 (*New-York Gazette and General Advertiser*, November 28, 1810, p. 3, col. 1). This may or may not be an error for W. *B*. Astor. On the other hand, it is possible that this item is an incorrect reference to George Astor, son of John Jacob Astor's brother, George Peter, who had come to New York some time before the War of 1812.

26. "William Backhouse Astor," *Appleton's Cyclopaedia of American Biography*.

27. Howe, Julia Ward, *Reminiscences, 1819–1899* (1899), pp. 73–76.

28. Ms. book, Baker Library, Astor Papers, Letter Book i, 1813–15, p. 102, John Jacob Astor, N. Y., November 11, 1813, to A. B. Bentzon; pp. 355–356, John Jacob Astor, N. Y., November 23, 1814, to John Dorr, Boston; p. 502, John Jacob Astor, N. Y., March 6, 1815, to George Ehninger, Canton.

29. Ms., New York Historical Society, Astor Papers, Letters of William B. Astor.

30. William B. Astor is said to have inherited from his father a proper consciousness of the value of money. The story is told that at one time John Jacob Astor "sent William to Europe to perfect himself in travel. He gave him permission to spend just as much money as he chose. He was absent a year. To a personal friend he expressed surprise that William should have spent so little. 'He spent only ten thousand dollars,' said the old man, 'I thought he would certainly spend fifty thousand dollars.'" (Smith, Matthew Hale, *Sunshine and Shadow in New York* (1868), p. 120.) This anecdote probably refers to William B. Astor's European trip of 1815–16. One of a speculative turn of mind might wonder what would have happened if William B. Astor had failed to show his knowledge of the value of money. Perhaps in that case he would have been permitted to

devote his life to literary and scholarly pursuits instead of taking over the management of his father's business. But it would be difficult to imagine a child of John Jacob Astor and Sarah Todd in the rôle of a spendthrift.

31. *New-York Gazette and General Advertiser*, July 11, 1815, p. 2, col. 3; January 25, 1816, p. 2, col. 2; March 30, 1816, p. 2, col. 3.

32. Morse, Hosea Ballou, *The Chronicles of the East India Company trading to China, 1635–1834*, 4 vols. (1926), vol. iii, p. 244.

33. *New-York Gazette and General Advertiser*, May 31, 1816, p. 2, col. 2.

34. "The Shipyard of America," *New York Herald*, December 31, 1852; ms. book, New York Custom House, New York Register, no. 162, May 30, 1816.

35. Ms. book, Baker Library, Astor Papers, Letter Book i, 1813–15, p. 470, John Jacob Astor, N. Y., February 13, 1815, to Megrath & Jones, Charleston, S. C.; *New-York Gazette and General Advertiser*, March 20, 1815, p. 2, col. 3; October 21, 1815, p. 2, col. 3.

36. *Ibid.*, October 1, 1816, p. 2, col. 2.

37. *Ibid.*, July 8, 1816, p. 2, col. 2. It is possible that one of the most popular of the many stories of Astor's occasional closeness was based upon an incident connected with this voyage. "On one occasion," the story goes, "a ship of his arrived from China, which he found necessary to dispatch at once to Amsterdam, the market in New-York being depressed by an over supply of China merchandise. But on board this ship, under a mountain of tea-chests, the owner had two pipes of precious Madeira wine, which had been sent on a voyage for the improvement of its constitution.

"'Can you get out that wine,' asked the owner, 'without discharging the tea?'

"The captain thought he could.

"'Well, then,' said Mr. Astor, 'you get it out, and I'll give you a demijohn of it. You'll say it's the best wine you ever tasted.'

"It required the labor of the whole ship's crew for two days to get out those two pipes of wine. They were sent to the house of Mr. Astor. A year passed. The captain had been to Amsterdam and back, but he had received no tidings of his demijohn of Madeira. One day, when Mr. Astor was on board the ship, the captain ventured to remind the great man, in a jocular manner, that he had not received the wine.

"'Ah!' said Astor, 'don't you know the reason? It isn't fine yet. Wait till it is fine, and you'll say you never tasted such Madeira.' The captain never heard of that wine again." It was, then, quite literally true that he "never tasted such Madeira." (Parton, James, *Life of John Jacob Astor* (1865), pp. 55–56.)

It is hard to tell what foundation there is for this story. The *Beaver* actually made such a voyage as is described, going to Amsterdam with teas after having returned to New York from a Canton voyage; so far as we know, she was the only Astor vessel to do this. It is also quite true that there were two pipes of Madeira wine sent from New York on the outward voyage of the *Beaver*, from which she returned only to go to Amsterdam. One of these, however, was for the benefit of Governor Baranoff. (Ms., Baker Library, Astor Papers, Letters, John Jacob Astor, N. Y., October 16, 1811, to Count Baranoff.) James Clark, who commanded the *Beaver* on the Amsterdam voyage, was later in Astor's employ for many years. This does not prove that the tale as narrated actually happened, but it indicates that something of the kind might conceivably have occurred, and this is much more than can be said of most traditions having to do with Astor.

38. *New-York Gazette and General Advertiser*, February 10, 1816, p. 2, col. 2; September 16, 1816, p. 2, col. 2; June 20, 1816, p. 2, col. 1; August 6, 1816, p. 2, col. 3.

39. Ms., Essex Institute, Salem, Massachusetts, American Trade at Canton, June 6, 1816–May 25, 1817.

40. Latourette, Kenneth Scott, "The History of Early Relations between the United States and China, 1784–1844," *Transactions of the Connecticut Academy of Arts and Sciences*, vol. 22 (1917–18), pp. 1–209, 72–73.

41. Ms., Girard College, Philadelphia, Girard Papers, 1817, no. 85, John Jacob Astor, N. Y., January 26, 1817, to Stephen Girard, Philadelphia; *ibid.*, Letter Book no. 15, letter 36 [Stephen Girard], Philadelphia, January 28, 1817, to John Jacob Astor, N. Y.

42. *New-York Gazette and General Advertiser*, January 27, 1817, p. 2, col. 3.

43. Ms., Library of Congress, New York Customs Records, John J. Astor, brig *Macedonian*, April 12, 1817.

44. Ms., Essex Institute, Salem, Massachusetts, American Trade at Canton, June 6, 1816–May 25, 1817.

45. *New-York Gazette and General Advertiser*, January 27, 1817, p. 2, col. 3; December 2, 1817, p. 2, col. 3; March 15, 1817, p. 2, col. 2; April 29, 1817, p. 2, col. 2; January 20, 1817, p. 1, col. 5; November 6, 1816, p. 2, col. 2.

46. Ms. book, Whitehall, London, East India Office, East India Company Records, China Factory Records, Diaries, vol. 210, 1817–18, p. 134.

47. *New-York Gazette and General Advertiser*, January 28, 1818, p. 2, col. 2; April 28, 1818, p. 2, col. 1.

48. *Ibid.*, August 26, 1818, p. 2, col. 3; August 31, 1818, p. 2, col. 6. On September 26, 1818, the *Boxer* was owned by G. G. & S. Howland and Peter Harmony (ms. book, New York Custom House, New York Register, no. 250, September 26, 1818). The brig *Boxer*, which arrived at New York on September 29, 1818, 76 days from Smyrna, with a cargo of "white wine, brandy, nuts, furs, &c. to Rhind & Turnbull, owners," and to vari-

ous other mercantile firms among whom were John Jacob Astor & Son, cannot, of course, be Astor's brig *Boxer*, offered for sale late in August of the same year (*New-York Gazette and General Advertiser*, September 30, 1818, p. 2, col. 2).

49. *Ibid.*, October 17, 1816, p. 2, col. 1.

50. Ms., Department of State, Washington, D. C., Consular Letters, Smyrna, vol. i, 1802–38, March 18, 1818. While at Smyrna, a serious mutiny took place on board the *Pedler*, which was only suppressed by the assistance of marines from a French frigate. Six members of the crew were involved, the alleged reason being insufficient food.

51. *New-York Gazette and General Advertiser*, March 11, 1818, p. 2, col. 3.

52. Ms., Library of Congress, New York Customs Records, Permission, ship *William and John*.

53. Ms., Baker Library, Astor Papers, Account of Shipments abroad, June 10, 1818.

54. *New-York Gazette and General Advertiser*, June 3, 1819, p. 2, col. 1.

55. *In the Superior Court of the City of New York, Transferred from the Supreme Court in Equity: Samuel G. Ogden, Administrator, Etc., of Nicholas G. Ogden, Deceased, vs. William B. Astor and William A. Astor and others, Executors, Etc., of John Jacob Astor, Deceased. Answer of the Complainant to the Petition of the Defendants for the Correction and Amendment of the Decree heretofore entered in this Cause* (1855), p. 11.

56. *Longworth's American Almanac, New-York Register, and City Directory* (1817–18).

57. *New-York Gazette and General Advertiser*, March 31, 1817, p. 3, col. 2.

58. Astor's brig *Macedonian* may have been sold to J. S. Ellery of Boston, since a brig of that name and ownership is mentioned as having been on the North West Coast in 1818, commanded by Captain Smith. It would be impossible, however, to state their identity as a fact unless their respective tonnages also coincided, and that of the Ellery brig is unknown. A Boston brig *Macedonian*, considerably smaller than Astor's vessel, later visited Canton at least once. The same list which mentions a brig *Macedonian* on the North West Coast also curiously speaks of a "Brig Savage, W. Coast Alex^a, Perry, N. W. Coast, J. J. Actor [*sic*]." "J. J. Actor" is evidently a form of "J. J. Astor," for this list also refers to the "Brig Sennica, New York, Clark, Canton, J. J. Actor." It is not clear what the compiler of this list meant by "W. Coast Alex^a" (apparently the port from which the vessel was supposed to hail), unless he was referring to Alexandria, Virginia, when "W. Coast" becomes inexplicable. This list also contains the "Ship William and John, New York, Brevert, Canton." The only brig Astor had in the Pacific in 1818 was the *Pedler*, and it may be that the name *Savage* was written in error for *Pedler*, possibly

through carelessness or a lapse of memory on the part of the British agent who framed this list. At any rate we have no other record of a brig or any other vessel named the *Savage* operating in the Pacific in 1818 under the command of Captain Perry and the ownership of Astor or "Actor," or under any other captaincy or ownership whatsoever. (*Parliamentary Papers*, vol. vii (1821), pp. 88–91. List of ships absent from the United States for Ports beyond the Cape of Good Hope. Secured by Robert Richards, from an American agent.)

59. Morison, Samuel Eliot, *The Maritime History of Massachusetts, 1783–1860* (1921), pp. 277–278.

60. Ms., Library of Congress, New York Customs Records, J. J. Astor, brig *Macedonian*, April 1, 1816.

61. Ms., Essex Institute, Salem, Massachusetts, American Trade at Canton, June 6, 1816–May 25, 1817.

62. Briggs, L. Vernon, *History and Genealogy of the Cabot Family, 1475–1927*, 2 vols. (1927), p. 561.

63. Morse, *op. cit.*, vol. iii, pp. 72–73, 339, 359.

64. About 1823 the American Fur Company sent more than $5,000 worth of furs to Marseilles and received returns in opium (ms., Baker Library, Astor Papers, Foreign Shipments and Consignments, American Fur Cº., Nº. 2). Late in April, 1826, John Jacob Astor & Son advertised three cases of Turkey opium (*New-York Gazette and General Advertiser*, April 29, 1826, p. 2, col. 7). Late in December, 1833, William B. Astor, writing for his father, announced to Frederick Bunker that he had just entered "some Opium received by the American Fur Company, and also a few cases received by myself from your House at Constantinople." In April of the next year he was giving instructions for its sale at $3.62½ per lb. (Ms. book, Baker Library, Astor Papers, Letter Book ii, 1831–38, p. 118, William B. Astor for John Jacob Astor, N. Y., December 27, 1832, to Frederick Bunker, Mansion House; pp. 142, 144, William B. Astor, N. Y., April 2, 5, 1833, to George W. Sumner.) Although it is obvious from the above that, up to its latest connection with the China trade, the Astor firm was trafficking in opium at New York, we have no evidence that the Astors were simultaneously engaged in sending the drug to China, though it would not be surprising to learn that they were.

65. Ms. book, Baker Library, Astor Papers, Letter Book i, 1813–15, pp. 493–494, John Jacob Astor, N. Y., March 3, 1815, to Daniel Stansbury, Canton.

66. Barnard, Charles H., *A Voyage round the World during the Years 1812 . . . 1816* (1829), p. 253.

67. Ms., Baker Library, Astor Papers, Canton Copartnership Concern, Account No. 1, Interest to 31ˢᵗ Decʳ 1818.

68. *Samuel G. Ogden vs. William B. Astor et al.*, p. 4.

69. Ms. book, Whitehall, London, East India Office, East India Company Records, China Factory Records, Diaries, vol. 215, 1818–19, p. 103.

70. *New-York Gazette and General Advertiser*, February 12, 1819, p. 2, col. 3.

71. Ms. book, Whitehall, London, East India Office, East India Company Records, China Factory Records, Diaries, vol. 215, 1818–19, p. 103.

72. *New-York Gazette and General Advertiser*, March 30, 1819, p. 2, col. 2; July 26, 1819, p. 2, col. 3.

73. Ms. book, Whitehall, London, East India Office, East India Company Records, China Factory Records, Diaries, vol. 215, 1818–19, p. 103.

74. *New-York Gazette and General Advertiser*, July 23, 1819, p. 2, col. 2.

75. Ms., Department of State, Washington, D. C., Consular Letters, Amsterdam, 1818–19; ms., The Hague, Royal Archives, Dutch East India Company and Colonial Records (Oost Indien Archiv); *Parliamentary Papers*, vol. vii (1821), pp. 38, 409.

76. *New-York Gazette and General Advertiser*, April 17, 1820, p. 2, col. 4.

77. Ms., Department of State, Washington, D. C., Consular Letters, Amsterdam, 1819–20; ms., The Hague, Royal Archives, Dutch East India Company and Colonial Records (Oost Indien Archiv).

78. A document which records foreign exportations out of various China cargoes brought to New York confirms this impression. No exportations from the cargo secured at China on the *William and John's* third voyage are mentioned as having taken place from New York. (Ms., Baker Library, Astor Papers, Canton Copartnership Concern.) Moreover, John Jacob Astor & Son on September 23, 1819, insured "five thousand dollars on Ship William and John, and fifteen thousand dollars on effects on board at & from Amsterdam to Canton & at & from thence to her port of discharge in Europe or the United States: with liberty to stop at Gibraltar on the homeward voyage for orders or to discharge in whole or in part; and at the usual places for refreshments." In this document the master's name was given as Bunker and the vessel valued at $20,000. The premium was 4 per cent. (Ms. book, Massachusetts Historical Society, Boston, Boston Marine Insurance Company Records, vol. &, no. 5929, September 23, 1819.)

79. Ms. book, New York Custom House, New York Register, March 22–August 28, 1819, no. 122, May 19, 1819.

80. *New-York Gazette and General Advertiser*, March 15, 1820, p. 2, col. 3; July 1, 1820, p. 1, col. 7; May 8, 1820, p. 2, col. 3. John Jacob Astor & Son on October 13, 1819, also made insurance of $20,000 "on property on board Ship Acasta at & from New York to Canton & at & from thence to her port of discharge in Europe or the United States: with liberty to stop at Gibraltar on the homeward voyage, for orders or to discharge in whole or in part, & at the usual places for refreshments. Acasta saild from Sandy Hook 13 Octo 1819." Her master was named Keene, the

premium was 4 per cent. (Ms. book, Massachusetts Historical Society, Boston, Boston Marine Insurance Company Records, vol. &, no. 5936, October 13, 1819.) The ship had returned to the United States within a year. She seems to have belonged to John Whetten. (*New-York Gazette and General Advertiser*, January 13, 1821, p. 2, col. 3.) Although the insurance was made by John Jacob Astor & Son, it seems probable that the goods insured were furs belonging to the American Fur Company; at least furs belonging to the Company were so shipped on the *Acasta*. (Ms., Baker Library, Astor Papers, Foreign Shipments and Consignments, American Fur C°. N° 1.) Furs belonging to the Company were frequently shipped abroad on vessels belonging to John Jacob Astor & Son, though usually as freight on vessels not owned by that firm.

The goods which came to John Jacob Astor & Son on the *Seneca* had been insured on February 18, 1820, for $20,000 from Canton to New York at a premium of 2¼ per cent (ms. book, Massachusetts Historical Society, Boston, Boston Marine Insurance Company Records, vol. &, no. 6026, February 18, 1820).

81. Ms. book, Whitehall, London, East India Office, East India Company Records, China Factory Records, Diaries, vol. 218, p. 108.

82. *New-York Gazette and General Advertiser*, September 18, 1820, p. 2, col. 3.

83. *Ibid.*, April 17, 1820, p. 2, col. 4.

84. Ms. book, Whitehall, London, East India Office, East India Company Records, China Factory Records, Diaries, vol. 222, 1820–21, pp. 149, 151.

85. *New-York Gazette and General Advertiser*, September 30, 1818, p. 2, col. 2; October 14, 1818, p. 2, col. 3; October 30, 1818, p. 4, col. 1; November 9, 1818, p. 3, col. 3; July 15, 1819, p. 2, col. 3; November 24, 1819, p. 2, col. 3; December 22, 1819, p. 2, col. 2.

86. *Ibid.*, November 29, 1820, p. 2, col. 3.

87. Morrison, John H., *History of New York Ship Yards* (1909), p. 47.

88. *New-York Gazette and General Advertiser*, November 20, 1820, p. 2, col. 3. The vessel and cargo were insured for $25,000, seven-eighths on the cargo, one-eighth on the vessel, at a premium of 4 per cent (ms. book, Massachusetts Historical Society, Boston, Boston Marine Insurance Company Records, vol. Aa, no. 6259).

89. *New-York Gazette and General Advertiser*, February 26, 1820, p. 1, col. 3; May 7, 1821, p. 2, col. 2; May 30, 1821, p. 1, col. 2. The *Ariadne* may have gone to Gibraltar, and possibly to other Mediterranean ports, in the course of this voyage. At least on March 30, 1821, $25,000 was insured "on property on board Schooner Ariadne, at & from New York to her port or ports of advice & discharge in the Mediterranean including Gibraltar." The premium was 1¼ per cent. (Ms. book, Massachusetts Historical Society, Boston, Boston Marine Insurance Company Records,

vol. &, no. 6078, March 30, 1820.) Part and perhaps all of the *Ariadne's* cargo consigned to Hamburg consisted of furs belonging to the American Fur Company, invoiced at $73,743.10 (ms., Baker Library, Astor Papers, Foreign Shipments and Consignments, American Fur C°. N° 1).

90. Ms. book, Whitehall, London, East India Office, East India Company Records, China Factory Records, Diaries, vol. 222, 1820–21, p. 151, 1821–22, p. 185; *New-York Gazette and General Advertiser*, May 28, 1821, p. 2, col. 3.

91. *Ibid.*, January 3, 1821, p. 2, col. 4; January 9, 1821, p. 2, col. 5; April 7, 1821, p. 3, col. 4; April 10, 1821, p. 2, col. 2; April 30, 1821, p. 2, col. 4; May 16, 1821, p. 2, col. 3. One of these items is of special interest in that it mentions the receipt by the Astor firm of Italian silks. Hitherto that fabric had been supplied to Astor entirely from China.

92. Ms. book, Whitehall, London, East India Office, East India Company Records, China Factory Records, Diaries, 1821–22, p. 185; ms. book, Essex Institute, Salem, Massachusetts, Log of the Schooner *Eagle*, March 8, 1822, "spoke the ship . . . Enterprise . . . bound home."

93. *New-York Gazette and General Advertiser*, December 5, 1821, p. 2, col. 3; January 7, 1822, p. 2, col. 4; August 13, 1822, p. 2, col. 2.

94. Ms. book, Whitehall, London, East India Office, East India Company Records, China Factory Records, Diaries, vol. 228, 1822–23, p. 167; ms. book, Essex Institute, Salem, Massachusetts, Log of the Schooner *Eagle*, at Whampoa, May 28, 1820, "Arrived Ship . . . Henry Astor." It seems likely that this vessel did not have much quicksilver, as only one vessel bringing this commodity to consignees, who included the Astor firm, had, so far as we know, arrived at New York in the latter part of 1821 (*New-York Gazette and General Advertiser*, June 22, 1821, p. 2, col. 2). The cargo, however, undoubtedly included some of the American Fur Company's furs, invoiced at over $20,000 (ms., Baker Library, Astor Papers, Foreign Shipments and Consignments, American Fur Company, N° 1).

95. Ms., Library of Congress, New York Customs Records, Henry Astor, 2^d Voyage, 1823–24.

96. *New-York Gazette and General Advertiser*, August 13, 1822, p. 2, col. 2; August 20, 1822, p. 2, col. 3; October 21, 1822, p. 2, col. 4; August 12, 1822, p. 2, col. 3; September 28, 1822, p. 2, col. 2; October 4, 1822, p. 2, col. 3. We know that part of the *William and John's* cargo on this voyage consisted of furs belonging to the company of which John Jacob Astor was the head (ms., Baker Library, Astor Papers, Foreign Shipments and Consignments, American Fur Company N° 2).

97. *Ibid.*, March 28, 1823, p. 3, col. 2; April 7, 1823, p. 2, col. 5; August 18, 1823, p. 2, col. 4; December 8, 1823, p. 2, col. 2.

98. Ms. book, Whitehall, London, East India Office, East India Company Records, China Factory Records, Diaries, vol. 230, 1823–24.

99. Ms., Department of State, Washington, D. C., Consular Letters, Canton, March 28, 1792–April 20, 1834, Richard R. Thompson, Consul, to John Quincy Adams, Secretary of State. The death of Astor's Canton agent has been the inspiration of a flock of legends, none of which can be literally true, although some of them may possess some actual basis in fact. One of these states that a certain captain, who had formerly been in Astor's employ, "had the opportunity of rendering the great merchant a most signal service. The agent of Mr. Astor in China suddenly died at a time when the property in his charge amounted to about seven hundred thousand dollars. Our captain, who was not then in Astor's employ, was perfectly aware that if this immense property fell into official hands, as the law required [*sic*], not one dollar of it would ever again find its way to the coffers of its proprieter [*sic*]. By a series of bold, prompt, and skillful measures, he rescued it from the official maw, and made it yield a profit to the owner. Mr. Astor acknowledged the service. He acknowledged it with emphasis and a great show of gratitude. He said many times:

"'If you had not done just as you did, I should never have seen one dollar of my money: no, not one dollar of it.'

"But he not only did not compensate him for his services, but he did not even reimburse the small sum of money which the captain had expended in performing those services. Astor was then worth ten millions, and the captain had his hundred dollars a month and a family of young children."

The author who tells this story adds later on that after John Jacob Astor's death his son, William B. Astor, "had the justice to send a considerable sum to the brave old captain who saved for Mr. Astor the large property in China imperiled by the sudden death of an agent." (Parton, *op. cit.*, pp. 54–55, 83.) Now this tale as given cannot be true. There is no authority for the statement that the death of an agent in China would legally result in the property under his care falling into "official hands" (presumably referring to Chinese officials), and thus almost inevitably becoming a total loss to its owners. It is, however, true that the death of an agent might cause considerable difficulty to his firm's next ship arriving in China after his death, especially if the captain were not experienced in the trade. Rossiter, the *Henry Astor's* captain, was new to the firm's service and possibly to the trade. Assistance from some captain experienced in business at Canton would doubtless be welcomed by him. It is possible, then, that the story we have recorded is merely an expansion of some event which actually did take place. Some former Astor captain, present at Canton late in 1823, may actually have assisted Rossiter in the difficulties caused by Ogden's death, and not received from Astor the financial recognition to which he felt himself entitled. Was there such a captain at Canton? The captain who is said to have performed this service was, we are told, styled by Astor his "king of captains." The man usually mentioned as bearing this title was Captain Cowman, but it is possible that Astor at various times conferred the distinction on different captains. Astor had a very high regard, as we have already seen, for F. A. De Peyster. The *Beaver*, formerly owned by Astor, and usually at that time commanded by De Peyster, was at Canton at the time of Ogden's death. It is therefore at least a possibility that De Peyster did some service to Rossiter and was not rewarded in the manner which he felt he deserved. Moreover, De Peyster was still alive at the time the tale was committed to print. ([Scoville, Joseph A.], *The Old Merchants of New York City*, 5 vols. (1889), vol. i, pp. 210–213.) However, the story as usually told is utterly impossible.

Another tale of a similar nature deals with this same captain. "He [Astor]," records the early biographer whom we have previously quoted, "once lost seventy thousand dollars by committing a piece of petty injustice toward his best captain. This gallant sailor, being notified by an insurance office of the necessity of having a chronometer on board his ship, spoke to Mr. Astor on the subject, who advised the captain to buy one.

"'But,' said the captain, 'I have no five hundred dollars to spare for such a purpose; the chronometer should belong to the ship.'

"'Well,' said the merchant, 'you need not pay for it now; pay for it at your convenience.'

"The captain still objecting, Astor, after a prolonged higgling, authorized him to buy a chronometer, and charge it to the ship's account; which was done. Sailing day was at hand. The ship was hauled into the stream. The captain, as is the custom, handed in his account. Astor, subjecting it to his usual close scrutiny, observed the novel item of five hundred dollars for the chronometer. He objected, averring that it was understood between them that the captain was to pay for the instrument. The worthy sailor recalled the conversation, and firmly held to his recollection of it. Astor insisting on his own view of the matter, the captain was so profoundly disgusted that, important as the command of the ship was to him, he resigned his post. Another captain was soon found, and the ship sailed for China. Another house, which was then engaged in the China trade, knowing the worth of this 'king of captains,' as Astor himself used to style him, bought him a ship and dispatched him to Canton two months after the departure of Astor's vessel. Our captain, put upon his mettle, employed all his skill to accelerate the speed of his ship, and had such success, that he reached New-York with a full cargo of tea just seven days after the arrival of Mr. Astor's ship. Astor, not expecting another ship for months, and therefore sure of monopolizing the market, had not yet broken bulk, nor even taken off the hatchways. Our captain arrived on a Saturday. Advertisements and hand-bills were immediately issued, and on the Wednesday morning following, as the custom then was, the auction sale of the tea began on the wharf — two barrels of punch contributing to the *éclât* and hilarity of the occasion. The cargo was sold to good advantage, and the market was glutted, Astor lost in consequence the entire profits of the voyage, not less than the sum named above. Meeting the captain some time after in Broadway, he said,

"'I had better have paid for that chronometer of yours.'

"Without ever acknowledging that he had been in the wrong, he was glad enough to engage the captain's future services."

Perhaps the best comment upon this story is the sentence with which the author concludes: "This anecdote we received from the worthy captain's own lips." (Parton, *op. cit.*, pp. 52–54.)

Even were this tale entirely authentic, the statement must be made in justice to Astor that his refusal to buy the chronometer was not necessarily such a piece of stinginess as it would on first sight appear, though of course he should not have gone back on his promise if he at any time agreed to pay for the instrument. In 1823 the great Boston firm of Bryant & Sturgis reprimanded one of their East India shipmasters for purchasing a chronometer for $250, and informed him that he must pay for it himself. "Could we have anticipated that our injunctions respecting economy would have been so totally disregarded," they wrote, "we would have sett fire to the Ship rather than have sent her to sea." (Morison, *op. cit.*, p. 116.) But it is impossible to prove either the truth or falsity of this tale without exhaustive research, which it is hardly worth while to undertake. If F. A. De Peyster is the "king of captains" referred to in this story, it is true that he was the captain of the Astor ship *William and John*, which arrived at New York from Canton on March 28, 1817, that the *William and John* cleared for Canton under the command of Curtiss Blakeman exactly a month later, that in that year De Peyster left the Astor employ and took charge of the ship *Ontario*, owned by Thomas H. Smith & Son, which cleared for Canton on July 10, 1817, or a little over two months after the sailing of the *William and John*, and that the *Ontario* returned to New York on May 4, 1818, *exactly a week* after the *William and John's* arrival. It is also a matter of record that later — not, however, till about ten years had passed — De Peyster re-entered Astor's service. (*New-York Gazette and General Advertiser*, March 29, 1817, p. 2, cols. 1 and 2; April 29, 1817, p. 2, col. 2; July 11, 1817, p. 2, col. 5; April 28, 1818, p. 2, col. 1; May 5, 1818, p. 2, col. 1; April 16, 1827, p. 2, col. 4.) These points of similarity between the traditional "chronometer-voyage" and one actually made by probably the best of Astor's China captains seem to constitute something more than a series of mere coincidences. Of course, however, they prove nothing definitely. The importance of the chronometer story lies in the fact that its details are not inherently impossible and that it reveals the sort of tales which were narrated — and believed — about Astor by his contemporaries.

But to return to the legends arising out of the death of Astor's agent

Nicholas G. Ogden. A contemporary records this tradition. "Mr. Samuel G. Ogden," he says, ". . . had a brother who was a leading merchant in Canton, China, and very extensively mixed up in business transactions with the late John Jacob Astor. He had been sent out to China by Mr. Astor, and was a partner in business with him. He had been abroad many years, and had acquired, as every one supposed, a very large fortune. His letters to his brother Sam, and other relatives, had conveyed that idea, and it was probably so. At any rate the Canton Ogden had determined to retire from business, and go to New York. He embarked at Whampoa on board of one of the ships belonging to John Jacob Astor, that was bound to New York. He had with him in the ship all his books and papers. On the passage he died. All his papers went into the possession of Mr. Astor. His relatives applied to Mr. Astor for a settlement, but they could get no satisfaction. I believe that Samuel G. Ogden bought up all the claims of other relatives, and then commenced a suit against John Jacob Astor. This suit lasted many years, and was going on when Mr. Astor died. After that event, Mr. W. B. Astor took the matter in his own hand, and made an offer for a settlement. I believe the amount was over $200,000." (Scoville, *op. cit.*, vol. ii, pp. 214–215.) Scoville, though he usually manifests toward John Jacob Astor a manner almost reverential, and in token of his esteem dedicates the fourth volume of his work to Astor's memory, still does not seem to have called in question the authenticity of this story, that Astor pilfered the papers of his dead agent in order to defraud the man's heirs, or to have found in the alleged action anything necessarily inconsistent with his character. As a matter of fact, however, this tale as told is undoubtedly false. We know from the letter of the United States consul at Canton (the reference to which is given at the head of this note) that Ogden did not die aboard an Astor ship, and that his papers were not left in the hands of Astor's agents, but were on the contrary taken charge of according to law by the consul. The suit against John Jacob Astor, arising out of his partnership with Ogden, arose from other circumstances than the agent's mythical death on an Astor vessel. It will be remembered that according to an agreement of March 2, 1819, Ogden's one-fifth share of the profits of the concern was to be computed on the basis of the market price of the goods in New York, and that shipments to other ports in the United States or to ports outside the United States were to be for the profit or loss of John Jacob Astor & Son. These shipments seem to have usually turned out unfavorably, and it was alleged by Samuel Ogden, in a suit entered in January, 1842, that, where a loss occurred through a foreign shipment, the Astor firm had finally credited Ogden with the amount for which the goods were sold and not for the value of the goods at the New York market price. John Jacob Astor's executors, who carried on the defence in the suit after his death, replied that all goods shipped had been on the account of both Ogden and the Astors, and that the agreement of 1819 had never gone into effect. The decision of the court was in favor of Ogden. (*Samuel Ogden vs. William B. Astor et al.*, p. 11.) However, see below, vol. ii, pp. 1252-1255.

100. Ms. book, Whitehall, London, East India Office, East India Company Records, China Factory Records, Diaries, vol. 230, 1823–24.

101. *New-York Gazette and General Advertiser*, March 24, 1824, p. 2, col. 3; April 24, 1824, p. 2, col. 3; April 14, 1823, p. 2, col. 2; April 16, 1823, p. 2, col. 3; June 14, 1823, p. 2, col. 5; September 1, 1823, p. 2, col. 5; November 19, 1823, p. 2, col. 4; March 25, 1824, p. 2, col. 2.

102. Ms., Baker Library, Astor Papers, Foreign Shipments and Consignments, American Fur Company N° 2.

103. *New-York Gazette and General Advertiser*, February 10, 1823, p. 2, col. 4; July 14, 1823, p. 2, col. 3.

104. Ms., Library of Congress, New York Customs Records, Exam^d. *Enterprise* 3^d Voyage, 1822–23, *Henry Astor* 2^d Voyage, 1823–24.

105. Ms., Baker Library, Astor Papers, Foreign Shipments and Consignments, American Fur Company N° 2.

106. *New-York Gazette and General Advertiser*, September 10, 1823, p. 3, col. 2; January 9, 1824, p. 1, col. 3. The *Pedler* made a voyage for her new owners to Gibraltar in 1823, leaving New York under the command of Phineas Stuart on October 15 (ms. book, New Haven Colony Historical Society, Captain James W. Goodrich Collection, Log of the *Pedler*, October 15, 1823–January 12, 1824). The *William and John* was registered under the ownership of James Magee on February 27, 1824 (ms. book, New York Custom House, New York Register, no. 69, February 27, 1824).

107. Ms. book, Whitehall, London, East India Office, East India Company Records, China Factory Records, Diaries, vol. 232, 1824–25, p. 159.

108. *New-York Gazette and General Advertiser*, March 11, 1825, p. 2, col. 1; April 29, 1825, p. 1, col. 2; July 1, 1825, p. 2, col. 3; December 20, 1825, p. 2, col. 2. On June 30, 1825, Peter Destebecho, Jr., was described as both master and owner of the *Henry Astor* (ms. book, New York Custom House, New York Register, no. 232, June 30, 1825).

109. Scoville, *op. cit.*, vol. i, pp. 31–33, 87–89. Scoville went on to say that soon after this Thomas H. Smith also "failed, owing the Government the sum of three millions of dollars. . . . This failure upset the tea business for five years, and ruined nearly every person engaged in it. It did not affect John Jacob Astor, for his tea business was a sort of secondary affair to his great Northwest fur business. His ships traded on the Pacific coast for furs and skins, and then went to China, were [*sic*] the fur cargoes were exchanged for teas, and these were brought to New York. Astor probably made by the voyages of his ships four times as much as the regular tea merchants even in the most prosperous days of the tea trade." (Scoville, *op. cit.*, vol. i, pp. 90–91.) It is probably true that one

reason for Astor's great success in the China trade was that it was carried on in connection with the North West Coast fur trade and other forms of commerce characteristic of the Pacific. However, it is an error to regard his China trade as "secondary" to the North West Coast fur trade, which was indeed a part of, and dependent upon, the commerce with Canton. Neither was the fact that Astor did not fail in company with Smith altogether due, as would seem to be implied, to the circumstance of his being simultaneously engaged in the Pacific trade. Even aside from Astor's unusually large capital, he had been too shrewd to overexpand his trade in teas, and had, indeed, practically withdrawn from trade with China in his own vessels before the failure of Thompson and Smith unsettled the tea market.

110. Briggs, *op. cit.*, p. 575.

111. Ms., Baker Library, Astor Papers, Statement of Shipments made by American Fur Company Concern of 1823.

112. *New-York Gazette and General Advertiser*, July 19, 1824, p. 2, col. 3; October 21, 1824, p. 2, col. 3; November 2, 1824, p. 1, col. 6; November 26, 1824; December 2, 1824, p. 2, col. 2; January 1, 1825, p. 2, col. 7; November 7, 1825, p. 2, col. 5; December 24, 1825, p. 2, col. 3; January 11, 1826, p. 2, col. 4; April 15, 1826, p. 2, col. 3; April 29, 1826, p. 2, col. 7; August 29, 1826, p. 2, col. 4; February 27, 1827, p. 1, col. 7.

113. Ms. book, Massachusetts Historical Society, Boston, Boston Marine Insurance Company Records, vol. Gg, no. 7674.

114. *New-York Gazette and General Advertiser*, April 16, 1827, p. 2, col. 4; March 26, 1828, p. 2, col. 3.

115. Ms. book, Widener Library, Harvard University, Bryant and Sturgis Papers, Letter Book, September 17, 1818–March 20, 1829, Bryant & Sturgis, Boston, January 24, 1829, to John Jacob Astor.

116. Ms. book (copy), Detroit Public Library, Burton Historical Collection, Letters of Ramsay Crooks, John Jacob Astor, and the American Fur Company, 1813–43, John Jacob Astor, N. Y., September 29, 1827, to Ramsay Crooks, St. Louis.

117. Ms., Baker Library, Astor Papers, Letters, John Jacob Astor, N. Y., April 1, 1831, to D. W. C. Olyphant; D. W. C. Olyphant, N. Y., April 1, 1831, to John Jacob Astor; John Jacob Astor, N. Y., April 8, 1831, to Mr. Olyphant (see below, vol. ii, pp. 1209–1210); John Jacob Astor, N.Y., April 9, 1831, to F. & N. G. Carnes; F. & N. G. Carnes, N. Y., April 9, 1831, June 5, 1832, to John Jacob Astor; *ibid.*, Letter Book ii, 1831–38, p. 3, John Jacob Astor, N. Y., October 8, 1831, to Charles N. Talbot, Canton; p. 4, John Jacob Astor, N. Y., October 28, 1831, to J. P. Sturgis & Co., Canton; p. 46, John Jacob Astor, N. Y., April 19, 1832, to J. P. Sturgis & Co., Canton; p. 47, John Jacob Astor, N. Y., April 19, 1832, to Charles N. Talbot, Canton; p. 55, John Jacob Astor, N. Y., May 25, 1832, to Charles N. Talbot, Canton; pp. 57–58, John Jacob Astor, N. Y., June 8, 1832, to

Charles N. Talbot, Canton; pp. 60–61, John Jacob Astor, N. Y., June 13, 1832, to Charles N. Talbot, Canton; p. 62, John Jacob Astor, N. Y., June 15, 1832, to Charles N. Talbot, Canton; p. 102, William B. Astor for John Jacob Astor, N. Y., October 20, 1832, to Olyphant & Co., Canton; pp. 100–101, William B. Astor for John Jacob Astor, October 23, 1832, to J. P. Sturgis & Co., Canton; p. 117, John Jacob Astor, Paris, November 9, 1832, to Charles N. Talbot, N. Y.; p. 117, John Jacob Astor, Paris, November 9, 1832, to J. P. Sturgis & Co., Canton; p. 153, William B. Astor for John Jacob Astor, N. Y., May 3, 1833, to Olyphant & Co., Canton (see below, vol. ii, p. 1223); p. 178, William B. Astor for John Jacob Astor, N. Y., September 10, 1833, to J. P. Sturgis & Co., Canton; p. 177, William B. Astor for John Jacob Astor, N. Y., September 11, 1833, to Talbot, Olyphant & Co., Canton; pp. 193–194, William B. Astor for John Jacob Astor, N. Y., December 2, 1833, to J. P. Sturgis & Co., Canton; p. 192, William B. Astor for John Jacob Astor, N. Y., November 25, 1833, to Bryant & Sturgis, Boston; p. 248, William B. Astor for John Jacob Astor, N. Y., July 16, 1834, to Olyphant & Co., Canton; p. 318, John Jacob Astor, Hell Gate, July 30, 1835, to Talbot, Olyphant & Co., Canton; ms. book, Massachusetts Historical Society, Boston, Boston Marine Insurance Company Records, no. 8526, April 27, 1831.

118. Ms., Baker Library, Astor Papers, Agreement with Bryant & Sturgis for Young Hyson Tea pr Sultan; *ibid.*, Letter Book ii, 1831–38, pp. 1, 57, John Jacob Astor, N. Y., September 30, 1831, June 8, 1832, to Welles & Greene, Havre; pp. 115, 130, William B. Astor, N. Y., December 15, 1832, February 7, 1833, to Welles & Greene, Havre; pp. 8–9, John Jacob Astor, N. Y., November 11, 1831, to Ellmaker, Philadelphia; p. 15, John Jacob Astor, N. Y., December 7, 1831, to A. & G. Ralston, Philadelphia; pp. 104, 265, John Jacob Astor per William B. Astor, N. Y., November 3, 1832, November 13, 1834, to A. & G. Ralston, Philadelphia; p. 19, John Jacob Astor, N. Y., January 4, 1832, to Benjamin French, Boston; pp. 108, 173, John Jacob Astor per William B. Astor, N. Y., November 27, 1832, August 11, 1833, to Haggerty, Austen & Co.; p. 112, William B. Astor for John Jacob Astor, N. Y., December 6, 1832, to Olyphant & Co., Canton; p. 109, John Jacob Astor per William B. Astor, N. Y., November 30, 1832, to Bulaid & Caswell; p. 142, William B. Astor, N. Y., April 1, 1833, to Joshua Moses; pp. 144, 243, William B. Astor for John Jacob Astor, N. Y., April 5, 1833, July 1, 1834, to Josiah Dow; p. 207, William B. Astor, N. Y., February 1, 1834, to L. M. Hoffman & Co., pp. 134, 168, William B. Astor, N. Y., March 5, July 22, 1833, to Hoffman & Sons.

119. *Hone, Philip, The Diary of, 1828–1851*, Allan Nevins, ed., 2 vols. (1927), vol. ii, pp. 847–848, vol. i, pp. viii–ix.

120. Ms., Massachusetts Historical Society, Boston, Perkins MSS., Thomas G. Cary, N. Y., November 2, 1831, to Samuel Cabot.

CHAPTER XIII

THE CHINA TRADE AND THE PACIFIC
1814–1828

In the previous chapter we considered the trade between New York and Canton, especially as it included various ports in Europe.[1] This trade was simultaneously being conducted in connection with an almost equal number of ports in the Pacific Ocean, and the details of this type of commerce are perhaps even more interesting than are those which relate to that side of the China trade more closely connected with Europe. The first Astor vessel to be engaged in the Pacific trade was the *Enterprise*, commanded by John Ebbets, which left New York in November, 1809, for the North West Coast and did not return to New York until the summer of 1812, just after the declaration of war. In the interval she had made two voyages from the Russian settlement of New Archangel at Sitka, on Norfolk Sound, to Canton, each time with a cargo of peltries to be exchanged for Chinese goods, with the last returns of which she sailed for New York. In the succeeding years, the trade in furs between the North West Coast and Canton, for which the ill-fated settlement of Astoria was to have been the headquarters, suffered a series of reverses. The first vessel to be sent out was the *Tonquin*, which left New York in 1810, and was blown up after an Indian massacre. The last vessel, the *Lark*, which cleared from her home port in the spring of 1813, was wrecked off the Hawaiian Islands. Only the second vessel, the *Beaver*, which sailed in the fall of 1811, got safely to the North West Coast and from thence with a cargo to Canton, where she was blockaded for the term of the war.

The failure of Astoria did not cause Astor to lose the interest which he had felt in that region since 1809, when he had first dispatched a ship to it. He concluded from the example of others that it was altogether possible to ply the fur trade of the North West Coast without the advantage of a post on the Columbia. One of Astor's characteristics was his ability to snatch a certain amount of profit even from the jaws of an apparently calamitous failure. A conspicuous illustration of this is to be found in the fact that his interest in another exceedingly important side of the Pacific trade — the sandalwood trade of the Hawaiian Islands [2] — seems to have been a product of his unsuccessful Astoria enterprise. As far as we can discover, Astor's first definite connection with the sandalwood trade was through the captain of one of the vessels employed in the Astoria venture. This vessel, whose part has been quite overlooked by chroniclers of that important chapter in the history of the North West Coast, was the brig *Forester*, fitted out in London early in 1813. She sailed under British colors to supply the colony at Astoria[3] and arrived at the Hawaiian Islands in November, 1813, under the command of John Jennings.[4] Here William J. Pigot, formerly the supercargo, became captain as one of the results of an attempted mutiny, and under his command the vessel sailed for the Russian settlement at Bodega on the coast of California. She also touched at various other points along the coast, at all of which places her captain carried on trade. Pigot had learned some time before that Astoria had been sold out to the North West Company [5] about the time he had arrived at the Islands,[6] and that the British had taken possession of the fort on December 13, 1813;[7] consequently he knew it would be of no avail to go to the Columbia River, which had been the original objective of the voyage.

Having wintered in the Gulf of California, Pigot started northward with his vessel in March, 1814,[8] and the next month was at New Archangel in Russian America, where he met Astor's agent, Wilson Price Hunt, in the *Pedler*. There Pigot received the news that the true nationality of his vessel had unfortunately become known at the Hawaiian Islands. He was thus forced to give up certain plans he had formed for trading to China, including one of purchasing a cargo of sandalwood from the king of Hawaii, since he could hardly hope to run the British blockade at Canton. From Sitka he returned to California, where he wintered again, starting north in April, 1815, and arriving at Norfolk Sound once more in June.

Here Captain Pigot conceived the idea of disposing of the cargo at Okhotsk and sending the brig herself to the Hawaiian Islands under the command of her former clerk, Richard Ebbets,[9] possibly a brother of John Ebbets (Astor's first North West Coast captain), accompanied by the sailing master, Alexander Adams. Leaving Norfolk Sound on the last day of July, 1815, the *Forester* sailed for Okhotsk, but was forced to put in to Kamchatka. On November 4, 1815, Pigot sent Ebbets in the *Forester* with a small cargo for California and the Hawaiian Islands, where it was hoped the brig might be sold for sandalwood. Pigot himself stayed behind for the winter with the seal skins for which most of his original cargo had been traded.[10] The *Forester*, accordingly, traded in California during December [11] and returned to Hawaii in January, 1816, where, in April, King Kamehameha conceived a strong passion for the brig and purchased it [12] for a price which has been stated as $9,000 and 8,000 "sticks" of sandalwood.[13] This description is, of course, quite indefinite, and the price is really unknown, though, because of the King's anxiety to purchase the vessel, it was probably a large one. It was undoubtedly paid mainly or entirely in sandalwood, and we shall later see how this wood was conveyed to market.

It proved that Pigot had been happier in his decision to send the *Forester* to the Hawaiian Islands for sale than in his plan of remaining behind at Kamchatka with the seal skins. Soon after Ebbets' departure a "M^r. Eudin, agent for the Russian American Company," offered to buy the seal skins, 61,140 in number, "for 900.000 roubles (assignats), payable as follows. 200,000 roubles, three months after sight. the remainder Eighteen months after date." A historian of the Russian company gives this account of the transaction. "By some means Pigot succeeded in selling his furs to the Kamtchatka Commissioner of the Company at the rate of 15 roubles per skin (having purchased them at Novo-Arkhangelsk at 2r. 50k.), amounting to 61,000 roubles. The General Administration justly objected to paying 35,000 roubles for carrying the furs to Kamtchatka and then to be compelled to ship them to Okhotsk in one of their own vessels."[14] Pigot seems either to have overreached himself or to have allowed himself to be maneuvered into a difficult position by the wily Eudin. The Russian American Fur Company not only refused to honor the bills which Eudin had drawn on it in favor of Pigot, but, utilizing an obscure ukase forbidding the importation of seal skins, tried to throw upon Pigot's shoulders the burden of transportation from Okhotsk (whither they had been conveyed by Eudin) back to Kamchatka. Pigot made a journey overland to St. Petersburg in order to seek more satisfactory terms, but in vain. He was able to regain possession of the seal skins only by paying the transportation charges. On account of these unforeseen difficulties Pigot was not able to sail from Kamchatka for the Hawaiian Islands with the seal skins till late October, 1818, when he made the voyage on the schooner *General San Martin*, commanded by Eliab Grimes.[15]

The *Forester* was not the only Astor vessel trading in the Pacific at the time when news of peace reached New York. On January 8, 1814, Astor, through his agent and fellow partner in the Pacific Fur Company, Wilson Price Hunt, had become the owner of a Boston brig of 225 tons, the *Pedler*, then at the

Hawaiian Islands, which Hunt purchased on learning of the wreck of the *Lark*, in order to carry out Astor's orders for the transportation of the property at Astoria to the Russian settlements, away from the menace of British capture. The *Pedler* sailed from the Islands late in January, 1814, and arrived on the last day of February at the Columbia River, where Hunt discovered that the post had already been transferred to the North West Company and formally declared a British possession. He spent more than a month at Astoria, or Fort George as it was then called, winding up the affairs of the recently dissolved Pacific Fur Company, and sailed for Norfolk Sound on April 2.[16]

Soon after the *Pedler* reached the settlement of New Archangel, the Astor brig *Forester* also arrived, on June 25, under command of William J. Pigot. This was a fortunate occurrence for the *Pedler's* company, since Hunt was thus enabled to add to his probably inadequate supply of goods. From the *Forester's* captain, Hunt received $1,099.26 in goods, $2,000 in cash, $757.25 in sundries, and 5,000 small seal skins to be sold in Canton, "all which on his arrival he will acct for —" How long the *Pedler* remained at Sitka we do not know, but it was probably not for any considerable period.[17]

The *Pedler* seems to have gone from Norfolk Sound to the Hawaiian Islands, having secured a contract while at New Archangel to take a cargo, including provisions from the Islands, to the Russian settlement of Ross on the coast of California, located on Bodega Roads not far from where San Francisco now is. Part of the cargo was delivered there, but on August 26, 1814, the *Pedler* was captured at San Luis Obispo by a Spanish corvette and held on the charge of having been engaged in illegal trade. The story told in court by the crew of the prize was that they had entered the bay to procure fresh meat and had mistaken their captor for a Russian vessel to which they were to deliver part of their cargo.

The cargo consisted of "flag-stones, looking-glasses, tea, sugar, coffee, glass beads, Russian canvas, cotton goods, colored thread, colored coating, blankets, sail-cloth, materials for trousers & shirts, trousers, jackets, shirts, skins, flannel, velveteen, hats, taffetas, etc."[18] The charge of smuggling could not be proved and the vessel was released after a detention of some two months.[19]

Evidently Hunt did not intend to return to Astor empty-handed after the collapse of the Astoria enterprise. He doubtless reasoned that half a loaf was better than a large baker's bill and that Astor would not look with any great kindness on his bringing an empty vessel back to New York solely for the purpose of transporting a few clerks to their homes. We do not know what the *Pedler* did immediately after her release, some time in October, 1814, but it may be strongly suspected that she revenged herself for this detention, followed though it was by acquittal, by justifying the suspicions of the Spanish authorities and engaging in illicit trade along the California coast. We know, at least, that one Astor vessel, the *Forester*, was so occupied about this time. After wintering in California, the *Pedler* probably sailed for the Hawaiian Islands and took on a cargo of provisions for New Archangel. I say "probably." As a matter of fact we do not know the brig's movements for nearly a year following her release in the fall of 1814. A visit to the Hawaiian Islands would, however, have been a logical procedure, as would trade along the coast, both of California and farther north.

At any rate, in the summer of 1815 the *Pedler* was again at New Archangel. Here she got into serious trouble, late in July, for she was "seized by the Russians for selling powder to the natives in the Sound, but was given up before . . . October 17, 1815."[20] She must have sailed soon afterwards, for about December 11, 1815, she arrived at Hawaii from the North West Coast, and on December 27 reached Oahu, accompanied by another Astor vessel, the *Enterprise*, direct from New York.[21]

On January 9, 1816, the *Pedler* sailed from Oahu for China, and at Canton took on a cargo of Oriental goods for New York, clearing late in March. Her arrival at New York with a cargo of silks, china, etc., was announced in the New York newspapers of October 17, 1816, and some of the teas on board were advertised as late as January, 1817.[22] Doubtless Astor was glad to receive some salvage from the wreck of his Astoria venture. The return of the *Pedler* not only marked the end of one of the last chapters in the history of Astoria, but also was a not unimportant event in his early post-war attention to the trade of the Pacific.

While the *Forester* and the *Pedler* were trading on the California coast and at Norfolk Sound, another Astor vessel had been sent to join them in this form of commerce. The ship *Enterprise*, commanded by John Ebbets, sailed from New York late in June, 1815, her destination being announced as the Columbia River,[23] and arrived at Oahu on December 27, 1815, in company with the *Pedler*.[24] From Oahu she sailed to the North West Coast by way of some of the other islands. By July, 1816, she was again at Oahu, where she celebrated Independence Day[25] and whither, after some cruising among the Islands, she returned. Here, on September 21, 1816, Ebbets bought the ship *Albatross* from Nathan Winship for "the sum of Two thousand dollars in Specie," and on the 16th of the next month sold the vessel to the king of the Hawaiian Islands for "Four hundred Piculs Sandal Wood,"[26] worth about $4,000 in Canton. The *Enterprise* sailed for Canton on October 27,[27] and arrived at that port on December 1,[28] with the first known cargo of Astor sandalwood,[29] 2,800 piculs (one picul equals 133⅓ pounds), which, with 5,000 seal skins from the North West Coast, made up her known cargo.[30] Part of this sandalwood was probably that which had been received in payment for the *Forester*.

On April 13, 1817, the *Enterprise* returned to Honolulu, and six months later she was still there,[31] but her movements in the interval are somewhat uncertain.[32] On December 1, 1817, she sailed for the "Spanish Main,"[33] arrived at Coquimbo in February, 1818, with a cargo of sundries, loaded there with copper, and, leaving this port on July 9, returned to the Hawaiian Islands,[34] where she arrived on August 23, 1818.[35]

James Hunnewell refers [36] to the loading of some sandalwood on the *Enterprise* in September, 1818. She sailed, apparently, the latter part of November, for Canton, where she disposed of her cargo, probably copper, sandalwood, and otter skins, and took on a load of teas, nankeens, silks, satins, crêpes, handkerchiefs, and other China goods. This merchandise was entered on September 6, 1819, at the Custom House of New York,[37] the port from which the vessel had sailed late in June, 1815, more than four years before. During this period she had been trading alternately in the Hawaiian Islands and along the West Coast, and twice, late in the years 1816 and 1818, she had visited Canton.

The *Enterprise's* voyage seems to have been so successful as to cause the firm of John Jacob Astor & Son to resolve upon making the Pacific trade, and especially the sandalwood trade of the Hawaiian Islands, a very important phase of its commerce with Canton. This decision was made while John Jacob Astor himself was in Europe, where he had gone in the early summer of 1819.

It was not surprising that Astor should recognize the opportunities offered by the sandalwood trade. Its profitable character was largely due to certain features in the economic and political organization of the Hawaiian Islands. Sandalwood was a royal monopoly [38] and was cut for the king by the chiefs on shares,[39] the common people doing the work, for which they received little or no compensation.[40] Since the wood cost the king and chiefs almost nothing, they were willing to buy enormous quantities of expensive goods at a price in sandalwood which, when reduced to dollars, was extremely high.[41] Canton offered a ready market for the wood, which was principally used as incense in the Chinese joss houses, and since the sandalwood trade could be readily carried on in connection with the North West Coast fur trade,[42] its advantage to the American merchants was obvious.

Although John Jacob Astor was not personally present in the New York office during much of the period of the firm's interest in this trade, still it was his policies which were carried out. Great as was the need for efficient, resourceful captains in the trade between New York and Canton alone, in which captain and ship-owner were cut off from any reciprocal communications for at least a year, still more important was the quality of ship-masters in the type of trade projected by Astor, in which a longer voyage would bring with it more than a proportionate increase of difficulties and of necessities for quick and independent decisions. It was Astor's policy to take into consideration every situation which might conceivably arise and give minute instructions as to his captains' conduct in each contingency, but he also strove to secure ship-masters who would not only follow his instructions to the letter in all cases for which he had made provision, but could also, when need arose, take measures on their own initiative and carry these to a successful conclusion. It is therefore necessary, in reading the account of the movements of an Astor vessel, the decisions and business transactions of her captain, to see behind each important measure the figure of the owner and employer, giving specific directions, while behind less important actions he also appears, through his selection of captains who could be safely trusted to handle successfully these questions of detail as they arose.

We have observed how the Pacific trade, originally intended to take in only the North West Coast in addition to New York and Canton, had been expanded, through the voyages of the *Forester* and the *Pedler*, to include California and the Hawaiian Islands. The reader will also remember how, in 1818, the *Enterprise*, the first vessel to make a Pacific voyage from New York since the conclusion of the war, visited Coquimbo, Chile, where China goods were exchanged for copper, thus bringing a new continent within the scope of the Pacific trade. But this project was one which had already occurred to Astor's mind, for in 1817, when Ebbets, in the *Enterprise*, was at Honolulu, preparing for a voyage which would include a visit to Chile, his employer at New York was independently engaged on plans for a very similar enterprise.

Early in 1817, a revolution had occurred in Chile, and as a result the restrictions on commerce, which had previously prevented trade in other than Spanish vessels, had been abolished. An experienced captain, Richard J. Cleveland, who had some knowledge of that part of the world, suggested that John Jacob Astor should load a vessel for a voyage thither.[43] Astor was favorably impressed with the project, and had his favorite ship, the *Beaver*, repaired at an expense almost equivalent to that of building a new vessel, a process which her experiences on the North West Coast had rendered necessary. This task was performed under the supervision of John Whetten, who had an interest of one-eighth in the voyage.[44] A cargo, consisting principally of European manufactures, was put on board. The ship was valued at $50,000 and the cargo at $140,000, "an aggregate," said Cleveland, "which, it is probable, no other individual in the United States would have risked on a voyage so full of dangers and uncertainty." Among the cargo were some arms and ammunition which Cleveland himself did not wish to take, but in this matter he was overruled by the owners.[45] On July 1, at 4 o'clock in the morning, Cleveland called on Astor, who, at that early hour, was up and waiting for him, and after a short interview took leave and went on board. Cleveland was to act both as captain and as first supercargo, while Francisco Ribas was to undertake the duties of assistant supercargo, probably chiefly as interpreter. The ship had ostensibly cleared for "Canton and North West Coast"[46] that her owners might not be accused of intending to engage in contraband trade at places still under Spanish control, but the cargo had evidently been definitely selected for the South American market, and on November 15 Astor had the cargo insured for $80,000 against all risks, specifically including those arising from participation in illegal trade.[47]

About the middle of October, the *Beaver* was forced to put into the port of Talcahuana for wood and water. The place was found to be in the hands of the Royalists, but vigorously besieged by the Patriots. The local officials determined to declare the vessel and cargo to be good prize, under the pretext that her arrival at Talcahuana had not been caused by any necessity and that the arms and ammunition on board evidenced her intention of trading with the enemy. Early in January this decision was formally announced and about $100,000 worth of the cargo taken out of the ship. A daring plan formed by Cleveland for seizing with his crew a Royalist war vessel, delivering her to the Patriots, and thus securing their aid in the recovery of the *Beaver*, was thwarted first by an unfavorable wind and on the second attempt by an attack of typhus. Captain Cleveland, though just recovering from a severe illness, entered an appeal to the court of appeals at Santiago and also wrote to the viceroy of Peru, which was still under Spanish control, laying the circumstances before him and requesting that the case should be judged at Lima, and not be postponed till the Royalists should succeed in establishing their authority over Chile — an event which, indeed, never took place.

In the meantime the assistant supercargo, Francisco Ribas, had escaped from Talcahuana and was endeavoring to bring influence to bear for the release of the *Beaver*. On November 18,

1817, he wrote from Concepción to Thomas Lloyd Halsey, the American consul at Buenos Aires, informing him of the circumstances of the vessel's capture, and even declaring that the *Beaver* had been intended not for any part of South America but for the "N. W. coast of America, island of Japam [!] & Canton." On January 2, 1818, he wrote Astor from Santiago that there was no market for anything on the *Beaver* and that "iron can't be sold at any price," which was true enough, owing to the lack of funds in the country, but must have proved cold comfort. He also wrote from Valparaiso on February 3 to James Biddle, who was then at that place in command of the U. S. sloop-of-war *Ontario*, in which he and J. B. Prevost had left the United States in the previous September for the purpose of regaining possession of the Columbia River.[48] In this letter Ribas urged Prevost to attempt to recover the *Beaver*,[49] and consequently on February 9 Prevost wrote to the secretary of State, John Quincy Adams, from "Sant Jago de Chile," informing him of the facts in the case, and about a month later wrote again, this time from Valparaiso, that he hoped, through the capture of Talcahuana by the Republicans, to be able to regain possession of the *Beaver*, though the cargo had been confiscated.[50] John Quincy Adams in his turn instructed George W. Erving, minister plenipotentiary to Madrid, to protest against the *Beaver's* unjustifiable seizure and condemnation.[51] It is to be hoped that Erving did not allow the irritation aroused by the fact that some years before Astor's daughter and son-in-law had ousted him from his own cabin to affect the vigor of his representations in this cause. Ribas wrote to Astor on March 10 from Santiago de Chile that he intended to set up in that city as a general agent and commission merchant. He forwarded the various letters he had written in Astor's interests to New York by means of Astor's agent at Buenos Aires, David C. Deforest.[52]

In the meantime Cleveland's letter to the viceroy of Peru had borne fruit and on May 7 word arrived at Talcahuana that he was to proceed at once in another confiscated American ship, the *Canton*, to Lima, where justice would be done. They arrived at Callao on the 25th and went on the next day to Lima, where the viceroy promised to examine the case. On June 25 Captain Biddle, in the *Ontario*, sailed from Valparaiso to Lima, taking with him Jeremy Robinson to act as his agent in claiming the American vessels which had been confiscated, because, as Robinson said, "I was the friend of John Jacob Astor . . . and knew all the circumstances of the case."[53] Cleveland began to feel confident that the vessel would be restored and that he would be awarded compensation for the confiscated cargo, and consequently on July 25 wrote Astor his plans for a voyage when the proceedings were over. He told Astor that he intended to suggest that he should be allowed to introduce some cargoes into Peru and receive compensation from the duties. His first choice was for a voyage to China on shares, but this was certain to be opposed by the Philippine Company; his next choice would be to go to Guayaquil, load with cocoa, return to the United States, and there load a cargo for Peru. In order to insure the recovery of the vessel, Cleveland went to Valparaiso early in August on a secret mission for the viceroy, which was successful only in that the viceroy was convinced that the captain had not come to Chile as an agent of the Patriots, and was therefore induced to show him friendship. Leaving Valparaiso late in October, Cleveland returned to Callao, where he found that Captain Biddle had been making every exertion to secure the release of the *Beaver* and other confiscated American vessels. His object was finally accomplished on November 20, 1818,[54] when the *Beaver* was ordered to be restored with whatever of her cargo was still available, and the owners were directed to seek compensation for the rest wherever they might think proper.

Cleveland then spent several months preparing the *Beaver* for sea, procuring a crew, which he finally obtained from among certain English and American prisoners of war at Callao, captured by the Royalists while serving in the Chilian navy, and obtaining a license from the viceroy allowing him to trade on the coast. The project of a China voyage had been defeated, just as Cleveland had anticipated. Early in March he was able to sail from Callao, and in four days arrived at Pisco, one of the places with which he was licensed to trade. Here he took on board 600 jars of wine and brandy, purchased out of the funds which had not been confiscated, and sailed for Guanchaca, where he sold the cargo for enough wheat and rice to fill half the vessel, and was able nearly to complete her lading with freight. Proceeding to Malabrigo, he there received enough offers for freight, to be taken on board at Pacasmayo, to fill up the vessel completely. On May 19, Cleveland sailed for Callao, where he arrived on June 9. There the cargo was sold at such a price as to bring in a profit of $20,000 for the voyage. Cleveland now determined to make a voyage to Lima, and sailed again for Pisco on June 25, arriving on the first of the next month. There he loaded 4,000 jars of brandy and a deckload of wheat, and returned to Callao on August 1. This cargo brought a profit of about $10,000.

He then chartered the vessel to some English merchants for $40,000, "to proceed to three ports to leeward, and there lade with the produce of the country, and proceed with it to Valparaiso; there deliver it, and relade with wheat for Callao." The *Beaver* sailed from Callao near the end of September, 1819, and after visiting a number of ports finally accomplished the voyage and unloaded at Callao by February 19, 1820. Cleveland now had enough property to justify his leaving for New York, and, moreover, this move was made necessary by the state of the rigging, etc. On March 13, then, the *Beaver* sailed for Guayaquil, where she arrived on the 25th. Here she was

Astor's Ship "Beaver" on the Coast of Peru in 1819

loaded with cocoa and sailed on April 18 for Callao. On June 11 Cleveland sailed for Rio de Janeiro for supplies, and left that port on August 21, 1820, for New York, where he arrived on October 6, after an absence of more than 3 years, with a cargo of 840,456 lbs. of cocoa and $5,000 or $6,000 in specie to John Jacob Astor and the National Insurance Company,[55] to which the vessel had long since been abandoned, as Cleveland had been notified as early as June, 1819, since the owners had considered her lost at the time of her condemnation.[56]

Some of this cocoa was being offered for sale by John Jacob Astor & Son and by the National Insurance Company in the same month,[57] and in the next month 17,927 lbs. were shipped to Havana by John Jacob Astor & Son.[58] Cleveland seems to have been treated rather shabbily by the National Insurance Company, receiving no recognition for his exertions and their extraordinary success, but Cleveland himself expressly exonerated Astor, who was in Europe at the time. The *Beaver* was sold by the National Insurance Company to Thomas H. Smith & Co., and made many China voyages in later years.[59]

The difficulties which the *Beaver* encountered in endeavoring to trade on the west coast of South America under war-time conditions seem to have terminated any intention which the Astors may have formed of carrying on a direct trade with that continent from New York City. As we shall see, however, the west coast of South America became increasingly important to the Pacific trade as the advancing revolutionary movement threw open the ports to the ships of foreign nations, a process which was complete by 1826.

The next Astor vessel in the Pacific trade was the *Pedler*, a brig which was not new to the Hawaiian Islands, the North West Coast, California, and Canton. Early in December, 1819, she was being fitted out at New York for the North West Coast under Captain John Meek, taking on board gin, brown sugar, cloth, and other goods suitable for that market.[60] On May 23,

1820, the *Pedler* arrived at Oahu,[61] where John Meek encountered William J. Pigot, who had left Kamchatka in October, 1818, in the *General San Martin*, sometimes known merely as the *St. Martin*, with a quantity of seal skins belonging to Astor, which Pigot had collected while in the *Forester*. Pigot had been in the Islands since late in 1818, probably doing some business for himself,[62] and had doubtless accumulated experience which, added to that derived from the time he had previously spent in the Islands, on the North West Coast and on the coast of California, and in the Siberian ports as captain of the *Forester*, would make his services of considerable value. Meek consequently engaged him as the *Pedler's* agent. During June the *Pedler* was cruising among the Islands,[63] and on June 23, 1820, "Tamoore" or Kaumalii, vassal king of Kauai, with his son George, signed a note to Pigot and Meek for 191 piculs of sandalwood, due them for goods purchased from the *Pedler's* cargo.[64] The *Pedler* left the Islands for the North West Coast, Norfolk Sound, and Kamchatka in the summer of 1820, with Meek and Pigot in charge.[65] We know few of the details of the voyage save that at New Archangel Pigot bought 2,620 fur seals for goods valued at the almost incredibly small amount of $302.60,[66] and that he was at Kamchatka in September.[67] The *Pedler* returned to Oahu on December 5,[68] and soon after sailed for Canton, which she reached on February 9, 1821, and whence she departed on March 25 [69] for the Hawaiian Islands and Oahu, arriving by April 20.[70] Pigot had left the brig, on her return to Oahu in December, for on February 5, 1821, the "Brig St Martin, Picket [*sic*] bound to Fanning's Islands" was described as being at Maui.[71]

In the fall of 1820 the Boston firm of Bryant & Sturgis, who were extensively engaged in the Pacific trade, wrote to their various captains and supercargoes at the Hawaiian Islands to be on the lookout for Captain Ebbets, whom we last saw at New York in the *Enterprise* early in September, 1819, since he was "fitting out at N York in Astors large ship the Wᵐ. & John. He will carry out the frame of a small vessel to be set up, & perhaps take out a schooner also. If from any cause you are desirous of getting wood or freight," the letter concluded, "you should lose no time in securing it before it is known that Ebbets is coming" — a remarkable testimony to the position held by this Astor captain. The Bryant & Sturgis employees were also warned that they must expect competition from an Astor vessel on the Coast as well as at the Islands since Ebbets had "been buying up some Blankets &c. & we think intends sending the Pedler, or perhaps a Schooner on the Coast."[72]

Captain Ebbets sailed from New York in the late fall of 1820 [73] and arrived at Oahu in April, 1821, a week earlier than the date of the *Pedler's* return, in the *William and John*,[74] with a full cargo. On April 20 the ship reached Kauai.[75] Ebbets succeeded in reaping a profit from the misfortune of one of his competitors, who had made a contract to furnish certain goods to the royal family, but whose vessel with the promised merchandise had failed to arrive on time.[76] On May 19 the "Ship Wᵐ. & John, Abbot [*sic*] of New York," was at Oahu, "taking in Wood."[77] By May 25, King "Tamooree," or more properly Kaumalii, impressed by the "fine cloths" on the *William and John*, had purchased nearly the entire cargo.[78] Not only the quality of Captain Ebbets' goods and their unusual cheapness (he is described as selling them "at first cost"), but also his "most gentlemanly manner towards all concerns," rendered him popular both with the natives and with his competitors, and made him a strong opponent in the commercial rivalry.[79] By July Ebbets had disposed of nearly all his goods and had nearly finished "building a beautiful pilot boat." The *Pedler*, however, had been unable to do anything at the Islands and had returned to the Coast.[80]

Early in October, 1821, the *William and John* had about 5,000 piculs of sandalwood on board and Ebbets had succeeded in selling the cargo of the *Pedler*, which had by this time returned to the Islands, having arrived at Oahu on September 18 and "sailed for Wyaroore" on the 24th.[81] His prices were so low that his competitors found it very difficult to make sales. He had also completed the "pilot boat of about 45 tons," for which at first he refused an offer of 1,200 piculs [82] or $5,000,[83] though later, before sailing, he agreed to sell at that price,[84] and thus, "from the liberality and good cheer he has shown to these people, he . . . made himself popular. . . ." On November 6 the *William and John*, with her 5,000 piculs (more than 666,000 lbs.) of wood, sailed for China,[85] where she arrived on December 12,[86] leaving the *Pedler* behind to collect and bring on an additional 3,000 piculs (nearly 400,000 lbs.), though originally the brig had been expected to leave before the *William and John* and return at once with a cargo of China goods.[87] By January 4, 1822, the 5,000 piculs on the *William and John*, which had been purchased for only a little over $4.00 per picul in goods, had been "sold in exchange for Teas at abt 10$."[88] With a China cargo on board, the ship *William and John* headed back for New York on March 25.[89] Part of her cargo was entered on August 21, 1822, at the Custom House of New York,[90] whence she had sailed something less than two years before.

The *Pedler* [91] sailed for Canton on December 25,[92] and arrived on February 9, 1822,[93] bringing not only the sandalwood, but some otter skins belonging partly to the ship *Paragon* and the brig *Arab* and partly to the *William and John*. These furs had been secured as follows. During the past summer J. C. Jones, Jr., agent of the Boston firm of Marshall & Wildes, had sent Captain Eliab Grimes to the Gulf of California in the schooner *Eagle*. In order to make up a full cargo for this voyage, Ebbets of the *William and John* and Davis of the *Arab* had gone together and "shipped $6,000 on half profits."[94] These otter skins were part of the proceeds, and though invoiced at only $881.75 were sold at Canton for about $2,000 in March, 1822.[95] Late in March, 1822,[96] the *Pedler* sailed "for the Russian settlements" with a China cargo,[97] part of which was disposed of for 10,000 seal skins.[98] Late in June she was back at Honolulu,[99] where in August she was disposing of the rest of her Canton goods.[100] Early in October it was believed that she would not get much wood,[101] but, nevertheless, late in December she had about 2,000 piculs (266,000 lbs.).[102] With these she sailed for Canton, arriving at that port on February 6, 1823.[103] Insurance had been made for her voyage from Canton to Norfolk Sound and thence back to Canton "with liberty on both passages to stop & trade at the Sandwich Islands," the insurance amounting to $4,000 on the vessel, which was valued at $14,000, and $8,000 on the cargo, which was valued at $20,000.[104] The *Pedler* sailed from Canton on April 6, 1823, for New York,[105] where she arrived in August with a cargo of teas and silks.[106] She had been gone from the home port more than three and a half years, during which time she had been to the Islands, New Archangel, Kamchatka, the Islands, Canton, the Islands and the Coast again, the Islands and Canton, New Archangel again, the Islands and Canton once more, and had finally sailed for New York.

In the Pacific, the place of John Meek and the *Pedler* was taken by our old friend John Ebbets, who appeared with the *Enterprise* at Oahu in April, 1824.[107] The agents of Bryant & Sturgis had been warned of this event in the previous fall. "We learn that Capt. Ebbets is about sailing for the Islands in the Enterprise," wrote the Boston office, "& is to be *followed* in a few weeks by Meeks, in the new Brig."[108] The indications are that Ebbets came prepared to act more or less as Astor's resident agent. On April 17, 1824, "at 5 Capt. Ebbets brought his coach ashore and put it up in Navarro's yard."[109] This was certainly evidence that he was not expecting to spend all his time in the near future on the ship's deck.

In September, 1824, the *Enterprise* was still at Oahu waiting for a cargo, in the collection of which her captain was apparently not meeting with the success which had distinguished him aforetime,[110] though among his transactions had been the sale of a parcel of blankets to his rival, Dixey Wildes.[111] By the latter part of the month Captain Ebbets had succeeded in collecting only the paltry amount of 400 piculs, which he thereupon shipped to Canton by the *Sultan* on September 27.

In the meantime "the new brig Tamaahmaah fitted out by J Astor, W Roberts & Capt J Ebbets . . . expressly to sell these people [the natives of the Islands]"[112] had arrived at the Islands August 9, 1824, under the command of Captain Meek,[113] after a passage of 115 days from New York,[114] with a cargo of lumber and spirits.[115] She had been built by Henry Eckford [116] and was variously described as "the beautiful brig Tamaahmaah" (by a missionary)[117] and as "nothing more than common I was disappointed in her, I doubt whether they will be able to sell her she leaks badly" (by Captain Dixey Wildes, a rival trader).[118] Let the reader judge which spoke with the more authority. At any rate Wildes was right in one respect. Although Captain Ebbets and Meek "tried hard to sell her," they "could not succeed;" so early in November she sailed "for the Spanish Main and Norfolk sound,"[119] intending to "touch on the coast,"[120] presumably that of California, where we know she was some time during 1825.[121]

At the Islands, Ebbets varied the monotony of collecting sandalwood by attempting, in association with Dixey Wildes and a Mr. Hammatt, a Bryant & Sturgis agent, to purchase "a fine lot of seal skins here belonging to Pitt about 6000," the latter being a prominent native chieftain. The white traders offered "one dollar in Cash or two dollars on account the old debts," which gives some idea of the prominence of credit in this trade. Wildes expected to offer $1.25 before leaving, though he stated, compassionately and regretfully, "I doubt

Astor's Brig "Tamaahmaah" at the Hawaiian Islands in 1825

whether they will sell them, they do not know the value of them and very likely they will lose the whole."[122] Whether they finally succeeded in purchasing these skins does not appear certain, though we know that Eliab Grimes, a Marshall & Wildes captain, shipped some skins of some kind to Canton in the *Enterprise* in March, 1825.[123] Ebbets did not go to Canton in his ship, but sent her under the command of "young Mr. Halsey, of New York,"[124] while he himself remained behind "for the purpose of closing his business."[125] Ebbets seems to have been pretty well established in Honolulu by this time, as on New Year's Day, 1825, he and Hammatt prepared a dinner "at which most of the residents partook in great pleasantness and mirth."[126] On July 16, 1825, he entertained at his residence a number of European and American residents, among them several missionaries, one of the guests being a "Mr. Halsey, of New York,"[127] which would seem to indicate that the *Enterprise* had by this time returned to the Islands. We know that Halsey and the *Enterprise* had arrived at Canton on May 4 and sailed on June 16,[128] but the vessel could not have tarried long at the Islands on her return, for she had reached the United States by December.[129]

In the meantime the brig *Tamaahmaah*, which, after the *Enterprise's* departure, was to be the only Astor vessel in the trade, and which had left the Islands early in November, 1824, for Norfolk Sound, the Spanish Main, and the Coast, had returned to Oahu by the latter part of March, 1825, and was preparing to sail for Lima.[130] She was at that port for an unknown length of time during the summer, arriving in ballast, and sailed for California on August 24.[131] Ebbets had again remained behind, probably to continue his activities as Astor's agent, for from the prominence of Astor vessels in the Islands in the period 1822–25, and from Ebbets' remaining much of the time at Honolulu, where he had a residence, instead of voyaging about the Pacific, it seems evident that the firm of John Jacob

Astor & Son was one of the "four American mercantile houses . . . which have establishments at this port, to which agents and clerks are attached." One of these firms, the missionary C. S. Stewart says, was of New York, but he mentions the names of none.[132]

The brig *Tamaahmaah*, which in the latter part of August, 1825, had sailed from Lima for California, had returned to Oahu by January of the next year, and on the 10th of that month Captain Ebbets was planning to proceed "for China in the Brig Tamaahmaah for the purpose of procuring a cargo for the Spanish Main." Apparently the brig's previous voyage to that region had proved profitable, and one of Marshall & Wildes' agents remarked concerning the projected voyage, "I think he will do extremely well while I am fearful I shall make a broken voyage."[133] Evidently John Meek was still in command of the brig, and Ebbets was acting merely as agent, or supercargo when on a voyage, for another Marshall & Wildes correspondent states that "Capt Meek sailed . . . in the Tamaahmaah for Canton [January 18, 1826] which Brig is to return to these Islands and land a part of her cargo & then proceed to the Coast of California."[134] The largeness of the profits which could be made on the west coast of South America are indicated by the fact that through the *Superior's* supercargo laying in a supply of "the best patterns and colours" he "cleared near one hundred thousand dollars."[135] The *Tamaahmaah* was mentioned in a list of vessels "visiting the Port of Honorura" between February 1 and May 1, 1826. This may have been on her return from the Canton voyage inaugurated on January 18. At this time the vessel was described as worth $20,000 and the cargo was valued at $15,000.[136] This cargo was presumably then taken, as previously planned, to California.

On April 29, 1826, Eliab Grimes, who was on the coast of California, stated that "Capt. Ebbets will be out in the Brig Tamaahmaah in the fall but he will labour under many disadvantages, not knowing at this time the kind of China goods in demand."[137] Ebbets was back at Honolulu on December 9, 1826. The brig was still there on March 2, 1827,[138] but must have gone to China soon after this to get goods for South America, since on May 8, 1827, Eliab Grimes had "obtained some freight" at Lima (probably for Guayaquil) and intended to "sail as soon as possible for that port being anxious to get there before the Brig Tamaahmaah."[139] Ebbets, however, must have remained at the Islands and let Meek take the brig, for on July 20, 1827, J. C. Jones, Jr., wrote to Dixey Wildes that "Capt. Ebbets has been at Atoi [Kauai] ever since you left, is doing well."[140] The *Tamaahmaah*, under Meek, was on the coast of California at some time during 1827.[141] At the end of September Ebbets was still at Kauai, where he had been, we are told, since February, while the *Tamaahmaah* had returned to the Islands and was "cruising for wood."[142] On Christmas, 1827, the brig was in Honolulu Harbor "bound to Manilla."[143]

The brig, however, did not sail under her original ownership, but instead was sold to the king on February 19, 1828, for 3,400 piculs of sandalwood, with interest at 5 per cent after 6 months.[144] On July 20, 1828, it was said that "the Brigs Tamahamah and Inore belonging to these people are loading with Sandal Wood for Manilla on their own account." The American traders were of the opinion that the venture would not turn out well, the wish apparently being the father of the thought, since, should the Islanders begin a profitable sandalwood trade in their own vessels and on their own account, much of the white traders' profits would, of course, disappear.[145] It would seem, then, that, by using as a lever the prospect of avoiding the payment of tribute to the middleman, Ebbets and Meek had finally been able to persuade Governor Boki to purchase the vessel which they had unsuccessfully tried to sell four years previously. With the sale of the *Tamaahmaah*, Astor's connection with the sandalwood trade and with the

Pacific seems to have come to an end. This last vessel, which had been without a consort since the *Enterprise* left the Pacific in the summer of 1825, had probably done more cruising than any of the others. Since her arrival at Oahu in August, 1824, she had been to "the Spanish Main," "Norfolk sound," and California, had returned to Oahu in the spring of 1825, sailed to Lima and thence to California, returned to the Islands and gone a little later to Canton, returned to Honolulu, gone on to California, and come back again to the Islands in the spring of 1826. After this she probably went to Canton, South America, and California, and by the fall of the year was back at the Islands, where she was sold in the next spring.[146]

With the sale of the last Astor-owned vessel engaged in the Pacific trade, we may pause for a moment and consider the relations of Astor's Pacific trade to his trade with China through Europe, and also the influence which the fur trade had on both the European and the Pacific aspects of the China trade. Let us imagine, then, that in some particular year after the end of the War of 1812 Astor finds himself in possession of a considerable quantity of assorted furs. Some of these are sold in the fur market of New York; a few are shipped to other ports in the United States. Those in which we are particularly interested are, however, sent as freight to various ports in England and on the Continent, of which London, Hamburg, and Le Havre are typical examples.

In return for these furs, from London come drygoods and hardware, such as blankets, cutlery, and muskets. From Hamburg, perhaps, are received iron, lead, and gin. Le Havre gives drygoods of a somewhat finer quality than those furnished by London. At New York some of these goods are, perhaps, offered in the open market. Some of the blankets, cutlery, muskets, lead, iron, gin, and other suitable articles are sent into the interior to be sold to the Indians for furs. But those which we are especially concerned in following are loaded on a vessel, intended for the Pacific Ocean. This vessel, perhaps, touches first at one of the Hawaiian Islands, where a miscellaneous assortment of goods from her cargo is sold on short credit because of the low prices made possible by Astor's large capital. Rum is popular, as are the fine textiles from Le Havre. Leaving the natives to collect the sandalwood for which the goods are exchanged, the vessel sails next for Norfolk Sound to trade with the Russians for seal skins and the fur of the sea otter. At Norfolk Sound, also, rum is popular, but there is a demand for general merchandise of all kinds. Perhaps some muskets and ammunition will be sold to the natives, if this can be done without arousing the suspicions of the Russians. Then the vessel may drop down to the vicinity of the Columbia River [147] and sell guns, powder, shot, knives, rum, and all sorts of metalwork to the natives. On the coast of California general merchandise again meets a ready market among the inhabitants, though before 1818 one must be on the lookout for the Spanish authorities. Having pretty well disposed of the cargo they took on board at New York, the captain and supercargo decide to return to the Islands. Here they take on the sandalwood which has been cut for them in their absence on the Coast, and with this and the furs from Norfolk Sound, Columbia River, and California — perhaps some silver and pearlshell from the last-named place — they sail to Canton.

Here sandalwood and furs are bartered for teas, silks, nankeens, chinaware, sugar, spices, etc. — a cargo sure to meet with a ready sale at New York. But there are markets nearer to Canton than any city of the United States. Back to the Hawaiian Islands they head. The wives of the chiefs are impressed by the beautiful Chinese silks. What matter that their storehouses are already piled with goods sufficient to last a generation? There is plenty of sandalwood on the mountains, plenty of commoners to cut and carry it to the seashore free of charge. Soon a part of the Canton cargo has been sold and the ship's sails are again set for the coast of the Americas. This time the cargo is not so suitable for the Indian trade, but the Russians at New Archangel and the Spaniards of California are ready to purchase teas, silks, and nankeens in exchange for seal skins, sea-otter furs, silver, and pearl-shell. Moreover, farther to the south are Ecuador, Peru, and Chile, which have recently cast off the Spanish yoke and thrown open their ports to the trade of the whole world. So ho for Guayaquil, for Callao, for Coquimbo, where the rest of the cargo taken on board at Canton may be sold for red copper and white specie! Then back to the Islands to stow away odorous sandalwood beside the bales of glossy skins of the seal and the otter, the copper ingots, and the kegs of specie.

Once again at Canton, a China cargo is taken on board, but this time the vessel at last clears for her home port from which she sailed three or four years ago. At New York the China cargo is unloaded. Some of the goods are sold at auction, some over the counter of Astor's own shop, some are shipped as freight to other ports in the United States and to the West Indies. Some, perhaps in company with furs from the Great Lakes and the Missouri, are shipped to Hamburg and Le Havre. We, however, shall devote our attention to those which are loaded on brigs and schooners, sometimes belonging to John Jacob Astor or to the Astor firm. The vessels clear for the Mediterranean, and sail away through the Straits of Gibraltar and on to the eastern end of the great inland sea. Here at Smyrna part of the China cargo is exchanged for Turkey opium. The brig then turns back on her course to Gibraltar, where the remainder of her China cargo is exchanged for quicksilver, specie, and lead, and the vessel clears once more for her home port.

At New York the vessels are unloaded. Some of the opium and quicksilver may be advertised for sale in the New York newspapers, but a large proportion of the products of this

Mediterranean cruise — opium, quicksilver, lead, and specie — is loaded on board an Astor vessel. Beneath the hatches are also stowed away bales of the choicest furs from the interior of North America, red-fox skins, beaver, and land-otter furs, much inferior in value to the sea otters and seals of the North West Coast, but still of a type to meet with a ready sale in the Canton fur market. There are also a number of kegs of ginseng and perhaps a little cotton and cochineal. This time the vessel proceeds directly to Canton, sells her cargo for the usual teas, nankeens, silks, chinaware, and cassia, and returns at once to New York, having been gone for less than a year. There her cargo is dispensed in much the same way as the cargo of the ship which we followed on her return from the Pacific.

So the process went on, involving the interior and the west and east coasts of North America, the west coast of South America, the Hawaiian Islands, Canton, England, the Mediterranean, both Northern and Southern Europe — indeed all parts of the commercial world. Is it surprising, in view of the number of times that goods were turned over between the departure and the return to New York, and the unsophisticated character of at least two of the races from whom Astor obtained the most important types of the commodities utilized in this commerce — from the Indians furs and from the Hawaiians sandalwood—that Astor became a multimillionaire of commerce at a time when simple millionaires were a rarity? Of course we must not forget that all this process was not as simple as it may sound. This program itself required careful planning based on long and hazardous experience, wise selection of subordinates, and a large capital which had been amassed from literally nothing by means of hard labor and the same foresight and willingness to venture on a small scale which he was now exhibiting in a large field. Otherwise Astor would not have emerged from the ruck of China merchants.

The probable reason for Astor's giving up the Pacific trade was his withdrawal from the China trade, on which the other was dependent, about 1825, though he unexpectedly re-entered the trade with Canton for a brief period in 1827.[148] This withdrawal of his interest from the China trade was, in turn, probably due merely to the intention of Astor, who was then well over sixty and in poor health, to concentrate upon the fur trade, upon land investments in New York City, and upon money-lending on good security.

Whether his decision to withdraw from the China trade was, in turn, influenced somewhat by the decline of the sandalwood trade is problematical, but it is at least a suggestion worthy of consideration. The trade, which was at its height between 1812 and 1825,[149] was by 1826 already quite distinctly on the down grade.[150] During the eighteen months of 1821 and the first half of 1822, sandalwood exports amounted to from $350,000 to $400,000 at $10 per picul;[151] in 1836, to only $26,000 worth at $7.00. No exports at all were made in 1840 and 1841.[152] This decline was primarily due to the destruction of the sandalwood forests through disregard of the first Kamehameha's policy of conservation.[153] The reckless new methods of collection involved the cutting of young saplings as well as mature trees, and even the digging up of the roots.[154] Wanton destruction by axe and fire on the part of the forced laborers is also said to have been a factor.[155] The quality of the wood had always been inferior to that of India;[156] and as the best trees were destroyed and small crooked wood began to become more conspicuous, and as its popularity in the Chinese joss houses began to diminish, the price declined.[157] The decisive blow to the trade was an edict by the king and chiefs on December 27, 1826, which provided for the liquidation of debts amounting to $150,000 owed by members of the royal family to citizens of the United States.[158] To satisfy this sum in sandalwood would have required a total of 15,000 piculs, or 2,000,000 lbs. In order to pay this debt "a tax of one half a pickul of sandal wood or four dollars in money" was levied "on every native of the Sandwich Islands;" 25,000 piculs of wood and $8,000 in money were collected, of which about 10,000 piculs reached the creditors, the rest being diverted by the chiefs. The sandalwood cut under this edict included nearly all that was still available.[159] Astor shared in the tax of 1827 through his agents. We learn that on July 18, 1827, the brig *Kamelolani*, apparently belonging to the king, had arrived with "about 750 piculs sandalwood on board of tax wood to pay old debts, to be divided into four parts," one each to the four principal firms in Honolulu. Of these one part was to go "to Manini, agent for T. Meek and Capt. Ebbets."[160] In the fall of 1829 the agents of the four firms were still trying to collect the balance.[161] At this time John Ebbets had received only 1,161 piculs of sandalwood and $400 in specie of the 3,400 piculs of wood for which he had sold the *Tamaahmaah* early in the previous year, and was endeavoring to collect the 2,165 piculs of sandalwood still due, with interest, which debt was acknowledged by "the King, Regent, and Chiefs of the Sandwich Islands," who promised to pay within nine months from November 2, 1829.[162] The collapse of the sandalwood trade, in which the tax of 1827 was a decisive factor, was doubtless a grievous blow to the Hawaiian nobility and the white traders, but to the commonalty, as can be readily seen, it was an unmixed blessing.[163]

It is evident that Astor got out of the trade at the proper time, immediately after the great tax collection of 1827 had struck a mortal blow at the business, but it is probable that in any event he would not have stayed in it much longer. The sandalwood trade could not exist without the China trade — of which, indeed, it was a part — and when Astor withdrew from the latter, as conducted in his own vessels, the former went too as a matter of course. Since Astor had successfully pursued the China trade for sixteen years before becoming interested in sandalwood, it is not likely that the abrupt decline in importance of the Hawaiian side of the trade would in itself have been an important factor in causing him to cease his connection with the commerce between New York and Canton. Indeed he had decided to cease sending vessels to China even before the tax of 1827 dealt irreparable injury to the sandalwood trade. We can therefore state with some assurance that Astor's withdrawal from the Pacific trade was principally inspired by his decision to abandon the China trade in general and only secondarily by the decline in the sandalwood trade.

It would seem, from what we know of the movements of such Astor vessels as the ships *Enterprise* and *William and John*, the brigs *Pedler* and *Tamaahmaah*, that a definite policy was in process of being worked out by Astor and his captains for the Pacific trade after the war. A ship and a brig would go from New York to the Hawaiian Islands. The first would remain in the Islands and collect a cargo, then sail to China and return to New York with China goods; the second would work a wider field, stay in the Pacific longer, and perhaps partly load her consort at the Islands with goods for China secured by trading on the west coast of North and South America and elsewhere, to be sold at Canton for merchandise suitable to the New York market. But this policy — if policy it actually was — is not by any means the most important reason for Astor's twelve successful years in this trade. He picked as captains experienced men, who were qualified not only as sailors but as traders, and who could be congenial to the natives and avoid undue friction with their competitors. It is possible, too, that the friendliness of Astor's captains toward the Boston missionaries,[164] who had great influence with the natives — a friendliness not shared by certain of the other firms engaged in business on the Islands [165] — may have also given them some advantage over their rivals. A somewhat less laudable factor in success on at least one voyage is revealed in a letter of instruction to a Bryant & Sturgis agent. "It has been proved in the voyages of the W^m & John & the Pedler (both of New York) that a cargo can be collected (tho perhaps in some measure a clandestine trade) as you make sale of your goods to the chiefs & others, & this is done with more expedition than when Sales are made to the King — — We recommend this trade particularly to your consideration, & at the same time advise its being done (if resorted to) in such way as to avoid offending the ruling authorities." [166] Since the king owned the wood but the chiefs cut it for him on shares, an ingenious captain and an unscrupulous chief could get together and divert some of the royal wood into illegitimate channels to their mutual profit. The advantage to the chief is obvious, and the captain got the wood at a minimum of time and expense, as there was not so much haggling in a clandestine operation of this kind.

Astor's large capital enabled him to sell goods of a superior quality at a very low price, so that his captains could dispose of all their goods before their rivals had a chance. Sometimes it was impossible for their competitors to make any sales worth mentioning at all. But these low prices were accepted on condition of receiving the payment in sandalwood at once. [167] A minimum time was thus expended at the Islands in selling the goods and taking on the proceeds in sandalwood. This, in turn, enabled the Astor captains to arrive at Canton early in the season, secure the best price in the market, and get their China goods back to New York in time to sell in a favorable market there also.

It was this policy which made Astor successful in the sandalwood trade between 1816 and 1828, and therefore in the Pacific trade in which this commodity was of such great importance, and which doubtless would have enabled him, had he so desired, to maintain a comparatively profitable trade for the brief period to elapse before the time when the sandalwood tree and the commerce in sandalwood came to an untimely end together. However, he chose rather to withdraw from this business as soon as it was evident that its best days were over and to concentrate upon other more congenial interests.

NOTES

1. From December 8, 1817, to June 10, 1818, 11 shipments of China goods were made from New York on Astor's account, 4 to New Orleans, 2 each to Charleston, Havana, and St. Thomas, and one to Gibraltar (ms., Baker Library, Astor Papers, Account of Shipments abroad). During the years 1819 to 1825 about 140 similar shipments were made to ports in the United States, the West Indies, and Europe (ms., Baker Library, Astor Papers, Canton Copartnership Concern). Trade with England was only remotely connected with the commerce to Canton, owing to the East India Company's monopoly. Astor never, so far as we know, sent a ship of his own to England. However, from the end of the war till 1827 at least 55 ships came to the Astors from England, usually from London, frequently from Liverpool, bringing drygoods and other merchandise (sometimes specified as iron, brandy, gin, and rum) as freight (*New-York Gazette and General Advertiser*, 1815–27, *passim*). The only connection between the China trade and these vessels is that they brought goods to be bartered with the Indians for furs, some of which would later be sent to Canton. However, from 1818 to 1828, inclusive, the American Fur Company sent only 12 consignments of furs to Canton, as compared with 45 to London, 24 to Hamburg, 10 to Le Havre, 4 to Smyrna, 2 to Marseilles, one each to St. Petersburg, Antwerp, and Leghorn, 4 to Boston, 2 to Montreal, and one to Philadelphia (ms., Baker Library, Astor Papers, Foreign Shipments and Consignments, American Fur C°. N°. 1; *ibid.*, N°. 2; *ibid.*, Statement of Shipments made by American Fur Company Concern of 1823 — with Gain or Loss on same). From 1815 to 1826, inclusive, also, a great many vessels from the continent of Europe — 52 at least — brought freight to the Astors. They came from France and ports of Northern Europe. Thirty-four vessels from Hamburg, Amsterdam, Antwerp, St. Petersburg, and Bremen, in the order named, brought hardware and drygoods of various kinds, iron, steel, lead, gin, specie, glassware, linens, oil-cloth, etc. Eighteen vessels from Le Havre, Bordeaux, and Nantes, the great majority from the first, brought principally drygoods, such as silks and ribbons, also wine, brandy, specie, and burr-stones. (*New-York Gazette and General Advertiser*, 1815–26, *passim*.) Some of these goods were doubtless in return for furs, others for China goods. Some of this European merchandise, drygoods, glassware, burr-stones, etc., would be sold by Astor in New York. Iron, steel, lead, some types of drygoods, and gin would go to the Indian country to be traded for furs. Some of the lead and specie might be sent to China, while the Pacific — the Hawaiian Islands, South America, Russian America, and California — would furnish, as we shall later see, a market for all these types of European goods. We have already noted the very intimate relation between the Mediter-

ranean and the China trade, both because that region furnished a good market for the silks and teas of the Orient and because of the importance which opium from Smyrna and lead and quicksilver from Cadiz and Gibraltar assumed in the cargoes of vessels to Canton.

Astor also had relations, though definitely minor ones, with ports on the Caribbean. From 1817 to 1823, inclusive, a vessel or two a year — we know of at least ten, nearly all schooners and brigs — came bringing freight, part of which was consigned to John Jacob Astor or John Jacob Astor & Son. Most of these vessels were from St. Thomas in the Danish West Indies and brought sugar, specie, hides, and rum chiefly, also a little cotton, mahogany, molasses, wine, cocoa, and tallow. One vessel, which arrived July 30, 1819, "the schooner Combine, Boyd, 14 days from St. Thomas, with sugar, cotton, &c.," and three passengers, was consigned to John Jacob Astor & Son alone. One came from Rio de Janeiro by way of St. Thomas with hides, sugar, wine, rum, etc. Another brought coffee, indigo, cork, etc., from La Guayra, still another was loaded with coffee from Port au Prince, and a ship from Havana had a cargo of sugar, molasses, and fruit. (*New-York Gazette and General Advertiser*, June 20, 1817, p. 2, col. 2; April 18, 1818, p. 2, col. 3; April 21, 1818, p. 2, col. 2; April 17, 1819, p. 2, col. 2; July 31, 1819, p. 2, col. 3; November 29, 1819, p. 2, col. 2; April 12, 1820, p. 2, col. 3; April 25, 1821, p. 2, col. 2; August 13, 1823, p. 2, col. 3; November 15, 1823, p. 2, col. 3.) Such of these goods as came to the Astors were doubtless the returns of China goods. At one time Astor had an agent at St. Thomas to whom parts of his Canton cargoes were consigned. It is doubtful that any furs were shipped to that quarter of the world. It is probable that the specie which formed such a large element in these West Indian cargoes was employed in Astor's trade with Canton.

The trade of John Jacob Astor and the Astor firm with ports in the United States was much more important. From 1815 to 1827, inclusive, we know of over four-score vessels which brought freight to John Jacob Astor & Son, among other New York firms and merchants, from a number of ports in the United States. More than half the vessels bringing goods to the Astors from other United States ports came from New Orleans, the merchandise on board these vessels consisting chiefly of peltries, hides, furs, deer skins, buffalo robes, lead, cotton, sugar, tobacco, molasses, flour, and specie. The reason for the importance of this port is that the returns from Astor's Western Department headquarters were shipped to New York by way of New Orleans. These arrivals from New Orleans would continue so long as Astor remained in the fur trade. Charleston was next in importance, with perhaps a dozen vessels over that period, bringing cargoes consisting chiefly of cotton, rice, and specie. Baltimore and Philadelphia tagged along with perhaps half a dozen vessels each, the former concentrating on flour, with rum, gin, tea, tobacco, etc., as minor commodities, while the latter went in for extraordinarily assorted cargoes in which flour, brandy, molasses, and steel seemed perhaps most conspicuous. Boston was on an equality with Philadelphia, with similarly miscellaneous cargoes, in which teas and piece-goods appeared to stand out a trifle beyond the rest. Alexandria, like Baltimore, emphasized flour. (*New-York Gazette and General Advertiser*, 1815–27, *passim*.) It is impossible to say exactly which of these commodities actually reached the Astors. Were they interested in the cotton, sugar, and rice which bulked so largely among the southern commodities? Astor had at one time sent cotton to China, though it never formed a very prominent part of his exports to that country, owing to the competition of Indian cotton. Tobacco, molasses, and the various forms of alcoholic drinks could, of course, be employed in the Indian trade of the interior and the North West Coast. It is probable that part of the flour and rice was used in provisioning his ships. Tea from Boston and Philadelphia may have been brought to New York in a move to dominate the market. Lead from New Orleans could be employed both in the China trade and in traffic with the Indians, while the specie from that port and from Charleston would always be welcomed for its importance as an essential element in cargoes to Canton. Some of the goods from Boston and Philadelphia may have been the returns of fur shipments, as a portion of those from all ports probably was the proceeds of China goods. Thus it will be seen how Astor's coastwise trade, conducted entirely in the vessels of others, linked up closely with his two main and intimately related commercial interests, the trade with the Indians and with Canton.

2. My article "John Jacob Astor and the Sandalwood Trade of the Hawaiian Islands, 1816–1828," in the *Journal of Economic and Business History*, vol. ii, no. 3 (May, 1930), pp. 495–519, contains a good deal of the same material as that included in this present chapter, but I have made various additions and corrected some errors of detail in the latter.

3. Ms., Baker Library, Astor Papers, Letters, Wm. J. Pigot and R. Ebbets, London, September 28, 1812, to John Jacob Astor, N. Y.; Wm. J. Pigot, London, February 8, 1813, to John Jacob Astor, N. Y.; ms., Department of State, Washington, D. C., Miscellaneous Letters, March–April, 1813, John Jacob Astor, Philadelphia, April 4, 1813, to the Department of State (see above, vol. i, pp. 523–526).

4. Corney, Peter, *Voyages in the Northern Pacific*, Prof. W. D. Alexander, ed. (1896), pp. 38–41. Reprinted from the *London Literary Gazette*, 1821.

5. Ms., Baker Library, Astor Papers, Letters, Wm. J. Pigot, Coast of California, March 22, 1814, to John Ebbets, N. Y.

6. Franchere, Gabriel, *Narrative of a Voyage to the Northwest Coast of America* (1854), p. 193; Ross, Alexander, *Adventures of the First Settlers on the Oregon or Columbia River* (1923), p. 275.

7. Coues, Elliott, ed., *Henry-Thompson Journals*, 3 vols. (1897), vol. ii, p. 770.

8. Ms., Baker Library, Astor Papers, Letters, Wm. J. Pigot, Coast of California, March 22, 1814, to John Ebbets, N. Y.

9. Corney, *loc. cit.*

10. Ms., Baker Library, Astor Papers, Letters, Wm. J. Pigot, St. Peter and St. Paul, Kamschatka, January 7, 1816, to [John Ebbets, N. Y.].

11. Alexander, W. D., "The Relations between the Hawaiian Islands and Spanish America in Early Times," *Papers of the Hawaiian Historical Society*, no. 1 (1892), p. 8.

12. Adams, Capt. Alexander, "Extracts from An Ancient Log. Occurrences on board the brig Forester, of London, from Conception toward the Sandwich Islands," *Hawaiian Almanac and Annual, 1906* (1905), pp. 66–74. Selections from Adams' log book, January 16, 1816–December 26, 1818.

13. *New-York Gazette and General Advertiser*, November 15, 1816, p. 2, col. 2.

14. *Istoritcheskoe Obosranie Obrazovanie Rossiysko-Amerikanskoi Kompaniy, i deistvia eya do nastoyashtchavo vremeny. sostavil P. Tikhmeneff*: Chast 1 (Historical Review of the Origin of the Russian American Company and its doings up to the present time, compiled by P. Tikhmeneff, part 1, St. Petersburg, 1861), pp. 189–190, translation in the Bancroft Library, Berkeley, California.

15. Ms., Baker Library, Astor Papers, Letters, William J. Pigot, St. Peter and St. Paul, Kamschatka, January 7, 1816, to [John Ebbets, N. Y.]; William J. Pigot, Ochotzk, August 1, 1817, to Meyer and Bruxner [St. Petersburg]; Meyer and Bruxner, St. Petersburg, October 23, 26, 1817, to [one of Astor's London agents]; William J. Pigot, St. Peter and St. Paul, Kamchatsk, October 14/26, 1818, to John Jacob Astor, N. Y.

16. Irving, Washington, *Astoria* (1836), chap. lviii; Ross, *op. cit.*, chap. xvii; Franchere, *op. cit.*, pp. 224, 226; Coues, *op. cit.*, pp. 841–863, *passim.*

17. Franchere, *op. cit.*, p. 368; ms., Baker Library, Astor Papers, Letters, William J. Pigot, St. Peter and St. Paul, Kamschatka, January 7, 1816, to [John Ebbets, N. Y.].

18. Ms., Bancroft Library, Berkeley, California, Archivo del arzobispado, Cartas de los misioneros de California, tomo ii, p. 101; *ibid.*, Provincial State Papers, tomo xix, p. 383; *ibid.*, Provincial Records, tomo xix, p. 136; *ibid.* (copy), Provincial State Papers, Benecia, Military, tomo xlv, p. 3–6.

19. Bancroft, Hubert Howe, *The Northwest Coast*, 2 vols. (1884), vol. i, pp. 332–333, vol. ii, p. 235; Franchere, *op. cit.*, p. 368.

20. Corney, *op. cit.*, pp. 41–46. The journal of John Suter gives an account of this episode and contains frequent mention of the *Pedler* and

the *Forester* (ms. book, Massachusetts Historical Society, Boston, Log of the *Atahualpa*, July 29, August 2, October 2, 1815).

21. Barnard, Charles H., *A Voyage round the World during the Years 1812 . . . 1816* (1829), pp. 218–219, 221, 253–254.

22. *New-York Gazette and General Advertiser*, October 17, 1816, p. 2, col. 1; December 24, 1816, p. 3, col. 2.

23. *Ibid.*, June 29, 1815, p. 2, col. 4.

24. Barnard, *op. cit.*, p. 221.

25. *Niles' Weekly Register*, vol. xxii (April 5, 1817), p. 96.

26. Ms., Archives of Hawaii, Honolulu, F. O. & Ex., Bill of Sale of the *Albatross* from Nathan Winship to John Jacob Astor and John Ebbets, September 21, 1816, and from John Ebbets to the King of the Hawaiian Islands, October 16, 1816 (see below, vol. ii, pp. 1146–1150).

27. Adams, *op. cit.*, pp. 67–68.

28. *New-York Gazette and General Advertiser*, June 29, 1815, p. 2, col. 4.

29. For a mythical account of an earlier interest of Astor in sandalwood, see Chapter VI, which deals with his trade with the Orient prior to the War of 1812.

30. Ms., Essex Institute, Salem, Massachusetts, American Trade at Canton, June 6, 1816–May 25, 1817.

31. Hunnewell, James F., "Voyage in the Brig Bordeaux Packet, Boston to Honolulu, 1817, and Residence in Honolulu, 1817–1818," *Papers of the Hawaiian Historical Society*, no. 8 (1895), pp. 5, 8.

32. She may have made a voyage to the North West Coast in the interim, though it is more likely that she was trading for sandalwood.

33. The term "Spanish Main," though properly applied only to the Caribbean, was used by Pacific traders as a general term referring to the sea bordering on any Spanish-speaking country.

34. Ms., Department of State, Washington, D. C., Consular Records, Omoa, Arrivals and Departures from Coquimbo, April, 1817–July, 1819. There is a good deal of confusion in the records in regard to this voyage of the *Enterprise* to Coquimbo. One account says that she arrived in January (ms., Department of State, Washington, D. C., Consular Records, Valparaiso). This, however, is a minor matter. Somewhat more serious is a reference to the arrival on February 25, 1818, from the North West Coast, of the schooner *Enterprise*, commanded by Captain Ebbets (ms., Department of State, Washington, D. C., Consular Records, Omoa, vol. i). Again, we find the statement that in January, 1818, the ship *Eagle*, commanded by Captain Ebbets, arrived from the North West Coast (ms., Department of State, Washington, D. C., Consular Records, Valparaiso, vol. i). It is evident that the schooner *Enterprise* should be the ship *Enterprise* and that the ship *Eagle*, commanded by Captain Ebbets, is an error for the schooner *Eagle*, in charge of Davis and Meek, which was at Coquimbo at the same time as the *Enterprise* (ms., Depart-

ment of State, Washington, D. C., Consular Records, Valparaiso). The statement as given in the text is the most complete and most consistent and therefore the most likely to be correct in the main.

35. A reference in Kotzebue (Kotzebue, Otto Von, *A Voyage of Discovery into the South Seas and Beering's [sic] Straits . . . in . . . 1815–1818*, 3 vols. (1821), vol. ii, pp. 195, 198, 203) may explain her movements during the past year. He states that Taracanof, agent of the Russian American Company, during October, 1817, "concluded a contract with M. Hebet, the owner of two ships lying here [Honolulu Harbor], by which he bound himself to maintain and clothe the Aleutians [belonging to the *Kadiak*] a whole year, on condition that he shall bring them to California, where they should employ themselves in catching sea-otters on the islands there. After the expiration of this year, Hebet brings them to Sitka, and gives the Company half of the skins obtained." There is no certainty that the reference is to John Ebbets, but this is at least an interesting possibility.

36. Hunnewell, James, "Reminiscences," *The Friend* (Honolulu, January, 1867), quoted in Thomas G. Thrum's "The Sandalwood Trade of Early Hawaii," *Hawaiian Almanac and Annual, 1905* (1904), p. 55.

37. Ms., Library of Congress, New York Customs Records, *Enterprise*, 1st voyage; *New-York Gazette and General Advertiser*, September 6, 1819, p. 2, col. 3.

38. Kamakau, S. M., etc., "Early Sandal-Wood Trade: Hawaiian Version," *Hawaiian Almanac and Annual, 1906* (1905), pp. 105–108.

39. *Supplement to Report of* [Hawaiian] *Minister of Foreign Relations, 1856*, pp. 6–30.

40. Mathison, Gilbert Farquhar, *Narrative of a Visit to Brazil, Chili, Peru and the Sandwich Islands* (1825), p. 451; Arago, J., *Voyage round the world in the Uranie and Physicienne, 1817–1820* (1853), p. 125.

41. *Supplement to Report of* [Hawaiian] *Minister of Foreign Relations, 1856*, pp. 6–30; Alexander, W. D., "The Story of Cleopatra's Barge," *Papers of the Hawaiian Historical Society*, no. 13 (1906), p. 29; Mathison, *op. cit.*, p. 457.

42. Arago, *loc. cit.*

43. Except where other sources are specified, all the information concerning the *Beaver's* protracted voyage has been drawn from two closely related sources. The first of these is the narrative of her captain, Richard J. Cleveland's *A Narrative of Voyages and Commercial Enterprises*, 2 vols. (1842), vol. ii, pp. 80–223; the second is the work of his son, who not only drew profusely from the work just mentioned but also presented some of the original letters upon which it had been based. It is by Horace William Shaler Cleveland and is entitled *Voyages of a Merchant Navigator* (1886), pp. 167–224.

44. Ms., Department of State, Washington, D. C., Claims on Spain,

Convention, 1819, vol. xiii, Schr. Beaver, Ship Beaver, Schr. Boston, Schr. Baltimore, Memorial of Wm. B. Astor for J. J. Astor in Europe, September 7, 1821.

45. The only arms and ammunition invoiced were 125 muskets with bayonets and 8,600 lbs. of powder (ms., Department of State, Washington, D. C., Claims on Spain, Convention, 1819, vol. xiii, Schr. Beaver, Ship Beaver, Schr. Boston, Schr. Baltimore, Invoice of the Beaver, June 30, 1817, see below, vol. ii, pp. 1150-1153).

46. *New-York Gazette and General Advertiser*, June 30, 1817, p. 2, col. 3.

47. Ms., Library of Congress, Miscellaneous Personal Collections, John Jacob Astor, N. Y., November 15, 1817, to Captain Cleveland and Mr. Ribas.

48. Greenhow, Robert, *The History of Oregon and California* (1845), pp. 307-310.

49. Ms., Library of Congress, Jeremy Robinson Papers, Letters, Francisco Ribas, Conception, November 18, 1817, to Thomas Lloyd Halsey, American Consul, Buenos Ayres; Francisco Ribas, Santiago, January 2, 1818, to John Jacob Abstor [sic], N. Y.; Francisco Ribas, Valparaiso, February 3, 1818, to James Biddle.

50. Ms., Department of State, Washington, D. C., Letters of J. B. Prevost, J. B. Prevost, Sant Jago de Chile, February 9, 1818, to J. Q. Adams, Secretary of State; J. B. Prevost, Valparaiso, March 8, 1818, to J. Q. Adams, Secretary of State.

51. *House Executive Documents*, 28th Cong., 2nd sess. (1844-45), vol. ii, no. 42, p. 16, John Quincy Adams, Department of State, May 2, 1818, to George Erving, Minister Plenipotentiary, Madrid.

52. Ms., Library of Congress, Jeremy Robinson Papers, Letters, Francisco Ribas, Santiago de Chile, March 10, 1818, to John Jacob Abstor [sic], N. Y.

53. *Ibid.*, Jeremy Robinson's Diary, May 22-June 30, 1818, June 25, 1818.

54. *Ibid.*, Diary iv, November 25, 1818. Cleveland, while acknowledging the assistance of Captain Biddle, and the good intentions of J. B. Prevost, was by no means willing to give them that credit for the *Beaver's* recovery which the New York press conferred upon them (*New-York Gazette and General Advertiser*, January 4, 1819, p. 2, col. 3; June 1, 1819, p. 2, col. 2; June 2, 1819, p. 2, cols. 1-3; June 30, 1819, p. 2, col. 1).

55. *New-York Gazette and General Advertiser*, October 7, 1820, p. 2, col. 3.

56. The memorials of Astor, Captain Cleveland, and of the insurance companies concerned, the Firemen Insurance Company and the National Insurance Company, are to be found in: ms., Department of State, Washington, D. C., Claims on Spain, Convention, 1819, vol. xiii, Schr. Beaver, Ship Beaver, Schr. Boston, Schr. Baltimore.

57. *New-York Gazette and General Advertiser*, October 30, 1820, p. 1, col. 3.

58. Ms., Library of Congress, New York Customs Records, November 3, 1820.

59. Hunter, William C., *The 'Fan Kwae' at Canton before Treaty Days, 1825–1844* (Shanghai, etc., 1911), p. 1; ms. book, Whitehall, London, East India Office, East India Company Records, China Factory Records, Diaries, 1821–22, p. 185; *ibid.*, vol. 228, 1822–23, p. 167; *ibid.*, vol. 230, 1823–24; *ibid.*, vol. 232, 1824–25, p. 159; *ibid.*, vol. 235, 1825–26, p. 141; *ibid.*, vol. 239, 1827–28, p. 204; *ibid.*, vol. 241, 1828–29, p. 198.

60. Ms., Library of Congress, New York Customs Records, J. J. Astor & Son, brig *Pedler*, December 1, 1819.

61. Gulick, The Rev. and Mrs. Orramel Hinckley, *The Pilgrims of Hawaii* (1918), p. 83. Extract from the journal of Elisha Loomis.

62. Roquefeuil met Pigot at the Islands in January, 1819 (Roquefeuil, Camille de, *Voyage autour du Monde*, 2 vols. (Paris, 1843 [?]), vol. ii, p. 350). On December 15, 1819, Pigot bought the *St. Martin*, the vessel in which he had come from Kamchatka, from William H. Davis and Thomas Meek, for $10,000. The schooner *St. Martin* arrived at Manila on March 21, 1820, in company with the *Sylph*, and sailed for the Hawaiian Islands on June 11 (ms., Department of State, Washington, D. C., Consular Records, Manila, vol. i). She arrived on August 19, in distress. However, Pigot had not himself commanded the vessel on this voyage, but had sent her in charge of Captain Dean. (*Missionary Herald*, vol. xvii (1821), p. 243.) He is mentioned as having been at Honolulu on April 19 and May 20, 1820 (Gulick, *op. cit.*, p. 82; Bingham, Hiram, *A Residence of Twenty-One Years in the Sandwich Islands* (1849), pp. 82, 95).

63. *Missionary Herald*, vol. xvii (1821), pp. 138–141.

64. Ms., Archives of Hawaii, Honolulu, F. O. & Ex., 1820, Promissory note from Tamooree and George Tamooree to William J. Pigot and John Meek, Oahu, June 23, 1820; Lydecker, Robert C., "The Archives of Hawaii," *Papers of the Hawaiian Historical Society*, no. 13 (1906), p. 21.

65. *Missionary Herald*, vol. xvii (1821), p. 141.

66. *Zapiski K. Khlebnikova o Americe* (Letters of K. Khlebnikoff on America; St. Petersburg, 1861), pp. 116–117. Translation in the Bancroft Library, Berkeley, California.

67. Bingham, *op. cit.*, p. 118.

68. *Missionary Herald*, vol. xviii (1822), p. 202.

69. Manuscript notes of Edwin B. Hewes on the trade between the North West Coast and China. The statement that Pigot was in command of the *Pedler* on her voyage to Canton in 1821 is inconsistent with his presence at the Islands about that time as recorded in the journals of men on the spot.

70. Ms. book, Widener Library, Harvard University, Josiah Marshall,

Letters Received from Sandwich Islands and Canton, 1820–32 [hereafter in this chapter referred to as ms. book, Marshall Letters], William Babcock by B. Elwell, Oahu, May 3, 1821, to Messrs. Marshall and Wildes, Boston.

71. Ms. book, Essex Institute, Salem, Massachusetts, Log of the Schooner *Eagle*, 1820–22, February 5, 1821.

72. Ms. book, Widener Library, Harvard University, Bryant and Sturgis Papers, Letter Book, September 17, 1818–March 20, 1829, pp. 161–162, Bryant & Sturgis, Boston, October 12, 1820, to Charles B. Bullard; pp. 164–166, Bryant & Sturgis, October 12, 1820, to Captain John Suter; p. 163, Bryant & Sturgis, October 12, 1820, to Captain Lemuel Porter.

73. Ms., Library of Congress, New York Customs Records, Permission, ship *William and John*.

74. Ms. book, Marshall Letters, William Babcock by B. Elwell, Oahu, May 3, 1821, to Messrs. Marshall and Wildes, Boston.

75. Ms. book, Essex Institute, Salem, Massachusetts, Log of the Schooner *Eagle*, 1820–22, April 18, 1821.

76. Ms. book, Marshall Letters, Thomas Brown, Oahu, May 21, 1821, to Josiah Marshall, Boston.

77. Ms. book, Essex Institute, Salem, Massachusetts, Log of the Schooner *Eagle*, 1820–22, May 19, 1821.

78. Ms. book, Marshall Letters, John Bragg, Maui, May 25, 1821, to Josiah Marshall; William Coles, Jr., Maui, May 25, 1821, to Messrs. Marshall and Wildes, Boston.

79. *Ibid.*, Eliab Grimes, Oahu, July 5, 1821, to Messrs. Marshall and Wildes; John Coffin Jones, Jr., Honolulu, Oahu, July 6, 1821, to Messrs. Marshall and Wildes.

80. *Ibid.*, John Coffin Jones, Jr., Honolulu, Oahu, July 6, 1821, to Messrs. Marshall and Wildes. Pigot had by this time left the *Pedler* and gone with a company of Americans in the *St. Martin* to settle Fanning's Island. The log of the brig *Arab*, which was on the North West Coast in 1821, mentions the presence of the *Pedler*, Captain Meek (Bancroft, *op. cit.*, vol. i, p. 340).

81. Ms. book, Essex Institute, Salem, Massachusetts, Log of the Schooner *Eagle*, 1820–22, September 24, 1821.

82. Ms. book, Marshall Letters, John Coffin Jones, Jr., Oahu, October 2, 1821, to Josiah Marshall; the same, October 5, 1821, to the same.

83. "The New York Boat sold $5000" (ms. book, Essex Institute, Salem, Massachusetts, Log of the Schooner *Eagle*, 1820–22, September 29, 1821).

84. This boat was named the *John Jacob Astor* and was launched August 2, 1821 (*New-York Gazette and General Advertiser*, May 20, 1822, p. 2, col. 1).

85. Ms. book, Essex Institute, Salem, Massachusetts, Log of the Schooner *Eagle*, 1820–22, November 6, 1821.

86. Ms. book, Whitehall, London, East India Office, East India Company Records, China Factory Records, Diaries, 1821–22, p. 185.

87. Ms. book, Marshall Letters, John Coffin Jones, Jr., Oahu, November 5, 1821, to Josiah Marshall; Thomas Brown [?], Oahu, November 20, 1821, to Josiah Marshall, Esqr. and Captain Dixey Wildes; Robert Ellwell, Oahu, October 10, 1821, to Josiah Marshall [?]. Although Meek was apparently hardly so successful a trader as Ebbets, he did distinguish himself at some time during his stay in the Islands on the *Pedler* by selling an old cannon, which had been brought from New York in the *William and John*, to Kamehameha II. "It was paid for in sandal wood — one hundred and fifty piculs — worth in China five thousand dollars." (*Pacific Commercial Advertiser*, Honolulu, October 22, 1857.) At this time 150 piculs of sandalwood would probably have been worth no more than $1,500 in China, rather than $5,000, but even this price gives some idea of the high rates at which American traders sold goods to the Hawaiian king and chiefs.

88. *Ibid.*, William French, Canton, January 4, 1822, to Josiah Marshall.

89. Ms. book, Whitehall, London, East India Office, East India Company Records, Diaries, 1821–22, p. 185; ms. book, Essex Institute, Salem, Massachusetts, Log of the Schooner *Eagle*, 1820–22, March 22, 1822.

90. Ms., Library of Congress, New York Customs Records, W. B. Astor, ship *William and John*, May 19, 1823; "143 days from Canton" (*New-York Gazette and General Advertiser*, August 20, 1822, p. 2, col. 3).

91. A good deal about the movements of the *Pedler* from August 19 to December 26, 1821, and from March 6 to December 7, 1822, can be found in the Log of the *Arab*, 1821–25, in the Bancroft Library, Berkeley, California. The *Arab*, which was in company with the *Pedler* for much of the time, was commanded by W. H. Davis, who seems to have frequently cooperated with captains of Astor vessels in business transactions.

92. Ms. book, Essex Institute, Salem, Massachusetts, Log of the Schooner *Eagle*, 1820–22, November 26, December 25, 1821.

93. Ms. book, Whitehall, London, East India Office, East India Company Records, China Factory Records, Diaries, 1821–22, p. 185.

94. John Ebbets and William H. Davis had been earlier associated in transactions connected with the Pacific trade. In June, 1818, the schooner *St. Martin*, then lying at Coquimbo, was described as belonging jointly to John Ebbets and William H. Davis (ms., Department of State, Washington, D. C., Consular Records, Manila, vol. i, Andrew Steuart, Consul, Manila, June 18, 1820, to John Quincy Adams, Secretary of State). Both these captains were at Coquimbo at the same time, Ebbets in the *Enterprise*, William H. Davis, accompanied by Thomas Meek, in the *Eagle* (ms., Department of State, Washington, D. C., Consular Records, Val-

paraiso). Whether the purchase by Ebbets of a share in the *St. Martin* was made on Astor's account or for that of the captain alone, we do not know. However, he did not long retain any interest in the vessel, for in December, 1819, the owners were William H. Davis and Thomas Meek, who had been in charge of the *Eagle* at Coquimbo when the *St. Martin* and Ebbets in the *Enterprise* were also at that port (ms., Department of State, Washington, D. C., Consular Records, Manila, vol. i). In view of certain instances of confusion we have previously observed in the consular records connected with this port, the question may arise whether Ebbets actually was ever interested in the *St. Martin*. At any rate, his connection with this vessel was negligible so far as the business activities of his employer were concerned.

95. Ms. book, Marshall Letters, John Coffin Jones, Jr., Oahu, December 23, 1821, to Messrs. Marshall and Wildes; Eliab Grimes [Oahu, December 23, 1821] to Messrs. Marshall and Wildes; John Coffin Jones, Jr., Oahu, October 5, 1821, to Josiah Marshall, Esq. and Capt. Dixey Wildes; Pitman & French, Canton, March, 1822, to Josiah Marshall.

96. Ms. book, Essex Institute, Salem, Massachusetts, Log of the Schooner *Eagle*, 1820–22, March 22, 1822.

97. Ms. book, Marshall Letters, Thomas Brown, Canton, March 22, 1822, to Josiah Marshall; ms. book, Whitehall, London, East India Office, East India Company Records, China Factory Records, Diaries, 1821–22, p. 185.

98. It is recorded that in 1822, John Meek, of the brig *Pedler*, purchased at New Archangel 4,361 fur seals at $1.75, payment being made in goods (*Zapiski K. Khlebnikova o Americe*, pp. 116–117).

99. Ms. book, Bancroft Library, Berkeley, California, Log of the *Arab*, June 29, 1822.

100. Ms. book, Marshall Letters, John Coffin Jones, Jr., Oahu, August 10, 1822, to Marshall & Wildes. Two missionaries mention that on August 15, 1822, "on board the Piddler, captain Meek, we saw a curious sledge from Kamschatka" (Tyerman, Rev. Daniel, and Bennet, George, *Journal of Voyages and Travels . . . in the South Sea Islands, China, India . . . 1821 . . . 1829*, 3 vols. (1832), vol. ii).

101. *Ibid.*, John Coffin Jones, Jr., Oahu, October 10, 1822, to Josiah Marshall & Capt. Dixey Wildes.

102. *Ibid.*, John Coffin Jones, Jr., Oahu, December 21, 1822, to Josiah Marshall and Capt. Dixey Wildes.

103. Ms. book, Whitehall, London, East India Office, East India Company Records, China Factory Records, Diaries, vol. 230, 1823–24.

104. Ms. book, Massachusetts Historical Society, Boston, Boston Marine Insurance Company Records, vol. Cc, no. 6614, September 3, 1822.

105. Ms. book, Marshall Letters, Pitman & French, Canton, April 25, 1823, to Josiah Marshall; ms. book, Whitehall, London, East India Office, East India Company Records, China Factory Records, Diaries, vol. 230, 1823–24.

106. Ms., Library of Congress, New York Customs Records, *Pedler*, August 18, 1823; *New-York Gazette and General Advertiser*, August 18, 1823, p. 2, col. 4.

107. Ms. book, Marshall Letters, Dixey Wildes [?], Oahu, April 29, 1824, to Josiah Marshall.

108. Ms. book, Widener Library, Harvard University, Bryant and Sturgis Papers, Letter Book September 17, 1818–March 20, 1829, p. 297, Bryant & Sturgis, Boston, November 24, 1823, to C. B. Bullard.

109. "Reynolds, Stephen, Journal of," *Hawaiian Almanac and Annual, 1909* (1908), p. 153.

110. Ms. book, Marshall Letters, Pitman & French, Canton, November 5, 1824, to Josiah Marshall.

111. *Ibid.*, Dixey Wildes, Oahu, July 2, 1824, to Josiah Marshall.

112. *Ibid.*, Dixey Wildes, Oahu, November 5, 1824, to Josiah Marshall.

113. Stewart, C. S., *Private Journal of a Voyage to the Pacific Ocean and Residence at the Sandwich Islands in the Years 1822 ... 1825* (1828), pp. 310–311.

114. Ms. book, Marshall Letters, Dixey Wildes, Oahu, September 7, 1824, to Josiah Marshall.

115. *Ibid.*, Dixey Wildes, Oahu, November 5, 1824, to Josiah Marshall.

116. Ms., Department of the Navy, Washington, D. C., Archives, Capt. Finch's Cruise in the U. S. S. *Vincennes*, John Ebbets, Oahu, October 26, 1829, to William B. Finch (see below, vol. ii, pp. 1195–1197).

117. Stewart, *op. cit.*, p. 313.

118. Ms. book, Marshall Letters, Dixey Wildes, Oahu, September 7, 1824 to [?].

119. *Ibid.*, Dixey Wildes, Oahu, November 5, 1824, to Josiah Marshall.

120. *Ibid.*, E. Grimes, Oahu, November 5, 1824, to Josiah Marshall.

121. Davis, William Heath, *Seventy-five years in California*, Douglas S. Watson, ed. (1929), pp. 397, 400–401. "Records of ships arriving from 1774 to 1847 ... at California ports ... 1825 ... Tamaahmaah (Am. brig) John Michi [*sic*], master."

122. Ms. book, Marshall Letters, Dixey Wildes, Oahu, December 7, 1824, to Josiah Marshall.

123. *Ibid.*, Eliab Grimes, Oahu, March 13, 1825, to Josiah Marshall.

124. Stewart, *op. cit.*, p. 300; ms. book, Marshall Letters, Russell & Co., Canton, June 14, 1825, to Josiah Marshall.

125. *Ibid.*, William H. McNeil, Oahu, March 21, 1825, to Josiah Marshall.

126. "Reynolds, Stephen, Journal of," *Hawaiian Almanac and Annual, 1909* (1908), p. 156.

127. Stewart, *op. cit.*, p. 300.

128. Ms. book, Marshall Letters, Russell & Co., Canton, June 14, 1825, to Josiah Marshall; ms. book, Whitehall, London, East India Office, East India Company Records, China Factory Records, Diaries, vol. 235, 1825–26, p. 141.

129. *New-York Gazette and General Advertiser*, December 20, 1825, p. 2, col. 2; ms. book, Marshall Letters, letters from Oahu to Boston, January–March, 1825, *passim*.

130. *Ibid.*, Eliab Grimes, Oahu, March 22, 27, 1825, to Josiah Marshall.

131. Ms., Department of State, Washington, D. C., Consular Letters, Lima, vol. i, 1823 to June, 1827, no. 4, Report of American shipping at the Port of Chorrillos for the six mos. ending December 31st 1825.

132. Stewart, *op. cit.*, pp. 154, 326.

133. Ms. book, Marshall Letters, William Henry McNeil, Oahu, January 10, 1826, to Josiah Marshall.

134. *Ibid.*, A. B. Thompson, Oahu, January 26, 1826, to Josiah Marshall.

135. *Ibid.*, Eliab Grimes, Lima, May 8, 1827, to Josiah Marshall.

136. Ms., Department of State, Washington, D. C., Consular Letters, Honolulu, vol. i, 1820 to June, 1843, List of vessels visiting the Port of Honorura Island of Woahoo from the 1st day of February to the 1st day of May 1826.

137. Ms. book, Marshall Letters, Eliab Grimes, Maria Island, April 29, 1826, to Josiah Marshall.

138. Thrum, Thomas G., ed., "Honolulu in Primitive Days" (extracts from the journal of a pioneer merchant, 1826–29), *Hawaiian Almanac and Annual, 1901* (1900), pp. 74–87.

139. Ms. book, Marshall Letters, Eliab Grimes, Lima, May 8, 1827, to Josiah Marshall.

140. *Ibid.*, J. C. Jones, Jr., Oahu, July 20, 1827, to Capt. Dixey Wildes.

141. Davis, *op. cit.*, pp. 401–402. "1827 . . . Tamaahmaah, J. Michi [*sic*], master." Elsewhere it is stated that Robert J. Elwell was "master or sup[ercargo]" of the *Tamaahmaah* while on the California coast in 1827. Evidently he held the latter position. (Bancroft, Hubert Howe, *California*, 7 vols. (1885), vol. iii, pp. 145, 149.)

142. Ms. book, Marshall Letters, John C. Jones, Jr., Oahu, September 30, 1827, to Capt. Dixey Wildes.

143. *Ibid.*, J. C. Jones, Jr., Oahu, December 25, 1827, to Josiah Marshall.

144. Kuykendall, R. S., "Some Early Commercial Adventures of Hawaii," *Report of the Hawaiian Historical Society, 1928* (1929), pp. 15–33. On November 2, 1829, the king, Governor Boki, Kaahumanu, and

other chiefs signed a note for 2,165 piculs of sandalwood at $7.00 per picul, the amount still due on the brig.

145. Ms. book, Marshall Letters, Eliab Grimes, Oahu, July 20, 1828, to Josiah Marshall; J. C. Jones, Jr., Oahu, July 20, 1828, to Josiah Marshall.

146. The *Tamaahmaah*, still commanded by Meek, was on the California coast in 1829 (Davis, *op. cit.*, p. 402).

147. The dangerous bar at the mouth of the Columbia and the fact that the Hudson's Bay Company had a post at Fort George (abandoned in 1824 for Fort Vancouver) kept American vessels from actually entering the river for the purpose of trade. According to the Hudson's Bay Company factor, Dr. John McLoughlin, "the first American vessel that entered the Columbia River to trade since 1814 was the Oahee, Captain Dominis, in February, 1829" (McLoughlin, Dr. John, "Document," *Oregon Historical Quarterly*, vol. ii, no. 2 (June, 1900), pp. 193–206).

148. Briggs, L. Vernon, *History and Genealogy of the Cabot Family, 1475–1927*, 2 vols. (1927), p. 575. "Feb. 15, 1827 . . . Mr. Astor having entered it [the China trade] anew was unexpected to us."

149. Alexander, W. D., *Brief History of the Hawaiian People* (1891), p. 156; Mathison, *op. cit.*, p. 458.

150. Paulding, Lieut. Hiran, *Journal of Cruise of United States Schooner Dolphin* (1831), p. 232.

151. Mathison, *op. cit.*, p. 457.

152. Wilkes, Charles, *United States Exploring Expedition, 1838 to 1842*, 5 vols. (1845), vol. v, Appendix lx, p. 527.

153. Dibble, Rev. Sheldon, *History of the Sandwich Islands* (1909), p. 60.

154. *Supplement to Report of* [Hawaiian] *Minister of Foreign Relations, 1856*, pp. 6–30.

155. Wilkes, *op. cit.*, vol. iv, p. 214.

156. Mathison, *op. cit.*, p. 458; Beechey, Capt. F. W., *Narrative of a Voyage to the Pacific*, 2 vols. (1831), vol. ii, p. 418.

157. *Ibid.*

158. The debt is sometimes said to have amounted to $500,000 (Alexander, W. D., *Brief History of the Hawaiian People*, p. 196).

159. *Report of the* [Hawaiian] *Minister of Foreign Relations, 1855*, pp. 2–4; *Supplement to Report of* [Hawaiian] *Minister of Foreign Relations, 1856*, pp. 6–30; ms., Department of the Navy, Washington, D. C., Archives, Capt. Finch's Cruise in the U. S. S. *Vincennes*, John Coffin Jones, Jr., and Thomas Meek by John Meek, to William B. Finch.

160. Thrum, *loc. cit.* Manini, who was a Spaniard and one of the Europeans occupying high rank in the Hawaiian kingdom, had probably been appointed as Ebbets' understudy while the latter was at Kauai. There were at that time five Meeks, all brothers and shipmasters, some of

whom were in the Pacific trade. John was the one who had hitherto been connected with Astor and Ebbets, but Thomas and John occasionally acted one for the other; Manini may have been the sub-agent for representatives of two or more firms (Brewer, Charles, *Reminiscences* (1884), pp. 27–31).

161. Ms., Department of the Navy, Washington, D. C., Archives, Capt. Finch's Cruise in the U. S. S. *Vincennes*, John Coffin Jones, Jr., and Thomas Meek by John Meek, Oahu, October 28, 1829, to William B. Finch.

162. *Ibid.*, John Ebbets, Oahu, October 26, 1829, to William B. Finch (see below, vol. ii, pp. 1195–1197); *ibid.*, Acknowledgment of indebtedness from the King, Regent, and Chiefs of the Sandwich Islands to John Ebbets, Honolulu, November 2, 1829 (see below, vol. ii, p. 1197).

163. Wilkes, *op. cit.*, vol. iv, p. 37; Simpson, Sir George, *Journey round the World during 1841–42*, 2 vols. (1847), vol. ii, pp. 13–14.

164. "Extracts from Missionary Letters," *Honolulu Mercury*, April, 1930, p. 454; *Missionary Herald*, vol. xvii (1821), pp. 131–141, *passim*; vol. xviii (1822), pp. 92, 202, 212, 277, 279.

165. Ms. book, Marshall Letters, *passim*, especially those from John Coffin Jones, Jr., and Eliab Grimes.

166. Ms. book, Widener Library, Harvard University, Bryant and Sturgis Papers, Letter Book, September 17, 1818–March 20, 1829, pp. 265–268, Bryant & Sturgis [October 3, 1822], to Charles Hammatt.

167. Ms. book, Marshall Letters, Thomas Brown, Oahu, November 24, 1821, to Josiah Marshall.

CHAPTER XIV

THE AMERICAN FUR COMPANY FROM THE WAR TO THE ESTABLISHMENT OF THE WESTERN DEPARTMENT
1815–1822

THERE is no doubt that Astor's intention in 1808, and probably for some years before that date, was to monopolize the fur trade both within the boundaries of the United States as they were then defined and also beyond them in as much of the North American territory then unclaimed as he could possibly compass. The incorporation of the American Fur Company in April, 1808, was one step in that direction; the establishment of the Pacific Fur Company in June, 1810, was another. Astor's arrangement with the Montreal Michilimackinac Company to become interested in the proportion of one-half in a firm to be known as the South West Fur Company, which was ratified in January, 1811, was at least a half-step. The Pacific Fur Company branch of Astor's organization was lopped completely off during the war by his rivals of the North West Company, but the South West Fur Company limb, though its productivity was impaired by the unseasonable blasts from the battlefield, was rendered only partially and temporarily sterile. The first outfit prepared by the South West Fur Company was made up in the spring of 1811 while peace still reigned, but the outfit of the succeeding year was hardly ready for the interior before war had broken out. Hampered by the difficulty of securing trade-goods and by the Indians' desertion of the trap line for the war-path, the trade during the years 1812, 1813, and 1814 shrank to a mere fraction of its former extent. However, shipments of furs from the Great Lakes region were made from Quebec to England by the Canadian partners in 1812 and 1813, and other peltries were brought from Canada into the United States by various means, as we have already observed, and sold by Astor for the Company's account. But during this period of war the fur trade was in a dormant condition, as is shown by the poverty and uninformative character of the correspondence carried on between John Jacob Astor and McTavish, McGillivrays & Co., of Montreal, concerning the Company's affairs.[1]

The agreement for the South West Fur Company would expire with the returns from the outfit to be made up in the spring of 1815. In the meantime Astor was making plans for his conduct when the arrangement should lapse. When he sent John Day to Montreal in the fall of 1813 to bring out some furs he warned him, "do not forget to sound them of, how they would like to sell to me their Interest in the Indian Country."[2] Here we have a hint that Astor was considering taking advantage of the provision that the Company could be dissolved by mutual consent. About the same time he told Ramsay Crooks, who was on a similar mission in the Great Lakes region, that he intended to "take hold of the whole," that is, of the fur trade in that area. In February, 1814, he encouraged Crooks with the assurance that "if we get peace . . . we shall make as much money as you want by the Indian trade."[3]

It is a curious fact that there seems to have been no provision in the South West Fur Company agreement forbidding any of the associates to conduct an independent trade in furs. It will be remembered that Crooks was sent to buy furs in the Great Lakes region during the war; and it was even suggested that, if goods could be obtained, he might make up some outfits for responsible traders. Robert Stuart seems to have been engaged in similar transactions on the Canadian frontier. Consequently it is not surprising that, with the arrival of peace, Astor should begin to consider how he might take to himself even greater power over the fur trade than he had achieved prior to the outbreak of war. He was encouraged by a letter from Charles

Gratiot, of St. Louis, who had written late in May, 1814: "The Indian trade will have in future to be carried on by a Comp^y to become profitable as it stand now it is too precarious for any body to hazard anything unless the factories were to be abolished."[4] Just three days before the news of peace arrived Astor wrote in answer to a letter from Henry Forrest of Mackinac, who had offered his services for the fur trade, that the risk was too great so long as war continued, but that "I cannot but help thinking but that in less than 6 months we must have peace when most assuredly there will be an entire change in the Indian trade, it is a trade by which I have lost money yet I prefer it to any other & I have not lost my hopes, but that ere long I shall participate to a considerable extent of its goods & its evils."[5] Six days later Astor ordered Crooks to return to New York as soon as possible, since he intended to engage in the Indian trade with goods which would arrive in about two months, just in time to make up an outfit for 1815.[6] A week after this, he expressed in a letter to one of his London correspondents, Thomas Wilson, couched in studiously noncommittal terms, the importance which he expected the fur trade hereafter to assume in his business life. "I have partly resolved," he said, "not to engage in any european business unless something would occasionally be done in Exchange, my object will be to the Canton trade & perhaps something in Furs on that I have not yet fix'd."[7]

On March 21, 1815, Robert Stuart, Crooks's friend, fellow Scot, and fellow Astorian, wrote him an exuberant letter explaining Astor's plans for the future and the part which the two friends were to have therein. "I . . . have only time," he wrote, "to give you the purport of a short tete-a-tete I had with the old Cock this morning Viz:—That he is digesting a very extensive plan for establishing all the Indian Countries within the line demarkation between G. B. and the U. S. and the probability is that a considerable time may elapse before that object can be brought to full maturity, as he wants an exclusive grant or privelege &c. &c. he added that it would be a pity, we should in the meantime be altogether inactive, therefore as he expects a parcel of Indian goods out in the Spring it is his wish that . . . you and myself would come to some arrangement either to purchase the goods and try the S. W. on our own Acct, or take them to Mackinac and give him a certain share of the profits (as might be agreed upon) These are the general outlines, from which you can very readily draw your own conclusions regarding his views, which I really believe are as friendly toward us all, as his own *dear* interest will permit, for of that you are no doubt aware, he will never loose sight *until some kind friend will put his or her fingers over his eyelids.*"[8] The italics in this letter are Stuart's. Astor himself wrote to Crooks early in April, "I wish you to be here to see if we cannot make some arrangements for something more important."[9]

Crooks probably returned to New York soon after this, and entered into a mutually satisfactory agreement with Astor for trading in the Indian country during 1815. James H. Lockwood states that on July 10, 1815, Crooks was his fellow passenger on a steamer for Mackinac, though Lockwood, writing forty years after the event, was doubtless in error when he stated that Crooks's reason for the journey was "to receive the property of the South-West Fur Company, which had been recently purchased by JOHN JACOB ASTOR of New York."[10] Crooks's activities at Mackinac were probably not unlike those in which we saw him engaged during the War of 1812, save that they were wider in scope and doubtless much more productive.

In the meantime, the agreement for the South West Fur Company was on the point of expiring. The last outfit of the five for which the Company had been established had been made up, and with its returns in the spring of 1816 the arrangement between Astor and the two Montreal firms would come to an end. If both parties agreed, there was no reason why the

Company should not be reconstituted for another term of years. Astor was not yet quite ready to throw himself into open competition with the Canadians, while they, now that the war was over, were not much better off than they had been in 1810 and 1811, when Astor's competition had forced them to compromise. Consequently, some time in the fall of 1815, William McGillivray seems to have gone to New York and arranged that the agreement of January, 1811, should be extended till the return of the 1820 outfit, that is, for five years beyond its original term. We have no copy of the agreement of 1815, but we do possess a copy of the 1811 document, somewhat revised and annotated, which probably formed the basis of the new arrangement. Aside from the removal of certain clauses which concerned only the original merging of the two companies, the principal changes were small omissions, such as that of the section concerning the annual sending of agents to Mackinac, and part of another granting the American Fur Company a $2\frac{1}{2}$ per cent commission on the proceeds of furs sold through that organization.[11]

On February 6, 1815, just before the coming of peace, an agreement had been made between the firms of Forsyth, Richardson & Co., McTavish, McGillivrays & Co. — Astor's Canadian partners — and Pierre de Rocheblave, all partners in the North West Company. The agreement, doubtless made in the belief that the war would continue, provided that the partnership was to carry on trade from Mackinac for nine years, while others could be admitted if necessary.[12] The coming of peace, of course, put matters on a different footing. On October 7, 1815, William McGillivray wrote to Astor from Montreal that he had "submitted the agreement entered into between us for the South Trade to Mess.rs Forsyth Richardson & Co, and to Pierre De Rocheblave Esq.r. I have the pleasure to inform you that they approve of the same."[13] De Rocheblave could not be left out of this agreement in view of the arrangement he had entered into with the two Montreal firms in February. Doubtless he was allowed to become a participant in their half-share of the Company.

In a letter written on December 30, 1816, to James Monroe, the secretary of State, Astor accounted for his arrangement with the Canadians in the following words: "Soon after the late War I found that the Canada Traders had pretty well established themselves in the Indian Country within the Boundary of the United States and that a Trade could not be carried on by Americans without an Opposition from the Canada Traders and that a heavy loss would probably be the result of such opposition. to prevent which I made an agreement with the Principles of them to carry on that Trade for joint Acc[ount] for the Term of Five years, unless the Government of the United States should in the meantime pass such Laws or Regulations, which would render it incompatible for me or the American Fur Company to be so interested with them I agreed to this in Order to get a hold in part of the Trade and under the firm belief that such law or Regulation would be passed by Our Government, as soon as We are in a Situation of carrying on that Trade to the full extent, and which I think We are now prepared to do, provided We can have the use of Canadian Boatmen, as Our Citizens will not submit to the hardships and habits of living which they have to endure."[14] Thus Astor had made an arrangement with the Canadians which he never expected would go into full effect, hoping that in this way he would be able, quietly and without conflict, to succeed in the fullness of time to the entire business.

At about the same time that Astor was sending Crooks to trade from Mackinac, and was arranging with his partners at Montreal for a renewal of their association, he was also throwing out roots toward St. Louis. It seems that, soon after the cessation of hostilities, the St. Louis trader, Cabanné (who, it will be remembered, was one of those who had become involved

in difficulties with the United States government at the outbreak of war, and for whom Gratiot had asked Astor to inter-
cede with Gallatin), had made arrangements with the New
York merchant to furnish him with trade-goods.[15] He later
wrote to Astor, who gives the substance of the letter as follows:
"that if I would not Suply anny other with goods to trade in
the part of this Cauntry Where he Dos he would preferr it &
would take a muish Larger quantity of goods than what he had
ordered." Few Indian goods were available, so it would be
greatly to Cabanné's advantage that he should be the only
trader in Upper Louisiana to be supplied by Astor. But Astor
had already, so he said, been engaged by Stuart and Crooks
"Last Year to Import Some goods for tham for the purpose of
trading with Indians & & in your quater of the Cauntry," and
therefore he was "Sorry to Say that I am under Several Engagements. Which being made thy must be complyd with on
my part but for the futher I will mak no more which can pos-
sebly tend to Injure any of my frinds." Astor therefore suggested, late in May, 1816, that Gratiot should persuade
Cabanné to have him take over the goods furnished Stuart and
Crooks, giving them "Some Compensation for time Lost." At
the same time Astor wrote, "I have tought a good Deal on the
proposition made me Some time Since by your frinds to make
Some genral arrangement for the Indian Trade & if our Government Do exclude Canada traders from aur Cauntry as I
belive thy will the trade will becom an object & I would Licke
to cam to the arrangement of which I will thank you to Inform
tham." A month later he mentioned the possibility of making
"Some arrangement with your frinds for Caring an the Indian
trade."[16] Gratiot in September, 1816, wrote to Astor, "it
appears to me that all rivalls for the Indian Trade will soon be
over, & fore see a disposition in all those who are conserned to
come together to Some understanding. I mean with Cabanné,
B[erthold] & Chouteau &c."[17]

Crooks had gone to St. Louis, probably late in the summer of 1816, and certainly without Astor's orders.[18] His purpose seems to have been to assist Stuart [19] in coming to an arrangement with certain St. Louis traders, which he, as a former resident of that region, was well qualified to do. Some sort of agreement was attained. Gratiot wrote Astor early in January, 1817, "the difficulties he [Crooks] meet with where [sic] almost insurmountable, but his indefatigable activity conquered most every difficulties [sic]."[20] Something of the nature of this agreement is revealed in a letter from Astor to Gratiot early in December, 1816: "I have made Some arrangement with aur frinds in your plaise & tho there is no copt [complete] understanding yet thy will Recie Some advantage if I Do not by anny Skins in your market & as thy Seem to be excallent men I wish to please tham it is on this account that I Do not now Give you an order for Skins."[21] Evidently Gratiot, now sixty-five years of age, was to be left out in the cold; but at any rate, no arrangement with him could have long endured, since he died on April 20, 1817. From the context, it would seem that this arrangement was with Cabanné & Co., and with Berthold & Chouteau, and that it provided that Astor was to furnish these companies with trade-goods and was to deal with no other company or trader in that area. Presumably they were also bound to trade exclusively with Astor so long as his prices were fair, and there seems to have been a tacit understanding that Astor would not himself send outfits to the Missouri so long as he was furnishing these St. Louis traders with goods.[22] Astor evidently did not feel strong enough as yet to enter into direct competition with the Missourians or to endeavor to force them into definite co-operation with his Company. It was not until 1822 that this tenuous commercial relationship was discarded in favor of open competition, begun by the establishment of a branch of the American Fur Company at St. Louis.[23]

It would seem that, during the period of the war, the agreement between Astor and his Montreal partners in the South West Fur Company and between the South West Fur Company and the North West Company for the division of trade had been regarded as more or less suspended, and that the North West Company, doubtless with at least the tacit consent of its agents (who were the Montreal firms associated with the South West Fur Company), had proceeded to re-establish certain posts within the limits of the United States. Doubtless the Nor'Westers reasoned that British successes had made boundaries exceedingly indefinite. At any rate, on March 22, 1816, B. J. Berthelot wrote Louis Grignon of Green Bay, Wisconsin, from Michilimackinac, that "the Company of the North has succumbed" to "Mr. Astor's Company,"[24] while Henry Schoolcraft spoke of the North West Company's withdrawing from the territory south of the Great Lakes after the boundary of 1783 had been reaffirmed by the Treaty of Ghent.[25]

On April 29, 1816, a law was passed which struck an even harder blow at Canadian interests in the United States fur trade than did the Treaty of Ghent, a law the passage of which has previously appeared in Astor's correspondence as an event anticipated and hoped for. This was an act which provided that "licenses to trade with the Indians within the territorial limits of the United States shall not be granted to any but citizens of the United States, unless by the express direction of the President of the United States, and upon such terms and conditions as the public interest may, in his opinion, require." Goods taken by an unlicensed foreigner into the Indian country for trade were to be forfeited, and other severe penalties were provided for violation of the several related sections of this act.[26]

It is usually said that Astor was the instigator of this measure, but we have no direct evidence for the truth of this altogether probable statement. The superintendent of Indian

Trade had informed him in the June of the year before the passage of this act that "it is the intention of the Government to prevent altogether the British Indian traders from coming within the United States."[27] This information had been received several months before his agreement with the Montreal merchants for the continuance of the South West Fur Company. There was no opposition to the bill in either house of Congress, and therefore no occasion for debate which might bring out the motives and personalities behind it. Congress was doubtless glad to strike a blow at the Canadians, who had on occasion handled the United States troops so roughly during the late war. The most conspicuous of these militant Canadians, especially in stirring up the Indians, had been the directors and agents of the Canadian fur companies. The act, then, had behind it the twin sanctions of revenge for the past and protection for the future, both cloaked with the sacred fabric of patriotism. Thus at one stroke all the forces of the United States were placed behind Astor's purpose of eliminating the Canadians from the United States fur trade. His next step was to secure an advantage over his American rivals. With this end in view, he wrote late in May, 1816, to Monroe, the secretary of State, expressing his approval of the act, which he said "ought to have been . . . [passed] some years ago," but stating that without "some few Canadian traders" experienced in the Indian country it would be impossible that year to supply the natives, especially those of the interior. This would result in "great distress among the Indians," and also, of course, in financial loss to Astor. He therefore requested Monroe to speak to the president and ask him to "give six to nine Licenses" for Astor's use, which "might be sent in blank & filled at Michilimackinac."[28] It seems, however, that President Madison did not accede to this cool request, even when transmitted through a man who was his personal friend as well as a member of his cabinet.[29]

Astor succeeded, however, in obtaining from George Graham, the chief clerk of the War Department, and at the direction of the then secretary of War, W. H. Crawford, who had succeeded James Monroe, a letter to the commanding officer at Michilimackinac and to William H. Puthuff, the Indian agent at that place, requesting these officials to give Astor's agents, Crooks, W. W. Matthews, and Joseph B. Varnum, "every possible facility and aid in the prosecution of their business, that may be compatible with your public duties."[30] This recommendation contained potentialities of great service to Astor's representatives, since the president had decided that the granting of licenses for the Indian trade to foreigners should be vested in "the Governor of the Michigan territory, and in the agents for Indian affairs at Michilimackinac, Green Bay, and Chicago,"[31] these officials being under the direction of the Department of War.

It is evident that it was particularly to Astor's interest that Puthuff, the agent at Michilimackinac, should receive such a letter, for on June 20, 1816, Puthuff wrote to Governor Lewis Cass that he had

seen a letter addressed by J. J. Astor to a Mr. Franks a British trader now at this place in which Mr. Astor expresses surprise and regret at the passage of a law forbidding British subjects from trading with Indians, within the American limits etc. but observes that power is vested in the President to grant special license for that purpose and that he Astor dispatched a messenger to the President from whom he entertains no doubt that some may be procured and will be immediately forwarded to Mr. Franks and Mr. Astor's friends in the North west trade. I wish to god the President knew this man Astor as well as he is known here. Licenses would not be placed at his discretion to be distributed among British subjects, Agents or Pensioners. I hope in god no such license will be granted, his British Friends here calculate confident on his success in this matter, that they may be disappointed is my most sincere wish, should they succeed incalculable evil will assuredly grow out of the measure.[32]

In consequence, when Crooks, for the South West Fur Company, applied for licenses to be used in the trade west of the

Mississippi and north of Prairie du Chien, Puthuff would agree to grant them only to persons "whose characters were unexectionable [*sic*]" and on condition that they should not trade at any post or place where Americans were already established. Crooks and the South West Fur Company found "the condition to be inadmissible," though they agreed to take two or three licenses, and Crooks was consequently referred to Governor Cass,[33] who advised that all agents of the South West Fur Company who could "be safely admitted to trade in the Indian Country" should be licensed unconditionally.[34] By August 4, 1816, Puthuff had licensed only three traders, and strenuously objected to licensing certain of those presented by the South West Fur Company who had been in "the British Indian Department during the War," a descriptive list of whom he sent to Governor Cass.[35]

Nevertheless, Astor seems to have secured enough licenses for the necessary Canadian employees to enable the South West Fur Company outfits for 1816 to proceed to their several locations. "The Goods which I have sent to that place [Michilimackinac] last fall and this spring," Astor wrote late in May, 1816, "amount to at least $150M."[36] It is possible that this refers to the whole amount of goods to be employed in 1816 by the South West Fur Company, since in another place it was stated that "Messr. F. R. & Co. half of the Invoices amount to £8000 Stg." Forsyth, Richardson & Co. were interested in the South West Fur Company in the proportion of one-fourth, which would make the total amount of goods in the invoices come to £32,000, or about $150,000.

The South West Fur Company's greatest difficulty in 1816 was not the reluctance of the United States Indian agents to grant licenses to British subjects, but rather the rivalry between the two great Canadian companies, the North West Company and the Hudson's Bay Company. In September, 1816, some employees of the latter organization, under the commands of the Earl of Selkirk, seized goods, "amounting in value to Several Thousand pounds," which were under the charge of James Grant, who was to manage the South West Fur Company's trade in "the Department of Fond du Lac within the Territories of the . . . United States," located "on the head waters of the Mississippi." Selkirk's men then arrested Grant and one of his clerks, William Morrison, and likewise detained another clerk, Eustache Roussin, together with "Seventy Kegs of Liquor and various other articles of Merchandize" at Fort William. Selkirk's motive for this illegal act was said to have been desire for revenge on the North West Company for certain of its actions against himself, while he also wished to monopolize the trade of that region for the Hudson's Bay Company. The result, according to the injured parties, was that the trade of the department, the returns from which in the previous year had been $25,000, was ruined, and that most of the seized goods were probably lost; also that the concern was bound "to pay to Eight Clerks & thirty to forty Canadians" a "large Sum" for services which would now prove of no avail. Astor urged Monroe, as secretary of State, to take steps to punish this insult and take revenge for the confiscation of the goods by sending a military expedition against Selkirk's post from Michilimackinac, Prairie du Chien, or Green Bay to seize the goods which Selkirk had illegally brought into the United States. Astor further suggested that the foray could be directed and assisted by Indian guides and Canadian *voyageurs* and interpreters furnished by the South West Fur Company.[37] However, the government did not see fit to adopt such drastic measures.

The act of April 29, 1816, had put the Canadian section of the South West Fur Company into the position of existing only by Astor's favor. At any moment he could dissolve the partnership, and by utilizing his influence with the United States government prevent the Montreal firms from carrying on an

independent trade with the Indians. The assistance of the
Montreal merchants had been of value to him during the transi-
tional year of 1816, but now he was ready to carry on the trade
entirely upon his own responsibility, basing it upon his own
capital and acting through his own personal agents. Consequently, some time early in 1817, Astor "purchased the whole
of the interest in what is termed the South West Company."[38]
We do not know at what price he bought out his partners'
shares, but the general belief is that he took advantage of the
opportunity to recoup himself for part of the losses inflicted on
him by the North West Company on the Columbia River.[39]
The price was probably not large, since Astor was in a position
to name his own terms; and anything beyond the bare value of
goods and buildings on United States territory belonging to the
Montreal partners was paid rather to retain their good will in
the Montreal fur market than because they had any legal
rights to convey south of the Canadian line. Probably the
greatest part of the purchase price represented payment for
the South West Fur Company posts on Canadian soil. Simply
to oust the Canadians from the field was worth much more
than any profit Astor could make through a forced purchase of
their flimsy trading posts. The only idea of the price at which
Astor bought out his partners is found in an account which
states that in October, 1817, Astor paid McTavish, McGillivrays & Co. $23,233.07, " 2nd. payment on acct. of their Intst
in S. W. Co. purchased & Interest."[40] How many payments,
if any, were made after this one, we do not know. Presumably
the first payment was for an equal amount. Moreover, Forsyth, Richardson & Co. would be entitled to as much compensation as the other Montreal firm. A fair guess would be that
Astor bought out his partners for about $100,000. On April 8,
1817, Ramsay Crooks, acting as Astor's agent, purchased from
Pierre de Rocheblave, who had been associated with Astor in
the South West Fur Company during the past year, a lot of

land, "with two houses two Stores and other dependancies thereon erected," located in the village of Michilimackinac, for which Astor paid £400 currency. Evidently these were the buildings used by the South West Fur Company when de Rocheblave was its agent at Mackinac.[41]

After the purchase, Astor immediately prepared for a vigorous campaign in the fur trade during the year 1817. On March 17 he offered Ramsay Crooks a position as one of the "two agents to conduct hereafter said business [the fur trade] at Montreal, New York, Michilimacinac, and at all other places, who are to give their whole time and attention to said business, and not to trade for account of themselves or any other person whatsoever." If Crooks accepted the offer, he was "to recieve as a compensation, Two Thousand Dollars per annum, and your expenses while absent on business of the Company . . . in addition to which you are to have the profit or loss on five shares (out of one hundred shares in said business). The profit or loss is to be deducted after all interest and expenses are paid and deducted as well as two and a half per cent commission which is to be charged by me, on the sale, or exportation on furs recieved as returns or otherwise. You are to continue to be Agent for three years should the business be so long continued, it being understood that you are to recieve and attend to all the goods comprehended in the outfit, 1816."[42] The other agent, as might be expected, was Crooks's friend and fellow Astorian, Robert Stuart. Another Astorian, William W. Matthews, seems to have been the Company's Montreal representative. He had been operating between that city and New York since as early as February, 1816. At Montreal he was engaged in buying skins and procuring Spanish dollars for Astor, having such goods as "6000 Ear *boobs* Round" manufactured for the Indian trade, and selling, both at Montreal and at Albany, such peltries as deer skins and muskrat skins. Mink, otter, beaver, especially red-fox skins, were the furs which he was particularly desired to secure in Montreal. The Spanish dollars were probably for Astor's China trade. Matthews continued to perform such functions for at least three years, or till the spring of 1819.[43]

The year 1817 was very important for the American Fur Company. Though the Company had been chartered nine years before, in 1808, it was not till 1817 that it assumed for the first time the form under which it was to be best known, and under which it was to endure for seventeen years. Astor was now in alliance with no other commercial organization. He was the sole head and director of the Company, furnishing all the capital and the general supervision of the organization, as well as personally handling the purchase of trade-goods and the sale of the furs received as returns. In the spring of 1817 a number of clerks and *voyageurs*, who had been hired by W. W. Matthews,[44] left Montreal on May 13 and arrived at Michilimackinac a month later.[45] Here various brigades were made up, each of which was put in charge of an experienced trader, furnished with an invoice of goods and a complement of clerks, *voyageurs*, and perhaps an interpreter, and dispatched for a specified region to trade with the Indians. "The American Fur Company, as had been the practice of the Mackinaw and South-West Companies, made their outfits to Lake Superior, to the Mississippi, the head of St. Peters, and the Missouri."[46] According to a contemporary, in these early days of 1816 and 1817 Astor "fitted out two hundred and forty boats, each one containing two traders and from four to six hands."[47] This would bring the total force of American Fur Company employees to the impossible number of about 1,500, and must be heavily discounted. For this year, indeed, we know of only nine outfits leaving Mackinac, the names of which it is not necessary to rehearse.[48]

During 1817 the American Fur Company had to meet the opposition not only of other traders, such as those of the Hudson's Bay Company, Bostwick, who was an agent of David Stone, Franks, Dousman, Berthelot, and half a dozen others,[49] but also of the military officers, factors, and Indian agents of the region. The military men looked with suspicion and enmity upon a company whose traders had fought on the British side in the late war, some of them, it is said, having been seen with scalps at their belts; the factors knew that it was the Company's aim to abolish the government trading posts over which they presided, and, either out of a sincere desire for the Indians' welfare or for a more selfish reason, they were anxious to combat the Company's influence; the Indian agents, who were closely associated both with the factors and with the army officers, and many of whom had been drawn from the ranks of the latter, naturally fell into line with the other opponents of the Company.

But Astor had powerful allies. On his stating that he had bought out the other South West Fur Company partners, George Graham, the acting secretary of War, wrote to Governor Cass requesting him to "afford to him [Astor] and his agents, every facility in your power consistent with the laws and regulations."[50] Governor Cass interpreted the recommendation in as broad a fashion as possible, and wrote to Puthuff, the Indian agent at Mackinac, to this effect: "From a correspondence, which Mr. Crooks has submitted to me, it is the intention of the Government that Mr. Crooks as the agent of Mr. Astor should have the selection of such persons to enter the Indian Country and conduct the business as he may require. To such persons therefore as Mr. Crooks may designate you will please grant licenses. . . . On mature reflection upon the subject I would recommend that as few licenses as may be consistent with those regulations be granted, rather reducing than exceeding the number."[51] Cass could hardly have found a more obvious way of saying to Puthuff, "Give Crooks all the licenses he may need or desire, but when that has been done, the fewer you grant to others, the better."

We have ample proof that we are not being unfair to Lewis Cass in our judgment of his intentions in an exquisitely naïve letter from Ramsay Crooks to John Jacob Astor, probably written at Montreal in the early spring of 1817. Says Crooks, "the Canadian Boatmen . . . are indispensable to the successful prosecution of the trade, their places cannot be supplied by Americans, who are for the most are [sic] too independent to submit quietly to a proper controul, and who can gain any where a subsistence much Superior to a Man of the interior and although the body of the Yankee can resist as much hardship as any Man, tis only in the Canadian we find that temper of mind to render him patient docile and persevering in short they are a people harmless in themselves whose habits of submission fit them peculiarly for our business and if guided as it is my wish they should be, will never give just cause of alarm to the Government of the Union. It is of course your object," Crooks concluded with touching frankness, "*to exclude every foreigner except those for whom you obtain licenses.*"[52] The italics are mine.

Late in June Crooks again took up the tale, writing in a tone of something not far from exultation. "Governor Cass," he stated, "although positively instructed to be guided by the orders of the war Department of last year in regard to the granting of licenses to foreigners; and having no directions from acting Secretary Graham to bestow any specific indulgencies on your Agents, has written Major Puthuff to attend particularly to our wishes; and should he act as the discretionary nature of his orders will allow, he can serve our purpose almost as effectually as if foreigners had been excluded geneally [sic] and we had obtained the number of licenses in blank you at one time so confidently expected — With this knowledge of the disposition evinced by [the] Governor of the Michigan Territory for our success you may well suppose no effort shall be wanting on our part to engage the Indian Agent here in our cause but his not being bound to pursue any particular system will leave all we obtain to be acquired by our own exertions, so conflicting will be the claims on his indulgence and so many stratagems will be tried to thawrt [sic] our views that it would be the extreme of folly to hazard an opinion of the result, but if he only remains true to the line of conduct we may prevail on him to adopt, we flatter ourselves with getting hold of a larger share of the trade than last year."[53] This last letter can only signify that Cass had gone so far beyond his instructions in favoring the American Fur Company that even Crooks, one of the beneficiaries, was surprised, and that Crooks himself expected by some unspecified means to persuade the Indian agent at Michilimackinac to follow the lofty example of the Governor. Apparently Crooks notified Astor of anything in the way of special favors desired in the Indian country, whereupon Astor secured from some government official a letter of recommendation to Cass which would be capable of very liberal interpretation. Then Astor would write to Cass in detail just what he desired should be done, and the Governor would transmit his wishes, in the form of requests or orders, as might seem most fitting, to his subordinates.[54]

These orders from Cass to Puthuff, in regard to the issuing of licenses to those whom Crooks should designate, resulted, as might be expected, in protests, especially from those connected with the Indian Department. John W. Johnson, factor at Prairie du Chien, complained that Major Puthuff was licensing "the blackest of characters" for trade in that region.[55] Major Matthew Irwin, factor at Green Bay, complained bitterly to Colonel McKenney, the superintendent of Indian Trade, of the way in which British traders, licensed at Michilimackinac, were ruining both American traders and government factories by their opposition. Nearly all these British traders had been active in stirring up the Indians against the Americans in the late war. "It was not expected," said Irwin, rather as an interrogation than as a statement, "that Mr. Astor would engage to do business with the Indians with none but British subjects, and those, too, so exceptionable in every particular."[56]

Russell Farnham, the Astorian, came into conflict with military officers while he was on his way to trade on the Des Moines River, accompanied by Daniel Darling. Lieutenant-Colonel Talbot Chambers, the commanding officer at Prairie du Chien, declined to recognize the validity of their Mackinac licenses and ordered them to proceed to St. Louis, without trading on the way, to get licenses from Governor Clark. But they disobeyed the injunction against trading and were arrested, their boats and goods being seized. This occurred in September. Astor complained directly to President Monroe early in November.[57] The American Fur Company sued Chambers, and some years later won an award of $5,000.[58] It was later found necessary to rule that only in certain special cases could an Indian agent grant licenses for trade with Indians beyond the limits of his own agency.[59]

During 1817 Astor had also been busy in closing up the affairs of the South West Fur Company, and in the late summer had been in Montreal, where he had offered to take "the Residue of the N. W. Martin skins of the Present years outfit not exceeding forty thousand Skins at the Price agreed on Say five shillings & three pence prskin," in order to maintain the price.[60]

The year 1817 was not profitable, despite the favoritism shown the Company by such an official as Cass. Such untoward incidents as the arrest of Farnham and his companion had increased the losses which would naturally be expected in a pioneer year. Goods had been sold at low prices in order to drive away competing traders. As a consequence, the accounts drawn up on February 1, 1818, presumably for the preceding year, bore a "very reproving aspect." The South West Fur Company appeared to have gained $27,202.07, but the American Fur Company's gain was only $9,475. Moreover, said

Ramsay Crooks, "the interest now due you is not yet against the Company and you will recollect we are not to change [charge?] any of the people who *bought goods* of us last summer." Here he was evidently referring to some policy of winning over traders to co-operation with the Company. Most of the Company's assets, too, were in unsold merchandise and furs.[61] It is not surprising, therefore, that all the outfits for the year finally resulted in losses — at least on paper.[62] Indeed, little or no profit could be expected for the first year in such a campaign designed to monopolize the fur trade.

With a year of experience as agents of an independent company behind them, with a consciousness that the governor of Michigan Territory was their friend, with a knowledge of the backing both in capital and prestige which Astor could furnish, Crooks and Stuart were ready for the campaign of 1818. It will be remembered that in the summer of 1817 they had mentioned their intention of winning over the Indian agent at Michilimackinac, Major Puthuff. Apparently they did not succeed, for on January 24, 1818, they wrote Astor a long letter which was chiefly an attack on Puthuff, whom they accused of charging $50 apiece for licenses, of favoring other traders as against the American Fur Company, of failing to check smuggling and the sale of liquor to the Indians, and of generally lacking single-mindedness in the performance of his duties.[63] Puthuff was in a bad position. He had angered other Indian agents and factors and even the superintendent of the Indian Department by the apparently reckless fashion in which he had scattered licenses among British subjects active in stirring up the Indians during the late war. It was not known that he had done this at the direct command of Governor Cass.[64] Puthuff himself, who seems to have been an honest and possibly even an over-zealous official,[65] could not deny that he had charged $50 apiece for the licenses, though in this he had merely followed the custom of other Indian agents,[66] and had been backed

up by the encouragement of the commanding officer at Michilimackinac. He made no attempt to conceal the fact, but justified his action on the ground that increased labor was needed
to make out the licenses required by the new regulations, and
that $5.00 had previously been charged for preparing docu-
ments of a much slighter character. It is certain that Puthuff's
motives were not entirely mercenary, for he would not have
objected, as he did, to the lavish fashion in which Cass wished
him to grant licenses to the American Fur Company traders if
he had been interested only in the $50 fee. He also asserted
that the American Fur Company agents in 1816 had paid the
sum voluntarily, long after the licenses had been granted, and
that he had always given a receipt for the amount.[67] It is hard
to convince oneself that Puthuff had been guilty of any worse
crimes than indiscretion and excess of zeal. But the position
into which he had been forced by Cass prevented his associates
and superiors from taking up the cudgels in his defence, and he
was removed from his position. The man who was appointed
in his place, George Boyd, was so pliable, at least in the early
portion of his term of service, that on July 17, 1819, we find
him authorizing the American Fur Company trader, William
Morrison, to seize goods illegally "introduced within the American limits in the neighbourhood of the Fond du Lac and Red
Lake Settlements" and to "destroy all spirituous liquors."[68]
The advantage which these powers would confer upon the company whose agent was so equipped is obvious. The American
Fur Company had undoubtedly been victorious on the Mackinac front, and of this triumph the Company's agents spoke
with exultation, boasting that it was the representations of
Crooks and Stuart which had caused Puthuff's dismissal, and
threatening the Indian agents at Green Bay and Prairie du
Chien with a similar fate. Emphasis was lent to their menaces
by the fact that, in the spring of 1818, Cass had actually commissioned Ramsay Crooks, a British subject, to make a tour of

the posts of Mackinac, Green Bay, Prairie du Chien, and St. Louis, to examine the conduct of the agents there.[69]

An important feature of the campaign of 1818 was that it began with the total prohibition by the president of "the trade of foreigners with the Indians living in the United States." Indian agents were therefore forbidden to issue a "licence to any foreigner to trade with the Indians,"or to"permit an american Citizen licenced to trade to take with him or to send into the Indian Country any foreigner."[70] This step had undoubtedly been taken at the instance of the superintendent of the Indian Trade, T. L. McKenney, who had been kept informed by his factors of the detrimental activities of British traders among the Indians, and especially of the way in which the trade of American citizens was being ruined. The president's action would chiefly affect Astor, whose Company was the largest in the field and the one which employed the greatest proportion of British subjects. The factor at Green Bay mentioned in a single letter ten or twelve British subjects, employed by Astor, who were competing both with independent American traders and with those employed by the government within his district.[71] The president's action was received with gratitude by factors and Indian agents,[72] and not with too much apprehension by the outlawed traders. Superintendent McKenney said, "foreigners are . . . now inoperative, and cannot oppose you [the Green Bay factor] in future,"[73] but Jacob Franks, British subject and fur trader of Green Bay, remarked that "M[r]. Stone who was here [Montreal] but a few days ago is of opinion that we can go on with our Trade. . . . M[r] Stone [an American fur trader] also says if M[r]. Astor has any advantage with the American Government he is sure he will be intitled to *as much* from the Interest of his friends who are Members of Congress which information has in some measure made my mind more Easy."[74] Similarly Michael Dousman, also of Green Bay, remarked, "there Is a report that British Subjects are totaly Excluded, but I presume there will be Some other arangement that Is Expecting with[out] Doubt that J. J. Astor & .D Stone will have Intrest Suficent to mack Sum Satisfactory arangements."[75] The Green Bay traders were right, for it was not many weeks until the president decided, doubtless upon the representations of such fur-trade capitalists as Astor and Stone, "that permits may be granted to American traders, to employ in their trade with the Indians foreign Boatmen and Interpreters."[76] This simply put matters back where they had been since April 29, 1816, since once in the Indian country a British subject licensed as a boatman could not be prevented from acting as a clerk or trader. As the concession just mentioned was made before the licenses previously granted to foreign traders had expired, the effect of the president's earlier prohibition was practically nil.[77]

Early in 1818 Astor's agents had gravely informed him that unless the government factories were abolished "it will in our opinion be imprudent in you to continue interested in the trade."[78] However, although these trading houses continued to stand, the American Fur Company, by dint of underselling, by the use of British subjects, frequently related by marriage to the Indians, and also, as we shall see, by the sale of liquor, succeeded in making such progress that in March, 1819, the arrangement between Ramsay Crooks and the Company, originally made on March 17, 1817, to continue for three years, was extended for one additional year, to March 16, 1821.[79] Affairs looked so promising to Astor that he felt able to leave for Paris in the summer of 1819, expecting to be absent for some time,[80] and leaving all matters connected with the American Fur Company in the capable hands of his agents, Crooks and Stuart, and of his son and partner, William B. Astor. He left with his son a memorandum containing detailed instructions for the trade, telling him, among other things, where and how each particular type of skin should be sold, counselling him to "retrensh the buisness as mush as possible," and stating that all orders for goods from Europe and all furs shipped to Europe should be sent to Astor.[81] Under the leadership of Crooks and Stuart, the Company pushed the trade with such vigor that on December 4, 1819, Crooks was able to write to Astor that "Buttelot [Berthelot] of Mackinac has quitted the trade. Ermatiser [Ermatinger] of St. Marys is crippled and D. Stone & Co. appear wavering. Should they withdraw the smaller importers must soon give in to our views and we at least for the time have the power of retrenchment to make the business excellent." It seems that Crooks made this encouraging statement as an offset to Astor's less optimistic attitude, which led him to advocate a partial withdrawal from the trade as a preliminary to its complete cessation with the returns from the outfit for 1820. Crooks, however, said that, though the posts they occupied on the British side of Lake Huron might be given up, it was from them that the best returns of the year had come.[82]

From the time when the American Fur Company had been first organized Astor had held in mind the abolition of the government trading houses.[83] This intention he had mentioned in 1808 to De Witt Clinton, and it had been provided in the South West Fur Company agreement of 1811 that, should the factories be closed, Astor would be entitled to two-thirds instead of one-half of this Company's trade. When the American Fur Company was reorganized in 1817, an attack on the factories was conspicuous among its plans of campaign. The factories were government trading houses, first established in 1796, supplied with the usual types of Indian goods, and selling to the natives at cost, with the intention of protecting the Indians against the exorbitant charges and raw alcohol of the private trader, and of attaching them by ties both of commerce and of friendship to the government of the United States. This system was unquestionably an "experiment noble in motive."

Indeed, so shrewd and careful a student of the fur trade as Hiram Martin Chittenden believes that, given a fair chance, it would have changed the entire course of our relations with the Indians into much more honorable and pacific channels. Its only chance for success, however, lay in making the fur trade a government monopoly, and against this the capitalists interested in the extravagant profits of that trade were able to put up a completely successful resistance. But, despite the severe handicap of being forced to compete against hordes of experienced, unscrupulous private traders, the factories carried on their trade with considerable success until the American Fur Company entered the field with its heavy capital of money, brains, experience, and political influence.[84]

In 1814, three years before that event had taken place, Gratiot, it will be recalled, wrote from St. Louis: "The Indian trade will have in future to be carried on by a Comp^y to become profitable, as it stand now it is too precarious for any body to hazard anything unless the factories were to be abolished."[85] His statement indicated that at least in the St. Louis trade area the factories were performing the functions for which they had been established, and clearly foreshadowed the only means by which their activity could be stifled. In their report to Astor on the transactions of 1817, Crooks and Stuart violently and bitterly attacked the trading houses, which they seemed to think should act merely as outposts against British influence, and, when the latter had been weakened, should withdraw in favor of the private American traders. It seems to have entirely escaped the comprehension of Astor's agents that the factories had been established to benefit the Indians as well as to oppose the British. They concluded, "we cannot check the extension of the System lately pursued by the public trading-Houses in situations affecting our commerce most materially and which on the most mature deliberation, gives us every reason to fear, and but little to hope from even the most active exertions on our part."[86] Crooks and Stuart may have exaggerated the aggressiveness displayed by the factories, but this very exaggeration goes to show that these institutions were furnishing some effective competition.

The first attack upon the factory system by the American Fur Company, as the most powerful of the private trading corporations engaged in this campaign, was "on the western front," that is, in the Indian country. It was essentially an attempt to prove the system an impracticable and uneconomic device. The Company's agents found some support for their thesis in certain shortsighted policies of the system, such as the omission of the usual ceremonial presents to the Indians, and the restrictions upon credit. The private traders followed up these advantages by the use of British employees, who utilized their great experience in the Indian trade to warn the Indians against the Americans, and especially to stir up prejudice against the factories. The British employees also directed the trade to themselves by underselling the factories on certain staple articles, later recouping themselves for this loss by raising the prices on other types of merchandise. The private traders also sold whiskey, which could not be secured by the Indians at the factories, or indeed legally anywhere. Through these devices the factories at Green Bay and Chicago were by 1821 well-nigh reduced to inactivity.[87]

When this end had been achieved, the next step was to attack the trading houses on the eastern or political front, advancing as a proof of their inutility the very condition which their assailants had been principally responsible for bringing about. Lewis Cass, who had already proved a valiant ally to the Company, wrote to J. C. Calhoun, the secretary of War, in 1818, advocating the abolition of the factories.[88] However, the report of McKenney, the superintendent of Indian Trade, won over Calhoun to favor the factories,[89] and in 1819 he ordered that licenses should be refused to those French-speaking inhabitants of Michigan Territory who had previously considered themselves British subjects and had conducted themselves accordingly, until they had been naturalized as American citizens, even though they had been born on United States soil. Licenses previously granted to such individuals were to be revoked.[90] Calhoun also seems to have projected other steps favorable to the factories, for on May 30, 1820, Crooks wrote to Astor of a bill favored by Calhoun, the passage of which would probably mean that there would be so few licensed traders that the factories would be sure to revive. The employees of the American Fur Company, he said, would probably not be among those licensed, because of the Company's independent attitude, as Crooks ingeniously described it. He appealed to Astor to "interest some of your numerous friends to obtain if possible the abolition of the Factory system."[91]

One of these "numerous friends" was Thomas Hart Benton, newly elected as a senator from Missouri, who spoke for his fur-trading constituents in attacking their government-supported rival.[92] An attack on the factory system in the second session of the sixteenth Congress proved inconclusive, but in the next Congress the battle was joined with redoubled fury, Benton leading the assailants of the trading houses. In November, 1821, Crooks wrote to Astor, "I shall follow your advice in again visiting Washington, and will use every fair means to obtain a decision on the Public Trading House system."[93] Presumably his intention of lobbying was carried out. At any rate, on April 1, 1822, Crooks was able to write these words of commendation to Benton: "You deserve the unqualified thanks of the Community for destroying the pious monster [the factory system] . . . the country is indebted for its deliverance from so gross and holy [sic] an imposition."[94] The bill, however, did not actually pass the Senate till May 2, and the House not till May 4. It was approved two days later.[95] The main argument used against the system was its stagnation during the last few years, which, however, was largely the work of those who were now using it as a pretext for the abolition of the system. Thomas L. McKenney, in a refutation made on February 27, 1822, of the attacks on the factory system, recognized this situation when he wrote: "no man knows better than Mr. Crooks the causes of this decline and the means which it is necessary to adopt at any time to produce the same results elsewhere."[96] Some light is thrown upon lobbying practices of a century ago by the fact that Benton was retained as an attorney for the American Fur Company in the same year in which he pushed through this bill so favorable to its interests.[97]

The American Fur Company went so far as to object to the factories' disposing of the goods still left on hand, and in November, 1822, Stuart wrote to Crooks, quoting Joseph Rolette, of Prairie du Chien, who stated that "the young man Ghant who has been sent to close the Factory concern, in place of doing so has opened it with as much eclat as ever. . . . Would it not be well for Mr Astor to communicate with Mr. Graham on the subject — and if he does not order it to be closed, Benton ought to give them an-other *rap* —"[98] Accordingly, Crooks wrote to Benton late in the next month objecting to the policy of continuing the factories in order to close them out, instead of sending the goods to trading posts to be sold.[99] He certainly showed colossal effrontery in demanding that the goods of the institution which the American Fur Company had been responsible for destroying should be to all practical purposes inherited by that Company. Such was the end of the institution of government trading houses, a system which possessed great possibilities for national benefit, and which probably would have enjoyed a reasonable measure of success and undoubtedly a much longer term of existence had it not been for the opposition of Astor's powerful American Fur Company.

Thus by the end of 1822 the agents of the American Fur Company had won their battle against the factory system.

But it must not be supposed that, while the fight was going on, they had slackened in their opposition to rival private traders. At the close of the 1820 season the American Fur Company had succeeded in making an arrangement with David Stone & Co., the firm described in the previous year as "wavering," by which the Astor company bought out the residue of Stone's goods, the English portion at 50 per cent advance, the rest at cost and charges, on condition that this Company should for the next five years "abandon altogether the trade of Michilimackinac."[100] Encouraged by this victory against the American Fur Company's most formidable opponent on one front, Crooks went to Paris in the spring of 1821 to make arrangements with Astor for the renewal of the American Fur Company's agreement with its agents. The earlier agreement, which had once already been extended, was to expire on March 16, 1821.

On March 27, 1821, Astor offered to renew his agreement with Crooks for the term of five years, beginning with the outfit of 1821, that is, until March 1, 1826. All the conditions of Crooks's agency were to be the same as before, except that he was to share, if he so desired, in the gain or loss of the concern in the proportion of one-fifth instead of one-twentieth. No change was to be made in Robert Stuart's position as agent, but Benjamin Clapp, their fellow Astorian, who had previously been employed by the Company, was now to be associated with that organization as the holder of five shares, or one-twentieth of the whole concern, receiving in addition a salary of $1,200 per annum. Stuart and Clapp were to decide whether to accept or reject the above terms within ten days after the offer had been made known to them. The whole of the agreement was to be considered null and void in the event of Crooks's death [101]— an evidence of the reliance which Astor placed in Crooks.

These terms were accepted by Crooks, who at once returned to America by way of England, stopping at London *en route* to inspect the fur market there. He wrote to Astor: "While in London I visited the great Fur-Brokers Row & Co. They and the merchants of that place concerned in trade expressed to me great anxiety that you would consent to make London the general place of sale for all your Furs, saying they were confident that were all the skins sold at and [sic] place with the certainty of now [not?] being shipped to any other point the buyers would necessarily come there and having nothing to dread from diffused shipments to the continental ports, they would buy with confidence, and this being the only market greater competition would be created, and better prices obtained — House of Bainbridge & Brown were particularly anxious."[102] Arrived at Mackinac, Crooks found Stuart ready to accept the arrangement proposed by Astor for the next five years, "altho much disappointed at the terms allowed him." Clapp, however, declined, though he would consent "to remain for his former salary, with the difference, that at New York he will attend only and solely to the American fur Company business . . . unless . . . you will make him a partner; a thing I very much desire."[103] Apparently Clapp meant that he would no longer act as an employee of John Jacob Astor & Son, as distinct from the American Fur Company, unless made a partner in the former firm. Astor, however, set aside the suggestion, much to Crooks's regret, and Clapp consequently decided to go into business for himself.[104]

With Crooks and Stuart still in the field the Company was ready for another five years' campaign. One step which had to be taken was to withdraw the Company's traders from the Canadian territory east of Lake Huron, which they had previously occupied as heirs of the South West Fur Company. This move was necessitated by an act of the British Parliament passed on July 2, 1821, "which virtually excluded American traders from Canadian territory." It seems rather surprising, in view of the act of Congress of April 29, 1816, that such a retaliative measure had not been put into effect long before. However, the American company "promptly made a counter move along the frontier from Lake Superior to the Lake of the Woods by establishing three posts there in competition with the Hudson Bay Company."[105] Late in 1821 Crooks was preparing to abandon the posts on British territory.[106]

But the question of these posts on British territory was a comparatively insignificant matter, and, indeed, their abandonment had been considered even before the action by Parliament. The event which distinguished the year 1822 was the establishment of a branch of the American Fur Company at St. Louis. Hitherto Mackinac had been the Company's sole distribution point and fur-buying center, and its trade had been confined to the Great Lakes and Upper Mississippi. Its relations with the Missouri area, by an agreement formed late in 1816, had been merely that it supplied certain of the St. Louis traders with goods, and received the preference in purchasing the returns. For some time the St. Louis firm of Berthold, Chouteau & Co. had been dallying with the idea of purchasing an interest in Astor's company, possibly to postpone the evil day when that organization would decide to enter into open competition with them, but nothing definite had been done.[107] Late in 1821, however, Crooks grew tired of waiting for a decision and announced to Astor: "Preliminary arrangements are made for prosecuting the Trade of the Missouri & St. Louis next season — Berthold & Chouteau with all their advantages has suffered the Concern of Stone & Co. to get the better of them more effectually than could have been believed, and as there is no injunction to the contrary we may as well come in for a share of the Business. . . . you now do no business with them worth attending to, and any scruples we have heretofore entertained in regard to embarking in their portion of the Trade ought not to be indulged in any longer."[108] In the spring of the next year Crooks wrote to Astor: "I regret beyond measure that our fastidiousness about interfering with our St. Louis friends; induced us to postpone till the present time any attempt at participating in the Missouri trade," because, owing to lack of opposition, David Stone & Co. had secured a strong footing in that district.[109]

Astor seems to have returned to the United States in the fall of 1821,[110] gone back to Europe in the spring of the next year, accompanied by his daughter Eliza,[111] and again come back to New York later in the year, perhaps to assist in establishing the western headquarters at St. Louis. Samuel Abbott, who had been managing the Company's business at Prairie du Chien, was put in charge of affairs at St. Louis, which was henceforth to be the headquarters for the posts on the Missouri and the lower posts on the Mississippi and the Illinois, while the whole area was to be known as the Western Department. Mackinac, presided over by Stuart, remained the headquarters for the trade of the Lakes and the Upper Mississippi, and this area was christened the Northern Department. Late in 1822 Astor sent to Abbott, at St. Louis, a letter containing instructions for the purchase of furs, which showed that Abbott was firmly established in the Missouri city.[112]

NOTES

1. Ms. book, Baker Library, Astor Papers, Letter Book i, 1813–15, pp. 26, 33, 43, 70–71, 74–76, 220–221, 292–293, 321–323, 340–341, 376–377, 405, 423, 450, 469, John Jacob Astor, N. Y., July 17, August 10, 24, October 9, 18, 1813, May 24, September 26, October 22, 26, November 30, December 24, 1814, January 6, 30, February 11, 1815, to McTavish, McGillivrays & Co.

2. *Ibid.*, p. 85, John Jacob Astor, N. Y., October 26, 1813, to John Day.

3. *Ibid.*, pp. 107–108, 180, John Jacob Astor, N. Y., November 15, 1813 (see above, vol. i, pp. 543–545), February 14, 1814, to Ramsay Crooks.

4. Ms. book, Missouri Historical Society, St. Louis, Gratiot Collection, Charles Gratiot's Letter Book, 1798–1816, pp. 165–166, Charles Gratiot, St. Louis, May 29, 1814, to John Jacob Astor, N. Y. (in English).

5. Ms. book, Baker Library, Astor Papers, Letter Book i, 1813–15, pp. 465–466, John Jacob Astor, N. Y., February 11, 1815, to Henry Forrest.

6. *Ibid.*, pp. 471–472, John Jacob Astor, N. Y., February 14, 1815, to Ramsay Crooks.

7. *Ibid.*, p. 480, John Jacob Astor, February 21, 1815, to Thomas Wilson, London.

8. Ms. book (copy), Detroit Public Library, Burton Historical Collection, and Missouri Historical Society, St. Louis, Letters of Ramsay Crooks, John Jacob Astor, and the American Fur Company, 1813–43, Robert Stewart, Brooklyn, March 21, 1815, to Ramsay Crooks, Pittsburg.

9. *Ibid.*, John Jacob Astor, N. Y., April 5, 1815, to Ramsay Crooks, Pittsburg.

10. Lockwood, James H., "Early Times and Events in Wisconsin," *Wisconsin Historical Collections*, vol. ii (1855), p. 101.

11. Ms., Baker Library, Astor Papers, Agreement between William McGillivray and John Jacob Astor for the South West Fur Company, January 28, 1811 (see above, vol. i, pp. 461–469).

12. Ms., Bibliothèque Ste. Sulpice, Montreal, Samuel Gerrard Papers, Baby Collection, Agreement between Forsyth, Richardson & Co., McTavish, McGillivrays & Co., and Pierre de Rocheblave, February 6, 1815.

13. *Ibid.*, William McGillivray, Montreal, October 7, 1815, to John Jacob Astor, N. Y.

14. Ms., Department of State, Washington, D. C., Miscellaneous Letters, December, 1816, John Jacob Astor, December 30, 1816, to James Monroe.

15. Ms. book, Missouri Historical Society, St. Louis, Gratiot Collection, Charles Gratiot's Letter Book, 1798–1816, pp. 175–177, 179–180, Charles Gratiot, St. Louis, June 26, August 28, 1815, to John Jacob Astor, N. Y. (in English).

16. Ms. (photostat), Missouri Historical Society, St. Louis, Bernard P. Bogy Collection, John Jacob Astor, N. Y., November 16, 1815, May 26 (see below, vol. ii, pp. 1143–1144), June 25, 1816, to Charles Gratiot, St. Louis.

17. Ms. book, Missouri Historical Society, St. Louis, Gratiot Collection, Charles Gratiot's Letter Book, 1798–1816, pp. 194–195, Charles Gratiot, St. Louis, September 9, 1816, to John Jacob Astor, N. Y. (in English).

18. Ms. book (copy), Detroit Public Library, Burton Historical Collection, and Missouri Historical Society, St. Louis, Letters of Ramsay Crooks, John Jacob Astor, and the American Fur Company, 1813–43, John Jacob Astor, N. Y., September 20, 1816, to William W. Matthews, Albany, "what has induced Mr Crooks to go to St. Louis;" ms. book, Missouri Historical Society, St. Louis, Gratiot Collection, Charles Gratiot's Letter Book, 1798–1816 [a few letters dated 1817 are included], pp. 194–195, Charles Gratiot, St. Louis, January 7, 1817, to John Jacob Astor, N. Y. (in English).

19. *Ibid.*, p. 194, Charles Gratiot, St. Louis, September 16, 1816, to John Jacob Astor, N. Y. (in English).

20. *Ibid.*, pp. 194–195, Charles Gratiot, St. Louis, January 7, 1817, to John Jacob Astor, N. Y. (in English).

21. Ms. (photostat), Missouri Historical Society, St. Louis, Bernard P. Bogy Collection, John Jacob Astor, N. Y., December 10, 1816, to Charles Gratiot, St. Louis.

22. Chittenden, Hiram Martin, *The American Fur Trade of the Far West*, 3 vols. (1902), vol. i, pp. 318–319, note, p. 318, quoting a letter from Crooks to Astor, November 30, 1821, and one from Crooks to Russell Farnham, December 28, 1818. Something of the amount of goods sent by Astor to St. Louis by this arrangement is indicated by the fact that on June 21, 1818, Cabanné & Co. sent John Jacob Astor & Son bills of exchange amounting to $20,508.91, to be passed to their credit for goods ordered the previous fall. Among these bills was one for $10,508.91, drawn by Ramsay Crooks on John Jacob Astor & Son, which probably represented the price of furs sold by the St. Louis firm to that in New York. (Ms. book, Missouri Historical Society, St. Louis, P. Chouteau Collection, Letter Book of Cabanné & Co., 1817–19, pp. 1–4, 5, 6, Cabanné & Co., St. Louis, September 9, 25, 1817 (in French), June 21, 1818 (in English), to John Jacob Astor and John Jacob Astor & Son, N. Y.)

23. Chittenden, *op. cit.*, vol. i, p. 320.

24. Thwaites, Reuben Gold, ed., "The Fur-Trade in Wisconsin —

1815–1817," *Wisconsin Historical Collections*, vol. xix (1910), pp. 404–405,
J. B. Berthelot, Michilimackinac, March 22, 1816, to Louis Grignon,
La Baye Verte (ms., Wisconsin Historical Society, Madison, Wisconsin
MSS., 3 B 52, original in French).

25. Schoolcraft, Henry Rowe, "Memoir of John Johnston," *Michigan
Pioneer and Historical Collections*, vol. xxxvi (1908), pp. 73–74, 80.

26. *United States Statutes at Large*, vol. iii, 1813–23, chap. 165, pp. 331–
333, 14th Cong., 1st sess., April 29, 1816.

27. Ms. book, Department of the Interior, Washington, D. C., Indian
Office Letter Book C, June, 1812–April, 1816, pp. 362–364, J[ohn]
M[ason], Indian Office, Georgetown, June 12, 1815, to John Jacob Astor,
N. Y.

28. Ms., New York Public Library, Monroe Papers, John Jacob Astor,
N. Y., May 27, 1816, to James Monroe (see below, vol. ii, pp. 1145–1146).

29. Ms. (photostat), Wisconsin Historical Collection, Madison, Ramsay Crooks' Letter Book, Mackinac, etc., 1816–20, p. 29, Ramsay Crooks,
Michilimackinac, June 23, 1817, to John Jacob Astor, N. Y.

30. Thwaites, *op. cit.*, p. 414, George Graham, Department of War,
June 5, 1816, to the commanding officer and William H. Puthuff, Indian
agent, Michilimackinac (ms. book, Department of the Interior, Washington, D. C., Indian Office Letter Book C, p. 374).

31. *Ibid.*, pp. 405–407, William H. Crawford, Department of War,
May 10, 1816, to Lewis Cass, Governor of Michigan Territory, and to
Major William H. Puthuff, Charles Jouett, John Bowyer, Agents at
Michilimackinac, Chicago, and Green Bay (ms. book, Department of the
Interior, Washington, D. C., Indian Office Letter Book C, p. 344).

32. *Ibid.*, pp. 417, 423, 424, William Henry Puthuff, Indian Agent,
Michilimackinac, June 20, 1816, to Lewis Cass, Governor, Michigan
Territory (ms. book, Department of the Interior, Washington, D. C.,
Indian Office Letter Book i, p. 239).

33. *Ibid.*, pp. 425–427, William Henry Puthuff, Indian Agent, Michilimackinac, July 12, 1816, to Governor Lewis Cass (ms. book, Department
of the Interior, Washington, D. C., Indian Office Letter Book i, p. 271).

34. *Ibid.*, pp. 427–428, Lewis Cass, Detroit, July 20, 1816, to Major
William Henry Puthuff, Indian Agent, Michilimackinac (ms. book, Department of the Interior, Washington, D. C., Indian Office Letter Book i,
p. 278).

35. *Ibid.*, pp. 430–432, William Henry Puthuff, Indian Agent, Michilimackinac, August 4, 1816, to Governor Lewis Cass (ms. book, Department of the Interior, Washington, D. C., Indian Office Letter Book i,
p. 290).

36. Ms., New York Public Library, Monroe Papers, John Jacob Astor,
N. Y., May 27, 1816, to James Monroe, Secretary of State (see below,
vol. ii, pp. 1145–1146).

37. "Summary of Evidence in the Controversy between The Hudson's Bay Company and the North-West Company. Reprinted from Papers relating to the Red River Settlement, 1815–1819. Ordered by House of Commons to be printed July 12, 1819," *State Historical Society, North Dakota,* vol. iv (1913); ms., Department of State, Washington, D. C., Miscellaneous Letters, December, 1816, John Jacob Astor, N. Y., December 30, 1816, to James Monroe, Department of State, with an affidavit from James Grant, York, Upper Canada, November 23, 1816, a letter from William McGillivray, York, Upper Canada, November 23, 1816, to John Jacob Astor, and a plan for the seizure of the Earl of Selkirk's goods, imported illegally into the United States; ms., Bibliothèque Ste. Sulpice, Montreal, Samuel Gerrard Papers, Baby Collection, William McGillivray, Montreal, December 17, 1816, to J. J. Astor. For further details of this episode, see Porter, Kenneth W., "John Jacob Astor and Lord Selkirk," *North Dakota Historical Quarterly,* vol. v, no. 1 (October, 1930), pp. 5–13.

38. Thwaites, *op. cit.,* pp. 457, 458, George Graham, Acting Secretary of War, May 4, 1817, to Governor Cass (ms. book, Department of the Interior, Washington, D. C., Indian Office Letter Book D, p. 294).

39. Chittenden, *op. cit.,* vol. i, pp. 310–311.

40. Ms., Bibliothèque Ste. Sulpice, Montreal, Samuel Gerrard Papers, Baby Collection, "Sketch of Acc^t. between Mc Tavish Mc Gillivrays & Co. & John Jacob Astor to Decr. 20. 1817."

41. Ms., Palais de Justice, Montreal, Notarial Records of N. B. Doucet, no. 4188, Sale by Pierre de Rocheblave to John Jacob Astor, April 8, 1817.

42. Thwaites, *op. cit.,* p. 451, Agreement between Ramsay Crooks and John Jacob Astor, N. Y., March 17, 1817 (ms. book (copy), Detroit Public Library, Burton Historical Collection, and Missouri Historical Society, St. Louis, Letters of Ramsay Crooks, John Jacob Astor, and the American Fur Company, 1813–43).

43. Ms. book (copy), Detroit Public Library, Burton Historical Collection, and Missouri Historical Society, St. Louis, Letters of Ramsay Crooks, John Jacob Astor, and the American Fur Company, 1813–43, John Jacob Astor, N. Y., once at Philadelphia, February 17, September 20, 1816, December 20, 1817 (see below, vol. ii, pp. 1158–1159), January 6, 10, 20, 23, February 24, March 5, 13, 21, 1818, February 15, April 19, 1819, to William W. Matthews, usually at Montreal, once or twice each at New York, Albany, and Quebec.

44. Kelton, Dwight H., *Annals of Fort Mackinac* (1888), p. 72.

45. Ms. book, Public Archives of Canada, Ottawa, Journal, American Fur Company, Montreal, 1817–34.

46. Lockwood, *op. cit.,* p. 108.

47. Biddle, James W., "Recollections of Green Bay in 1816–17," *Wisconsin Historical Collections*, vol. i (1854), p. 51.

48. Ms. book, Public Archives of Canada, Ottawa, Ledger, American Fur Company, 1817–34, pp. 119, 139, 140, 141, 142, 146, 147, 152, 158, 384.

49. Ms. (photostat), Wisconsin Historical Society, Madison, Ramsay Crooks' Letter Book, Mackinac, etc., 1816–20, p. 34, Ramsay Crooks and Robert Stuart, Michilimackinac, July 21, 1817, to John Jacob Astor, N. Y.

50. Thwaites, *op. cit.*, pp. 457–458, George Graham, Department of War, May 4, 1817, to Governor Cass (ms. book, Department of the Interior, Washington, D. C., Indian Office Letter Book D, p. 294).

51. *Ibid.*, pp. 460–461, Lewis Cass, Detroit, June 8, 1817, to Major W. H. Puthuff, Indian agent (ms. book, Department of the Interior, Washington, D. C., Indian Office Letter Book ii, p. 69).

52. Ms. (photostat), Wisconsin Historical Society, Madison, Ramsay Crooks' Letter Book, Mackinac, etc., 1816–20, p. 12, Ramsay Crooks [Montreal, March?], 1817, to John Jacob Astor, N. Y.

53. *Ibid.*, p. 29, Ramsay Crooks, Michilimackinac, June 23, 1817, to John Jacob Astor, N. Y.

54. There is an impression among some who have written on the fur trade of Michilimackinac in this period that Lewis Cass was bribed with the sum of $35,000 to allow Astor's agents and employees special privileges in the Indian country, of the type indicated in the text. The statement upon which this belief is based first appeared in the *New York Press*, November 2, 1892, in a description of six American Fur Company account books owned by Ford H. Rogers of Detroit. The passage runs as follows: "The blotter is begun on the first page, the opening entry being made on April 1, 1817, at Montreal. . . . Among other entries is one showing that Lewis Cass took certain money from Montreal to Michilimackinac on May 3, 1817, amounting to £7,238. There are two columns used in the blotter for figures, one for pounds sterling and one for dollars and cents." The next reference occurs in the *New York Times*, March 7, 1909, in an account of six American Fur Company books then on display at the Anderson Galleries in that city. It reads: "An entry, May 3, 1817, shows that Lewis Cass, then Governor of Michigan Territory . . . took about $35,000 of the Astor money from Montreal to Detroit, in consideration of something which is not set down." The Catalogue of the Anderson Auction Company, no. 739, p. 11, auction of Thursday and Friday, March 18 and 19, 1909, contains practically the same statement. "On May 13, 1817, an entry shows that Lewis Cass took about $35,000 of the Astor money from Montreal to Detroit in consideration of something not set down." It will be noted that the two earlier accounts make the date of the entry May 3 instead of May 13. These books were sold by the

Anderson Galleries for the account of Ford H. Rogers and were evidently the same as those described by the *New York Press* as belonging to Rogers in 1892. Gustavus Myers in his *History of the Great American Fortunes*, 3 vols. (1907–10), vol. i, p. 130, takes it for granted that this $35,000 was a payment to Cass for some corrupt purpose. "The $35,000 that Astor paid to Cass, the very official who, as Secretary of War, had jurisdiction over the Indian tribes and over the Indian trade . . . were, it may well be supposed, only the merest parts of the total sums he disbursed to officials and politicians, high and low." These six account books were sold by the Anderson Galleries to Arthur H. Clark, of the Arthur H. Clark Company, a publishing house of Cleveland, Ohio, and were sold by this Company on December 1, 1909, to Dr. James Douglass of New York. On September 4, 1914, Dr. Douglass donated them to the Public Archives of Canada, Ottawa, Ontario, where they are now deposited. Thus the chain of evidence which identifies the account books now in Ottawa with those in the possession of Ford H. Rogers back in the last decade of the nineteenth century is complete. We now come to the inexplicable part of the story. Upon a visit to the Archives, I made an attempt to look up in the blotter the entry above referred to, but could find it under neither May 3 nor May 13, 1817. A search through the entire month of May, then through the entire blotter, revealed no entry answering to that description. The other account books containing entries for 1817 were no more fruitful. Several careful investigations by members of the research staff at the Archives, taking in all six volumes, revealed the name of Lewis Cass only once, and then as United States commissioner and in connection with the sum of $138.60. This entry occurs in September, 1820. The volumes are all intact, no pages being missing for the year 1817. It is almost impossible to find an explanation for the way in which this entry, which apparently never existed, has cropped up again and again in three apparently independent sources, over a period of seventeen years. It may be that the account of 1892 was somehow responsible for the error and that later writers copied from it without question. Mr. George B. Catlin, a Detroit historian, states that an accusation of this character was levelled against Cass in 1848 when he was running for the presidency against Zachary Taylor, but that nothing was ever proved. It has been suggested in Cass's behalf that $35,000 might have been paid to him as governor of Michigan Territory, for license-bonds or duties on goods, but licenses were granted by Indian agents, and bonds, of course, necessitated no cash payment, while the collector at Mackinac would handle all matters pertaining to duties. To make matters even more confusing, the Burton Historical Collection of the Detroit Public Library possesses an account book, described as "Blotter, American Fur Company, Montreal, April 1, 1817–May 12, 1817, Mackinac, June 15, 1817–June 25, 1817, October 18, 1818–June 28, 1819." This covers practically the same period as the volume which is supposed to have contained the Cass entry, and which is said to have run at Montreal from April 1, 1817, to May 13, 1817, and at Michilimackinac until October 6, 1819 — and which apparently does not, by the way, exactly correspond with the dates of that in the Public Archives of Canada. Moreover, in the Burton Historical Collection blotter, *a page is torn out after the entry of May 12, 1817!* What significance there is in this interesting fact it is impossible to state without further information, which it is rather unlikely will ever appear. At any rate, we do not at present have any definite evidence that Lewis Cass ever touched $35,000 belonging to Astor, as a bribe or fee, or for any other reason. Such a crude form of persuasion would be foreign to the natures of both men. It is doubtful whether Cass would require any more material reason for granting Astor special favors than the knowledge that Astor was a wealthy man, well-affected politically, the friend of Jefferson, Madison, Monroe, and Gallatin, a strong supporter of the government during the war, and had been recommended to Cass's consideration by the secretary of War. That a man of such distinction should be favored above the ordinary rabble of independent traders and undercapitalized companies would seem self-evident. We have evidence that Cass did grant Astor's company privileges which went beyond all reason. It is not necessary to prove that he did so because of corrupt financial inducements.

55. Thwaites, *op. cit.*, p. 452, Thomas L. McKenney, Superintendent, Indian Trade, Georgetown, March 19, 1817, to George Graham, Acting Secretary of War (ms. book, Department of the Interior, Washington, D. C., Indian Office, Letter Book D, p. 258).

56. "The Fur Trade and Factory System at Green Bay 1816-21," *Wisconsin Historical Collections*, vol. vii (1873-76), p. 275, Major Irwin, Green Bay, September 29, 1817, to Colonel McKenney.

57. Ms., New York Public Library, Monroe Papers, John Jacob Astor, N. Y., November 7, 1817, to James Monroe. In this connection something should be said of the personal relationship subsisting during the formative years of the American Fur Company between its founder and president and the chief executive of the United States. Immediately after the war, when the American Fur Company had not yet assumed its independent and characteristic form, the president of the United States was James Madison, and between him and Astor there undoubtedly existed something more than a purely formal friendship. (Adams, Henry, ed., *The Life of Albert Gallatin* (1880), pp. 487-488, Mrs. Madison, July 29, 1813, to Mrs. Gallatin; ms. book, Baker Library, Astor Papers, Letter Book i, 1813-15, pp. 265, 280, John Jacob Astor, N. Y., August 25, September 13, 1814, to Richard Forrest, Washington, D. C.) However, it was James Monroe who as chief executive had the greatest opportunity from 1817 to 1825 — the critical years for the American Fur Company — to assist the Company in reaching and maintaining its position of su-

premacy. With Monroe, Astor had even closer connections than with Madison, and to him he wrote with the utmost fullness whenever any menace to the fur trade or to his own position therein appeared to be in view among the acts of government. For example, in January, 1821, Astor, then in Paris, seems to have feared that Congress might have in mind some measure unfavorable to his company, which was even then locked in conflict with the dragon of the Factory System. Accordingly he wrote to Monroe in the following words: "I observed in your Excellent Measuage of the 14 Na^r. you recomend congress to Dercit there attention to the trade with aur Indians If any Change is contemplated I hope it will not be to oprate against Citzons who are at present engagd in that trade under the System which government adopted Some years ago. I may confidently asert that the Trade has been muesh extended & Chiefly So by the american furr Compay of whom I am principle relyng on that we shall be permiteted to trade under that Syesterm we have made many and extensive engagements Some of which will not expire for Some years to cam in fact aur men for the canducting of that trade are genrally engagd for 4 to 5. years & whether the trade is good or bade thy must bee paid & must be fead at a great expence aur property too becams so engagd that it taks years to retire I have at present not Less than than [sic] 400000 Say faur hundred thousand Dollars Engagd in this particular trade no fav^r. iss askd but I trust that no [interlineated: new] measure will be adopted by government to the Injury of us or other Privert traders & that if congress who perhaps may not bee fully Informd as to the nature of the trade pass any act thy will Leave it to the Discression of the executive to Carry the Same in to effect as the good of aur Country may Require." (Ms., New York Public Library, Monroe Papers, John Jacob Astor, Paiis, January 10, 1821, to James Monroe, President, see below, vol. ii, pp. 1169–1170.) It does not appear exactly what action of Congress Astor feared. Perhaps it was some unusually rigid restriction on the employment of foreigners in the trade. In any case the danger failed to materialize. We see that Astor felt himself entitled to write with great freedom to the president and to be made the subject (in spite of his disclaimer) of special favor on the part of officials of the government in the Indian country. The reason for his attitude may be connected with certain financial transactions between himself and Monroe. During the previous year Astor had concluded a letter to Monroe from Rome in this fashion: "under standing that Landed proper[ty] in the US. is at present not verry Saleble I presume you have not. Sold any of your estates & there for it may not bee convenient to repay me the Sume Lend to you nor am I particularly in want of it it will hawever bee agreable to have the Intrest paid & have taking the Liberty to Drow an you for 2100$ fav^r. of my Son at 90 Days, being equil to 3 years Intrest." (Ms., New York Public Library, Monroe Papers, John Jacob Astor, Rome, April 5, 1820,

to James Monroe, President, Washington, D. C.)   The further history of
this debt appears in a letter from Monroe to Madison, written in the
spring of 1828, from the former's estate of Oakhill: "I have sold my slaves
in that [Albemarle] county, to Col: White of Florida, who will take them
in families, to that territory.   He gives me for them, (with the exception
of a few sold there) five thousand dol^{rs}., which are paid by obtaining for
me a release in that amount from J. J. Astor, for a loan obtained of him
in the late war, offerd by himself, on hearing that I was pressd for money."
(Ms., Library of Congress, Madison Papers, vol. lviii, Writings to Madison, March 17–July 30, 1816, James Monroe, Oak hill, March 28, 1828, to
[James Madison].)   From the above we learn that for twelve years and
more Monroe was indebted to Astor for $5,000, and that he found it im-
possible to repay this sum, save by the sale of his slaves, and that during
much of this period he held such influential posts in the government as
secretary of State, secretary of War, and even chief executive.   During
this period, also, Astor was in constant communication with the government in search of favors and considerations of one kind or another, during
the war, for example, asking — and securing — permission to have one of
his vessels employed as a flag of truce, and after the war requesting special
consideration for his agents in the Indian country.   I do not suggest for a
moment that Monroe would, against his own better judgment, allow
Astor favors which would be injurious to the country, but it does seem
altogether natural that whenever Monroe received an application
for some consideration of a nature to which the president could accede without undue strain on his conscience he would be much more
likely to give a favorable response to Astor than to someone toward whom
he did not feel the same sense of obligation.   This situation does much
more to explain Lewis Cass's compliant attitude toward the demands of
Astor's agents than does any shadowy bribe of $35,000.   But what would
be the repercussions should a similar situation be made public today?

   58.   Thwaites, *op. cit.*, pp. 477–479, 483–484, Lieut. Col. T. Chambers,
Fort Crawford or Armstrong, September 18, 19, 1817, to Major Morgan;
Major Willoughby Morgan, Fort Armstrong, September 27, 1817, to ?;
John O. Fallon, Acting Assistant Adjutant General, "Bellfontain," Oc-
tober 6, 1817, to General William Clark (ms. (copy), Wisconsin Historical
Society, Madison, Street Papers); Thwaites, Reuben Gold, ed., "The
Fur-Trade in Wisconsin — 1812–1825," *Wisconsin Historical Collections*,
vol. xx (1911) [hereafter in this chapter referred to simply as Thwaites,
"The Fur-Trade in Wisconsin — 1812-1825"], pp. 17–31, Ramsay Crooks
and Robert Stuart, N. Y., January 24, 1818, to John Jacob Astor (ms.
book, Department of the Interior, Washington, D. C., Indian Office
Letter Book ii, p. 269); Chittenden, *op. cit.*, vol. i, pp. 312–313.   It
appears, however, that the American Fur Company did not succeed
in collecting the amount which it had been awarded in the Cham-

bers case. In 1826 Astor stated that no money had been received. The award of $5,000 had been made in 1822, but in November, 1825, a jury, after what agents of the War Department described as a singular charge by the judge, found against Chambers in $200 damages. This may have been an appeal from the earlier decision or may have been in connection with a new suit brought by the Company (ms., Department of the Interior, Washington, D. C., Indian Office Records, Miscellaneous, John Jacob Astor, N. Y., May 26, 1826, to James Barbour, Secretary of War; H. S. Geyer, George F. Struther, and A. L. Magenis, November, 1825, to the Secretary of War).

59. Thwaites, "The Fur-Trade in Wisconsin — 1812–1825," pp. 47–49, Lewis Cass, Detroit, April 22, 1818, to Major Puthuff, Colonel Bowyer, Messrs. Jouett, Stickney, and Johnston, Agents for Indian Affairs (ms. book, Department of the Interior, Washington, D. C., Indian Office Letter Book ii, p. 343).

60. Ms., Bibliothèque Ste. Sulpice, Montreal, Samuel Gerrard Papers, Baby Collection, McTavish, McGillivrays & Co., Forsyth, Richardson & Co., Montreal, March 29, 1817, to John Jacob Astor; John Jacob Astor, St. Johns, September 1, 1817, to McTavish, McGillivrays & Co., Montreal.

61. Ms. book (copy), Detroit Public Library, Burton Historical Collection, and Missouri Historical Society, St. Louis, Letters of Ramsay Crooks, John Jacob Astor, and the American Fur Company, 1813–43, Ramsay Crooks, N. Y., February 7, 1818, to John Jacob Astor, Baltimore, with statements of the affairs of the South West Company and the American Fur Company to February 1, 1818. Late in August, 1817, a schooner and a sloop had arrived at Buffalo bringing "the largest and most valuable lot of furs ever seen before in this village. They consisted of beaver, otter, muskrat and bear skins and buffalo robes. Three hundred and twenty-two packs were consigned to Hart & Lay, and owned by John Jacob Astor, of New York; and one hundred packs were consigned to Townsend & Cort, belonging to several owners. The value of these furs is figured at one hundred and fifty thousand dollars." Astor's share of this consignment, some of the first fruits of the trade of the reorganized American Fur Company, must have been valued at more than $100,000. (Sheldon, James, "Fifty Years Ago," *Publications of the Buffalo Historical Society*, vol. ii (1880), pp. 357–374, quoting from the Buffalo *Gazette*, September 2, 1817; *Niles' Weekly Register*, vol. xiii, p. 48, September 13, 1817.)

62. Ms. book, Public Archives of Canada, Ottawa, American Fur Company, Ledger, 1817–34, pp. 119, 139, 140, 141, 142, 146, 147, 152, 158, 384.

63. Thwaites, "The Fur-Trade in Wisconsin — 1812–1825," pp. 17–31, Ramsay Crooks and Robert Stuart, N. Y., January 24, 1818, to John

Jacob Astor (ms. book, Department of the Interior, Washington, D. C., Indian Office Letter Book ii, p. 269).

64. *Idem.*, "The Fur-Trade in Wisconsin — 1815–1817," *Wisconsin Historical Collections*, vol. xix (1910) [hereafter in this chapter referred to simply as Thwaites, "The Fur-Trade in Wisconsin — 1815–1817"], p. 452, T. L. McKenney, Superintendent, Indian Trade, Indian Office, Georgetown, March 19, 1817, to George Graham, Acting Secretary of War (ms. book, Department of the Interior, Washington, D. C., Indian Office Letter Book D, p. 258).

65. Major Puthuff had formerly been the commanding officer at Detroit, and on his retirement from that position was presented with a highly complimentary address signed by fifty-one of the town's most prominent citizens (ms., Detroit Public Library, Burton Historical Collection, J. R. Williams MSS., vol. xix, p. 150, Detroit, August 9, 1815).

66. Thwaites, "The Fur-Trade in Wisconsin — 1815–1817," p. 441, Licenses from John Bowyer, Indian Agent, Green Bay, October 3, 1816, to Messrs. Bouthillier and Rolette (ms., Detroit Public Library, Burton Historical Collection, vol. 112, p. 224).

67. *Idem.*, "The Fur-Trade in Wisconsin — 1812–1825," pp. 88–90, William Henry Puthuff, Detroit, October 15, 1818, to Governor Lewis Cass (ms. book, Department of the Interior, Washington, D. C., Indian Office Letter Book iii, p. 52).

68. *Ibid.*, p. 116, George Boyd, Indian Agent, Michilimackinac, July 17, 1819, to William Morrison (ms., Wisconsin Historical Society, Madison, Wisconsin MSS., 1 D 82).

69. "The Fur Trade and Factory System at Green Bay 1816–21," *Wisconsin Historical Collections*, vol. vii (1873–76), pp. 269–288, pp. 276–277, Major Irwin, Green Bay, 1818 or 1819, to Colonel McKenney.

70. Thwaites, "The Fur-Trade in Wisconsin — 1812–1825," pp. 16–17, Lewis Cass, Detroit, January 22, 1818, to Colonel John Bowyer, Indian Agent, Green Bay (ms. book, Department of the Interior, Washington, D. C., Indian Office Letter Book ii, p. 247).

71. "The Fur Trade and Factory System at Green Bay 1816–21," *Wisconsin Historical Collections*, vol. vii (1873–76), pp. 277–278.

72. Thwaites, "The Fur-Trade in Wisconsin — 1812–1825," pp. 32–33, William Henry Puthuff, Indian Agent, Mackinac, March 4, 1818, to Lewis Cass, Governor, Michigan Territory (ms. book, Department of the Interior, Washington, D. C., Indian Office Letter Book ii, p. 292).

73. *Ibid.*, p. 34, T. L. McKenney, Office of Indian Trade, Georgetown, March 6, 1818, to Matthew Irwin, United States Factor, Green Bay (ms. book, Department of the Interior, Washington, D. C., Indian Office Letter Book D, p. 505).

74. *Ibid.*, pp. 34–36, Jacob Franks, Montreal, March 11, 1818, to John Lawe, Green Bay (ms., Wisconsin Historical Society, Madison, Wiscon-

sin MSS., Martin Papers). The unusual favors granted to Astor's company by Indian agents and others at the request of Governor Cass quite understandably led many traders to believe that the American Fur Company was at least a quasi-official institution. For example, the trader Frederic Oliva, applying to Colonel John Bowyer, Indian agent at Green Bay, for a couple of licenses, offered to "Give . . . Satisfaction that the Goods I have imported from Michil^a Were purchased from the House of David Stone & C° Who have obtained the Same privilege as the American Fur Comp^y." The nature of the "privilege" was not specified, but was evidently supposed to be of a character which would favorably impress an Indian agent. (Thwaites, "The Fur-Trade in Wisconsin — 1815-1817," pp. 476-477, Frederic Oliva, Green Bay, September 16, 1817, to Colonel Bo[w]yer, ms., Wisconsin Historical Society, Madison, Wisconsin MSS., 1 D 38.) The British had early become convinced that Astor's fur-trade activities were of a more or less official character. On August 19, 1815, a British officer stated in a letter that "ever since the Peace the Americans have been bestowing uncommon pains to perfect and complete their plan of entirely gaining the Western Indians — They are aware of its Vital importance in the event of another War — as one great means of effecting this the whole Trade of Michilimackinac is to be monopolized by the House of John Jacob Astor who will soon distance all competitors in consequence of being enabled by the favor of his Government to send his goods into the Indian Country free of all duties whatever. The English traders are in a manner prohibited by being saddled with the enormous duty of 35 and 40 p cent: after this year, it will exclude them wholly, and in times of Peace, to them it has chiefly been owing, that our connection and influence with the Indians has been kept up. —" (Ms., Public Archives of Canada, Ottawa, Series C. 258, p. 212, Lieutenant Colonel Robert McDouall, Drummond's Island, August 19, 1815, to Major General Sir Frederick P. Robinson.) Of course Lieutenant-Colonel McDouall was mistaken in stating that Astor was allowed to import goods duty-free, but his analysis of the relation of the fur trade to Indian affairs helps somewhat to justify certain of the special favors actually granted Astor by the War Department and its subordinates.

75. Thwaites, "The Fur-Trade in Wisconsin — 1812-1825," pp. 55-56, Michael Dousman, Mackinac, May 10, 1818, to John Lawe, Green Bay (ms., Wisconsin Historical Society, Madison, Wisconsin MSS., 1 C 24).

76. *Ibid.*, pp. 42-47, Lewis Cass, Detroit, April 23, 1818, to the Agents at Mackinac, Green Bay, and Chicago (ms. book, Department of the Interior, Washington, D. C., Indian Office Letter Book ii, p. 347).

77. *Ibid.*, pp. 32-33, William Henry Puthuff, Indian Agent, Michilimackinac, March 4, 1818, to Lewis Cass, Governor, Michigan Territory (ms. book, Department of the Interior, Washington, D. C., Indian Office Letter Book ii, p. 292).

78. *Ibid.*, p. 31, Ramsay Crooks and Robert Stuart, N. Y., January 24, 1818, to John Jacob Astor (ms. book, Department of the Interior, Washington, D. C., Indian Office Letter Book ii, p. 269).

79. Ms. book (copy), Detroit Public Library, Burton Historical Collection, and Missouri Historical Society, St. Louis, Letters of Ramsay Crooks, John Jacob Astor, and the American Fur Company, 1813–43, John Jacob Astor, Paris, March 27, 1821, to Ramsay Crooks.

80. Ms. (copy), New York State Library, Albany, Peter Sailly Palmer Papers, John Jacob Astor, N. Y., May 31, 1819, to William H. Crawford, Secretary of the Treasury.

81. Ms. book, Office of the Astor Estate, N. Y., Untitled memorandum book.

82. Ms. book (copy), Detroit Public Library, Burton Historical Collection, and Missouri Historical Society, St. Louis, Letters of Ramsay Crooks, John Jacob Astor, and the American Fur Company, 1813–43, Ramsay Crooks, N. Y., December 4, 1819, to John Jacob Astor, Europe.

83. Of course Astor's opposition to the factories had not kept him from having some business relations with them. We find him in 1810 and 1815 trying to buy deer skins from the superintendent of Indian Trade and in the latter year unsuccessfully endeavoring to sell him some tobacco. In 1816 he congratulated T. L. McKenney on his appointment as superintendent of Indian Trade and succeeded in selling him some scarlet cloth. In 1821 he bought at auction at Georgetown a little over a hundred dollars' worth of skins from the Prairie du Chien factory, 100 wolf, cat, and fox skins for $41, 53 fisher skins for $60.95, and 19 ground-hog skins for $10.45. It is evident, however, that his relations with the government trading houses were not at all extensive. (Ms. book, Department of the Interior, Washington, D. C., Indian Office Letter Book B, June, 1809–June, 1812, pp. 110 and 114, J[ohn] M[ason], Superintendent of Indian Trade, Georgetown, March 20, 27, 1810, to John Jacob Astor, N. Y.; *ibid.*, Letter Book C, June, 1812–April, 1816, pp. 362–364, J[ohn] M[ason], Indian Office, Georgetown, June 12, 1815, to John Jacob Astor, N. Y.; pp. 367–368, W. H. Crawford, War Department, May 27, 1816, to John Jacob Astor, N. Y.; pp. 374–412, George Graham, Chief Clerk, War Department, June 5, August 27, 1816, to John Jacob Astor, N. Y.; *ibid.*, Letter Book D, April, 1816–April, 1818, pp. 28, 279, 291, T. L. McKenney, Indian Office, April 29, 1816, April 17, 29, 1817, to John Jacob Astor, N. Y.; *Senate Documents*, 17th Cong., 1st sess. (1821–22), vol. i, no. 60, table 9.)

84. Chittenden, *op. cit.*, vol. i, pp. 12–16.

85. Ms. book, Missouri Historical Society, St. Louis, Gratiot Collection, Charles Gratiot's Letter Book, 1798–1816, pp. 165–166, Charles Gratiot, St. Louis, May 29, 1814, to John Jacob Astor, N. Y. (in English).

86. Thwaites, "The Fur-Trade in Wisconsin — 1812–1825," pp. 17–

31, Ramsay Crooks and Robert Stuart, N. Y., January 24, 1818, to John Jacob Astor (ms. book, Department of the Interior, Washington, D. C., Indian Office Letter Book ii, p. 269).

87. "The Fur Trade and Factory System at Green Bay 1816–21," *Wisconsin Historical Collections*, vol. vii (1873–76), pp. 269–288, Major Irwin, Green Bay, March 10, September 29, 1817, June 18, August 10, 1818, no date, 1818 or 1819, February 15, 1820, October 6, 1821, to Colonel McKenney; Colonel McKenney, Office of Indian Trade, May 28, 1817, July 5, 1821, to Major Irwin; M. Irwin, U. S. Factor [1820], to Dr. J. Morse, Green Bay.

88. Thwaites, "The Fur-Trade in Wisconsin — 1812–1825," pp. 82–86, Lewis Cass, St. Mary's, September 14, 1818, to J. C. Calhoun, Secretary of War (ms. book, Department of the Interior, Washington, D. C., Indian Office Letter Book iii, p. 30).

89. *Ibid.*, p. 66, note 42.

90. *Ibid.*, pp. 127–128, Lewis Cass, Detroit, October 11, 1819, to the Agents at Michilimackinac, Green Bay, Chicago, Fort Wayne and Piqua (ms. book, Department of the Interior, Washington, D. C., Indian Office Letter Book iii, p. 137).

91. Ms. (photostat), Wisconsin Historical Society, Madison, Ramsay Crooks' Letter Book, Mackinac, etc., 1816–20, Ramsay Crooks, N. Y., May 30, 1820, to John Jacob Astor.

92. Ramsay Crooks and Russell Farnham spent the winter of 1820–21 at Washington, lodging in the same hotel as Thomas Hart Benton, who mentioned having many conversations with them. It is probable that the Astorians did not select their residence entirely by accident and that the inutility of the factory system was a frequent subject of discussion. (Benton, Thomas Hart, *Thirty Years' View*, 2 vols. (1854), vol. i, p. 13.)

93. Ms. (photostat), Wisconsin Historical Society, Madison, Ramsay Crooks' and Robert Stuart's Letter Book, Mackinac, Detroit, New York, etc., 1820–25, pp. 175–178, Ramsay Crooks, N. Y., November 30, 1821, to John Jacob Astor, Europe.

94. *Ibid.*, Ramsay Crooks, N. Y., April 1, 1822, to Thomas Hart Benton, Washington, D. C.

95. Thwaites, "The Fur-Trade in Wisconsin — 1812–1825," p. 240, note 39.

96. *Senate Documents*, 17th Cong., 1st sess. (1821–22), vol. i, no. 60, pp. 39–43, Thomas L. McKenney, Office of Indian Trade, February 27, 1822, to Henry Johnson, Chairman of the Committee of the Senate on Indian Affairs.

97. Ms. (photostat), Wisconsin Historical Society, Madison, Ramsay Crooks' and Robert Stuart's Letter Book, Mackinac, Detroit, New York, etc., 1820–25, pp. 381–382, Ramsay Crooks, N. Y., December 31, 1822, to Thomas Hart Benton, Washington, D. C.

98. *Ibid.*, pp. 437–438, Robert Stuart, Mackinac, November 10, 1822, to Ramsay Crooks.

99. *Ibid.*, pp. 381–382, Ramsay Crooks, N. Y., December 31, 1822, to Thomas Hart Benton, Washington, D. C.

100. *Ibid.*, Ramsay Crooks, N. Y., December 4, 1821, to Munson & Barnard, Boston.

101. Ms. book (copy), Detroit Public Library, Burton Historical Collection, and Missouri Historical Society, St. Louis, Letters of Ramsay Crooks, John Jacob Astor, and the American Fur Company, 1813–43, John Jacob Astor, Paris, March 27, 1821, to Ramsay Crooks.

102. Ms. (photostat), Wisconsin Historical Society, Madison, Ramsay Crooks' and Robert Stuart's Letter Book, Mackinac, Detroit, New York, etc., 1820–25, pp. 83–84, Ramsay Crooks, Liverpool, April 18, 1821, to John Jacob Astor, Paris.

103. *Ibid.*, Ramsay Crooks, Mackinac, July 11, 1821, to John Jacob Astor.

104. *Ibid.*, pp. 175–178, Ramsay Crooks, N. Y., November 30, 1821, to John Jacob Astor, Europe; pp. 184–187, Ramsay Crooks, N. Y., December 5, 1821, to Robert Stuart, Mackinac.

105. Chittenden, *op. cit.*, vol. i, p. 319.

106. Ms. (photostat), Wisconsin Historical Society, Madison, Ramsay Crooks' and Robert Stuart's Letter Book, Mackinac, Detroit, New York, etc., 1820–25, pp. 184–187, Ramsay Crooks, N. Y., December 5, 1821, to Robert Stuart, Mackinac.

107. Chittenden, *op. cit.*, vol. i, pp. 316–320.

108. Ms. (photostat), Wisconsin Historical Society, Madison, Ramsay Crooks' and Robert Stuart's Letter Book, Mackinac, Detroit, New York, etc., 1820–25, pp. 175–178, Ramsay Crooks, N. Y., November 30, 1821, to John Jacob Astor, Europe.

109. *Ibid.*, pp. 261–265, Ramsay Crooks, N. Y., April 23, 1822, to John Jacob Astor, N. Y.

110. Ms., Syracuse University, Gerrit Smith Miller Collection, Letters, John Jacob Astor & Son, N. Y., July 16, 1821, to Peter Smith, Peterboro.

111. *New-York Gazette and General Advertiser*, April 29, 1822, p. 2, col. 2.

112. Ms., Newberry Library, Chicago, Edward E. Ayer Collection, John Jacob Astor, N. Y., December 23, 1822, to Samuel Abbott, St. Louis.

CHAPTER XV

THE AMERICAN FUR COMPANY FROM THE ESTABLISH-
MENT OF THE WESTERN DEPARTMENT TO RETIREMENT
1822-1834

AFTER his return from Europe in 1822, Astor remained in the United States long enough to put through another important arrangement in the fur trade, in addition to the establishment of the Western Department, namely, a consolidation with David Stone's company, sometimes known as Stone, Bostwick & Co., for the term of three and one-half years from April 1, 1823, to October 1, 1826. Apparently this consolidation was to affect only the trade of the Western Department, since in 1820 Stone had agreed not to trade from Mackinac for five years. Astor's agreement with Crooks and Stuart, formed in March, 1821, was due to expire in the spring of 1826, and it was therefore desirable to extend it till October of that year. Crooks's share of the business was still to be one-fifth of Astor's interest, unless he wished to increase it to one-fifth of the profit or loss of the whole concern, in which case he must, however, give security by May 1 for any loss which might result.[1] Robert Stuart, on being notified of the arrangement, wrote to David Stone saying, "Permit me to welcome you as member of the American Fur Company & I think you have all acted wisely, but if the junction had been formed five years ago there would have been cause of mutual congratulation."[2] According to the arrangement Stuart was to remain in charge of the Northern Department, while Bostwick, one of the new partners, was to co-operate with Abbott at St. Louis. Crooks was also to assist on this new western front,[3] while William B. Astor was to handle affairs at New York as the president of the Company, after his father had returned to Europe,[4] whither he was again accompanied, in the early summer of 1823, by Eliza, his youngest and only unmarried daughter.[5]

The American Fur Company had also been engaged in eliminating competition in the Green Bay district. If the Company's agents had entered into open rivalry with the traders here, they would have been forced to meet the powerful Grignon-Lawe-Porlier combination, the members of which, by long residence in the country and intercourse with the natives, would be unusually formidable antagonists. Consequently, the Company utilized the device previously employed against the St. Louis traders and furnished the traders at Green Bay with their outfits under the threat of open competition unless the traders would agree to purchase from the American Fur Company. Goods were furnished at such high prices that losses resulted to the Green Bay men; so in order to eliminate competition, Crooks induced the five principal traders, in the late summer of 1821, to form the Green Bay Company, which was to endure for three years from August 1, 1821, any partner being allowed to withdraw at the end of a year, provided that he gave two months' notice.[6] Apparently, however, the Green Bay Company did not prove very successful, except for the American Fur Company. The agents of that organization seem to have opposed the Green Bay traders in an unprincipled manner, though Stuart disclaimed all responsibility for any unfair tactics on the part of his subordinates.[7] John Lawe's characterization of the Green Bay Company, a year after its formation, was as follows:

they made us form a Company at the Bay but it is a Mere Burlesque for to throw us into misery & trouble & they pretend it is for our own Good it's true it would be if we had the privelege of others (that is to get our Goods as low as they [interlineated: really] could give them, [interlineated: with a good profit]) and at least to get enough to try & clear our

Expences & have at least liberty to go where we please but no it is quite the contrary they dont wish I believe to ruin us for fear an opposition might form & come into the Country.

According to Lawe, the American Fur Company opposed the Green Bay Company on all fronts, yet restricted the Green Bay agents from trading outside a specified area;

so [he wrote] I leave it for you to Judge what can we do I say oppose it is their own Equipment that they have to oppose as I do not mean people on their own accounts it is their agents they send so far to have more profit where did you ever hear of an instance that people that is on their own account that there should be such heavy restrictions & tax is laid on them that they cannot go where they please but must go where these Gentlemen should please . . . they take the Peltries low . . . & they would after all wish to keep us in a small Circular [region] did you ever hear any thing like this. The Mississippi they are drawing our Indians there so that they would work to fix us completely but you would perhaps say why do you take goods from them when we cannot better ourselves. . . .[8]

The only thing entirely clear about this diatribe is Lawe's low opinion of the American Fur Company. By the fall of 1823 the Green Bay Company seems to have pretty well gone under, for Robert Stuart wrote: "I have just returned from Green Bay . . . I went in order . . . to Close our old concerns. Money was not to be had but we are secured by mortgages on real estate for the most of what the people in that quarter owed us."[9] Ramsay Crooks, a little earlier in the same fall, had taken occasion gently to reprove Joseph Rolette of Prairie du Chien, trading on shares with the Company, for too vigorous opposition to Green Bay traders deriving their goods from Astor — an attempt to temper the wind to the shorn lamb.[10] In view of the fact that Rolette was strongly suspected of having stirred up the Indians to burn the store of one of the Green Bay men, a modest warning of this kind was not inappropriate.[11] By the fall of 1824 the number of the Green Bay traders had been reduced to two, John Lawe and Michael Dousman, trading on shares, differently stated as two-thirds and one-half.[12]

At the beginning of the 1824 season, then, seven years after the reorganization of the American Fur Company, the situation was as follows: in New York William B. Astor was acting as president of the Company in place of his father, who was again in Europe; Robert Stuart, with headquarters at Mackinac, was in charge of the Northern Department, the Great Lakes and Upper Mississippi, an area from which the competition of Stone, Bostwick & Co. had been eliminated in the fall of 1820; a Western Department had been formed with headquarters at St. Louis, and including the Missouri, the Lower Mississippi, and the Illinois, and an arrangement had been made with Stone, Bostwick & Co. to carry on the trade in this area on joint account, Bostwick, Abbott, and Crooks acting as the agents of the associated companies for this purpose; the Company's posts on British territory had of necessity been abandoned, but on the other side of the border the government factories had been eliminated; the outfits in the Northern Department had not greatly increased in number, but they had become larger and better organized through such consolidations as had taken place at Green Bay, and, from consistently showing at least a book loss, had come in most cases to bring a profit, whether they were made up for the Company's account or on shares.[13]

We are now ready to consider the American Fur Company's further history. In 1824 an act of Congress was passed which required the "Indian agents to designate from time to time Certain Convenient & Suitable places for Carrying on trade with the different Indian tribes, and to require all traders to trade at the place thus designated and at no other place."[14] This regulation, according to the general opinion of the time, had been established

through the influence of John Jacob Astor ... to favor the American Fur Company for if a license was granted to some adventurous trader not connected with that Company he was only permitted to trade at some designated point already occupied by that opulent and formidable Company; and the consequence was, that the Company would sell goods at half their real value, and thus drive away the new opposition trader who could not compete with them, and then the Company would again put up their goods to the old prices, and soon make up for the little loss sustained while performing the necessary process of breaking down all show of opposition.[15]

Such a law, if enforced, would unquestionably benefit a company with sufficient capital to carry on a price-cutting campaign against ordinary poorly financed private traders. It would therefore seem altogether probable that Astor or his agents should have been behind this measure. If this was so, however, the act was not at first administered in the manner which had been anticipated, for in the summer of 1825 William B. Astor, as president *pro tempore* of the American Fur Company, wrote to Thomas L. McKenney at the Office of Indian Affairs protesting against the locations assigned to Company traders. McKenney, agreeable to William B. Astor's request, suggested to William Clark, the superintendent of Indian Affairs at St. Louis, that the locations suggested by the Company's president be adopted if suitable.[16] Although the difficulty was thus adjusted, either the effects of the act continued in other ways to fall short of what had been expected by any sponsors it may have had in the ranks of the Company, or else, after a year and six months of operation, all the desired results had been achieved; for on January 28, 1826, Bernard Pratte, one of the partners in the Western Department, and Robert Stuart wrote a joint letter to James Barbour, the secretary of War, petitioning for the repeal of the location law, on the grounds that the uncertainty of the Indian trade made the assignment of definite trading stations a distinct disadvantage to those engaged in the business, and also that the regulation worked to the advantage of the Hudson's Bay Company along the border and of the lawless trader everywhere. Lewis Cass, as might have been expected, sponsored their appeal, but upon

Thomas L. McKenney's insistence that the location law was a necessary weapon in the campaign against the liquor trade with the Indians the obnoxious law was left in effect,[17] and was, indeed, reaffirmed ten years later.[18] It seems probable, however, that the American Fur Company's influence prevented the location law from working it any particular injury. When an American Fur Company trader named Crafts was warned off from a certain district by Wolcott, the Indian agent at Chicago, Stuart merely got into touch with Governor Cass, who probably instructed his subordinate to allow the trader to return to his previous station, in view of the fact that preparations had already been made for the year's business.[19]

During 1824 Robert Stuart was also interested in tariff lobbying. He wrote to Crooks, "You will of course make every exertion to get a duty laid on *Neutra Skins*, Cony Wool, Russia Hares, &c."[20] (goods which came into competition with the Company's beavers and muskrats for hat-making); while at the same time he urged John Jacob Astor to induce McKenney of the Indian Bureau and his friends to work on Congress to "lessen the duties on at least, Strouds, Indian Blankets & Guns," which could be brought in from Canada at a price twenty to thirty per cent below the American rate. Stuart suggested that a plea for "the poor red children of the Forest" might be utilized to good effect upon the Congressmen.[21]

Although John Jacob Astor was in Europe for the sake of his health, he kept in almost as close touch with the situation at Mackinac and St. Louis from his residence in Geneva, by frequent correspondence, as he could from New York. The result was that the American Fur Company had for all practical purposes a European agent, since it was not in Astor's nature to avoid taking a keen interest in the fur trade of England and the Continent. Indeed, despite the primary purpose of his residence in Europe, he seems to have alternated periods of feverish activity in the fur market with severe sieges of illness.

Astor's constant warning was "that no more goods be bought or imported than can well be sold this season." In view of the situation in the European fur market he seemed to favor contraction rather than expansion, and warned the Company, "We must absolutely give less for the skins we take or do less business if we do not wish to lose more money." In the fall of 1824, perhaps rendered more than usually pessimistic by his ill-health, he repeated, "the more I see of it, the more I am convinced that we have even [ever] imported too many goods and been induced to give them too freely to people who are not able to pay for them. . . . It appears to me that even the last year you had too many goods. I hope this year you will not order so many rather fall short than to have over . . . I repeat don't order too many and be not too sanguine in so loosing a trade as that in which we are engaged." Later he wrote Crooks: "you have always been too sanguine as to the result of our trade, I am sure that to this day it has not paid interest for the money."[22] Astor communicated this opinion also to Stuart, who, dissenting from his superior's gloomy opinion of the trade, replied: "You intimate a wish that we should contract our business: to this Sir, I can have no *personal* objection, but rest assured of its being bad policy, unless you mean *imperceptibly*, (if I may use the expression) to withdraw altogether."[23]

To the stock counsel to contract the business, by ordering less goods, buying fewer skins [24] and at lower prices, and keeping out of debt, Astor added more concrete instructions, as to what types of peltries to purchase, with reference to their prices in Europe, and whether to dispose of them in New York, London, or Germany. It was evidently Astor's policy to support the market by buying up all or practically all of certain types of skins much in demand.[25]

It seems that the American Fur Company had experienced some difficulty with its new associates in the Western Department. It is not at all clear what the trouble was, but it would appear that Munson of C. W. Munson & Co., probably one of the "others" included in "the agreement . . . between the American Fur Company and Stone Bostwick and Co and others," had, with the knowledge of Stone and Bostwick, "been pleased to break the agreement" by buying some furs from "the *Mesurie* Co.," apparently on their own account, which was evidently a violation of the contract with Astor's company. They seem to have done this to "secor" [secure] a debt owed to them by the persons from whom the furs were purchased, but though for this reason Astor did not "consider the act of buying the skins as a dishonest act," he was still so aroused that he wrote: "I think this will afford a good reason for displacing Bostwick and even Mr Stone from their Agency." However, he expressed himself as willing to forgive them if they would "indemnify the Company . . . bust [*sic*] they must indemnify the Company first, and if this can be done to mutual satisfaction, so much the better, you are on the spot and can judge better than I can." He suggested that one means of indemnification might be "to take the skins and furs of Munson & Co. at such price as that the Company may gain 5 or 10 per cent on them. . . . We certainly have a claim on them it will be better to have the skins in one hand." Apparently, however, his anger finally cooled, and in the fall he had nothing to say more than the following: "I presume nothing has been got from Munson. I only wish these gentlemen may act with strict integrity & ocanency [economy?]," and "From Messrs Stone & Co. I see as I expected we got nothing for the supposed great damage done by Mr Munsons contract I thought at the time better to settle the matter at New York, and take what might be got, be it more or less, its now done with." Forgivingly he added: "I rather suppose you will find Mr Stone a useful member and I hope Mr Bostwick will turn out better than we expected."[26]

Early in 1825 Astor was looking forward to the expiration in

October, 1826, of the agreement made with Stone, Bostwick
& Co. and their associates for the trade of the Western Department; also the agreement with Stuart and Crooks as agents of
the American Fur Company. "I as Chief agent of the Company," he wrote, "consider it my duty to act . . . as shall appear to me for the interest of the Company till the termination
of the agreement and consequently I will order goods for 1826,
for be the agreement extended or not, the trade will be carried
on by some one, and be it who it may they must have goods —
what will be prudent if not necessary [will be] to make no engagement which will extend beyond Oct. 1826, if it can be
avoided of which you and the other Agents can judge better
than me." He continued: "it appears to me that our new
friend[s] will prefer to sell out, and excepting Stone, I should
as leave be without them, though I may also wish to sell out,
but whether I do or not, it will be of great satisfaction to me to
see the Companys affairs in a good state at the exporation of the
[illegible — agreement?] or winding up of the concern." Astor
seemed at this time to be unusually optimistic, a mood which
soon passed. However, he admitted that 1824 had been "a
good year," and this probably inspired William B. Astor as
president *pro tempore* to renew "the agreement with our new
partners for one year longer," that is, to October, 1827. But
Crooks and Stuart did not agree to the extension of their own
agencies for another year as promptly as they had on a previous similar occasion. It would not be surprising were they
somewhat disgruntled by the way in which those "concerns"
in which they had been associated with Astor had so uniformly
appeared to lose money, while on the other hand the firm of
John Jacob Astor & Son had not seemed to lack prosperity.
But this is a subject which deserves separate treatment. Astor
assured him and Stuart:

With regard as to whether I continue in the trade I really cannot now
tell . . . but whether I do or not I never had any other thought than that

I did retire, I would like you and Mr Stuart to be fully satisfied. I must say that I never intended to make an arrangement contrary to your interest. Quite otherwise, nor did I contemplate that you or Mr Stuart would ever separate from the concern while I continued. I hope that both of you on reflection have come in the late agreement. You tell me indeed that you will at all events go on as if you had come into it —

that is, that they would continue for the additional year without a formal contract.[27]

Astor returned to the United States in the spring of 1826, and on May 11 succeeded in making an agreement with Robert Stuart to the effect that he should act as agent for five years from October 1, 1826, at a salary of $2,500 per year, "fifteen percent of the net profits which shall have arisen during the said period . . . the profit to be ascertained after all expenses, saleries, commissions, interest on the Capital stock etc. shall have been paid," with travelling expenses if "required to go to a distance from your usual station on the business of the Company." Crooks was considerably harder to persuade. On May 16 he was undecided whether he would make an arrangement with Astor. Stuart's agreement he "did not think . . . so plain and explicit as such documents ought always to be." He pointed out that in his opinion Astor's proposed agreement with himself and Stuart did not clearly define the share of the profits which they were to receive, and he declared that no way of closing the firm was specified; so that they might be forced to wait ten years for any profits due to them. He concluded in a burst of Highland indignation, "if Mr. A. maintains the ground he took with me five days ago, we will part as sure as the sun shines on the poor as well as the rich."[28] One party or the other must have reconsidered and a mutually agreeable arrangement must have been achieved, for long after the expiration of the earlier agreement Crooks was still acting as the American Fur Company's agent. However, Crooks's attitude towards Astor after this controversy seems to have been always slightly edged with antagonism.

The year 1826 was important in the history of the American Fur Company for other reasons besides those just mentioned. The extension of the agreement with Stone, Bostwick & Co. had been granted not by John Jacob but by his son, and the older man does not seem to have altogether approved. Quite early in the history of the partnership he had considered breaking the agreement, not without cause. Consequently, soon after his return to the United States, he had considered the advisability of buying out his present partners and taking into the business of the Western Department the St. Louis firm of Bernard Pratte & Co., who would probably be more efficient in the trade of that area than the New Englanders with whom he was then connected. It will be remembered that for more than a quarter of a century it had been Astor's desire to associate himself with the St. Louis fur traders, and he had now reached the point where he could bring about such a result by main force. The St. Louisans had been in competition with Astor since 1822, and knew his strength. Consequently, Bernard Pratte & Co. were probably only too glad to accept Astor's offer of a partnership in the Western Department. The agreement was made by January, 1827, according to which the St. Louis company was to share equally with Astor's organization in the profits or losses of those posts on the Mississippi below Prairie du Chien and all those on the Missouri and its dependencies.[29] In order that this arrangement might go into effect Astor was, of course, obliged to buy out the interests of his existing partners for the unexpired portion of the agreement with them. He had succeeded in purchasing the interests of Munson and Stone by at least April, 1827, and on May 25 he wrote to Crooks: "You will have seen long since the arrangements made with Stone Bostwick & Co., & Munson & Barnard for all their interest, and that in consequence of this, and the arrangement with Pratte & Co. he, Mr. Bostwick is no longer our agent, say not after the first of July," on which date, it would appear, the agreement with Bernard Pratte & Co. was to go into effect.[30] As Crooks took pains to point out, however, "Mr. Munson in announcing the arrangement to him says he hopes Mr. B. will accede to it. — this he is not inclined to do, for he says his partners sold out too cheap; and so long as he retains his interest I cannot (unless he behaves improperly) deprive him of his agency before 1 Oct next."[31] Consequently Astor wrote Bostwick: "they [Bostwick's partners] have no doubt informed you that I was willing to have you continue interested, if you will be stock holder, I will give you what stock you may wish at an advance of 10 say ten percent."[32] Apparently, however, Bostwick did not feel that the position of stockholder was any compensation for the loss of a partnership and agency. Some other arrangement seems to have been made with him for the relinquishment of his interest, as he does not appear as a Company agent after July 1.

Even before the arrangement with Bernard Pratte & Co. had been consummated, a campaign had been inaugurated to crush a formidable opposition which had arisen in the Upper Mississippi region between the Great Lakes and the Missouri. This rival concern, known as the Columbia Fur Company, had been established, after the union of the North West and Hudson's Bay Companies in 1821, by Joseph Renville, a trader who had been thrown out of employment by this amalgamation. He gathered about him some of the most experienced of those in a situation similar to his own, the most prominent being Kenneth McKenzie and William Laidlaw, and evaded the United States law of 1816 by bringing in certain citizens of the United States, such as Daniel Lamont and a Mr. Tilton (who gave his name to the company as its legal title), to act as the nominal heads of the organization. The Company did not have a large capital, but made up for this deficiency by the superabundant energy and experience displayed by its members. In a few years they had posts along the Missouri River from

Council Bluffs, their most southerly station, to the Mandan country. Another post was situated between the headwaters of the St. Peter's and the Red River of the North, while still others were at Prairie du Chien, on the Mississippi, and Green Bay, as far east as Lake Michigan. Through most of this area the Columbia Fur Company was in active competition with the American Fur Company, principally the Western Department, as most of the Columbia Fur Company's posts were on the Missouri. However, Astor's company had no post so far north as the Mandan country, the northernmost area exploited by its rival. According to Crooks, the Columbia Fur Company, of which Kenneth McKenzie was now president, did the American Fur Company "an annual injury of ten thousand dollars at least."[33]

Astor had two policies toward his rivals in the fur trade. Individual traders, and small, weak companies, would be speedily, ruthlessly crushed by means of all the tremendous forces of financial and political power which he had at his disposal. After that, the more efficient of the vanquished might become employees of his company or be allowed to trade on shares. But, if a company put up a stubborn fight, it was not in Astor's nature to waste money, time, and effort in achieving its complete destruction. Business was business, and though he probably enjoyed its struggles for their own sake, he never regarded trade as a game in which a sweeping victory was in itself the principal end. Consequently a rival group who he realized could not be easily conquered would usually be bought out or admitted to the American Fur Company on fairly generous terms. Such had been his policy with Stone, Bostwick & Co. and with Bernard Pratte & Co., and such it would be with the Columbia Fur Company.

As early as August 30, 1826, Ramsay Crooks at Prairie du Chien was carrying on negotiations by correspondence with Kenneth McKenzie and Daniel Lamont at their headquarters on Lac Travers and the St. Peter's River. The Columbia Fur Company seems to have proposed some plan for the division of the trade so as to prevent competition from St. Croix upwards; this plan would involve the American Fur Company's abandonment of the St. Peter's from the Travers des Sioux upwards, as Crooks expressed it. Crooks declined the proposal, but suggested a conference at Prairie du Chien or Fort Snelling in April, 1827, or earlier, and advised McKenzie and Lamont to avoid making engagements for the future if there was a chance for an understanding.[34] However, by April, 1827, little had been done. Crooks said: "From McKenzie I have a letter of the 9th January last, but their expectations are two [sic] unreasonable to permit me to hope that we can make an equitable arrangement with them; I will nevertheless try."[35] On the last day of the month, he was on his way to Prairie du Chien, where he intended to consult with Rolette and the other traders of that place before negotiating with McKenzie. The situation seemed somewhat more hopeful. "At St. Louis, and on my way here I heard that the house which supplies his [McKenzie's] concern is sick of the business and somewhat cramped in its means, but whether this be true or otherwise, it will not prevent, my offering him fair terms, and if we do not agree, the negociations will only be broken by his unreasonable pretentions."[36]

Late in the next month Crooks, then back at St. Louis, wrote to Astor that the prospects for an arrangement with McKenzie seemed even more promising than before. McKenzie's arrangements with his eight partners were to expire in the summer of 1827, but some of these he would not leave to shift for themselves, and consequently, should he enter the American Fur Company, they would have to be provided for unless their demands were unreasonable, when he would probably abandon them. "To secure even Mr. McKenzie," Crooks wrote, "would be very desireable for he is certainly the sole [*sic*] of his concern: but I would prefer taking with him such of his partners as are efficient traders, and might continue to annoy us so as to annihilate their opposition entirely, for it is the only sure way of improving our affairs if we arrange with them at all." Nothing could be done until McKenzie saw his partners, and probably nothing then unless the American Fur Company would take all their goods on hand, about $20,000 worth, apart from the importations for 1827.[37]

Astor encouraged Crooks in his negotiations, writing, "I trust you will arrange with the people called the Columbia fur Company to do way the opposition," and "I still hope you will succeed in arranging with McKeney [*sic*] — as it will be better than to carry on one opposition after another." He felt that Crooks was right in thinking "that those who seized [?] him [McKenzie] are sick of the business . . . if they are not now, I take it they will be so before very long, for surly the business is bad under an opposition, and indeed not very good with it."[38]

Early in June, Crooks was still at St. Louis negotiating with McKenzie and awaiting the arrival of the partners. He wrote: "I have uniformly consulted all the four members of B. Pratte & Co., who fortunately are now assembled here, and shall act on our joint determination in regard to the terms and conditions on which we will admit Mr. McKenzie and his friends." Late in June, McKenzie's partners had arrived. "The business with McKenzie & Co. is drawing to a close," Crooks wrote to Astor on the 22nd, "and the negotiation will terminate in 2 or 3 days at fartherest when you will be advised of the result."[39] But it seemed as if this discussion of nearly a year was to prove fruitless. On June 26 Crooks wrote to Stuart, head of the Northern Department, that the terms of McKenzie and his friends had been too exorbitant and that it had been agreed with Bernard Pratte & Co. that peace under such conditions was worse than war. "I have therefore only to add," he concluded grimly, "that I trust you will compel Mr. Aitkens to act as he ought above the Falls of St. Anthony, and I am very sure Mr. Rolette will not suffer them to triumph on the River of St. Peters."[40] On the following day Crooks announced to Rolette that the arrangements with the Columbia Fur Company had proved abortive and that "we must now fight harder than ever."[41]

But apparently the refusal of McKenzie and his friends to agree to the terms proposed by Crooks had been very largely a bluff, and when they faced the prospect of competition with an alliance composed of the American Fur Company and Bernard Pratte & Co. their hearts failed them and they acceded to Crooks's offers. Consequently on July 6, 1827, Crooks was able to write to Astor in triumph: "It affords me pleasure to inform you that after an almost useless negociation, I have, at last succeeded in agreeing on preliminaries with the Columbia Fur Company to give up their trade entirely and take a share with us in that of the Upper Missouri. . . . We have to take all the goods on hand in the Indian Country at their cost and transportation to the Col. Fur Co."[42] Also, according to the agreement, the

Columbia Fur Company withdrew altogether from the region of the Great Lakes and the upper Mississippi, which thus reverted to the Northern Department without opposition. On the Missouri a sub-department was created including all the valley above the mouth of the Big Sioux and the Columbia Fur Company took charge of this department almost without change of organization. The partners of the retiring company became partners or proprietors of this sub-department, and McKenzie, Laidlaw, and Lamont conducted the affairs of the upper Missouri quite as independently as if they had remained a separate company.

This new sub-department was known as the Upper Missouri Outfit, and the transfer of property and other arrangements were completed by the end of 1827.[43] It is of interest, as showing of the attitude of the American Fur Company toward their rivals in the Columbia Fur Company before the consolidation, to note the comment on this transaction of Lawrence Taliaferro, the Indian agent at St. Peter's, who wrote that the American Fur Company had "purchased out, and given *places* to a number of the late Columbia Fur Company — tho confining *these exclusively* to the *Naturalized* Scotchmen, whom they have vilafied and abused ever Since they enterd the Indian Country." [44]

THE AMERICAN FUR COMPANY, 1808–1834

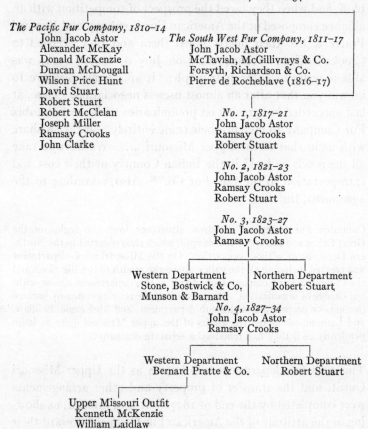

The Pacific Fur Company, 1810–14
   John Jacob Astor
   Alexander McKay
   Donald McKenzie
   Duncan McDougall
   Wilson Price Hunt
   David Stuart
   Robert Stuart
   Robert McClelan
   Joseph Miller
   Ramsay Crooks
   John Clarke

The South West Fur Company, 1811–17
   John Jacob Astor
   McTavish, McGillivrays & Co.
   Forsyth, Richardson & Co.
   Pierre de Rocheblave (1816–17)

No. 1, 1817–21
   John Jacob Astor
   Ramsay Crooks
   Robert Stuart

No. 2, 1821–23
   John Jacob Astor
   Ramsay Crooks
   Robert Stuart

No. 3, 1823–27
   John Jacob Astor
   Ramsay Crooks

Western Department
   Stone, Bostwick & Co.
   Munson & Barnard

Northern Department
   Robert Stuart

No. 4, 1827–34
   John Jacob Astor
   Ramsay Crooks

Western Department
   Bernard Pratte & Co.

Northern Department
   Robert Stuart

Upper Missouri Outfit
   Kenneth McKenzie
   William Laidlaw
   Daniel Lamont

(An attempt has been made to indicate, very roughly, the relationship in time and space of the various units concerned.)

At the same time as Crooks succeeded in making the above-mentioned agreement with the Columbia Fur Company, he also was able to eliminate the competition of another less formidable opponent, of which we know little. This was the firm of Collier & Powell, of which Crooks wrote as follows: "I have, at last succeeded in agreeing . . . with Collier & Powell to desist from all interference whatsoever in the trade with the Indians for 4 years. We have to . . . pay Collier & Powell 1/2 per cent profit on the importation of this year, the English part of which was bought for cash, and most of that from Philadelphia also."[45] Doubtless this firm realized that, though it might succeed in making fair profits in competition with the American Fur Company, Bernard Pratte & Co., and the Columbia Fur Company separately, it would have no chance against a coalition of these three organizations.

While the American Fur Company was negotiating with McKenzie and his associates in an attempt to eliminate competition, it was also having difficulty with the firm of Menard & Vallé, the senior member of which was probably Pierre Menard of Kaskaskia, Illinois, who had been concerned in a number of the Missouri fur companies. Apparently the arrangement with Menard & Vallé was similar to that which Crooks had established late in 1816 with certain of the St. Louis traders, namely, that Menard & Vallé were to buy all their goods from the American Fur Company, or perhaps from John Jacob Astor & Son, and give the latter the first opportunity of buying the returns, on condition that the American Fur Company should not compete with them or furnish other competitors with goods. Of course the temptation, when competition from the American Fur Company had been eliminated, was to try to secure goods elsewhere at a lower price. On March 16, 1827, Astor wrote to Crooks at St. Louis that he had "recieved 2 days ago an order for goods from Mr Bastwick for Messrs Marard [Menard] and Vallé for blankets and some few stroud

& cloth, the whole will cost £400 say four hundred pounds. Whether this is all they mean to order or all they will want or whether this is merely a favor I know not, nor do I know what the arrangement with them is. If we are to give up any advantage in consequence of importing such triffel goods for them you will know best. I wrote to Mr Bastwick that I have ordered the goods without reference to any agreement or understanding with them. You will judge whether they play fair with us and act accordingly." Nearly a month later he added: "Valle is here and tells me he wants no more good than the triffling order they gave us, so I suppose gets them by other means."[46] To this Crooks replied: "Our agent here has no understanding with Menard and Valle as to the terms on which we were to import the goods they recently ordered, and I am not quite able to give an opinion whether or not they treat us fairly, or make this triffling demand merely to cover their requisitions elsewhere."[47] Late in April, Astor repeated: "as to Menard & Valle. I think they do not act fair, and you must see to it, Valle says they want no goods." Early in the next month the mystery was revealed. Astor wrote: "Valle is here shipping his Deer skins, their goods are ordered without any understanding," adding in a postscript: "I find this moment that Manard and Valle shipped furs and skins to Gillispie here and ordered goods from them. You will know what to do, and that we ought at once to oppose them in this country." This information had been derived, said Astor, from the fact that "by accident I saw a letter from Gillispie & Co. to them [Menard & Vallé] in which they stated that they received his letter and some skins which they were to sell for them & to ship goods for the Indian Trade either for this or next year. I do not remember [sic] the small quantity ordered from us is evidence that they must get goods elsewhere." So, repeated Astor, "I take that Valle left us, and we must meet him in the Indian Country if we can."[48] To this Crooks cheerfully replied: "I am

truly glad you have detected Valle at last, and shall not fail to
bear in mind your orders relative to opposing our quondam
friend of St. Genevieve."[49] We are not left in doubt as to the
final result of Menard & Vallé's attempt to befool the Company. There is in existence a book of accounts, marked
"Ledger-Bk A, Am. Fur Co., Menard & Valle, James Fork,
White River, October 7, 1829–March 20, 1832,"[50] which indicates that by at least the fall of 1829 Menard & Vallé had been
forced, like so many other independent traders, into the position of trading on shares for the American Fur Company.
Their field of operations was in the region of the White River
in southwestern Missouri, and there they could use the ability
at dissimulation, by which they had once expected to trick the
Company, in that organization's interests.

John Jacob Astor, after his return from Europe in the spring
of 1826, did not spend his whole time during that and the succeeding year in assisting with the negotiations between the
American Fur Company and its various rivals. On his arrival
in New York he plunged vigorously into those routine processes of the fur trade which were no less important than the
more spectacular transactions of forming coalitions, buying
out rivals, and crushing opposition.

It will be remembered that Astor's constant refrain for several
years had been retrenchment, that is, withdrawal from certain
of the less productive districts and ordering fewer goods. His
idea seemed to be that, as the Company pushed west to the Missouri and beyond that river toward the Rockies, the trade
farther east, around the Lakes, might gradually be contracted
and attention concentrated on the Western Department. Late
in October, 1826, he wrote to Stuart, remarking, "in comparing
your order of this yeare with that of last the amount Dos not
Differ mush & I have Some toughts of ordering about 10 pct
Less an the whole than Your order but Will not Determine till I
See Mr Crooks who has ben very Ill at St Louis & is not yet

arrivd I exspt him in 15 Days —" Astor seemed especially determined to make retrenchments at Detroit. Samuel Abbott, who was a Detroit man but had been sent to St. Louis in 1822 to assist Bostwick and Crooks in organizing the Western Department, had subsequently been transferred back to his native city in an attempt to hold matters there in line.[51] Detroit was the most easterly of Astor's posts, and had naturally suffered most from the rapid westward march of civilization. Then, too, that city had always been a center for individual traders, no one large firm ever having acquired a dominant position there.[52] Accordingly, in this same letter Astor remarked, "abuet our Detrot concern it must be lessond or Giveng up I presum to Lesson will be best."[53]

As to Astor's suggested retrenchment, Stuart had this to say: "Your intention of curtailing the order for our next year's supplies will not I trust be put into execution for rely upon it that for every per Cent you take off; at least a proportionate diminution of percentage on the profits will be the consequence; and it may involve a much more ruinous result."[54] But despite Stuart's protests Astor seems to have been still of the opinion that some move at least should be taken toward withdrawing from the Detroit area. He wrote to Crooks, late in May, 1827, "I am quite at a loss about our matters at Detroit, as I can give no directions about outfits or what to do with our goods there;" and early in the next month, "I think to send Clupp [Clapp] to Detroit to see what he can do to wind up and perhaps send a few outfits or sell what we have there."[55]

Crooks backed up his fellow agent and warned Astor: "It will never do to abandon Detroit altogether for if you leave our opponents there free to act as they please, they will annoy the Northern Department most seriously in the district of Chicago particularly and make enough in their own country to balance the loss they may sustain in Stuart's territory. I would not do much at Detroit but still enough to hold our adversaries in check, and keep them busy nearer home."[56] Crooks's and Stuart's counsel at this time prevailed, for in June, 1830, in giving Crooks instructions for an expedition in the Lake district, Astor said, "At the Detroit, you will do the best you can to sell out, would be most agreeable provided it can be done to safe people." [57] By 1831 Detroit seems to have become the headquarters of a definite department similar to but much less important than those whose headquarters were at Mackinac and St. Louis.[58] In 1834, when the American Fur Company passed out of Astor's hands, James Abbott, Samuel Abbott's brother, was acting as Detroit agent.[59]

Meanwhile, Robert Stuart at Mackinac was at his old occupation of exerting political influence for the benefit of the American Fur Company. He had apparently initiated a campaign against Major Lawrence Taliaferro, the Indian agent at St. Peter's, and early in April, 1826, informed Joseph Rolette, of Prairie du Chien, that there was no longer any need to work for Taliaferro's removal, as Governor Cass had informed him that the agent was applying for another office.[60] Stuart's action against the agent had been taken at the instance of Rolette, who seems to have found in Taliaferro an exception to his favorite maxim that any officer of the United States could be bought for a quarter-keg of wine. Taliaferro was one of the most determined opponents of the Company among the ranks of those United States officers of whom Rolette had such a low opinion. He had good reason for his hostility, which may, indeed, have been largely due to the fact that Rolette himself was the representative of the Company with whom he most frequently came into contact. Rolette seems to have been laboring during many of his later years under the delusion that the War of 1812, in which he had been a prominent commander of Indians on the British side, was still in progress; and Major Taliaferro's account of his experiences as an Indian agent is one unrelieved narrative of lawlessness on the part of Rolette and other agents of the Company.[61] Among Rolette's exploits, according to another contemporary authority, was the provocation of the Indians by means of whiskey to attack boats bringing provisions to Fort Snelling. Another American Fur Company trader, William A. Aitkin, has been quoted as saying "that the Indian agents made Laws & restricted him, but the moment that he Mr. Aitkin got into the interiour would do as he thought proper, and that he did not care a damn for their Laws no further than the time being, or whilst at St. Mary's." This statement is alleged to have been made in 1825, and in 1827 this same trader threatened that, if the Indian agent at St. Peter's (Major Taliaferro) tried to seize his liquor, he would arm the Indians against him.[62] It would not, then, be surprising if Taliaferro agreed heartily with the judgment of Zachary Taylor, who had acted as an officer of infantry on the Upper Mississippi during the 'twenties and had thus had many opportunities of judging the American Fur Company's employees from such unfavorable specimens as Rolette: "Take the American Fur Company in the aggregate, and they are the greatest scoundrels the world ever knew."[63]

Stuart might privately feel that Rolette was at times a little over-zealous in his dealings with the opposition, but he nevertheless felt compelled to back up an agent of the Company whenever he came into conflict either with other commercial organizations or with the government. It appeared that Cass had been mistaken in his prediction that Taliaferro would disappear without the necessity for an open clash. Taliaferro continued in his agency, and accordingly in March, 1827, Robert Stuart wrote to Astor suggesting that he should lodge against Colonel Snelling and his Indian agent a general complaint of unfriendly conduct toward the agents of the American Fur Company.[64] Soon after this, Ramsay Crooks transmitted to General Clark, the superintendent of Indian Affairs on the Mississippi and Missouri, the complaints of Rolette and Stuart against the Indian agent at St. Peter's. Clark replied by requesting Crooks to furnish evidence in support of these charges. Crooks promised to do so at Prairie du Chien, and notified "Taliofeno" to be there.[65]

But Major Taliaferro was of a mettle much superior to that of the luckless Major Puthuff. He had been guilty of no indiscretions in the matter of licenses, such as had proved to be the Achilles' heel of the Mackinac agent, and in general was "armed so strong in honesty" that the American Fur Company's complaints apparently passed by him "like an idle wind" which he did not need to regard too seriously. In reporting "upon the charges preferred by the agents of the American Fur Company," Taliaferro wrote: "I will do M^r. Stewart the justice to say that his groundless exceptions were formed from the report of Joseph Rolette the Company's agent at Prairie du Chien, a man of very bad character, and one reputed for his want of principle — and *policy* alone compels the Company to continue him as their agent — for he could destroy all their prospects of gain in this country if discharged — of this fact there is no doubt." Stuart and Crooks seem soon to have recognized the insubstantial character of the accusations levelled against Taliaferro, which had been inspired by such traders as Rolette and Alexis Bailly, and, once having become aware of their nature, realized that further proceedings would be of disadvantage to the Company. They therefore withdrew their charges, and in the middle of June, 1827, William Clark was able to write to the secretary of War concerning Taliaferro that "no evidence has been produced by the company in support of their charges or Statements, and it is believed they do not wish to go into further investigation."[66] In consequence, as late as 1840 Taliaferro was still performing the duties of his office at the same agency, among which duties the first and foremost, in his opinion, was the annoying of the American Fur Company by the strict and impartial enforcement of all laws relating to trade with the Indians.[67]

Stuart was more successful in his attempt to win the support of Colonel T. L. McKenney, who had found it hard to forgive the Company for its part in the overthrow of his favorite factory system. As early as 1824 an attempt had been made to win McKenney's support for a lower duty on certain goods for the Indian trade, by persuading him that in this endeavor, as in all others, the American Fur Company was motivated by a desire to assist "the poor red children of the Forest." In 1824, Tipton, an Indian agent on the Wabash, had seized some of the American Fur Company's property and secured its condemnation on account of an alleged violation of the liquor law, although, according to Stuart, "nothing but the strong prejudices which exist in that country against what they call a Monopolizing Company could have brought about the first condemnation."

Here one would have expected McKenney, with his hatred of liquor and of the American Fur Company, to take a leading part in securing the confiscation of the Company's goods. But McKenney, it seems, had seen the light and changed his attitude toward the Company; he now approved its conduct and declared himself willing to assist in recovering the condemned property.[68] Astor, in commenting on this affair, remarked, "I thinke it not Improveble that government will give tham [the goods] up & I Shall consult with Mr Crooks — McKensy [McKenney] Dind with me & I Do belive he is better inclind."[69] Stuart, in a letter to Crooks written late in November, stated that McKenney had suggested a petition to the president of the United States as a means of recovering the goods seized by Tipton. His conclusion was that, if McKenney were really friendly, they had Cass to thank for his change of attitude.[70] Cass had, on June 30, 1825, written a letter to McKenney in which he said that the agents of the American Fur Company had co-operated with the public officials in Indian affairs. "I consider the gentlemen composing this company," Cass declared, "highly honorable men and zealous and faithful citizens."[71]

It would be pleasant to be able to state that McKenney's apparent change of heart had been due to an actual reformation of the Company's business methods, but Stuart was not under any such illusion for even a moment. McKenney's new attitude, in Stuart's shrewd opinion, was probably due to his wish to "establish an independent Dept for Indian affairs, the full control of which he aspires to, — and I *know*. that he is very much afraid of your opposition to the measure — this I told him I was confident he need not apprehend," probably with the implied addition of the words "so long as he continued to work for our interests." Stuart concluded by characterizing the Indian superintendent as good-hearted, vain, and feather-headed, but, he declared, "we are pretty sure of him at present," and he would be useful in such matters as the Tipton case and the securing of a revenue cutter on the Lakes for the prevention of smuggling by Astor's rivals.[72]

At New York Astor was devoting himself assiduously to operations in the fur market.[73] Late in 1826 he was more than ordinarily pessimistic. Sugar, buffalo robes, muskrats, beaver, raccoons, martens, and deer skins were all low or unpromising, "aur atter the only articl are well Sold here — an the whole Prospects for furrs is Bade."[74] But by the spring of 1827 fur prices, as revealed in Astor's letters of instruction to Ramsay Crooks at St. Louis, were somewhat more promising, though the news from Europe was still not very good. "We have no good accounts from Europe," wrote Astor, "not for any one article." Astor was at first inclined to order Crooks to purchase only good deer, beaver, and muskrat at a low rate, and also to get all the otter available at reasonable prices. Astor himself, on February 27, 1827, tried to buy the Hudson's Bay Company's Canadian muskrat skins, with what success is not known.[75] However, later in the season matters began to appear so promising that Astor's orders were to purchase heavily of nearly everything save raccoons and deer skins, and the latter were also to be purchased if at a good market. Astor's policy throughout this year was to corner such desirable skins as beaver, buffalo, muskrat, bear, and otter. The results of this policy upon the sales of one type of skins alone are revealed in a letter of late September, 1827. "Yesterday," Astor wrote, "we had our Sale and you will be surprised to learn the quantity of Muskrats I sold in less than 24 hours by Private and Public Sale. Say at Public Sale 200,000 at Private Sale 350,000 altogether 550,000, so many have never in the world been sold in one day. We have still *200,000* on hand the average price is about 36 Cents. those you and what Bostwick sent are included. . . . This year I had to arrange as to have nearly all in our own hands, as I bought some lots and made a good profit on them. . . . Our Sale was uncommonly well attended and all were pleased." This sale of well over half a million muskrat skins in a single day — and these by no means all that were in Astor's possession — gives us some idea of the proportions of the American Fur Company's business a decade after its actual organization.[76]

Crooks, at St. Louis, found that to his mind "the Indian Trade of this whole region according to present appearances will turn out badly," owing to such disturbing factors as Indian wars. He thought that Farnham's and Rolette's trade would probably result badly, although later he learned that, though his fear for the former was justified, Rolette would come out better than had been expected, and Lake Superior would give an unexpectedly large number of muskrats.

Crooks, in accordance with Astor's orders, intended to buy all the muskrats and buffalo robes belonging to McKenzie and his associates; he succeeded in purchasing all the muskrats, and also all their other skins except robes, raccoon, and beaver. McKenzie and his friends, with Collier & Powell, had nearly half the buffalo robes, but demanded too high a price. Bernard Pratte & Co. had held the other half of the robes, but had already sold them. Bernard Pratte & Co. also had half the beaver, which Crooks hoped to get, as well as their otter. He had bought some Rocky Mountain beaver, and intended to get all the deer, beaver, and otter in the market. Bernard Pratte & Co., and also McKenzie, demanded too much for their beaver, and early in August Bernard Pratte, head of the former company, left for New York to sell his beaver and otter.

Thus all that Crooks had managed to do was to buy nearly all the muskrats in the market and all the Columbia Fur Company's peltries save robes, raccoon, and beaver, and also some Rocky Mountain beaver.[77] Astor regretted Crooks's failure to get more beaver, but comforted him over his lack of success in purchasing robes by stating that, as it would be impossible to dominate the market, because of the large supply, it was as well that none had been purchased.[78]

It will be remembered that all the time that Crooks had been trying to buy skins from these various companies he had also been engaged in negotiating with Collier & Powell and the Columbia Fur Company. I described earlier in the chapter his attempts to buy them out or form an alliance, and his final success in purchasing the interest of the first firm and taking the other into the Company. Bernard Pratte & Co., as we have seen, had become partners earlier in the year. When we note that half the buffalo robes at the important fur-trade center of St. Louis were owned by Bernard Pratte & Co., and most of the rest by Collier & Powell and McKenzie's company, and also that the latter firm had nearly all the muskrats in the market and Bernard Pratte & Co. more than half the beaver, the importance of extinguishing the opposition of these three firms and making allies of the two most important becomes strikingly evident.

For 1828, the first year of the association of the American Fur Company, Bernard Pratte & Co., and the former Columbia Fur Company, certain rearrangements were found necessary. John Jacob Astor, assisted by his son, remained at the head of the Company and in special charge of matters at New York. Ramsay Crooks retained his position as principal agent of the Company, with special attention to the Western Department. Robert Stuart continued to head the affairs of the Northern Department. Pierre Chouteau, Jr., who with Bernard Pratte, J. P. Cabanné, and B. Berthold made up the firm of Bernard Pratte & Co., became the agent at St. Louis. Samuel Abbott, formerly clerk at St. Louis, then at Detroit, was considered as Chouteau's assistant; but, though Astor agreed to raise his salary from $1,000 per year to $1,300, he found Abbott's further demand for "lodgings in the Company's Buildings" to be "extravagant," and apparently decided not to accede to it, since in 1830 Samuel Abbott was at Mackinac, where he had probably been sent to assist Stuart in the place of Currie, a clerk who had absconded in 1826. Wilson P. Hunt, formerly of Astoria and of the *Pedler*, then a resident of St. Louis, was considered as a probable ally in fur-buying, etc., on occasion. Kenneth McKenzie was, of course, in charge of the Upper Missouri Outfit, and probably was subjected to very little oversight by his technical superiors in the firm of Bernard Pratte & Co., who were in general charge of the Western Department. This merger seems to have resulted in the casting adrift of certain employees, though it must be said that Astor usually appeared to manifest a sense of responsibility for any man who had once been prominent in the service of the Company. However, Gabriel Franchere, Jr., Astorian and historian of the Astoria enterprise, seems to have superseded his fellow Astorian W. W. Matthews as agent at Montreal,[79] for which position Franchere, being a native of the place, was especially well qualified. Wilson P. Hunt's comment on this incident in a letter to Ramsay Crooks was: "I regret what you

say about poor Matthews it is terrible to first spoil an useful
good fellow in his way and then cast him off; which you will
agree, has in a great degree been the fact in this case."[80]

Near the end of 1827, relations between the principals of the
American Fur Company and of Bernard Pratte & Co. seemed
to be in some ways not perfectly amicable. Bernard Pratte, as
Crooks had said, left St. Louis for New York early in August,
1827, to sell his otter and beaver. For the otter skins, according to Astor, "Mr Pratte by my means got 4$ or 2/ per skin
more . . . than he asked." Then, Astor went on, "[I] made
him the first offer for the Beaver at 4 1/8$, on his promise that
unless he could get more I was to have it. I am now told that
he sold it at some [same] price, contrary to what he stated."
The result was, the beaver being thus sold to Astor's opponents
a day or so before Astor's own beaver was to be put up for sale,
"these people come in the market with this Beaver against us."
Another reason for Astor's wish to get Pratte's beaver was to
"enable me to keep up the price of all we may get the next
year. It was on this account that I wished so much to have the
Beaver which Gen. Pratte had here, but which I could not get
unless I paid more than others — Had I gotten it I would have
sent it out of the country to China."

Astor's estimate of Pratte's action was that he "did not be-
have well in the sale." He continued: "I am quite at a loss to
account for the conduct of Generl. Pratte, he did everything to
prevent our getting his Beaver. . . . he has forfeited every
thing with me, and even those who bought his fur think no
better of him. . . . Had Mr Pratte acted candidly with me, it
would have been greatly to our mutual benefit. I am sorry to
say I lost all confidence in him."

The reason both for Pratte's action and for Astor's chagrin
is revealed in the price at which the beaver skins which Astor
did possess were disposed of a few days after Pratte had demanded $4⅜ per lb. for his. Astor himself says, "The Beaver

you sent sold at 5 to 5 1/8$ per #. Our Lake Superior 5 1/2; nearly all our Beaver sold."[81] In other words, had Pratte sold his beaver to Astor at $4⅛ per lb., the price which Astor offered, the latter would have made in a few days an extra profit of about $1.00 per lb!

Astor had mentioned Pratte's alleged dishonorable conduct on September 26, 28, and 29 in letters to Ramsay Crooks, his wrath increasing day by day as he learned what profits he had missed by his failure to secure the Missourian's beaver. In these letters he had made at least three errors: first, in accepting hearsay evidence of individuals who may have been glad to sow dissension in the ranks of the powerful Company by misrepresenting the price at which Pratte had sold his beaver; second, in most astoundingly neglecting to take into account the well-known fact that Ramsay Crooks, two years before, had married a Mlle. Emilie Pratte, of St. Louis; and third, in recording his low opinion of Pratte's conduct in three successive letters.

Crooks, knowing as he did his employer's anguish at any unforeseen commercial misfortune, would probably have overlooked a single burst of disappointment, but he had not yet fully forgiven Astor for his resistance to Crooks's terms in the contract of the preceding year, and he now took advantage of the occasion to administer a stinging rebuke in the following words: "I cannot close this letter without adverting to your remarks on the conduct of Mr. Pratte, and must be permitted to say that whatever reason you may have to find fault with him as relates to the sale of his Beaver (which he did *not* dispose of at $4 1/8) I do think you might have recollected he is my father-in-law and not have forced the subject upon me in all of your last three letters."[82] There spoke the proud and clannish Highlander, to whom the ties of kinship, if only by marriage, were of much greater strength than any commercial bonds.

Be it said to Astor's credit that he was hardly the man to take offence at such plain language, especially when it was called forth by a reflection on the writer's kin; nor was Crooks a man whom it was safe to anger. Astor never actually apologized, or even made any reference to the misunderstanding, and this was undoubtedly the wiser course, but his next letter to Crooks, which was full of solicitude for his health and the welfare of his "good family,"[83] was equivalent to a formal expression of regret, and was probably so received. Consequently no feud between the American Fur Company's New York headquarters and its Western Department operated to bring solace to its opponents as the campaign of 1828 began.

The West was now, as it had been almost from the first establishment of the Western Department, by far the most active front. In the Northern Department, the region of the Great Lakes and Upper Mississippi, the American Fur Company already possessed a practical monopoly. According to George Boyd, the Indian agent at Mackinac, the headquarters of the Northern Department, "the Amount of furs & peltries brought yearly to this Island, are supposed to be worth from 250 to 300,000 dollars — nineteen twentieths of the same being for and on account of the American Fur Co. — "[84] It is probable that by this statement the agent merely meant that this proportion of the peltries brought to Mackinac was held either by the American Fur Company or by traders associated with it on shares, the Company, of course, having the refusal of the traders' share of the returns. The various outfits were now consistently making profits, though often very small ones,[85] and so far as opening up new territory or crushing opposition was concerned, Robert Stuart had nothing more to do than to preserve the Company's already overwhelmingly dominant position.

The situation in the Western Department, however, was altogether different. In 1822, the very year in which the American Fur Company established western headquarters at St. Louis, the Rocky Mountain Fur Company was founded by William H. Ashley and Andrew Henry for the purpose of exploiting the virgin beaver-territory of that great area. This company was so successful that within five years Ashley, its founder, was able to sell out to his ablest lieutenants and retire on a fortune to take up politics. The American Fur Company, through its new partners, Bernard Pratte & Co., had been concerned in the proportion of one-half in Ashley's expedition of 1827,[86] which brought in net profits of seventy per cent. It was, then, the very formidable opposition of the new Rocky Mountain Fur Company partners, Jedediah S. Smith, David E. Jackson, and William L. Sublette, that the Western Department, and especially McKenzie's Upper Missouri Outfit, would be forced to meet.

McKenzie, remembering the profits of the last Ashley expedition, was quite ready to inaugurate an immediate campaign against his rivals of the Rocky Mountains, but Pierre Chouteau persuaded him to postpone such a move until more thorough preparations had been made. Accordingly, 1828 was spent in establishing "a permanent post at the mouth of the Yellowstone, which would afford a safe and convenient base for the operations of the upper country." In the fall of that year McKenzie sent Etienne Provost, a former member of the Rocky Mountain Fur Company, to look up the free trappers and bring them to the new post, Fort Floyd, and in the next spring dispatched Henry Vanderburgh with goods to a *rendezvous* with these trappers after the spring hunt of 1829. "This was the beginning of the American Fur Company's participation in the fur trade of the Rocky mountains. . . . It did not," says Chittenden, "prove to be an advantageous branch of the trade, but rather a source of infinite annoyance in the fierce competition which it engendered."

The American Fur Company had hardly entered the Rocky

Mountain trade before the contracts, each for four years, with Bernard Pratte & Co. and with McKenzie and his associates had expired. Both were renewed for the same period of four years. The original contract with Bernard Pratte & Co. came to an end with the outfit for the year 1829, that with McKenzie, Laidlaw, and Lamont with the outfit for the succeeding year. The terms of the new agreements were practically the same as the old, save that McKenzie had his annual salary, which he received in addition to his share of the profits, raised from $1,500 to $2,000. During his first term of service he had not only entered the Rocky Mountain trade, but had maintained the Company's monopoly on its original territory by crushing all attempts at opposition. One of the defeated rivals was the French Fur Company, which was established in 1829 and sold out to the Company in the fall of the next year, some of its partners entering the employ of the dominant organization.

The history of the Western Department's Upper Missouri Outfit during its second term, and especially of that side of its business which pertains to the Rocky Mountain fur trade, is by no means pleasant reading. True, McKenzie distinguished himself by the utmost daring and efficiency in forming a connection in 1831 with the hitherto hostile Blackfeet, bringing about a treaty in the same year between them and the Assiniboines, and also establishing a post in the Blackfeet country at the junction of the Marias River with the Yellowstone. In 1832 he established a post among the Crows on the Yellowstone near the mouth of the Bighorn, which was appropriately christened Fort Cass, after the Company's most consistent ally in governmental circles, then occupying the influential position of secretary of War. McKenzie was also responsible in 1831 for putting a steamboat, the *Yellowstone*, on the Missouri, to make the journey between St. Louis and Fort Union (the successor of Fort Floyd) at the mouth of the Yellowstone. The voyage was first completed in June, 1832, and did much to turn the Indians along the Canadian border from the Hudson's Bay Company to its great American rival. Another ingenious contrivance to win over the Indians on the border from British influence was the striking off of medals (though Crooks wrote, "Remember they are ornaments, not medals") bearing the likeness of John Jacob Astor, for distribution to the chiefs, in imitation of the British custom of distributing medals with the image of the reigning monarch! This was done with the consent of the always complaisant Lewis Cass, then, as we have noted, secretary of War.

There was, of course, nothing objectionable in these broad strokes of the American Fur Company, but both the Company's agents and their rivals, when once in the Indian country, were guilty of activities some of which would doubtless have horrified the Astors, in the comparatively civilized surroundings of New York or of France, whither John Jacob had returned in the summer of 1832. The Rocky Mountain fur trade was carried on much more by parties of white trappers who brought their returns to an annual *rendezvous*, where they were met by representatives of the various companies with supplies of goods,[87] than by outfits of traders, clerks, and *voyageurs* who bartered for furs secured by the Indians. Consequently, it was the policy of the American Fur Company's employees, among whom Vanderburgh, Drips, and Fontenelle were the most conspicuous, to follow the Rocky Mountain Company partners, who now, since August 4, 1830, were Thomas Fitzpatrick, Milton G. Sublette, Henry Fraeb, Jean Baptiste Gervais, and James Bridger, into the Rocky Mountain region in an attempt to learn where the best beaver country was. Finally, in 1832, Fitzpatrick and Bridger deliberately led Vanderburgh and Drips into the heart of the Blackfeet country until Vanderburgh was attacked and killed, while Bridger himself was wounded before he could escape from the dangerous region into which he had lured his rivals. In the next year the American Fur Company retaliated by stirring up the Crows to rob Fitzpatrick, later buying his peltries, marked plainly with the initials of his Company, from the guilty parties. In 1834 the Rocky Mountain Fur Company was dissolved. But their rivals in the American Fur Company had not profited by the mountain trade,[88] having always been late at the annual *rendezvous*, and the trade in the mountains had been continued largely to maintain the Company's prestige among the Indians and the free trappers. Then, too, as Chouteau wrote Astor in the spring of 1833, "I am convinced that these expeditions have been an annual loss. But we have hoped for improvement from year to year. *Generally the loss falls upon the traders.*" The italics are mine.

Meanwhile upon the Upper Missouri, McKenzie, who, owing to his distance from the legal code of civilization, was always the most unscrupulous of the Company's agents, had been throttling opposition in his usual ruthless style. Among his exploits was the arrest by his agents of an ex-employee of the Company, one Narcisse Leclerc, for taking liquor into the Indian country, as absolutely forbidden by an act of July 9, 1832. As Leclerc had received permission from the superintendent of Indian Affairs at St. Louis to take the liquor with him up the Missouri, owing to the fact that the act of July 9, 1832, had not yet been officially promulgated, this arrest was utterly without legal sanction. Leclerc promptly instituted criminal proceedings against the responsible agent, J. P. Cabanné, and likewise sued the Company, recovering $9,200, but the Upper Missouri Outfit probably profited much more than this amount by being freed from competition with a trader possessing liquor.

A much more formidable opposition was offered by the firm of Sublette & Campbell, formed on December 20, 1832, and backed by General Ashley, then a member of Congress. This company intended to oppose the American Fur Company at all points on the Upper Missouri. But by dint of paying four

times the usual price for furs McKenzie soon weakened the
opposition, and would probably have extinguished it entirely
had not his superiors at St. Louis become frightened and bought
out their rivals early in 1834, on condition that Sublette &
Campbell should retire for one year from the Upper Missouri,
while the American Fur Company should similarly withdraw
from the mountain trade.[89] It may be that the St. Louis house
was partly influenced by the fact that the Company was just
then in very bad odor at Washington, owing to Fitzpatrick's
robbery, Leclerc's illegal arrest, and finally, in 1833, McKenzie's scheme of dodging the liquor law by *distilling whiskey in
the Indian country*, thus, as he professed to believe, avoiding
the penalty attached to "bringing" liquor into the Indian
country.[90] This device was, of course, discovered, and it was
only by some strenuous pleading with the friendly secretary of
War, Lewis Cass, that the Company avoided being barred from
the trade. But had such a result actually taken place, it would
not have greatly affected Astor, for in 1833 he had definitely
decided to withdraw from the fur trade, and took the final step
in the following year.[91]

It will be well at this point to stop and consider how far
Astor's ambition to monopolize the fur trade of the North
American continent, at least within the territory claimed by
the United States, had been fulfilled. On the Pacific Coast, of
course, he had met with a prompt and decisive defeat, but
within that area over which the United States possessed more
undoubted dominion his success had been much greater. In
the region of the Upper Mississippi and of the Great Lakes,
save for the Detroit district, which, as we have seen, he had
been inclined to neglect as of comparative unimportance, he
did have a position of unchallenged supremacy.[93] On the
Lower Mississippi and on the Missouri, the company of which
he was the guiding spirit possessed, if possible, an even greater
measure of control over the trade.[93] It will be remembered, how-

ever, that this control had been obtained only by an alliance
with Bernard Pratte & Co., and with the ex-members of the
Columbia Fur Company who were now in charge of the Upper
Missouri Outfit. However, the year which saw Astor's withdrawal from the Company had also witnessed, as we have already stated, an agreement whereby the Company had withdrawn from the trade of the Rocky Mountains in order to
eliminate competition on the Upper Missouri. The dominance
which Astor possessed over the principal fur-trade areas of the
United States naturally brought with it a corresponding supremacy in the New York fur market, which has already been
developed elsewhere in this chapter.[94] Even in London, where
he had to meet the competition of the Hudson's Bay Company,
his position was a commanding one,[95] and in Canton, it would
seem, he was actually in virtual control of the market.[96] Thus,
though Astor never fully attained to the goal which he had
once set for himself in the fur trade, he came surprisingly near
to it. Certainly no other individual in the trade could even
compare with him in importance.

We have for some time omitted all reference to the Northern
Department, but largely because no important campaign or
change of policy had taken place in that area since Astor's return from Europe in 1826, when he had made new five-year
contracts with Stuart and Crooks. The only excitement had
been furnished by the abortive attack on the Indian agent at
St. Peter's. The Northern Department had continued its
normal course under the charge of Robert Stuart, whose contract had been renewed after the expiration of the five years'
agreement of 1826. On the Canadian border might be mentioned the withdrawal of William A. Aitkin, of the Department
of Fond du Lac, "from the frontiers of Lake Superior, Lac la
Pluie, Winnipeg and Red River Districts conformably to the
terms of an engagement entered into between Governor Simpson and Mr. Aitkin as per correspondence dated 'Red River

21st March 1833,'" for which the outfit received £300 annually.[97] The usual instructions as to fur prices had gone out
from New York to Mackinac, and matters on the whole, as
indicated in these letters, seem to have been as nearly satisfactory as Astor would ever admit. In 1828, for example,
Astor had written to Stuart: "I think you can well aford to
give good Pricess porticularly to aur pepol or those Who have
goods from us."[98] In 1830 Ramsay Crooks had been sent to
Mackinac and Detroit to purchase skins and make new contracts, since those formed in 1826 were about to expire. He was
exhorted to conduct himself in a "fair and liberal manner
toward our friends and connections," but with due regard to
the interests of the Company.[99] With this letter Astor's personal interest in the Northern Department becomes very obscure, and we find no reference to his attention to it until his
retirement in 1834.

However, we do have some knowledge of his activities in the
fur markets of New York and London. As usual, conditions
were very discouraging, although now an element other than
the usual one of too high prices for too many furs had entered
the situation. Astor wrote in November, 1831: "the bad state
for Furs is owing to the Cholera-Morbus in Europe — Mills &
Co will lose much and so will the Company — Beaver and
Muskrats are again falling." Earlier in the letter he had written: "the Otters [are] the only article that sell well."[100] In the
same month he wrote to David Stone at Dayton, Ohio: "No
Sale of Racoons in London — all looks bad there."[101] Early in
the next year he wrote in an even gloomier strain and in greater
detail to Wilson Price Hunt: "You will be sorry to learn that
our Fur business, as also the trade with the interior has taken
a very unfavorable turn — The Company (I suppose) will lose
not less than $60 to 70m$ by last year's business — Mills & Co.
I put down at 40m loss and Mr. Halsey [the Astorian] 15 to
20m. There is no sale in Europe for any one article, except

Otter. The Hudson's Bay Company have an immense quantity of Furs and are coining — had we succeeded in keeping Astoria, ere now we should all have made great fortunes there, and even more and much more than the Hudson's Bay Company now do." In February, 1832, he wrote again: "We have late accounts from Europe — the prospect for Furs is very bad, but I am glad to understand that Mr. Halsey will not lost so much as I mentioned in my former letter, but the American Fur Company will lose even more than what I supposed."[102] More credit could be given to Astor's insistence upon his losses in the fur trade, were not his complaints upon this subject a constant refrain throughout his connection with the American Fur Company. To take them at their face value would be to conclude that Astor carried on a losing trade throughout his seventeen years in that organization — a judgment inconsistent with his unchallenged business ability.

The demand for otter skins caused Astor throughout the fall of 1831 and the spring of the following year to urge his London agents, Gillespies, Moffatt, Finlay & Co., to make purchases of from 2,000 to 4,000 of that article for his account. He hoped they would be able to secure from one-half to the whole of the otter skins held by the Hudson's Bay Company. In the middle of December, 1831, he wrote: "if what are called good seasoned can be had at 20/, about 1500 will answer the purpose." Late in January, 1832, Astor had as yet received no otter skins, but was ready to buy 8,000 or more, since if more than that number "come out, it will affect the market, unless they were in one hand." On February 7 he was willing to buy one-half or one-third of the entire importation at private sale at from 22/6 to 23/-, good and bad, or to "buy 2 or 3000 at Public Sale — the large seasoned skins at about 24 to 25/ would do me." It was late in April, however, before Astor received word of the purchase of an inadequate number of otter skins.

For a while during this same period Astor was also attempting to purchase muskrat skins in London. In the middle of November, 1831, he wrote: "if they are equal to York-Fort skins and you can obtain them at $7\frac{1}{2}^d$ say seven pence half penny you may buy them for me say 150.000." Later in the same letter he added: "I have rather a better opinion of Muskrat Skins and if the Hudson's Bay selection does not exceed 250,000 I would be willing to advance on my last limits and give 8^d for York Fort, kittens thrown out." By the middle of December, however, Astor's desire for muskrat skins had nearly reached the vanishing point, and by the end of January, 1832, it had disappeared. Throughout this same period Astor was constantly urging the sale of some raccoon skins which had been sent to his agents in 1830, but this was not achieved till the late summer of 1832.

Astor also sowed between sentences relating to the purchase and sale of furs various casual remarks which were intended to lower the standing of certain of his rivals. Late in October, 1831, he wrote: "The trade is extremely heavy just now, and I will not be surprised if some of our exporters will be obliged to suspend operations in which case the Company and myself will suffer more or less; as you say some good may hereafter follow, but the present loss seems to be certain, the future not." In the middle of the next month he informed his agents: "I believe you will have competitors [in the purchase of otter skins]. M^r. Halsey if he can find means will buy, and M^r. C. Mills of C. Mills & Co is going in this Packet and will (as I understand from one of his friends) be also a buyer, I doubt somewhat his abilities to do so and suppose his object would be more to arrange his affairs, which I hope he may be able to effect." Late in that month he enquired: "what is friend Mills doing in your market, I think he will be less inclined to the fur trade than he has been." Finally, late in March, 1832, came these two closely related remarks: "Muskrats we do not want — some that came from your city quite lately, belong (I believe) to Mills & Co.

were offered yesterday and only two casks could be sold at 14 to 15 cents — I believe you will not regret having closed with C. Mills & Co., they are engaged in a business which they do not understand (how many Racoons have they in your market)."[103]

During the spring of 1832 Astor was engaged in various operations in the New York fur market, always, according to his own account, at a considerable loss. On April 20 he wrote to Martin Bates at Boston: "We have to day the fur sale. Red Foxes as well as cross and grey sold badly — Minks sold so as to leave no loss. Fishers and Martens 30 per cent loss — Bears & Racoons the same." Astor at the same time seems to have been buying skins from the Boston fur merchant, for early in the next month he wrote: "Your Bill at sight for Fox Skins is paid (rather short credit.) The skins are not yet arrived hope they are a good lot — You say nothing about the Beaver — I have now an application for a parcel to go to Europe and if you could let me know which kind you prefer I will endeavour to reserve for you — I think both are cheap. I think of going to Europe in a few weeks and before I go. I propose to sell all the furs now on hand — I expect to sell to two or three of our Buyers all we have say all our Muskrat Skins and the Beaver — If you want, now will be the time — please let me know if you are coming and when? . . . If you can get me 1 or 200 cross fox, pretty fair quality at $2 I will take them — If you were to buy all our Beaver and Muskrats you would do well."[104] Astor did not specify for whose interests the Boston fur merchant "would do well" by a purchase of beaver and muskrat skins from the American Fur Company. A hint as to his actual meaning, however, appears in a letter written a week later to Andrew Mitchell of Pentaguishin: "I suppose you have accounts of the Fur Sales in London: they were not good, but better than was expected here they have fallen much; both beaver & muskrat are lower. For beaver there is no sale and I would not advise you to send any here Otter Skins are also fallen. I think your beaver would not bring over $4 here. Muskrats 15 Cents Otter $5."[105] certainly for Astor to advise the purchase from his Company of furs for which there was otherwise no sale could not be regarded as entirely disinterested.

At the same time Astor was making or planning to make various minor foreign shipments. In the middle of November, 1831, he wrote to his partner, Bernard Pratte, at Philadelphia: "I find the Buffalo Tongues do not go off. If you approve I will put 10 Boxes to auction with a view to buy and sent them to London on my own account."[106] In April, 1832, he wrote to Charles N. Talbot at Canton, saying: "By some other opportunity I propose to ship to you some Otter and Red Fox Skins,"[107] and in the next month he wrote to Churchill, Bunker & Co., at Constantinople: "I . . . have the pleasure to enclose herewith Bill Lading and Invoice over five casks containing 1500 Red fox skins, they are of better quality than what I sent to you before, and I hope will yield profit — please send returns in Opium. If you make good sales we can supply you with good quantity. As they are subject to damage by worms in warm weather I recommend speedy sale."[108]

Astor's departure on June 20 for Europe,[109] whence he did not return until April 4, 1834, only two months before his final and definite withdrawal from the American Fur Company, brought to an end activities of the type we have just examined. Astor had for some time been considering at intervals the propriety of his withdrawal from the fur trade, but, as Crooks commented in 1833, "the business seems to him like an only child and he can not muster courage to part with it."[110] Early in 1825 Astor had remarked, "I may also wish to sell out." In the latter half of the 1820's he had begun to sell his ships and withdraw from foreign trade conducted in his own bottoms; and, when he had ceased to be a ship-owner, the American Fur

Company's peltries had, of course, to be sent as freight and at a consequently lessened profit to Astor. Still, in the spring of 1830, Robert Stuart wrote to John Lawe of Green Bay stating: "Pray, give yourself no concern about M^r. Astors retiring from the trade &c: — my opinion is that he will never retire *until he is called* —"[111] In view of the fact that Stuart had informed Lawe in the previous autumn that Astor had ordered that no more credit should be given to the whites at Green Bay,[112] it seems likely that Lawe's enquiry was inspired by hope rather than apprehension. In the fall of 1831 and again in the spring of the following year, Astor wrote of being "about to retire from all mercantile or money transactions, my health," as he said, "being feeble."[113] In 1832 there was another epidemic of cholera, not only in Paris and in New York, but also as far west as St. Louis. One of the victims in the last-named city was the Astorian Russell Farnham, one of Astor's most trusted agents in the western fur trade. In Paris both Astor's daughter, Eliza, and her husband, Viscount Vincent Rumpff, were attacked, but recovered. Furs being a common carrier of contagion,[114] the epidemic had a bad effect on the fur trade. Astor said: "It is a pity there is so little demand for Beaver and I fear the distress from Colera will make matters worse," adding a few sentences farther on, "I very much fear Beaver will not sell well very soon unless very fine, it appears that they make hats of silk in place of Beaver."[115]

It seems very doubtful whether the substitution of silk for beaver skins in the manufacture of high hats actually had, as has been claimed, any great influence on Astor's withdrawal from the fur trade. It is hardly more likely, despite the discouraged tone with which Astor spoke of market conditions, that some more generally unfavorable aspect of the trade was primarily responsible for his retirement. His attitude of disappointment at the profits, or lack of them, in the trade had been one which he had consistently maintained since at least as early as the war. Moreover, those associated with him in business gave no evidences of any intention to withdraw, and surely his opportunities were not inferior to theirs. The American Fur Company's New York charter, granted in 1808 for twenty-five years, expired in April, 1833, though no notice seems to have been taken of that fact. Another anniversary was of much greater significance; on July 17, 1833, Astor would celebrate his seventieth birthday, but the ill-health which had been more and more afflicting him during the last decade or so [116] was probably the greatest factor in his decision, which, indeed, he had been considering for some years, and, according to his own account, for the reason we have just mentioned. His retirement from the American Fur Company was the culmination of a process of withdrawal from commercial transactions which had definitely commenced when he began, a decade before, to dispose of his fleet of China vessels. It may, perhaps, be asked why William B. Astor, who had been president of the Company, did not carry on the Astor fur-trade tradition, but the son, though an excellent business man, certainly lacked the interest in commerce,[117] and probably the commercial ability as well, which his father had so conspicuously displayed. The true scope for William B. Astor's business talent was to be found in the administration of the great real-estate holdings which his father had built up on Manhattan Island.[118] But, for whatever complex of reasons,[119] the decision was made, and first found definite expression in a letter from Geneva, of June 25, 1833, addressed to Bernard Pratte & Co., St. Louis. The letter read: "Wishing to retire from the Concern in which I am engaged with your House, you will please to take this as notice thereof, & that the agreement entered into on the 7th. May 1830 — between your House & me on the part of the American Fur Company will expire with the outfit of the present year on the terms expressed in said agreement."[120] Letters to the same effect from William B. Astor, later in the year, confirmed this decision.[121] In 1834 Astor sold out his interest in the Western Department to Pratte, Chouteau & Co., which had succeeded Bernard Pratte & Co., and disposed of the Northern Department to a group headed by Ramsay Crooks, which was allowed to retain the Company's distinctive title.[122] Robert Stuart at Mackinac was notified of this agreement on June 4, 1834.[123] Astor's sale of his interests had included only the property in the interior. He had reserved the furs at New York, London, and elsewhere. A few months were spent in disposing of these in New York, London, Smyrna, and other fur-trading centers; an operation which also involved making some purchases for the good of the market. This period in the liquidation of Astor's interest in the Company was probably pretty well over by the early part of 1835.[124] Thus ended — save for the final winding up of debts due to the Company and similar inevitable long-drawn-out activities — Astor's connection with the Company which he had founded and which he had headed for more than a quarter of a century, and with the trade in which he had been engaged for nearly twice that length of time.

NOTES

1. Ms. book (copy), Detroit Public Library, Burton Historical Collection, and Missouri Historical Society, St. Louis, Letters of Ramsay Crooks, John Jacob Astor, and the American Fur Company 1813–43, John Jacob Astor for the American Fur Company, N. Y., January 27, 1823, to Ramsay Crooks (see below, vol. ii, pp. 1171–1172).

2. Ms. (photostat), Wisconsin Historical Society, Madison, Ramsay Crooks' and Robert Stuart's Letter Book, Mackinac, Detroit, New York, etc., 1820–25, Robert Stuart, Mackinac, May 19, 1823, to David Stone, Detroit.

3. Chittenden, Hiram Martin, *The American Fur Trade of the Far West*, 3 vols. (1902), vol. i, p. 322.

4. Ms. (photostat), Wisconsin Historical Society, Madison, Robert Stuart's Letter Book, Mackinac, 1823–30, p. 5, Robert Stuart, Mackinac, July 19, 1823, to William B. Astor, N. Y.

5. *New-York Gazette and General Advertiser*, June 3, 1823, p. 2, col. 2.

6. Thwaites, Reuben Gold, ed., "The Fur-Trade in Wisconsin — 1812–1825," *Wisconsin Historical Collections*, vol. xx (1911), pp. 206–210, Agreement for the Green Bay Company between Augustin Grignon, Pierre Grignon, Louis Grignon, John Lawe, and Jacques Porlier, Sr., Michilimackinac, August 24, 1821 (ms., Wisconsin Historical Society, Madison, Wisconsin MSS., 61 B 66).

7. *Ibid.*, pp. 254–255, Robert Stuart, Mackinac, May 16, 1822, to Jacques Porlier, Green Bay (ms., Wisconsin Historical Society, Madison, Wisconsin MSS., 10 B 59).

8. *Ibid.*, pp. 277–278, John Lawe, Michilimackinac, August 26, 1822, to Jacob Franks (ms., Wisconsin Historical Society, Madison, Wisconsin MSS., 1 C 128).

9. Ms. (photostat), Wisconsin Historical Society, Madison, Ramsay Crooks' and Robert Stuart's Letter Book, Mackinac, Detroit, New York, etc., 1820–25, Robert Stuart, Mackinac, October 1, 1823, to John Jacob Astor & Son, N. Y.

10. *Ibid.*, Robert Stuart's Letter Book, Mackinac, 1823–30, pp. 17–18, Ramsay Crooks, Mackinac, September 5, 1823, to Joseph Rolette, Prairie du Chien.

11. Thwaites, *op. cit.*, pp. 257–260, Jacques Porlier, Green Bay, June 8, 1822, to Governor Cass, Michigan Territory (ms., Wisconsin Historical Society, Madison, Wisconsin MSS., 54 B 83, and Department of the Interior, Washington, D. C., Indian Office, Letters Received, 1822, no. 1, p. 400).

12. Ms. (photostat), Wisconsin Historical Society, Madison, Robert Stuart's Letter Book, Mackinac, 1823–30, pp. 112, 129–132, Robert

Stuart, Mackinac, September 17, 1824, to William B. Astor, N. Y., and October 20, 1824, to John Jacob Astor, Europe.

13. *Ibid.*, p. 124, Robert Stuart, Mackinac, October 15, 1824, to John Jacob Astor, Europe (see below, vol. ii, pp. 1176–1177).

14. Thwaites, *op. cit.*, pp. 339–340, War Department, Office of Indian Affairs, June 5, 1824, to Lewis Cass, Detroit (ms., Wisconsin Historical Society, Madison, Wisconsin MSS., 72 C 25).

15. Childs, Colonel Ebenezer, "Recollections of Wisconsin since 1820," *Wisconsin Historical Collections*, vol. iv (1857–58), pp. 156–157.

16. Ms. book, Department of the Interior, Washington, D. C., Indian Office Records, Miscellaneous, William B. Astor, N. Y., June 28, 1825 to James Barbour, Secretary of War; *ibid.*, Indian Office Letter Book ii, 1824–25, Thomas L. McKenney, Department of War, Office of Indian Affairs, July 22, 1825, to William B. Astor, President *pro tempore* of the American Fur Company; Thomas L. McKenney, July 22, 1825, to William Clark, Superintendent of Indian Affairs, St. Louis.

17. *American State Papers: Indian Affairs*, vol. ii, pp. 657–661, Bernard Pratte and Robert Stuart, Washington, D. C., January 28, 1826, to James Barbour, Secretary of War; Lewis Cass, Washington, D. C., February 2, 1826, to James Barbour, Secretary of War; Thomas L. McKenney, Department of War, Office of Indian Affairs, February 14, 1826, to James Barbour, Secretary of War.

18. *United States Statutes at Large*, vol. iv, 1824–35, p. 729, June 30, 1834.

19. Ms. (photostat), Wisconsin Historical Society, Madison, Robert Stuart's Letter Book, Mackinac, 1823–30, pp. 89–90, Robert Stuart, Mackinac, August 26, 1824, to Governor Cass.

20. *Ibid.*, p. 29, Robert Stuart, Mackinac, October 26, 1823, to Ramsay Crooks, N. Y.

21. *Ibid.*, pp. 122–125, Robert Stuart, Mackinac, October 15, 1824, to John Jacob Astor, Europe.

22. Ms. book (copy), Detroit Public Library, Burton Historical Collection, and Missouri Historical Society, St. Louis, Letters of Ramsay Crooks, John Jacob Astor, and the American Fur Company, 1813–43, John Jacob Astor, Geneva, February 16 (see below, vol. ii, pp. 1173–1175), March 13, 19, 19, June 12, September 21, November 10, December 4, 1824, to Ramsay Crooks, N. Y.

23. Ms. (photostat), Wisconsin Historical Society, Madison, Robert Stuart's Letter Book, Mackinac, 1823–30, pp. 122–125, Robert Stuart, Mackinac, October 15, 1824, to John Jacob Astor, Europe.

24. In October, 1824, the American Fur Company announced that the "greatest quantity of furs ever before offered for sale at one time in the United States, will be put up at auction, in the city of New York on the

11th instant. . . . It consists of 12,500 *lbs.* beaver, 120,000 muskrat skins, 72,000 Racoon ditto, 60,000 hare and nutria ditto, and 10,000 buffalo robes from different regions, and will be sold in lots to suit purchasers." (*Niles' Register*, vol. xxvii, p. 68, October 2, 1824.)

25. Ms. book (copy), Detroit Public Library, Burton Historical Collection, and Missouri Historical Society, St. Louis, Letters of Ramsay Crooks, John Jacob Astor, and the American Fur Company, 1813–43, John Jacob Astor, Geneva, February 16 (see below, vol. ii, pp. 1173–1175), March 13, 19, 19, April 17, June 12, September 21, November 10, December 4, 1824, January 10, 1825 (see below, vol. ii, pp. 1176, 1178), to Ramsay Crooks, N. Y.; John Jacob Astor, Geneva, March 24, 1824, to W. B. Clapp, N. Y.

26. *Ibid.*, John Jacob Astor, Geneva, March 19, 19, April 17, September 21, November 10, 1824, to Ramsay Crooks, N. Y.

27. *Ibid.*, John Jacob Astor, Geneva, January 10 (see below, vol. ii, pp. 1176, 1178), March 11, May 20, 1825, Schentznach, July 5, 1825, Geneva, August 20, 1825 (see below, vol. ii, pp. 1179–1180), to Ramsay Crooks, N. Y.

28. *Ibid.*, Ramsay Crooks, N. Y., May 16, 1826, to Mr. Mathews, Detroit and Mackinac, to Joseph Rolette, Mackinac, and to Robert Stuart, Buffalo.

29. Chittenden, *op. cit.*, vol. i, pp. 322–323, note 2.

30. Ms. book (copy), Detroit Public Library, Burton Historical Collection, and Missouri Historical Society, St. Louis, Letters of Ramsay Crooks, John Jacob Astor, and the American Fur Company, 1813–43, John Jacob Astor, N. Y., April 12 (see below, vol. ii, pp. 1190–1192), 16, May 25, June 4, 1827, to Ramsay Crooks.

31. *Ibid.*, Ramsay Crooks, St. Louis, June 22, 1827, to John Jacob Astor, N. Y.

32. *Ibid.*, John Jacob Astor, N. Y., June 4, 1827, to O. N. Bostwick, Agent, American Fur Company, St. Louis, Missouri.

33. Chittenden, *op. cit.*, vol. i, pp. 323–327.

34. Ms. book (copy), Detroit Public Library, Burton Historical Collection, and Missouri Historical Society, St. Louis, Letters of Ramsay Crooks, John Jacob Astor, and the American Fur Company, 1813–43, Ramsay Crooks, Prairie du Chien, August 30, 1826, to Kenneth McKenzie and Daniel Lamont, Lac Travers and St. Peter's.

35. *Ibid.*, Ramsay Crooks, St. Louis, April 13, 1827, to John Jacob Astor, N. Y.

36. *Ibid.*, Ramsay Crooks, Steamboat *Indiana*, Mississippi River, 75 miles below Prairie du Chien, April 30, 1827, to John Jacob Astor, N. Y.

37. *Ibid.*, Ramsay Crooks, St. Louis, May 24, 1827, to John Jacob Astor, N. Y.

38. *Ibid.*, John Jacob Astor, N. Y., April 25, May 7, 25, June 4, 1827, to Ramsay Crooks, St. Louis.

39. *Ibid.*, Ramsay Crooks, St. Louis, June 8, 11, 22, 1827, to John Jacob Astor, N. Y.

40. *Ibid.*, Ramsay Crooks, St. Louis, June 26, 1827, to Robert Stuart, Mackinac.

41. *Ibid.*, Ramsay Crooks, St. Louis, June 27, 1827, to Joseph Rolette, Cincinnati.

42. *Ibid.*, Ramsay Crooks, St. Louis, July 6, 1827, to John Jacob Astor, N. Y.

43. Chittenden, *op. cit.*, vol. i, pp. 325-327.

44. Ms., Department of the Interior, Washington, D. C., Indian Office Records, Miscellaneous, Lawrence Taliaferro, St. Peters, October 1, 1827, to Gen. William Clark, St. Louis.

45. Ms. book (copy), Detroit Public Library, Burton Historical Collection, and Missouri Historical Society, St. Louis, Letters of Ramsay Crooks, John Jacob Astor, and the American Fur Company, 1813-43, Ramsay Crooks, St. Louis, July 6, 1827, to John Jacob Astor, N. Y.

46. *Ibid.*, John Jacob Astor, N. Y., March 16, April 12, 1827 (see below, vol. ii, pp. 1190-1192), to Ramsay Crooks, St. Louis.

47. *Ibid.*, Ramsay Crooks, St. Louis, April 13, 1827, to John Jacob Astor, N. Y.

48. *Ibid.*, John Jacob Astor, N. Y., April 25, May 7, June 4, 28, 1827, to Ramsay Crooks, St. Louis.

49. *Ibid.*, Ramsay Crooks, St. Louis, June 8, 1827, to John Jacob Astor, N. Y.

50. Ms. book, Chicago Historical Society, Menard and Vallé Papers.

51. Ms., New York State Library, Albany, John Jacob Astor, Office, American Fur Company, October 31, 1826, to Robert Stuart, Agent, American Fur Company, Michilimackinac, Territory of Michigan.

52. Johnson, Ida Amanda, *The Michigan Fur Trade* (1919), pp. 143-144, 152-153.

53. Ms., New York State Library, Albany, John Jacob Astor, Office, American Fur Company, October 31, 1826, to Robert Stuart, Agent, American Fur Company, Michilimackinac, Territory of Michigan.

54. Ms. (photostat), Wisconsin Historical Society, Madison, Robert Stuart's Letter Book, Mackinac, 1823-30, Robert Stuart, Mackinac, January 18, 1827, to John Jacob Astor, N. Y.

55. Ms. book (copy), Detroit Public Library, Burton Historical Collection, and Missouri Historical Society, St. Louis, Letters of Ramsay Crooks, John Jacob Astor, and the American Fur Company, 1813-43, John Jacob Astor, N. Y., May 25, June 4, 1827, to Ramsay Crooks, St. Louis.

56. *Ibid.*, Ramsay Crooks, St. Louis, June 22, 1827, to John Jacob Astor, N. Y.

57. *Ibid.*, John Jacob Astor, N. Y., June, 1830, to Ramsay Crooks (see below, vol. ii, pp. 1204–1205).

58. *Senate Documents*, 22nd Cong., 1st sess., vol. ii, no. 90, pp. 77–78, William B. Astor, N. Y., November 25, 1831, to the Secretary of War.

59. Ms. book, Baker Library, Astor Papers, Letter Book ii, 1831–38, p. 237, John Jacob Astor for the American Fur Company, N. Y., June 24, 1834, to James Abbott, Detroit.

60. Ms. (photostat), Wisconsin Historical Society, Madison, Robert Stuart's Letter Book, Mackinac, 1823–30, pp. 282–285, Robert Stuart, N. Y., April 4, 1826, to Joseph Rolette.

61. "Taliaferro, Maj. Lawrence, Autobiography of: Written in 1864," *Minnesota Historical Collections*, vol. vi (1887–94), pp. 189–255.

62. Ms. book, Library of Congress, George Johnston's Journal in the North West, August 3, 1824–May 16, 1827, August 4, 1825, February 15, 1827.

63. Neill, Rev. E. D., "Occurrences in and around Fort Snelling, from 1819 to 1840," *Minnesota Historical Collections*, vol. ii (1864), pp. 21–56. It is rather amusing to note that in 1848 Lewis Cass, the American Fur Company's steadfast friend, ran unsuccessfully for the presidency of the United States against Zachary Taylor, who had so sweepingly characterized all those connected with that organization as a pack of scoundrels. It does not appear, however, that their respective attitudes toward the Company was an important issue in the campaign.

64. Ms. (photostat), Wisconsin Historical Society, Madison, Robert Stuart's Letter Book, Mackinac, 1823–30, pp. 416–417, Robert Stuart, Mackinac, March 10, 1827, to John Jacob Astor, N. Y.

65. Ms. book (copy), Detroit Public Library, Burton Historical Collection, and Missouri Historical Society, St. Louis, Letters of Ramsay Crooks, John Jacob Astor, and the American Fur Company, 1813–43, Ramsay Crooks, April 30, 1827, to John Jacob Astor, N. Y.

66. Ms., Department of the Interior, Washington, D. C., Indian Office Records, Miscellaneous, Lawrence Taliaferro, St. Peters, May, 1827, to Gen. William Clark, St. Louis; William Clark, St. Louis, June 16, 1827, to James Barbour, Secretary of War.

67. Thwaites, *op. cit.*, p. 258, note 97.

68. Ms. (photostat), Wisconsin Historical Society, Madison, Robert Stuart's Letter Book, Mackinac, 1823–30, p. 358, Robert Stuart, Mackinac, August 28, 1826, to John Jacob Astor, N. Y.

69. Ms., New York State Library, Albany, John Jacob Astor, N. Y., October 31, 1826, to Robert Stuart, Michilimackinac.

70. Ms. (photostat), Wisconsin Historical Society, Madison, Robert

Stuart's Letter Book, Mackinac, 1823–30, pp. 402–405, Robert Stuart, Mackinac, November 29, 1826, to Ramsay Crooks.

71. Ms. (copy), Department of the Interior, Washington, D. C., Indian Office Records, Miscellaneous, Lewis Cass, Michilimackinac, June 30, 1825, to Thomas L. McKenney.

72. Ms. (photostat), Wisconsin Historical Society, Madison, Robert Stuart's Letter Book, Mackinac, pp. 469–471, Robert Stuart, Mackinac, September 26, 1827, to John Jacob Astor, N. Y.

73. The following furs were disposed of at public sale in New York by the American Fur Company on April 13, 1826: "1670 Mackinac and lake Superior *beaver* . . . at $5 3-8 a $6 per lb.— 1486 Missouri at $4 3-8 a $4¾— 1090 Rocky Mountain at $5¼ a 6— 11,200 northern *muskrats* at 34 to 38½ cents — 79,000 Kankikee at 35½ to 40 — 9000 Mississippi at 33 a 37½ — 3755 assorted at 21 to 22 cents — 3600 Northern *raccoon* at 30 to 34 — 16000 Mississippi at 30½ a 33½, and 2400 Detroit at 34 to 36 cents per skin: at 4 and 5 months." (*Niles' Register*, vol. xxx, p. 156, April 29, 1826.)

74. Ms., New York State Library, John Jacob Astor, Office, American Fur Company, October 31, 1826, to Robert Stuart, Agent, American Fur Company, Michilimackinac, Territory of Michigan.

75. Ms., Hudson's Bay Company House, London, John Jacob Astor, N. Y., February 27, 1827, to George Simpson, Montreal; George Simpson, Montreal, March 13, 1827, to John Jacob Astor.

76. Ms. book (copy), Detroit Public Library, Burton Historical Collection, and Missouri Historical Society, St. Louis, Letters of Ramsay Crooks, John Jacob Astor, and the American Fur Company, 1813–43, John Jacob Astor, N. Y., March 16, April 12 (see below, vol. ii, pp. 1190–1192), 25, May 7, May 25, June 4, 28, July 9, September 26, 28, 29, 1827, to Ramsay Crooks, St. Louis.

77. *Ibid.*, Ramsay Crooks, St. Louis, etc., April 13, 30, May 24, June 8, 11, 22, August 10, 1827, to John Jacob Astor, N. Y.

78. *Ibid.*, John Jacob Astor, N. Y., April 16, May 25, June 4, 28, September 26, 29, 1827, to Ramsay Crooks, St. Louis.

79. Ms., Palais de Justice, Montreal, Notarial Records of P. Lukin, no. 1439, Engagement of J. Bᵗᵉ Gibeau to Gabriel Franchere, Jr., Agent of the American Fur Company, February 9, 1828 (see below, vol. ii, pp. 1192–1194).

80. Ms. book (copy), Detroit Public Library, Burton Historical Collection, and Missouri Historical Society, St. Louis, Letters of Ramsay Crooks, John Jacob Astor, and the American Fur Company, 1813–43, Wilson P. Hunt, St. Louis, April 17, 1828, to Ramsay Crooks, N. Y.

81. *Ibid.*, John Jacob Astor, N. Y., September 26, 28, 29, 1827, to Ramsay Crooks, St. Louis.

82. *Ibid.*, Ramsay Crooks, St. Louis, October 19, 1827, to John Jacob Astor, N. Y.

83. *Ibid.*, John Jacob Astor, N. Y., November 26, 1827, to Ramsay Crooks, Lancaster, Pa.

84. Ms., Wisconsin Historical Society, Madison, Wisconsin MSS., 3 D 122, George Boyd, Mackinac, August 18, 1830, to James B. Gardiner, Mackinac (see below, vol. ii, pp. 1206–1209).

85. Ms. book, Public Archives of Canada, Ottawa, Ledger, American Fur Company, Northern Department, June 23, 1827–March 28, 1835, *passim*.

86. Ms. book (copy), Detroit Public Library, Burton Historical Collection, and Missouri Historical Society, St. Louis, Letters of Ramsay Crooks, John Jacob Astor, and the American Fur Company, 1813–43, Ramsay Crooks, St. Louis, April 13, 1827, to John Jacob Astor, N. Y.

87. These *rendezvous* have been described by the New England fur trader Nathaniel Wyeth. On July 8, 1832, he wrote that he found at the *rendezvous* "a company of trappers of about 90 under Mr. Dripps of the firm of Dripps & Fortenelle connected with the American Fur Co."; also many independent hunters and a hundred from the Rocky Mountain Fur Company. On July 18 of the following year he wrote from Green River: "I arrived here on the 16th. . . . I should have been proud of my countrymen if you could have seen the American Fur Co. or the party of Mr. S. Campbell. For efficiency of goods, men, animals and arms, I do not believe the fur business has offered a better example or discipline. . . . Mr. Wm Sublette and Mr Campbell have come up the Missouri and established a trading post at each location of the posts of the Am. Fur Co. with a view to a strong opposition. Good luck to their quarrels." Elsewhere Wyeth tells something of conditions at these Missouri River posts of Astor's organization. ("Wyeth, Captain Nathaniel, The Correspondence and Journals of, 1831–6," *Sources of the History of Oregon*, vol. i (1899), pp. 69, 73–78, 159, 210.)

88. On November 8, 1833, Nathaniel Wyeth, who had been at the *rendezvous* that summer, wrote from Cambridge, Massachusetts: "Since the commencement of this species of business [conducting the Rocky Mountain fur trade through trapping parties] severall persons have attempted it, but all are now out of the way except Mess Dripps & Fortenelle fitted out by the Am. Fur Co. and Mess. Bonneville & Co. fitted out by men in New York. Neither of these last named Companies as far as I can ascertain have made money to any great extent, owing to enormous prices paid for goods." (Wyeth, *op. cit.*, pp. 73–78. See also Chittenden, *op. cit.*, vol. i, chap. xxiv, and Irving, Washington, *The Adventures of Captain Bonneville* (1st ed., 1843; 1873), especially p. 22.)

89. Charles Larpenteur, who was a clerk of Sublette & Campbell in 1833, said of this rivalry: "The Indians had no confidence in his [Mr.

Campbell's] remaining, so that the bulk of the trade went to the big American Company" — an example of the position which Astor's organization had attained among the natives. He also said: "Sublette . . . sold out during the winter of 1833–34, to the American Fur Company — as I learned afterward, very much to the displeasure of Mr. McKenzie, who wished to break us down completely." Larpenteur was later employed by McKenzie. (Larpenteur, Charles, *Forty Years a Fur Trader on the Upper Missouri* . . . *1833–1872*, Elliott Coues, ed., 2 vols. (1898), vol. i, pp. 9–10, 56, 59, 62, 63–64.)

90. As a matter of fact, setting up a still in the Indian country had been expressly forbidden in 1815 by an act of Congress. Perhaps McKenzie preferred to subject himself to the penalty of a $5,000 fine, in such a case provided, rather than to the confiscation of all his goods as prescribed in the act of 1832. Or more likely he was merely ignorant of the earlier law. (*United States Statutes at Large*, vol. iii, 1813–23, chap. c, sec. 20, pp. 243–244, 13th Cong., 3rd sess., 1815.)

91. Chittenden, *op. cit.*, vol. i, pp. 246–365, *passim*. Except where another source is specified, the information concerning activities in the Western Department has been drawn from Chittenden.

92. Ms., Wisconsin Historical Society, Madison, Wisconsin MSS., 3 D 122, George Boyd, Mackinac, August 18, 1830, to James B. Gardiner, Mackinac (see below, vol. ii, pp. 1206–1209); *Hubbard, Gurdon Saltonstall, The Autobiography of* (1911), pp. 23–24.

93. *Senate Documents*, 22nd Cong., 1st sess., vol. ii, no. 90, pp. 11–18, Joshua Pilcher, St. Louis, December 1, 1831, to Lewis Cass, pp. 70–90, Thomas Forsyth, St. Louis, October 24, 1831, to the Secretary of War.

94. [Scoville, Joseph A.], *The Old Merchants of New York City*, 5 vols. (1889), vol. iii, p. 38: "Those sales of the American Fur Company . . . used to bring crowds of fur dealers from all parts of Europe to this city, in the spring and in the fall, to attend them."

95. Ms. (photostat), Wisconsin Historical Society, Madison, Ramsay Crooks' and Robert Stuart's Letter Book, Mackinac, Detroit, New York, etc., 1820–25, pp. 83–84, Ramsay Crooks, Liverpool, April 18, 1821, to John Jacob Astor, Paris.

96. Ms., Massachusetts Historical Society, Boston, Perkins MSS., Thomas G. Cary, N. Y., November 2, 1831, to Samuel Cabot.

97. "The Minutes of the Council of the Northern Department of Rupert's Land 1830 to 1843," *North Dakota Historical Collection*, vol. iv (1913), pp. 644–865, especially pp. 720, 735, 752, 768, 783, 816; ms., Hudson's Bay Company House, London, Hudson's Bay Company, Hudson's Bay House, London, March 5, 1834, to George Simpson; George Simpson, London, November 15, 1837, to Ramsay Crooks, President of the American Fur Company, N. Y. It is possible that some earlier agreement of this type was responsible for the rumor which reached the Indian country

in the spring of 1825. "There is News here from Red River, that the Hudson Bay Company have paid (probably last year) to the American Furr Company the immense sum of half a Million of dollars not to extend their Trade to the River Columbia." (Thwaites, *op. cit.*, pp. 374–375, Thomas Forsyth, Rocky Island, April 22, 1825, to General William Clark, Superintendent of Indian Affairs, St. Louis, ms., Wisconsin Historical Society, Madison, Draper MSS., 4 T 222, 223.) Of course, Astor actually had no intention of reviving his Astoria experiment of a decade before.

98. Ms., Chicago Historical Society, Atwater Collection, Autograph Letters, vol. ii, pp. 175–178, John Jacob Astor, N. Y., June 3, 1828, to Robert Stuart, Michilimackinac.

99. Ms. book (copy), Detroit Public Library, Burton Historical Collection, and Missouri Historical Society, St. Louis, Letters of Ramsay Crooks, John Jacob Astor, and the American Fur Company, 1813–43, John Jacob Astor, N. Y., June, 1830, to Ramsay Crooks (see below, vol. ii, pp. 1204–1205); conversation with J. J. Astor, July 28, 1830.

100. Ms. book, Baker Library, Astor Papers, Letter Book ii, 1831–38, p. 8, John Jacob Astor, N. Y., November 10, 1831, to Joseph Rolette.

101. *Ibid.*, p. 9, John Jacob Astor, N. Y., November 12, 1831, to David Stone, Dayton, Ohio.

102. *Ibid.*, pp. 25–26, 30, John Jacob Astor, N. Y., January 21, February 7, 1832, to Wilson Price Hunt, St. Louis.

103. *Ibid.*, pp. 5, 10, 13, 14–15, 16, 17, 18, 20–21, 26–27, 29–30, 31, 36–37, 42, 48, John Jacob Astor, N. Y., October 31, November 15, 24, 30, December 15, 16, 30, 1831, January 6, 21, 31, February 7, March 23, April 7, 23, 1832, to Gillespies, Moffatt, Finlay & Co., London; p. 81, William B. Astor, N. Y., July 31, 1832, to Gillespies, Moffatt, Finlay & Co., London.

104. *Ibid.*, pp. 47, 50–51, John Jacob Astor, N. Y., April 20, May 8, 1832, to Martin Bates, Boston.

105. *Ibid.*, p. 51, John Jacob Astor, N. Y., May 15, 1832, to Andrew Mitchell, Pentauguishin.

106. *Ibid.*, p. 11, John Jacob Astor, N. Y., November 14, 1831, to B. Pratte, Philadelphia.

107. *Ibid.*, p. 47, John Jacob Astor, N. Y., April 19, 1832, to Charles N. Talbot, Canton.

108. *Ibid.*, p. 51, John Jacob Astor, N. Y., May 14, 1832, to Churchill, Bunker & Co., Constantinople.

109. *Ibid.*, p. 81, William B. Astor, N. Y., August 4, 1832, to John P. Van Ness, Washington.

110. Chittenden, *op. cit.*, vol. i, p. 362.

111. Ms., Wisconsin Historical Society, Madison, Wisconsin MSS., 25 B 11, Robert Stuart, N. Y., April 1, 1830, to John Lawe, Green Bay, Wisconsin.

112. *Ibid.*, 24 B 22, Robert Stuart, Mackinac, September 4, 1829, to John Lawe, Green Bay, Wisconsin.

113. Ms. book, Baker Library, Astor Papers, Letter Book ii, 1831–38, p. 9, John Jacob Astor, N. Y., November 12, 1831, to Joseph McGillivray, Montreal; p. 40, John Jacob Astor, N. Y., April 3, 1832, to Benjamin Mooers, Plattsburgh.

114. *Minutes of the Common Council of the City of New York, 1784–1831,* vol. xiii, p. 520, February 2, 1824, pp. 582–583, March 1, 1824.

115. Ms., Missouri Historical Society, St. Louis, P. Chouteau Collection, Pierre Chouteau Papers, John Jacob Astor, Paris, August, 1832, to Pierre Chouteau, Jr., St. Louis.

116. In the month before Astor finally sold out his interest in the Company, his friend Philip Hone committed to his diary his opinion that Astor would not live to see the completion of the hotel, preparations for the erection of which were then in progress (*Hone, Philip, The Diary of, 1828–1851,* Allan Nevins, ed., 2 vols. (1927), vol. i, p. 126).

117. Smith, Matthew Hale, *Sunshine and Shadow in New York* (1868), p. 188: "He has none of that love of trade and enterprise of his father. . . . His business is with investments."

118. Scoville, *op. cit.*, vol. iii, p. 38: "William B. Astor never made a dollar in his life. He always stood by his father. William B. is the best man in the United States to have charge of a colossal fortune."

119. In this connection we might set down for what it is worth another account of Astor's reason for withdrawing from the American Fur Company. "A surviving daughter of Mr. Crooks has given some sketches of her father's life as she remembers it. . . . The American Fur Company became involved owing to the extensive exportation of furs to London. Mr. Astor retired from the Company, but Mr. Crooks took hold of it and in the face of great difficulties succeeded in winding it up, paying everybody one hundred cents on the dollar." (Ms., Detroit Public Library, Burton Historical Collection, Robert J. Hoguet, 487 Broadway, N. Y., February 17, 1908, to C. M. Burton, Detroit.) The above is an example of the untrustworthiness of family tradition, especially three-quarters of a century after the events dealt with. There is not the slightest evidence for the statement that Astor retired because the Company had become "involved," nor is there the least likelihood that in such an event Crooks would succeed in winding up the Company's affairs where Astor had failed. This story probably has to do with the final collapse of the American Fur Company, after a group headed by Crooks had bought out its Northern Department, retaining the original name, but, deprived of Astor's personal and financial backing, had failed of success.

120. Ms., Missouri Historical Society, St. Louis, P. Chouteau Collection, Pierre Chouteau Papers, John Jacob Astor, Geneva, June 25, 1833, to Bernard Pratte & Co., St. Louis (see below, vol. ii, p. 1224).

121. *Ibid.*, William B. Astor, N. Y., August 26, 1833, to Bernard Pratte & Co., St. Louis; William B. Astor, President, American Fur Company, November 1, 1833, to Messrs. Bernard Pratte, Pierre Chouteau, Jr., J. P. Cabanné, St. Louis.

122. Chittenden, *op. cit.*, vol. i, p. 364.

123. Ms. book, Baker Library, Astor Papers, Letter Book ii, 1831–38, pp. 232–233, John Jacob Astor, N. Y., June 4, 1834, to Robert Stuart (see below, vol. ii, pp. 1226–1227).

124. *Ibid.*, pp. 242, 260, 272, 274, 275, John Jacob Astor, N. Y., June 30, September 30, 1834, January 7, 15, 16, 1835, to Gillespies, Moffatt, Finlay & Co., London; p. 250, William B. Astor, N. Y., July 28, 1834, to A. H. Center; p. 266, John Jacob Astor, N. Y., November 22, 1834, to John Dorr, Boston; p. 270, John Jacob Astor, N. Y., December 27, 1834, to H. L. Dousman, Mackinac or Prairie des Chiens; p. 306, John Jacob Astor, N. Y., June 18, 1835, to P. Chouteau, Jr., St. Louis.

CHAPTER XVI

POLICIES AND PRACTICES OF THE AMERICAN
FUR COMPANY

THE attitude of the American Fur Company toward the traffic in liquor with the Indians is, for an obvious reason, of surpassing interest to residents of the United States at the present time, but it was of scarcely less importance to John Jacob Astor's contemporaries. The question most frequently asked by those who have only a casual interest in John Jacob Astor or in the fur trade is: "Did Astor sell whiskey to the Indians?" If by this the questioner means: "Did Astor, at any time after his first few years in the fur trade, go out personally among the natives with a jug of rum under his arm to trade for peltries?" the answer is obviously in the negative. If, on the other hand, he means: "Did the American Fur Company, that organization of which all the capital and most of the management was furnished by Astor, sell liquor to the Indians?" the reply is most emphatically "Yes!" The question of liquor and the Indians was of such tremendous importance to those officials of government who had the welfare of the natives in charge during the period covered by Astor's connection with the American Fur Company, and that Company possessed such overwhelming influence in the Indian country during the same period, that the attitude of Astor and his agents toward the liquor traffic in the Indian country, the policy advocated by them toward this question, the practice actually adopted, and the reasons behind both, are worthy of detailed consideration.

The effect which liquor, even in small quantities, had upon the Indian is well known to all readers of the journals of those traders or explorers in the Indian country who have recorded the scenes which ensued when intoxicants had found their way down the gullets of the natives. The immediate effect was to turn the drinker into a homicidal maniac, ready to stab and scalp his best friend or closest relative. Moreover, it was not long until the Indian who had for a few times partaken of the trader's liquor had become, when not under the direct influence of the intoxicant, a pitiful sot, so enslaved to the habit as to be willing to trade his gun or his last blanket for a swallow of alcohol. Alcohol in its various forms left in its wake intertribal wars, hostility between the natives and the border settlements, disease, poverty, starvation, and death.[1] But it also left, here and there, fur traders with weighty packs of furs and well-filled pocketbooks, the fruits of the ruin which their greed and their kegs of rum had brought upon the natives. It was inevitable that government officials, inspired not merely by feelings of humanity for the Indians but also by a desire for the safety of the frontier, should endeavor to prevent liquor from reaching the Indians, and no less inevitable that a certain type of trader, anxious only for his own immediate financial profit, should use every means in his power to see that the Indians had personal freedom to use intoxicants whenever they so chose.

In 1802, by an act of Congress, the president of the United States was "authorized to take such measures, from time to time, as to him may appear expedient to prevent or restrain the vending or distributing of spirituous liquors among all or any of the . . . Indian tribes."[2] It will be observed that this act did not actually forbid the sale of intoxicants to the Indians, but merely empowered the president to do so, should he see fit. At the conclusion of the War of 1812 the government became conscious that more attention must be paid to the welfare of the Indians, if they were to be attached to the United States. Accordingly, in 1815, an act of Congress forbade the setting up of a still in the Indian country under pain of a fine of $5,000.[3] It does not appear, however, that any definite action was taken by the president against the liquor trade with the Indians under the authority of the law of 1802. If any such was taken at an early date, it certainly never received wide currency even among those whom it principally concerned. In 1818 Major Puthuff, the Indian agent at Mackinac, defended himself against an accusation by agents of the American Fur Company in these words: "As respects my having sent ardent spirits into the Indian Country to purchase corn, I beg leave to remark, that not having any instructions to that effect from my Government, or your Excellency [Governor Lewis Cass], the introduction of ardent spirits into any part of the Indian Country by an American Citizen, was not prohibited, nor was any prohibition imposed to that effect until 1817."[4] Late in 1822 Lieutenant-Colonel Willoughby Morgan, commanding officer at Fort Crawford, Prairie du Chien, on the Upper Mississippi, complained of the lack of clarity in the instructions given to him for his guidance in connection with liquor and the Indians, and, referring to the act of 1802, remarked: "If any regulations have been adopted under the authority vested in this section, I should think it highly important, that the officers directed to inforce the laws, should be furnished with them . . . the President might remove all the difficulties, attending the execution of the laws, to the introduction of spiritous liquors among the Indian Tribes, by a regulation adopted under the authority . . . before mentioned."[5]

But in spite of the lack of definite instructions, such officials in the Indian country as Ninian Edwards, the territorial governor of Illinois, took it on themselves to forbid the sale of liquor to the Indians at such posts as Green Bay and Prairie du Chien,[6] and when licenses began to be granted under the law of 1816, which forbade foreigners to trade with the Indians, the provision was always inserted that the trader should not deal in spirituous liquor, the Indians being authorized to seize all the goods of those who violated this law.[7]

It may now be asked: "What was the attitude of Astor and the agents of the American Fur Company toward measures adopted for the purpose of keeping liquor from the Indians?" The answer is that at first they were heartily in favor of such measures and were constantly urging that more rigid laws be adopted and enforcement made more effective. This policy was inspired by no particular humanitarian feelings or consideration for the welfare of Indians or frontiersmen — though neither Astor and his associates nor their rivals could be imagined as taking any pleasure in the debauching of the natives — but was purely the result of a shrewd long-range business viewpoint. It was to Astor's interest that the Indians should remain keen, successful hunters and trappers, and this they could not do if ruined by liquor. True, a drunken Indian could be cheated with much greater ease than a sober one, but this argument in favor of rum appealed only to the small fly-by-night trader, whose little capital brought about a corresponding lack of vision. His aim was to make two or three big killings in successive years, and then retire, altogether unperturbed by the fact that he had ruined the trade for his more scrupulous successors.

But such methods had no appeal for Astor, who preferred a score of years of comparatively low but steady profits to half a dozen of more extravagant gains. He could afford to take profits only half as great as those of his comparatively insignificant rivals. He needed no whiskey to attract the Indians to his trading posts so long as his competitors were also unsupplied with that article. The sober Indian was a shrewd creature who could well compare prices and qualities of goods, and Astor's capital was large enough to allow of price-cutting, by which means, without the added attraction of alcohol, he could speedily drive out his rivals and win a monopoly of the Indian trade, after which his motto could be, "all the traffic will bear." A proof of Astor's disapproval of furnishing liquor to the Indians is the fact that the leaders of his Astoria expedition were ordered to sell no intoxicants to the natives—an order which, for a marvel, they seem to have in general obeyed.[8] If an effective blockade could have been established about the Indian country at the time when the American Fur Company first entered the fur trade of the interior, and in this way all liquor could have been barred *save that belonging to the American Fur Company*, I do not believe that Astor would have utilized his favored position to introduce intoxicants in any quantity.

Unfortunately, his theories could not be put into practice. There were always some traders to be found who desired quick profits and found that whiskey, when applied to the Indian, had many of the virtues of that philosopher's stone long sought after by the alchemists. Moreover, certain more honorable traders, who under other circumstances might not have employed intoxicants, discovered that alcohol was the only effective weapon within their reach which could be used to prevent Astor, with his superior money power, from forming a great monopoly. A vicious circle was in the process of formation. The Company, owing to its financial strength, had no need for whiskey so long as no other trader was using it. Opposing traders, however, discovered that without whiskey they could not compete with the heavily capitalized Company. It was inevitable that the Company should sooner or later decide that price-cutting was not a sufficient substitute for alcohol and that both must be brought into play in order to crush the opposition. This would not necessarily have happened had it not been for the fact that the Indian's passion for intoxicants was more like that of a drug fiend for his narcotic than the fondness of the alcohol-habituated white for his dram. Among the Indians there was no such thing as a "moderate drinker." Cass said: "Their attachment to ardent spirits is a moral phenomenon, and to it they sacrifice every consideration public or private";[9] while Thomas L. McKenney, the superintendent of the Indian Bureau, testified to the results of this passion in the statement: "The trader with the whiskey, it must be admitted, is certain of getting most furs."[10]

In one section of its territory, the vicinity of the Canadian border, the American Fur Company was exposed not only to the smuggled liquor of private American traders but also to that which was furnished by special permission to the Hudson's Bay Company posts for use in competition with the Americans, though the latter disadvantage was probably stressed more than its importance justified. It was consequently in this district that Astor first gave up his objections to the use of liquor in the Indian trade. "Seventy Kegs of Liquor," intended for the trade of the department of Fond du Lac, were among the merchandise seized by Selkirk's agents at Fort William in 1816, as described in a previous chapter. Selkirk followed up this action by sending a party of Hudson's Bay Company men to that department "with Goods — a part of which . . . consists of about fifty Kegs of Rum." William McGillivray, Astor's partner in the South West Fur Company, who informed Astor of this incident, went on to give his opinion that this "accounts for his detaining our liquor destined for the outfit of Fond du Lac, at Fort William — and would have given his people every advantage in the trade, even if our Posts had not been molested —"[11]

Although it is probable that agents of the American Fur Company introduced liquor into the Indian country outside the department of Fond du Lac, we have no direct evidence to show that they did so for some time after the Company's reorganization, in 1817. On the contrary, among the charges made by that Company against Major Puthuff, the Indian agent at Mackinac and scapegoat-in-ordinary to the American Fur Company for all the sins of his colleagues, was that he had failed to take any steps against violators of the liquor law within his jurisdiction.

The first thing we learned on arriving at Mackinaw last June [wrote Crooks and Stuart in January, 1818], was the injury our outfits had sustained at Sagina Bay on Lake Huron, and at Grand River, of Lake Michigan; from the clandestine introduction of Spirituous liquors . at the first place, by Jacob Smith from Detroit; and at the latter, by Mrs. Laframboise (a half breed) from Mackinaw. These acts were made known to Major Puthoff, and evidence offered in support; but we are not aware that he ever took the trouble to investigate their merits: and indeed it ought hardly to have been expected that the Agent who was himself the first to brake the law prohibiting the introduction of this pernicious liquid, should show much, *if any zeal* in the detection of other Violation.[12]

By this they meant that in 1816 Puthuff had purchased some corn for whiskey, as has already been mentioned, which act he claimed was at that time in violation of no regulation. By the above denunciation, of course, Crooks and Stuart meant to insinuate into their attack on Puthuff an assurance of their own innocence in the matter of the liquor trade.

On March 2, 1819, Ramsay Crooks, continuing his efforts to bar liquor from the Indian country, wrote to J. C. Calhoun, the secretary of War, suggesting that the regulation against bringing liquor into the Indian country should be extended to include the Mississippi River region as well as the Lakes.[13] Here we have another indication of the vagueness of the liquor regulations, since the ban on intoxicants certainly must have already applied to the Mississippi. Later in the same year the Company's agents persuaded the pliable George Boyd, who succeeded to the recalcitrant Puthuff as the Mackinac Indian agent, to grant the Company trader, William Morrison, the power to "destroy all spirituous liquors as soon as detected" which had been "introduced within the American limits in the neighbourhood of the Fond du Lac and Red Lake Settlements."[14] One may be sure that Morrison would see to it that, in the department of Fond du Lac, Company traders would have to meet liquor competition from none but their British rivals.

To judge from the letters of factors and Indian agents, all

attempts to keep liquor out of the Indian country proved in a large degree unsuccessful.[15] To the natural difficulty — or rather impossibility — of guarding a wild and extensive border was added the uncertainty of the regulations, which has been mentioned several times. For example, the Indian agent at Green Bay "prohibited the landing of every discription of spirits in this agency, for the purpose of trade or Barter,"[16] but his superior, Lewis Cass, though admitting that "there is no treaty or law which extinguish the Indian title in the vicinity of Green Bay," yet believed that, considering the nature and duration of the settlement, the district could not be classed as "Indian country," and that therefore "the sale of such liquors to the Inhabitants of the Country ought not to be wholly prohibited, but only limited or guarded in such manner as to prevent their subsequent transfer to the Indians."[17] This was obviously impossible, and it was no wonder that it seemed to factors and agents that the flood-gates had been opened.

It was not long until American Fur Company traders were as merrily engaged in the liquor trade as any in the ranks of the opposition. James H. Lockwood, the Company trader at Prairie du Chien, was described as one of "the principal venders in that article" during the winter of 1819,[18] while in 1821 "Mr. Kinzie, son to the Indian Sub-Agent at Chicago, and agent for the American Fur Company," was "detected in selling large quantities of whisky to the Indians at and near Milwalky of Lake Michigan; in consequence of which, the Indian Agent at Chicago, directed him to close his concerns at Milwalky in sixty days and then leave the place."[19]

In 1822, as a result of the lawlessness prevalent among traders in the Indian country, Congress was influenced by the representations of such men as Lewis Cass [20] and T. L. McKenney to pass a law forbidding traders to carry ardent spirits into the Indian country under penalty of forfeiting all their goods.[21] It will be observed that this was merely a reaffirmation, in statute form, of the regulations which had already been in force for some five years under authority of the act of 1802. It was not likely that the mere approval by Congress of the exclusion of liquor from the Indian country would make it much easier to put such a regulation into effect. In November, 1822, Major Willoughby Morgan, the commanding officer at Fort Crawford, Prairie du Chien, wrote a long letter to his superior, Major-General Gaines, explaining why he was finding it impossible to prevent "ardent spirits . . . in . . . considerable quantities" from entering the Indian country. The principal difficulty was to decide whether Prairie du Chien, located in the heart of the Indian country and "resorted to by some powerful tribes of Indians," was itself actually "Indian country." Another question was whether American citizens who were not Indian traders could pass through the Indian country with ardent spirits. If the former question were decided in the negative and the latter in the affirmative, the law of 1822 became practically a dead letter in Prairie du Chien and the Indian country supplied from it. Morgan thought that the new law could be enforced only by the absolute prohibition of the entrance of ardent spirits, brought by any person for any purpose whatsoever.[22]

It is unfortunate for the reputation of the American Fur Company that its agents did not even wait to see how strictly the new law would be interpreted and enforced before taking steps to evade its provisions. In July, 1822, Robert Stuart wrote to the pliable George Boyd, the Indian agent at Mackinac, requesting permission to take twelve barrels of whiskey into the Indian country on the Canadian border, to be bartered solely for provisions, which otherwise, Boyd was assured, could not be obtained, owing to the lavish use of liquor by the Hudson's Bay Company.[23] We are not told whether Boyd felt able to accede to this particular request, but he probably did, for in the next summer Lewis Cass, on his own responsibility, suspended the act of 1822 so far as the territory "west of Lake Superior, and adjoining the trading posts of the Hudson's Bay company" was concerned, for the very reason previously advanced by Stuart.[24] Of course, once in the Indian country with whiskey, the Company's traders would have nothing but their sensitive consciences to restrain them from employing whiskey for the purchase of beaver skins rather than buffalo beef.

It is even more regrettable that the Company's agents did not attempt to secure a ruling that Prairie du Chien and other similar posts were to be considered as Indian country so far as the importation of liquor was concerned, thus restricting their rivals in the whiskey trade of this area, instead of joining in the headlong rush to run intoxicants into the Indian country through that knot-hole. In the summer of 1822 boats containing whiskey consigned to Prairie du Chien were granted permits to proceed thither by the collector at Mackinac. It may be noted in passing that the collector at this post from 1818 to 1833 was one Adam D. Steuart,[25] who during that period also acted on occasion as the Company's representative in Washington.[26] These boats, however, were stopped at Green Bay by the Indian agent, Major John Biddle, who, as a newcomer to the country, had not yet learned flexibility where the Company was concerned. Robert Stuart protested against this action on the grounds that Prairie du Chien, though located, as we have seen, in the midst of the Indian country, was not itself "Indian country" and that therefore the ban against liquor did not hold in this case.[27] J. C. Calhoun, the secretary of War, on the other hand, was much surprised at the collector's action, and addressed a communication to the Treasury Department on that subject.[28] In the end Stuart's view of Prairie du Chien's status seems to have prevailed, for in 1825 William Clark, the Indian superintendent at St. Louis, remarked: "Permit me to observe, that in relation to the scenes of intoxication and vice at Prairie des Chiens, neither the Agent at that place, or the Officer in command, has the power to prevent the sale of spirits to the Indians; that being a Town and settlement without the Indian limits, over which the Government and Laws of Michigan Territory are extended, and where the Laws in relation to that subject are but little regarded by the civil authority at that place."[29] At this time Cass was still the governor of Michigan Territory.

Still another excuse was soon found for introducing liquor into the Indian country. "Whisky," wrote George Boyd in 1830, referring to a practice then long established, "is allowed in small quantities to each Outfit for the use of the Engagés or men Employed in the laborious part of the Trade, with an explicit assurance that no part of the same be given under any pretences to Indians."[30] It may easily be imagined how well this assurance was carried out.

The result was that the Indian country was flooded with liquor. Colonel Josiah Snelling, the commanding officer of the fort of that name, is the author of a classic description of the evils of the trade. Taking up the plea that "our traders cannot enter into successful competition with the British traders without it [liquor]," he replied, concisely and accurately, "If the sales of whisky could be restricted to the vicinity of the British line, the mischief would be comparatively trivial, but if permitted *at all*, no limits can be set to it." He gave a graphic and disgusting account of the scenes caused by the traffic at Prairie du Chien, Mackinac, and Green Bay, but again stated, "If the evil could be confined to the places I have mentioned, it would be of little importance." His opinion, allegedly based on admissions of traders themselves, was that certain Indian agents on the Lakes were conniving at "spreading it through all those extensive regions within the American boundaries," and that they were thus going beyond even the liberal construction which had been put officially or semiofficially on the already badly mangled act of 1822. Apparently section four in the act of 1824, providing for the location of all traders at specific places, had availed little or nothing to make the restriction of the liquor trade more easy.

It seems that Colonel Snelling was correct in believing that intoxicants were entering the Indian country in considerable quantities and with the tacit consent of certain Indian agents. It also seems that the American Fur Company was almost certainly the greatest offender in this respect. Colonel Snelling himself stated:

> The present year there has been delivered to the Agent of the North American fur company at Mackinac, (by contract,) three thousand, three hundred gallons of whisky, and two thousand, five hundred of high wines. The practice of using high wines is a favorite one with the traders, as it saves transportation, and the quantity of liquor can be increased at pleasure. . . . I will venture to add that an enquiry into the manner in which the Indian trade is conducted, and especially by the N American fur company is a matter of no small importance to the tranquillity of the borders.[31]

It is evident that Snelling did not exaggerate the amount of liquor delivered to the Company at Mackinac, for a few years later something over 5,000 gallons came to be the smallest amount ever delivered to the Company's outfits there in one year.[32]

Apropos of Snelling's comment on the reason for the favored position of "high wines," a parenthetical statement may be inserted as to the fashion in which this intoxicant could be "increased at pleasure." Chief Pokagon, who had been familiar with the fur trade, made this statement.

> "Let me tell you," he said, "some things I have seen at some of our trading posts; even Mackinaw, where Astor got rich and we very poor. The most profitable trade and the most ruinous trade Mackinaw ever had was in whisky." He then gave the formula . . . used on Mackinaw island 1817–18, for making whisky for the Indians. Actual cost not to exceed five cents a gallon and retailed to the Indians for fifty cents a bottle, of which thousands of bottles were sold every year. . . . Take two gallons of common whisky or unrectified spirits [high wines], add to thirty gallons

of water and to this add red pepper enough to make it fiery and tobacco enough to make it intoxicating, and you have a decation that will cause the Indian to give everything he possesses into the hands of the white man.[33]

There is reason to believe that not all this liquor delivered to Robert Stuart at Mackinac was used on the Canadian border nor for the refreshment of the Company's employees. The unenviable reputation acquired by Joseph Rolette and William Aitkin, of the Upper Mississippi and Fond du Lac outfits, respectively, as brazen traffickers in liquor has already been described.[34] The seizure on the Wabash of liquor belonging to the Company by the Indian agent, Major Tipton, is a case in point. This episode, which has been previously mentioned, took place in 1824. Its sequel was of sufficient importance to invite further examination. Tipton later declared: "From the time of my comeing into the agency complaints were frequently [interlineated: made] to me of the improper conduct of the Clerks of the [American] fur Company . . . as soon as they arrived among the Indians of this agency this fall I was informed of thier selling liquor . . . of which I have ample proof." He consequently reported the Astorian William H. Wallace, who was one of the clerks involved. When William B. Astor heard of this action, early in 1824, he wrote to Tipton, assuring him that there must be some mistake and demanding an investigation, to which letter Tipton made no reply. In September, 1824, Tipton made the seizure already mentioned; and, when William B. Astor heard of it, he tried to secure the release, on bond, of the goods among which the liquor had been found, which thereby were forfeited to the government. A few weeks later, William B. Astor, aroused by the report that Tipton had made another seizure, wrote to the secretary of War accusing Tipton of being "more actuated by a desire to injure our Company than to discharge his duty to the public faithfully." Tipton defended his conduct and the motives behind it in letters to the secretary of War, and early in 1825 the goods were condemned. An appeal was taken by the Company and attempts to have the goods released on bond continued. Robert Stuart insisted that the liquor seized on the Wabash had not been intended for the Indians, though without giving any particular evidence for his assertion. The agents of the Company displayed little further energy in this cause, however, until John Jacob Astor returned from Europe in 1826. Upon his arrival the situation speedily changed. There was now a secretary of War in office who had not been in charge when the Fort Wayne case first came up, and upon Astor's application to him that the goods be given up on bond to prevent their complete destruction, which petition was backed by a personal letter from Albert Gallatin, praising Astor's patriotism and public spirit as manifested in the Astoria enterprise, an order was procured, in July, 1826, that the goods should be released to the Company, satisfactory security being given.[35] As we have seen in a previous chapter, Astor did not despair of ultimately obtaining possession of the goods without conditions, and in view of the personal and political influence he had demonstrated himself as possessing thus far in the case his sanguine attitude may be understood.

The attack on the American Fur Company for liquor-selling which Colonel Snelling had made late in August, 1825, was followed up early in the next month by a letter which asserted: "I have been informed from good authority, that . . . a merchant of this place [Detroit] has sold them [the American Fur Company] two hundred barrels [of whiskey] this present season." Robert Stuart replied to these accusations in February, 1826, in a letter to the secretary of War. According to him, the American Fur Company was in possession of three-fourths of the Missouri trade, and any liquor brought in by the Missouri route must pass Fort Snelling, where Colonel Snelling was in charge. He declared that it was difficult to introduce liquor by way of the Sault Ste. Marie, and asserted that, at any rate, the liquor at Mackinac was not intended for the Indians. Colonel Snelling was accused of having given personal testimony to the rectitude of the Company through his attempt to procure his son a job with it. Stuart's refutation of Snelling's charges was supported by Adam D. Steuart, collector at Mackinac, who, as we have seen, combined his duties as a government official with those of a special agent for the Company on occasion. Steuart testified that the strict inspection at the Sault Ste. Marie made it impossible to use liquor on the St. Peter's River and in the Lake Superior region. He, too, asserted that the spirits imported by way of Mackinac were intended for Mackinac and Green Bay and were not sold to the Indians, save a little on the border. Both Stuart and Steuart coolly ignored the question of where the drunken Indians seen by Snelling at Mackinac, Green Bay, and Prairie du Chien had obtained the facilities for intoxication.

These aspersions upon his veracity and powers of observation naturally aroused Colonel Snelling's ire. The agents and allies of the American Fur Company insisted that its traders could not have brought liquor into the Indian country. To Colonel Snelling the best answer to this insistence was to prove that, regardless of possibilities, they had actually done so, and the best proof would be the seizure in the Indian country of liquor in the possession of Company agents. Consequently, it was not long until word reached the New York office that Colonel Snelling was sending out troops to examine Company trading posts. Had all the officials of the Company been as sure as Robert Stuart that their consignments of Indian goods were free from liquor, this news would have caused little perturbation. On the contrary, it resulted in John Jacob Astor himself writing an extraordinary letter to the secretary of War in which it was requested that Company goods among which liquor was found should be released on bond. In support of this request Astor informed the secretary that the capital of the Company was $600,000, and that under his predecessor the commandants had been ordered "not to interfere with the Indian traders." The secretary was further informed that a verdict of $5,000 had been obtained against Lieutenant-Colonel Chambers for his activities against the Company's agents in 1817, and it was strongly hinted that further suits might be brought in view of the prejudice against the Company manifested by such government officials as Snelling and Taliaferro. Astor's letter had the desired effect, and on May 29, 1826, McKenney wrote to Clark at St. Louis that the president had ordered him to release any property which might be seized on bond, so that the furs might not spoil. On the same day he wrote to Astor that he hoped no liquor would be found, but that, if it were, the property might be released on bond. The anxiety manifested by Astor on learning that the Company posts were to be searched for liquor is significant.[36]

For ten years after the passage of the law of 1822 no particular change of attitude toward the liquor traffic appeared among the Company's policies. The agents continued to run liquor into the Indian country under the usual subterfuges, or without any explanation whatsoever, and continued to attack all over-zealous Indian agents who took exception to this highhanded procedure. Something of the situation during this period is indicated by such items as a letter from Robert Stuart to Auguste Grignon in 1829 stating that the Indian agent (whether at Mackinac or Green Bay is not specified) would allow Grignon to take ten gallons of whiskey per man into the Indian country, but warning him to beware of the less agreeable Major Twiggs at the Portage,[37] and an invoice of fifty-five barrels of whiskey ("enough to half drown all the Indians you deal with"[38]) shipped by Stuart in 1831 to Porlier and Grignon at Green Bay.[39] Of greater importance are the records which indicate the quantity of liquor delivered to the various outfits

at Mackinac Island. In 1830, for example, wine, brandy, and
shrub, but principally whiskey and high wines, to the amount
of 5,985 gallons were delivered to the various outfits of the
Northern Department; in the next year this quantity was increased to 6,173¼ gallons; in 1832 it rose to 8,776 gallons. The
small quantities of wine, brandy, and shrub in the above invoices may have been intended for the consumption of *bourgeois* and clerks, but the whiskey and high wines were undoubtedly for sale to the natives. If any proof is required for this
statement, I may mention a very unusual entry by a certain
trader showing the specific destination of part of his goods,
which revealed that he had sold eight gallons of high wine, or
practically pure alcohol, to an Indian.[40]

Late in 1829 William B. Astor, then president of the American Fur Company, did make an effort to form an agreement
with the Hudson's Bay Company for the exclusion of liquor
from the territory along the border. In a letter of December 15,
1829, to James Keith, a chief factor of the Hudson's Bay Company, he stated that the people of the American Fur Company
should "not in the future, either directly or indirectly, carry in,
or in any way give ardent spirits to the Indians of that region,
or vicinity; provided the Honbl[e]. The Hudson Bay C[o]. pledge
themselves to the same effect." In case of such an agreement
"the United States Indian Agent at the Sault de S[te]. Marie,
has promised that . . . he will not permit any individual traders to take Liquor into the country under any pretence whatever." This letter was communicated to the Governor and
Committee of the Hudson's Bay Company at London, and on
March 3 the secretary wrote to William B. Astor a rather stiff
and frigid note in which he stated:

The Governor and Committee have this Season confirmed and repeated
the orders given last year by Gov[r] Simpson, that in the event of the American Traders discontinuing the practice, those in the Service of the Company should do the same; But the Governor and Committee do not feel

justified in leaving their trading Posts on the Frontier totally deprived of Spirits, at the same time I am directed to assure you, that the Governor and Committee have the means of strictly enforcing the instructions given to their Traders; the discontinuance of the Practice will therefore entirely depend on the conduct of the American traders, to which I am to call your attention.[41]

This suggestion of a vague and qualified prohibition of liquor, the entire responsibility for initiating such a program to be thrown upon the American company, was manifestly an unfair and unequal arrangement, and William B. Astor evidently decided that its uncertainty was too great to warrant a test of its results. So matters continued for another two years as they had been for ten or more.

As an indication of how little the situation had changed during the past decade, a letter from Robert Stuart to George B. Porter, governor of Michigan, is worthy of note. This letter, which was dated July 6, 1832, stated that the Company intended.

to extend our posts of trade, this season along the boundary line to the west of Red River; this will require the establishment of *three* new posts, exclusive of the *four* we now have on that frontier, which will enable us to engross all the trade within the limits of our own Territory; but . . . this is impracticable unless he [William A. Aitkin, the agent of the Company] be permitted to take in An additional quantity of ardent spirits; say as much for each of the new posts, as is allowed by the War department, for each of the four old ones: . . . that is, two barrels for each post — making in all 14 barrels — believe me Sir [went on Stuart plaintively], that it is not because we wish to give liquor to the Indians, I make the present request; but thro' sheer necessity — for the British Hudson Bay Company carry in large quantities all along our frontier: and unless our people have *a little*, to induce the Indians to visit them, we will not only lose the trade; but all the influence we have hitherto managed to retain over the frontier tribes

— an appeal to that emotion which Dr. Johnson has described in such an uncomplimentary fashion. In a postscript Stuart continued, with the intention of indicating the comparative righteousness of the Company's agents: "Our traders of Lake

Superior, have taken no liquor for the last two years; but the people of Prairie du Chien, St. Peters and Green Bay, having found this out, send large quantities into the Chippawa Country so that the Indians are but little benefitted by the exertions of Mr. Schoolcraft, even combined with that of our people, to keep away this bane of Indians."[42]

This accusation against the traders of Prairie du Chien, St. Peter's, and Green Bay may be balanced against one of Colonel Snelling's charges against the American Fur Company traders and the traders from Mackinac generally, that through the connivance of Indian agents they were supplied with liquor, while the traders from St. Louis, who supplied some of these posts on the Upper Mississippi, had their boats strictly searched at Fort Snelling and were thus put at a disadvantage in the commercial competition.[43] Of course it is rather doubtful whether the Company's Lake Superior traders were as innocent of trading in liquor during "the last two years" as Robert Stuart asserted. True, the Sault Ste. Marie invoices for 1831 and 1832 contain no reference to liquor, and no Chippewa or Lake Superior outfits for the same years are mentioned. However, the Lake Superior outfit received 463 gallons of liquor in 1830, while the outfit of Fond du Lac — the one with which Aitkin was associated — had been furnished with 434½ gallons in 1831 and 478 gallons in 1832.[44] It is, therefore, doubtful whether the region of Lake Superior was so free from Company liquor as Stuart wished Governor Porter to believe.[45] At any rate Stuart's request came too late, for in that very month Congress was to pass another and a more stringent law against the introduction of liquor into the Indian country. This we shall consider later.

This survey of the American Fur Company's policy toward the liquor trade with the Indians has been illustrated almost entirely with incidents occurring in that portion of the Company's territory which was known, after 1822, as the Northern

Department. It might be well also to examine conditions in the Western Department. The situation there was practically the same as in the Great Lakes and Upper Mississippi area, save that smuggling and other devices for evading the law were probably even more rife, owing to the less settled character of the country and the necessity felt by the Upper Missouri Outfit of winning over the powerful and usually hostile Blackfeet from the strong British influence by which they had so long been dominated. One of the favorite devices was to secure permission to take along liquor for the use of boatmen, and to pad the list with the names of all the employees anywhere in the country. As each boatman was allowed one gill per day for twelve months, one can imagine how much alcohol could reach the Indians by this subterfuge. Pierre Chouteau, Jr., in 1828, wrote to Kenneth McKenzie of having utilized this method.[46] The guilelessness of certain officials of the Indian Bureau seems to have still further opened up the Indian country to intoxicants. The superintendent of Indian Affairs at St. Louis, on November 20, 1831, wrote to Lewis Cass that, "relying on their [the traders'] good faith, it was not deemed necessary to examine their outfit [for liquor]." The result was that thousands of gallons of alcohol passed by Fort Leavenworth into the Indian country. It was doubtless such conduct as this which led Andrew S. Hughes in 1831 to report to the secretary of War, Lewis Cass, that "the agents and engagees of the American Fur Trade Company [sic] . . . entertain, as I know to be the fact, no sort of respect for our citizens, agents, officers or the Government, or its laws or general policy." His chief accusation concerned the amount of alcohol illegally employed in the trade, and he estimated that on the Missouri River alone, that year, a clear gain of $50,000 had been made in selling whiskey at $25 to $50 per gallon.[47]

In 1832 a new bill was presented, intended completely to

seal up the many legal rat-holes by which liquor had been allowed to stream into the Indian country. It provided "that
no ardent spirits shall be hereafter introduced, under any pretence, into the Indian country."[48] In other words, the law of
1822 had provided that liquor should be excluded; the law of
1832 was to state that liquor should really be excluded. Certainly such a law was needed. That of 1822 had been so riddled
with exceptions that it could be said: "No distinct, substantial
provision, forbidding the introduction of spirituous liquors into
the Indian country, exists in our statute book."[49]

It is interesting and perhaps regrettable to note that John
Jacob Astor, who had begun his career in the American Fur
Company in 1810 by forbidding his agents on the Columbia to
give spirits to the Indians, should now, a score of years later,
for the first and only time so far as I can discover, have definitely exerted his great personal influence against this anti-
liquor law. Ordinarily such matters were handled by his subordinates, but now in a letter to Congressman W. H. Ashley,
formerly of the Rocky Mountain fur trade, he stated: "If the
Hudson's Bay Company did not employ ardent spirits against
us, we would not ask for a single drop. But without it competition is hopeless." At the same time he admitted that in competition between American traders "the uniform and complete
enforcement of such a law will be beneficial both to the Indians
and the traders." However, in this crisis even Lewis Cass, who
as the secretary of War felt better able to take a strong stand
for the welfare of the Indians than he could as the governor of
Michigan Territory, deserted the Company, and the bill became a law. Robert Stuart and Ramsay Crooks attempted to
secure some relaxation of its stringency on the Canadian border
through Lewis Cass, but in this they failed, though the secretary of War consented to ask the president and the secretary
of State to do all in their power to have the British also ban

liquor on their side of the line, and promised to take steps to enforce the law against the Company's rivals on the Upper Mississippi.[50]

We have observed that the prohibitory act of 1822 did not actually prohibit. We may now ask whether the far more stringent law of a decade later worked any better, at least so far as checking the American Fur Company's liquor trade was concerned. There is little doubt that in the Northern Department the amount of liquor taken into the Indian country was considerably decreased by the passage of this law, though it was by no means entirely cut off. For example, in 1832 liquor to the amount of 8,776 gallons was delivered at Mackinac to ten outfits; in 1833, after the passage of the new law, the quantity turned over to the same number of outfits had decreased to $5,573\frac{1}{4}$ gallons,[51] a decline of more than 3,000 gallons, or about 40 per cent. Still it is obvious that the Indians did not have to go entirely thirsty.

It was in the Western Department that the most desperate methods of resistance to the law were taken by Company agents. Some of these we have already touched upon. In 1832, for example, J. P. Cabanné, a partner in the Company, illegally seized upon and confiscated liquor belonging to an opposition trader who had been permitted to take 250 gallons of alcohol into the Indian country just before the promulgation of the new law. The opposition trader, Leclerc, later collected damages. In the next year, Kenneth McKenzie, in charge of the Company's Upper Missouri Outfit, determined that he must have liquor to combat the Sublette & Campbell opposition. Crooks, who had taken the high ground that, once the law had been passed, he "would . . . rather abandon the trade, than violate the statute," urged McKenzie to abandon both the plans which he had formed for this purpose. McKenzie, however, paid no attention, and when an attempt to smuggle liquor had failed, he decided to carry out the alternative measure and distil liquor in the Indian country with corn to be grown there. Thus he thought to evade the law of 1832, apparently not knowing or caring that there was a law of 1815 which forbade such a procedure. The distillery worked well, but a rival trader reported it to the government, and it took all the ingenuity of McKenzie and Pierre Chouteau to prevent the Company from being barred from the Indian trade. The still, according to their account, belonged to one of McKenzie's friends in Canada; on the way to its owner it had been set up and used to manufacture "wine" from the "fruits of the country" more for amusement than for any other purpose. At times it also seemed that a scientific purpose lay behind the distillery. The only thing certain was that it had nothing whatsoever to do with the Indian trade! By dint of hard pleading to the Company's old friend, Lewis Cass, the matter was patched up, but the affair ended McKenzie's usefulness to the Company.[52]

In 1833, William B. Astor, the president of the American Fur Company, wrote to Lewis Cass stating that the Hudson's Bay Company, in addition to the advantage they enjoyed of being able to import goods from England without duty, also made "unlimited use of spirituous Liquors," which, he said, "is a curse to them (the Indians), and an injury to the trade." Hitherto, he said, the American Fur Company had been allowed to import a limited amount of liquor for competitive purposes, but this privilege had been abolished by the new law. The result would be to stifle competition unless liquor was excluded everywhere. Cass was urged to petition the president to persuade the British government to prohibit the use of liquor by the Hudson's Bay Company. William B. Astor concluded by painting a gloomy picture of the results of the use of liquor among the Indians, and declared that the American Fur Company used it only in self-defence.[53] From the reaction of the Hudson's Bay Company to his earlier attempt at the exclusion of liquor from the border, there would seem to have been some truth in William B. Astor's statement. Astor withdrew from the fur trade in 1834; this indeed seems to have been the last public statement on the subject by a representative of the Company under his control.

The policy of John Jacob Astor toward the sale of liquor to the Indians, as developed through the history of his American Fur Company, was, then, very largely the result of his commanding financial position in the fur trade. If liquor could have been entirely excluded from the Indian country, Astor's business would not have suffered, but would rather have improved, owing to the favorable position in which his large capital placed him as compared with individual traders and small companies. But there was a certain element in the fur trade who would always insist on using liquor; and in addition to this factor, Astor's policy of price-cutting forced other more honorable traders to employ intoxicants as a means of defence against his capital. At first Astor made an attempt to meet this menace by urging strict enforcement of the laws against liquor; but soon he himself plunged into the game of law violation, and, by his large capital and strong influence with the government, succeeded in beating his rivals both at his own game of price-cutting and at theirs of rum-selling. To such lengths did Astor's agents go that the American Fur Company gained an unenviable reputation for lawlessness among Indian agents, army officers, and others connected with the Indian Bureau. It is possible that if Astor had been as energetic in endeavoring to bar liquor from both sides of the Canadian boundary as he was in securing liquor for his agents on that border, and had used as much influence in securing the strict enforcement of the liquor law by Indian agents upon his rivals as he used in himself circumventing the regulation, he might not have been forced to contribute to a condition which he probably found very distasteful. But the policy he did adopt was simple, direct, ingenious, and effective, and therefore altogether in harmony with his character as evidenced by past achievements.[54]

We have observed how under the direction of John Jacob Astor the American Fur Company moved westward from Mackinac Island, during the years between 1817 and 1834, crushing and absorbing the independent traders and the less formidable fur companies, buying out or forming alliances with their more dangerous rivals, establishing a Western Department with headquarters at St. Louis in 1822, entering the Rocky Mountain fur trade in 1830, bringing into play all the weapons of price-cutting, large quantities of liquor, and political influence to overwhelm their opponents. It is obvious that this steady policy of expansion was founded to a great extent upon the profits acquired through the fur trade, and was inspired by the prospects of even greater gains in the future. Some consideration of these profits and of some of the general business policies from which they resulted is essential to an understanding of the American Fur Company and John Jacob Astor's connection with it.

It must always be remembered that John Jacob Astor in his own proper person was, to a very large extent, the American Fur Company. He it was who furnished every cent of the capital used in carrying on the business of the Northern Department (the territory occupied by the Company as first established), and he it was who took the profit or loss on 90 out of the 100 shares of stock in the original Company. His agents, Ramsay Crooks and Robert Stuart, each had five shares, in addition to their salaries of $2,500 and $2,000 per year. In the Western Department, however, and especially after the alliance with Bernard Pratte & Co. and the Columbia Fur Company, part of the funds employed in carrying on the trade probably came from Astor's partners, since the proportion in which Bernard Pratte & Co. were interested, namely, one-half of the Department's business, was larger than would have been conferred on a mere agent, who furnished no capital. It was John Jacob Astor, or the firm of John Jacob Astor & Son, who purchased the goods used in the Indian trade and who disposed of the furs for which these goods were bartered. In other words, every piece of merchandise, every fur, used in or derived from the Indian trade passed through the hands of John Jacob Astor or the firm of John Jacob Astor & Son.

Despite the steady expansion of the American Fur Company, which must have been based on the profits of the trade, Astor for a long time steadfastly insisted upon the bad state of the business. It might be expected that at first the business would not be particularly profitable, and early in 1818 Ramsay Crooks admitted that matters bore a "very reproving aspect."[55] Early in 1824, Astor, referring to the agreement which had ended on March 16, 1821, said, "I am sorry to see so great a loss to be sustained by the concern of 1817 which I fear will prove still more when the sales of furs are received." Later in the year he repeated:

I hope that some of the debts due to the old concern will have been collected as well as of that of 21 or we shall make a business rather worse than I even contemplated. I am sorry to see that so large a sum of money is likely to be lost by our former concern, the more I see of it, the more I am convinced that we have even [ever] imported too many goods and been induced to give them too freely to people who are not able to pay for them the less so, when skins and furs are so very cheap, but even in years when they sold *we* we [*sic*] made to say nothing by the trade our expenses have been too great and we had too much Dead Capital on hand.

Late in the year he stated to Crooks, "you have always been too sanguine as to the result of our trade, I am sure that to this day it has not paid interest for the money. Our old concerns will prove very bad ones." This same tone continued in the next spring, though prospects for the future seemed to Astor slightly more promising.[56]

In 1828, William Clark, the Indian superintendent at St. Louis, and Lewis Cass, the governor of Michigan Territory, in a letter which advocated placing American fur traders on an equality with the British by means of a duty on furs or a drawback on goods sent into the Indian country, spoke of the uncertain character of the Indian trade and asserted: "We are satisfied that the average profits of the fur trade are not in proportion to the enterprise and skill required to prosecute it and to the risk attending it. We believe it is conducted upon as fair principles as other branches of business in the United States, and we know many of the persons engaged in it, who are honorable, intelligent men."[57] John Jacob Astor himself in the following year wrote to Benton:

> I very much fear, that unless a duty is imposed on foreign furs, the American Fur Company, the only respectable one of any capital now existing in the country, will be obliged to suspend their operations. I believe I am safe when I say that all our Indian traders for these 20 years past, with very few exceptions, have been losing time and property in that trade. . . . The American Fur Company have for years past, and do now employ a capital of a million or more of dollars. They have not yet been able to declare a dividend. . . . The Hudson Bay Company divide 10 per cent. per annum, and have a large surplus on hand. Their stock is at a premium of 150 per cent. above par.[58]

Of course Astor's statement can hardly be taken at face value, since it is the inevitable convention for a company applying for government assistance to insist upon its extreme poverty. It may help us to check Astor's estimate of conditions in the fur trade if we give some attention to what various contemporary authorities on the fur trade had to say concerning the profits in that business. We have already noted that William Clark and Lewis Cass tended to support Astor in his assertion of the fur trade's unprofitable condition. But not all who were qualified to judge agreed with Clark and Cass on this point. John Dougherty, the Indian agent at Leavenworth, wrote to William Clark in the fall of 1831, estimating that in "the Fur Trade on the Missouri and its waters, including the Rocky Mountains, commencing 1815, and ending 1830," the "total amount of expenditures" had been $2,100,000 and the returns in furs had come to $3,750,000. "Profit brought down" amounted to $1,650,000, or something over $100,000 per year. To put it in another way, the profits in the trade had amounted to only a little less than half the value of the returns.[59] Joshua Pilcher, an experienced Missouri River fur trader, commenting upon the above estimate, stated: "This was a random guess on his [Dougherty's] part, and the returns may have greatly exceeded that amount; possibly they may have fell short of it, if they could be correctly ascertained." It seems clear, however, despite the caution of this statement, that Pilcher inclined to the belief that Dougherty had underestimated the profits.[60]

It will be remembered that Astor did not actually enter the Missouri River fur trade till 1822; but, when he did so, his Company made a speedy conquest of that territory, culminating in the arrangements of 1827 with Bernard Pratte & Co., the Columbia Fur Company, and Collier & Powell. Pilcher said on this subject:

About this time [1823], the American Fur Company had turned their attention to the Missouri trade, and, as might have been expected, soon put an end to all opposition. Backed as it was by any amount of capital, and with skilful agents to conduct its affairs at *every point*, it succeeded, by the year 1827, in monopolizing the whole trade of the Indians on the Missouri, and has maintained that monopoly up to this time, and I have but little doubt will continue to do so for years to come, as it would be rather a hazardous business to small adventurers to rise in opposition to it.[61]

In 1831 Thomas Forsyth wrote: "This trade [the fur trade of the Missouri] continues to be monopolized by the American Fur Company."[62] It is evident that during the last three years of the period covered by Dougherty's figures practically all the returns from the Missouri River had been on the account of the American Fur Company. These annual returns, in view of the elimination of competition, were probably higher, on the average, than the annual average for the entire period.

Dougherty's estimate of these profits, of course, pertained only to the Western Department. A somewhat similar estimate has been given for the Northern Department. George Boyd, the Indian agent at Mackinac, said that in 1826 "the sum of $67,408.07 was forwarded to the Indian Country" in trade-goods, while the "Amount of furs & peltries brought yearly to this Island, are supposed to be worth from 250 to 300,000 dollars — nineteen twentieths of the same being for and on account of the American Fur Co. —"[63] We can check his estimate of the trade-goods to a certain extent by use of a later invoice book, which reveals that in 1831 goods valued at Mackinac at $82,593.50 were sent into the Indian country by the Company. Probably, then, Boyd's judgment was not very far out of line with the facts. In the Northern Department there were also 400 or 500 *engagés* who received something like $100 each per year and whose wages must have been added to the trade-goods as a large component of the annual investment.[64] Let us say, then, that in the Northern Department $125,000 was expended annually for trade-goods and wages, and returns of $250,000 or $300,000 in furs were received. This would make the profits conform to Dougherty's standard, that is, they would equal about half the returns. Dougherty's estimate made the annual value of the Western Department's furs amount to $250,000; Boyd estimated the Northern Department's returns as about the same: taking the judgment of these men together, the annual profits on the trade for both areas would come to something over $200,000. William B. Astor also made an estimate upon the same subject. Late in 1831 he wrote: "The capital we annually employ in the trade of the interior . . . is . . . upwards of one million of dollars," thus agreeing with his father's statement of 1829. He went on, "You may . . . estimate our annual returns at about half a million of dollars."[65] In other words, William B. Astor, George Boyd, and John Dougherty, making independent estimates from locations on the Missouri River, at Mackinac, and in New York, reached fundamentally the same conclusions as to the volume of business.

Unfortunately, the books of the American Fur Company kept at the New York office, the only ones which could give us information concerning the profits of the whole business, have been destroyed. We do, however, have some definite information as to profits in Astor's personal letter book, in which, writing to Robert Stuart, he said: "On settlement in April 1830, a dividend was paid you on that concern [the one known as no. 3, running from April 1, 1823, to April 1, 1827] of $450 per share profit, being an estimated profit of $450,000, on the Capital." The capital stock amounted to $300,000. This dividend, it seems, should actually have been somewhat smaller. Evidently, then, the actual dividend declared for these four years was something over $100,000 per year, or about 10 per cent on the actual capital employed, the same as that which Astor had described as being annually divided by the Hudson's Bay Company. He also wrote: "The amount of profits realized [in the concern known as no. 4, April 1, 1827–June, 1834] appears to be $845,593$\frac{14}{100}$ less $191,864$\frac{24}{}$ Notes & not yet paid say $653,729$\frac{10}{100}$," indicating that the profits from number 4 would, if realized, be in proportion approximately the same as those from number 3.[66]

Although Astor received the lion's share of these dividends, declared for the period from 1823 to 1834, this was not the only income he derived from the American Fur Company. In the first place, he received interest on the capital furnished by him, which capital for much of the time amounted to more than a million dollars. This in itself was a considerable item. Astor was also responsible for furnishing the goods employed in the trade. It is probable that he did not make a profit on their sale to the Company which he headed, since such a practice was forbidden in the articles of agreement both of the Pacific Fur Company and of the South West Fur Company. However, we know of no provision which would have prohibited his doing this if he had chosen. Chittenden assumes that he did, and says definitely: "They [the goods] were generally furnished by Mr. Astor at a fixed advance upon cost and charges."[67]

From New York the goods were shipped in the spring to Mackinac and St. Louis, in the latter case usually by way of New Orleans,[68] and from these headquarters were given out to the various outfits at an advance which was supposed to cover the cost of transportation from England to New York and from New York to the fur country. At Mackinac this advance was, in 1830, $83\frac{1}{2}$ per cent on the "sterling cost of blankets, strouds, and other English goods,"[69] and $13\frac{1}{2}$ per cent on articles purchased in New York City. William B. Astor said that nearly all the woolens, cutlery, and other goods used by the American Fur Company, except the gunpowder, were imported from Europe.[70] These advances varied somewhat. In 1833 the advance on the sterling cost of goods dropped sharply from 81 per cent to 70 per cent. The advance on New York prices remained more nearly constant, the low point being 13 per cent. To the whole sum, cost plus advance, was added a commission of 5 per cent, and it was with this total amount that the clerk or trader employed by the Company was charged.[71] We shall elsewhere consider the various classes of traders receiving goods from the Company, and the different policies adopted toward them at certain times in the organization's history.

In the following spring, a year after the goods had been shipped to the fur country, the furs for which they had been traded were brought to the departmental headquarters and the profits or losses of the outfits were decided. The traders, of course, received credit for the furs at the Mackinac price, rather than the price they would bring in New York. William

Johnston, son of the fur trader John Johnston and brother-in-law of Henry Rowe Schoolcraft, said: "on the receipt of the Furs they [the fur company's agents] generally gave what they thought proper for them; this is at the outfitting-post, at which places, they seldom have any one to compete with, on the prices for the furs, on which they calculate to make as much profit, as they did on the merchandize."[72] From this circumstance, as well as from the heavy advances on the cost price of goods through the charges and the commission,[73] it frequently happened that the prices of furs at Mackinac fell short of the invoice price of the goods for which they had been bartered, and a book loss resulted, whereas actually the Company was not a loser.

These furs, then, were shipped to New York to John Jacob Astor or to the firm of John Jacob Astor & Son, for sale in the city [74] or for exportation. From a memorandum it appears that between March 1, 1818, and March 1, 1823, furs to the amount of $842,419.16 were sold by Astor in New York.[75] From 1818 to 1822, furs invoiced at $499,489.06 were shipped to Europe and to Canton,[76] and between 1822 and 1824 furs valued at $247,923.84 were also sent abroad.[77] During these two periods, foreign shipments brought about losses of $58,858.41 and $22,167, respectively. Of course these were not necessarily real losses, since the peltries were invoiced at what seemed a suitable value, and the low price paid for them in merchandise helped to cover any apparent loss. However, from 1824 to 1829 foreign shipments began to bring paper profits. During that period furs were sold abroad for $544,829.87 at a profit of $20,596.19, most of which began to accrue from the beginning of 1826 on.[78] But no matter whether fur sales, at home and abroad, showed a profit or not, Astor was entitled to a commission of $2\frac{1}{2}$ per cent on all furs sold. Many years later a claim was made against his estate by Crooks and Stuart, on the charge that Astor had based his commission on the invoice price rather than on the sales price of certain shipments.

William B. Astor once estimated the annual returns of the Company at $500,000 per year, which would mean a commission to Astor of $12,500 on sales, and helped to swell his income from interest and dividends. There was a chance for profit, too, in Astor's taking to his own account furs at New York at the market rate and holding them for a rise or sending them abroad for his own benefit. We know, for example, that he did ship 2,190 fox skins to Canton on the *Enterprise* in 1820, while this ship is not mentioned in the list of vessels carrying furs on the Company's account.[79] We also know that he sometimes took to himself funds derived from the sale of furs, allowing the Company interest, and invested this money in goods for the account of his own firm.[80] He also received benefits in the way of freights when furs belonging to the Company were exported in his ships. Of course an estimate, in a case of this kind, when only scattered pieces of material are available, is rather risky. It is likely that Astor did not make much money from the Company during the years between 1817 and 1823, though it is unlikely, in view of the heavy advances charged on goods, that he lost anything. But after 1823, and for more than a decade, we know that the Company did make profits and declared dividends of well over a million dollars. It seems safe to say that during his seventeen years as head of the American Fur Company Astor cleared in dividends, interest, commissions, etc., not less than a million dollars, and probably nearer two million.

For the time this was a large amount to be acquired in commerce. It might be well to inspect more closely the process by which this fortune was accumulated. Of course the profits were derived from selling furs for an amount much greater than the cost of the goods for which they had been bartered, but the exact source of this profit requires more careful consideration. In buying his trade-goods in London or New York, Astor had no great advantage over others; this was also true when he sold his furs in London, Hamburg, or Canton. His great opportunities for profit came in the Indian country. We have seen that at Mackinac Astor's agents made an advance on the cost price of goods purchased in London of about 80 per cent, and on that of goods bought in New York of 13 per cent, adding a commission of 5 per cent on the whole amount. These invoices were now ready to be dealt out to the heads of the various outfits.

Those to whom these goods were advanced, on credit, belonged to several different classes. Early in the history of the Company the trade had been carried on almost entirely by outfits operating on the account and at the risk of the Company. A historian of Mackinac Island has said: "the plan of the company was to arrange and secure the services of old traders and their voyageurs, who, at the (new) organization of the company were in the Indian country, depending on their influence and knowledge of the trade with the Indians; and as fast as possible secure the vast trade in the West and Northwest, within the district of the United States, interspersing the novices brought from Canada so as to consolidate, extend and monopolize, as far as possible, over the country, the Indian trade. The first two years they had succeeded in bringing into their employ seven-eighths of the old Indian traders on the Upper Mississippi, Wabash, and Illinois Rivers, Lakes Michigan and Superior, and their tributaries as far north as the boundaries of the United States extended. The other eighth thought that their interest was to remain independent; toward such the company selected their best traders, and located them in opposition, with instructions so to manage by underselling to bring them to terms."[81]

Of course under this early severe competition it was almost impossible to make profits. Consequently most of the outfits were handled by clerks on a salary of from $180 to $500 for the account and at the risk of the Company. If the year's trading resulted in a loss, the deficit was merely charged to profit and loss, the Company's agent reflecting that the goods had been invoiced at a rate so high that the loss was more nominal than real. In 1817 every outfit showed a loss, but the real sufferers were the two traders who had been indiscreet enough to take goods on shares. Consequently John Johnston and Alexis Luc Reaume found themselves charged with one-half the loss on the year's outfit. Johnston finally had to secure the amount charged to him by a mortgage on his Sault Ste. Marie property.[82] During the next year or so the salaried clerk still continued to be the principal figure in the trade, and two or three gains per year out of a dozen or so outfits were all that seemed to be expected. Only men of unusual ability, such as Russell Farnham and James H. Lockwood, found it at all profitable to trade on shares, receiving one-half the profit or being charged with the same proportion of loss.[83]

In the next few years, however, matters had somewhat changed. Price-cutting had driven many of the opposition traders out of business or into the ranks of the Company, and underselling, with its resultant losses, was no longer such a necessary weapon. Consequently profits became more possible. In 1823 ten outfits (exclusive of the retail store at the Island, which though classed as an outfit is really a unique case) were made up at Mackinac. Of these, five were for the account and at the risk of the Company, the others being managed by traders on shares. All of the outfits on shares proved more or less profitable, but two of those on the account of the Company met with a loss.

A third class of traders, receiving goods from the Company, had also appeared. These were men who had sufficient ability to attain some success in competition with the Company, but who had nevertheless been forced into a position of semidependence and had to purchase all their goods from the Company at the usual advances on the London and New York cost prices plus a profit of $33\frac{1}{3}$ per cent.[84] In some cases the free trader would agree to purchase half his goods from the American Fur Company and half from one of the Company's competitors, giving each "the preference in purchasing half of his furs," but being "at perfect liberty to sell them to the highest bidder, on payment in cash, [of] such advances as the respective parties may have made on his account."[85] But the Company did not enjoy the existence of even such semi-independent traders as these, and endeavored to reduce them to the position of complete dependence in which they would be required to take the whole of their goods from the Company and give the Company the refusal of all their returns. We have already observed John Lawe's complaints regarding the treatment of the Green Bay traders by the Company's agents.

The Company's aim, then, was to eliminate both the semi-independent trader and the salaried clerk, and conduct the business entirely on shares. By this arrangement the Company would secure three advantages: all the goods employed would be furnished and all the returns purchased by the Company; the outfits would be in the hands of men with a strong personal interest in their success; and half of any loss which might ensue would be charged to the traders. To attain this end the Company brought into play its usual methods. "It is believed to be the policy of the Company [to] control the Indian trade within the limits of the U. States —," wrote George Boyd, "Either by purchasing out any opposition which may at any time arise contrary to its interest — or by the mere power of money to Crush the individual trader. —"[86] Gurdon S. Hubbard, one of the earliest and most successful of American Fur Company traders, confirmed Boyd's opinion. "It was the policy of the American Fur Company," he wrote, "to monopolize the entire fur trade of the Northwest; and to this end they engaged fully nineteen-twentieths of all the traders of that territory; and with their immense capital and influence succeeded in breaking up the business of any trader who refused to enter their service."[87] By 1824, of the nine outfits made up at Mackinac, three were on the Company's exclusive account, two others were still furnished with part of their goods by one of the opposition companies, and two of the traders were of sufficient ability to secure the payment of a salary from the outfit in addition to their share of profits.[88] In the last years of Astor's connection with the Company, the typical outfit was managed on shares, with an occasional trader of outstanding ability receiving a salary in addition to his proportion of any profits which might appear. Only one or two outfits comparatively near to civilization were managed by salaried clerks.[89]

This virtual elimination of independent traders, and the subjection of those who had formerly occupied that position to the influence of the Company, were doubtless advantageous to that organization, but certainly constituted a distinct step-down for the traders. They now had to buy all their goods from the Company at whatever price the latter thought proper, and to receive credit for their returns on the same principle. Sometimes, indeed, they made a profit, but the next year might see a loss which would swallow up all their previous gains.

William Johnston, who was not only the son of an American Fur Company trader, the grandson of an Ojibway chief, and the brother-in-law of an Indian agent, but was also himself a clerk in the fur trade, and consequently entitled to speak with some authority, described in confused but unmistakably indignant tones the situation in which the traders found themselves under the Company's monopoly. He said: "eastern merchants . . . furnish goods or merchandize and all other necessary articles for the trade, at a certain per centage, with the priviledge of having the first refusal of the furs obtained." The system of advances has already been described. Johnston continued:

They [the eastern merchants] had to receive half of the profits made on the outfits, and on the receipt of the Furs they generally gave what they thought proper for them; this is at the outfitting post, at which places, they seldom have any one to compete with, on the prices for the furs, on which they calculate to make as much profit, as they did on the merchandize.[90] At these exorbitant charges, the traders were through necessity compelled to take the merchandize, the consequence was, and is still; that for them to pay for the goods, and barely to obtain a livelihood; they are in part compelled to use fraud and deceit towards the men they have in their employ; but the whole weight of this extortion, fraud and deceit falls on the poor Indians. All the blame attached to the manner in which the fur trade has been conducted, and in which it is still carried; and the baneful effects of which it has been the cause; first to the Indians in keeping them destitute from any moral good . . . in place of it they have been taught to practice fraud and deceit, in fact all the vices of the whites they have imbibed; and to crown the efforts of the trader, to cheat them more completely he brings to his aid ardent Spirits . . . which has sent, more to the grave . . . then [sic] all the wars they have waged with the whites, or among themselves, even sickness and decease added to it. . . . Next comes the men employed in the trade, they feel its effects; but they also can be allowed an excuse, which is ignorance and which those who employ them take advantage of. They will have to lead always a life of want and dissipation, as long as the present system of trade is followed. The trader feels the effects more keenly, he sees the ruination of his character, health and fortune; but circumstances are such that he cannot remedy the evil, and their brightest prospects are crumbled in the dust; and many promising young men, have been driven to dissipation, from which it is impossible to extricate themselves. the blame rests on the heads of the principals, and they will have to answer for it some day or other.[91]

By "the principals," of course, he meant the "eastern merchants," that is, so far as our purpose is concerned, John Jacob Astor.

At a much later date, Reuben Gold Thwaites stated the situation more concisely when he wrote:

The American monopoly [the American Fur Company] . . . merely outfitted its traders, charging them the highest market price for goods, and taking over their furs at rates that made due allowance for possible declining values. The sphere of each individual trader's activities being limited they were forced into combinations or partnerships, and the great company took security from them in the form of mortgages on their lands. There was not a year after the close of the War of 1812–15 that the Green Bay traders, for instance, did not suffer a heavy deficit.[92]

It will be remembered that Robert Stuart took a mortgage for the Company on property belonging to certain of the Green Bay traders as security for debts due to losses in the trade. The result of these mortgages, as described by Henry S. Baird, a man who long acted as one of Astor's agents, was that the

land [in Green Bay] . . . originally owned by JOHN LAWE and the GRIGNON family. Together with other real estate . . . was taken in payment of balance[s] due [from] the old Green Bay Company to the former company [the American Fur Company]; the debt having accrued by loss in the Indian trade — for in this business, it generally happened that the small traders who purchased their goods at high prices, after years of toil and privation spent in the trade, came out with nothing — leaving to the great monopoly the lion's share of the profits.[93]

Joseph Rolette, of Prairie du Chien, one of the most active and unscrupulous of Company traders, also lost his property to the Company, and similar instances might be multiplied.[94] In view of this situation, Astor's probably quite accurate statement "that all our Indian traders . . . with very few exceptions, have been losing time and property in that trade . . ." takes on a note of unconscious and ironic humor. Even Thomas Hart Benton, to whom this letter was addressed, would probably have been at no loss to name one of the "very few exceptions."

It might be logically asked: "Why did these traders continue in an occupation which brought them nothing but losses?" This question is not difficult to answer. Thwaites says: "That the business continued at all, was apparently due to sheer inertia, and the unfitness of the traders for any other form of occupation."[95] He doubtless reached this very proper conclusion from a study of the letters of the unusually, though sometimes incoherently, articulate Green Bay trader, John Lawe, who wrote :

The first Year after the War was the last year I saved myself for every year since I have been loosing Money & not a little in that cursed Indian Trade that I have allways persisted and do Still persist to continue which will soon put me a beggar (but you may well say or ask the question why do you still continue since you find it a loosing business) I will say I do not know what to do else as I am not capable of doing or following any other kind of business I have always lived in hopes but I am at last beginning to despair the old times is no more that pleasant reign is over & never to return any more.[96]

The traders who had been brought up in the old independent traditions of the early fur trade, which was based to a large extent on the existence of ties of friendship, and even of marriage, between the traders and the Indians, found it impossible to accommodate themselves to this new and rigid system, and, knowing no other occupation, continued to endure annual losses secured by mortgages on their land, receiving in return for their exertions only a bare livelihood, and existing in the hope that somehow some change would take place in their situation.

William Johnston, quoted above, was, as the son of a fur trader, particularly impressed by the evils which the system had brought upon this class of individuals. As a half-breed, the misfortunes of the Indians also aroused his sympathy and indignation. Sufficient has been written concerning the miseries which such aspects of the fur trade as the liquor traffic brought down upon the heads of the natives, and we need discuss this question no further. Johnston, however, also mentioned the condition of another group of men connected with the trade, to which not much attention has been given, and which will repay some discussion. These were the *engagés* of the Company, the *voyageurs*, who acted as subordinates to the clerks and traders and performed all the dangerous, difficult, and exhausting manual labor of the trade. William Clark and Lewis Cass testified to the hardships of their life.[97]

The Men who manage the boats [said William Johnston] are obliged to perform all that is required of them, to row the boats, to carry the baggage on their backs, across the portages. When at the trading post, they perform all the menial services, such as fishing, chopping wood, and cooking, etc. . . . their labour is very hard for in a few years they are completeatly broken down in constitution, they have to work more like beasts of burden than men, and when they can procure the means they will go into all kinds of excesses; exposed constantly to change of heat and cold; which soon brings them to an untimely grave.[98]

These *engagés* were all drawn from the ranks of the docile, hardy French-Canadians, since the more independent Americans refused to undergo the strict discipline enforced upon the *voyageurs*. They were usually engaged for a term of three or five years, and for their labors, which were confined to no particular number of hours per day, but continued as long as there was work to do, they received about $100, more or less, per year, which was, however, not required to be paid until a month after the expiration of their term of service, though they received a small advance on being hired.[99] Johnston said, "at present they are seldom allowed perquisites, formerly it was an indespensible rule; but it is gradually losing ground. Some now get a few trifling articles of clothing; tobacco, soap, salt, etc."[100] The American Fur Company gave its *engagés* no perquisites whatsoever save a ration of "blé d'Inde," that is, Indian corn, which was the only food the Company was required to furnish to its common workmen, though once in the Indian country they often had game, sometimes for want of anything else. Moreover, the Company's wages were rather below than above the norm of $100, and frequently the *voyageur* would receive only $250 for the three years.[101]

It was natural for the trader, who had to depend upon his own exertions to avoid loss and to acquire any possible profits, "to use," in Johnston's words, "fraud and deceit towards the men they have in their employ." If the trader could by any device avoid having to pay the *voyageur* his full wages, that was so much to the credit of the outfit. Any goods which the *engagé* might wish or need to purchase, such as clothing, tobacco, or liquor, would be sold to him on credit at a tremendous advance. At Mackinac Island in the year 1823–24, the retail store, which of course sold most of its goods to the *engagés* of the Company, made a net gain of $7,200 on goods invoiced at only $8,300, and this after a heavy charge had been added to the cost price of the merchandise.[102] If this was the profit at Mackinac, the prices in the Indian country may only be estimated with the assistance of a good deal of imagination. The *engagé*, since little or no risk was involved in selling him goods on credit, was probably not charged so heavily for his goods as were the Indians, the classic example of the prices paid by the natives being "*Fifteen Dollars for a pound of Tobacco; and one Dollar and an half for a thimble!*"[103] but even at a lower price it is obvious that the Company could make a large profit from selling to the *engagé*. As a result, it was not unusual for an *engagé* to end his three years' term as a debtor to the Company and be forced to re-engage for another term.[104]

Chittenden, who is, on the whole, more an admirer of John Jacob Astor than otherwise, is inclined to give credence to almost unbelievably horrifying tales of the treatment of the Company's *engagés* in the Indian country. He writes of the Western Department, where competition was much more desperate and ruthless than in the Great Lakes region.

> It is difficult to exaggerate the state of affairs which at times prevailed. "The company," by which is always meant the American Fur Company, was thoroughly hated even by its own servants. Throughout its career it was an object of popular execration as all grasping monopolies are. Many are the stories, largely exaggerated, no doubt, that have come down to us of its hard and cruel ways. Small traders stood no show whatever and the most desperate measures were resorted to without scruple to get them out of the way. Many an employe, it is said, who had finished his term of service and had started for St. Louis with a letter of credit for his pay fell by the way and was reported as killed by the Indians. These harsher features of a heartless business it is difficult to believe, but the fact that such traditions have persisted even to the present day is not compatible with the theory of entire innocence.

It is impossible to imagine Crooks or Stuart, to say nothing of their superiors, giving the slightest sanction to the assassination of an employee in order to save the expense of his wages. It is almost equally difficult to conceive of McKenzie sponsoring such an atrocity, even though the story is told that on a certain occasion, "when news came of an Indian attack upon a party of hunters, he was heard to inquire if the horses had been saved. On hearing that they had all been lost and that only the men had escaped, he exclaimed: 'D—n the men! If the horses had been saved it would have amounted to something!'"[105] But it is possible that in the ranks of subordinate traders there might here and there be found a man rendered so desperate by misfortune and debt as to be willing to authorize the destruction of an obscure *engagé* for the two or three hundred dollars which his death might save to the outfit in wages.

It is not, however, necessary to be convinced that assassination by his superiors was a normal risk of the *voyageur's* existence in order to believe that the *engagé* was frequently the victim of oppression and injustice. George Boyd, immediately upon taking up the duties of Indian agent at Mackinac as successor to Major Puthuff, who had been dismissed through the machinations of the American Fur Company, had been persuaded by Robert Stuart to make a sweeping statement to the effect that the conduct of the American Fur Company through its agents had been fair and honorable to the government, the Indians, and the public. In this eulogy he had been joined by Adam D. Steuart, collector of customs for the District of Michilimackinac,[106] who later combined the duties of that office with the position of American Fur Company lobbyist at Washington. A decade's experience seems to have sown the seeds of doubt in Boyd's mind as to the uniform righteousness of the Company's conduct. In a letter written in 1830, in which he made suggestions, as he had been requested, for the better management of Indian affairs, this statement occurs:

Suffer the Indians in particular ([*sic*] cases as in Robbery or Murder) to give testimony in our courts, and it will go far to do away many of the

Evils they at present suffer from our violence & our avarice — and at the same time give the poor Canadians, hirelings for a term of years to hard task-masters, an assurance that there is a power vested somewhere in the Government, to Call this great monied Aristocracy to account, not only for aggressions practised on the red man, but for any maltreatment of any free man trading by their permission within these limits, and under the sanction of their laws, and you will at once divest them of a great portion of that power, which is but too often used to grind down & oppress all within the circle of their influence:

To effect this let a Board of Comptrol, or of accounts, be established, under the authority of the War Dept., composed; say of the principal Agent of the American Fur Co., the Ind. Agent, & the Commanding officer of the post; whose duty it shall be, to see that justice is rendered to all &a Every Canadian, Employed by the Company, & receiving his discharge — [107]

What a decline had the universally fair and honorable American Fur Company experienced during those ten years, to have become at last a "great monied Aristocracy" against whose rapacity the Indian, the small trader, and the Canadian employee alike all required government protection!

As a matter of fact, the consolidation of the fur trade under one company had resulted in a sort of pyramidal system. The partners of the Company charged the goods to the traders at a price sufficient to insure a heavy profit for themselves, and the trader, in order even to balance his accounts, had to use every one of his bag of tricks. The temptation to cheat and debauch the Indians and to defraud his *engagés* therefore became almost irresistible. For this situation the reasonably honest and frequently good-natured John Jacob Astor, in his country home at Hellgate or among the mountains of Switzerland, cannot escape the responsibility.

Yet in some ways Astor and his Company, in intention at least, occupied higher ground than certain of the other traders. Astor and his partners, for example, were at first reluctant to use alcohol in the trade, though their agents ended by becoming the most brazen and successful of liquor-law violators. It is also alleged that, while some traders cheated the Indians twice on every transaction, not only charging them inordinately high prices, but giving them worthless goods, Astor was content with a single profit and saw to it that the Indians at least received first-class merchandise for their furs. It is certain that he did make every effort to secure suitable goods.[108]

Hercules L. Dousman, who managed Astor's trading post at Prairie du Chien for a number of years, is quoted as having once said that if by any accident a gun, a blanket, or any other article sold to an Indian was not up to standard, the policy, regardless of trouble or expense, was to replace it with a perfect article as soon as possible. This was a strict rule within [sic] Astor's dealings with the Indians and to it is undoubtedly due much of the success which rewarded his enterprise in the wilderness.[109]

If this statement is true, even though competition with other traders, especially the British, may be a sufficient explanation for this policy, it is nevertheless very creditable to Astor.

It is also undoubtedly true that Astor's method of carrying on the fur trade involved something more than a mere bludgeoning of competitors by the weight of superior capital. It must not be forgotten that there had been a day when Astor was less well endowed with funds than the most poverty-stricken of the individual traders competing with the American Fur Company in the Indian country, though with this difference, that he had no well-organized company to confront. It had been through sheer perseverance, foresight, and a process of profiting by the mistakes of himself and of others that Astor had become the wielder of this tremendous capital which now made him king of the fur trade. These qualities did not desert him with the coming of prosperity. Probably the most striking testimony to the ability which made Astor almost as successful in the sale of his furs as he was in their collection is found in the letter of one of his former business rivals, William G. Ewing, senior partner in the firm of W. G. & G. W. Ewing, written in 1846 to Messrs. Suydam and Sage of New York. In this letter Ewing contrasted the plan of selling all furs and skins through a London agent, which after seven years' trial had proved itself a failure, with Astor's successful policy. The London agency, he said, was defective:

1ˢᵗ Because it *exposes* to the world all of the transactions of the trade.— —

2ᵈ Because a *Second* stock is purchased, before the first is disposed of — — thereby doubling the hazzard, — —

3ᵈ It stimulates early collections, beyond the consumption, and gluts the market & the losses on *large* amounts, exceed the profits in *small* supplies that occasionally happen; these are the results of these Public Sales made 2 or 3 times a year. //

Mr. Astor managed the trade different & made it *profitable* — (No Yankee or Humbuggery about it)

1ˢᵗ He collected a large amount of skins in New York, and retailed the Muskrat & poor Deer Skins, as the consumption on *this side* called for it in New York; sold at a small profit. — —

2ᵈ He assorted his *shipping* skins for the different European markets; sent his *Deer Skins* to Germany with his poor Raccoon — — 2ᵈ Sent his *Fine* Raccoon to *Russia*

3ᵈ Sent his *Otter Martin* & some of the other *fine* Northern skins to *China*

4ᵗʰ Sold Mink, Beaver & some other skins in London.

And thus *directly* supplied the markets, where these articles are consumed

The *supply* & *consumption* kept pace with each other; and the result was mostly *only known* to *himself!* The collective result was profitable. And he did not make his purchases until *June* & *July* in Detroit & other places; after he had heard from the past years business. — —

The effect of Mr. Lampsons plan [that of Ewing's London agent] requires a sett of *intermediate speculators*, who purchase at his London *Auctions* & sell in those countries where Astor shipped to.¹¹⁰

The result of Astor's policy in the sale of furs is perhaps even more graphically revealed in a letter from Thomas G. Cary to Samuel Cabot in 1831, suggesting that they collect a cargo of furs for export to Canton, *provided that John Jacob Astor dies or that he does not propose to send any furs in the coming year* — certainly a powerful revelation of his dominating influence in the Canton fur market.¹¹¹

ASTOR IN HIS PRIME

A brief recapitulation of those policies and practices by which the American Fur Company was enabled to achieve and maintain its supremacy from the Great Lakes to the Rockies during the height of the fur trade may be appropriately inserted here. In the first stage Astor's organization endeavored, through financial power and political influence, to drive from the field or into alliance with the Company all rival traders, whether financed by the government or by private individuals. When this had been almost achieved, the territory was carefully divided to avoid competition and duplication of effort, and the responsibilities were definitely allocated. Stuart, Crooks, and to a certain extent even the St. Louis partners, were responsible to John Jacob Astor; the heads of each outfit were in turn responsible to those in charge of the Department to which they belonged; the clerks at each trading post were under control of the trader who managed that outfit; and the *engagés*, finally, were the humble servitors of that particular clerk who was their *bourgeois*. All combined to get as many furs as possible from the Indians for the least possible amount of goods. Their efforts were rendered more effective because of the fact that experienced traders had been forced into the Company's ranks, and because in most cases the country had already been opened up by private traders. Few of Astor's enterprises were marked by a pioneering spirit. He excelled in profiting by the successes and failures both of others and of himself. Astor, at the New York office, utilized his two-score years or more of experience in foreign trade to buy goods in the cheapest and sell furs in the highest market. He also saw to it that goods sent into the Indian country were charged at such rates that all the risk was thrown upon the individual traders.

This system was successful for Astor, and in a lesser degree for some of his partners and principal agents. Many, and perhaps most, of the traders who had been employed by the Company for a decade or more found themselves in debt when that corporation closed up its affairs, though the habits of hospitality, which it was necessary for those engaged in the Indian trade to form, were doubtless at least partly responsible for this result. It is probable, too, that very few *voyageurs* acquired a competency by saving up what was left of their $83⅓ a year wages after they had bought tobacco, soap, and clothing at a heavy advance on the cost price. The Indians, after making treaties by which their land was yielded up for a payment from the government, found the Company ready to put in a claim for old debts owed by individual members of the tribes to certain Company traders.[112] William W. Warren, whose father was an American Fur Company trader of New England stock, while his mother was of French and Chippewa descent, summed up the attitude of both the better class of fur traders and of the Indians when he wrote:

When John Jacob Astor entered into arrangements with the British Fur Companies for the monopoly of the Ojibway trade within the United States territory, a new era may be said to have occurred in the fur trade. ... To some degree the Indian ceased to find that true kindness ... which he had always experienced from his French traders ... as a general fact, which redounds greatly to the honor of this class of fur traders [those who had married Ojibway wives and imbibed the "generous and hospitable qualities of the Indians"] they died poor. The money which has been made by the fur trade has been made by the sweat of their brows, but it has flowed into the coffers of such men as John Jacob Astor.[113]

NOTES

1. Thwaites, Reuben Gold, ed., "The Fur-Trade in Wisconsin — 1812–1825," *Wisconsin Historical Collections*, vol. xx (1911), pp. 66–79, Thomas L. McKenney, Office of Indian Trade, Georgetown, August 19, 1818, to John C. Calhoun, Secretary of War (ms., Department of the Interior, Washington, D. C., Indian Office Records, Miscellaneous).

2. *United States Statutes at Large*, vol. ii, 1800–13, chap. xiii, sec. 21, p. 146, 7th Cong., 1st sess., 1802.

3. *Ibid.*, vol. iii, 1813–23, chap. c, sec. 20, pp. 243–244, 13th Cong., 3rd sess., 1815.

4. Thwaites, *op. cit.*, pp. 88–90, William Henry Puthuff, Detroit, October 15, 1818, to Governor Lewis Cass (ms. book, Department of the Interior, Washington, D. C., Indian Office Letter Book iii, p. 52).

5. *Ibid.*, pp. 291–297, Lieut. Col. Willoughby Morgan, Fort Crawford, November 15, 1822, to Major-General Gaines (ms., Department of the Interior, Washington, D. C., Indian Office Records, Miscellaneous).

6. Thwaites, Reuben Gold, ed., "The Fur-Trade in Wisconsin — 1815–1817," *Wisconsin Historical Collections*, vol. xix (1910) [hereafter in this chapter referred to simply as Thwaites, "The Fur-Trade in Wisconsin — 1815–1817"], pp. 395–396, 398, 399 (mss., Wisconsin Historical Society, Wisconsin MSS., 3 B 42, 60 B 51, 60 B 53, translated from the French).

7. Thwaites, Reuben Gold, ed., "The Fur-Trade in Wisconsin — 1812–1825," *Wisconsin Historical Collections*, vol. xx (1911) [hereafter in this chapter referred to simply as Thwaites, "The Fur-Trade in Wisconsin — 1812–1825"], pp. 87–88, Instructions of Lewis Cass to Daniel Bourassa, Indian Trader, October 9, 1818 (ms., Detroit Public Library, Burton Historical Collection, vol. 115, p. 37); pp. 107–108, License Bond of Andrew Leiphant, Robert Irwin, Jr., and Lewis Morgan, Green Bay, April 24, 1819 (ms., Wisconsin Historical Society, Madison, 89 C 2); p. 118, License of James H. Lockwood, Mackinac, July 27, 1819 (ms., Wisconsin Historical Society, Madison, Wisconsin MSS., 55 B 72).

8. Ross, Alexander, *The Fur Hunters of the Far West*, 2 vols. (1855), vol. i, p. 15.

9. Thwaites, "The Fur-Trade in Wisconsin — 1812–1825," pp. 82–86, Lewis Cass, St. Mary's, September 14, 1818, to J. C. Calhoun, Secretary of War (ms. book, Department of the Interior, Washington, D. C., Indian Office Letter Book iii, p. 30).

10. *American State Papers: Indian Affairs*, vol. ii, pp. 659–661, T. L. McKenney, February 14, 1826, to James Barbour, Secretary of War.

11. Ms., Department of State, Washington, D. C., Miscellaneous Letters, December, 1816, Affidavit of James Grant, Fort William, No-

vember 23, 1816; William McGillivray, York, Upper Canada, November 23, 1816, to John Jacob Astor.

12. Thwaites, "The Fur-Trade in Wisconsin — 1812–1825," pp. 17–31, Ramsay Crooks and Robert Stuart, N. Y., January 24, 1818, to John Jacob Astor (ms. book, Department of the Interior, Washington, D. C., Indian Office Letter Book ii, p. 247).

13. Ms. (photostat), Wisconsin Historical Society, Madison, Ramsay Crooks' Letter Book, Mackinac, etc., 1816–20, Ramsay Crooks, Washington, D. C., March 2, 1819, to J. C. Calhoun, Secretary of War.

14. Thwaites, "The Fur-Trade [in Wisconsin — 1812–1825," p. 116, Authorization from George Boyd, Indian Agent, Mackinac, July 17, 1819, to William Morrison (ms., Wisconsin Historical Society, Madison, Wisconsin MSS., 1 D 82).

15. "The Fur Trade and Factory System at Green Bay 1816–21," *Wisconsin Historical Collections*, vol. vii (1873–76), pp. 271, 272, 278, 279.

16. Thwaites, Reuben Gold, ed., "The Fur-Trade in Wisconsin — 1815–1817," pp. 466–467, 487–488, John Bowyer, Indian Agent, Green Bay, July 22, December 15, 1817, to Governor Lewis Cass (ms. book, Department of the Interior, Washington, D. C., Indian Office Letter Book ii, pp. 147, 225).

17. Thwaites, "The Fur-Trade in Wisconsin — 1812–1825," pp. 16–17, Lewis Cass, Detroit, January 22, 1818, to Colonel John Bowyer, Indian Agent, Green Bay (ms. book, Department of the Interior, Washington, D. C., Indian Office Letter Book ii, p. 247).

18. *Ibid.*, p. 167, John W. Johnson, Indian Agent pro tem., Prairie du Chien, April 19, 1820, to Governor Cass, Detroit (ms. book, Department of the Interior, Washington, D. C., Indian Office, Letters Received, 1831, no. 1); pp. 168–170, F. Barnard, Prairie du Chien, May 14, 1820, to Colonel John Hunt, Detroit (ms., Detroit Public Library, Burton Historical Collection, vol. 259, p. 104).

19. "The Fur Trade and Factory System at Green Bay 1816–21," *Wisconsin Historical Collections*, vol. vii (1873–76), p. 280, Major Irwin, Green Bay, October 6, 1821, to Colonel McKenney.

20. Thwaites, "The Fur-Trade in Wisconsin — 1812–1825," pp. 82–86, Lewis Cass, St. Mary's, September 14, 1818, to J. C. Calhoun, Secretary of War (ms. book, Department of the Interior, Washington, D. C., Indian Office Letter Book iii, p. 30).

21. *United States Statutes at Large*, vol. iii, 1813–23, chap. 58, sec. 2, pp. 682–683, 17th Cong., 1st sess., May 6, 1822.

22. Thwaites, "The Fur-Trade in Wisconsin — 1812–1825," pp. 291–297, Lieut.-Colonel Willoughby Morgan, Fort Crawford, November 15, 1822, to Maj.-Gen. Edmund P. Gaines (ms., Department of the Interior, Washington, D. C., Indian Office Records, Miscellaneous).

23. Ms. (photostat), Wisconsin Historical Society, Madison, Ramsay Crooks' and Robert Stuart's Letter Book, Mackinac, Detroit, New York, etc., 1820–25, pp. 307–308, Robert Stuart, July, 1822, to George Boyd, Indian Agent, Mackinac.

24. Thwaites, "The Fur-Trade in Wisconsin — 1812–1825," pp. 306–307, Lewis Cass, Detroit, June 10, 1823, to Henry R. Schoolcraft, Indian Agent, Sault Ste. Marie (ms. book, Department of the Interior, Washington, D. C., Indian Office Letter Book iv).

25. Kelton, Dwight H., *Annals of Fort Mackinac* (1888), pp. 122–123.

26. Ms. book (copy), Detroit Public Library, Burton Historical Collection, and Missouri Historical Society, St. Louis, Letters of Ramsay Crooks, John Jacob Astor, and the American Fur Company, 1813–43, Adam D. Steuart, Washington, D. C., February 14, 1827, February 2, 1828, to Ramsay Crooks, N. Y.

27. Ms. (photostat), Wisconsin Historical Society, Madison, Ramsay Crooks' and Robert Stuart's Letter Book, Mackinac, Detroit, New York etc., 1820–25, Robert Stuart, Mackinac, August 11, 1822, to the Indian Agent, Green Bay.

28. Thwaites, "The Fur-Trade in Wisconsin — 1812–1825," p. 297, J. C. Calhoun, Department of War, December 6, 1822, to William H. Crawford, Secretary of the Treasury (ms. book, Department of the Interior, Washington, D. C., Indian Officer Letter Book E, 1820–23, p. 365); p. 305, J. C. Calhoun, Department of War, June 3, 1823, to Colonel Ninian Pinkney, Fort Howard, Green Bay (ms. book, Department of the Interior, Washington, D. C., Indian Office Letter Book E, 1820–23, p. 448).

29. *Ibid.*, pp. 385–387, William Clark, Superintendency, St. Louis, October 19, 1825, to James Barbour, Secretary of War (ms., Department of the Interior, Washington, D. C., Indian Office Records, Miscellaneous).

30. Ms., Wisconsin Historical Society, Madison, Wisconsin MSS., 3 D 122, George Boyd, Mackinac, August 18, 1830, to James B. Gardiner, Mackinac (see below, vol. ii, pp. 1206-1209).

31. Thwaites, "The Fur-Trade in Wisconsin — 1812–1825," pp. 382–385, Colonel Josiah Snelling, Detroit, August 23, 1825, to James Barbour, Secretary of War (ms., Department of the Interior, Washington, D. C., Indian Office Records, Miscellaneous); *American State Papers: Indian Affairs*, vol. ii, p. 661.

32. Ms. book, Public Archives of Canada, Ottawa, Invoices Outward C, American Fur Company, Northern, September, 1829–May, 1834, *passim*.

33. Hoyt, Mrs. Mary M. Lewis, "Life of Leonard Slater, Pioneer Preacher and Missionary," *Michigan Pioneer and Historical Collections*, vol. xxv, p. 150.

34. Neill, Rev. E. D., "Occurrences in and around Fort Snelling, from 1819 to 1840," *Minnesota Historical Collections*, vol. ii (1864), pp. 30–31, 34; "Taliaferro, Maj. Lawrence, Autobiography of: Written in 1864," *Minnesota Historical Collections*, vol. vi (1887–94), pp. 189–255; ms., Library of Congress, George Johnston's Journal in the North West, August 3, 1824–May 16, 1827, August 4, 1825, February 15, 1827, etc.

35. Ms., Department of the Interior, Washington, D. C., Indian Office Records, Miscellaneous, William B. Astor, January 24, 1824, to John Tipton, Indian Agent, Ft. Wayne; William B. Astor, N. Y., October 29, November 13, 1824, to J. C. Calhoun, Secretary of War; John Tipton, Fort Wayne, November 20, December 21, 1824, January 25, 1825, to John C. Calhoun, Secretary of War; Robert Stuart, Washington, February 24, 1826, to James Barbour; John Jacob Astor, July 5, 1826, to James Barbour, Secretary of War; Albert Gallatin, N. Y., June 30, 1826, to James Barbour, Secretary of War (see below, vol. ii, pp. 1183–1184); *ibid.*, Indian Office Letter Book i, March 18, 1824–May 3, 1825, p. 218, Thomas L. McKenney, Department of War, Office of Indian Affairs, November 3, 1824, to William B. Astor, President pro tem., American Fur Company; *ibid.*, Indian Office Letter Book iii, April 1, 1826–March 31, 1827, p. 139, James Barbour, Department of War, July 5, 1826, to Gen. John Tipton, Indian Agent; p. 140, James Barbour, Department of War, July 6, 1826, to John Jacob Astor; *American State Papers: Indian Affairs*, vol. ii, pp. 659–661, T. L. McKenney, Superintendent of the Indian Bureau, February 14, 1826, to James Barbour, Secretary of War. It should be noted, however, that the condemnation of the Company's goods for possession of liquor was reversed in 1829 by the United States Supreme Court, on the grounds that the lower court's instructions as to the meaning of the term "Indian country" had not been clear. (Curtis, B. R., *Reports of Decisions in the Supreme Court of the United States* (1881), vol. viii, January term, 1829, pp. 137–143.)

36. Ms., Department of the Interior, Washington, D. C., Indian Office Records, Miscellaneous, Colonel John Snelling, Detroit, September 5, 1825, to James Barbour, Secretary of War; Robert Stuart, Washington, February 24, 1826, to James Barbour; Adam D. Steuart, Washington, February 25, 1826, to Robert Stuart, Agent of the American Fur Company, Washington; John Jacob Astor, N. Y., May 26, 1826, to James Barbour, Secretary of War; *ibid.*, Indian Office Letter Book iii, April 1, 1826–March 31, 1827, p. 107, T. L. McKenney, May 29, 1826, to Gen. William Clark, Superintendent, Indian Affairs, St. Louis; p. 107, T. L. McKenney, May 29, 1826, to John Jacob Astor.

37. Ms., Wisconsin Historical Society, Madison, Wisconsin MSS., 24 B 21, Robert Stuart, Mackinac, September 4, 1829, to Auguste Grignon, Green Bay.

38. Neville, Ella Hoes, Martin, Sarah Greene, and Martin, Deborah Beaumont, *Historic Green Bay* (1893), p. 268.

39. Ms., Wisconsin Historical Society, Madison, Invoice, Robert Stuart, Mackinac, August 12, 1831, to Porlier & Grignon, Green Bay.

40. Ms. book, Public Archives of Canada, Ottawa, Invoices Outward C, American Fur Company, Northern, September, 1829–May, 1834, *passim*, esp. pp. 270–271.

41. Ms., Hudson's Bay Company House, London, William B. Astor, President, American Fur Company, N. Y., December 15, 1829, to James Keith, Agent, Hudson's Bay Company (see below, vol. ii, p. 1198); W. S., Secretary, Hudson's Bay Company, Hudson's Bay House, London, March 3, 1830, to William B. Astor, N. Y. (see below, vol. ii, pp. 1203–1204).

42. Fox, J. Sharpless, ed., "Territorial Papers, 1831–1836," *Michigan Pioneer and Historical Collections*, vol. xxxvii (1909–10), pp. 236–238, Robert Stuart, Mackinac, July 6, 1832, to Governor George B. Porter (ms., Smithsonian, Washington, D. C., Schoolcraft Papers, File Case A, no. 117). This letter had been preceded, a month before, by one of a similar nature to Lewis Cass, the secretary of War (ms., Department of the Interior, Washington, D. C., Indian Office Records, Miscellaneous, Robert Stuart, Mackinac, June 6, 1832, to Lewis Cass, Secretary of War).

43. Thwaites, "The Fur-Trade in Wisconsin — 1812–1825," pp. 382–385, Colonel Josiah Snelling, Detroit, August 23, 1825, to James Barbour, Secretary of War (ms., Department of the Interior, Washington, D. C., Indian Office Records, Miscellaneous).

44. Ms. book, Public Archives of Canada, Ottawa, Invoices Outward C, American Fur Company, Northern, September, 1829–May, 1834, *passim*.

45. In view of the prominence of Robert Stuart in shipping thousands of gallons of liquor every year into the Indian country, and of his plea to Governor Porter for permission to increase the quantity used on the Canadian border, a sidelight on his private and personal attitude toward the whiskey trade may be of interest. It seems that about 1828 Robert Stuart went through a religious experience which changed his attitude toward life considerably. He had always had a quick temper — his handiness with a pistol aboard the *Tonquin* is a case in point — and it is told of him that once he felled two drunken and insolent *voyageurs* with a stick of wood, fracturing the skull of one. He later sat up all night with the injured man until assured that he would recover. It was always a word and a blow with him — and indeed often he decided to omit the word. Consequently when he was heard in a subdued voice instructing a careless *voyageur* to fish out a pack of furs he had dropped in the water, instead of clubbing the man over the head with the most readily available bludgeon, everyone was willing to believe that he had either "got religion" or some

wasting disease. It was natural, then, that he should begin to wonder whether the debauching of Indians by means of liquor was altogether consistent with his position as a man who had been born again and elected as a ruling elder in the Presbyterian church. His procedure is thus described by a friend and admirer. "Whiskey was one of the principal articles of exchange in the fur trade. Before his conversion, Mr. Stuart had joined the temperance society and was trying to do something to suppress the evil. But after this change his conscience troubled him. He felt that it was inconsistent for a temperance man and Christian to send whisky by the barrel to the Indians. The company would put this branch of the trade into other hands and relieve him; but then the evil would be increased four-fold. His best friends persuaded him to hold his position, even if he was reproached, and lessen the evil he could not cure. He finally consented, but not," as his biographer concluded with entirely unconscious humor, "till he had obtained the opinion and advice of the most eminent men in the country." Conscious of not having played an entirely courageous part in this matter, Stuart salved his conscience by forbidding all Sabbath work for the Company on Mackinac Island, and rigidly adhered to this prohibition, much to the bewilderment of the *engagés*. (Heydenburk, Martin, "Incidents in the Life of Robert Stuart," *Michigan Pioneer and Historical Collections*, vol. iii (1879–80), pp. 56–61.) In short, Stuart realized that though the fur trade could, at a pinch, be carried on without working during a certain specific twenty-four hours per week and without breaking in the skulls of refractory or careless *voyageurs*, still, when it came to ruining the Indians with liquor, business was business and both Christianity and the United States Statutes at Large must give way. His exertions to "lessen the evil he could not cure" were so successful that between 1830, a year or so after his conversion, and 1832, the year in which we find him pleading for more whiskey on the border, the liquor he delivered to the outfits at Mackinac only increased from 5,985 gallons per year to 8,776 gallons — an increase of a little less than 3,000 gallons, or about 50 per cent, in two years!

46. Chittenden, Hiram Martin, *The American Fur Trade of the Far West*, 3 vols. (1902), vol. i, pp. 25–26.

47. *Senate Documents*, 22nd Cong., 1st sess., vol. ii, no. 90, pp. 5–11, Superintendent of Indian Affairs, St. Louis, November 20, 1831, to Lewis Cass; pp. 18–26, Andrew S. Hughes, October 31, 1831, to General William Clark, Superintendent of Indian Affairs, St. Louis; Myers, Gustavus, *History of the Great American Fortunes*, 3 vols. (1907–10), vol. i, pp. 118–120.

48. *United States Statutes at Large*, vol. iv, 1824–35, chap. 174, p. 564, 22nd Cong., 1st sess., July 9, 1832.

49. *House Documents*, 20th Cong., 2nd sess., no. 117, p. 40.

50. Chittenden, *op. cit.*, vol. i, pp. 22–29; ms., Department of the Interior, Washington, D. C., Indian Office Records, Miscellaneous, Robert Stuart, Mackinac, June 6, 1832, to Lewis Cass, Secretary of War; William B. Astor, N. Y., July 25, August 4, 1832, to Lewis Cass, Secretary of War; *ibid.*, Letter Book ix, July 5, 1832–January 27, 1833, pp. 93–94, 162, John Robb, Acting Secretary of War, July 26, August 15, 1832, to Robert Stuart, Mackinac; p. 96, John Robb, Acting Secretary of War, July 28, 1832, to William B. Astor; pp. 152–153, Lewis Cass, Detroit, August 17, 1832, to William B. Astor; pp. 450–451, Elbert Herring, Department of War, Office of Indian Affairs, December 27, 1832, to Robert Stuart, Mackinac.

51. Ms. book, Public Archives of Canada, Ottawa, Invoices Outward C, American Fur Company, Northern, September, 1829–May, 1834, *passim*.

52. Chittenden, *op. cit.*, vol. i, pp. 355–362.

53. Ms., Department of State, Washington, D. C., Territorial Papers, B I A, Miscellaneous, William B. Astor, President, The American Fur Company, N. Y., May 27, 1833, to Lewis Cass, Secretary of War, Washington, D. C.

54. It might be objected that the liquor policy which we have just examined belongs not to John Jacob Astor but to the American Fur Company, that Astor was absent in Europe for nearly half the duration of the reorganized American Fur Company (1817–34) and that therefore he does not deserve the odium or credit for his Company's circumvention of government liquor regulations. It is quite true that not until the bone-dry law of 1832 was in agitation have I observed any statement by John Jacob Astor, or, indeed, even by Ramsay Crooks, justifying the use of liquor in the Indian country, but it would be impossible to convince anyone acquainted with Astor's methods of doing business that he was not pretty well informed of what was going on in the Indian country. It was to John Jacob Astor or John Jacob Astor & Son that the ships from England, the Continent, the West Indies, and various ports in the United States, with their cargoes of wine, brandy, gin, rum, and whiskey, were consigned (*New-York Gazette and General Advertiser*, Marine News, *passim*). According to agreement it was John Jacob Astor who was to be personally responsible for the purchase of the goods employed by the Company in its trade, including those thousands of gallons of intoxicants which were delivered each year to the Company's traders at Mackinac. It might be remarked, parenthetically, that Astor's elder sister, Catherine, owned a distillery. Of course neither Astor nor Crooks, out of mere worldly wisdom if for no more lofty reason, would approve of such crude work on the part of their employees as Rolette's incitement of the Sioux against one of the Grignons, the action of another agent in stirring up the Crows to rob Fitzpatrick, and the futile attempt to drive out the ex-clerk Wil-

liam Farnsworth from his location (Martin, Morgan L., "Sketch of William Farnsworth," *Wisconsin Historical Collections*, vol. ix (1880–82), pp. 397–400; Childs, Colonel Ebenezer, "Recollections of Wisconsin since 1820," *Wisconsin Historical Collections*, vol. iv (1857–58), pp. 156–157). In fact it will be recalled that Crooks urged McKenzie not to engage in his fatal distillery experiment. Nevertheless, Astor felt bound to back up his agents whenever their labors for their own and the Company's welfare brought them into conflict with unsympathetic government officials. The impossibility of Astor's not knowing in something more than a general way of what his agents were doing among the Indians is shown by a rather amusing extract from a letter from Robert Stuart to William B. Astor. Stuart said: "shall I put up *by themselves*, the very inferior Rats or rather such as it may be doubtful whether they are Rats or Kittens? I do not know whether you are aware that Mr. J. J. Astor objected to this mode, which may be seen by his letter to me of 22ᵈ Novbr. 1822." (Ms. (photostat), Wisconsin Historical Society, Madison, Robert Stuart's Letter Book, Mackinac, 1823–30, pp. 49–50, Robert Stuart, Mackinac, April 26, 1824, to William B. Astor, N. Y.) Evidently Astor had no intention of losing an opportunity of securing full price for an undersized or otherwise inferior rat skin. But it is evident that a man who would pay such minute attention to the details of packing furs could hardly be oblivious to such an important matter of policy as that presented by the liquor trade.

55. Ms. book (copy), Detroit Public Library, Burton Historical Collection, and Missouri Historical Society, St. Louis, Letters of Ramsay Crooks, John Jacob Astor, and the American Fur Company, 1813–43, Ramsay Crooks, N. Y., February 7, 1818, to John Jacob Astor, Baltimore.

56. *Ibid.*, John Jacob Astor, Geneva, February 16 (see below, vol. ii, pp. 1173–1175), September 21, November 10, 1824, March 11, May 20, 1825, to Ramsay Crooks, N. Y.

57. *House Documents*, 20th Cong., 2nd sess., no. 117, pp. 108–113, William Clark and Lewis Cass, Washington, D. C., December 27, 1828, to Senator Thomas H. Benton.

58. *Senate Documents*, 22nd Cong., 1st sess., vol. ii, no. 90, pp. 61–62, John Jacob Astor, N. Y., January 29, 1829, to Colonel Benton.

59. *Ibid.*, pp. 51–53, John Dougherty, Indian Agent, Leavenworth, October 25, 1831, to William Clark, St. Louis.

60. *Ibid.*, pp. 46–48, Statement of Joshua Pilcher.

61. *Ibid.*, pp. 11–18, Joshua Pilcher, St. Louis, December 1, 1831, to Lewis Cass.

62. *Ibid.*, pp. 70–90, Thomas Forsyth, St. Louis, October 24, 1831, to the Secretary of War.

63. Ms., Wisconsin Historical Society, Madison, Wisconsin MSS.,

3 D 122, George Boyd, Mackinac, August 18, 1830, to James B. Gardiner, Mackinac (see below, vol. ii, pp. 1206–1209).

64. Ms. book, Public Archives of Canada, Ottawa, Invoices Outward C, American Fur Company, Northern, 1829–34, *passim*.

65. *Senate Documents*, 22nd Cong., 1st sess., vol. ii, no. 90, pp. 77–78, William B. Astor, N. Y., November 25, 1831, to the Secretary of War.

66. Ms. book, Baker Library, Astor Papers, Letter Book ii, 1831–38, pp. 560–561, 578–579, 590, John Jacob Astor, N. Y., February 5, March 31, June 2, 1838, to Robert Stuart, Detroit.

67. Chittenden, *op. cit.*, vol. i, pp. 376–377.

68. *Senate Documents*, 22nd Cong., 1st sess., vol. ii, no. 90, pp. 70–90, Thomas Forsyth, St. Louis, October 24, 1831, to the Secretary of War.

69. *Ibid.*, pp. 41–46, Henry R. Schoolcraft, Sault Ste. Marie, October 24, 1831, to Lewis Cass.

70. Ms., Department of State, Washington, D. C., Territorial Papers, B I A, Miscellaneous, William B. Astor, President, The American Fur Company, N. Y., May 27, 1833, to Lewis Cass, Secretary of War, Washington, D. C.

71. Ms. book, Public Archives of Canada, Ottawa, Invoices Outward C, American Fur Company, Northern, September, 1829–May, 1834, *passim*.

72. Johnston, William, "Letters on the Fur Trade 1833," *Michigan Pioneer and Historical Collections*, vol. xxxvii (1909–10), pp. 132–207, no. 1, pp. 133–138, William Johnston, Sault Ste. Marie, July 23, 1833, to Mrs. Jane Johnston Schoolcraft. (Ms., Smithsonian, Washington, D. C., Schoolcraft Papers, "Manners and Customs.")

73. An interesting sidelight is thrown upon these advances by a statement of Ramsay Crooks made at the time when he was leading the attack on the factory system. One of his accusations was that the factories were charging exorbitant advances on the cost price of their goods. In support of the justice of his attack he declared: "the transportation from any of the Atlantic cities . . . to any of the Northwestern factories, *does not* cost ten per cent. on the invoice of a regular assortment of Indian goods." (*Senate Documents*, 17th Cong., 1st sess., 1821–22, vol. i, no. 60, pp. 9–17, Ramsay Crooks, Washington, January 23, 1822, to [Thomas Hart Benton?].) In this statement Crooks was supported by John Biddle, the Indian agent at Green Bay, who asserted: "This rate [for transportation from New York to Green Bay] would produce a charge of less, certainly, than ten per cent, on the original cost of an invoice of goods for the Indian trade" (*Senate Documents*, 17th Cong., 1st sess., 1821–22, vol. i, no. 60, pp. 3–6, John Biddle, Washington, January 19, 1822, to the Chairman of the Committee on Indian Affairs). Yet the Company of which Crooks was a representative regularly charged a 13½ per cent advance (sometimes, it is said, even one of 15⅓ per cent), plus a commission of 5 per cent,

upon the cost price of goods purchased in New York (*Senate Documents*, 22nd Cong., 1st sess., vol. ii, no. 90, pp. 41–46, Henry Schoolcraft, Sault Ste. Marie, October 24, 1831, to Lewis Cass). Either Crooks was insincere in his attack on the factory system or else the accusation levelled against the American Fur Company that its agents charged an exorbitant price for goods was well-founded. It is not necessary, indeed, that these alternatives should be regarded as mutually exclusive.

74. Many advertisements wherein John Jacob Astor (in 1818 and after, John Jacob Astor & Son) offer furs, peltries, and castoreum for sale, frequently in conjunction with goods from Europe, China, and South America, appear in the New York press of that period. See the *New-York Gazette and General Advertiser*, October 31, 1815, p. 1, col. 5; June 28, 1817, p. 2, col. 5; December 31, 1817, p. 1, col. 6; January 28, 1818, p. 4, col. 7; November 28, 1818, p. 3, col. 4; November 29, 1819, p. 1, col. 5; December 2, 1819, p. 2, col. 7; October 30, 1820, p. 3, col. 5; November 21, 1820, p. 1, col. 2; December 23, 1820, p. 1, col. 2; May 12, 1821, p. 3, col. 3; August 26, 1822, p. 1, col. 4; January 3, 1823, p. 4, col. 1; May 31, 1824, p. 1, col. 6; etc., etc.

75. Ms., Baker Library, Astor Papers, Crooks' and Stuart's Account of Commissions, Fur Company.

76. *Ibid.*, Foreign Shipments and Consignments, American Fur Co. No. 1.

77. *Ibid.*, No. 2.

78. *Ibid.*, Statement of Shipments made by American Fur Company Concern of 1823 — with Gain or Loss on same.

79. Ms. book, Whitehall, London, East India Office, East India Company Records, China Factory Records, Diaries, vol. 222, p. 149.

80. Ms., Baker Library, Astor Papers, Daniel Lord, N. Y., August 7, 1848, to Ramsay Crooks for Robert Stuart and himself.

81. Kelton, *op. cit.*, pp. 72–73.

82. Ms. book, Public Archives of Canada, Ottawa, Ledger, American Fur Company, 1817–34, pp. 119, 152, 384, *passim*; *ibid.*, Journal, American Fur Company, 1817–34, pp. 331, 363.

83. *Ibid.*, Ledger, American Fur Company, 1817–34, *passim*.

84. Ms. (photostat), Wisconsin Historical Society, Madison, Robert Stuart's Letter Book, Mackinac, 1823–30, p. 124, Robert Stuart, Mackinac, October 15, 1824, to John Jacob Astor, Europe (see below, vol. ii, pp. 1176–1177); *Senate Documents*, 22nd Cong., 1st sess., vol. ii, no. 90, pp. 41–46, Henry R. Schoolcraft, Sault Ste. Marie, October 24, 1831, to Lewis Cass.

85. Thwaites, "The Fur-Trade in Wisconsin — 1812–1825," pp. 340–342, Affidavits of William A. Aitkens and Truman A. Warren, July 24, 1824 (ms., Wisconsin Historical Society, Madison, Wisconsin MSS., 90 C 4, 68 B 118).

86. Ms., Wisconsin Historical Society, Madison, Wisconsin MSS., 3 D 122, George Boyd, Mackinac, August 18, 1830, to James B. Gardiner, Mackinac (see below, vol. ii, pp. 1206–1209); see also George H. White's "Sketch of the Life of Hon. Rix Robinson; A Pioneer of Western Michigan," *Michigan Pioneer and Historical Collections*, vol. xi, p. 189.

87. *Hubbard, Gurdon Saltonstall, The Autobiography of* (1911), pp. 23–24. One of the few inside accounts of the fur trade in the Northern Department.

88. Ms. (photostat), Wisconsin Historical Society, Madison, Robert Stuart's Letter Book, Mackinac, 1823–30, pp. 112, 129–132, Robert Stuart, Mackinac, September 17, October 20, 1824, to William B. Astor, N. Y.

89. Ms. book, Public Archives of Canada, Ottawa, Ledger, American Fur Company, Northern Department, 1827–35, *passim*.

90. An agreement between Robert Stuart, for the American Fur Company, and Jacques Vieaux, a Green Bay fur trader, reveals with great clarity the profits which the Company expected to make by charging goods to their traders at high prices and taking the returns at a low rate. The Company was to furnish Vieaux the necessary goods, all said property to belong "exclusively to the American Fur Company" and "all the returns of which, the said Jacques agrees to bring, or send to the Agent of the American fur Company at Mackinac . . . where they shall be taken to account by the said Company at the current prices of that place, at that period — and in consideration of the said Jacques giving all his time and attention to said trade, and defraying all expenses attending it; he shall in lieu of wages, receive all the profits arising thereon." Stuart evidently expected to make so much on the sale of merchandise to Vieaux and the purchase of furs from him that any difference in value between the invoice of merchandise and that of the furs would amount to no more than wages. (Thwaites, "The Fur-Trade in Wisconsin — 1812–1825," p. 342, Agreement between Robert Stuart and Jacques Vieaux, Michilimackinac, August 4, 1824, ms., Wisconsin Historical Society, Madison, Wisconsin MSS., 88 C 11.)

91. Johnston, *op. cit.*, pp. 135–136.

92. Thwaites, "The Fur-Trade in Wisconsin — 1812–1825," pp. xviii–xix.

93. Baird, Hon. Henry S., "Recollections of the Early History of Northern Wisconsin," *Wisconsin Historical Collections*, vol. iv (1857–58), pp. 197–221, p. 215.

94. *Wisconsin Historical Collections*, vol. ix (1880–82), pp. 466–467.

95. Thwaites, "The Fur-Trade in Wisconsin — 1812–25," p. xix.

96. *Ibid.*, pp. 351–353, John Lawe, Michilimackinac, September 12, 1824, to [Mrs. Robert Hamilton, Niagara?].

97. *House Documents*, 20th Cong., 2nd sess., no. 117, pp. 108–113, William Clark and Lewis Cass, Washington, D. C., December 27, 1828, to Senator Thomas H. Benton.

98. Johnston, *op. cit.*, pp. 137–138.

99. Ms., Palais de Justice, Montreal, Notarial Records of P. Lukin, no. 1439, Engagement of J. B^te Gibeau to Gabriel Franchere, Jr., Agent of the American Fur Company, February 9, 1828 (see below, vol. ii, pp. 1192–1194).

100. Johnston, *op. cit.*, pp. 137–138.

101. Ms., Palais de Justice, Montreal, Notarial Records of P. Lukin, no. 1439, Engagement of J. B^te Gibeau to Gabriel Franchere, Jr., Agent of the American Fur Company, February 9, 1828 (see below, vol. ii, pp. 1192–1194).

102. Ms. (photostat), Wisconsin Historical Society, Madison, Robert Stuart's Letter Book, Mackinac, 1823–30, p. 124, Robert Stuart, Mackinac, October 15, 1824, to John Jacob Astor, Europe (see below, vol. ii, pp. 1176–1177).

103. Thwaites, "The Fur-Trade in Wisconsin — 1812–1825," pp. 66–79, p. 71, Thomas L. McKenney, Superintendent of Indian Trade, Georgetown, August 19, 1818, to John C. Calhoun, Secretary of War (ms., Department of the Interior, Washington, D. C., Indian Office Records, Miscellaneous). Compared to these prices, the charge of $1.00 for a pint of salt and $8.00 for a two-and-one-half-gallon tin kettle, sold by Company traders to Missouri Indians in 1831, seems trifling (ms., Department of the Interior, Washington, D. C., Indian Office Records, Miscellaneous, Statement of Prices of Merchandise, Sold to the Sauk, Fox, and Ioway Indians of Missouri, by Traders belonging to the American Fur Company, August 19, 1831). See also price schedule in Neill, *op. cit.*, pp. 30–31, 34.

104. An excellent synopsis of this aspect of the fur trade is found in Henry Colin Campbell's *Wisconsin in Three Centuries, 1634–1905*, 4 vols. (1906), vol. ii, pp. 70–72.

105. Chittenden, *op. cit.*, vol. i, pp. 344–345, 386.

106. Ms., Wisconsin Historical Society, Madison, Wisconsin MSS., 1 D, George Boyd, United States Indian Agent, and Adam D. Steuart, Collector, District of Michilimackinac, Mackinac, November 14, 1820, to Robert Stuart, Agent American Fur Company, Mackinac.

107. *Ibid.*, 3 D 122, George Boyd, Mackinac, August 18, 1830, to James B. Gardiner, Mackinac (see below, vol. ii, pp. 1206–1209).

108. Lockwood, James H., "Early Times and Events in Wisconsin," *Wisconsin Historical Collections*, vol. ii (1855), pp. 98–196, pp. 130–131; ms. book (copy), Detroit Public Library, Burton Historical Collection, and Missouri Historical Society, St. Louis, Letters of Ramsay Crooks, John Jacob Astor, and the American Fur Company, 1813–43, John Jacob

Astor, Office, American Fur Company, November 26, 1827, to Ramsay Crooks, Lancaster, Pennsylvania.

109. Campbell, *op. cit.*, vol. ii, p. 78.

110. Ms., Indiana State Library, Indianapolis, Ewing Papers, William G. Ewing, May 4, 1846, to Messrs. Suydam and Sage, N. Y. The minute attention which Astor paid to the fur market is especially well revealed in his letters from Geneva in 1824 and 1825, and from New York in 1826 and 1827. Interesting from the fashion in which it confirms W. G. Ewing's description of his policy in the shipping of furs is this letter of May 8, 1828, to Astor's agent in New York. "I think you best have at least 10,000 of the very poor Racoon put up and sent to Hamburgh, those that have little *or no* fur on them, those that were baled of better kind, I kept will go to London, and you will be so good as to tell Custer to have his martin and mink skins, as also about 150 to 200 of his best Red Fox, and some Cross Fox put up to be sent, and next packet to London. . . . If application for deer skin, you will of course sell. . . . Muskrat you will of course sell, also Beaver." (Ms. book (copy), Detroit Public Library, Burton Historical Collection, and Missouri Historical Society, St. Louis, Letters of Ramsay Crooks, John Jacob Astor, and the American Fur Company, 1813-43, J. J. Astor, Albany, May 8, 1828, to Ramsay Crooks, N. Y.)

111. Ms., Massachusetts Historical Society, Boston, Perkins MSS., Thomas G. Cary, N. Y., November 2, 1831, to Samuel Cabot.

112. Ms., Department of the Interior, Washington, D. C., Indian Office Records, Miscellaneous, Ramsay Crooks for William B. Astor, N. Y., March 17, 1828, to Thomas L. McKenney, Washington; John Jacob Astor, N. Y., April 10, 1828, to Thomas L. McKenney; *ibid.*, Indian Office Letter Book iv, April 1, 1827-June 5, 1828, p. 344, Thomas L. McKenney, March 19, 1828, to William B. Astor, President, American Fur Company; Thomas L. McKenney, April 5, 1828, to William B. Astor; ms. book, Baker Library, Astor Papers, Letter Book ii, 1831-38, p. 238, William B. Astor, N. Y., June 18, 1834, to General Gratiot, sending a power of attorney to receive $41,260, belonging to the Company and others under the Chicago Treaty; pp. 313-314, John Jacob Astor, N. Y., July 20, 1835, to Robert Stuart, Detroit, "I am glad to see that you have finally arranged so that we shall receive our money from the Treaty."

113. Warren, William W., "History of the Ojibways," *Minnesota Historical Collections*, vol. v (1885), pp. 381-386.

CHAPTER XVII

WESTERN REAL ESTATE

THROUGHOUT Astor's business career, we can trace a close relation between the fur trade and land investment. In 1792 Astor had attempted to gain possession of part of the waste lands of the Crown in Lower Canada. It was through his annual fur-buying trips to Montreal that he had become acquainted with this field of investment, in which many of the Montreal fur magnates were largely concerned. His early fur-trading expeditions into the backwoods of New York and his connection with Peter Smith in the fur business had led him, at about the same time as he became interested in Canadian lands, to invest, both alone and in company with this old partner of his in the Indian trade, in lands in the Mohawk Valley and elsewhere in the backcountry of New York. His interest in western lands did not become of any importance until much later in his life, and consequently, compared with the great enterprises in which he had previously been engaged, appears of much less significance than his early attention to real estate in Canada and New York State. However, this interest in western land was, similarly, a product of his fur trade, this time in the Mississippi Valley, and was principally due to his position at the head of the American Fur Company. The western land in which Astor became concerned, unlike that in New York and Canada, was never deliberately purchased by him as an investment.[1] It usually came into his hands in one of two other ways: either it was purchased in connection with the establishment of trading posts, or it was taken over as the result of mortgages made to the American Fur Company or to its president as security for debts incurred by some of the luckless traders who obtained their supplies of goods on credit from the Company.

Inasmuch as St. Louis was an important fur-trade center, and the headquarters of the American Fur Company's Western Department, we naturally expect to find Astor concerned in some land in its vicinity. In this we are not disappointed. Astor's first connection with St. Louis land came through a transaction related to the fur trade which we have already noted. Astor was given a power of attorney from Schneider & Co., of London, to collect a debt of £1,000 due to that firm from the St. Louis fur trader, Charles Gratiot. In the spring of 1800 Astor took over the debt, and received a note for the amount from Gratiot, payable in April, 1804. Gratiot was disappointed of the sale of some lands, and was consequently unable to pay the note when it was due. By 1806 he had remitted Astor only $1,000. Gratiot was under great apprehension that the New York merchant would sue to recover the balance, and when Astor reassured him on that point the gratitude of the St. Louisan was touching.[2] On December 13, 1813, Gratiot, rather for his own satisfaction than because of any insistence on Astor's part, sent the New Yorker a mortgage for $5,544.35 on a lot of land in St. Louis with a dwelling-house and other buildings, payable on October 21, 1815. Gratiot died in 1817, leaving the mortgage still unpaid, but on January 31, 1818, the St. Louis merchant and philanthropist, John Mullanphy, bought the mortgaged property from Gratiot's widow for 6,000 silver gourdes (dollars), and satisfied the mortgage by paying Astor $5,935.33, principal and back interest.[3] This ended Astor's connection with St. Louis lands for some time.

On November 4, 1822, John McKnight became indebted to the American Fur Company for the sum of $2,400, due on June 15, 1823. He was killed by Comanches in 1823, near a post he had established on the Upper Arkansas.[4] Consequently the mortgage he had offered as security was not settled by the time specified, the land was put up for sale on September 11, 1824, and was bought in by John Jacob Astor for $1,450. It seems probable that John McKnight's debt to the Company was for goods with which he had stocked his fur-trading post. On March 21, 1829, Astor disposed of this lot to the Astorian and American Fur Company trader Russell Farnham, for $2,000,[5] not enough to cover the debt as security for which the lot had originally been offered. Although the Company apparently lost money on this transaction, it is probable, considering the high price charged for trade-goods, that this loss was more nominal than actual, and Astor himself evidently made a profit.

On February 4, 1819, and on March 5, 1825, Astor lent $10,000 and $10,971 respectively to Wilson Price Hunt, once his partner and agent in the Astoria enterprise, who had later moved to St. Louis, where Astor's influence had won him the postmastership. This money seems to have been lent to Hunt in order that he might purchase and develop two tracts of land near St. Louis, which had been mortgaged as security for repayment of the amount. Hunt's investment apparently turned out to be unprofitable, and in December, 1831, Hunt owed Astor $29,390.91, on which Astor requested him at least to pay the interest. In the next month Astor offered to accept the mortgaged property in full payment for the loan and to deed back to Hunt 300 acres of improved land. If Hunt agreed to this proposition, as seems to be implied, he certainly made no haste to fulfill its conditions. Some question as to his title to part of this land, and a consequent lawsuit, appears to have been his excuse for the long delay. In 1835 and 1836 Astor felt called upon to write Hunt some rather pressing — even sharp — letters, and on November 7, 1836, Hunt finally succeeded in getting a conveyance of the two tracts of land made out to Astor. The promised 300 acres were later reconveyed to Hunt, who was also put in charge of the management of the whole.

On July 20, 1840, Hunt managed to sell all the land conveyed by him to Astor, about 4,674 acres, to Kenneth McKenzie, another of Astor's former partners in the fur trade, who had been in charge of the Upper Missouri Outfit of the American Fur Company's Western Department, for $23,375. McKenzie paid $4,000 down and gave Astor a mortgage on the land to secure the rest. This mortgage he succeeded in paying off by August 8, 1845.[6] From the difference between the amount owed by Hunt to Astor and the amount which the latter received for the land deeded him in satisfaction for the mortgage, it is evident that this time Astor lost money through his willingness to lend to his friend and former associate.

This was the end of Astor's attention to lands in the vicinity of St. Louis, which was evidently almost entirely the result of his interest in the fur trade of that region. Astor's withdrawal from the American Fur Company left him, however, in possession of other pieces of land in the vicinity of his former trading posts. In 1835 he was enquiring of Wilson P. Hunt concerning the value of lands which he owned in Illinois. A decade later he was still paying taxes on these same lands, having apparently failed to meet with a satisfactory offer for their purchase.[7] These lands were probably the 700 to 1,000 acres at Cahokia which Astor valued at $10,000 in the late 1830's and at $14,000 in 1846.[8] Astor also owned a lot in Chicago which had been bought from George Cicot by F. Comparet for the American Fur Company. It was probably this land which Astor told Robert Stuart he might sell to a Mr. Beaubien for $4,000, if he wished. This sale was probably made.[9] David Stone and Astor together owned land on the St. Joseph River and on the Wabash, of which Astor's share was 216 and 167 acres. Stone offered to pay $3.00 per acre for the former tract and $4.00 for the latter, that is, $1,316 for the whole. Astor countered with an offer to sell the whole for $2,000, though he instructed Stuart to sell for $1,600 if he thought it worth no more. He soon decided, however, not to do anything with the lands before consulting Ramsay Crooks.[10] We hear nothing further of these lands on the St. Joseph and the Wabash. Probably they were finally sold to Stone, on the advice of Ramsay Crooks. As late as 1845 an acre lot at Mackinac belonging to Astor came to his attention, and was finally sold to a Mr. Scott for $500.[11] Astor also seems in some way to have acquired lands in Florida, which in 1836 he sold to Captain William Henry Chase, of Philadelphia, for $4,500.[12]

Another interesting little case involved lands in Ohio.[13] On September 20, 1826, Thomas Worthington, governor of that State from 1814 to 1818, had borrowed $11,449 from Astor, with interest at 7 per cent, secured by a deed of trust to 700 acres of land. Worthington died in 1827 without having paid this debt. The United States also had a claim on the Worthington estate for $10,000, with interest at 6 per cent from July 20, 1826. There were three additional judgments against the estate, of $1,700, $2,152, and $960, respectively.

Astor decided that it would facilitate matters if he bought the claim of the United States, and also the three minor claims if necessary. Therefore, on August 14, 1830, he made an agreement with Albert Gallatin, son of the statesman of the same name, to go to Ohio and collect the amount due to him, first buying up any other claims against the estate which might impede the collection of the debt to Astor. If Gallatin succeeded in collecting anything on account of the claims of Astor, the latter was first to receive in full and with interest all money used in purchasing the above-mentioned judgments against Worthington. Whatever amount remained over was to be equally divided between Astor and Gallatin, after legal expenses had been deducted. Gallatin was to pay his own personal expenses. Evidently Astor was not very sure of collecting anything like the full amount of his claim against the Worthington estate.

Gallatin accordingly went to Ohio, and in the meantime Astor purchased the claim of the United States for $12,510.94. When Gallatin reached Ohio he was approached by representatives of the Bank of Chillicothe, which also had claims against the Worthington estate. These representatives wished to buy Astor's claims, and offered $21,000 for the two. As an alternative, the Bank's representatives proposed that Astor should receive payment in cash for the full amount of the claim of the United States and a satisfactory amount of land for Astor's own claim. Gallatin advised him to accept one offer or the other, since, if he did not, there was a likelihood that the estate could not pay all the claims against it, and Astor (as well as Gallatin) would receive less than either offer would bring.

When Astor perceived a chance for a settlement at an earlier date and at less trouble and expense than he had anticipated, he began to mention *one-third* instead of *one-half* as the share which should be Gallatin's compensation. Gallatin insisted that one-half had been agreed upon, but said that he would be contented with the smaller amount. On December 17, 1830, the Bank purchased both claims for $22,000, giving two checks, one payable at sight and the other in six months from date with interest from date. These checks were given to Astor on December 28, and on December 31 Gallatin acknowledged the receipt of $3,111.12 in payment for his services, stating that he considered the amount very liberal. It was certainly a very generous compensation for services of only three months' duration, even though less than he would have received had Astor adhered to the original agreement. This is an example of a case in which money-lending on western real estate was not based upon the fur trade, and in which the transaction caused Astor a loss. It is noteworthy that he preferred cash payment at a definite loss to the uncertainty of a possible profit through payment in lands.

Both more important and more typical than any of the foregoing examples was Astor's connection with land in the vicinity of his two principal fur-trading posts in Wisconsin, Prairie du Chien and Green Bay. The former, being the least complex, may be examined first. Upon Astor's retirement from the fur trade in 1834, Joseph Rolette of Prairie du Chien, on the Upper Mississippi, one of the most conspicuous among the traders associated with the American Fur Company, found himself, like most of his class, indebted to the organization of which Astor was the head. Late in August, 1835, Astor was requesting Rolette to pay his note and expressing surprise that he had not already done so.[14] The matter was settled in the customary manner, by Rolette's agreeing to convey to Astor a sufficiently large amount of land to cover his indebtedness. Accordingly, on August 29, 1836, Joseph Rolette and his wife conveyed to Astor and to James Duane Doty a tract of land containing something less than 200 acres, probably about 160 acres. Doty, who was a speculator and politician, then resident at Green Bay, a member of the legislative council of Michigan Territory, and formerly a judge at Prairie du Chien, probably had a part in this deed as Astor's agent, receiving a share in the land in return for his services in managing and disposing of the property. The consideration mentioned in the deed was $10,881, which was doubtless the amount of Rolette's note to Astor, with interest.

On January 11, 1837, Doty wrote to Astor that he would probably be able to sell the Rolette farm for what it had cost.[15] Some sales had already been made, one even before the conveyance from the Rolettes had been signed. Robert Stuart purchased $\frac{2}{20}$ of the lot for $1,100, and John F. Schermerhorn of Utica in the next month bought as much more for $1,200. Early in the year 1837 Aaron Vanderpool became the owner of $\frac{1}{20}$ for the consideration of $500, the value apparently rapidly advancing, and F. R. Tillon invested $2,000 in $\frac{2}{20}$ of the tract.

If all the land could have been sold at the same rate as that purchased by Vanderpool and Tillon, Astor and Doty would have made a good profit, or if it could all have been sold even at the rate which Stuart and Schermerhorn paid, Astor's books would have shown little or no loss. By the spring of 1839, however, no more had been sold than that already mentioned, — 32½ per cent of 160 acres for $4,800,[16] and additional sales could hardly be expected. The Panic of 1837 had caused a cessation of almost all sales of land in the Wisconsin area, especially of land intended, as was that at Prairie du Chien, to be laid out in town lots. So completely did the owners lose interest in what had once been the Rolette farm that in 1845 it was sold for taxes [17] (though later it was recovered by the Astor estate). Less than a year before Astor's death, Joseph G. Cogswell, his secretary and companion, enquired in a letter to Robert Stuart, then located at Lockport, Illinois, "How is it with our lands at Prairie du Chien, are they worth anything?"[18] Had Stuart replied, the answer could only have been, "At present, practically nothing." Astor's Prairie du Chien connection, however, can hardly be classed as a definite enterprise which failed. It was merely an attempt to squeeze the last drop of profit out of the assets of the American Fur Company.

Similar to the Prairie du Chien transaction, but much more important, both because of the amount of property involved and because the enterprise was pressed with incomparably greater spirit than was devoted to Prairie du Chien, was Astor's attempt to found a town near his other Wisconsin trading post at Green Bay, on an arm of Lake Michigan. It may be remembered that on October 1, 1823, Robert Stuart wrote from Mackinac Island to John Jacob Astor & Son in these words: "I have just returned from Green Bay . . . I went in order . . . to close our old concerns. Money was not to be had but we are secured by mortgages on real estate for the most of what the people in that quarter owed us."[19] These mortgages were from Jacques

Porlier, John Lawe, and Augustin and Louis Grignon, and involved a little over 5,000 acres on the banks of the Fox River near Green Bay. In October, 1828, these same persons gave further mortgages, partly to the same tracts covered by the conveyances of five years before, partly to additional pieces of land. These mortgages were not paid off, and in November, 1834, enough of the mortgaged lands were conveyed to John Jacob Astor, Ramsay Crooks, and Robert Stuart, who were the owners of the fur company to which these mortgages had been made, to satisfy the claims against the Green Bay residents. The portions of lots thus conveyed, with another tract which Lewis Rouse had sold to Robert Stuart under similar circumstances five years before, contained about 2,790 acres. The amounts of the mortgages satisfied thereby came to a total of about $35,000.[20]

The circumstances under which this transfer was made were described only a few years after Astor's death by Henry S. Baird, one of Astor's agents and at one time president of the council of Wisconsin Territory, as follows:

The land was originally owned by JOHN LAWE and the GRIGNON family. Together with other real estate, it was taken in payment of balance[s] due [by] the old Green Bay Company to the former company [the American Fur Company], the debt having accrued by loss in the Indian trade — for in this business, it generally happened that the small traders who purchased their goods at high prices, after years of toil and privation spent in the trade, came out with nothing — leaving to the great monopoly the lion's share of the profits. The consideration received by the former owners was trifling compared with the present value of the property.[21]

Of course this last sentence does not necessarily signify that the "former owners" had received less than their land was worth at the time, that is, in 1834, twenty years before this statement was made.

The face value of mortgages extinguished through the conveyance of these lands by the Green Bay settlers was — not to go behind these documents — probably rather above than be-

low the actual immediate value of the tracts ceded. An indication of this is found in the articles of agreement drawn up and
signed at New York City on March 5, 1835, between John
Jacob Astor, Ramsay Crooks, and Robert Stuart of the first
part and James Duane Doty of the second, in which for the
purposes of the agreement the value of the lands at Green Bay
jointly owned by the first three was stated as $10,000. In this
document it was provided that James Duane Doty was to become interested in the proportion of one-fourth in the Green
Bay lands, and was to pay the sum of $2,500 in return for this
share "out of the first avails of the said estate." He was also to
act as agent for the partnership at Green Bay, and in return
for his services he was to receive one-fourth of the net proceeds
from the land, after the $2,500 had been paid. He might not
sell his share without permission.[22] It was the intention of the
associates to lay out a town at Green Bay on the east side of the
Fox River and dispose of the land in this area either by shares
to other capitalists or by lots to individuals desiring to locate in
the community. It was to be Doty's business to act as local
agent, and he was given minute instructions as to how the interests of the town were to be advanced. In order to attract
the "offices of the Register and Receiver of public monies" to
the town, Doty was given permission to deed one or two lots to
each of these officers. He was to endeavor to get the county
seat located at the town, and to have the post-offices abolished
at Navarino and Shanty-town (two communities already established at Green Bay, the first of which had been laid out in 1830
by Daniel Whitney, as a speculation, while the other had grown
up in the vicinity of Fort Smith from 1820 to 1822)[23] and one
in lieu thereof established at Astor, as the new town was shortly
to be christened. Every effort was to be made to secure settlers,
through cheap lots and other inducements.[24]

Doty spent most of the remaining months in 1835 in endeavors to attract to Astor settlers who would locate perma-

nently and carry on their trades or professions. To this end he gave away some lots and sold others at a very low rate, as was the custom among land speculators there at that time. Astor, used to real-estate conditions on Manhattan Island, and with a mind not so flexible as it had been twenty years before, could not help feeling that Doty, in his anxiety to secure settlers, was showing undue generosity in disposing of Astor lots. In June he wrote that it would be "*best not to sell*, unless a few lots to persons who will at once build and reside there." In the next month he expressed the opinion that $100 per lot was very cheap, but gave permission to sell some at that price.[25] In October he wrote to Stuart that he considered Doty's sale of 100 lots at $130 was made at a very low rate. He also stated that he feared Doty did not have sufficient time to spend on Green Bay.[26] He had more justification for this opinion than for his dissatisfaction with the prices at which Astor lots had been sold, since Doty had been absent at the time of an important land sale late in the summer.[27] But to any criticism of the time he was devoting to political matters Doty might have replied that the success or failure of a newly laid out town in Wisconsin at that period was more a matter of politics than anything else, and that anything which he did to increase his political influence would be to the benefit of the town in which he was interested. Astor, in the meantime, had also become concerned to a small extent with he in some of the latter's multifarious investments in Wisconsin bank stocks and lands, especially near the site of Madison, which became the State capital largely through Doty's efforts.

Astor's high opinion of the value, actual or prospective, of his municipal namesake at Green Bay was evidenced by his refusal of the offers made by various speculators to buy out the interests of himself and his associates. Daniel Whitney, the proprietor of the neighboring town of Navarino, offered to buy the town of Astor for $20,000 ($4,000 down, and the balance in four annual payments of $4,000 each, with interest), secured by mortgages on the property.[28] In July Astor wrote to Doty that he had already refused offers ranging from $25,000 to $40,000, and in the next month he stated that Crooks had been offered $50,000 but that he himself would not sell for $100,000. Astor repeated this estimate of the town's value in the next month,[29] although Doty said, "I think $50,000 the fair value of the property *at present.* . . . At this price I should be willing to sell my interest." However, should money continue to pour into the West during the next year as it had in the past six months, the value of Astor would probably go to $100,000. On the other hand, any serious derangement of the currency after the expiration of the charter of the Bank of the United States would at once send its value below $50,000.[30] Stuart was not so sanguine as Astor, and the latter wrote him: "You think $50,000 a great price. At present I believe much more can be got for it."[31]

In January, 1836, Astor, still impressed with the belief that Doty was disposing of more lots and at a lower rate than was advantageous, rather sharply ordered him to cease sales for the future and to report on those which had already been made.[32] He also enquired what would be a proper price to take for the town. Doty replied, denying that his sales had been inconsistent with any previous understanding, as he felt sure Astor would realize on reflection. It was his opinion that any offer of $120,000 or more for the land at Green Bay should be accepted.[33]

Accordingly in the spring of 1836 sales to speculators began to be made of the lands at Green Bay owned by Astor, Crooks, Stuart, and Doty. These lands had originally belonged 75 per cent to Astor, 20 per cent to Crooks, and 5 per cent to Stuart. When Doty associated himself with them he became the owner of ¼ of the whole amount of land, that is, each of the other 3 gave up ¼ of his original holdings. On February 29, 1836, the 4 associates sold $\frac{1}{4}$ of the Green Bay lands to Samuel Stocking of Utica for $40,000, 10 per cent down and the residue in 9 equal annual installments with interest at 6 per cent. As before, the lands were to be left to Astor's management. On March 31, Stocking was visited with another burst of enthusiasm which caused him to purchase an additional $\frac{1}{16}$ of the Green Bay lands for $18,750. It will be observed how much these lands seem to have increased in value within the space of one month. In the meantime Washington Irving had purchased 5 of John Jacob Astor's original 75 shares for $4,000, but this transaction did not concern the other associates and the shares remained in Astor's name. This may have been intended as an indirect way of compensating Irving for writing *Astoria*. Sales to speculators now became rapid. On April 6, the 4 associates sold $\frac{1}{32}$ of the lands to Norris M. Woodruff of Watertown, New York, for $13,000, $3,000 down and the balance in 9 equal annual installments with interest at 7 per cent. On April 14, $\frac{1}{64}$ was sold to James Watson Webb for $7,830, $783 in cash, otherwise on the same conditions as those found in the first contract of sale to Stocking. On April 30, the same proportion was sold to Chester Jenings for $9,375, $2,343.75 down and the balance in 4 annual installments with interest at 7 per cent. Finally, on May 6, $\frac{1}{16}$ was sold to Charles Butler for $37,500, $9,375 down and the rest in 4 equal annual installments with interest at 7 per cent.[34]

When this last sale had been made, the respective proportions of the various owners, upon a basis of 320 shares, stood as follows: Astor owned 57.417; Crooks, 21; Stuart, 5.25; Doty, 70; Stocking, 100; Irving, 21.33; Woodruff, 10; Webb, 5; Jenings, 5; and Butler, 25. Thus it will be observed that between the last day of February and the sixth of May the estimated value of the whole Green Bay estate had increased from $160,000 to $600,000. Leaving out Irving's proportion, we see that the 4 original associates had succeeded in disposing of 28/64 of their interests, originally estimated as worth $10,000, for $126,455, on which, however, they had received down payments of only about $21,376.75. It is evident that the 4 original associates would come out of this affair very well, regardless of the actual sales of lots in Astor, if they could only succeed in collecting the amounts still due from the later speculators. It now remains to be seen whether these conditions were fulfilled.

Even while these sales at high rates were being made, Astor was far-seeing enough to observe the prospects of difficulties in the near future. On March 12, 1836, he wrote to Robert Stuart, "The land fever seems to run high. I fear there will be a blow up by and by."[35] Nevertheless, during 1836 and 1837 Doty sold some lots; leased others, rent free, on condition that buildings should be erected on them; endeavored to secure, through grants of lots, the location of the Bank of Wisconsin, the land office, the receiver's office, the post-office, and other similar institutions, at Astor; assisted in similar fashion the establishment of various churches in the town; laid out roads and erected bridges; projected a steamboat connection between Chicago and Green Bay; and pushed the erection of a hotel. The projects of the bank, land office, and hotel went through successfully, but the Panic of 1837, which Astor had foreseen in the spring of the previous year, abruptly halted the progress of the town of Astor. Early in January, Astor informed Doty of the great pressure for money then existing. In March, Woodruff unsuccessfully endeavored to sell Astor his share in the town. In July, Butler had to be dunned for an installment on his share, and in September Astor repeated, "here matters are very bad." By the end of the year sales and collections at Green Bay had come to a standstill.

On February 22, 1838, the total amount which had been received from the speculators, Stocking, Woodruff, Webb, Jenings, and Butler, in payment for their shares in the lands at Green Bay, principal and interest, was $35,857.04. Webb and Butler had been able to pay practically nothing beyond the first installment.

Matters at Green Bay continued bad. "The times are no better here," wrote Doty on June 12, 1839, "but rather worse. There is no money in this country and we are living by barter."[36] On January 11, 1838, Astor and Navarino had been "united under the name of the Borough of Green Bay,"[37] probably to enable the citizens of Navarino to tax property in Astor. In 1838, and again in 1839, Doty was elected territorial delegate to Congress, and while there he used his position to further the interests of his land speculation at Green Bay by removing the Navarino postmaster and having the office transferred to Astor,[38] and by inducing the government to make expenditures in that vicinity for river improvements and roads. On December 12, 1840, Charles Butler, being unable to satisfy more than the first cash payment on the one-sixteenth interest in the town of Astor which he had purchased for $37,500, made over all his interest in the lands to the four original owners.

In 1841 President Tyler appointed Doty to the governorship of Wisconsin Territory, an office which he held till 1844, and this, of course, necessitated the appointment of an agent to take charge of affairs at Green Bay. Indeed, since 1838 Doty had usually been absent from the vicinity of that town, attending to his political duties. Consequently, Nathan Goodell was made agent at Green Bay in 1842.[39] On December 28, 1844, Doty sold out all his one-fourth interest in the lands at Green Bay to Astor for $4,000 — a striking evidence of the great decline in the property's value. There may have been a number of reasons for this action. As commissioner for public buildings and as governor, Doty had involved himself in various scandals connected with banks, the location of the State capital, and the erection of a State house, which had resulted in a demand for his removal by the territorial delegate and finally in his failure to be reappointed in 1844. His withdrawal from the partnership may have been taken on the initiative of the others concerned, being possibly inspired by the feeling that his connection with the enterprise would add little to its respectability, though quite as probably he was merely disgusted with the unprofitable character of the lands and wished to rid himself of all responsibility for them.

Others had also severed their connection with the enterprise. Webb had gone bankrupt in 1842. Irving had sold back the interest which he had bought from Astor at $4,000 for $2,100, that is, for what he had paid less receipts he had received on the shares sold to later speculators.[40] The account of Jenings seems to have been carried by Astor, who may have felt responsible for having brought Jenings — once the manager of Astor's City Hotel — into the speculation. Stocking, the largest shareholder in the lands, had paid nothing after the first two installments, and consequently his proportion was taken over in 1846 by foreclosure. Only Woodruff had kept up his payments, thereby, as it turned out, throwing more good money after that which had already been lost.

The bill filed in the suit against Stocking gives a clear picture of the situation at that time. It was alleged that Stocking not only owed the associates $53,016.64, principal and interest on his purchase of five-sixteenths of the lands, but also five-sixteenths of $23,198.15 which had been expended over and above receipts from land sales, for taxes, agent's salary, improvements, etc. It was also stated that "the lands . . . have greatly depreciated in their estimated value, and cannot be sold at any other than nominal prices, and the whole value of the interest purchased by . . . Samuel Stocking is not worth and will not bring the amount remaining unpaid thereon."

In the meantime Nathan Goodell acted as agent at Green Bay. He got most of Astor vacated, so as not to be responsible for town taxes; paid such taxes on the property as it was impossible to avoid; bought in lots which had been sold for nonpayment of such assessments; and endeavored to collect the amounts still due on lots which had been previously sold, or to persuade those purchasers who were unable to complete their payments to sign away their interests. Every now and then he actually succeeded in selling a lot for some nominal price or in leasing a building for little or nothing more than its upkeep. Three years after he had assumed the agency, it was his opinion that matters were worse than ever, though in 1841 he would not have imagined it possible. Only about two-thirds of the houses in the town were occupied. In Goodell's opinion the only thing which could improve conditions would be the establishment of regular steamboat communication with Buffalo, which would bring to Green Bay some of the thousands of immigrants who were annually going to other parts of Wisconsin.

Accordingly, on September 8, 1845, Astor agreed with Augustus Walker that the latter should run a good steamboat fortnightly from Buffalo to Green Bay during the season of navigation from 1846 to 1848, inclusive, for which he was to receive $1,000 the first year and $500 each for the other two, one-half payable on the first of July and of October of each year. Doty had advocated making such an arrangement much earlier in the history of the enterprise. The prospects for steamboat communication with the East caused a temporary revival of prosperity, which speedily passed when the boat made a few rather irregular visits and then, soon after the payment of the first installment of consideration money, completely ceased to run, while the suspension of the service was accompanied by suspicions of collusion with some other land company. Astor declined to take any further steps toward the establishing of transportation facilities between Green Bay and the East, and at his death, late in March, 1848, no such service had been opened.

It is hardly necessary to state, after what has gone before, that Astor's attempt to found a town at Green Bay resulted in a financial loss to him, at least on paper. The expenses of managing the investment exceeded by several thousand dollars the amount received from the sale of lots, while Astor's proportion of the sums paid in by speculators for shares in the investment did not exceed the face values of the mortgages under which the lands had been secured. Others of those concerned in the town of Astor probably lost more heavily in proportion than did the man after whom the community was named. Woodruff, for example, after paying out $13,000 in ten installments, to say nothing of interest, for his one thirty-second interest in the town, later sold out his share to Astor's executors for $3,000. It becomes especially plausible that Astor's actual loss was comparatively light when we consider that the mortgages under which these lands had been secured were given to cover debts owed for trade-goods furnished to Green Bay traders at high prices by Astor's American Fur Company.

The immediate and most obvious reason for the failure of the projected town was, of course, the general financial Panic of 1837. This, however, does not furnish an entirely adequate explanation. Though the investment would probably have succeeded but for the panic, still this occurrence need not have ruined forever the chances of establishing the town on a profitable basis. Another reason for failure was that the lands were chiefly owned by non-residents who could not be constantly on hand to attend to the welfare of their property; and a third was that the management was divided between individuals at a great distance one from another. Even when Doty was concerned in the lands, he was frequently absent on one or another of his multitudinous political and financial speculations. Nor can Astor be altogether absolved from responsibility. He was more than seventy years old at the time this enterprise was begun, and his mind had lost the elasticity of his prime. Not only did he have no personal knowledge of conditions in the West or of the methods which had there been found effective in land development, but he seemed psychologically incapable of allowing his agent, who was on the spot and knew the circumstances, a free hand in the local management of the enterprise. He could not avoid thinking of the Green Bay lands in terms of New York City, and the prices at which Astor lots were being sold seemed to him insanely low, while to convey lots gratis appeared almost sacrilegious. This exaggerated idea of the value of Astor held by its principal owner not only hampered the agent at Green Bay in making sales of individual lots, but also made it impossible for Astor, who was handling the New York end of the business, to secure purchasers for the town as a whole before the crash came — though had he succeeded this would have only resulted in transferring the loss to the new speculators.

Even after the effects of the panic had partly died away, Astor did not display his usual energy in pushing the enterprise. It was not that he had lost interest in the project because of any belief that it was too insignificant to occupy his attention. A bill for eighty-seven cents, charged him for a deed which he thought should be paid for by someone else, could still rouse his interest and resentment.[41] But the establishment of steamship communication between Buffalo and Green Bay, which showed excellent prospects of not only being a good investment in itself but also of greatly increasing the value of his lands, was an enterprise far beyond the vigor which remained to him. So the Green Bay land investment must be classed as one of Astor's few financial failures. To be sure, the lands concerned had been merely a by-product of his fur trade, and his attempt at their development had consequently been only a side-interest, probably handled in his last years almost entirely by his son. The attempt to establish a town at Green Bay was the last definite business enterprise of Astor's life, undertaken when he had already retired from an active share in commerce, and the fact that it was unsuccessful largely because of Astor's age causes to stand out in stronger colors the initiative and energy which he had displayed under similar circumstances when he still possessed full vigor of mind and body.

NOTES

1. In this connection a legend or myth preserved by Joseph A. Scoville might be appropriate. "Some one," he writes, "once asked John Jacob Astor about the largest sum of money he ever made at any one time in his life. He said in reply that the largest sum he ever missed making was in reference to the purchase of Louisiana, in connection with De Witt Clinton, Governeur [sic] Morris, and others. They intended to purchase all of that province of the Emperor Napoleon, and then sell it to President Jefferson at the same price, merely retaining the public domain, charging 2½ commission on the purchase. It fell through, for some trifling cause or other. Had they succeeded, Mr. Astor estimated that he should have made about thirty millions of dollars." ([Scoville, Joseph A.], *The Old Merchants of New York City*, 5 vols. (1889), vol. iii, p. 37.) It is rather hard to understand how Astor and his associates could sell the Louisiana Territory to President Jefferson — presumably meaning the United States — and yet retain "merely . . . the public domain." Perhaps the narrator means that the associates intended to retain the right to quit rents. This question is not very important, for there is little doubt that this story belongs in the same category as that of "East Indian Pass No. 68." The ascription of such tales to Astor makes one wonder whether that merchant actually did amuse himself in his later life by inventing wild romances concerning the foundations of his fortune for the delectation of inquisitive questioners. On the other hand, some of Astor's best-authenticated and most successful exploits — that involving the "Chinese mandarin," for example — are almost as fantastic as any of his fictional enterprises.

2. Ms. book, Missouri Historical Society, St. Louis, Gratiot Collection, Charles Gratiot's Letter Book, 1798–1816, letters from Charles Gratiot, St. Louis, to John Jacob Astor, N. Y., *passim.*

3. Ms. book, City Hall, St. Louis, General Records, D 349, G 35, O 194.

4. Chittenden, Hiram Martin, *The American Fur Trade of the Far West*, 3 vols. (1902), vol. ii, p. 501, note.

5. Ms. book, City Hall, St. Louis, General Records, M 243, V 212–213.

6. *Ibid.*, H 189, M 238, Z 193–5, C² 282, N² 452, O² 376, T³ 238; ms. book, Baker Library, Astor Papers, Letter Book ii, 1831–38, letters from John Jacob Astor (chiefly) and William B. Astor to Wilson P. Hunt, St. Louis, *passim.* It must be this land which in the late 1830's Astor described as 4,000–5,000 acres near St. Louis, cost $45,000, worth $35,000 (ms. book, Office of the Astor Estate, N. Y., Untitled memorandum book).

7. Ms. book, Baker Library, Astor Papers, Letter Book ii, 1831–38, pp. 287, 337, John Jacob Astor, N. Y., March 9, October 12, 1835, to Wilson P. Hunt, St. Louis; Letter Book iii, 1845–48, p. 34, John Jacob Astor by William B. Astor, N. Y., October 28, 1845, to Benjamin Clapp, St. Louis.

8. Ms. book, Office of the Astor Estate, N. Y., Untitled memorandum book; *ibid.*, Valuation of Houses & Lands, October, 1846.

9. Ms. book, Baker Library, Astor Papers, Letter Book ii, 1831–38, pp. 299, 313–314, 318, William B. Astor and John Jacob Astor, N. Y., May 12, July 20, 30, 1835, to Robert Stuart, Detroit.

10. *Ibid.*, pp. 319, 322, John Jacob Astor, N. Y., August 8, 12, 1835, to Robert Stuart, Detroit; p. 319, John Jacob Astor, August 8, 1835, to David Stone, Detroit.

11. *Ibid.*, Letter Book iii, 1845–48, pp. 32–33, 114, 276, 282, William B. Astor for John Jacob Astor, N. Y., October 25, 1845, to Robert Stuart, Lockport, Illinois; Robert Stuart, Lockport, Illinois, September 1, 1846, to John Jacob Astor; John Jacob Astor by William B. Astor, N. Y., September 9, 1846, to David Stuart, Detroit, Michigan; William B. Astor, N. Y., March 13, April 6, 1848, to David Stuart, Detroit, Michigan.

12. *Ibid.*, Letter Book ii, 1831–38, pp. 362, 365, William B. Astor, N. Y., January 5, 11, 1836, to Captain W. H. Chase, Philadelphia.

13. Ms. book, New York Historical Society, an untitled memorandum book, devoted to an account of Albert R. Gallatin's activities as John Jacob Astor's agent for the collection of monies due from the estate of Thomas Worthington, former governor of Ohio.

14. Ms. book, Baker Library, Astor Papers, Letter Book ii, 1831–38, p. 327, John Jacob Astor, N. Y., August 27, 1835, to Joseph Rolette, Prairie des Chiens [*sic*].

15. *Ibid.*, Letters, James Duane Doty, Green Bay, January 11, 1837, to John Jacob Astor, N. Y.

16. *Ibid.*, Copies of Deeds, etc. relating to Lands at Prairie Du Chien, *passim*; *ibid.*, James D. Doty's a/c, 23 March '39.

17. *Ibid.*, Certificate from Seth Hill, Treasurer, Crawford County, Wisconsin Territory, December 8, 1845, to E. W. Pelton.

18. *Ibid.*, Letter Book iii, 1845–48, pp. 181–182, Joseph G. Cogswell, N. Y., May 20, 1847, to Robert Stuart, Lockport, Illinois (see below, vol. ii, pp. 1256–1257).

19. Ms. (photostat), Wisconsin Historical Society, Madison, Ramsay Crooks' and Robert Stuart's Letter Book, Mackinac, Detroit, New York, etc., 1820–25, Robert Stuart, Mackinac, October 1, 1823, to John Jacob Astor & Son, N. Y.

20. Ms. book, Baker Library, Astor Papers, Green Bay Land Book, p. 1; ms., Chicago Historical Society, John Lawe Papers, vol. ii, pp. 527–530.

21. Baird, Hon. Henry S., "Recollections of the Early History of Northern Wisconsin," *Wisconsin Historical Collections* (vol. iv), 1857–58, pp. 197–221, p. 215.

22. Ms., Baker Library, Astor Papers, Agreement between J. J. Astor, R. Crooks & Robert Stuart and James D. Doty of Green Bay, in relation to the lands at that place — New York 5 March 1835.

23. Neville, Ella Hoes, Martin, Sarah Greene, and Martin, Deborah Beaumont, *Historic Green Bay* (1893), pp. 166–167, 237.

24. Ms., Baker Library, Astor Papers, Letters, John Jacob Astor, Ramsay Crooks, Robert Stuart, N. Y., March 5, 1835, to James Duane Doty, Present.

25. *Ibid.*, Letter Book ii, 1831–38, pp. 307, 312, John Jacob Astor, N. Y., June 22, July 16, 1835 (see below, vol. ii, pp. 1230–1231), to James Duane Doty, Green Bay.

26. *Ibid.*, p. 338, John Jacob Astor, N. Y., October 15, 1835, to Robert Stuart.

27. *Ibid.*, p. 330, John Jacob Astor, N. Y., September 8, 1835, to James Duane Doty, Green Bay.

28. *Ibid.*, Memorandum from Daniel Whitney, Navarino, May 18, 1835, to J. D. Doty, enclosed in a letter from J. D. Doty, Green Bay, May 19, 1835, to J. J. Astor, N. Y.

29. *Ibid.*, Letter Book ii, 1831–38, pp. 312, 322, 330, John Jacob Astor, N. Y., July 16 (see below, vol. ii, pp. 1230–1231), August 11, September 8, 1835, to James Duane Doty, Green Bay.

30. *Ibid.*, Letters, J. D. Doty, Detroit, August 19, 1835, to J. J. Astor, N. Y.

31. *Ibid.*, Letter Book ii, 1831–38, p. 331, John Jacob Astor, N. Y., September 11, 1835, to Robert Stuart.

32. *Ibid.*, p. 367, John Jacob Astor, N. Y., January 13, 16, 1836, to Judge Doty, Green Bay.

33. *Ibid.*, Letters, J. D. Doty, Astor, February 9, 14, 1836, to J. J. Astor, N. Y.

34. *Ibid.*, Green Bay Land Book, pp. 6–9.

35. *Ibid.*, Letter Book ii, 1831–38, p. 381, John Jacob Astor, N. Y., March 4, 1836, to Robert Stuart.

36. *Ibid.*, Letters, J. D. Doty, Astor, June 12, 1839, to J. J. Astor, N. Y.

37. Neville, Martin, and Martin, *op. cit.*, p. 260.

38. Ms., Baker Library, Astor Papers, Letters, J. D. Doty, Washington, May 10, 1840, to J. J. Astor, N. Y.

39. The history of Astor's Green Bay land investment under the local management of Nathan Goodell is of such slight importance and is drawn from such a number and variety of documents that exact references to all those consulted for the purpose would be of little value. All the information on this phase of Astor's western real estate investments, unless another source is specified, is to be found in the Astor Papers, Baker Library, Soldiers Field, Boston.

40. See also Pierre M. Irving's *The Life and Letters of Washington Irving*, 4 vols. (1862–64), vol. iii, pp. 86–87.

41. Ms. book, Baker Library, Astor Papers, Letter Book iii, 1845–48, p. 58, John Jacob Astor by William B. Astor, N. Y., February 5, 1846, to Nathan Goodell, Green Bay, Wisconsin (see below, vol. ii, pp. 1250–1252).

CHAPTER XVIII

THE PUTNAM COUNTY LAND CLAIMS
(THE MORRIS CASE), 1803-1832

ONE of Astor's less important transactions, which is of such an interesting nature as to justify attention out of all proportion to the value of the property involved, arose out of his claim to certain lands situated principally in Putnam County, New York. Astor's part in this affair has made him the subject of more criticism than almost any of his other activities except his presidency of the American Fur Company. For this reason, if for no other, this matter is worthy of our attention.

Astor, from his early years in the United States, had been interested in the backcountry of New York State as a field for land investment. It will be remembered that during the last decade of the eighteenth century he had invested in several tracts, of which the most important were the two Mohawk Valley areas known as the Charlotte River and Byrnes Patent tracts, formerly owned by Sir William Johnson, in which Astor had become concerned with Peter Smith and William Laight. Their title turned out to be incomplete, and there ensued a process of litigation and private negotiation, extending over a period of nearly a decade, before their claim to most of the acreage in these tracts was legally established, about the year 1802. Astor's disappointment in this matter cured him for all time of investment in lands in the backcountry of New York, to be rented or sold to private individuals, but, as we shall see, he was still ready to involve himself in even more extensive land litigation if there appeared to be a chance of making a good lump profit. Consequently, in 1809, though his mind was mostly occupied with plans for the recently incorporated American Fur Company and the establishment of Astoria, he nevertheless devoted some time and attention to purchasing the claims of the Morris heirs to about 50,000 acres of confiscated land in Putnam and Dutchess counties, New York.

It is necessary to go back a century and more to examine the circumstances which gave birth to Astor's project. On June 17, 1697, a grant including the land in question was made by William III to Adolph Philipse. His nephew and heir, F. Philipse, in a will dated June 6, 1751, left the property to his son, Philip Philipse, and to his son's daughters. In 1754 the land was divided among the heirs, one of whom was Mary Philipse, who married Major Roger Morris in 1758, having, according to tradition, two years earlier rejected the suit of a Virginia colonel of militia named George Washington.[1] In 1779 the property of Roger Morris and his wife was confiscated by the New York legislature because of their adherence to the loyalist cause, and from 1782 to 1784 the property, amounting to nearly 50,000 acres, was sold to various individuals for £23,915 17s. Roger Morris died in September, 1794, being survived by his wife and by four children, Johanna, Amherst, Maria, and Henry Gage, of whom Amherst died in 1802, intestate and a bachelor. In 1787 Joanna Philipse, the mother of Mrs. Morris and a trustee of the estate, had applied to the legislature, on behalf of the Morris heirs, for compensation, and a committee of the legislature had replied that the courts were open to their claim and that the legislature need not interpose.[2] The Morris heirs seem to have felt that to press their claim in the courts would be futile, and they made no attempt to pursue the case any further. So matters remained for more than twenty years, during which time the heirs seem to have relinquished all expectation of the recovery of the confiscated land or of compensation for it.

However, some time in 1809, Astor made the discovery that, according to the marriage settlement of Mary and Roger

Morris, they possessed only a life interest in the property and that upon their death it would descend to their children. The most important of Astor's recent biographers, Arthur D. Howden Smith, hazards the guess that Aaron Burr, who had previously acted for Astor in land cases and who was prowling about London at this time, was responsible for bringing the matter to his attention.[3] Because of the existence of this settlement, Astor reasoned, the confiscatory act of New York State could operate only against the life interest of Roger and Mary Morris, and, after their death, their children, under the terms of the treaty of peace, would be legally entitled to the land with all its improvements. Astor at once saw that here was a chance for a man possessed of some ready money and a venturesome spirit to make a good profit by buying out at a low rate the rights of the Morris heirs, who would look on such a payment almost in the light of money dropped from heaven. Mrs. Morris, who had been born about 1730, could not live much longer. Upon her death, the owner of the heirs' rights could force New York State to pay a handsome sum in order to make good the claims of the occupants, since the State would be in honor bound to secure to those who had purchased property from it in good faith the full legal ownership of their holdings. Accordingly, about the 18th or 19th of December, 1809, an agent of John Jacob Astor purchased from the three surviving children of Roger and Mary Morris their rights in the confiscated property for the sum of £20,000.[4]

Astor could not make any attempt to eject the present occupants of the land until the death of Mrs. Morris, but he had no idea of instituting suits against the individual owners, save as a last resort. It was his intention to collect from the State. Should Astor's claim to the land be substantiated, the present occupants, even prior to Mrs. Morris' death, would be unable to furnish a clear title to the land for purposes of mortgage or sale. It was Astor's hope that the State, on being notified of his claim, would immediately take steps to extinguish it, without his taking any legal measures. To this end, it was necessary for his claim to be widely known; consequently in the summer of 1810 Astor sent an agent, H. Livingston, on a tour of several days through the tract in question, to notify the occupants of the situation. According to his own statement, the agent "found a friendly personal reception every where" — a testimony either to the extraordinarily courteous nature of the inhabitants of Putnam and Dutchess counties or to the confidence they had in the superiority of their own rights. All put their confidence in the legislature under which they held their land, and none seemed to have any desire to open immediate negotiations, though some enquired, perhaps rather idly, at what price Astor would be inclined to sell. Astor had instructed his agent to state that he would dispose of his interest "on reasonable terms," but this was probably a mere cloak for his real intention of applying to the legislature.[5]

Astor could also endeavor to insure some immediate profits, as well as winning himself useful allies, by selling part of his claim to other moneyed men of a speculative turn of mind. As early as June 30, 1810, he had sold one equal undivided fourth part of the lands to John K. Beekman for $50,000. This brought him a profit of 100 per cent on that proportion of his investment, since he had originally paid only approximately $100,000 for all the land. Beekman, however, probably because he had run short of funds, sold back half of his one-fourth share to Astor within a year at the same rate as he had purchased it, that is, for $25,000.[6] In this transaction Beekman made no profit, and even lost nearly a year's interest on his investment, but later he cashed in by selling his remaining one-eighth, for which he had paid only $25,000, to Theodosius Fowler for $55,000.[7] When the case came to trial nearly a score of years later, those concerned with Astor were Theodosius Fowler, Cadwallader D. Colden, and Cornelius I.

Bogert,[8] though Astor's interest amounted to well over nine-tenths of the whole.[9] Any others who may have been concerned from time to time had probably been forced by the delay to sell out to Astor.[10]

Astor did not long delay offers of a compromise. On September 29, 1813, he enclosed a letter to the commissioners of the land office with one to Jacob R. Van Rensselaer in which he made use of the fiction that he was acting largely as the agent of other gentlemen interested with him. They had decided "that at the rate at which they purchased the estate ought to produce $300,000 to make them whole, including Interest." The amount demanded was about half the estimated value of the land. This letter was intended to create the impression that those interested in the Morris estate had purchased at so high a rate that payment of $300,000 would not do much more than compensate them for their original expenditure, with interest. This was true in this sense, that Astor, who had purchased a claim to these lands at only one-third of that amount which he now demanded, had in the meantime sold part of his interest to various individuals, and they to others, at so high a rate of profit that a 200 per cent advance on the original purchase price would not give the last purchasers much more than their original investment with reasonable interest. Astor also remarked that he found that the rights of reversion were "getting more and more divided," so that some early arrangement was imperative; and surely he must have spoken with authority on this subject, since he had been the one principally responsible for the wider dissemination of these reversionary rights. Astor at this time seems to have scrupulously abstained from allowing one hand to be aware of the other's activities.[11]

The State officials, however, do not seem to have taken Astor's claim and offer of compromise very seriously. They took no definite action for some years; and, since Mrs. Morris was still alive, Astor could not force the officials to any steps in regard to the matter. On January 16, 1819, however, Astor again brought his claim before the legislature and repeated his previous offer to compromise for $300,000. "I am still willing," he said, "to receive the amount which I then stated, with interest on the same, payable in money or stock, bearing an interest of — per cent, payable quarterly. The stock may be made payable at such periods as the hon. the Legislature may deem proper." Astor asserted that his offer was quite reasonable, in view of the value of the property, which he estimated as being about 50,000 acres and worth perhaps $450,000. He had once spoken of the value of the land as being over $1,000,000. He also declared that the same amount of money invested otherwise would have probably yielded him better profits. This latter argument probably did not much impress the members of "the hon. the Legislature," who must have wished that Astor had spared them trouble by utilizing these other more profitable fields of investment. Astor's offer in 1819 was, then, that he would compromise for a total of $415,000, including interest; he had long since shed his rôle of agent for certain unspecified "other gentlemen."[12] However, though a bill in regard to his claim was under consideration in the spring of 1819, nothing was done toward extinguishing his rights in the land.[13]

The reason for the legislature's inactivity was that Mrs. Morris' continued survival estopped Astor from taking any steps toward the assertion of his reversionary right to the land in question; and naturally enough, each legislature preferred to pass on such a ticklish question to the next. Astor may have felt occasional stabs of irritation as the lady reached her ninetieth year and still showed no intention of departing for a better world. When Astor had made the bargain in 1809 he must have calculated that a woman who was then four-score years of age would in all probability shortly pass on, at the decent, conservative age of eighty-four or eighty-five at the most. Otherwise he would probably not have made her three children what, so far as they were concerned, practically amounted to a gift of £20,000, since had it not been for him there was little likelihood of their ever receiving a farthing for their rights. Astor had some experience with longevity, since his own father had in 1816 at the age of ninety-two ceased to draw the pension supplied by his son's filial piety. But Mrs. Morris was of a still more hardy stock, and 1822 passed with no news from England, as did the next year and the next. Astor may well have wondered whether she would reach the century mark — might perhaps outlive him, since he was himself over sixty and not enjoying the best of health. He knew that his death before bringing the matter to a successful conclusion would be a source of immense amusement to a good share of the population of the State, and particularly to the farmers of Putnam County, though he could comfort himself with the thought that his son, at least, would get the benefit, sooner or later. However, in 1825 Mrs. Morris finally died, sincerely mourned by that legislature of the State of New York which was thus forced to decide on ways and means of meeting Astor's claims to what had once been her estate.[14]

Astor began operations on January 15, 1827, by offering to accept a "*moderate sum*, compared with the actual value of the lands, *exclusive of Improvements*; and to transfer his title to the State; or he is willing to submit the question of title, and all questions appertaining to his rights, to the judgment of the Supreme Court of the United States by an amicable suit; or, that the matter be submitted to the final decision and award of three competent, unbiassed, and independent arbitrators, to be agreed on by the President of the United States."[15]

On February 15, 1827, a committee of the senate reported that 48,472 acres of land, worth more than $600,000, were affected by Astor's claim. They stated that Astor and his associates asserted that their claim had cost $350,000. The committee believed that an offer of payment in 5 per cent stock, redeemable after 1850, might be accepted. The committee also stated that Astor wished "an amicable arrangement" and had assisted the committee in its investigation.[16] Accordingly on April 6, 1827, a bill was passed whereby the legislature offered to pay Astor $450,000 in State stock with interest at 5 per cent per annum, payable quarterly, redeemable at the pleasure of the State, should the United States Supreme Court decide that he was entitled to recover the land claimed by him without payment for buildings and permanent improvements, or $250,000 if the Supreme Court decided that he could recover *with* such payment. It was provided, however, that Astor must first be victorious in three out of five ejectment proceedings in the circuit court of the Southern District of New York before the case should be brought to the Supreme Court of the United States, while if he should be defeated in three out of five his title should be relinquished. It was further provided that the title to the lands must be conveyed to the State before any stock certificates should be issued, and that Astor (or his heirs) must accept the conditions of the act within six months and bind himself to abide by the compromise therein proposed.[17] Gustavus Myers hints that the legislature may have been corruptly influenced to pass this bill, but it is hard to see what else they could have done which would have been a better safeguard to the State's interests.[18]

Astor had until October 6, 1827, to accept the terms laid down in the act of April 6. However, there was nothing to prevent him from continuing any ejectment suits which he might already have inaugurated, regardless of whether he accepted or rejected the legislature's offer. But the trial of certain cases, which had been set for early in June, was postponed because of a "want of some agreement between the counsel,"[19] and later Astor was prevented from accepting the offer of compromise because some doubt arose as to whether the Morris heirs had released their claims completely to Astor. Representatives of the State professed to believe that there might be a flaw in the conveyance, in which case Astor might receive payment and at the same time the Morris heirs might also be enabled to claim compensation from the State.[20]

The six months within which Astor's acceptance must be filed in order for the act of April 6 to go into effect had passed and no agreement had been reached. Nevertheless in November, 1827, an ejectment suit connected with the Astor claim went to trial. Astor was represented principally by David B. Ogden and Thomas Addis Emmet, but also by Jonas Platt, T. J. Oakley, and probably Murray Hoffman, perhaps assisted outside the court room by Aaron Burr. Against this formidable array of legal talent the State pitted not only the attorney-general but also two of the most gifted representatives of the bar then in public life, Daniel Webster and Martin Van Buren, with Ogden Hoffman, Talcott, and Cowles. The State argued that there had never been a marriage settlement, and that, if there had been, the remainders had been destroyed by the act of attainder. Astor's counsel produced witnesses to the marriage settlement, and declared that no act of attainder against an individual or individuals could affect a right already belonging to another. The high points in this case were the speeches of the leading lawyers involved, Daniel Webster for the State and Thomas Addis Emmet for Astor. An early Astor biographer, who is by no means consistently sympathetic with his subject, described the speeches as follows:

Mr. Webster's speech on this occasion betrays, even to the unprofessional reader, both that he had no case and that he knew he had not, for he indulged in a strain of remark that could only have been designed to prejudice, not convince, the jury.

"It is a claim for lands," said he, "not in their wild and forest state, but for lands the intrinsic value of which is mingled with the labor expended upon them. It is no every day purchase, for it extends over towns and counties and almost takes in a degree of latitude. It is a stupendous speculation. The individual who now claims it has not succeeded to it by inheritance; he has not attained it, as he did that vast wealth which no one less envies him than I do, by fair and honest exertions in commercial enterprise, but by speculation, by purchasing the forlorn hope of the heirs of a family driven from their country by a bill of attainder. By the defendants, on the contrary, the lands in question are held as a patrimony. They have labored for years to improve them. The rugged hills had grown green under their cultivation before a question was raised as to the integrity of their titles."

A line of remark like this would appeal powerfully to a jury of farmers. Its effect, however, was destroyed by the simple observation of one of the opposing counsel:

"Mr. Astor bought this property confiding in the justice of the State of New York, firmly believing that in the litigation of his claim his right would be maintained."[21]

All that Webster said concerning the character of Astor's claim was doubtless true, but ethics and legality are seldom exactly synonymous. Consequently the judge, in his charge to the jury, restated the facts, and instructed the jurors that, if they found the facts to be as enunciated, the law would authorize a verdict for the plaintiff, that is, in favor of Astor. The jury accordingly brought in such a verdict.[22]

The legislature soon saw from this decision in Astor's favor that some compromise agreement must be reached, or the State would not only lose the land to Astor, and thus have to compensate the holders under the State, but would in the process become involved in legal expenses of considerable amount, and all to no avail. Consequently, during March and April, 1828, a bill to revive and amend the act of April 6, 1827, was before the legislature; it was finally passed on April 19, 1828. Astor was to have thirty days to accede to its terms. Amendments to the bill were that the claims of the Morris heirs were to be completely extinguished and that the decision in Astor's favor in the preceding November was not to be counted.[23]

Upon this basis an agreement was reached, and ejectment suits against certain tenants holding from the State were brought by one of those who claimed under Astor. As these were decided in Astor's favor in the circuit court, they were appealed by the State to the United States Supreme Court. By the fall of 1829 matters had progressed so far and so well for Astor that he considered the affair virtually settled in his favor, though he characteristically asserted that "it had cost him more bother than it was worth."[24]

But despite the series of decisions in Astor's favor,[25] his triumph was not to be complete for some years, and during the intervening period several persons endeavored vainly, and probably never with very much hope of success, to check his triumphal progress. It was to be expected that many people would resent the spectacle of a multimillionaire making another half-million dollars out of his adopted State — even though he had established a residence at Hoboken, in order, it was asserted, to make his lack of loyalty to the State somewhat less conspicuous. Green C. Bronson, the attorney-general, was aggrieved by his failure to thwart Astor's claim, and complained that Astor and some of his counsel had communicated with the governor and the judiciary committee of the senate, during the course of the case, commenting on the actions of the attorney-general.[26] Considerably more impressive but no less ineffectual was Edmond Charles (Citizen) Genêt's entrance into the lists to do battle for the rights of his adopted State. In a tremendously learned and manifestly vindictive memorial of December 9, 1830, he mustered an awe-inspiring host of authorities in support of his contention that the people of the State of New York possessed an absolute title in the disputed lands, that Astor's procedure throughout had been highly irregular and the acts of the legislature and the federal courts not much less so, and finally that the legislature's acts in connection with this claim should be repealed, and he laid a petition to that effect before the legislature. In a memorial of March 10, 1831, he made some additions to his previous document.[27] It may be that, had the legislature followed Citizen Genêt's counsel, or perhaps had he conferred his advice upon that body considerably earlier in the day, Astor would have been discomfited. However, the unprejudiced observer with a full knowledge of the relations between Astor and Genêt will probably be impelled to the conclusion that the Citizen was motivated in his attack fully as much by the fact that Astor had some time previously foreclosed mortgages on certain property belonging to Genêt as by an unselfish solicitude for the prosperity of the State of New York.

However, despite all the efforts of attorney-general and State's counsel, and even the assistance of Citizen Genêt, Astor's final triumph was near. During January and February of 1832 Astor was constantly urging his counsel, David B. Ogden and William Wirt, to have the third and decisive case speedily brought before the United States Supreme Court. "The fact is," he wrote to Wirt, "all my associates are very far advanced in years, as well as myself, and all wish to see an end to the business, and I understand that the State are also desirous." He continued: "You know that the title of the Lands in question has been transferred by the 'Act of Compromise' to the State some years ago and is completely in the state, so that having gained the 3 suits the matter is settled."[28] The third case, too, was decided in Astor's favor, and he was thus entitled to the payment specified in the Act of Compromise. The legislature therefore prepared to pay Astor $450,000 in 5 per cent stock with interest from April 16, 1827, payable quarterly, redeemable at the pleasure of the State. The interest would amount to more than $100,000.[29]

Consequently, on April 6, William B. Astor was able to write to his brother-in-law, Viscount Vincent Rumpff, that his father had "at length successfully gotten through with his large Land Claim." Astor himself wrote to the Viscount that $560,000 was to be paid for the land, of which sum Astor owned all but

$40,000. As usual, he concluded: "I had much trouble and little profit by this transaction, though people think I made a fortune by it." Since this was Astor's professed attitude toward the transaction, it is not surprising that he soon lodged a protest against the statement found in the stock certificates that the interest was payable on the first *Monday* in April, July, etc., thus causing Astor a loss of interest, since it had originally been agreed that payment should be made on the first *day* of these months.[30]

Thus Astor's connection with the Putnam County land once owned by the Morrises came to an end — save that for some years to come the people of New York State continued to make, and Astor to receive, payments of principal and interest on the more than half a million dollars which he had been awarded in recompense for his claims. In spite of Astor's assertion that he had made very little profit out of the affair, and certainly not so much as would have been derived from the investment of a similar sum in Manhattan Island real estate, the fur trade, or commerce with China, it is not likely that he came out of this transaction without some slight recompense for his trouble. His original investment had been $100,000, his expenses in the suits about $50,000;[31] he received $520,000 in payment for the surrender of his rights, 23 years after their original acquisition. Most of the expenses involved in pressing his claims had come in the last few years of the negotiations, and consequently not much interest on these expenditures had been lost. A return of more than 350 per cent on the original investment within a period of less than a quarter of a century would not be bad business — at least not for anyone other than Astor. But even were it true that Astor had actually lost money in this case, it would be difficult to muster up much regret, such as it is quite possible to feel over his losses in the Astoria enterprise. This affair could not have benefited anyone but Astor and his associates, save the Morris heirs, who had already been compensated by the British government for the loyalty of their ancestors.[32] It certainly resulted in a loss to the people of the State in which Astor had made his home for more than two-score years. It must therefore remain on a lower plane than his other interests, the fur trade, European and Oriental commerce, and Manhattan Island real estate, in all of which a certain amount of general public benefit accompanied his private profit.

NOTES

1. *Appleton's Cyclopaedia of American Biography*, vol. iv, p. 418; *The National Cyclopaedia of American Biography*, vol. iv, pp. 43–44.

2. *New-York Gazette and General Advertiser*, February 26, 1819, p. 2, col. 2.

3. Smith, Arthur D. Howden, *John Jacob Astor* (1929), pp. 261–265.

4. Ms. book, Hall of Records, N. Y., Liber Conveyances 137, p. 401; *New-York Gazette and General Advertiser*, February 26, 1819, p. 2, col. 2; *Niles' Weekly Register*, vol. xvi (February 27, 1819), p. 6.

5. Ms. (copy), New York State Library, Albany, Letters, H. Livingston, Poughkeepsie, August 1, 1810, to John Jacob Astor (see above, vol. i, pp. 445–447).

6. Ms. book, Hall of Records, N. Y., Liber Conveyances 137, p. 401.

7. Ms. book, New York Public Library, brief of part of Morris trial in United States Circuit Court, November, 1827.

8. *Supreme Court of the United States of America: James Carver, Plaintiff in Error, vs. James Jackson on the Demise of John Jacob Astor, Theodosius Fowler, Cadwallader D. Colden, Cornelius I. Bogert, Henry Gage Morris, Maria Morris, Thomas Hincks and John Hincks, Defendants in Error* (1829).

9. Ms. book, Baker Library, Astor Papers, Letter Book ii, 1831–38, p. 441, John Jacob Astor, N. Y., April 9, 1833, to Vincent Rumpff, Paris.

10. We get a hint of the way ownership of this land shifted, with a constant tendency to be concentrated in Astor's hands, from a memorandum of 1819 in which Astor is described as owning $\frac{3}{4}$, and $\frac{2}{5}$ of $\frac{1}{8}$, of the disputed lands in Putnam County, these holdings being valued at $190,000, and as having recently purchased $\frac{1}{8}$ from S. Jones in May, 1819, valued at $28,150. In 1819, then, Astor owned $92\frac{1}{2}$ per cent of these lands in Putnam County, his share of which was estimated as worth $218,150. (Ms. book, Office of the Astor Estate, N. Y., Untitled land book, about 1819.)

11. Ms. book, Baker Library, Astor Papers, Letter Book i, 1813–15, p. 58, John Jacob Astor, N. Y., September 29, 1813, to the Commissioners of the Land Office; John Jacob Astor, N. Y., September 29, 1813, to Jacob R. Van Rensselaer; *New-York Gazette and General Advertiser*, February 26, 1813, p. 2, col. 2; *Statement and Exposition of the Title of John Jacob Astor to the Lands Purchased by him from the Surviving Children of Roger Morris and Mary his Wife* (1827), pp. 44–45.

12. *Ibid.*, pp. 44–46; *New-York Gazette and General Advertiser*, February 26, 1819, p. 2, col. 2.

13. *Ibid.*, April 10, 1819, p. 2, col. 1.

14. Pumpelly, Josiah Collins, "The Old Morris House, Afterwards the Jumel Mansion: Its History and Traditions," *New York Genealogical and Biographical Record*, vol. xxxiv (1903), p. 83; *Report of the Trial before Judges Thompson and Betts in the Circuit Court of the U. S. For the Southern District of New-York, in the case of James Jackson, ex dem. Theodosius Fowler and others, vs. James Carver; involving the claim of John Jacob Astor to Lands in Putnam County* (1827), p. 6.

15. *Statement and Exposition of the Title of John Jacob Astor to the Lands purchased by him from the Surviving Children of Roger Morris and Mary his Wife* (1827), p. 54.

16. *Journal of the Senate of the State of New-York*, 50th sess., February 15, 1827, pp. 197–199.

17. *Supreme Court of the United States of America: James Carver, Plaintiff in Error, vs. James Jackson on the Demise of John Jacob Astor, Theodosius Fowler, Cadwallader D. Colden, Cornelius I. Bogert, Henry Gage Morris, Maria Morris, Thomas Hincks and John Hincks, Defendants in Error* (1829), pp. 101–106; *New-York Gazette and General Advertiser*, April 9, 1827, p. 2, col. 2.

18. Myers, Gustavus, *History of the Great American Fortunes*, 3 vols. (1907–10), vol. i, pp. 139–141.

19. *New-York Gazette and General Advertiser*, June 2, 1827, p. 2, col. 1; *Niles' Register*, vol. xxxii (June 9, 1827), p. 245.

20. *Journal of the Senate of the State of New-York*, 50th sess., October 6, 1827, pp. 36–40.

21. Parton, James, *Life of John Jacob Astor* (1865), pp. 64–65.

22. *Report of the Trial before Judges Thompson and Betts in the Circuit Court of the U. S. For the Southern District of New-York, in the case of James Jackson, ex dem. Theodosius Fowler and others, vs. James Carver; involving the claim of John Jacob Astor to Lands in Putnam County* (1827), pp. 3, 66; ms. book, New York Public Library, brief of part of the Morris trial in the United States Circuit Court, 1827; *New-York Gazette and General Advertiser*, November 12, 1827, p. 2, col. 3; November 13, 1827, p. 2, col. 1; *Niles' Register*, vol. xxxiii (December 1, 1827), p. 215, quoting from the New York *Commercial Advertiser*.

23. *New-York Gazette and General Advertiser*, March 24, 1828, p. 2, col. 2; April 12, 1828, p. 2, col. 2; April 15, 1828, p. 2, col. 2; *Niles' Register*, vol. xxxiv (June 7, 1828), p. 235.

24. Ms., Detroit Public Library, Burton Historical Collection, Gilkison Papers, Lieut. Col. J. T. Gilkison, Brantford, Ontario, November, 1895, to John Jacob Astor (the grandson of John Jacob Astor 1).

25. *New-York Gazette and General Advertiser*, November 10, 1829, p. 2, col. 1; *Supreme Court of the United States of America: James Carver, Plaintiff in Error, vs. James Jackson on the Demise of John Jacob Astor, Theodosius Fowler, Cadwallader D. Colden, Cornelius I. Bogert, Henry Gage*

Morris, Maria Morris, Thomas Hincks and John Hincks, Defendants in Error (1829); *Supreme Court of the United States of America: Nathaniel Crane, Plaintiff in Error, vs. James Jackson, Ex Dem. John Jacob Astor and Others, Defendant in Error: Samuel Kelly, vs. The Same* (1831); Curtis, B. R., ed., *Reports of Decisions in the Supreme Court of the United States* (1881), vol. ix, pp. 1–19, January term, 1830; *Documents of the Senate of the State of New-York*, 54th sess., no. 2, p. 3; no. 24; *Webster, Daniel, The Writings and Speeches of*, Fletcher Webster, ed., 18 vols. (1903), vol. xv, pp. 290–304.

26. *Documents of the Senate of the State of New-York*, 54th sess., no. 28, pp. 1–19.

27. *Ibid.*, no. 29, pp. 1–35; no. 77, pp. 1–3.

28. Ms. book, Baker Library, Astor Papers, Letter Book ii, 1831–38, pp. 23, 24, 25, 28, and 29, John Jacob Astor, N. Y., January 13, 15, 18, 28, and 29, 1832, to David B. Ogden, Washington; pp. 24, 32, and 34, John Jacob Astor, N. Y., January 15, February 17, 24, 1832, to William Wirt, Baltimore and Washington.

29. *Documents of the Assembly of the State of New-York*, 55th sess., vol. ii, no. 149, pp. 1–5; *Documents of the Senate of the State of New-York*, 55th sess., vol. ii, no. 81, pp. 1–10.

30. Ms. book, Baker Library, Astor Papers, Letter Book ii, 1831–38, p. 41, William B. Astor, N. Y., April 6, 1832, to Vincent Rumpff; p. 44, John Jacob Astor, N. Y., April 9, 1832, to Vincent Rumpff, Paris (see below, vol. ii, pp. 1214–1215); p. 50, John Jacob Astor, N. Y., May 7, 1832, to Silas Wright, Albany.

31. *Documents of the Senate of the State of New-York*, 55th sess., vol. ii, no. 81, pp. 1–10.

32. *Appleton's Cyclopaedia of American Biography*, vol. iv, p. 418; *The National Cyclopaedia of American Biography*, vol. iv, pp. 43–44.

CHAPTER XIX

MONEY–LENDING, PRINCIPALLY ON REAL–ESTATE SECURITY: THE GERRIT SMITH CASE

ABOUT 1825 Astor disposed of the last of those ships in which for a quarter of a century he had carried on commerce with various parts of the world and especially with China. In 1834 he retired from the American Fur Company and at the same time withdrew entirely from foreign and domestic trade. It was then necessary for him to decide upon some other field of investment. For a third of a century he had been steadily making purchases of real estate on Manhattan Island, but purchases of land in New York City could not be made with the even rhythm which had characterized the conduct of his various commercial interests. Some other disposition must be made of as much of the accumulated profits of his half-century of commerce as were not absorbed by land investments, and of that proportion of his income from real estate which did not go back again into land purchases. In a city like New York, however, there was always a demand for ready money. For years, Astor had been making occasional loans from his surplus cash to responsible citizens who could offer him substantial security, preferably in land, and now, about 1835, money-lending on real-estate security began to be a significant feature of his business life.

There were two — possibly three — classes of land on which Astor had made loans. The most important class was land in the city of New York; the second was land in New York State, but outside Manhattan Island; the third, land outside New York State, within the area which had been the field of activity of the American Fur Company. We have already considered

Astor's interest in western land; his loans on land in New York City will be discussed elsewhere in connection with his activities in acquiring real estate on Manhattan Island. However, when Astor took a mortgage on land in New York State, outside of Manhattan Island, it was purely a money-lending proposition. Astor most emphatically did not want any more land in the backcountry of New York. In the last decade of the eighteenth century, when he was gaining experience even more rapidly than money, Astor had invested heavily in the backcountry land of New York, and during the next ten years had frequently regretted that he had ever done so. Consequently, when he lent money upon the security of land in New York State, he did it simply with an eye to the interest to be received upon the loan, and not at all to any possibility of profits from the foreclosure of a mortgage.

We have no source from which we can derive complete information concerning the extent and character of Astor's money-lending on real-estate security. We know from the letter books which still remain to us, covering the last sixteen or seventeen years of Astor's life, that he was engaged in many transactions of that character. These volumes are full of isolated pieces of information on the subject, agreements to lend money, acknowledgments of payments on the interest and principal, refusals to accept the security offered, and notifications that installments on the principal or interest were due, sometimes accompanied by threats of foreclosure, outright or implied.[1] Moreover, this gives us information concerning only one side of these transactions, and even that information is of a sketchy nature.

It happens, on the other hand, that we have nearly all the essential facts of one of the largest of Astor's loans, and one, too, which links up with certain aspects of his earlier life. Astor's original interest in New York backcountry land had been an outgrowth from the fur trade he had conducted in that area in partnership with Peter Smith. Several of his early land investments, including the one which has been discussed at some length in a previous chapter, had been made in connection with this partner. Now, in his last years, probably the largest of his money-lending transactions was to spring out of these earlier connections in the fur trade and in land investments.

It will be remembered that in 1829 Astor sold out his one-fourth share in the two extensive tracts of Mohawk Valley land, known as Charlotte River and Byrnes Patent, to Peter Smith, who already owned the proportion of one-half of these same pieces of property. Astor received $14,500 for his share in the form of a bond from Peter Smith, secured by the land involved; and he also lent Smith the same amount with which to purchase the one-fourth interest held by the heirs of William Laight. This sum was similarly secured by a bond and mortgage. This transaction had been preceded, and seems to have been partly inspired, by a disagreement between Smith and Astor as to whether the former should receive compensation for his services in managing the partnership's lands. The dispute seems to have had an unfortunate effect on the friendly relations which had existed between them for more than forty years. But any hard feelings which may have remained were thrust out of sight after the land partnership had been liquidated in 1829; and in any case the disagreement had never extended to Peter Smith's son and heir, Gerrit Smith, who had been born in 1798, and to whom his father, following Astor's advice, had made over much of his property in 1819. Gerrit, with his uncle, Daniel Cady, had signed the bond of 1829 jointly with Peter Smith. Thus, at the beginning of 1830, Astor held mortgages in New York State to the amount of $29,000 from one family alone. In the next year Astor purchased a bond and mortgage for $12,000 given by Gerrit Smith to a certain Rudolph Bunner.[2]

For several years the matter rested thus, Peter and Gerrit Smith paying the interest and part of the principal on their two bonds to Astor. But in 1836 Peter Smith died, leaving his property to Gerrit. Peter Smith's wealth had been chiefly in land, of which he owned nearly a million acres. Its potential value was very great, but a large proportion was still unproductive or was productive only to a small degree. It was Gerrit's wish to furnish financial assistance to some of his relatives and to extend indulgence to certain creditors, but he found it difficult to raise money on his extensive property, especially since the country was then in the throes of the financial panic of 1837. In this situation his thoughts turned to the man who had been his father's friend and to whom he was already indebted in the amount of several thousand dollars.

On July 21, 1837, Smith wrote to Astor requesting the loan of $200,000 or $300,000, secured by a bond and mortgage on his land at Oswego. After considering the matter for a little less than a week, Astor replied that the amount desired was too great but that he might be able to lend $100,000 or $200,000 at 7 per cent, payable quarterly. If Smith wished this amount on the terms mentioned, Astor would let him have it in payments of $10,000 or more, over a period of from 3 to 4 months or less. In fact, if Astor received some money then due to him, he might be able to lend Smith the full amount of $200,000 at once.[3]

Astor received the sum he had mentioned, and on August 5 he was able to name the terms on which he would lend Smith the $200,000. Two days before, Smith had offered to pay the amount still due on the two bonds to Astor, and this assisted in making Astor feel that he could lend the desired amount. Smith was to draw on Astor for the sums which the latter would from time to time specify. As security, Smith was to pledge his Oswego property, supplemented by a sufficient amount of bank stock to make the loan safe. The loan was to be for 3 years for the whole amount, after which it was to be paid off in 7 installments.[4] The interest was to be, as previously stated, 7 per cent, though apparently payable semiannually rather than quarterly.[5]

Gerrit Smith commented on this offer through an entry in his diary, dated August 10, in these words:

> I this week receive a letter from my friend, and my father's friend, John Jacob Astor, in which he consents to loan me for a long period the large sum of money which I had applied for to him. This money will enable me to rid myself of pecuniary embarrassments, and to extend important assistance to others, and especially to extend indulgence to those who owe me. This is a great mercy of God to me. It relieves my mind of a great burden of anxiety. My pecuniary embarrassments, growing out of my liabilities for —— and out of my liabilities for, and advances to —— have often, and for hours together, filled me with painful concern.[6]

The next four months or so were spent in completing this transaction. Astor disclaimed any desire to investigate the value of Smith's Oswego property offered as security, but requested him also to pledge $28,000 of bank stock. About the middle of September, Smith accordingly sent Astor 200 shares of the Canal Bank, 200 of the Mechanics and Farmers Bank, 200 of the New York State Bank, and, a month later, 25 shares of the Commercial Bank of Oswego and 131 of the Bank of Utica, a total of $27,800. In the meanwhile, from time to time, Astor had been giving Smith permission to draw upon him for various amounts, and Peter Smith's bond and that to Bunner had both been satisfied. By November 8 a balance of $29,349.37 was still due to Smith. The mortgage he was to have given on his Oswego land had, however, not yet appeared, owing to the carelessness of a clerk in the county registry office, and on December 1 Astor enquired about it. It was received by him on December 18.[7] The preliminaries of this transaction were now completed, and the loan was ready to run for its specified period of ten years.[8]

Nothing further of interest occurred in this connection for about two years, but the summer of 1839 again saw Gerrit Smith in financial straits. He had found it necessary to give a bond to his brother, and early in June, 1839, he asked Astor to take it up, to which request the latter replied noncommittally, "at present there is a very great call for money, nevertheless if your bond to your brother, mentioned in your letter, should be offered to me I may possibly negotiate for the same."[9] Smith then fell six months behind on his interest to the amount of $7,000, but early in December he sent Astor two stock certificates of the Rochester City Bank and one of that of Utica, to the amount of $11,000, as security for his overdue interest and for a further loan of $4,000 which he requested Astor to make. If necessary, Astor might sell the stock, though it was preferable that he should not do so.[10] Astor, however, declined with deep regret to give Smith any further financial assistance, stating that he had been disappointed in the "Collection of monies," had many engagements to fulfill, and must make sacrifices to comply with them. He enquired whether Smith wanted the stock to be sold for interest due, and, if so, in what manner he wished this to be done.[11] We do not know positively whether this stock was sold or not, but next spring saw Smith again behindhand with his interest, and Astor wrote to him: "I must request, my Dear Sir, that you will send me the balance of interest due on your bond as soon as you can —"[12] By June Smith seems to have been able to accede to this request, for on the 8th he sent Astor a check for $140 "for interest on the interest of your bond & also an allowance for having paid the interest in several Sums and because money has been worth more than 7 percent." Astor, however, declined to charge Smith more than the bare interest on interest.[13] But late in July William B. Astor, at the request of his father, was dunning Smith for the interest due on the first of that month.[14]

A year or so later, in the spring of 1841, Smith became indebted to Astor for an additional sum. Astor owned stock in the Commercial Bank of Oswego to the amount of $16,500 and had heard unfavorable rumors about its solvency. Being anxious, as he said, "in the feeble state of my health . . . to avoid ale causes of trouble & anxiety as much as possible," he offered to sell Smith his stock "at its fair value, & give as long a credit as you may require" at 7 per cent interest.[15] Smith would offer only 27 per cent on the par value of the stock, while Astor at first insisted that he could not sell at less than one-third and that the stock was worth much more than that.[16] When Smith would bid no higher, however, Astor revised his ideas of the value of the stock and accepted the offer.[17] In payment, Smith gave Astor his bond for $12,000, representing 27 per cent on the par value of Astor's stock and an assessment of 50 per cent on the par value, due from each shareholder as part of a campaign to bolster up the tottering institution. This sum was advanced by Astor to Smith.[18] Late in the year the bank went under,[19] which indicated that Smith had come nearer than Astor to gauging its future, though both were far enough out.

The first installment of principal on Smith's bond was due on January 1, 1842. A week before this date Astor enquired what plans he had made regarding the payment of the $28,-571.43 represented by this installment.[20] Smith apparently replied that it would be impossible to make the payment at the time designated, but Astor merely commented: "I note your remarks respecting the instalment of principal on your bond — I sincerely trust that we may ere long have a favorable change in the Commercial affairs of the Country, it is indeed greatly needed—"[21]

More than a year later, however, Astor's attitude was not quite so disinterested. He had his son write to Smith on May 10, 1843, "that the general and great depreciation in the value of personal and real property may have very considerably affected the value of the lands, which you mortgaged to him as security for your bond," and that he therefore requested Smith to furnish him further security.[22] Smith replied that he regretted that the failure of the Commercial Bank of Oswego left Astor with only $2,500 stock in the Rochester City Bank — probably the same stock which Smith had offered some years before as security for overdue interest — as collateral security for his $12,000 bond. He would consequently give Astor an order on the Safety Fund for $9,500 and interest, being the sum which Smith had lent the Commercial Bank of Oswego in an attempt to bolster up that unstable institution, the payment of which sum had been provided for. As to the large bond, he could, if Astor insisted, give him a mortgage on 2,500 acres of land and some stock in the Oswego Canal Company. Smith also presented an account of his assets and liabilities and suggested that Astor should purchase the latter.[23] William B. Astor replied for his father that he would receive the order in his favor on the comptroller for the amount lent to the Commercial Bank of Oswego, and also a mortgage on 2,500 acres of land lying between the Erie Canal and Oneida Lake, and 87 shares of stock in the Oswego Canal Company.[24]

Gerrit Smith had offered to give the security mentioned above, if Astor insisted; but evidently he hoped that Astor would not insist. Smith would, he now said, give the mortgages and canal stock if Astor would take over his other debts up to $75,000; but out of consideration for his other creditors he felt that he could give Astor no further security unless the latter would advance him the money for his other debts.[25] To this Astor replied by a personal letter in which he stated that Smith had promised further security, should it be needed, at the time when the loan was made; that his other creditors were already well secured, the debts to them being small compared to the debt to Astor, and already partially paid off; that Astor would release any property Smith wished to sell on receiving a just consideration; and that Smith still had "a very large

amount of unincumberd property." He therefore requested
the mortgage and canal stock, and stated that if Smith's present
debt were satisfactorily secured "it would give me great satisfaction to afford you . . . a farther loan . . . if the security you
offerd for it should be found sufficient."[26] On June 13 and 20
Astor wrote to William L. Marcy, former governor of New
York, at Albany, requesting information as to the value of the
canal stock and real estate which Smith wished to employ as
security.[27]

Smith, in the meantime, assuming that the $75,000 addi-
tional loan was assured, prepared to complete arrangements for
the loan and pay off his creditors, but in reply to a letter written on June 6 he received one from Joseph G. Cogswell, Astor's
secretary and companion, stating that the feeble condition of
Astor's health made it impossible for him to reply personally,
but that he wished Smith to understand that he had not intended to bind himself to make the loan but rather merely to
express the pleasure it would give him to do so if he should find
it possible.[28] A second letter from Smith brought another reply
from Cogswell, acknowledging the receipt of canal stock, expressing Astor's regret that the desired loan could not be made
at the time required, and requesting Smith in the future to
write to William B. Astor.[29] Smith was persistent, and his next
letter drew a reply from Astor's son to the effect that his father
could make no future loan without more complete knowledge
of the value of the land offered as security.[30] Smith again returned to the charge by requesting a loan for only $26,000.
Astor, who had by this time probably heard from Marcy, finally agreed to furnish Smith with that amount if he would give
him as security not only the mortgage on 2,500 acres of land
and the Oswego Canal stock but also mortgages on some property in Schenectady and Oswego, and on additional property
to the amount of the new loan.[31] Smith had already sent Astor
the mortgage on 2,500 acres of Madison County land, a certifi-

cate for canal stock, and mortgages on property in Oswego and Schenectady, partly as additional security for the loan of $26,000. He declined to furnish further security, however, and requested the return of his bond for $26,000 and of the mortgages on Oswego and Schenectady property.[32] William B. Astor then returned these, though he expressed the opinion that if Smith had adopted his suggestion of coming to New York he might have arranged for the loan.[33]

The disagreement over the loan did not cause any hard feelings, at least on Astor's side, for about the middle of August, 1843, he instructed his son to inform Smith that he might, if necessary, postpone the interest payment due on January 1, 1844, until the spring of that year [34] — apparently as a gesture of regret that no agreement could be reached about the loan. In the next spring he also offered to let Smith postpone the interest due on July 1 for two or three months.[35]

In the fall of 1844 a dividend of 25 per cent was declared on the debts due from the Oswego Commercial Bank, and this enabled Smith to reduce his small bond to $9,136.[36] By the fall of 1845 further payments on the debt due to Smith from the Commercial Bank of Oswego had enabled him to pay off this bond.[37]

In the meantime, in the summer of 1845, Smith, whose financial condition seems to have improved, had sent Astor a mortgage for $25,000 on an Oswego hotel property as additional collateral security for his large bond.[38] In this year, too, he began to make payments on this bond for $200,000; and, as the debt decreased, the mortgages given as security for it were cancelled. By 1846 the debt had been reduced to $190,000 and in the next year to $170,000. By 1848 it had declined to $160,000.[39] Early in January, 1848, Smith made a payment of $25,600 and requested that a mortgage for $50,000 on lands in Madison County, and also his bank stocks, should be released to him. William B. Astor accordingly satisfied the mortgage, but his father declined to return the bank stocks until a further payment had been made.[40]

It would probably be well at this point to pause and consider what this case has so far revealed to us concerning Astor's methods in money-lending on real-estate security. It might be objected that this is not a typical case, that Astor extended indulgences to Gerrit Smith which would not have been granted to an individual of lower standing or to one not bound to him by ties of friendship. It is possibly true that this particular transaction is not typical, though it may be for that very reason more worthy of our attention than one of a more obscure character. But we have no reason to think that this loan was made purely as a matter of friendship. Astor's insistence on adequate security and his determination to secure complete information on the value of property offered for that purpose are evidences to the contrary. It may be said, then, that in lending money on real-estate security it was Astor's policy to assist only men of a responsible and trustworthy character who could furnish adequate security and increase it if necessary. When these conditions had been satisfied, Astor worried very little if they failed to pay the principal on time, and was even ready to grant some indulgence on the interest. Foreclosure was a last resort. Astor's concern, after the ultimate repayment of the principal had been assured, was purely with his seven per cent interest.[41]

Although Smith's bond was not to be finally paid off until 1862, John Jacob Astor's connection with it was soon to be ended by his death from old age, late in March, 1848. Gerrit Smith, in his letter of condolence to William B. Astor, wrote: "You have lost an affectionate father. I have lost a fast friend —a friend, too,–who had the ability, as well as the disposition to render me very important Services."[42] And this statement brings up a curious indirect result of Astor's money-lending connection with Gerrit Smith, which makes the study of this relationship valuable from a personal standpoint as well as for its illustration of some of Astor's business methods and policies. As Astor was the complete business man, so Gerrit Smith was the complete reformer, interested in the abolition of slavery, the prohibition of the liquor traffic, the elimination of land monopoly, women's rights, the peace movement, and rational religion. Apparently all the pietistic zeal of his father, Peter Smith, which had found vent in the distribution of tracts and in loud and dolorous epistolary outcries concerning the state of his soul to the bewildered and slightly disgusted Astor, had in the son been directed into the channels of social readjustment. We have no evidence that Astor was ever in the slightest degree sympathetic with the younger man's radical schemes for the regeneration of society. When Smith urged the New York capitalist to ban liquor from a hotel he was building, Astor replied: "I admire much your ideas on the subject of temperance; but I fear our folk here are not good enough to admit of the introduction at the Hotel I am building of the temperance principles."[43] It would have been difficult to bring together two men whose characters were more diametrically opposed, yet despite this fact — or because of it — they seem to have had a genuine feeling of liking and respect one for the other. John Jacob Astor always enjoyed a joke, and I wonder whether this great landowner and supporter of Henry Clay did not occasionally chuckle to himself when he thought that his money was making it possible for Peter Smith's boy to carry on what probably appeared to Astor an utterly absurd campaign for the abolition of slavery and of private property in land.

NOTES

1. Some of the great ones of the land were among those who resorted to Astor for temporary financial assistance. We have previously noted that James Monroe was indebted to Astor, both while he was a cabinet member and after he had become president. Henry Clay needed but to apply to Astor for a $20,000 loan in order to receive a most cordial accession to his wishes (ms. book, Baker Library, Astor Papers, Letter Book ii, 1831–38, letters from John Jacob Astor to Henry Clay, *passim*, esp. p. 281, February 16, 1835), and a later request for an extension of the time of payment met with an equally ready and favorable reply (ms. book, Baker Library, Astor Papers, Letter Book iii, 1845–48, p. 171, William B. Astor, N. Y., April 8, 1847, to Henry Clay, Ashland, Ky.). A future president, however, was not so fortunate as the former "Mill Boy of the Slashes," and Millard Fillmore's attempt to raise money encountered the cold reply that "it will not be convenient for me to make the loans, at least for some time to come" (ms. book, Baker Library, Astor Papers, Letter Book ii, 1831–38, p. 386, John Jacob Astor, N. Y., March 22, 1836, to Millard Fillmore, Buffalo).

2. Ms., Syracuse University, Gerrit Smith Miller Collection, Letters, John Jacob Astor, N. Y., February 22, 1830, to Gerrit Smith, Peterboro (see below, vol. ii, pp. 1201–1202).

3. Ms. book, Baker Library, Astor Papers, Letter Book ii, 1831–38, p. 505, John Jacob Astor, N. Y., July 28, 1837, to Gerrit Smith, Peterboro.

4. *Ibid.*, p. 507, John Jacob Astor, N. Y., August 5, 1837, to Gerrit Smith, Peterboro (see below, vol. ii, pp. 1234–1235).

5. The Boston merchant William Sturgis, who, as a member of the firm of Bryant & Sturgis, had been Astor's rival in the trade with China and the Pacific, it is said used to explain his own policy of never charging more than 6 per cent by a quotation from John Jacob Astor, who, he apparently thought, would be a good man to follow in financial matters. "I always remember a remark which old Mr. Astor once made to me," he is quoted as saying, "that the practice of taking usurious interest 'narrered the mind and 'ardened the 'art.'" (Loring, Charles G., "Memoirs of Honorable William Sturgis," *Proceedings of the Massachusetts Historical Society*, vol. vii (1863–64), p. 468.) This would seem to indicate, aside from its statement of business ethics, that Astor occasionally varied the German gutterals of his childhood with a cockney twang acquired in those London days when he used to be awakened by the sound of Bow Bells in time to go to his work in his brother's musical-instrument manufactory. Astor's own charge of 7 per cent, however, was the maximum

allowed by the law of New York State (Murray, J. B. C., *The History of Usury* (1866), pp. 81–83), though in this time of great financial stringency a higher rate would not have been usury in the moral sense.

6. Frothingham, Octavius Brooks, *Gerrit Smith* (1878), p. 34.

7. Ms. book, Baker Library, Astor Papers, Letter Book ii, 1831–38, pp. 507–508, 509, 515, 520, 535, 539, 545, John Jacob Astor per William B. Astor, N. Y., August 10, 17, September 1, 20, November 8, December 1, 18, 1837, to Gerrit Smith, Peterboro.

8. Gerrit Smith's official biographer gives an account of this transaction which differs in some more or less important respects from the narrative recorded above, which has been drawn from the original documents. "The sum requested," says this narrator, "was in all, two hundred and fifty thousand dollars. The application, in general terms, was made by letter. The letter was answered by an invitation to dinner. As the two sat at meat, the host was full of reminiscences of former years when he went in search of skins with his guest's father, now little more than three months deceased. There was no talk of business till the cloth was removed, and the two were by themselves. Then the visitor opened a tale of distress which was short, but heavy. It was a season of panic. The banks had suspended specie payments and could afford only feeble and precarious relief. Business was at a stand-still; real estate had fallen to a nominal value; land was unproductive. The legal adviser and brother-in-law of Peter Smith, his son's counsellor too, urged an assignment of property for the benefit of the creditors. How much do you need? asked the millionaire. The visitor named the sum. Do you want the whole of it at once? I do. Astor looked grave for a moment, then said: 'you shall have it.' A mortgage was pledged on the Oswego purchase, made ten years before, and the relieved guest went home to Peterboro. Astor's cheque for two hundred and fifty thousand dollars came in a few days. The mortgage was executed and duly recorded, and Smith went on with his affairs. Here comes the most remarkable part of the transaction. The country clerk neglected to transmit the papers to Mr. Astor. Weeks elapsed, and Smith's part of the bargain was unfulfilled. A letter from New York, sent Mr. Smith to Oswego. The clerk's stupidity was reprimanded, and the papers, with satisfactory explanations, were sent to their proper destination. Mr. Astor had parted with a quarter of a million dollars on the bare word of Gerrit Smith, and had been content with the bare word, for weeks!" (Frothingham, *op. cit.*, pp. 33–34.) The object of the probably quite sincere and unintentional errors in the above account seems to be to exaggerate the confidence of Astor in Smith's integrity and to make the transaction much more of an agreement *en famille* than it actually was. The sum in question was not a quarter of a million dollars but $200,000. The agreement was made entirely by letter and not under the immediate personal influence of Astor's memories of his early connection with Gerrit

Smith's father. The sum actually lent was supplied over a period of three months and not furnished in a single check. Astor was too good a business man to have $200,000 or $250,000 lying idle on the off-chance that some-one might come along wishing to borrow that sum. Moreover, though it is true that three months had passed before Astor enquired concerning the missing mortgage, it is hardly correct to state that he had "parted with a quarter of a million dollars on the bare word of Gerrit Smith, and had been content with the bare word, for weeks." As a matter of fact, Astor had received a bond for the amount, which would be sufficient evidence of the loan to enable him to recover from Smith's property should the latter default, and was also in possession of nearly $28,000 in bank stock as security. Undoubtedly Smith's honesty would have been sufficient security for even a million dollars, but it would not be like Astor to lend anyone any considerable amount on the security of his "bare word," if only out of mere regard for the forms of business.

9. Ms., Syracuse University, Gerrit Smith Miller Collection, Letters, John Jacob Astor per William B. Astor, N. Y., June 10, 1839, to Gerrit Smith, Peterboro.

10. *Ibid.*, Note Book, 1829–43, p. 69, Gerrit Smith, Peterboro, December 2, 1839, to John Jacob Astor, N. Y.

11. *Ibid.*, Letters, John Jacob Astor per William B. Astor, N. Y., December 5, 1839, to Gerrit Smith, Peterboro (see below, vol. ii, pp. 1236–1237).

12. *Ibid.*, John Jacob Astor per William B. Astor, N. Y., March 2, 1840, to Gerrit Smith, Peterboro.

13. *Ibid.*, John Jacob Astor per William B. Astor, N. Y., June 11, 1840, to Gerrit Smith, Peterboro (see below, vol. ii, p. 1238).

14. *Ibid.*, William B. Astor, N. Y., July 21, 1840, to Gerrit Smith, Peterboro.

15. *Ibid.*, John Jacob Astor, N. Y., March 15, 1841, to Gerrit Smith, Peterboro.

16. *Ibid.*, John Jacob Astor, N. Y., March 24, 1841, to Gerrit Smith, Peterboro (see below, vol. ii, pp. 1238–1239); John Jacob Astor per F. G. Halleck, N. Y., April 5, 1841, to Gerrit Smith.

17. *Ibid.*, William B. Astor, N. Y., April 26, 1841, to Gerrit Smith, Peterboro (see below, vol. ii, pp. 1240–1241).

18. *Ibid.*, John Jacob Astor per William B. Astor, N. Y., May 3, 1841, to Gerrit Smith, Peterboro.

19. *Ibid.*, William B. Astor, N. Y., August 26, 1841, to Gerrit Smith, Peterboro; John Jacob Astor per William B. Astor, N. Y., December 13, 1841, to Gerrit Smith, Peterboro (see below, vol. ii, pp. 1241–1242).

20. *Ibid.*, John Jacob Astor per William B. Astor, N. Y., December 24, 1841, to Gerrit Smith, Peterboro.

21. *Ibid.*, John Jacob Astor per William B. Astor, N. Y., January 4, 1842, to Gerrit Smith, Peterboro.

22. *Ibid.*, William B. Astor, N. Y., May 10, 1843, to Gerrit Smith, Peterboro.

23. *Ibid.*, Gerrit Smith, Peterboro, May 12, 1843, to William B. Astor.

24. *Ibid.*, William B. Astor, N. Y., May 22, 1843, to Gerrit Smith, Peterboro.

25. *Ibid.*, Gerrit Smith, Peterboro, May 26, 1843, to William B. Astor, N. Y.

26. *Ibid.*, John Jacob Astor, Hellgate, N. Y., May 31, 1843, to Gerrit Smith, Peterboro (see below, vol. ii, pp. 1242–1243).

27. Ms., Library of Congress, William L. Marcy Papers, vol. viii, 1842–43, November 28–December 6, John Jacob Astor, Hellgate, June 13, 20, 1843, to William L. Marcy, Albany.

28. Ms., Syracuse University, Gerrit Smith Miller Collection, Letters, Joseph G. Cogswell, Hellgate, June 9, 1843, to Gerrit Smith, Peterboro (see below, vol. ii, p. 1244).

29. *Ibid.*, Joseph G. Cogswell, Hellgate, June 17, 1843, to Gerrit Smith, Peterboro.

30. *Ibid.*, William B. Astor, N. Y., June 29, 1843, to Gerrit Smith, Peterboro.

31. *Ibid.*, William B. Astor, N. Y., July 11, 1843, to Gerrit Smith, Peterboro (see below, vol. ii, p. 1245).

32. *Ibid.*, Gerrit Smith, Peterboro, July 27, 1843, to William B. Astor, N. Y.

33. *Ibid.*, William B. Astor, N. Y., August 2, 1843, to Gerrit Smith, Peterboro.

34. *Ibid.*, William B. Astor, N. Y., August 14, 1843, to Gerrit Smith, Peterboro.

35. *Ibid.*, William B. Astor, N. Y., May 11, 1844, to Gerrit Smith, Peterboro.

36. *Ibid.*, William B. Astor, N. Y., September 20, 1844, to Gerrit Smith, Peterboro; John Jacob Astor per William B. Astor, N. Y., September 26, 1844, to Gerrit Smith, Peterboro; *ibid.*, List of Debt owing by Gerrit Smith Including All debts due from his late father — Principal only — no interest — no taxes —, p. 100.

37. *Ibid.*, Letters, T. Beekman, Oswego, June 23, 1845, to John Jacob Astor, N. Y.; John Jacob Astor per William B. Astor, N. Y., June 27, 1845, to Gerrit Smith, Peterboro; Gerrit Smith, Peterboro, July 5, 1845, to William B. Astor; ms. book, Baker Library, Astor Papers, Letter Book iii, 1845–48, p. 31, John Jacob Astor per William B. Astor, N. Y., October 17, 1845, to Gerrit Smith, Peterboro.

38. Ms., Syracuse University, Gerrit Smith Miller Collection, Letters, Gerrit Smith, Peterboro, July 5, 1845, to William B. Astor, N. Y.; ms.

book, Baker Library, Astor Papers, Letter Book iii, 1845–48, William B. Astor, N. Y., July 9, 1845, to Gerrit Smith, Peterboro.

39. *Ibid.*, p. 10, William B. Astor, N. Y., August 20, 1845, to Gerrit Smith, Peterboro; ms. book, Syracuse University, Gerrit Smith Miller Collection, List of Debt owing by Gerrit Smith Including All debts due from his late father — Principal only — no interest — no taxes —, p. 100.

40. Ms. book, Baker Library, Astor Papers, Letter Book iii, 1845–48, p. 254, William B. Astor, N. Y., January 4, 1848, to Gerrit Smith, Peterboro (see below, vol. ii, p. 1258); p. 263, John Jacob Astor per William B. Astor, N. Y., February 1, 1848, to Gerrit Smith, Peterboro.

41. In his late years Astor refused to make loans to non-residents of the State of New York or on property located outside of the State (ms. book, Baker Library, Astor Papers, Letter Book iii, 1845–48, pp. 30, 107, John Jacob Astor by William B. Astor, N. Y., October 16, 1845, to Levi E. Tell, August 17, 1846, to Orlow R. Coe, Aurora, Ohio).

42. Ms. book, Syracuse University, Gerrit Smith Miller Collection, Letter Book, 1843–55, Gerrit Smith, Peterboro, April 6, 1848, to William B. Astor, N. Y. (see below, vol. ii, p. 1259).

43. Ms. book, Baker Library, Astor Papers, Letter Book ii, 1831–38, p. 283, John Jacob Astor per William B. Astor, N. Y., February 18, 1835, to Gerrit Smith, Peterboro.

CHAPTER XX

MANHATTAN ISLAND REAL ESTATE

1800–1848

THE year 1800 was in several ways the beginning of a new era in John Jacob Astor's business life. At this time he was believed to be worth a quarter of a million dollars and had consequently decided that he might venture to establish a residence apart from his place of business.[1] Those best qualified to judge proclaimed that he had reached a position of undoubted supremacy among the citizens of the United States engaged in the trade with the North American Indians. Such was the standing to which Astor had attained sixteen years after his arrival in the United States, but he now showed no inclination to rest on his laurels. On the contrary, it was during this significant year that he definitely entered two fields which were to rank among the most important of his business activities. One of these was trade with Canton, conducted in his own vessels. The other was investment in real estate on Manhattan Island.

Manhattan Island real estate was a form of investment not entirely new to Astor in 1800. Within the space of twenty months in the years 1789, 1790, and 1791, he had purchased five pieces of land in New York. He then paid no further attention to New York City real estate until 1800, nearly a decade after his last investment of that type.[2] This interim period, however, did not indicate any cessation of interest in real estate in general as a field for investment, but only a shift of attention from lots on Manhattan Island to much more extensive tracts of largely uncultivated land in Lower Canada and the backcountry of New York State. Astor was not the first investor to be misled into the belief that property which could be secured at a price much below its potential value must necessarily be a good investment. Consequently, between 1792 and 1796, he wasted a good deal of time trying to acquire part of the waste lands of the Crown in Lower Canada, but without success, for it was not till 1801 that he finally secured some Canadian land through a mortgage, later selling it, as is noted elsewhere, sight unseen and at a profit, to his brother George in London.

At once more important and more successful was Astor's interest in land in New York State, which began about 1792. His most extensive investment, in partnership with Peter Smith and William Laight, involved him in expensive litigation, which, indeed, was fairly successful in the end, although it did not come to a conclusion until 1802; even then the property in question did not prove to be particularly profitable.[3] Astor was always ready to learn by experience, and by 1800 he had reached the conclusion that, during most of the last decade, he had been following the wrong track in land investment. His idea in acquiring land in New York State had been to make a quick turnover and sell out at a good profit, not to hold the tract as a permanent investment, but to dispose of it as soon as he could. It turned out, however, that in normal times uncultivated land could not be sold at much of an advance on the purchase price. There was too much of it within the indefinite boundaries of the United States. Astor was forced to take his returns in the form of rent from farmers. But here, too, the oversupply of unoccupied land made his income from this source rather small. Moreover, the distance of this land from Astor's headquarters in New York City made it impossible for him to give it that personal attention which any such project must have to be successful.

Astor realized that he had been right in his first purchase of land on Manhattan Island, where the progress of commerce would cause the value to increase much more rapidly than the value of backwoods areas. Moreover, on Manhattan Island agriculture was not the sole use to which his holdings could be put, while he would be on hand to manage his property personally and take immediate advantage of any opportunity to increase its extent. New York City at this time occupied only a small area at the southerly tip of Manhattan Island, the upper portions of the Island being still devoted to farming. The population of New York City, when Astor first arrived there in 1784, was about 23,000. In 1790, when Astor had become firmly established in the city of his choice, as a rising young merchant, the population had increased to 33,000. But by 1800 New York City had 60,000 inhabitants, having nearly doubled in population during the last decade.[4] Astor judged from this rapid growth in population during the past few years that the city must move northward. With these considerations in mind Astor began in 1800 the consistent program of investment in Manhattan Island real estate which was to continue for nearly half a century and make him the richest man in the country.

During the forty-eight years of his connection with Manhattan Island real estate, Astor participated in hundreds, even thousands, of transactions, buying, selling, leasing, renting, and lending money on real-estate security. In considering his interest in New York City land we must, then, confine ourselves to the general methods he employed at various periods in acquiring property and to his changing policies in the administration of his holdings, with perhaps an examination of typical or particularly important cases by way of illustration. The story of Astor's Manhattan Island real-estate investments unfortunately does not lend itself to treatment by periods quite so well as does his fur trade or his commerce with Canton. There are no definite points at which we can say that one policy was established or another discarded.

It is logical to determine, first of all, the circumstances and method of Astor's acquisition of lands, whether in fee simple or on long-term lease, in the 252 transactions in which he was concerned as grantee between the years 1800 and 1848.[5] Although we can here distinguish no definite lines of demarcation, marked off by changes of policy in his real-estate investment, still, for the sake of convenience, we may begin by dividing this part of his business career roughly into periods. These periods will run from 1800 to 1819, from 1820 to 1834, when Astor retired from commerce, and from 1835 to 1848, the year of Astor's death. The middle period was further distinguished by the fact that in 1819 Astor went to Europe for his health and spent most of his time on the Continent till 1826, returning to America only for short visits. Unlike his fur trade and his commerce with Canton, his real-estate interests did not require a constant process of buying and selling. As a consequence, this interim period, from 1820 to 1825 inclusive, was not rich in land conveyances to Astor. In fact, during these years, land conveyed to him was valued at less than one thousand dollars.

During the period from 1800 to 1819 he paid out for land conveyed to him in fee simple or on long-term lease over $715,000. In other words, at this period Astor's annual investment in Manhattan Island real estate was over $35,000. We are naturally eager to learn where he secured all this money paid out for real estate, since whatever land he bought he paid for in cash, nor was the property ever encumbered at any subsequent period.[6] We have seen that at the beginning of the nineteenth century his wealth was estimated at $250,000. At this time he owned a few lots and buildings in New York City, which at the time of their purchase, a decade before, had cost him about $7,000 and the value of which had probably increased considerably since then. He was also the owner of about 1,000 acres in Lower Canada, valued at something over

£1,000 in the currency of that province. He owned a good deal of land in the New York backcountry, where his largest holdings were his one-fourth interest in the Charlotte River and Byrnes Patent tracts, which originally contained 37,200 acres and were valued at about $4.00 per acre, and a tract of nearly 6,000 acres in Tioga County. He also owned stock of various kinds — for example, some 6 per cent stock of the United States,[7] a few shares in the Bank of New York,[8] and 100 or 200 shares in the Bank of Manhattan Company.[9] The rest of his property was probably in the form of bank deposits, debts and notes outstanding, and furs and other merchandise in his warehouse. It is evident that Astor's income from land, in the form of either sales or rents, was small and uncertain, and that his stock dividends were of no great significance. His income, then, must have been derived almost entirely from his activities as a dealer in furs and general merchandise, and, in view of his great prominence, in the former field especially, was doubtless considerable. By 1800, we know, he had enough capital to take the lead in buying and loading a ship for Canton. Had he gone into this enterprise alone, it would probably have required the expenditure of about $100,000. In that year and in the succeeding year together, he also invested a little more than $10,000 in New York City land. This sum was not much more than he had invested in the space of 20 months a decade before; but in 1802 he expended more than $20,000; and in 1803 his interest in Manhattan Island real estate assumed startling proportions, for in that year he paid out more than $184,000 in return for land conveyances.

The source of these funds is no less significant than their expenditure. It will be remembered that the *Severn*, the first ship in which Astor owned an interest, sailed from New York for China in April, 1800, and returned in May of the next year. The remaining months of 1801 and most of 1802 were spent in disposing of the goods brought by the *Severn*. Thus, it was not till late in 1802, at the earliest, that the cash returns of the voyage, which had been initiated in 1800, were available to those concerned. It seems evident that the funds invested in land in 1803 were part of Astor's share in the profits of the *Severn's* first voyage. It appears, indeed, that there is a close correlation between Astor's commercial profits in this period and his investments in land. Tradition coincides with our belief that Astor followed the policy of investing in lands a large proportion of his commercial profits. An article written while Astor was still alive stated that he had put two-thirds of his profits into land.[10] It seems evident, further, that it was principally the returns from the China trade which went into real estate, since during the first decade of the nineteenth century Astor's fur trade had undergone no expansion which would account for such heavy profits.

In 1804 and 1805 Astor invested about $80,000 each year in Manhattan Island real estate. An Astor vessel had gone to Canton in 1802 and had returned in the next year. The years 1803 and 1804 had probably been consumed largely in disposing of the cargo from the voyage of 1802 and 1803. It was probably not until 1805 that the returns from this voyage were all available. The land investments in 1804 may have been from some of the earlier returns of this voyage or from the remaining profits of the *Severn's* first Canton venture. Moreover, in 1805 Astor bought a new vessel, which cut down his funds for land investment. But in 1806, when the profits for the voyage inaugurated in 1803 had been received, Astor made up for the comparatively small investments of the two preceding years by expending nearly $125,000 in land. In 1807, however, his land investments sank to $37,000. The state of the China trade accounts for this decline also. An Astor vessel had gone to China in 1804 as usual, another in 1805, and two in 1806; but international difficulties kept Astor from sending a ship to Canton in 1807, though he did send one to Calcutta. Astor evidently thought that the prospects of commercial gain in that year were so small that he had better keep his funds in a readily accessible form. Accordingly, in 1808 he invested only a little over $6,000 in land, since the embargo of that year had put commerce in a more parlous state than ever. In 1809 his investments in Manhattan Island real estate hit rock-bottom, amounting to only a little more than $1,000. However, it should be said that very late in the year, cheered, probably, by the removal of the embargo in the spring and the return of the *Beaver* from the "mandarin voyage," Astor purchased lands in Putnam County for $100,000 — a transaction which has been dealt with previously. Thus it will be observed that during the first decade of Astor's interest in the China trade he had invested well over $500,000 in Manhattan Island real estate, probably to a large extent from the profits of the China trade, which in its turn had been based principally on the fur trade. This also gives us some idea of Astor's profits during this period in the commerce with Canton.

The next ten years showed a sharp drop in Astor's investments in Manhattan Island real estate. From 1810 to 1819, inclusive, he invested only a little over $170,000, considerably less than one-third of the amount similarly expended during the preceding period, and, indeed, less than he had invested during the single year of 1803. This decline in Astor's attention to real estate is easily explained. The Non-Importation Act was badly hampering his Great Lakes fur trade in the period prior to the war, and in the years from 1809 to 1813, inclusive, he was engaged in fitting out expeditions to the North West Coast, at great expense and with no prospects of early returns. Even so, his investments for 1810 and 1811 — over $27,000 and $45,000, respectively — were not small. Owing to the outbreak of war in 1812, he made no investments in real estate during that year. But he received two cargoes of China goods after the outbreak of the war. Prices went up and merchants began to fail; Astor increased his land purchases to over $30,000 in 1813 and $42,000 in 1814. However, during the next five years Manhattan Island real estate ceased to be important as a field of investment for Astor. In 1815 his expenditures amounted to $8,000, in 1819 to $5,400, and during the intervening period they never attained in any one year a larger amount than $5,000. Here again we need not search far for a reason. In 1815 Astor began a definite campaign for the monopoly of the United States fur trade. He also devoted more attention to the China trade than ever before. His profits from the China trade were no longer invested in Manhattan Island real estate, but were either turned back into the trade itself or employed in building up the million-dollar capital of the American Fur Company.

We are now able to state some conclusions as to the scope of Astor's investments in Manhattan Island real estate in the first score of years during which he was interested in it. The sum invested amounted to well over $700,000, of which by far the largest portion belonged to the pre-war period. The funds employed came almost entirely from the profits of Astor's China trade, which, in its turn, had been based principally upon his success as a dealer in furs, and also as a general merchant. It should be added, however, that during the years 1803–19 Astor made conveyances by sale or lease of lands on Manhattan Island valued at more than $191,000,[11] so that this amount became available for use in the purchase of other lands. This fact must be taken into consideration in determining the source of the funds employed in Astor's real-estate investments.

Most of the conveyances to Astor during this period involved land lying outside of the built-up portion of New York City, chiefly in what were then the sixth, seventh, and eighth (formerly seventh) wards. Very few of the lots conveyed to Astor, in consequence, had buildings on them. It was evidently

Astor's policy to buy unimproved lots which, with the growth of the city, would increase in value much more, in proportion, than the down-town lots, whose value at that time was much greater. Of the hundred-odd conveyances made to Astor in this period, only eight (which, however, amounted to a total of $137,628) were in the form of long-term leases rather than outright sales.[12] Seven of these leases occurred in the years 1803–05, and nearly all were to property which had been leased to Aaron Burr in 1797 by Trinity Church, a Protestant Episcopal institution of New York City. Later Burr, or his tenants under this lease, sold their rights in the property to Astor. Aaron Burr's part in this transaction will later be examined in detail. Astor's purchase of leases from Burr seems to have whetted his desire for land belonging to the Protestant Episcopal Church, and during the years from 1805 to 1814, but chiefly in 1807, he bought a number of lots from this organization to the total amount of nearly $100,000.[13]

Astor is traditionally supposed to have acquired most of his land through the foreclosure of mortgages. This is certainly not true of the period which we are now discussing. Of about 100 conveyances made to Astor during these 20 years, only 8 were made by the master in chancery, and one by a United States marshal. Astor appeared as complainant in only 5 of these conveyances; in the others he merely chanced to be the highest bidder in the auction sales at which the lots in question were sold to satisfy mortgages. It was not until the summer of 1813 that he secured possession of land through the foreclosure of a mortgage made to himself.[14] As a matter of fact, during the years 1803–16, Astor was concerned in only 24 mortgages, of which very few were, as we have seen, foreclosed by him. It is evident that, so far at least, the mortgage was playing a very small part in Astor's program for the acquisition of Manhattan Island real estate.

Astor was sometimes able to secure land by grant of water-lots from the city; that is, he was given the right to reclaim land under water below high-water mark, bordering on land owned by him. As his policy in regard to such lands did not change throughout his life, we may consider it as a whole. In 1806, 1807, 1808, 1811, 1814, 1825, 1828, and 1829, he applied for and received 12 or 15 such grants, for which he usually agreed to pay rent to the city at the rate of $32.50 annually. In many cases, however, not content with receiving the grant, he would petition later for better terms, such as the reduction of the rent, or its remission for a period of 30 years, usually with success. Also in 1826, 1829, and 1831 Astor bought gores bordering on his land, formed by closing old roads. Unfortunately, Astor was not always very careful about carrying out the terms of these grants. He would often insist that other owners of water-lots should complete streets adjacent to them, but even more often he would protest against being himself required to undergo expense for that purpose. Also, he was constantly being reported for tardiness in filling up the lots granted to him, some of which became public nuisances in consequence of his neglect.[15] Evidently Astor was by no means so eager to do his part in the improvement of the city as he was to acquire all the public lands which the corporation could give him; but of course he was not unique in this attitude.

Such, in general, were Astor's methods in acquiring Manhattan Island real estate. A few particular illustrations may serve to make these methods more clear. The connection with Aaron Burr, which began with Astor's first purchase of real estate in 1800, was of great importance.[16] We have noted the purchase of Burr's leases from Trinity Church. Trinity was a large owner of land on Manhattan Island, but its income from this land, it is said, was at that time restricted by law to $12,000 annually. In 1767 Trinity leased to one Abraham Mortier a parcel of 465 lots for 99 years at a total annual rental of only $269. According to one account, the lease reverted to Trinity because Mortier did not keep the conditions. All stories, however, agree that in 1797 Burr was appointed chairman of a committee from the New York legislature to enquire into the affairs of Trinity Church. For some reason the investigation was never made, but on May 11, 1797, the chairman emerged as owner of the remainder of the Mortier lease. Burr, as always, was financially embarrassed, and obtained a mortgage on this lease for $38,000 from the Manhattan Bank, whose charter he had been responsible for procuring.[17] Burr's extravagance, however, soon made it necessary for him to raise some more funds. He had long been acquainted with Astor and had done some legal business for him. Accordingly, it was to Astor he applied in the fall of 1803; and on October 22, 1803, Astor bought for $62,500 the remainder of the Trinity lease to 241 lots, subject to the mortgage, which he satisfied on July 20, 1804, by paying $41,783. During that autumn and the following year Astor bought other lots and lease-remainders from Burr to a total value of more than $12,000, an $8,000 purchase of a lease being made in the month after Burr's duel with Hamilton.[18]

At about the same time as the transaction with Aaron Burr, another famous real-estate operation was in progress. In 1797 Medcef Eden had inherited a piece of farm land on Manhattan Island, bounded on one side by the Hudson River, containing about 70 acres, with a dwelling-house thereon. We are told that he "frittered away" the value of this property until in 1801 it was sold by one of the masters in chancery. It was later pledged to one Benjamin Haskins, who sold a third of his interest in the mortgage to Astor, and finally on June 13, 1803, the property was sold by a master in chancery to John Jacob Astor and William Cutting for $25,000. Astor later bought out part of Cutting's share. Long after, certain heirs of Medcef Eden turned up, claiming some right in these lands, and Astor paid them $9,000 to quiet the title.[19]

Still more important was Astor's connection with George Clinton, formerly governor of New York, who was at this time vice-president of the United States. Clinton, like Burr, found politics an expensive amusement. Consequently in the summer of 1805 he sold to Astor a half interest in his lands in Greenwich Village, near New York City. For this interest Astor paid $75,000. The plan was that the two should divide up the property according to certain streets to be laid out by them. The division was made and the resultant blocks were apportioned by lot. However, before the two could complete their project by actually constructing the streets which they had planned, commissioners appointed by the New York legislature had laid out new streets which cut up the lots as originally apportioned in a very prejudicial manner. In 1812 Clinton died intestate, leaving a number of minor heirs who found it impossible to give satisfactory conveyances to property which Clinton had previously contracted to sell. For example, it was impossible for them to make a new distribution of the lots in which Clinton and Astor had each owned a one-half share, in such a manner as to increase their value. In the following year, however, an application to the legislature resulted in the heirs receiving the right to make conveyances through their representatives with the same validity as if they were of age. Consequently a new partition of lots was made, more equitable to all concerned.[20] Clinton's death and the final partition of his property did not cause Astor to lose interest in that portion which remained to his heirs. In 1816 Edmond C. Genêt ("Citizen" Genêt, who was Clinton's son-in-law) mortgaged some property to Astor, into whose hands it fell three years later, after a sale by the master in chancery. In the next decade Astor bought a number of lots from Clinton's executors and from the children of Edmond C. Genêt, to the total amount of more than $12,000.[21] At one time or another Astor invested well over $100,000 in land which was or had recently been the property of George

Clinton. His real-estate transactions with Burr, Clinton, and the Protestant Episcopal Church accounted for well over half of the $715,000 he invested in Manhattan Island real estate in the twenty years beginning in 1800.[22]

The next question we have to consider is how, during the period 1800–19, Astor administered the real estate which he had acquired on Manhattan Island. In order to answer this question, we must first put aside the hoary tradition that neither Astor nor any of his descendants have ever sold a lot once in their possession. As a matter of fact, Astor's chief care in regard to his New York City real estate, during his first twenty years of investment, was to sell it as soon after its purchase as possible, and at as large an advance as he could get on the original price. It was not until 1806 that leases from Astor, either for a long or for a short term, began to be recorded, and during the entire period of 20 years the amount paid to him for long-term leases did not reach $10,000, as compared with more than $180,000 received for property sold outright. We shall consequently turn our attention to Astor's sales policy from 1803, when he first began to dispose of real estate on Manhattan Island, up to and including 1819. In the main his methods have been well described by a contemporary.

When he [Astor] first trod the streets of New-York, in 1784, the city was a snug, leafy place of twenty-five thousand inhabitants, situated at the extremity of the island, mostly below Cortlandt street. In 1800, when he began to have money to invest, the city had more than doubled in population, and had advanced nearly a mile up the island. Now, Astor was a shrewd calculator of the future. No reason appeared why New-York should not repeat this doubling game and this mile of extension every fifteen years. He acted upon the supposition, and fell into the habit of buying lands and lots just beyond the verge of the city. One little anecdote will show the wisdom of this proceeding. He sold a lot in the vicinity of Wall street [which he had probably purchased in 1802], about the year 1810, for eight thousand dollars, which was supposed to be somewhat under its value. The purchaser, after the papers were signed, seemed disposed to chuckle over his bargain.

"Why, Mr. Astor," said he, "in a few years this lot will be worth twelve thousand dollars."

"Very true," replied Astor; "but now you shall see what I will do with this money. With eight thousand dollars I buy eighty lots above Canal street. By the time your lot is worth twelve thousand dollars, my eighty lots will be worth eighty thousand dollars;" which proved to be the fact.[23]

Whether or not this exact incident actually occurred and whether or not we should allow for some exaggeration in Astor's estimate of the speed with which he expected his land to multiply in value, this story nevertheless expresses with great clarity the policy of sell-and-buy which dominated Astor's real-estate activities in this period.

It should be of interest to ascertain the advance of Astor's selling price in each case over the amount which he had originally paid. His first conveyance of any importance took place on February 15, 1803, when he sold for $4,500 a water-lot which on January 5, 1791, had cost him only £200. On February 16, 1803, he sold for $2,500 20 lots which, together with a dwelling-house and lot and 4 other lots, had been sold to him 2 months before for $3,000. Late in January, 1803, Astor bought a lot with a three-story brick house for $11,500, and in a little over 6 weeks sold a mere third of the lot — not the part containing the house — for $2,150. Even more striking was the sale of a lot which Astor purchased in 1803 for $4,550, and for which he received $9,000 on March 31, 1806, thus nearly doubling his money. Still more important were the sales Astor made after dividing such tracts as the Eden estate into lots. On June 13, 1803, he and William Cutting bought the Eden estate, consisting of about 70 acres, for $25,000. Before the summer was over, a dozen lots of a little more than an acre apiece had been sold for more than $7,000. Another series of transactions also held promise of considerable profits. On June 29, 1803, Astor bought 32 lots from Edward Livingston for $12,500; during the next year half a dozen of these lots met a ready sale at $625 apiece. But perhaps Astor's greatest proportionate profits from land sales were made from the lots he had secured by his transaction with George Clinton. He had paid $75,000 for half of Clinton's Greenwich Village land, and in the division, on July 8, 1805, he received 243 lots, which meant that he paid only about $300 apiece. But during the next few years, from 1806 to 1814, Astor sold 32 of these same lots at an average price of more than $1,000 apiece, thus making a profit of more than 200 per cent. Since most of the lots were sold during the years 1806–08, Astor did not have long to wait for his returns. In some cases, Astor took a mortgage on the lots sold, for the full value of the purchase price, to be paid in 2 or 3 years with interest, and providing that if the grantee should default in either principal or interest Astor might have the property sold at auction and recompense himself out of the proceeds for principal, interest, and costs.[24] Examples could be multiplied, but these will suffice to show the profits Astor was able to make in a short time by buying and selling lots, or by purchasing larger tracts to be subdivided and sold.

We may now turn to an aspect of Astor's real-estate management which, in the period up to 1819, was of much less importance than his outright sales, but which was later predominant, namely, his leasing of real estate. His leases naturally fall into two classes: long-term leases, made on the payment of a lump sum; and short-term leases, at an annual rental. Both types first appeared in 1806, though from the many advertisements in the New York press of previous years offering buildings to let [25] we may infer that Astor rented some of his property without the formality of a lease. Practically all the long-term leases were made to land acquired through the Burr lease, which was to run from May 1, 1797, for 69 years, to May 1, 1866. Since Astor had only a leasehold to this land, he could not, of course, sell it outright, as otherwise he might have preferred to do. The next best recourse was to lease it for a long period of 57, 56, 52, 49, or 47 years, according to the length of time his own lease still had to run. Sometimes these leases covered the full time up to May 1, 1866, and once, indeed, a miscalculation sent a lease beyond that deadline; but nearly as often they terminated a year or two before the expiration of the lease to Astor. The extremes in this class are represented by a lease for the brief term of 18 years, and another — not to land belonging to Trinity Church — for 99 years.

A lease to a single lot for a term of about 50 years normally cost about $500, though it would sometimes come as low as $325, and again as high as $700. In addition, the lessee agreed to pay all taxes, duties, and assessments, except the nominal ground rent to Trinity Church, for which Astor was responsible. In one case the lessee agreed to erect and repair a board fence conforming to certain specifications. Among other conditions, we find that the lessee should be allowed to remove any buildings erected by him within a certain specific brief period before or after the expiration of the lease. In some cases the lessee, being unable to pay for the lease at the time of the conveyance, gave Astor a mortgage on the property for all or part of the amount of the lease, payable with interest, usually of 6 per cent and in 3 or 5 years, when any rate and term were specified, and with the provision that, if any default were made in the payment of principal or interest, the property might be sold at auction, any surplus going to the defaulting lessee.[26]

The short-term lease was usually made for 21 years on the basis of an annual rental, which was ordinarily payable quarterly, and ranged in normal cases from $45 or $50 to $100 per lot. As in the case of long-term leases, the lessee was responsible for all taxes, duties, and assessments, except that Astor agreed to pay the nominal ground rent on land belonging to Trinity Church. It was usually provided that within 2 years the lessee should build a dwelling-house with a brick front of at least 2 stories. When no such provision was explicitly made, it seems to have been assumed that such a building would nevertheless be constructed. The lessee, however, was not, as has been assumed by various writers dealing with Astor's real-estate policy, left entirely without compensation at the end of the lease for the building he had erected. In some cases it was provided that, on the expiration of the lease, the lessee might within 10 days remove any buildings on the property, or that he should be given a new lease for another period of 21 years, at a rent to be fixed. These provisions, however, do not appear to have been in themselves an adequate safeguard for the rights of the lessee, since the removal of the buildings would undoubtedly be an unsatisfactory expedient and the rent provided for in the new lease might, it would seem, be increased almost indefinitely. Somewhat more satisfactory was the provision, sometimes found, that any buildings erected by the lessee should be valued by competent persons and Astor should either pay the price so fixed or renew the lease. A method of determining the value of these buildings which was sometimes specified was the employment of an umpire chosen by a committee composed of a representative of each party. In at least one case it was provided that a renewal of the lease was to be preferred to a payment for the buildings at their estimated value.[27] In the cases when a new lease was an alternative, no very clear method of determining the yearly rent seems to have been specified, but we may assume that if no terms mutually agreeable could be fixed upon Astor would be forced to pay for the buildings. It is evident that the terms were on the whole favorable to Astor, as he got his lots built upon without trouble to himself and at the termination of the lease had only to pay the estimated value of the buildings or give a new lease, probably at a considerably increased rental.

One specific short-term lease may be mentioned as belonging to a different category from those described above and as illustrating the real-estate situation on Manhattan Island in the first decade of the nineteenth century. This lease, dated December 1, 1806, was the first, indeed, to appear in the records of conveyances by Astor. It was a lease for 7 years and at $800 annual rent to 21 acres "within four miles of the city," part of the Eden estate, with dwelling-houses, barns, and other buildings. This land was to be used for farming purposes; provisions were made that the lessee should spread 100 cart-loads of manure upon the land annually, and that, if he actually expended as much as $50 per year in repairs, he should be remitted an equal amount of his rent. While this part of the Eden farm was still being used for agricultural purposes, building lots were being laid out on the rest of Astor's share of its original 70 acres.[28]

Certain characteristics may be noted as marking Astor's real-estate policy from 1800 to 1819. During this period he purchased land in fee simple or on long-term lease, principally the former, to the amount of over $700,000, on that part of Manhattan Island which was outside of but not very far distant from the city. At this time land secured by Astor in mortgage sales was not a conspicuous element in his purchases. During this same period Astor disposed of land, in fee simple or on long-term lease, principally the former, to the amount of nearly $200,000. He also rented a number of lots on short-term leases, though this type of lease did not become significant till after 1809 and never, in this period, became a really important factor in the development of his real estate.

We may now go on to consider Astor's methods of acquiring Manhattan Island real estate during the period between his departure to Europe in 1819 and his death in 1848. These 29 years may be divided, for convenience, into 2 nearly equal periods, one extending from 1820 to 1834, and the other from 1835 to 1848. By the end of the first period, Astor had withdrawn from commerce of all kinds, and had moreover returned to the United States for good, after another sojourn in Europe from 1832 to 1834.

We have already observed that during the first 10 years in which Astor was engaged in purchasing land in New York City he had expended nearly $550,000, while during the next decade his land purchases had fallen to less than one-third of that amount. The reason for this discrepancy is that in the first decade a large part of Astor's income from the China trade was being employed in land investment, while at the beginning of the second the war had cut off nearly all foreign trade, and after its conclusion his commercial profits had largely been diverted to build up the American Fur Company and to expand his commerce with China. During his last 29 years, Astor's real-estate investments in New York City amounted to more than $1,250,000, raising the total for his entire lifetime to just over $2,000,000. His annual expenditures on land varied just as widely during these 29 years as they had during the previous 20 years. From 1820 to 1834 Astor invested $445,000 in Manhattan Island lands. During the 14 years from 1835 to his death, his investments came to a total of $832,000, nearly twice as much as he had invested in the previous 15 years, and considerably more than the total for the whole of the first 20 years after 1800.

Let us now consider where Astor secured the funds for this investment of more than $1,250,000 from 1820 to 1848. We have seen that during the period from 1820 to 1834 Astor invested $450,000; for all practical purposes, this sum was invested between 1826 and 1834, for Astor was almost continuously absent in Europe from 1819 to 1826, and therefore invested less than $1,000 during the years 1820–25. All this time, even while absent in Europe, Astor was actively pushing the fur trade, and was a prominent figure in the China trade. But another source of funds for Astor's land investments was probably of much greater importance than his profits from commerce. From 1800 to 1819 Astor had invested over $700,000 in land in or near New York City. During this period, less than $200,000 worth of this land had been conveyed by Astor in fee simple or on long-term leases. Not very much had been leased on yearly rental. But in 1826 Astor's yearly rents on 174 pieces of property amounted to more than $27,000. By 1831 the number of pieces of property rented had gone up to 244 and the rents to more than $46,000. From August 1, 1826, to May 1, 1831, Astor's income from rents alone amounted to $190,000.[29] Moreover, from 1820 to 1834 Astor disposed of land in fee simple or on long-term lease for more than $386,000. But during the whole period from 1820 to 1834 Astor's investments in land amounted to only $445,000. In other words, he could probably have obtained nearly all the funds he needed for his land investments from 1820 to 1834, from either his yearly income in rentals or the proceeds of his land sales and long-term leases, without having any recourse to his commercial profits for this purpose.

Between 1835 and 1848, Astor put $832,000 into lands on Manhattan Island. We may at once dismiss the possibility that profits from commercial enterprises went into land during this period. By 1834 both the fur trade and the commerce with China had passed out of Astor's business life. Whence, then, came the large sum which from 1835 to 1848 Astor invested in Manhattan Island real estate? In answering this question we may be guided by consideration of the source of funds used in real-estate investments from 1820 to 1834. It will be remembered that in 1831 Astor's income from the rental of land on Manhattan Island was $46,000. The number of separate pieces of property rented was 244. In the next 10 years, both the amount of property rented and rental values increased to such an extent that in the year from May 1, 1840, to May 1, 1841, 355 pieces of property brought in more than $128,000. During the year from May 1, 1847, to May 1, 1848, 470 pieces of property brought Astor an income of more than $200,000.[30] From May 1, 1840, to May 1, 1848, Astor's total income from rents was more than $1,265,000. In other words, his income from rents alone during the period 1835–48 was much more than the amount he invested in land during that same period. And in this period, as in the one from 1820 to 1834, we find that Astor also made conveyances for lump sums, sales, or long-term leases, which amounted to more than $608,000. It is not hard, then, to see where Astor secured the funds for investment in Manhattan Island real estate from 1835 to 1848, even though he had entirely withdrawn from commercial activities.

We have next to inspect the character of the conveyances by which, during the period from 1820 to 1848, Astor came into possession of his lands. It has been pointed out that, while in the period 1800–19 Astor acquired most of his land by outright purchase, still an important proportion of his investments was in long-term leases, usually of land belonging to Trinity Church, occurring chiefly in the years 1803 and 1804. During the remainder of Astor's real-estate activities, leases were by no means so important either in number or in significance. They represented a negligible element in his land purchases until the year 1840, when they represented nearly half the number of conveyances to him. But having said so much, we must avoid giving a false impression, and add that nearly all these leases were made to Astor by the master in chancery and were to lots to which Astor himself had previously given leases, taking mortgages on the lots for the payment of the consideration mentioned in the conveyances, which conditions the leaseholders had failed to pay.

This brings us to another question concerning Astor's methods of acquiring real estate, namely, what part the foreclosure of mortgages had in his policy. We have already seen that conveyances to Astor under mortgages were not conspicuous during his first 20 years in real-estate investment on Manhattan Island. Were they no more important in the later period? Of 95 conveyances to Astor from 1800 to 1819, only 8 were by the master in chancery; of 152 conveyances from 1823 to 1848, there were 58 by the master in chancery or the sheriff. All these, be it noted, occurred from 1832 to 1848, and 53 in the years after 1837. It may be definitely said, then, that it was only in Astor's last years that the mortgage became a significant element in the acquisition of property, since not a single foreclosure was recorded between 1819 and 1832, and only 8 before 1819. However, from 1835 onward, Astor was concerned as the grantee in mortgage sales to the amount of over $448,000; about $100,000 of these arose from conveyances which Astor himself had made, taking mortgages as security for the fulfillment of the conditions, which the purchasers had then failed to carry out. Consequently, these latter transactions cannot be used to prove that Astor gained his land on Manhattan Island chiefly by means of foreclosing mortgages on the old homesteads of widows with large families of minor children.

The records, moreover, do not justify the common opinion that Astor was utterly ruthless in foreclosing mortgages. As a matter of fact, during his entire career he was the mortgagee in nearly 500 separate transactions, but became the owner of less than 70 pieces of property by foreclosure. The terms of his mortgages were usually specified as 3 or 5 years, but Astor frequently carried the mortgages for several times the prescribed period. On the other hand, there is no doubt that, if a mortgagor failed to pay his interest, Astor would promptly foreclose and buy in the property at a very low price. When Astor on one occasion had bid in 7 lots for $5,650, the Court of Chancery considered the price so low that it intervened and required him to pay a bonus of $1,500.[31]

Nearly all of Astor's foreclosures took place during and after the Panic of 1837. Of this period Philip Hone, at one time mayor of New York, is quoted as saying: "Here, in the city of New York, trade is stagnant. Local stocks are lower than ever; real estate is unsalable at any price; rents have fallen and are not punctually paid, and taxes have increased most ruinously. The pressure is severe enough upon the owners of houses and stores who are out of debt, but if the property is mortgaged and the seven per cent interest must be regularly paid, God help the owners!"[32] Astor, having withdrawn from business and being possessed of a large capital, was able to profit immensely by this temporary decline in real-estate values and by the scarcity of money. But it was not only nor even principally through the foreclosure of mortgages that Astor profited by the Panic. An average annual investment in Manhattan Island real estate for one of the fourteen years from 1835 to 1848 would have been less than $60,000; but during the years 1837–39 the average was more than $160,000, and in 1838 more than $224,000 was invested. By 1840 investments had fallen off greatly.

Let us now examine Astor's methods of managing his real estate during this period. We have already seen that before 1820 his object was to dispose of his lands outright, at a good profit and as quickly as possible, and that leases, either long-term or short-term, were a side-issue and probably occurred largely because Astor's extensive leaseholds of land belonging to Trinity Church could not be handled in any other way. From 1820 on, however, matters changed radically. During this period Astor disposed of land in fee simple, or on long-term lease for a lump sum, to the amount of nearly a million dollars — a little less than $995,000, to be more exact. Of this amount the great bulk was disposed of in fee simple, only a little over $190,000 being conveyed on long-term leases. There is little to be said about these outright sales, since no particular policy appears in this connection which is distinguishable from that employed in the earlier period.

It may, however, be noted that Astor frequently took mortgages on lots sold, as security for the payment of the price agreed upon. One of these transactions involved a certain

Christopher Keyes, variously described as a cartman and as a contractor, the first probably being his occupation and the second his ambition. In 1836 and 1837 he bought several lots from Astor, half a dozen at $2,738.89 each and nine at $5,454.54. These lots were mortgaged to Astor for their full value for a term of 5 years and at 7 per cent interest, payable semiannually. Keyes also mortgaged half a dozen lots to Astor which had not been purchased from him, for $1,000 each. Keyes evidently intended to build on these lots and thus make enough to enable him to pay off the mortgages. However, he had chosen the wrong time for such a business venture, though he may have bought the land at a lower rate than usual on account of the depression caused by the Panic. On October 23, 1840, Astor sold William Tucker 2 of the $1,000 mortgages for $1,035.38 each, and one mortgage of $2,738.89 for $2,807.59. Keyes soon defaulted on his interest payments and on December 2, 1839, some of these lots were sold at auction. Astor bought in for a total of $48,350[33] the 9 lots he had sold for $49,090.86, at $5,454.54 apiece. Presumably Astor received compensation on the other mortgages through sales not made to himself. This may serve as an illustration of Astor's sales policy and the part mortgages played in it.

During the earlier period long-term leases had played a part only second to that of outright sales in Astor's program of real-estate management. Long-term leases now sank to a subordinate position, though from 1824 to 1835, and in the year 1840, they predominated numerically over outright sales. It is not very hard to determine the reason for this comparative decline. Astor had begun to lease land because he was concerned in certain areas in which he possessed only a leasehold. Conveyances by long-term lease, next to outright sales, which in this case were impossible, represented the most convenient way of handling his real-estate investments. But Astor had a lease on the Trinity Church land only to May 1, 1866. As the years passed, he found his rights in this property diminishing and consequently it was impossible to find outright purchasers for the comparatively few years of his leasehold still remaining. This factor, and others which we shall later mention, caused him to lease his New York City property for comparatively short terms, and for a rent payable annually or oftener, rather than for long periods on the outright payment of a lump sum.

We shall now investigate Astor's policy in granting long-term leases during his last thirty years of attention to Manhattan Island real estate. The provisions in Astor's long-term leases after 1820 did not differ materially from those of the previous period. The lessee still agreed to pay all taxes, duties, and assessments upon the lots, except for the trifling ground rent to Trinity Church, for which Astor, as before, was to be responsible. The lessee still had the nominal right to remove any buildings erected on the lots within ten days after the expiration of the lease. The principal changes appeared in the length of the leases and the consideration to be paid. Naturally, as Astor's lease from Trinity drew nearer and nearer to an end, the leases he himself made under it also became shorter. Astor's policy seems to have been sometimes to give a lease for the full remainder of his own term, that is, to May 1, 1866, but much more frequently the lease he granted fell short of that date by one, two, or three years. The reason for this was that Astor hoped the lessees would find that the trouble and expense of moving their buildings outweighed the profit and that thus they would either move out and waive their rights in this regard, enabling the leaseholder to rent the buildings for the remainder of his lease at what would probably be a good rate, or else would purchase at a heavy price the privilege of themselves remaining for the rest of the term. Astor, of course, expected no personal profit from this, but his heirs would benefit.[34] Consequently, from 1820 to 1840, the term for which leases were granted descended from 42 years or thereabouts down through the 30's to 25, after which no more leases were granted, save at a yearly rental. The monetary consideration in these leases also changed during this period, but the prices paid per lot for leases did not decline in proportion to the lessened periods for which these conveyances were given. On the contrary, the tendency was in the other direction. Real-estate values were advancing so rapidly, under the influence of such factors as the Erie Canal, completed in 1825, the development of steam transportation, and the increase of immigration, that a lot which just after the War of 1812 could have been leased for a period of 50 years by the payment of only about $500 would a decade later bring $1,000 for a term of only 40 years. After that, the advance in lease values increased even more rapidly, till leases for 30 or 25 years in some cases were valued at $2,000 and $4,000 per lot or even more.

A typical example of Astor's methods of handling real estate through the long-term lease is found in his dealings with Daniel H. Turner, which in many respects resemble his relations with Christopher Keyes in land sales. From 1832 to 1835 and in 1840 and 1841, chiefly in the spring, Astor sold to Turner a number of leases to May 1, 1866, for about $56,000. The price of these leases ranged from $900 in 1832 to more than $4,000 in 1841. In 1841 Astor also sold him outright property valued at more than $15,000, but this is apart from our present consideration. Almost all these leased lots were at once mortgaged to Astor for a much larger amount than their original price, more than $94,000 in all. Lots for which Astor had charged Turner about $900 were mortgaged for $2,400, and others which had sold for $1,200 or $1,600 were pledged as security for $3,000. These mortgages were to cover the value of the lots and the amount of funds advanced to Turner by Astor for the purpose of making improvements on them. Turner was a builder, and it was evidently his intention to erect houses on these lots and let them out to tenants. He was more fortunate

or more efficient than Christopher Keyes, and of 32 mortgages
made to Astor he succeeded in discharging 19. On the rest,
however, mortgages given as security for more than $42,000,
he defaulted, and the mortgages were presumably foreclosed.
Mortgages to Astor amounting to more than $33,000 were
bought in by him for about $10,000 less. Probably the im-
provements made by Turner were more than sufficient to compensate Astor for the funds advanced. It has been said that
Astor's last public act was to foreclose a mortgage. This occurred in the month before his death, and concerned one of the
leases which Turner had bought from him, giving a mortgage
as security.[35] Turner's case is only one of the many examples
which might be given of Astor's policy in managing and developing his land through long-term leases, secured by mortgages.[36]

　In managing his Manhattan Island real estate up to 1820,
Astor had stressed outright sales and, next to this method, had
emphasized leases for a long term of years. Leases for a comparatively short period, with payments on a yearly basis, had
occupied quite a subordinate position. From 1820 to 1848,
however, there was a considerable change in these conditions.
Outright sales were still a more important factor in real-estate
management than long-term leases, and neither was to be a
negligible aspect of Astor's land policy, but both were to be
definitely overshadowed by short-term leases on yearly rentals.
It was probably in part the rapid growth of the city [37] which led
Astor to lease rather than sell. People who could not afford to
buy a lot and build were able to lease and build at a rent payable quarterly. Astor also saw that, in view of the rise in real-
estate values, it would be well to retain ownership of his lands
and take his income in rentals rather than in profits from sales.
This policy was especially convenient because the great need
for houses relieved Astor of the necessity of improving his lots
himself in order to attract tenants. We have already observed

the conditions on which such leases were granted in the period before 1820. These provisions did not materially change from 1820 to 1848. The greatest dissimilarities between the leases in the two periods concerned the length of the leases and the amount of the rentals. At first 21 years was the normal period, and this was true until about 1825, when the term began to grow shorter, to be reduced to 19 and 17 years, to 16, 14, 13, 12, 11, and even 10. But, when the 1840's began, this downward progress in the length of leases came to a stop. A lessee would not build a house unless he could be assured of occupancy for at least ten years. It was the great need for building lots that made it possible for Astor to secure lessees for so short a term. This fact accounts in part for the process of reducing the period of leases; but there was also another reason for it. As has been said before, most of these leases were to lots of land belonging to Trinity Church, to which Astor's right expired on May 1, 1866. It was frequently found necessary to insert a provision in the lease that it should be renewed under certain conditions. Therefore, when only 40 years or less of this lease remained, of course no second term of 21 years could be granted, and the period must needs be reduced. After 1840, however, leases for 20 and 22 years returned, but with no provisions for renewal. During this period there was also a considerable advance in rent per lot, as had been the case with the prices of long-term leases. At first the yearly rent per lot for a 21-year lease, always payable quarterly, had been from $50 to $87.50, always less than $100, and as the period of the leases grew shorter, the rents, being on an annual basis, did not proportionately decrease but rather tended to advance, as indeed might have been expected, till the 1830's saw leases for 11 years at $100 per lot and for 21 years sometimes at $220, $275, etc. In the 1840's the normal annual rental for a 22-year lease was $175, though sometimes it was much more, these rates applying only to lots not yet built upon; and in those cases in which the use of a house was conveyed by a lease the rental was from $600 to $1,400.

The other terms of these leases remained much the same throughout the two-score years and more that Astor was concerned with such matters. It was always provided, as before, that the lessee should pay all taxes, duties, and assessments, save the ground rent to Trinity Church, and it was nearly always specified as a condition that he should within one year erect a substantial dwelling-house at least two stories high and fronted with brick. It was sometimes stated that the lessee might remove all buildings from the premises a short time before or after the expiration of the lease, but usually it was provided that at the end of the term Astor was either to pay a fair price for the buildings which had been erected or renew the lease for another term, frequently for a period rather shorter than the first, at a rental to be agreed upon. It does not appear that the rent varied with these provisions. Detailed methods of determining the fair value of the buildings, and, more frequently, a reasonable yearly consideration for a new lease, were occasionally features of these leases. The value of the building was sometimes to be determined by two unprejudiced persons, one chosen by each of the two parties, with power to agree on an umpire. It was sometimes provided that the rent in the new lease should be fixed by "indifferent parties," but more frequently the rent was specified as 5 per cent annually on the fee-simple value of the lot. Occasionally 5 per cent was the minimum, and the exact rent was to be fixed by an impartial committee of sworn appraisers.[38] After 1827 it was frequently provided that no industry or business likely to be offensive to the neighbors should be carried on by any of Astor's lessees. It is not hard to trace the way in which the necessity for this prohibition came into Astor's mind. In 1806 he had rented a farm of 21 acres, which the lessee had promptly converted into a glue factory. This was all very well at the time, but as the city pushed north the need for the exclusion of such industries from Astor's residential districts became obvious.[39]

We have already mentioned the annual income which Astor received from rent in our consideration of the source of the funds he invested in land, but the importance of the short-term lease in the last 20 years or so of his life may best be comprehended by a repetition of some of the facts. In 1826 Astor received an income of more than $27,000 from 174 pieces of property. By 1831 the number of short-term leases had increased to 244 and the income to more than $46,000. About ten years later, in 1840, his income from rents had reached the amount of more than $128,000, received from 355 pieces of property. During the last year of his life 470 leases brought him an income of more than $200,000.[40] During the last decade of his life his income from rent alone was, then, more than $1,250,000.[41]

At the time of Astor's death his wealth was estimated at from $8,000,000[42] to $150,000,000.[43] The lower extreme was the conservative estimate of his executors, the higher the wild guess of the populace; but those who knew him best, and who had no reason either to exaggerate or minimize the amount of his property, put his wealth at from $20,000,000 to $30,000,000.[44] All agreed that the greatest source of this wealth was to be found in the increase in value of his lands on Manhattan Island. These land holdings, as we have seen, were originally based on the profits from the China trade, but, as land values began to increase, Astor was able to make even more extensive investments out of the income from the lands previously purchased.

The position which Astor holds in the eyes of posterity, as the great symbol of early American wealth, is the result of his foresight and courage in purchasing land on Manhattan Island. In the China trade, he was, perhaps, *primus inter pares*, yet there were some, like Thomas Handasyd Perkins and Stephen

Girard, who might with reason challenge his supremacy; as the founder of the American Fur Company, he is remembered perhaps even more because of Washington Irving's *Astoria* than for his own outstanding ability in the fur trade. His success in both forms of commerce was due partly to the opportunities of the times, and partly to his policy of profiting by the initiative of others, his ability to learn from his own mistakes, and his gift of seeing how one form of commerce could be linked up with another to the advantage of both. In other words, he had the same genius for buying and selling that some men have for diplomacy, for science, or for sculpture. But there was a single field in which he had no rivals. It was through his almost unique vision of the future of New York City that he found the one place where the capital secured to him by his commerce could be finally invested so that, with a minimum of personal exertion, it would make him the richest man in America, and one of the five or six richest men in the world.[45] Thus it was that his name, and not that of one of his commercial rivals, finally became a household synonym for the possession of property incalculably great. Astor was fully aware of the situation, and is said to have given evidence of his knowledge in his answer to someone who "just before he died . . . asked him if he had not too much real estate. He replied, 'Could I begin life again, knowing what I now know, and had money to invest, I would buy every foot of land on the Island of Manhattan.'"[46] How he must have regretted the money and time wasted on lands in Canada and the New York backcountry during that last decade of the eighteenth century when for the first time he had money to invest!

CONVEYANCES OF MANHATTAN REAL ESTATE TO ASTOR

In Fee Simple		On Long-Term Lease		Total
1789–91	$6,898.75	1789–91		$6,898.75
1800–09	425,784.19	1803–05	$119,628.83	545,413.02
1810–19	152,447.00	1810	18,000.00	170,447.00
1822	10.00	1824	751.52	761.52
1826–34	438,650.80	1827, 30–32	6,876.00	445,526.80
1835–47	764,551.70	1835, 38, 40, 42–48	68,127.98	832,679.68
	$1,788,342.44		$213,384.33	$2,001,726.77

CONVEYANCES OF MANHATTAN REAL ESTATE BY ASTOR [1]

In Fee Simple		On Long-Term Lease		Total
1803–04, 06–09	$75,313.66	1806, 09	$1,025.00	$76,338.66
1811–12, 18–19	106,899.18	1812, 14–15, 18–19	8,745.34	115,644.52
1820, 22–23, 26–34	271,985.24	1824–34	114,682.39	386,667.63
1835–39, 41, 44, 46	531,931.28	1835–36, 40–41, 47	76,200.00	608,131.28
	$986,129.36		$200,652.73	$1,186,782.09

[1] This table leaves short-term leases by Astor, for an annual rental, out of account.

NOTES

1. Many anecdotes are told concerning this simplicity of taste which caused Astor, when already a wealthy man for his day, to continue both to live and to transact business at 149 Broadway from 1794 to 1800, when he moved his store to 71 Liberty Street and began using his former place of business solely for residence purposes (*Longworth's American Almanac, New-York Register, and City Directory*, for 1800). "He used to relate," said Parton, "that he was worth a million before any one suspected it. A dandy bank clerk, one day, having expressed a doubt as to the sufficiency of his name to a piece of mercantile paper, Astor asked him how much he thought he was worth. The clerk mentioned a sum ludicrously less than the real amount. Astor then asked him how much he supposed this and that leading merchant, whom he named, was worth. The young man endowed them with generous sum-totals proportioned to their style of living. 'Well,' said Astor, 'I am worth more than any sum you have mentioned.' 'Then,' said the clerk, 'you are even a greater fool than I took you for, to work as hard as you do.' The old man would tell this story with great glee, for he always liked a joke." (Parton, James, *Life of John Jacob Astor* (1865), p. 50, quoting from Frothingham, W., "Astor and the Capitalists of New-York," *Continental Monthly*, vol. ii (August, 1862), pp. 208, 213–215.) Apparently, too, he was not over-fastidious as to the quality of the jest. It may be that incidents of this kind led Astor to decide that he had better assume a style of living somewhat more in accordance with his financial position. Accordingly, in 1802, he moved out of his old store building to a house at 214 Broadway and in the succeeding year took up his residence at 223 Broadway, where he remained for many years. (*Longworth's American Almanac, New-York Register, and City Directory*, for 1802 and 1803.) He had purchased this lot and dwelling-house for $27,500 from Rufus King, so it was probably a more fitting habitation for a great merchant than was his old office building farther down Broadway, even though Parton described it as a "house . . . such as a fifth-rate merchant would now consider much beneath his dignity" (ms. book, Hall of Records, N. Y., Liber Conveyances 67, p. 15; [Scoville, Joseph A.], *The Old Merchants of New York City*, 5 vols. (1889), vol. iii, p. 232; Parton, *op. cit.*, pp. 49–50).

2. There are a considerable number of legends, in both oral and printed forms, concerning Astor's interest in Manhattan Island real estate — as is the case, indeed, with every other phase of his business activities. One of these stories is preserved by a Montreal family and is to the effect that among Astor's earliest acquisitions of land in New York City were some not secured by purchase. According to this account the widow of a loy-

alist left New York at the time of its evacuation by the British and remained in Montreal for several years. On returning to New York she discovered that John Jacob Astor had thrown a fence about the family property and laid claim to it by right of possession. (Personal information.) Vincent Nolte, one of Astor's contemporaries, published another account dealing with the alleged foundations of Astor's real-estate holdings on Manhattan Island. "Another circumstance [in addition to the fur trade]," he wrote, "contributed to the increase of his means. At the peace concluded in 1783, between England and her revolted provinces, the thirteen United States, many acres of land in the State of New York, some even in the neighborhood of New York City, were voted by Congress to the German soldiers who had fought in the American army. The latter were chiefly Hessians and Darmstadters. Most of them died in the course of the year [!], without having succeeded in converting this property into money; but the relatives and heirs they left behind them in Germany did not forget these little inheritances. Upon the occasion of a visit made by Astor to Heidelberg, in later years, most of the parties last referred to, as inheriting the allotments of the deceased German soldiers, and residing in Heidelberg, united and made our friend their legally authorized attorney, in order to realize something if possible, from their hitherto useless acres. But the hoped for increase of the value of this property was, on the whole, rather slow in coming, and the heirs wanted money, money quick and ready MONEY — Astor having been applied to on this score, told them that, in order to get ready money, they must reckon up the real present value of the cash itself, and not any imagined value of the land, and that only through pretty considerable sacrifice could they get cash for the same. Thereupon the parties advised with each other, and finally Astor received peremptory orders to sell, without further delay. Unknown speculators were found; the proceeds were small, but the heirs got what they wanted — money. At the present day many of these pieces of ground are among the most valuable and most important in the city, and have gradually passed through Astor into other hands: the unknown speculators, however," Nolte concluded significantly, "have faded from the memory of everybody." (Nolte, Vincent, *Fifty Years in Both Hemispheres* (1854), pp. 140–143.) This is another of those traditional tales which may have some basis in fact but which cannot be accepted at more than a small percentage of their face value. One would be inclined to think, for example, that most of those "Hessians and Darmstadters" who took part in the Revolution would belong to the category of that old gentleman who used to proclaim at patriotic gatherings, "Yes, I fought hard for this country — but I didn't get it" — to the class, indeed, represented by John Jacob Astor's own brother Henry. It seems probable that the lands to which they would be entitled would be much more likely to be located in Lower Canada than on Manhattan Island. It is, of course, true that some Germans did fight in the American army during the Revolution. Astor, as we know, once unsuccessfully endeavored to recover from Congress compensation supposed to be due to a Philip Liebert, one of these German soldiers. However, it is extremely doubtful whether they would be allotted military grants on Manhattan Island. We know that Astor did visit Germany in 1795 and that he was interested in buying up military land-warrants. It is possible, then, that while in Germany he was engaged as an attorney to dispose of lands due to deceased German soldiers for military service and that he utilized this position to secure these lands for himself at a low rate, but the existence of a transaction as extensive as Nolte implies or of one involving Manhattan Island real estate seems as doubtful as most of the legends which have clustered about John Jacob Astor's head, not altogether with a halo-like effect.

3. Although Astor's lands in the New York backcountry were never particularly profitable financially, the question might be raised whether the deficit may not have been partly compensated for by the satisfaction of owning several thousand acres of the surface of this globe. Astor had all the peasant's craving for the possession of land. He is said to have been attracted to the United States largely because he had heard that there everyone could hold land, and it may be that this feeling impelled him at first to buy land in quantity without carefully considering whether a profit could be made out of it. Of course if Astor ever was unduly influenced by a desire to own land purely for the sake of ownership, he speedily recovered from that obsession.

4. *Minutes of the Common Council of the City of New York, 1784–1831*, vol. x, p. 203.

5. *Index of Conveyances Recorded in the Office of Register of the City and County of New York Grantees A* (1858).

6. It has been said that John Jacob Astor never mortgaged a lot ("John Jacob Astor," *Hunt's Merchant's Magazine*, vol. xi (August, 1844), pp. 153–159). This probably comes nearer to being literally true than any other general statement ever made about him. Although he is several times mentioned as a mortgagor in the Index to Mortgages, found at the Hall of Records in New York City, in every case but one this was due to the fact that mortgages *to* Astor were later transferred *by* him to others. The sole exception is in the case of a tract of land which he purchased on April 30, 1804, and for which he paid $22,500. (Ms. book, Hall of Records, N. Y., Liber Conveyances 67, p. 27.) Astor seems to have been a little short of cash at that time, having several rather extensive deals in prospect, and so paid only $7,500 in cash, securing the remaining $15,000 with a mortgage on the property, which was paid off by the specified date of May 1, 1807 (ms. book, Hall of Records, N. Y., Liber Mortgages 13, p. 447).

7. "On the fifteenth day of July next, I promise to receive from Mr. Griffith Evans or order two thousand five hundred dollars, six per cent stock of the United States, and pay him or order at the rate of twenty-five shillings, one penny and three farthings on the pound. Philadelphia, the 4th January, 1792. JOHN JACOB ASTOR" ("The Astors Organize a Trust," *The Detroit Journal*, February 12, 1898).

8. Ms. book, Bank of New York and Trust Company Museum, N. Y., Stock Book, p. 41, January 30, 1792.

9. Ms. book, Bank of Manhattan Company, N. Y., "Cash received of the Subscribers to the Manhattan Company at the time of Subscribing," no. 59; "Dividend Book of the Bank of the Manhattan Company" (facsimile reprinted from *The Bankers Magazine*, n. d.).

10. "John Jacob Astor," *Hunt's Merchant's Magazine*, vol. xi (August, 1844), pp. 153–159.

11. The popular tradition that Astor never sold a lot of land on Manhattan Island is, as we shall later develop more fully, even less well founded than most of the other stories clustering about his name.

12. Though leases to Astor were ordinarily made for a long term and on the payment of a lump sum, a few of a different character appeared in which he was annually to pay $75 to $100 per lot, as well as all taxes, duties, and assessments, usually for the term of 21 years. It was also in most cases provided that the lessee, Astor, *might* build a house of a specified character on the lot, which, at the end of the lease, should either be paid for by the lessor or the lease renewed. (Ms. book, Hall of Records, N. Y., Liber Conveyances 119, p. 64; 135, p. 66; 350, p. 618.)

13. Ms. book, Hall of Records, N. Y., Liber Conveyances 75, p. 386; 79, pp. 221, 224, 227, 229; 88, p. 517; 138, p. 272.

14. *Ibid.*, 138, p. 287.

15. *Ibid.*, 158, p. 316; 159, p. 119; *Minutes of the Common Council of the City of New York, 1784–1831*, vol. iv, pp. 145, 178, 415, 612, 613, 618, 629, 652, 726; vol. v, pp. 95, 144–146, 613; vol. vi, pp. 315, 338, 528, 635–636, 664; vol. vii, pp. 358, 570, 582, 583, 601–602, 666; vol. viii, pp. 237, 314, 470, 534, 551, 585, 596, 648; vol. ix, pp. 110, 245, 266, 300, 447, 453, 478, 507, 663; vol. x, pp. 223, 224, 369, 455, 630; vol. xi, pp. 138, 226, 390, 638; vol. xii, p. 114; vol. xiii, pp. 758–759; vol. xiv, pp. 490, 508, 527; vol. xv, pp. 385, 388, 603, 604, 630; vol. xvi, pp. 65, 168, 182, 234, 431, 779, 780; vol. xvii, pp. 3, 58, 95, 643, 683, 728; vol. xviii, pp. 445, 481, 482, 530, 577; vol. xix, pp. 8, 9, 35, 36, 301, 302, 451, 452.

16. Ms. book, Hall of Records, N. Y., Liber Conveyances 138, p. 521.

17. Smith, Matthew Hale, *Sunshine and Shadow in New York* (1868), pp. 121–122; Myers, Gustavus, *History of the Great American Fortunes*, 3 vols. (1907–10), vol. i, pp. 167–168.

18. Ms. book, Hall of Records, N. Y., Liber Conveyances 67, pp. 2, 11, 411; 138, p. 518; 222, p. 43. It has sometimes been said that Astor

bought Burr's land, amounting to 160 acres, for $160,000 (Parton, *op. cit.*, p. 61). As a matter of fact the amount Astor expended in purchases from Burr, including his satisfaction of the Manhattan Bank mortgage, came to only a little over $116,000. The tale has also been told that the adroit Burr personally drew up the deed whereby he conveyed his lease-hold to Astor and thus managed to slip in a clause stating that under "certain conditions" the land should be restored to him. Burr later de-manded the return of the land and Astor had to pay him $50,000 to adjust the matter. ([Armstrong, William], *The Aristocracy of New York* (1848), pp. 5–6.) A more circumstantial account had its origin in a letter from a resident of New York to a friend in Richmond, dated June 29, 1817, in which it was said that Burr had sold this property on condition that he should be allowed to redeem it at any time within twenty years by paying the amount of the purchase price (said to be $40,000) and the interest on it. Accordingly, a few days before, he had tendered the amount to Astor and demanded his property, which had now greatly increased in value. Astor refused to receive the money, Burr demanded $150,000 compensa-tion, and Astor finally had to compromise for $100,000 in order to re-tain the property. When this account was broadcast among the public, Astor denounced it as an unqualified falsehood, which it probably was. (*New York Evening Post*, July 14, 1817, p. 2, col. 1.) The origin of the story seems to have been that when Burr sold his leasehold to Astor it was agreed that if Burr should by October 24, 1808, pay Astor the sum of $13,500, and in the meantime annually pay him 7 per cent interest on that amount, Burr should receive back his mansion-house at Richmond Hill, and in the meantime, or until he should default on the interest pay-ments, might continue to occupy the premises (ms. book, Hall of Records, N. Y., Liber Mortgages 13, p. 176). There is no doubt that Burr failed to pay both principal and interest, for in February, 1812, Richmond Hill was offered to let (*New-York Gazette and General Advertiser*, February 10, 1812, p. 4, col. 5). It is quite possible that when Burr returned in 1812 from the exile necessitated by his western plans he made some attempt at that late date to redeem his estate, under the plea, perhaps, that the circumstances had been so unusual that he should in fairness be given another opportu-nity. Of course Astor would disregard any such plea, Burr might complain, and the stories at once would probably begin to grow. This tradition, however, is much more revelatory of the popular high opinion held of Burr's astuteness than of any similar estimate of Astor's ability.

19. Ms. book, Hall of Records, N. Y., Liber Conveyances 64, p. 440; 67, pp. 20, 23; 207, p. 247.

20. "An Act for the Relief of the Heirs of the late George Clinton, Esquire, deceased. Passed March 12, 1813," *Laws of the State of New-York, Passed at the Thirty-Sixth, Thirty-Seventh and Thirty-Eighth Sessions of the Legislature, Commencing November 1812, and Ending April 1815,*

vol. iii (1815), chap. lix, pp. 47–54; ms. book, Hall of Records, N. Y., Liber Conveyances 70, p. 318; 220, p. 344; 145, p. 293; 106, p. 615; 145, p. 284.

21. *Ibid.*, Liber Mortgages 34, p. 467 (see below, vol. ii, pp. 1141–1143); *ibid.*, Liber Conveyances 141, pp. 281, 292; 237, p. 188; 248, pp. 180, 184, 187.

22. About 1819 Astor estimated the value of all his lands as $1,519,600. However, $256,150 of this represented lands not on Manhattan Island (ms. book, Office of the Astor Estate, N. Y., Untitled land book, about 1819).

23. Parton, *op. cit.*, pp. 60–61. Gustavus Myers states dogmatically that this story "bears all the impress of being undoubtedly a fraud," adducing in support of his judgment the assertion that "Astor was remarkably secretive and dissembling, and never revealed his plans to anyone" (Myers, *op. cit.*, vol. i, pp. 150–151). It might be of some interest to inspect the records and determine — not whether Astor made the remark quoted, which, of course, it would be impossible to ascertain — but whether he ever made such an investment at about the time mentioned. It is unfortunate that in 1810 Astor sold no real estate whatsoever. However, the exact year is not important. Examining his conveyances for the entire period, we find that in 1807 and 1814 he did become involved in transactions in each of which real estate was sold by him for $8,000. Here again, however, is a discrepancy. One of these transactions involved four lots, one eight, and both were concerned with land formerly belonging to George Clinton, outside the city. Perhaps, then, $8,000 was merely the approximate amount of the consideration in this conveyance. This assumption gives us a considerably wider scope for our investigation. It is possible, then, that this story has to do with the sale on April 30, 1814, of a dwelling-house and lot on Pearl Street to John Greenfield for $7,750, which he had purchased in 1802 from the master in chancery for $5,100. (Ms. book, Hall of Records, N. Y., Liber Conveyances 62, p. 251; 105, p. 422.) Pearl Street is in the section of New York below Wall Street and might be spoken of as being "in the vicinity of Wall street." It is evident, however, that it is impossible to confirm this story as it stands, but that, like many other Astor traditions, it probably does have some foundation in truth.

24. Ms. book, Hall of Records, N. Y., Liber Conveyances 217, p. 265; 49, p. 257; 174, p. 163; 223, p. 482; 63, p. 462; 103, p. 157; 64, p. 440; 66, pp. 355, 520; 209, p. 364; 194, p. 68; 155, p. 25; 81, p. 452; 64, p. 420; 70, p. 68; 127, p. 296; 70, pp. 73; 318; 106, p. 590; 84, p. 375; 79, p. 109; 128, p. 263; 105, p. 61; *ibid.*, Liber Mortgages 18, p. 148.

25. *New-York Gazette and General Advertiser*, February 24, 1802, p. 3, col. 1; January 30, 1804, p. 3, col. 4; February 2, 1804, p. 3, col. 4;

August 22, 1804, p. 3, col. 2; June 4, 1805, p. 4, col. 5; February 27, 1806, p. 4, col. 1.

26. Ms. book, Hall of Records, N. Y., Liber Conveyances 239, p. 151; 82, p. 325; 101, p. 176; 107, p. 386; 194, p. 287; 225, p. 6; 276, p. 341; *ibid.*, Liber Mortgages 20, p. 112; 29, p. 111; 47, p. 191.

27. *Ibid.*, Liber Conveyances 134, p. 498; 239, p. 416; 117, p. 206; 135, p. 66; 127, p. 248; 119, p. 64; 167, p. 145; 228, p. 204.

28. *Ibid.*, 78, p. 352; *New-York Gazette and General Advertiser*, December 1, 1806, p. 4, col. 1.

29. Ms. book, Office of the Astor Estate, N. Y., Lessees and Tenants.

30. *Ibid.*, Rent Roll 1840-48.

31. Ms. book, Hall of Records, N. Y., Liber Conveyances 424, p. 202, March 14, 1842.

32. Hendricks, Burton Jesse, "The Astor Fortune," *McClure's Magazine*, vol. xxiv (April, 1905), pp. 563-578.

33. Ms. book, Hall of Records, N. Y., Liber Conveyances 381, pp. 441, 444, 447; 382, p. 483; 384, pp. 83, 86, 92, 96, 99, 102, 105, 108, 111, 114; *ibid.*, Liber Mortgages 211, pp. 313, 316, 319, 322, 325, 328; 218, pp. 423-452; 222, pp. 62-77; 243, pp. 125-128.

34. Concerning these leases it has been said: "Persons who took the Astor leases supposed that they took them for the full term of the Trinity lease. Mr. Astor was too far-sighted and too shrewd for that. Every lease he gave expired in 1864, leaving him the reversion for three years, putting him in possession of all the buildings and improvements made on the lots, and giving him the right of renewal. When the fact was discovered, the lessees tried to buy from Mr. Astor the three years' reversion. He was, [*sic*] offered as high as a thousand dollars a lot. He refused all offers except in one case. . . . A Mr. Pell, a coach-builder, had his establishment on the corner of Wall Street and Broad. He was a great friend of Mr. Astor. When Mr. Pell made a fashionable coach, Mr. Astor generally took a ride in it to try the springs. This was in the humble days of Mr. Astor's mercantile career. As Mr. Astor increased in wealth their paths diverged, and after a while they saw nothing of each other. The son of Mr. Pell took one of the Astor leases, and when he found that it expired in '64, he went down to the office to see if he could not purchase Mr. Astor's three years' interest in the lease. William gave him a gruff and decided refusal. 'We don't want to sell,' was his laconic answer. As the young man was going out, some one stepped up to him, and quietly whispered, 'See the old man. Come to-morrow at precisely eleven, and you will find him in.' The young man said nothing, but went away, and returned the next day a little before the hour. It was very cold, and he took a seat by the fire in the outer office. Promptly on the time, Mr. Astor came in. He walked very slowly, doubled up, leaning on the head of his

cane in a stooping posture, taking short steps, so that he rather scuffed along than walked. He sat down and warmed himself, then turning to young Pell, he said, in a pleasant tone, 'Young man, what can I do for you?' The request was made. He immediately and decidedly replied, 'We don't wish to sell those reversions, young man. But what might your name be?' The young man replied, 'It is Pell.' 'Pell — Pell' — said Mr. Astor, 'I used to know a man by that name once; he was a dear friend of mine, but I haven't seen him for a great many years.' 'Yes,' said Mr. Pell, 'that man was my father.' 'Your father? Why, he used to give me rides in his coaches. How I should like to see him!' For a moment Mr. Astor was young again. 'You shall have the lease, young man. Go home, have the papers drawn, come here at eleven o'clock precisely, on Thursday, and I'll sign them. But don't put in any consideration.' The young man was prompt, so was Mr. Astor. 'Have you got the papers?' said the merchant. 'Did you put in the consideration? Well, let it be one hundred dollars. Have you got the money about you? Well, no matter, Bruce will keep the lease till you come and pay. I've given you two thousand dollars, young man. Don't you buy any more, for I shan't do it again. You tell your father that I remember him, and that I have given you two thousand dollars.'" (Smith, *op. cit.*, pp. 122, 124–125.)

There are several obvious errors in the above. The Mortier lease was to run not to 1867 but only to 1866, and a considerable number of leases were given for the full term, though more did fall short of that by from one to three years. It is incorrect to state that "every lease he gave expired in 1864," since most probably ended in 1865. It is also very doubtful that the lessees did not know how long their own leases were to run. In the main, however, the facts as to Astor's granting a renewal of the lease to Pell, for the full remainder of the Trinity lease, are probably as given in this story. We know positively that one Emmet T. Pell, holder of one of the Astor leases for thirty-nine years from May 1, 1826, did on February 27, 1840, come into the possession of the year's reversion to that property. The price he paid, however, was not $100 but $200. Moreover, his case was not unique as the above story would indicate, for various other lessees purchased a year's reversion for exactly the same price. (Ms. book, Hall of Records, N. Y., Liber Conveyances 403, p. 360; 496, p. 48.) We are not told whether the fathers of these lessees were also hospitable coach-makers, or by what act of paternal generosity they became entitled to Astor's special consideration. It is certain, however, that not many of these reversions were sold, and it is therefore possible that those which were disposed of constituted marks of rather special favor to the purchasers. This story may, then, be taken as evidence that there were contemporaries of Astor who had a more favorable opinion of his generosity than had those who purveyed the stories of the chronometer and the pipes of Madeira wine. Certainly it is a much better authenti-

cated tale than most of those with which we have previously been forced
to deal, and is not to be discarded merely because it presents Astor in a
somewhat more appealing light than that in which he usually seems to
have been portrayed.

35. Ms. book, Hall of Records, N. Y., Liber Conveyances 284, pp. 612,
615, 618, 620; 288, p. 478; 295, pp. 331, 334, 337, 340, 343, 346, 349, 352;
313, p. 328, 330, 333, 335, 337; 354, pp. 344, 347, 350, 353, 356; 407,
pp. 125, 127, 129, 131, 133; 406, pp. 270, 272; 412, pp. 504, 505, 507, 509,
510; 430, p. 1; 439, p. 596, 597, 599; 454, pp. 34, 35; 464, pp. 158, 631;
469, pp. 61, 316; 495, p. 400; 502, p. 242; *ibid.*, Liber Mortgages 153,
pp. 308, 311, 313, 316; 156, p. 87; 161, pp. 139, 142, 144, 146, 149, 151,
153, 156; 170, pp. 516, 519, 521, 523, 525; 202, pp. 34, 36, 39, 42, 44;
236, p. 636; 240, pp. 184, 186, 188, 191, 193; 241, p. 226; 245, pp. 271, 273,
275, 277, 279; 248, p. 591.

36. Astor insisted that all property pledged to him should be adequately insured against fire by the mortgagors. Many letters are to be
found in his letter books warning the lessees that their policies are about
to expire or informing them what insurance companies are on Astor's approved list. (Ms. books, Baker Library, Astor Papers, Letter Book ii,
1831–38, Letter Book iii, 1845–48, *passim.*)

37. The following table, from E. Porter Belden's *New-York, Past, Present, and Future* (1850), will give an idea of the growth in the population
of New York City during the period of Astor's residence:

1786	23,614	1820	123,706
1790	33,131	1825	166,086
1800	60,489	1830	202,589
1805	75,570	1835	270,089
1810	96,373	1840	312,852
1816	100,619	1845	371,223

38. A typical request to serve on a committee to value property for
this purpose is contained in a letter of December 30, 1835, from John
Jacob Astor to a Mr. Samuel Thompson (ms. book, Baker Library,
Astor Papers, Letter Book ii, 1831–38, p. 359).

39. Ms. book, Hall of Records, N. Y., Liber Conveyances 422, p. 449;
245, p. 358; 458, p. 465; 256, p. 447; 78, p. 352.

40. Ms. book, Office of the Astor Estate, N. Y., Lessees and Tenants;
Rent Roll, 1840–48. After Astor had withdrawn from the American Fur
Company in 1834, his only important business interest was his Manhattan
Island real estate, and all his attention was concentrated upon its care.
"The roll-book of his possessions," it has been said, "was his Bible."
This may have caused his individual holdings to assume an altogether
undue importance in his mind, which might not have been the case had

his interests been somewhat more diversified, and helps to account for such stories as the following. "When all else had died within him," wrote a contemporary, "when he was at last nourished like an infant at a woman's breast, and when being no longer able to ride in a carriage, he was daily tossed in blanket for exercise, he still retained a strong interest in the care and increase of his property. His agent called daily upon him to render a report of moneys received. One morning this gentleman chanced to enter his room while he was enjoying his blanket exercise. The old man cried out from the middle of his blanket:

"'Has Mrs. —— paid that rent yet?'

"'No,' replied the agent.

"'Well, but she must pay it,' said the poor old man.

"'Mr. Astor,' rejoined the agent, 'she can't pay it now; she has had misfortunes, and we must give her time.'

"'No, no,' said Astor: 'I tell you she can pay it, and she will pay it. You don't go the right way to work with her.'

"The agent took leave, and mentioned the anxiety of the old gentleman with regard to this unpaid rent to his son, who counted out the requisite sum, and told the agent to give it to the old man as if he had received it from the tenant.

"'There!' exclaimed Mr. Astor when he received the money, 'I told you she would pay it if you went the right way to work with her.'" (Parton, *op. cit.*, pp. 75, 80–81.)

Of course it must be remembered that this incident — if it actually occurred — took place at a time when Astor was both physically and mentally as far removed as imaginable from the young man in his 'twenties who had stridden along the Indian trails of late eighteenth-century New York, barely conscious of his heavy pack of furs and trade-goods. This story, if accurate, is, then, only of the same value in depicting Astor's usual character as a caricature is in representing its subject's physical appearance.

41. A "moderate estimate" of Astor's income, made in the last years of his life, put it at $2,000,000 a year (Armstrong, *op. cit.*, p. 7; [Beach, Moses Yale], *The Wealth and Biography of the Wealthy Citizens of the City of New York* (1846), p. 3).

42. Bristed, Charles Astor, *A Letter to the Hon. Horace Mann* (1850), p. 16. In October, 1846, Astor put a value of $5,184,343 upon his houses and lands, and in March, 1847, he valued his real-estate holdings at $5,188,943; at the same time William B. Astor estimated that they were worth $5,178,443 (ms. book, Office of the Astor Estate, N. Y., Valuation of Houses & Lands, Oct. 1, 1846; J. J. Astor's valuation of Real Estate. This valuation made March 1847). The significance of these estimates is decreased by the fact that several years before, in May, 1839, Astor estimated his real estate as worth $5,445,525 (ms. book, Office of the Astor

Estate, N. Y., Value of Real Estate in the City of New York May 1839 & Manhattan Island & elsewhere; Untitled land book; A Schedule of Real Estate made at H. Gate; Untitled land book, about 1839).

43. Smith, *op. cit.*, p. 115; Armstrong, *op. cit.*, p. 7.

44. *Hone, Philip, The Diary of, 1828–1851*, Allan Nevins, ed., 2 vols. (1927), vol. ii, p. 847; Beach, *loc. cit.*

45. Armstrong, *op. cit.*, p. 7.

46. Smith, *op. cit.*, p. 117.

CHAPTER XXI

MISCELLANEOUS BUSINESS INTERESTS: INSURANCE
AND BANKING

As an owner of ships and of buildings in New York City, John Jacob Astor naturally had to confront the problem of insurance. Unlike his youthful contemporary, Cornelius Vanderbilt, he made no boast that he could insure his own property, since, as Vanderbilt argued, if the companies could make money out of insurance, he could do so himself. Being thus brought into contact with insurance companies in order to secure protection for his property, he soon came to consider insurance as an opening for investment. His purchase in 1792 of a share in the Tontine Coffee House for his daughter Magdalen might perhaps be regarded as his earliest manifestation of interest in insurance.[1] However, the first evidence that Astor was showing attention of any significance to the possibilities of insurance appeared about 1816. From at least as early as that year until as late as 1834, Astor was occasionally a director of the Globe Insurance Company,[2] which had been incorporated in 1814.[3] Astor was elected on December 8, 1817, to a directorship in the New York Firemen's Insurance Company,[4] which had been incorporated in 1810;[5] in 1819 he was re-elected.[6] In December, 1821, Astor was elected a director in the Hope Insurance Company,[7] which had been incorporated in the same year.[8] The great fire of 1835 was especially hard on the insurance companies. William B. Astor wrote: "All here will eventually either directly or indirectly be losers by the fire. My father and myself lose heavily by the distruction of the Insᶜᵉ. Cos." Shares in the Globe Insurance Company, in which Astor had in March of the previous year purchased $5,000 worth of stock at 14 per cent premium,[9] were entirely lost.[10]

In the next year, 1836, Astor seems to have dabbled a little in the stocks of other insurance companies. Gallatin Brothers on February 3 were "authorized to make the transfer of the Eagle Fire Stock which no doubt stands in your name,"[11] and in April were ordered to buy 50 shares of American Marine Insurance Company stock at 144 per cent to 146 per cent, and 100 of Ohio Life Insurance and Trust Company at 123 per cent.[12] An order of March 3 to John Warren to buy 100 shares of Ohio Life Insurance and Trust Company stock at $121\frac{1}{2}$ per cent and sell again at $124\frac{1}{2}$ per cent at 60 or 90 days with interest at 6 per cent was cancelled two days later.[13]

In the meantime Astor had become considerably interested in the New York Life Insurance and Trust Company (organized in 1830[14]), in which he was a director at least by 1833, and in which office he continued until as late as 1839.[15] It may have been stock in this company of which he offered in May, 1832, to accept from $4,000 to $5,000 worth if his correspondent, N. Devereux, of Utica, thought well of it.[16] At any rate late in January, 1834, Astor's son, acting in his father's name, ordered Gallatin Brothers to purchase $5,000 of this stock at about 133 per cent.[17] Astor had probably bought largely of this company's stock. Some of the certificates he had sent to his correspondents in England, Gillespies, Moffatt, Finlay & Co. and Thomas Wilson & Co., for sale at his orders. Early in April, 1836, he informed the former company that "at present it is no time to sell them,"[18] and late in October he ordered the latter firm to return to him the certificates of that insurance company which they held.[19] At the same time he was making purchases of stock in the New York Life Insurance and Trust Company, in April, 1836, buying 50 shares from a professor at Columbia for $9,500.[20] The Panic of 1837 resulted in a great decline in the value of certain stocks, among them those of the life-insurance companies, though State stocks stood up pretty well. Astor accordingly instructed Gillespies, Moffatt & Co. to sell his New York Life Insurance and Trust Company certificates at from $86 to $87.50. Disregarding his instructions, the firm sold certain State stocks at a price below what Astor thought he should receive, and as a result, late in December, 1837, he withdrew all his stock from their hands.[21]

We hear little more of Astor's interest in insurance companies. In 1838 he was one of the trustees of the New York Life Insurance and Trust Company,[22] and in 1845 he must still have been a considerable holder of stock, especially in fire-insurance companies. In the summer of 1845 another "calamitous fire . . . affected some of the insurance Companies here so as to render their policies of little value." The Bowery, North River, and Greenwich Insurance Companies were the least severely affected.[23] William B. Astor commented upon the general effects of this conflagration and particularly upon the way in which it had affected his father. He wrote: "The fire has created much suffering here. Four or five of our insurance Companies have lost the whole of their capitals, and the rest, with the exception of two or three, have lost heavily, probably nearly half their capitals. . . . My father loses a considerable amount of fire stock."[24]

Although Astor was at various times from 1816 to 1838 sufficiently interested in four insurance companies to be elected a director, and though he held stock in other companies, it is evident that the attention he paid to this field of investment was not great and can hardly be compared even to such of his minor concerns as railroads and hotels, in which, as we shall see, he did take a more direct personal interest.

John Jacob Astor, unlike Stephen Girard, that other immigrant, China merchant, and millionaire with whom he has most frequently been compared, could not be classed as a

banker, but like most moneyed men of his time he was necessarily somewhat interested in banking. His first interest of
which we know appeared on December 24, 1791, and on January 12, 1792, when he sold 5 shares of stock of the Bank of New
York, valued at $2,500, 3 to Peter and Philip Curtinius and
2 to Leonard Bleecker, apparently covering the sale late in the
latter month by purchasing 5 shares from Brockholst Livingston.[25] On the last of March, 1793, Astor, who was considering
the purchase of a tract of land in the backcountry of New York,
remarked: "I Dont think I Can buy as I have nothing to get
Cash with un Less it be Bank Shares which Cost me 40 p Ct
& now Sell but at 15 p Cent advance which you knaw would be
making a very grate sacrificig. . . . Should Stocks Riss which
I Dont think they will Soon I woud in that Case be willing to
buy."[26] We do not know what bank shares these were to which
Astor referred, but a year later he bought the land in question.
Somewhat more important than Astor's known interest in the
Bank of New York was his investment in 1799 in 200 shares of
stock of the Bank of the Manhattan Company.[27] On July 16,
1800, Astor received $120 in dividends on 96 shares of stock in
the Bank of the Manhattan Company.[28] In 1805 his interest in
this bank was so great that he "proposed verbally to cede
eight lots of ground near Greenwich: being part of his purchase from Gov. Clinton" to use for a country office.[29] In 1806
Astor was invited to become a shareholder in the Detroit Bank.
He "declined, but he expresses much friendship," wrote Nathaniel Parker to Augustus B. Woodward, "for your attention
&c."[30] By this time Astor was evidently looked upon as a
promising prospective shareholder in any new bank, especially
in a city where his fur trade made him as well known as he was
in Detroit.

By 1811 Astor had become sufficiently interested in banking
to take a positive stand on the renewal of the charter of the
first Bank of the United States. It may seem strange to note

that he was strongly opposed to this institution, which most authorities, and especially Gallatin, the secretary of the Treasury and one of Astor's friends, regarded as indispensable to the financial well-being of the country.

On January 5, 1811, when the Bank's charter was on the point of expiration, Gallatin wrote Madison a letter concerning Astor's attitude.

> Mr. Astor sent me a verbal message that in case of nonrenewal of the charter of the Bank U. S., all his funds & those of his friends to the amount of two millions of dollars would be at the command of Government, either in importing specie, circulating any Govern^t. paper, or in any other way best calculated to prevent any injury arising from the dissolution of the Bank. Mr Bentson told me that in this instance profit was not his object, and that he would go great lengths, partly from pride & partly from wish to see the Bank down. As there will be no time to be lost, I think that I had better open a correspondence with him on the subject.[31]

Various reasons have been advanced to account for Astor's attitude toward the Bank. An explanation which is by no means complimentary to his public spirit is that he realized that the elimination of the Bank would put the wealthy men of the country, of whom he was not the least, in a strategic position. If this was an element in determining his attitude, his foresight was justified, for, upon the outbreak of war, Astor, with Girard and Parish, was able, as we have already seen, to loan large sums of money to the government upon terms exceedingly favorable to themselves.

An incident which took place late in 1810, however, is sufficient to explain Astor's hostility to the first Bank of the United States without taking into consideration any possible subsidiary factor. In October, 1810, Astor "purchased 50,000 l. sterling, in Bills of Exchange," and in November drew from the Branch Bank at New York " 200000 Dollars in specie, to be conveyed to Canada." This transaction was probably a step in the fulfillment of some contract which Astor had with the commander of the Forces in Canada for supplying "a large provision in specie to meet its [the army's] expences." We know that in the following year a tender of this kind on his part was accepted.[32] The directors of the Branch Bank, angered by this large withdrawal of specie, retaliated by closing his account at the Bank and informing him that the loans which he had at the Bank must be paid as they came due. The directors declined to give Astor any explanation for this action or to enter into any correspondence on the subject. Astor consequently published in a leading New York newspaper the several letters which had passed between himself and the cashier;[33] it would seem from these that Astor had rather the better of the argument, but, however this may be, it is not surprising that Astor, who was now a man of some standing in the community, should be anxious "to see the Bank down" which had insulted and inconvenienced him in such a manner.

Since Astor's enmity to the first national bank was a personal matter and not inspired by any constitutional or financial opposition to such an institution, he might be expected soon to advocate the establishment of a United States bank which should be more to his liking. The decline in the value of the United States stock, of which he was a large holder, convinced him of the immediate necessity for a national bank to prevent further loss to him in disposing of such of his shares as he was unable to retain permanently. The year 1814 began inauspiciously for proponents of a national bank. A petition from 150 citizens of New York presented to the House of Representatives on January 4, 1814, praying for the incorporation of a national bank with a capital of $30,000,000, half of which sum they offered in return to loan to the government, was rejected by the Committee of Ways and Means on the grounds that it was unconstitutional, and a substitute plan, proposed by Calhoun, appealed to none but the strict constructionists.[34]

Although Astor does not appear to have been active in these early attempts, in March, 1814, he was communicating with his large fellow stockholders, David Parish and Stephen Girard, in regard to the establishment of a bank and was described as "Still Sanguine" that his purpose would be accomplished;[35] perhaps having been warned of the intention of the adminis- tration spokesman to revive the matter. This attempt, how- ever, proved abortive.[36] We hear nothing further about the project until the middle of August, at which time Astor began to take a very active part in the movement for a national bank. At this time he wrote to Girard:

There is no doubt but congress will in the early part of the session tak up the subject of a national Bank which now apears to have becom indis- pensible the probability is that such Bank will be established its capital will probably be 30 Millions of Dollars or upwards – the notes are not to be made a tender except in payments to the government but the Bank must be protected from being obliged to pay Specie for their notes at Least till one or 2 years after the war —

It is contemplated to form an Association and to mak application to Congress for the Charter I mantian this to you in confidence and I wish to know whether you will Lick to becom Interested in such an Institu- tion.[37]

A day or two earlier Astor had mentioned both to Parish and to Dennis A. Smith of Baltimore that "Barker [the man with whom Astor had come into conflict over the war loans] is al- ready running about the streets with petition for signatures to Congress for a national Bank. I think our most respectable people will have nothing to do with it with him [*sic*]." On August 19 Astor again wrote Smith on the need for "a national Bank, *which we* must have or we are all gone." About a week later he informed him, "It is proposed to have a meeting of wealthy people at my house tomorrow to consider on the pro- priety of applying to Congress for a National Bank— When a plan is formed I will send it to you for approbation . . . no doubt the moment the National Bank gets in operation, prop- erty must come to its proper & fair value — Our Idea is to pledge real property for amount of the Bank stock." On the first of September he explained the plan somewhat more in detail. The "committee of whom I am," he wrote, "have yesterday agreed to a plan or outlines of a bank, it will be reported to morrow afternoon & if agreed on, I'll the next day send a copy to you. our Capital is to be in bonds & mortgages on good real security, it will answer the purpose of the country if congress will only pass it, the gentlemen here," he concluded optimistically, "are of opinion that they will pass it. . . ."[38] The next day he conveyed to James Monroe the encouraging information that "we are bussey in forming a plan for a national Bank which if adopted must Relive the Country in its Pecuneary matters —"[39] A letter from Rufus King, received about this time in reply to one from Astor relative to the proposed bank, was critical of the plan.[40]

The British capture, temporary occupation, and partial destruction of Washington late in September had precipitated the suspension of specie payments, outside of New England, and this aroused Congress, which met in special session on September 19, to the seriousness of the financial situation. Consequently, one of its first acts was to take up the discussion of a bank bill and refer to the Committee of Ways and Means a petition from New York praying for the establishment of a bank.[41] This petition was doubtless the one in which Astor had been concerned.

Shortly after Congress assembled, Astor wrote to Smith asking:

what is about the Bank, we must have one or we will never get on . . . my own opinion is that if congress will pass a bill for a Bank, the capital to consist of 1/4 in specie & 3/4 in 6 pCt Stock on liberal terms, the people from the east will in some shape and by degrees come in, the Specie cannot be paid at once, it cannot nor will there be need for it, by time & proper management The Land scheme I think will be attended with many difficulties, tho' I believe it's the best to inspire confidence, but there are so many objections of one kind & another that I believe that a Bank upon the plan of the last national Bank will pass the most readily, & if it can be made to answer Government it will do us.

By the "Land scheme" Astor probably meant the suggestion to "pledge real property for amount of the Bank stock." It is noteworthy that Astor, who had been so anxious to see the first Bank of the United States down in 1811, was now ready to welcome another bank on the same plan, which shows that his opposition to the earlier institution had been personal rather than political or financial.

Late in September Astor proposed another supplementary course of action in a letter to Parish: "with regard to the plan of a national Bank it's thought none can be agreed on here so as to meet peoples ideas at Washington & other parts, it's therefore calculated that we get here a petition signed by the most respectable people & then send one or two persons to Washington to join some of your city & Baltimore to do this we shall want your aid. . . ." Early in October Astor was still expounding his ideas of what the proposed bank should be like and reluctantly considering going in person to Washington to exert his influence toward the passage of a bank bill. He wrote to Smith on October 3:

Now about the Bank — I am pretty sure that the plan proposed by you is too much in favor of the Stockholders & that Congress can never pass it, and people this Way will have no confidence in it — Make a Bank to consist 3/4 6 pCt Stock & 1/4 Specie — of the last make the first payment only 5 pCt & let the Directors call in by instalments the remaining 25 pCt at such time and period as they deem prudent — You see they need not call for it till after the War is over, this will be the more readily agreed to as being like the old National Bank, and it will answer us & the Government all the purpose — If your friends will support such a Bank with branches I will come to Washington tho I cannot before 10 days — It will be very inconvenient for me to go but go I will if you say so — All our people here will support such a plan as will also Mr. King —

During October Astor kept in close touch with Smith. A meeting to discuss the bank was in prospect. On October 4 he wrote: "Mr. Parish is expected here tomorrow. Mr. Francis is here & some others from Philadelphia, when we shall have some further talk about the Bank. . . . I wish . . . that I might have time to write to some people there [at Washington] & that you would do the same, to ascertain as nearly as possible the prospect of success, no one here believes that a Bank as you last proposed can be obtained, but if 1/4 is cash which need not to be paid now then. I think some probability of its passing and people will subscribe."[42]

The unhappy financial situation brought one piece of good out of evil. It resulted in the resignation of George W. Campbell, the secretary of the Treasury, who was succeeded on October 5 by Alexander J. Dallas, a man approved by such capitalists as Astor,[43] who regarded him as favorable to a national bank. In this they were correct, for on October 17 he declared such an institution to be "the only efficient remedy for the disordered condition of our circulating medium." Astor consequently communicated his ideas on the subject to the new secretary, and received a request to come to Washington for a consultation.[44] On October 17 Dallas had communicated a plan for a national bank with a capital of $50,000,000, of which only $6,000,000 should be in specie and the rest in government stock and treasury notes, in which the government should hold stock, and which should lend $30,000,000 to the government.[45] Astor's comment on this plan was that "the payments . . . specially the Specie part is too prompt, would it not be better to give some discretion to the directors & will it not give too much advantage to those who are provided with Specie. If you think it will be of any good," he wrote to Smith, "I'll come to Washington & make any arrangements so as to leave here the day after I receive your letter." He had previously mentioned to Parish that it had been recommended "that some respectable say two Merchants of this & some from other Cities should come down — It is very inconvenient for me to go but I suppose I must do it."[46] It seems never to have occurred to him that some other New York merchant could have taken his place.

On October 24 the Committee of Ways and Means "reported a resolution declaring that it was 'expedient to establish a National Bank, with branches in the several States.' The House agreed to the resolution immediately and without debate."[47] Astor realized that the time was now ripe for him to go to Washington and see that the bank which it now seemed would inevitably be established was of a nature to meet with his approval. Accordingly, on November 3, Astor left for Baltimore and Washington, expecting to join Parish and Smith. On the 8th he wrote Girard from Baltimore, saying that "the federal gentlemen object to Mr. Dallas Bank Plan because he makes it a point that the President shall appoint 5 Directors I certainly will advise him to give up this point & I think it would do much good if you would writ to him your opinion to the Same effect." On the 10th Astor arrived in Washington, two days after a "bill drawn up on lines marked out by Secretary Dallas" had been reported by the Committee of Ways and Means. As Parish commented in a letter to Girard, "Mr. D.A Smith & Mr. Astor are here to attend to the Subject." Parish confirmed Astor's opinion that the bill could not pass, unless amendments should first be made providing "that the Government must give up the right of naming any directors & that the interest of the United States in the Bank is to be reduced to Ten Millions [as opposed to the original proposal of $20,000,000]. Without these alterations," he wrote, "not a federal vote will be obtained in favor of the Bank & without Some aid from that Side of the house the bill will not pass as many Democrats are opposed to it on constitutional grounds." Parish was of the "opinion that a Bill will pass, but with great difficulty," but according to Joseph Curwen, Girard's agent at Baltimore, the conduct of Smith was indicative of "an apprehension that the proposed Bank would not be carried into effect."[48]

Astor seems to have become discouraged at the opposition which the bill encountered even from those who favored a national bank, and especially by the action of Calhoun on November 16 in introducing an opposition bill, which had, immediately on its presentation, been substituted for that of Dallas.[49] At any rate he left Washington, and arrived at New York on the 18th, somewhat to Dallas's displeasure. In a letter to Smith, however, Astor stated: "I am now more than ever Satisfied, that I could not have done any good, it appears to me, that it will take some weeks before Congress get to pass the Bank bill & if they go on Mr. Calhoune's plan they must fail & ruin the country & themselves."[50] In support of this conviction he wrote on November 23 to a certain Theron Rudd that "stocks are fallen and public credit is going down fast in consequence of M[r]. Calhoune's amendment nor do I believe that a Bank can be establish'd on the plan as now proposed and I would hope that the old plan would be again revised."[51] On the same day he wrote Jonathan Fisk, member of Congress from New York, who had been on the bank committee in April, that "in a word the Amendment of M[r] Colhoun is to defeat the idea of a national Bank. It can never be carried into effect & what is worse will bring the nation to a complete bankruptcy in less than 6 months since the motion of M[r] Calhoun," he repeated, "stocks have fallen 3 pCt and to day there is no sale. I am satisfied if M[r]. C could know the dreadful effect of his plan, he would, if he is a friend to his country, regret the circumstance . . . all parties here are out of temper with govern[t]. and with Congress. . . . The best thing you can do now is to make delay."[52]

Astor on the same day put his expressed belief in Calhoun's open-mindedness to a practical test by writing to him a discreetly-worded letter casting some doubt upon the wisdom of certain features of his bank plan. He especially pointed out that the "public opinion here is against it and if the government should have no connectian with the Bank and the Notes are not to be received in all payments of taxes and pay[t]. to gover^t. generally I should doubt much whether the Bank will have *any Subscribers* for I do not see whence the advantages of this Bank are over that of any other whose stock is plenty in this city at 20 PC^t. below par and the U.S. Stocks at 24–25 Pc^t. under par and declining."[53]

For the next two months and more, Astor seems to have watched the fortunes of the bank bill without taking any very active part in the campaign. Indeed, the proceedings in regard to the bank bill were in so chaotic a state that there was little he could do. Calhoun's bill, after undergoing various vicissitudes, was voted on and defeated, Dallas being opposed to its passage.[54] Astor watched with interest and not too much optimism the career of another bill,[55] which had been reported in the Senate on December 2, "substantially incorporating the provisions desired by Dallas," and which in one week's time had passed the Senate and gone to the House. The debate in the latter body began on the 23rd. It seemed that the bill would pass, though by a very close vote. However, a Calhoun-Federalist coalition resulted in a tie and the casting vote of the speaker defeated the bill.[56] Astor's comment in a letter to Parish was, "I supposed with you that the Bank bill had passed, but you see that all parties are not yet satisfied & that there is no faith to be put in their doings." However, the narrow margin by which the bill had been lost led him to conclude, "I suppose however that the bill will at last pass."[57]

Some support was given to his optimism by a motion to reconsider the bill, which passed on January 3, 1815. It was recommitted to a select committee, which on January 6 reported it in a form similar to the bill previously proposed by Calhoun and defeated. This time, however, the bank supporters were ready to vote for almost any bill which would secure such an institution; the bill was passed overwhelmingly on January 7 and sent to the Senate, where amendments were attempted.[58] Astor commented: "The accounts which I have from Washington are that the Bank bill will probably be amended so as to make it near Mr. Dallas plan & that the lower house will finally agree to it."[59] In this expectation Astor's informants were misguided, for the Federalists in the House stood firm, the Senate gave way, and the bill went to the president, who after ten days returned it with his veto, based on the conviction that the proposed bank "would not fulfill the purposes for which a bank was then needed."[60] Astor had rather anticipated this result, since, as he said, "one of my friends wrote me from Washington that the President would not sign the present Bank bill but return it . . . and that another effort will be made for a 50 million Bank and without Specie. . . . whatever Bank we have we must work together. Several of the most wealthy here will go with us."

But despite the tone of this letter Astor was evidently disgusted and discouraged. On February 6, the very day when a "new measure drawn mostly along the lines of the original Dallas bill" was introduced into the Senate, he wrote Smith a letter sharply criticizing his conduct of the campaign for a national bank.

I would not give a cent for all the good of Mr Ps [probably David Parish] or any other person speaking to the president on the subject of a Bank for we all know that he is in fav^r but that he has no influence, you have begun at the wrong end had you agreed with me a Bank would have been made altho' I got a gentleman to go on purpose to confer with you, you not even so much as call'd to see him If a plan can be adopted to promise success & I am consulted & agree then I will agree to contribute otherwise not.

The "gentleman" to whom Astor referred and whom Smith had failed to see was a Mr. Rudd, evidently Astor's correspondent Theron Rudd, whom Astor had described early in December as able to "render more service to you and all of us in establishing a Bank than any other or all of us put together. . . . I repeat go and see him and take his advices . . ." later adding, "I am sorry to find you had not seen my friend at

Washington he can do more good than you and I would believe and I say again it is a pity you had not seen him as, if needed, he would have put everything to right."[61] The reason neither for Astor's astonishingly high estimate of Mr. Rudd's powers nor for Smith's equally curious failure to consult a man so highly recommended is revealed in their correspondence. Rudd was apparently connected in some way with William P. Van Ness,[62] judge of the Southern District Court of the State of New York and a prominent Democratic politician, who had been associated with Astor in getting some of the latter's goods out of Canada earlier in the war. It is probable from this connection, and from the cryptic way in which Astor referred to Rudd, that his function in Washington during the discussion of the bank bill was as an expert lobbyist in its interest.

On February 7 Astor exclaimed, "I wish to God we might get a national Bank & that quickly do you think," he wrote Smith, "it would do any good if I was now to go to Washington at all events I must meet you somewhere."[63] Astor's aroused interest probably came from the discussion of the bank bill then in the Senate, which soon after was passed and sent to the House. However, "the news of peace, promising an end to the most urgent necessities of the government, gave the whole question pause" and "the bill was indefinitely postponed."[64] Thus Astor's strenuous attempts to secure the incorporation of a national bank during the War of 1812 came to an inconclusive end with the termination of that war. The account of his endeavors is interesting chiefly in demonstrating the prominent place which he of necessity took in any campaign involving the financial interests of the country, and in revealing the characteristics regarded by this great merchant as proper to an effective national bank.

With the end of the war came an elimination of all cause for disagreement between the two wings of the bank party, since the question was not one of procuring loans but of settling the currency and resuming specie payments. On January 8, 1816, Calhoun, who had been appointed chairman of a select committee to consider "a Uniform National Currency," brought in a bill based on an outline prepared by Dallas; the president was able to sign it a little more than three months later.[65]

Astor had doubtless watched the progress of events with interest.[66] His large subscriptions to the war loans and his activity in the war-time attempts to establish a national bank were now recognized, in May, by an appointment (along with William Jones, Stephen Girard, Pierce Butler, and James Buchanan) as one of the government's five directors for the term ending January, 1817, and, in June, by appointment with Peter H. Schenck and Isaac Denison as one of the "Commissioners for superintending the subscriptions at New York, in the State of New York."[67] On July 1, 1816, Astor with the other commissioners was granted letters of attorney from certain prospective subscribers "to transfer in due form of law, the *Funded Debt*, whereof the Certificates are hereto annexed, to the President, Directors and Company of the Bank of the United States, as soon as the Bank shall be organized."[68]

Astor bought largely of the stock of the second Bank of the United States, though he was certainly not so heavy a purchaser as his friend and associate Stephen Girard, who, when more than $3,000,000 of stock remained unsubscribed, took over the entire deficit.[69] On August 27, Stephen Girard signed two papers, in each of which he promised "for value received . . . to transfer to John Jacob Astor or Order, One Thousand Shares of the Bank of the United States, on which the first Instalment has been paid, as soon as the Books for that purpose, Shall be opened by the Said Bank."[70] The value of the shares was $100 each. Astor, as one of the commissioners for the Bank subscriptions at New York, was occasionally found sending stock certificates to the cashier of the Bank in payment of an installment on bank shares "subscribed by the names on

List herewith marked," or referring in other connections to such transactions.[71] It is probable, however, that, in certain cases when he applied for stock certificates and mentioned no list of persons in whose names they were to be issued, the shares had been purchased on his own account. In one letter he requested "Certificates of 1299 Bank Shares — on which the Second payment has been made to you," accompanied by a request for 226 shares in the names of his wife and five children, "for all of which the 3 payment has been made here."[72]

The organization of the Bank followed immediately upon the closing of subscriptions to the capital stock, late in July. Much to the disgust of such men as Astor and Girard, "intrigue & Corruption . . . formed a ticket for twenty Directors of the Bank of the United States who I am sorry to say," to use Girard's words, "appear to have been selected for the purpose of securing the presidency to W[m]. Jones, the Cashier's office to Jon[n]. A. Smith & for other pecuneary views." It was with difficulty that Astor and Girard secured the election of two directors favored by themselves. When the incompetence of Jones as secretary of the Treasury is considered, his selection as president of the new Bank is easily detected as an attempt on the part of the government to insinuate politics into the management of that institution, a policy which Girard and Astor, business men first and Democrats afterwards, could not be expected to approve. Both consequently were active during the organization and early days of the Bank with the purpose of preventing or minimizing the ill results which might be expected from this injection of politics into a financial institution.[73] Astor took a leading rôle in drawing up a ticket for directors of the branch bank to be established at New York,[74] and the candidates approved by him were, with possibly one exception, elected early in December, with Astor himself heading the list. Shortly after this Astor was elected president of the New York branch.[75]

Astor's term as a director of the Bank of the United States was not an extended one. In January, 1817, when the time came for a new choice of directors, his name appeared neither on the list of those appointed by the president nor on that of those elected by the stockholders.[76] It is probable that he declined to allow his name to be considered, in view of his responsibilities as commissioner for Bank subscriptions and as president of the Branch Bank at New York. During his term of service his activities had been chiefly confined to attempts at procuring the election of proper men for directors both of the parent bank and of the branch at New York, though he also seems, ineffectually, to have opposed the establishment of more than a few branches. On November 2 he wrote to one of his choices for director of the New York branch, "you may make yourself quit Easey as to the Branches none will be fixd on unless Baltimore Nyk & Boston there are a 100 persons here from Defferient parts of the Country Applying but I should think it Strange if *any* of tham ware to Succd."[77] Nevertheless, strange though it may have seemed to Astor, by December 7, 1816, "directors were appointed for offices at Boston, New York, Baltimore, Charleston, and New Orleans, and by March sixteen cities had been selected as sites for offices in addition to Philadelphia."[78]

As president of the New York branch Astor continued his attempts to procure suitable directors for that institution.[79] He also engaged in one or two minor tilts with officials of the parent bank, insignificant in themselves, but, from what we know of Astor's attitude toward the motives which had inspired their selection, perhaps symptomatic of a more serious tendency toward conflict beneath the surface.[80] We know that Girard felt well-grounded apprehensions as to the manner in which the Bank was being run, which Astor probably shared.[81] Astor continued his duties as commissioner, and was re-elected as director of the Branch Bank in 1817 and 1818, but in the following year his absence in Europe necessitated the selection of someone else to fill his place.[82]

Although Astor's connection with the second Bank of the United States was not of long duration, it was nevertheless of considerable importance. He took a leading part in the agitation for a national bank during the war years which resulted in the establishment of such an institution soon after peace had arrived. He was a large stockholder, and for several months after the Bank's establishment he enjoyed the unusual distinction of being simultaneously a director of the parent bank, a commissioner for subscriptions to the Bank stock, and director and president of the branch at New York, which last position he held for three years. It seems evident that, if the establishment of the second Bank of the United States meant anything to the financial welfare of the country, Astor could claim a substantial share of the credit.[83]

Since most of Astor's time from 1819 to 1826 was spent in Europe, he had little opportunity during this period to display his interest in American banks and banking. The next definite evidence of attention on his part to any banking institution appeared in 1829. In 1821, Astor had renewed the offers to Albert Gallatin, then in Paris, which he had first made in 1815, but as before without effect.[84] Astor had, however, not given up his hope of being able to give Gallatin an opportunity to exert his financial talents, even though he himself should not be principally benefited thereby. Consequently when the projectors of a bank, who had secured in April, 1829, a charter from the New York legislature but had been unable to dispose of the stock, applied to Astor for assistance, he offered to make up the deficiency on condition that Gallatin should be the president. This was agreed to and Gallatin became the head of the "National (afterwards the Gallatin) Bank . . . a small corporation with a capital of only $750,000," from which "Mr. Gallatin drew . . . the very modest compensation of $2000 a year."[85]

After this, Astor did not take an active part in banking. During the years remaining to him (almost a score) he did interest himself, however, in the stock of something over a dozen banking institutions. In some cases he purchased stock as a matter of speculation, intending to dispose of it when it should rise in value; in others he intended to hold the stock as an investment. Among the institutions which seem to have belonged to the first category was the Louisiana Bank, the stock of which Astor apparently tried to dispose of abroad. In May, 1832, he sent 101 shares to Thomas Wilson & Co., at London, with instructions to sell at not less than £26 15s. per share. In April, 1835, Astor sent the same firm $3,400 worth of Louisiana Bank warrants to be put to his credit, and in October, 1836, requested the return of the Louisiana Bank stock in their charge.[86] In March, 1838, Astor sent Gillespies, Moffatt & Co., of London, $3,400 in Louisiana Bank warrants to be put to his credit.[87] In March, 1833, Clarkson & Co. were requested to return to Astor 50 shares of this stock.[88] It was perhaps some of this stock, described as selling at 109, which was referred to in a letter of March 8, 1848, to a correspondent in New Orleans.[89] On June 7, 1834, Astor wrote Gillespie, Moffatt, Finlay & Co., of London, "if U. S. Bank Shares can be obtained at about £22 . . . you will please buy 150 to 200 shares and send them to me," and two days later he instructed the same firm to take 400 or 500 shares of that stock "if to be had at or under 22£."[90]

In this country one of Astor's brokers was John Warren. To him William B. Astor on February 27, 1836, wrote, "My father requests you to sell 200 say two hundred shares of the Ohio Trust Co at 124 per cent say One hundred and twenty four per cent at 90 days with option to the buyer — interest at 6 per cent."[91] On October 6 Gallatin Brothers were instructed to buy 100 shares of the same stock.[92] In April of the next year Astor commented on this stock to a correspondent in

Paris. "I hold myself 300 shares," he wrote, "which I paid (within 12 months) 20 per cent advance — they gave a dividend of 9 per cent and I think the stock more safe than our local bank stocks being less liable to losses by commercial paper."[93] In September, 1836, Astor also requested Gallatin Brothers to purchase 250 shares of stock in the New York State Bank, and a month later ordered 50 more shares. In July, 1838, the same firm was instructed to purchase 150 shares in the Farmers' Loan and Trust Company (before April 30, 1836, the Farmers' Fire Insurance and Loan Company[94]) at not more than $112\frac{1}{2}$ per cent.[95]

When Astor purchased stock in a bank it was usually, however, to hold for dividends. Early in January, 1832, he wrote Thomas W. Olcott, at Albany: "I will have to receive in the course of this month from 20 to 30m dollars, which I would like to invest as a permanent investment in some safe stock — no objections to large dividends, but whether that be a little more or less is not so much a matter, as to have it perfectly safe." A few days later he added: "The many applications for New Banks have induced me to wait for a time — We have also several failures here which if they should increase may cause a a [sic] greater demand for money and lower the price of stocks — .... If any of your Bank Stock should offer on terms you think not too dear, please take for 5000 say Five thousand dollars worth for me."[96]

We have more knowledge of Astor's interest in banks outside of New York City than in those located on Manhattan Island, because of the greater amount of correspondence involved. However, we do get a few glimpses of his investments in New York City banks. On August 31, 1833, William B. Astor ordered Prime, Ward, King & Co. to transfer 100 shares of the Manhattan Bank to his father, adding, "the Phoenix Bank shares when purchased you will please transfer in like manner."[97] In May, 1834, Astor wrote, "I beg to subscribe for

(320) three hundred and twenty shares Phoenix Bank Stock, and enclose you herewith a check for $1600 being $5 on each share of my subscription."[98]

As far as the number of banks was concerned, Astor's greatest interest seemed to be in that region of New York State with which he had first become familiar as a tramping fur trader. We know he was interested to some extent in the Merchants and Mechanics Bank of Troy, for in January, 1833, his son wrote to the cashier requesting the payment of interest on bonds belonging to Astor.[99] On June 6, 1834, Astor wrote to the president of the Bank of Troy, saying:

> I will take the 30m$ stock you mention in your letter of yesterday, at the rate I paid to the Bank at Albany viz: 6½ per cent premium, and allow interest at 5 per cent per annum from the 20th April to the day of payment say the 1st of July. I take for granted the stock bears interest from the 15th April last.
>
> Owing to the fall in exchange, the stock has also declined since some days past. I expect your reply per return mail. . . . P.S. The stock not to be delivered until paid for.

The next day he added: "I expect the 30m dollars of stock mentioned in your's of the 5th inst: to be of the same I bought of M[r]. Olcott viz: not payable until after 1845 and also that the interest from April to July is to be received by me."[100]

In August, 1836, the cashier of the Bank of Utica was requested to transfer 100 shares to Astor, but we hear nothing further of this transaction save that in 1837 Astor expressed his gratification at learning that the bank was prosperous and in the next year requested the remittance of dividends.[101] Astor also had some stock in the Bank of Ithaca, which had been formed in 1829.[102] During 1832, 1833, and 1834, he was receiving semiannual dividends of $250, or 5 per cent on 250 shares of stock. In 1834 he purchased an additional $5,000 worth of stock, par value, for $6,250. This must have doubled his previous holdings, for from 1835 to 1838 he received semiannual dividends of 5 per cent, amounting to $500.[103] Presumably Astor continued to draw dividends from this bank until, in February, 1847, he sold his stock to the cashier at a premium of 5 per cent.[104]

Astor's investment in the Bank of Rochester, formed in 1824,[105] was not altogether successful. In November, 1831, he ordered a certificate for 200 shares to be transferred to him.[106] In May, 1834, William B. Astor made a similar request in regard to two certificates of 270 and 65 shares, respectively.[107] In the meantime William B. Astor had declined an offer from Thomas W. Olcott for his father's stock in the Bank of Rochester and said that he would not sell unless it was going to depreciate.[108] In 1846 the bank's charter expired and could be extended only on condition that the stockholders would assume a personal liability. Astor declined to accede to any such proposal and expressed his opposition in vigorous letters to the president [109] and to the comptroller.[110] The bank soon closed up, and Astor's interest in it came to be expressed only in enquiries as to what progress was being made in winding up its affairs and how much capital was to be divided. In September, 1846, he mentioned that he had heard it would pay seventy cents on the dollar and asked whether that result was still probable.[111] He made similar enquiries of H. S. Fairchild, writing in October, 1846, "I am a large holder of shares in the Bank of Rochester, and as I understand that you have the immediate care of the assets of the Bank, I would desire you to inform me what the present state of the Institution is — what the Stock is probably worth; and when it is likely that a dividend of the assets will be made among the stockholders."[112] In February, 1847, Astor informed Fairchild that he had no funds for cashing bonds and mortgages and thereby facilitating the closing up of the bank; and in August he was again enquiring, through his son, concerning the progress and prospects in the winding up of the bank's affairs.[113]

Astor's connection with another Rochester banking institution was somewhat more satisfactory. This was the Rochester City Bank, in which Astor owned 300 shares whose par value was $30,000. In May, 1837, he wrote to its cashier, "I am happy to learn that notwithstanding the very bad times, under which the whole country is so severely suffering, your Bank is likely to escape with out loss." The comparatively good condition of the bank was confirmed a year later by the declaration of a dividend of $7\frac{1}{2}$ per cent, probably for an entire year, amounting in Astor's case to $2,250.[114] In the next decade Astor seems to have regularly received a semiannual dividend of 3 per cent, amounting to $900.[115] The condition of the Bank of Rochester seems to have aroused Astor's apprehensions for the Rochester City Bank, and in consequence in August, 1847, he wrote A. B. Johnson of Utica, in these words: "I shall feel much obliged to you for any information you may give me respecting the present condition of the City Bank of Rochester. By a statement I have lately seen in a newspaper, it appears to me that the amounts of real estate, and bonds and mortgages held by the institution are very large and would seem to indicate that it had suffered much from bad debts."[116] In January, 1848, however, Astor wrote to the president of the bank: "Please accept my thanks for the account you give me of the prosperous condition of your Bank as before."

A New York backstate bank in which Astor was concerned was the Commercial Bank of Oswego. We have already had occasion to note some of his relations with this institution. It could not have been to this bank that Gerrit Smith referred in August, 1831 (when he wrote Astor that, not liking the Oswego bank, he had purchased no stock, either for Astor or for himself),[117] since the Commercial Bank was not formed till 1836. In November of that year Astor acknowledged the receipt of two stock certificates. In March, 1837, he enquired, "I have lately been offered some of your stock at par. What is it worth with you?" and a year later he sent the cashier fifteen shares to be transferred to him.[118] In 1841 the Oswego bank got into difficulties, due to wasting its funds through making excessive loans to favorites, mostly directors, and, in order to keep from suspending, levied a 50 per cent assessment on the stockholders.[119] Astor did not choose to pay this assessment and offered to sell his stock, worth $16,500 at par, to Gerrit Smith for $33\frac{1}{3}$ per cent on its par value.[120] Smith replied that the stock was selling at 25 per cent but that he would go as high as 27 per cent if Astor would lend him the money both to pay for the stock and to meet the 50 per cent assessment.[121] Astor declined this offer on the ground that "the assets of the Bank are worth from 50 to 60 per cent. The real estate I am told, is very valuable and will be more so. I believe the Bank is in good hands and if sustained will do well."[122] Gerrit Smith remained unconvinced and replied that he was "unprepared to make any better offer for your stock."[123] Astor, after thinking the matter over for a fortnight, finally, on April 26, accepted Smith's terms.[124] The bank failed some months later in the year, and Astor's expressed regret at the fact was doubtless tempered by the reflection that he had lost less by its downfall than otherwise might have been the case.[125]

We have observed that most of the bank stocks in which Astor invested were of institutions in the New York back-country. We get occasional glimpses, however, which reveal something of an interest in banks located elsewhere. On March 28, 1837, in the midst of the panic, he wrote to P. Chouteau, Jr., at St. Louis, in regard to the situation. "You no doubt are informed of all that took place since you left here which causes me to delay from writing to you on the subject of subscribing to the Bank as I had expressed a wish to do, provided you thought well of it. Matters are so bad here that I am still undecided to what amount to engage, until I can be informed how soon the payments are to be made and your opinion as to the stock itself."[126] The bank undoubtedly referred to in this letter was the Bank of the State of Missouri. Although Astor at this time seemed uncertain as to whether or not he should invest in this bank, it is recorded that on September 7 of the same year 3 bonds of the Bank of the State of Missouri, payable in 25 years, bearing interest at 6 per cent, were transferred to Astor. On January 17, 1846, Astor assigned them to his son William.[127]

There is some evidence that in 1838 Astor experienced a revival of interest in direct personal connection with banks and banking — an interest which, save for his sponsoring of the Gallatin Bank in 1829, had scarcely appeared since his retirement from the directorship of the New York Branch Bank in 1819.[128] On May 19, 1838, he wrote to C. C. Cambreleng, once, more than a score of years earlier, his commercial agent in Europe, then a member of Congress, concerning the banking situation. "There are several plans for banks, under the new law in contemplation. It is probable that I may take an interest in one of them, in which case I shall be happy to have you interested. . . . The idea is to have the capital in money and State stock."[129] It is probably to one of these contemplated banks mentioned by Astor that J. G. King referred in a letter of January 16, 1839, to Joshua Bates of Baring Brothers & Co., at London. He wrote:

You will see by the newspapers that the "Bank of Commerce" is now before the public — and the *directors*, who are among our strongest men in New York, having taken one million and a half dollars — the remainder (of the fixed capital to commence with, five millions) — say, three millions and a half dollars, are left for general subscription — and there is no doubt of its being filled — so far as can now be judged.

At this point — Mr. Astor has desired to come into the direction — and to take a large amount of the Stock, which is very desirable, on all scores — and will be probably managed — tho' not in time to advise p this packet. — In any event the business will be well and safely managed and the stock become of the most favorable character. — [130]

Later in the same month, however, King added:

The allusion to Mr. Astor's coming into the direction of the Bank of Commerce, was founded upon his application to do so — but some misunderstanding took place and he in a sort of pet — rejoined some other friends, with whom he had been in treaty, and made up a Trust Company — his new associates are

Mr Gallatin for	$100,000 —
— Kernochan —	100,000 —
Messrs Hunt of Mobile and Parish of N York }	500,000
Mr. Astor	1,300,000
	—————
	$2,000,000

and the public are not invited to participate with them, at least at par. — [131]

However, we learn nothing further concerning Astor's intention of establishing a stock company.

Some idea of the extent of Astor's interest in banks at his death may be gathered from the assets mentioned in his will. Among them were 500 shares capital stock of the Bank of North America, 1,000 shares of the Manhattan Company, 1,000 shares capital stock of the Merchants Bank,[132] and 1,604 shares capital stock of the Mechanics Bank.[133] Undoubtedly he had many other bank investments which were not mentioned. These large investments in bank stock were doubtless made principally because they promised a reasonable return with safety and without the necessity of personal attention. Those smaller investments, of perhaps $20,000 or $30,000 each, which we have examined in more detail, probably had the same primary motives behind them, but in a secondary way may have been partly inspired by the thought of assisting to build up the banking institutions of the country and particularly of New York State.

NOTES

1. [Scoville, Joseph A.], *The Old Merchants of New York City*, 5 vols. (1889), vol. iv, pp. 212–227.

2. *New-York Gazette and General Advertiser*, February 6, 1823, p. 2, col. 2; February 6, 1824, p. 2, col. 1; *Longworth's American Almanac, New-York Register, and City Directory* (1815), p. 91; *ibid.* (1816), p. 79; *ibid.*, for 1817–18, p. 78; *New York As It Is In 1833*, p. 104; *ibid.*, *1834*, p. 109.

3. Smythe, R. M., compiler, *Obsolete American Securities and Corporations* (1904), p. 316.

4. *New-York Gazette and General Advertiser*, December 9, 1817, p. 2, col. 2.

5. Smythe, *op. cit.*, p. 517.

6. *New-York Gazette and General Advertiser*, December 17, 1819, p. 2, col. 1.

7. *Ibid.*, December 14, 1821, p. 2, col. 2.

8. Smythe, *op. cit.*, p. 349.

9. Ms. book, Baker Library, Astor Papers, Letter Book ii, 1831–38, p. 213, John Jacob Astor per William B. Astor, N. Y., March 4, 1834, to J. G. Warren & Son.

10. *Ibid.*, p. 360, William B. Astor, N. Y., December 30, 1835, to Vincent Rumpff, Paris.

11. *Ibid.*, p. 372, William B. Astor, N. Y., February 3, 1836, to Gallatin Bros.

12. *Ibid.*, p. 395, John Jacob Astor by William B. Astor, N. Y., April 11, 1836, to Gallatin Brothers.

13. *Ibid.*, pp. 379, 381, William B. Astor, N. Y., March 3, 5, 1836, to John Warren.

14. Moody, John, *Moody's Manual of Investments* (1928), p. 340.

15. Ms. book, Baker Library, Astor Papers, Letter Book ii, 1831–38, pp. 446–447, William B. Astor, November 8, 1836, to Robert Neilson, c/o Arbuthnot & Latham, London; *New York As It Is In 1833*, p. 107; *ibid.*, *1834*, p. 113; *ibid.*, *1837*, p. 149; *ibid.*, *1839*, p. 149.

16. Ms. book, Baker Library, Astor Papers, Letter Book ii, 1831–38, p. 50, John Jacob Astor, N. Y., May 7, 1832, to N. Devereux, Utica.

17. *Ibid.*, p. 205, John Jacob Astor by William B. Astor, N. Y., January 25, 1834, to Gallatin Brothers.

18. *Ibid.*, pp. 394–395, John Jacob Astor, N. Y., April 8, 1836, to Gillespies, Moffatt, Finlay & Co., London.

19. *Ibid.*, p. 443, John Jacob Astor, N. Y., October 28, 1836, to Thomas Wilson & Co., London.

20. *Ibid.*, p. 398, William B. Astor, N. Y., April 22, 1836, to Prof. McVickar, Columbia College.

21. *Ibid.*, pp. 490, 550, John Jacob Astor, N. Y., May 10, December 30, 1837, to Gillespies, Moffatt & Co., London.

22. *New York Evening Post*, July 28, 1838, p. 4, col. 1. The story is told that "late in life by a gratuitous loan he [Astor] saved the New York Life Insurance Company, which had been robbed of its entire surplus of two hundred and fifty thousand dollars." (Faust, Albert Bernhardt, *The German Element in the United States*, 2 vols. (1909), vol. ii, p. 430.) This must refer to the New York Life Insurance and Trust Company; by a gratuitous loan is presumably meant one free of interest.

23. Ms. book, Baker Library, Astor Papers, Letter Book iii, 1845–48, p. 3, William B. Astor, July 22, 1845, to John B. Finlay.

24. *Ibid.*, p. 4, William B. Astor, N. Y., July 23, 1845, to Robert Neilson, Long Branch, N. J.

25. Ms. book, Bank of New York and Trust Company Museum, N. Y., Stock Book, pp. 38, 39, 41.

26. Ms., Syracuse University, Gerrit Smith Miller Collection, Letters, John Jacob Astor, N. Y., March 31, 1793, to Peter Smith, Old Fort Schuyler.

27. Ms. book, Bank of Manhattan Company, N. Y., "Cash received of the Subscribers to the Manhattan Company at the time of Subscribing," p. 59.

28. Facsimile of the dividend book of the Bank of Manhattan Company in *The Bankers' Magazine* (reprint, n. d.).

29. *Bank of the Manhattan Company* (n. d.), pp. 8–9.

30. "Miscellaneous Documents," *Michigan Pioneer Collections*, vol. viii (1885), pp. 573–574, Nathaniel Parker, N. Y., November 18, 1806, to Augustus B. Woodward.

31. Ms., Library of Congress, Madison Papers, vol. xli, Writings to Madison, December 23, 1810–April 13, 1811, Albert Gallatin, January 5, 1811, to Madison.

32. Ms., Public Archives of Canada, Ottawa, Series C, vol. 1218, p. 114, Noah Freer, Military Secretary, Quebec, December 31, 1811, to W. H. Robinson, Commissary General.

33. *Mercantile Advertiser* (N. Y.), December 21, 1810.

34. Catterall, Ralph C. H., *The Second Bank of the United States* (1903), pp. 7–8; McMaster, John Bach, *A History of the People of the United States*, 7 vols. (1911), vol. iv, pp. 292–293; Jenkins, John S., *The Life of John Caldwell Calhoun* (1850), pp. 80–81.

35. Ms., Girard College, Philadelphia, Girard Papers, 1814, nos. 192 and 213, David Parish, March 28, April 9, 1814, to Stephen Girard.

36. Catterall, *op. cit.*, pp. 8–9; McMaster, *loc. cit.*; Jenkins, *op. cit.*, p. 82.

37. Ms., Girard College, Philadelphia, Girard Papers, 1814, no. 354, John Jacob Astor, N. Y., August 15, 1814, to Stephen Girard, Philadelphia (see above, vol. i, pp. 561–563).

38. Ms. book, Baker Library, Astor Papers, Letter Book i, 1813–15, pp. 255, 260, 264, 269–270, 271, John Jacob Astor, N. Y., August 13, 19, 25, 30, September 1, 1814, to D. A. Smith, Baltimore; p. 256, John Jacob Astor, N. Y., August 13, 1814, to David Parish, Philadelphia.

39. Ms., Library of Congress, Monroe Papers, vol. xiv, Writings to Monroe, November, 1813–March 19, 1815, John Jacob Astor, N. Y., September 2, 1814, to James Monroe (see above, vol. i, pp. 563–564).

40. Ms., New York Historical Society, Astor Papers, Rufus King, Jamaica, L. I., September 1, 1814, to John Jacob Astor.

41. Catterall, *op. cit.*, p. 9.

42. Ms. book, Baker Library, Astor Papers, Letter Book i, 1813–15, pp. 276–277, 288–289, 289, 293, 300–301, 302, John Jacob Astor, N. Y., September 8, 22, 23, 27, October 3, 4, 1814, to D. A. Smith, Baltimore; p. 293, John Jacob Astor, N. Y., September 27, 1814, to David Parish, Philadelphia.

43. Dallas, George Mifflin, *The Life and Writings of Alexander James Dallas* (1871), pp. 128–129.

44. Ms. book, Baker Library, Astor Papers, Letter Book i, 1813–15, pp. 306–307, 308–309, 324, John Jacob Astor, N. Y., October 8, 10, 23, 1814, to D. A. Smith, Baltimore; p. 313, John Jacob Astor, N. Y., September 27, 1814, to David Parish, Philadelphia.

45. Dallas, *op. cit.*, pp. 237–239; Jenkins, *op. cit.*, pp. 82–83; Dewey, Davis R., *Financial History of the United States* (1920), p. 146.

46. Ms. book, Baker Library, Astor Papers, Letter Book i, 1813–15, p. 324, John Jacob Astor, N. Y., October 23, 1814, to D. A. Smith, Baltimore; p. 313, John Jacob Astor, N. Y., October 13, 1814, to David Parish, Philadelphia.

47. Catterall, *op. cit.*, p. 10.

48. Ms., Girard College, Philadelphia, Girard Papers, 1814, no. 428, John Jacob Astor, Baltimore, November 8, 1814, to Stephen Girard; nos. 431, 435, David Parish, Georgetown, November 9, 11, 1814, to Stephen Girard, Philadelphia; no. 439, Joseph Curwen, Baltimore, November 14, 1814, to Stephen Girard, Philadelphia.

49. McMaster, *op. cit.*, vol. iv, p. 237; Catterall, *op. cit.*, p. 12; Jenkins, *op. cit.*, pp. 84–87.

50. Ms. book, Baker Library, Astor Papers, Letter Book i, 1813–15, pp. 350–351, John Jacob Astor, N. Y., November 20, 1814, to D. A. Smith, Baltimore.

51. *Ibid.*, p. 366, John Jacob Astor, N. Y., November 23, 1814, to Theron Rudd.

52. *Ibid.*, p. 368, John Jacob Astor, N. Y., November 23, 1814, to Mr. Fisk.

53. *Ibid.*, pp. 368–369, John Jacob Astor, N. Y., November 23, 1814, to Calhoun (see above, vol. i, pp. 575–577).

54. Catterall, *op. cit.*, pp. 12–14; McMaster, *op. cit.*, vol. iv, p. 238; Jenkins, *op. cit.*, pp. 86–87; Dallas, *op. cit.*, pp. 244–248.

55. Ms. book, Baker Library, Astor Papers, Letter Book i, 1813–15, pp. 370–371, 378, 380–381, 390, 396, John Jacob Astor, N. Y., November 26, December 2, 4, 10–11, 16, 1814, to D. A. Smith; pp. 379, 401, John Jacob Astor, N. Y., December 4, 19, 1814, to David Parish.

56. Catterall, *op. cit.*, pp. 14–15.

57. Ms. book, Baker Library, Astor Papers, Letter Book i, 1813–15, p. 415, John Jacob Astor, N. Y., December 31, 1814, to David Parish.

58. Catterall, *op. cit.*, pp. 15–16.

59. Ms. book, Baker Library, Astor Papers, Letter Book i, 1813–15, p. 429, John Jacob Astor, N. Y., January 14, 1815, to David Parish.

60. Catterall, *op. cit.*, p. 16.

61. Ms. book, Baker Library, Astor Papers, Letter Book i, 1813–15, pp. 380–381, 390, 396, 438, 442–443, 448, 457–458, John Jacob Astor, N. Y., December 4, 10–11, 16, 1814, January 21, 25, 30, February 6, 1815, to D. A. Smith.

62. Ms., New York Historical Society, Astor Papers, John Jacob Astor, N. Y., November 27, 1814, to William P. Van Ness, Kinderhook, N. Y.

63. Ms., Baker Library, Astor Papers, Letter Book i, 1813–15, John Jacob Astor, N. Y., February 7, 1815, to D. A. Smith.

64. Catterall, *op. cit.*, p. 17; McMaster, *op. cit.*, vol. iv, p. 239; Jenkins, *op. cit.*, p. 88.

65. Catterall, *op. cit.*, pp. 17–21; McMaster, *op. cit.*, vol. iv, pp. 309–311.

66. Ms., Girard College, Philadelphia, Girard Papers, 1815, no. 132, David Parish, March 29, 1815, to Stephen Girard.

67. Ms., Library of Congress, Madison Papers, vol. lviii, Writings to Madison, March 17–July 30, 1816, John Smith, N. Y., April 5, 1816, to Albert Gallatin; Albert Gallatin, N. Y., April 19, 1816, to Mr. Madison; John P. Van Ness, Washington, April 24, 1816, to the President of the United States; *Niles' Weekly Register*, vol. x, pp. 197–198, May 18, 1816; *New-York Gazette and General Advertiser*, July 11, 1816, p. 4, col. 5.

68. Ms., Library Company of Philadelphia, Ridgeway Branch, Astor Papers, Letters of Attorney from Henry Thomas, Charles Gillerd, and Nicholas Fish, July 1, 8, 20, 1816, to John Jacob Astor, Peter H. Schenck, Isaac Dennison.

69. Catterall, *op. cit.*, p. 22.

70. Ms., Girard College, Philadelphia, Girard Papers, 1816, no. 731.

71. Ms., Library Company of Philadelphia, Ridgeway Branch, Astor Papers, John Jacob Astor, N. Y., June 4, 1817, to Jonathan Smith; ms., Pennsylvania Historical Society, Philadelphia, Society Collection, John Jacob Astor, N. Y., October 31, 1817, to John Vaughan, Philadelphia.

72. Ms., Chicago Historical Society, Atwater Collection, Autograph Letters, vol. xxxii, 1882, p. 543, John Jacob Astor, N. Y., July 8 [1817?], to Jonathan Smith, Cashier of the Bank of the United States, Philadelphia.

73. Ms. book, Girard College, Philadelphia, Girard Papers, Letter Book xiv, letter no. 336, Stephen Girard, Philadelphia, October 29, 1816, to John Stoney, Charleston.

74. Ms., Library of Congress, William Samuel Johnson Papers, John Jacob Astor, Philadelphia, November 2, 1816, to W. W. Woolsey, New Haven; ms., Girard College, Philadelphia, Girard Papers, 1816, no. 970, John Jacob Astor, N. Y., November 13, 1816, to Stephen Girard.

75. *Niles' Weekly Register*, vol. xi, p. 156, November 2, 1816; p. 176, November 9, 1816; pp. 238–239, December 7, 1816; p. 259, December 14, 1816.

76. *Ibid.*, vol. xi, p. 336, January 11, 1817; p. 351, January 18, 1817.

77. Ms., Library of Congress, William Samuel Johnson Papers, John Jacob Astor, Philadelphia, November 2, 1816, to W. W. Woolsey, New Haven.

78. Catterall, *op. cit.*, p. 23.

79. Ms. book, Girard College, Philadelphia, Girard Papers, Letter Book xv, letter no. 13, Stephen Girard, Philadelphia, January 14, 1817, to Jacob Astor; *ibid.*, Letters, 1817, no. 29, John Jacob Astor, N. Y., July 11, 1817, to Stephen Girard.

80. Ms., New York Public Library, Astor Papers, John Jacob Astor, President, Office of Discount and Deposit, N. Y., March 3, 1817, to William Jones, President, Bank of the United States; John Jacob Astor, November 25, 1817, to John Savage.

81. Ms. book, Girard College, Philadelphia, Girard Papers, Letter Book xvi, letter no. 87, Stephen Girard, Philadelphia, March 9, 1818, to John Jacob Astor, N. Y.

82. *New-York Gazette and General Advertiser*, November 29, 1817, p. 2, col. 1; December 13, 1819, p. 2, col. 1.

83. Astor apparently took no part in the difficulties of the second Bank of the United States in its last years. He was in Europe from 1832 to 1834, but it has been said that he "remained abroad till 1835, when he hurried home in consequence of the disturbance in financial affairs, caused by General Jackson's war upon the Bank of the United States" (Parton, James, *Life of John Jacob Astor* (1865), p. 76). As a matter of fact he had intended to return to New York in the fall of 1833, even before Jackson's withdrawal of government deposits from the Bank. His return (which took place in the spring of 1834 and not in 1835) may be sufficiently ac-

counted for by his desire to be present at the beginning of work on his proposed new hotel.

84. Gallatin, Count, ed., *A Great Peace Maker: The Diary of James Gallatin, Secretary to Albert Gallatin* (1914), pp. 174, 201, January 1, 1821, February 7, 1822. A year later Astor urged Gallatin "to accept the Presidency of the United States Bank," but he would not hear of it. When Astor learned of his friend's refusal he wrote to him, on October 18, in these words: "For the interest of the United States Bank I am sorry that you did not take it. For your own sake I am glad. It is, as you say, a troublesome situation, and I doubt if much credit is to be got by it. I have been to-day spoken to about your taking the situation, but I stated that you decline it, and I think you are right. Matters here go on irregular enough. It's all the while up and down. So soon as people have a little money they run into extravagancy, get in debt, and down it goes. Exchange is again 12½ to 13, and people will again ship specie, the banks again curtail discounts, bankruptcy ensues, exchange will fall for a short time, and then we have the same scene over again. You know so well this country and character of the people that I need say no more." (Adams, Henry, *The Life of Albert Gallatin* (1880), p. 584.)

85. Adams, *op. cit.*, pp. 642–643; Scoville, *op. cit.*, vol. iii, p. 37. Scoville makes the entire capital of the bank only $75,000, and adds the information that "the old Astor had an immense account with that bank. In the difficulties of 1834, William B. Astor drew out a balance of $10,000, and placed it in the United States Branch Bank, Mr. Gallatin never forgave it."

86. Ms. book, Baker Library, Astor Papers, Letter Book ii, 1831–38, pp. 49, 298, 443, John Jacob Astor by William B. Astor, N. Y., May 4, 1832, April 30, 1835, October 28, 1836, to Thomas Wilson & Company, London.

87. *Ibid.*, p. 580, John Jacob Astor by William B. Astor, N. Y., March 31, 1838, to Gillespies, Moffatt & Co., London.

88. *Ibid.*, p. 140, John Jacob Astor, N. Y., March 27, 1833, to Clarkson & Co.

89. *Ibid.*, Letter Book iii, 1845–48, pp. 274–275, William B. Astor, N. Y., March 8, 1848, to Ambrose Lanfear, New Orleans.

90. *Ibid.*, Letter Book ii, 1831–38, pp. 235, 236, John Jacob Astor, N. Y., June 7, 9, 1834, to Gillespies, Moffatt, Finlay & Co., London.

91. *Ibid.*, p. 376, William B. Astor, N. Y., February 27, 1836, to John Warren.

92. *Ibid.*, p. 436, John Jacob Astor by William B. Astor, N. Y., October 6, 1836, to Gallatin Brothers.

93. *Ibid.*, pp. 479–480, 480, John Jacob Astor, N. Y., April 7, 10, 1837, to C. W. Lutteroth, Paris.

94. Moody, *op. cit.*, p. 74.

95. Ms. book, Baker Library, Astor Papers, Letter Book ii, 1831–38, pp. 429, 436, 601, John Jacob Astor by William B. Astor, N. Y., September 5, October 6, 1836, July 14, 1838, to Gallatin Brothers.

96. *Ibid.*, pp. 21, 24, John Jacob Astor, N. Y., January 6 (see below, vol. ii, p. 1212), 18, 1832, to Thomas W. Olcott, Albany.

97. *Ibid.*, p. 176, William B Astor, N. Y., August 31, 1833, to Prime, Ward, King & Co.

98. *Ibid.*, p. 230, John Jacob Astor by William B. Astor, N. Y., May 21, 1834, to Delafield, Crary, and Bryce, Commissioners.

99. *Ibid.*, p. 121, William B. Astor, N. Y., January 5, 1833, to Mr. Douglas, Cashier, Merchants and Mechanics Bank, Troy.

100. *Ibid.*, pp. 234, 235, John Jacob Astor, N. Y., June 6, 7, 1834, to Stephen Warren, President, Bank of Troy.

101. *Ibid.*, pp. 421, 536, 585, John Jacob Astor by William B. Astor, N. Y., August 6, 1836, November 14, 1837, May 16, 1838, to William B. Welles, Cashier, Bank of Utica.

102. Smythe, *op. cit.*, p. 96.

103. Ms. book, Baker Library, Astor Papers, Letter Book ii, 1831–38. pp. 35, 90, 133, 174–175, 212–213, 255, 256, 268, 286, 330, 382, 589, 614, John Jacob Astor by William B. Astor, N. Y., March 3, September 1, 1832, March 2, August 30, 1833, March 3, September 2, 9, December 10, 1834, March 5, September 11, 1835, March 7, June 2, September 10, 1838, to Ancel St. John, Cashier, Bank of Ithaca.

104. *Ibid.*, Letter Book iii, 1845–48, pp. 91, 150, John Jacob Astor by William B. Astor, N. Y., June 5, 1846, to William B. Douglass, Cashier, Bank of Ithaca.

105. Smythe, *op. cit.*, p. 97.

106. Ms. book, Baker Library, Astor Papers, Letter Book ii, 1831–38, pp. 13, 96, John Jacob Astor by William B. Astor, November 28, 1831, October 3, 1832, to James Seymour, Cashier, Bank of Rochester.

107. *Ibid.*, pp. 228, 229, William B. Astor, N. Y., May 2, 5, 1834, to James Seymour, Cashier, Bank of Rochester.

108. *Ibid.*, p. 170, William B. Astor, N. Y., August 7, 1833, to Thomas W. Olcott.

109. *Ibid.*, Letter Book iii, 1845–48, pp. 33, 34, John Jacob Astor by William B. Astor, N. Y., October 27, 28, 1845, to John Seymour, President, Bank of Rochester.

110. *Ibid.*, p. 33, John Jacob Astor, N. Y., October 27, 1845, to A. C. Flagg, Comptroller, Albany; ms., Boston Public Library, Aldrich Collection, John Jacob Astor by William B. Astor, N. Y., October 27, 1845, to A. C. Flagg, Comptroller, Albany.

111. Ms. book, Baker Library, Astor Papers, Letter Book iii, 1845–48, pp. 59, 118, John Jacob Astor by William B. Astor, N. Y., February 10, September 17, 1846, to John Seymour, President, Bank of Rochester.

112. *Ibid.*, p. 124, John Jacob Astor by William B. Astor, N. Y., October 23, 1846, to H. S. Fairchild, Rochester.

113. *Ibid.*, pp. 154, 206–207, William B. Astor, N. Y., February 15, August 13, 1847, to H. S. Fairchild.

114. *Ibid.*, Letter Book ii, 1831–38, pp. 493, 581, John Jacob Astor by William B. Astor, N. Y., May 24, 1837, May 30, 1838, to Fletcher M. Haight, Cashier, Rochester City Bank.

115. *Ibid.*, Letter Book iii, 1845–48, pp. 9, 49, 98, 193, 255, John Jacob Astor by William B. Astor, August 5, 1845, January 6, July 6, 1846, July 3, 1847, January 5, 1848, to Thomas H. Rochester, President, Rochester City Bank.

116. *Ibid.*, p. 207, John Jacob Astor by William B. Astor, N. Y., August 13, 1847, to A. B. Johnson, Utica.

117. Ms., Syracuse University, Gerrit Smith Miller Collection, Letters, Gerrit Smith, Peterboro, August 19, 1831, to John Jacob Astor, N. Y.

118. Ms. book, Baker Library, Astor Papers, Letter Book ii, 1831–38, pp. 445, 469, 576, John Jacob Astor by William B. Astor, N. Y., November 4, 1836, March 10, 1837, March 28, 1838, to L. Jones, Cashier, Commercial Bank of Oswego.

119. Ms., Syracuse University, Gerrit Smith Miller Collection, Letters, Gerrit Smith, Peterboro, April 1, 1841, to John Jacob Astor, N. Y.

120. *Ibid.*, John Jacob Astor, N. Y., March 24, 1841, to Gerrit Smith, Peterboro (see below, vol. ii, pp. 1238–1239).

121. *Ibid.*, Gerrit Smith, Peterboro, April 1, 1841, to John Jacob Astor, N. Y.

122. *Ibid.*, John Jacob Astor by Fitz Greene Halleck, N. Y., April 5, 1841, to Gerrit Smith (see below, vol. ii, pp. 1239–1240).

123. *Ibid.*, Gerrit Smith, Peterboro, April 9, 1841, to John Jacob Astor, N. Y.

124. *Ibid.*, William B. Astor, N. Y., April 26, 1841, to Gerrit Smith, Peterboro (see below, vol. ii, pp. 1240-1241).

125. *Ibid.*, John Jacob Astor by William B. Astor, N. Y., December 13, 1841, to Gerrit Smith, Peterboro (see below, vol. ii, pp. 1241–1242).

126. Ms. book, Baker Library, Astor Papers, Letter Book ii, 1831–38, p. 475, John Jacob Astor, N. Y., March 28, 1837, to P. Chouteau, Jr., St. Louis.

127. Ms., Detroit Public Library, Burton Historical Collection, Banks and Banking.

128. On May 11, 1837, Astor, in a letter to Governor Marcy, denounced the suspension of specie payment and declared that "3 or 4 days more would have carried us safe" (ms. book, Baker Library, Astor Papers, Letter Book ii, 1831–38, p. 491, John Jacob Astor, N. Y., May 11, 1837, to Governor Marcy, see below, vol. ii, p. 1234).

129. Ms. book, Baker Library, Astor Papers, Letter Book ii, 1831–38, p. 586, John Jacob Astor by William B. Astor, N. Y., May 19, 1838, to Churchill C. Cambreleng, Washington.

130. Ms., Public Archives of Canada, Ottawa, Baring Papers, J. G. King, N. Y., January 16, 1839, to Joshua Bates, London. King is said, while in Liverpool, 1818–24, to have met John Jacob Astor and to have been invited by him to take charge of the American Fur Company. King declined, but, in 1823, Astor, on being consulted by Nathaniel Prime, of Prime, Ward, Sands & Co., as to a suitable partner, recommended King, who accepted. (King, Charles, "James Gore King," Hunt, Freeman, ed., *Lives of American Merchants*, 2 vols. (1856), vol. i, pp. 188–189.)

131. *Ibid.*, James Gore King, N. Y., January 25, 1839, to J. Bates, London.

132. On August 30, 1822, John Jacob Astor & Son had announced that "*the notes* and *acceptances* of the subscribers will be paid at the Merchants' and Branch Banks" (*New-York Gazette and General Advertiser*, August 31, 1822, p. 3, col. 5).

133. Youngman, Anna, *The Economic Causes of Great Fortunes* (1909), chap. ii, pp. 7–54, drawn from "The Will of John Jacob Astor," which is to be found in James Parton's *The Life of John Jacob Astor* (1865), pp. 90–121, and in ms., Baker Library, Astor Papers (see below, vol. ii, pp. 1260–1296).

CHAPTER XXII

MISCELLANEOUS BUSINESS INTERESTS: THE PARK THEATRE, HOTELS, CANALS AND RAILROADS, AND PUBLIC SECURITIES

ALTHOUGH Astor's chief business interests were the fur trade, foreign commerce, land investments, and money-lending, it was not to be expected that a man with his activity of mind and abundance of capital should not branch out into types of enterprise which, so far as he was concerned, were of lesser importance. We have just examined two fields of activity which fall under this classification, namely, insurance and banking. Some of his other activities, like the two just mentioned, were connected in a more or less tenuous fashion with his more important interests. Astor had always been interested in the theater from a cultural and recreational standpoint, and we are told that he "seldom missed a good performance in the palmy days of the 'Old Park.'"[1] The most noted example of this interest was his appearance at the theater upon the very evening that he received word of the loss of the *Tonquin*, which gloomy intelligence he determined should not cost him the loss of his favorite evening's amusement.[2] It is quite likely that his association with Peter Smith was brought about by their common interest in the drama, which in the latter's case was so strong that only religious scruples caused him reluctantly to discard his ambitions for the career of an actor.

It was, then, perhaps natural that, though most of Astor's investments in New York real estate were in the form of vacant lots, he should, on April 21, 1806, have bought for $50,000, in company with John K. Beekman, that Park Theatre in which he had spent so many enjoyable evenings.[3] The theater was rented to Thomas A. Cooper for $2,100 quarterly, an amount which during the depressed days of the War of 1812 he frequently found it difficult to pay, so that his security, Stephen Price, was regularly called upon to supply his deficiency. The situation was so severe that in September, 1814, Price informed Astor that unless the rent were reduced they would give up the theater, as he said they would have the right to do because of the war.[4] Astor, of course, did not agree.

In 1820 the Park Theatre was destroyed by fire, but was rebuilt by the owners and reopened in 1822.[5] During the interim Price sponsored the appearance of Edmund Kean in a theater on Anthony Street, and was so successful that in January, 1821, he threatened Astor and Beekman with building a new theater unless they complied with his proposals for the one then rebuilding. However, by May Price had "taken a lease of it ["our new Theatre"], at a net of 13000$ per annum. —" Henry Brevoort, Astor's nephew, gave as his opinion that "the Theatre will be beautiful, but I fear it will never support such an enormous rent charge."[6] In 1823 the Park Theatre was assessed at $80,000,[7] and five years later, on September 1, 1828, it was leased to Edmund Simpson for seven years at an annual rental of $16,000; the theater at that time was estimated as worth $150,000, Astor's share being still one-half.[8] Evidently Brevoort's pessimistic prophecy had not been fulfilled. Under Simpson's management the theater continued to prosper and to retain its place as the leading New York playhouse. The building was completely remodelled in 1834,[9] after which it was valued at $200,000.[10] In 1846, however, in an estimate by one of its owners, its value was placed at only $60,000, though perhaps this apparent depreciation need not be taken too seriously.[11] Simpson remained the manager till his death late in 1848. The theater was again burned soon after his death.[12] Astor's business connection with the Park Theatre after its purchase and rebuilding was confined to collecting the rent and seeing that the lessee maintained the building in good physical condition and kept up the insurance.

Another interest closely related to Astor's general activities in Manhattan Island real estate was his investments in hotels. On April 8, 1828, Astor bought the City Hotel, then the leading institution of its kind in the city,[13] at auction for $101,000. The consideration may have actually been more and is officially stated to have been made in two payments of $90,750 and $30,254.[14] The hotel was retained under the management of Chester Jenings, who had acted as manager since 1817.[15] On April 25, 1833, a fire did $20,000 worth of damage to the building.[16] Fortunately it was insured for that amount.[17] On October 8, 1838, Astor granted a 5-years lease of the hotel to John H. Gardner and Eldredge Parker for $12,500 annually, payable weekly, and an additional ten per cent yearly upon the amount of expenses, repairs, and alterations made by Astor, payable quarterly.[18] We have no record that this lease was renewed in 1843; it seems that Jenings again took charge of the hotel, and early in 1847 he was said to have concluded not to renew his lease, which was on the point of expiring.[19] We have little further definite information about Astor's connection with the City Hotel, save that some time in the late 1830's it was estimated as worth $250,000 — a valuation which had shrunk to $150,000 by 1846 [20] — and that Astor was said to be annually deriving $15,000 from it at the time of his death.[21]

Much more important was the erection of the Park Hotel (later the Astor House) by Astor in 1834. Many stories are told concerning the circumstances surrounding this project. Irving tells us that when Astor was "yet almost a stranger in the city, and in very narrow circumstances, he passed by where a row of houses had just been erected in Broadway, and which, from the superior style of their architecture, were the talk and boast of the city. 'I'll build, one day or other, a greater house than any of these, in this very street,' said he to himself."[22] When Astor had decided to retire from business he began to make preparations "to fulfill this vow of his youth and build on Broadway a house larger and costlier than any it could then boast."[23] But it was characteristic of Astor's thriftiness and simplicity that this house which he projected took the form not of a magnificent private mansion but of a hotel.

Astor decided to erect this hotel on the block then occupied, besides other buildings, by his own private residence, even though such a procedure was considered rash and wasteful. He already owned most of the lots, and the houses thereon were chiefly occupied by his tenants. There were, however, some buildings which were in the hands of others. One of these belonged to David Lydig, but on April 26, 1831, Astor succeeded in buying his property for $32,500.[24] Another neighbor was John G. Coster, a wealthy retired merchant, and his opposition nearly blocked Astor's plans. Astor offered him $30,000, or about the same price he had paid Lydig — probably more than the property was normally worth — but Coster refused to sell. He declared that he had planned to spend the rest of his days in the house and did not feel like revising his intentions.

It is said that Coster considered that he had once got the worst of a bargain with Astor — at one time they had been concerned together in a vessel — and was not sorry to have the opportunity of turning the tables. Moreover, his wife is said to have been strongly averse to a removal. Astor offered to pay $40,000, but in vain. Finally in desperation Astor said that he would add $20,000 to whatever value a committee of three, two chosen by Coster and one by Astor, should place upon the property. This offer was so extraordinarily lavish that Coster was tempted. At last he agreed to accept this offer, provided that Astor could secure Mrs. Coster's consent. The property was evaluated at $40,000 — two out of three on the committee, it should be remembered, being Coster's appointees — and Astor accordingly called on Mrs. Coster to see if she would accept $60,000 — from 50 per cent to 100 per cent more than its real value — for the coveted house and lot. "'Well, Mr. Astor,' said the lady in the tone of one who was conferring a very great favor for nothing, 'we are such old friends that I am willing for your sake.'" Later Astor was accustomed to repeat this story with great glee, "amused at the simplicity of the old lady in considering it a great favor to him to sell her house at twice its value."

However, if a story, published during Astor's lifetime, can be credited, he may have had another reason for looking back with amusement on the Coster transaction. This tale runs that on the first of May, 1834 — by which time the Costers, among others, had been warned, by a letter of November 29, 1833, to yield possession of their residence in order that construction might commence — Coster had not yet left the house for which Astor had paid such a high price. When Astor was informed of this fact he waited until noon. Coster was still in possession. "Has he left yet?" Astor enquired. "No? Well, never mind. Just start in tearing down the house anyhow. And — by the way — you might begin by taking away the steps!"[25] If this story is authentic, it indicates how Astor's love for a jest could triumph even over ill-health and domestic bereavement — the death of his wife and a number of other relatives during his absence in Europe.[26]

On April 4, 1834, Astor had "arrived in the packet ship *Utica* from Havre. . . . He comes," wrote Philip Hone, "in time to witness the pulling down of the block of houses next to that on which I live — the whole front Barclay to Vesey Street on Broadway — where he is going to erect a New York *palais royal*, which will cost him five or six hundred thousand dollars." On May 1 "Mr. Astor commenced . . . the demolition of the valuable building on the block . . . on which . . . his great hotel is to be erected. The dust and rubbish," Hone commented, "will be almost intolerable; but the establishment will be a great public advantage, and the edifice an ornament to the city, and for centuries to come will serve, as it was probably intended, as a monument of its wealthy proprietor." The writer was of the opinion that the building's entrance upon its function as a monument to its proprietor would probably not be long delayed. "I am sorry to observe," he wrote, "since Mr. Astor's return from Europe that his health is declining. He appears sickly and feeble, and I have some doubt if he will live to witness the completion of his splendid edifice." Hone's anticipations as to the discomfort from the dust consequent to the demolition of Astor's buildings were completely fulfilled, but by the middle of May nearly all this part of the work had been completed.[27]

As early as the spring of 1832, Isaiah Rogers, who had acted as architect for the Tremont Hotel in Boston,[28] had been employed to draw up the plans for the hotel. These had not been completed before the fall of the succeeding year.[29] Rogers and William W. Berwick of Newburgh, New York, had been appointed superintendents.[30] Late in December, 1833, Woodruff, Storms, Campbell & Adams had been awarded the contract.[31] All this had been done during Astor's absnece in Europe. Astor returned, however, in time to be present at the laying of the corner-stone of the hotel on July 4, 1834. The dimensions of the building on Broadway were to be 201 feet and one inch, on Barclay Street, 154 feet, on Vesey Street, 146 feet and 6 inches. It was to consist of 6 stories, and the height to the top of the cornice was to be 77 feet. In the center was to be a courtyard, 105 feet by 76, and 4 columns were to stand at the Broadway entrance. The fronts were to be of blue Quincy granite.[32] The hotel was completed by the spring of 1836, though the Astors were constantly forced to wave their contract in the faces of the contractors in order to enforce its provisions.[33]

Astor had never considered having the hotel managed for his own account [34] and early in 1835 it had been let to S. & F. Boyden, managers of the Tremont Hotel at Boston, who, being progressively minded, suggested that it might be well to increase "the number of bathing-rooms at the Hotel, at present 10, to 17."[35] The hotel was to contain "three hundred rooms each furnished with black walnut."[36] Astor did not object to this increase in the number of bathrooms if the Boydens would pay the extra expenses, and in various other connections he called on the Boydens to pay for certain fittings of the building. By the middle of April the Park Hotel was nearly ready for occupancy. The lower floor was to contain eighteen shops, of which five were to be occupied by tailors, one by barbers, one by a wigmaker and hairdresser, while the others were devoted to the sale of jewelry, hats, cutlery, books, pianofortes, trusses, soda-water, drugs, medicines, clocks, "fancy plated goods," gold leaf, and fancy drygoods.[37]

Although this hotel was built by John Jacob Astor, it did not long remain in his possession, for as early as January 28, 1834, he had conveyed the ground on which it was to stand to his son, William B. Astor, for "one Spanish milled dollar."[38] However, it was John Jacob Astor who on May 21, 1835, leased the hotel for seven years to Simeon and Frederick Boyden at $16,000 for the first year, $17,000 for the second, $18,000 for the third, and $20,500 for the rest, payable monthly.[39] They were also to pay for the furniture, part of the funds for which Astor would advance. Astor also rented the hotel shops, which were not included in the above lease, at about $1,250 yearly, to be paid quarterly, on a 5-years lease.[40] The Astor has been described as "at once a duplication and elaboration of the Tremont, made of the same materials, designed by the same architect, Rogers, and run by the Boyden family."[41] But though in this case, as in others, Astor showed that his mind was of an eclectic rather than an inventive nature, he also demonstrated that it possessed powers of combination which were truly creative in quality; consequently, though he copied the innovations of the Tremont, he improved on them and added certain "machine-age features" which were the wonder of the community and enabled the hotel to maintain till long past Astor's death the pre-eminence which at one bound it had assumed upon its opening on May 31, 1836.[42]

It is evident that Astor did not make a great deal of money out of the hotel, which, soon after its opening, he valued at $750,000, since during the term of the first 7-years lease he received an annual rent of only about $20,000. When the Boydens' lease expired, one of the clerks, Charles A. Stetson, became their successor. It is said that the success of his application was due to his boast that "he was a hotel-keeper, not a tavern-keeper, and would run the Astor House in first-class hotel style. When Astor asked him to define a hotel-keeper, he said: 'A hotel-keeper is a gentleman who stands on a level with his guests.'" This answer took Astor's fancy and Stetson was the leaseholder of the hotel up to and after Astor's death,[43] paying an annual rental of $30,000 for the hotel,[44] which was then estimated as worth $600,000.[45]

Astor's interest in transportation during the first forty years and more of his life in America had been rather casual. True, his vessels frequently conveyed goods as freight for other merchants and, more rarely, carried passengers, but under normal conditions his ships had not made freight or passenger service a major activity. In 1826, however, at about the same time that he disposed of the last of his China vessels, he became interested in advancing a form of inland transportation, the canal. On July 19, 1826, the New York newspapers announced that "the Ohio Canal Loan of one million dollars has been contracted for by Mr. J. J. Astor, who gave a premium for six per cent. stock." In 1830 he was one of the bidders for the Chemung Canal Loan, offering a premium of 10 27/100 per

The Astor House about 1871

cent for 5 per cent stock payable in 1830. However, he was outbid by several of the others, the highest premium, offered by the State Bank of Albany, being 12½ per cent.[46]

Much more definite and direct was his connection with a more recent form of land transportation, through the Mohawk and Hudson Railroad, the forerunner of the New York Central, which was incorporated in 1826. The original number of shares was 3,000, of which Astor held 500, being the second-largest shareholder. On May 29, 1828, he was elected as one of the nine directors, and on January, 1829, was appointed as a member of the committee "to report on the measures which will be proper to be taken preparatory to commencing the construction of the Rail Road." On account of ill-health, he declined to accept this latter appointment, but on May 25 was again elected a director. On July 14 and 21 he was present at directors' meetings, and on September 25 attended a meeting of the stockholders at which his motion carried that further proceedings in relation to the report of the committee "to examine and report a proper location for the railroad" be suspended until a future meeting.[47]

In the meantime Astor had been in correspondence with Gerrit Smith on this subject. On August 7, 1829, he wrote: "about the Rail Road I am in hopes it will be got in hands that will mak it go Mr. Fearsthon[haugh] has Resignd & nothng more to Do with it I will writ to you more fully ere long & hope you will be com Intrestd." On September 9 Astor wrote: "what will be Done about the Rail Road will your pepol of Schencetady give tham what Land thy may want as an Inducement. no Doubt it will benefit Schenectady. I Trust it will go on provited we can get money anoph to go on with & that those who will be benefited by it will act with liberality." It was evidently this consideration which led Astor later in the month to suggest that decision upon the location of the railroad be postponed.

On November 21 Astor wrote Smith urging him to become concerned in the railroad. "Mr. Featherstonehaugh," he wrote, "has no more Interest he is no langer dercitor nor even Stock holder and all the Stock except 30,000$ worth is taking up by good men who will pay the Deriction is agood ane & we are going to have agood Engineer and I think all promises well we have Secerd or nearly So all the Real property which we Shall have acation for an faire terms now if you are Still of the mind to take 20 or 25000$ worth of the Stock you can have it provited you writ Imedeally & I will loan you the Moy as you propasd — the stock can now Readely be Disposd off in Deed there is none for Sale that I knaw of."[48] Gerrit Smith accordingly, after consulting his father, agreed in a letter written December 3, 1829, to take $25,000 worth of stock in the railroad, the stock to remain in Astor's hands as security with Smith paying interest thereon for a certain term of years, when, if excess of dividends over interest had not earlier extinguished the debt, he was to pay the balance and receive the stock.[49] Astor replied on December 21 that " 250 Shares . . . are engag[d] for you of the parit which belongd to M[r]. Featherston hough . . . you Speck about Mismanagement So fare its Bade a nough but I Do belive there will now be an end to it thy Spend 8 or 9000$ not much for it — altho this is considerabl its not muh matter because I Do thnk that 10 or 20,000$ ane Way or other So as we com Right at Last is of no consequence the objict will bare it. I am quit of opinion with you that the Stock will be the best in the State & I exspect next Sprig we Shall get Seriously about it —" Astor informed Smith that they were "in treaty with Mr. White for engineer," stated that the board would be glad to have Smith a member, and asked for his confidential opinion of Mr. De Graff as the company's agent and what compensation he should receive if selected. On February 22, 1830, Astor had to write Smith that "nothing has ben Done of late about the Rail Road." White had accepted another offer, but the company hoped to secure an engineer within two or three weeks. No commissioner had as yet been selected, and Astor did not favor De Graff for that position, both because he considered his terms — $1,500 annually — as too high and because in "Some buississ of the Road" he thought De Graff had "Showd him self the off handed man which you Describd." Astor was also worried "about getting the proper quantety of land at the Dermination of the Road at Albany." Astor, as he said, had been unable to secure the 250 shares which he had originally intended for Smith, and so let him have that amount from his own subscription. On March 6 they were still "about to engage an Engeneer."

Within a week, however, matters had begun to develop with considerably greater rapidity. John B. Jervis was engaged as engineer, Astor wrote to Smith, "but we can only have half his time for the first year & Shall comence 1 May next . . . no Doubt our Rail Road will Do well—," he continued. "Can you tell me if we can find at this Season timber Ready Cutt—"[50] On May 22, 1830, Astor, Lynde Catlin, and James Renwick "were appointed a standing committee to carry into effect the objects of the incorporation. It would seem that Jervis mapped out the location and this committee approved it." On the same day, by Astor's motion, "Churchill C. Cambreling, of New York, then a member of Congress from that city, and a close business associate of Mr. Astor, was appointed commissioner of the Company, and Astor, Catlin, and Renwick were appointed a committee to confer with him 'with power to assign his duty and fix the terms of his engagement.'"[51]

During the construction period the stock experienced a rapid rise [52] and early in March, 1831, was "selling . . . at 60 pt advance — & is Susposed will go higher —"[53] "On March 31, 1831, on motion of Mr. Astor, the Board appointed C. C. Cambreling 'Commissioner of the Company with a compensation of two thousand dollars.'"[54] On August 9, 1831, the road was opened to the public,[55] and during that fall its stock rose to 174.[56] Astor, however, who had originally held 500 shares [57] and who "at one time during the construction period owned as many as seven hundred and forty-five shares, almost one-fourth of the entire capital stock,"[58] had by September 15, 1831, disposed of all but 180,[59] we might expect at a considerable advance, though late in January, 1832, he made the strange statement, "I was a large subscriber to the stock, but I am not so much interested, having given most of it to different persons at par."[60]

Astor took part in securing from the legislature in the spring of 1832 an act authorizing "the Mohawk and Hudson to construct a branch from its railroad at or near its intersection with the great western turnpike to Capital Square in albany and thence to the Albany base," in which branch the Albany and Schenectady Turnpike Company, which had threatened competition, was to be allowed to have an interest.[61] The threat of competition followed by "our Bargain with the Albany people" had, in Astor's opinion, as he wrote early in March, 1832, "reduced the Stock . . . very much indeed." A month before he had stated that "our Rail Road is down to 31 @ 32,"[62] meaning that much above par as compared to a previous high point of $196\frac{3}{4}$ in the middle of the previous Septebmer.[63] At the time that Astor expressed his misgivings of the Albany bargain the stock stood at 22 above par, but late in the month it was up to $28\frac{1}{2}$. This did not raise Astor's spirits very much, and on April 2 he made this comment in a letter to Gerrit Smith: "I note what you say about Rail Road — every thing does well, if well managed I wish yourself and some other clever men with you had it."[64]

As we have said before, however, Astor had already disposed of most of his stock, though in late August, 1832, he still had $20,000 worth at 15 per cent to $15\frac{1}{2}$ per cent premium, which was still on the rise, in spite of the fact that "no dividend has been made from the earnings of the Road." In October, 1835, Astor was offering 100 shares at $130 or more, and in February, 1836, he was trying to sell 50 shares at 112 per cent or more, cash. In July of the next year he declined to purchase any of the bonds of the company.[65] This seems to have ended his connection with the Mohawk and Hudson Railroad. Even had Astor not sold a large share of his holdings late in 1831, his departure for France on June 20, 1832, to be absent from New York for nearly two years, would have prevented his re-election as director in 1832.

The services which Astor performed for the first railroad in New York State may be summed up in the words of the historian of the New York Central: "John Jacob Astor . . . was one of the chief promoters of the Mohawk and Hudson; was elected a director in 1828, 1829, 1830, and 1831, and during this period he attended fifty-one meetings of the directors, thirty-eight of which were held at his house in New York City. He served upon committees and was chairman of the general or executive committee in charge of the construction of the road. Besides being a subscriber to a large number of shares of stock, he assisted the enterprise financially, at one time loaning it $35,000."[66] Though his connection with the project was brief in point of time, it was none the less valuable.

Astor was also concerned in a minor way with one of the railroads which later became part of the Pennsylvania system. The Delaware and Raritan Canal Company and the Camden and Amboy Railroad Company were both incorporated in New Jersey on February 4, 1830.[67] Astor became the owner of 80 shares of the canal company's stock and 70 of that of the railroad,[68] their total value being $15,000. On February 15, 1831, the two companies united to avoid competition, although "they kept up their separate organizations and kept separate accounts." The Philadelphia and Trenton Railroad Company was chartered by Pennsylvania on February 23, 1832, and "secured a majority of stock of the Trenton Bridge Company and the Trenton and New Brunswick Turnpike Company, and seemed to menace the monopoly between Philadelphia and New York." To overcome this, Captain Robert F. Stockton, president of the Delaware and Raritan Canal Company, "bought up sufficient stock in the Philadelphia and Trenton Company to control it and thus remove the menace."[69] The stockholders in the joint companies seem to have been invited to become interested to a certain proportion of their shares in the Philadelphia and Trenton Company; and accordingly Astor on May 23, 1836, sent John Naglee, president of the Philadelphia and Trenton Railroad Company, a check for $6,300 in payment for 50 shares of stock in his company.[70] By April 10, 1837, Astor had increased his holdings in the Camden and Amboy Railroad Company to $50,000, the stock selling at $135 and paying a dividend of 12 per cent, and was also "in treaty for . . . three hundred thousand dollars in Bonds" of that railroad. However, "in consequence of the suspension of specie pay[ts]. by our banks, the Camden & Amboy Co, declined carrying the agreement into effect, and my father," William B. Astor wrote, "did not get the bonds."[71] We learn nothing further concerning Astor's connection with the joint companies, but from early in 1837 to his death in 1848 he received semiannual dividend payments from the Philadelphia and Trenton Railroad Company of from $200 to $300, usually, it would seem, of $250 or $300.[72] This probably does not give anything like a complete picture of Astor's connection with these transportation lines. During 1838 he loaned the president of the Delaware and Raritan Canal Company $150,000, doubtless for the use of the Company, receiving 100 shares of stock in the Camden and Amboy Railroad Company as part security.[73]

It is evident that, after Astor had withdrawn from the directorship in the Mohawk and Hudson, he did not pay a great deal of attention to railroads. In October, 1834, he wrote to a man in Ohio, who seems to have been projecting a railroad to that section of the country, that he did not believe there was "enough of Public Spirit" in New York to make his enterprise successful. He also said that there was "a general want of Confidence in Rail Roads or Rail Road Stock which after more experience, more knowledge & better management may be restored — If the Rail Road to Utica succeeds or is likely to do so, which will soon be ascertained, it will help yours — much —."[74] The "Rail Road to Utica" to which Astor referred was that projected by the Utica and Schenectady Railroad Company, incorporated April 29, 1833, of which Erastus Corning was the leading spirit.[75] Astor showed his "Public Spirit" in assisting in the establishment of this road through lending it money. In 1835 he loaned Erastus Corning, president of the Company, and other directors, $100,000 at 6 per cent interest on their bond, taking 1,484 shares of stock as security. Nearly two-thirds of this bond had been paid off by August, 1838, but from 1845 to 1848 Astor was still receiving interest of $437.50 every three months from Corning on a bond from Corning and Alonzo C. Paige for which he held 371 shares as security. He also received interest of $176.89 at the same intervals from Paige on a bond from Paige and Corning for which his security was 150 shares.[76]

Astor did not restrict his connection with the Utica and Schenectady Railroad to lending money to its directors on the security of its stock. On October 26, 1835, he ordered the firm of Gallatin Brothers to purchase 100 shares of "Utica & Schenectady Rl. Stock, if at 11 per cent," and on the 30th ordered the purchase of "200 . . . shares Utica & Schenectady Rail Road Stock . . . at 13 per cent." On November 12 he ordered another 200 shares "if you can get them at a price not to exceed 10 per Ct."[77] Construction had begun early in the year and at this time "work was . . . being rushed."[78] On March 5, 1836, William B. Astor ordered another broker, John

Warren, to "buy for account of my father 200 . . . shares Utica at or about 25 per cent and sell them at 28 per cent or thereabout 60 d/s agreeably to your suggestion yesterday."[79] On August 26, 1837, Astor ordered Gallatin Brothers to purchase 100 shares for his account "at or about 16 1/4 per cent."[80] The road had been "opened for operation" on August 1, 1836.[81] It is easy to see that Astor's interest in this road was more or less speculative. In the early summer of 1847, however, he still owned 200 shares of stock, and was applying for that proportion of an increase in the stock to which his holdings would give him the right to subscribe. This would be 78 shares.[82]

After purchasing some shares in the Utica and Schenectady Railroad in 1835, Astor did not for some time show much further interest in railroads as a field of investment. On September 15, 1836, he wrote George H. McWhorter of Oswego: "I am much obliged to you for your polite invitation for me to become a subscriber to the railroad, but regret that I have not the means to avail myself of the opportunity of doing so."[83] The Panic of 1837 made Astor still less inclined to look with favor upon railroads. On June 24, 1837, William B. Astor wrote to a correspondent in Paris, whose investments the Astors seem to have been handling: "My father requests me to say that he cannot recommend you to purchase stock in any of our Rail Road Co⁸, as he is not satisfied that they would prove good investments and believes them to be rather uncertain as to profit and somewhat speculative in character."[84] In the late summer of 1841 Gerrit Smith called Astor's attention to "the Syracuse & Oswego Rail Road Stock," but the latter was "not disposed to invest in it."[85]

By 1847, however, Astor was more convinced of the possibility of railroads proving profitable investments and in that year subscribed for $10,000 worth of the stock of the Hudson River Railroad Company, expressing his willingness to purchase an additional $5,000 worth of stock, should it be necessary to do so in order to secure the building of the road. Consequently the extra amount was purchased for his account. He followed this up by suggesting that the Company lease some of his land for a depot.[86] This seems to have ended Astor's attention to railroads — a field of investment in which he had once manifested considerable interest but from which advancing age had caused him largely to withdraw, as indeed had been the case with many other forms of business enterprise.

Another form of investment in which Astor became interested, especially in his later years, was the stock of municipal and State governments as well as that of the United States. One of the earliest evidences of such an interest appeared in an agreement which ran: "On the fifteenth day of July next, I promise to receive from Mr. Griffith Evans or order two thousand five hundred dollars, six per cent stock of the United States, and pay him or order at the rate of twenty-five shillings one penny and three farthings on the pound. Philadelphia, the 4th January, 1792. JOHN JACOB ASTOR."[87] A little over a score of years later Astor was able to lend the government nearly a thousand times the amount of this early investment, in connection with the financial crisis caused by the War of 1812, which transaction we have already examined in detail.

Astor's interest in loans to the government of the United States continued to the end of his life. In the early 1830's he was trying to purchase United States stock through his London agents. In March, 1832, he wrote, "I have no doubt but our Government will very soon, perhaps on 1 July next pay off the 3 per cent Stock. If you can buy 1 or 200.000$ of them at 86 or 87 for joint account I would like it — charge no commission here or there —"[88] Concerning this same stock he wrote to his son-in-law, Vincent Rumpff, in April, saying, "The 3 per cent stock [of the United States] will be paid in October. . . . I think it safe, it is at least as much so as any local Stock we have – I take myself $250,000 of it."[89]   In August, 1834, he again requested the London firm to "purchase for me Some United States 5 pC^t. Stock, if to be had at 91 . . . in money be it 1/4 pr. Ct. more or less — to the extent of five or six thousand pounds worth."[90]   We have no record that the London firm succeeded in procuring the desired stock.   In March, 1836, Astor instructed Hottinguer & Co., of Paris, to "sell for me the 5 & 3 per cent stock of which I left certificates with you — say 220.000 francs 5 per cents and 200.000 francs 3 per cents.   I am willing to leave to your better judgement whether to sell on receipt of this, or wait some short time."[91]

Astor's interest in United States stock was much more active during the next decade.   In 1847 and 1848 he requested his Washington correspondent to "receive the interest due . . . on 5798\frac{30}{100}$ Stock in my name (Mexican claim) at 5 per cent $144.96," this being for six months.[92]   Through this same firm Astor tried to buy in June, 1847, from "$25,000 to $50,000 Treasury Notes of the last Loan," and later in the month wrote, "I . . . will take $20,000 say Twenty thousand Dollars Treasury notes of the last loan, at the price you name, 106. I take the notes as an Investment."   In the following month he offered to buy "from $80,000 to $100,000 United States six per cent Treasury notes of the last loan."[93]   It was probably some of the treasury notes purchased through Corcoran & Riggs which Astor sent, to the value of $25,000, in September, 1847, to the register of the Treasury to be exchanged for United States 6 per cent stock.[94]   His grandson, John Jacob Astor, Jr., in March, 1848, acting for his grandfather, sent $10,000 worth of treasury notes to the register of the Treasury to be exchanged for United States 6 per cent stock, payable in 1867.[95]   In September, 1847, Astor desired "$43000 @ 95000$ United States 6 with Interest from 1 July last payable on receipt of the Stock here immediately and also the lowest price for $100,000 receivable & payable 4th Octr prox."   Astor was able to purchase at least $20,000 of United States 6 per cent stock of 1867.[96]

It is probable that most, if not all, of these transactions in United States stock in the late 1840's were inspired by Astor's desire to establish trust funds for some of his children and grandchildren. In May, 1847, William B. Astor sent certificates of United States 6 per cent stock, loan of 1842 (redeemable in 1862), to the amount of $130,000, loan of 1846 (redeemable in 1856), $50,000, and loan of 1847 (redeemable in 1868), $25,000 — a total of $205,000 — to the register of the Treasury to be transferred from his father to himself.[97] In January, 1848, Astor sent $20,000 of United States 6 per cent stock, loan of 1842, payable in 1862, to Washington to be exchanged for fresh certificates, and the same amount of stock in the loan of 1847 for the same purpose. In the next month he had $100,000 of United States 6 per cent stock (redeemable in 1867) transferred to a trust fund for his grandchildren Mrs. Louisa D. Kane and Mrs. Eliza Wilks.[98] It will thus be seen that during the last year of his life Astor transferred well over $250,000 of United States stock, recently purchased, to some of his descendants, either directly or in trust. He probably also owned a good deal of United States stock not included in this amount.

It will be remembered that Astor in 1832 received more than $500,000 in New York State 5 per cent stock in payment for his rights in the Morris estate. Almost at once the State comptroller, Silas Wright, offered to buy from $70,000 to $80,000 of this stock and enquired of Astor what premium he would take.[99] Astor left this question to his agent, Dudley Selden, telling him that if the State Bank of Albany would give 6½ per cent or 7 per cent for $70,000 to $80,000 for two years the premium required for the stock might be decreased somewhat.[100] Three days later Astor agreed to sell $80,000 of stock at ¾ per cent premium [101] and late in the month sent Thomas W. Olcott, cashier of the Mechanics and Farmers Bank, Albany, a power to receive interest on the stock and to transfer it. Olcott accordingly collected the quarterly interest payments, which after the sale to Wright amounted to $5,627.77 on $450,221.88. In 1838 there was transferred to William B. Astor $200,000 of this stock, and in 1846 all the rest was similarly turned over to Astor's son and heir.[102]

Astor also invested in New York State stock other than that derived from the Morris claim. Some of this he endeavored to dispose of from time to time during the 1830's, usually in London. In September, 1834, he sent Thomas Wilson, in London, "$20,669.$\frac{15}{}$ State Stock," due in 1845, 1847, and 1850, to be sold at 7 per cent premium, expressing the hope that the stock which had longer to run might bring a higher price than the rest.[103] At the same time he sent to another London firm, Gillespies, Moffat, Finlay & Co., "sundry Certificates of 5 p^r C^t Stock of this State amounting to $20,000" to be sold at "about 107 p^r C^t," the other instructions being similar to those in regard to the other consignment.

During the next three years Astor occasionally wrote his London agent, giving instructions and urging sales. Late in November, 1834, he acknowledged "sales of $5000 New-York 5 per Cent Stock. The price is less than I expected. Prices being better here, I defer sending you any more at present."[104] This sale reduced the stock held by Gillespies, Moffat, Finlay & Co. to $15,000. Thomas Wilson & Co. did not meet with even the slight success of the other firm. Late in November, 1834, Astor wrote, "I . . . note that the demand for American stocks is lessened with you. I will therefore defer sending any New York fives for the present." In March of the next year he wrote, "I note you had not then [January 22] disposed of my 5 per cent stock. . . . I think you will do as well to sell my five per cent stock as soon as may be after the 1st. of April say dividend off," and in June repeated, "I wish you to make sale of my New York State 5 per cent Stock." In April of the next year his tone became more peremptory. "I regret to see you had not [February 13] disposed of my New York 5 per Ct State Stock. I will thank you to make sale of them, if even somewhat below par." Something over a year later, in the emergency caused by the Panic of 1837, he lost all patience and ordered Thomas Wilson & Co. to turn over his stock to Gillespies, Moffat, Finlay & Co.,[105] to whom he recommended "a speedy sale (if it can be done without too great a sacrifice)," not knowing that the other firm had about this time succeeded in disposing of the stock at 92.[106] About the same time, in April, 1837, and probably for the same reason, Astor informed a New York broker, John Warren, "you are authorized to sell for my account $30.000 New York State Fives of '45 at a price not less than 98 per cent."[107] We hear nothing more of this New York State stock.

Astor did not confine his investments in State stocks to those of his own commonwealth. He was probably most interested in Ohio. We have already mentioned his interest in Ohio canals. These improvements were financed by the State, and an interesting story which has at least some basis in fact is told by Scoville concerning the way in which Astor's investments in Ohio stocks came to be made. Speaking of one of Astor's friends in the business world, this author writes:

John Robins was once associated with John Jacob Astor, Nathaniel Prime and John Hone, as a committee to examine into the condition of a proposed loan asked for by the State of Ohio, to carry on her internal improvements. That great State had witnessed the success of the Erie Canal in this, and became anxious to follow in the track. Commissioners came on to Wall street to raise money. The subject was referred to the above persons. The true reason why Ohio state credit is to this day better than any other Western state, is doubtless due to the report of these financial gentlemen, and to the advice they gave the legislature of Ohio.

The Commissioners first applied to old Nat Prime, of the great house of Prime, Ward & King. He selected the other names, Robins, Hone and Astor. The Ohio agents left all their papers with these men, and they spent one night and day in a room together, carefully examining every document and with fidelity searching into the true condition of Ohio. . . . They reported unanimously in favor of loaning to Ohio every dollar she asked for, providing the legislature of that state would insert in the law creating said loan a clause prepared by them relative to taxation, such as had been agreed upon by the four rich men, who stated that if this suggestion was perfected, the money should be had — the loan should be made.

The Ohio agents called at the time appointed to hear the report. Old Mr. Prime told them what was wanted to be made a law. That night the agents started for the capital of Ohio. The legislature was in session. That body promptly amended the law, as suggested by the money kings of Wall street. The agents again returned to New York, and got all the money Ohio wanted; and her credit has been A 1 from that until now.[108]

Whatever may be the truth as to Astor's twenty-four hours' vigil spent in investigating the financial condition of Ohio, we know that he did invest heavily in her stock. On July 20, 1826, he purchased $800,000 of Ohio 6 per cent stock, payable in 1850, and on October 8, 1828, he became the owner of another $300,000.[109] That Ohio's credit was indeed "A 1" a few years later is revealed by letters of January, 1832, to one of the London firms in correspondence with Astor, accompanying $6,800 of Ohio stock to be sold at 121½ to 122; it was then on the rise, and in March of that year he stated that "Ohio 6 per ct Stock is at 126 per cent to 127." In the Panic of 1837 Astor decided to sell some of his stock-holdings and accordingly in April and May of that year sent this same firm $50,000 of Ohio 6 per cent stock to sell at any price above par, remarking in a letter of May 10, announcing the suspension of specie payments, that "Ohio 6 per cents are much in demand." According to custom, Astor had drawn certain bills on the firm to which he had sent the stock, and they, apparently alarmed by the financial situation in the United States, took it upon themselves to sell some of the stock at a lower rate than Astor had prescribed. In a letter of July he remonstrated with them for this action, saying, "I . . . note . . . that you had sold $5000 of Ohio at 98. I will be as well pleased if you have not sold any more unless at a much higher price." But the end was not yet, and a month later Astor was writing in a tone of somewhat stronger disapproval, "I am sorry to see that you had sold $10,000 of my Ohio Stock at 93½ which I think you had no authority to do, at least not for more than enough to put you in funds to pay the Bills I drew on you." Later in the month his tone became righteously indignant as he exclaimed, "you advise the sale of 10,000 6 per cent Ohio at 94 1/2. I cannot express to you my surprize at the sale, and I cannot but believe that . . . you will consider me entitled to some remuneration." Late in December he concluded, "I see no satisfactory reason . . . for having sold some of my Ohio six per cents as you have done. The $25m unsold you will please return to me."[110] Astor did not lose interest in Ohio stocks till the end of his life. In February, 1846, he wrote to the brokers Ebbets Brothers to "please purchase, for my account, Ten thousand dollars Ohio Six per cents,"[111] and in July, 1847, his son wrote to John Ward & Co., "By your Bill I see the last Ohio Stock is considered as bought for me. It is for account of my father and you will please have it transferred accordingly."[112]

Astor also invested largely in Pennsylvania stock. In August, 1836, he announced, "I purchased of the Bank of Philadelphia $90.000 5 per cents Pennsylvania Stock."[113] This, however, was by no means all he came to own of the stocks of this State. Ten years later, January, 1846, William B. Astor wrote to Robert Neilson, at Philadelphia, "my father desires you to be pleased to receive the interest due on his Pennsylvania stock . . . Six per cents $25,000 $750. Five per cents 223.090.54 $5577.26."[114] In other words, near the end of his life he owned little less than a quarter-million dollars of Pennsylvania stocks; nor did these satisfy him, for in February, 1846, he instructed John Ward & Co. to "please purchase for my account, ten thousand dollars Pennsylvania five per cents,"[115] though a year later, when, owing to financial difficulties, the interest had to be paid in relief notes, he remarked disgustedly through his son, "I am sorry to learn that they paid it in such trash."[116]   In April, 1847, less than a year before Astor's death, William B. Astor instructed the cashier of the Bank of Pennsylvania to transfer to him "Pennsylvania State stock standing in the name of my father."[117]

Astor invested lesser, yet quite substantial, sums in the stocks of other States. Late in March, 1832, he mentioned in a letter to Thomas Wilson & Co., London, "a Loan . . . about to be authorized by the State of Louisiana in which I contemplate (if here) to become interested, and count that you will the same." Early in May he wrote to the same firm, "you will receive by this, the Bonds for interest on $90,000 Louisiana Bonds (Wilson's) due the 1ˢᵗ July and 1ˢᵗ January next, which amount $4500 equal to £1012.10/ stg: you will please pass to credit of my account." In April, 1836, he sent this firm Louisiana bond warrants amounting to $3,400,[118] having in April, 1834, cashed twenty-two bonds of $1,000 each.[119]

Astor also owned £13,000 in Massachusetts 5 per cent sterling bonds, on which he semiannually received $1,560 interest, received through Josiah Quincy, Jr., treasurer of the Western Railroad Company, for the assistance of which these bonds had been voted.[120]

We also get a glimpse of investment in Indiana stocks. In August, 1834, Astor wrote to Prime, Ward & King, "I recᵈ. your communication of yesterday by which I understand that I am interested with you in the Indiana Loan Say one third of $200.000. The payment for it will be provided and ready on the day wanted."[121] Late in the next decade, less than a year before Astor's death, his son wrote to Robert Neilson, at Philadelphia: "I understand that no advance in money will be required on the Wabash and Erie Canal Bonds (of which your Indiana bonds form a part) by the state of Indiana in accepting the offer it makes for an exchange of new bonds paying interest for the present ones. I have almost concluded to exchange my father's bonds for the new ones."[122]

Astor on at least two different occasions purchased stocks and bonds of Missouri. In December, 1832, William B. Astor requested Pierre Chouteau, Jr., to collect dividends, probably for only half a year, due since July 1: "the amount due on the Stock held by my father is $2625 together with 5 months interest on the same, which please receive."[123] In the summer of 1838 Astor purchased from a Mr. Thomas 100 bonds of the State of Missouri, all of the same but unspecified denomination.[124] In October, 1846, he informed the governor of Missouri that the State of Missouri, having renewed its 10 per cent bonds for 5 years, had no right to pay them off till the end of the term. However, Astor would trade for 8 per cent bonds, bearing the guarantee of the Bank of Missouri, though if others were allowed to retain the 10 per cent bonds he would insist on the same privilege.[125] In June, 1847, he refused to take Missouri bonds.[126]

Astor was also in 1847 the owner of some Maryland sterling 5 per cent bonds on which the interest had remained unpaid from July 1, 1843, to July 1, 1847, or for four years, amounting to £900, or $4,236. Stock was issued to the amount of this unpaid interest and placed in a trust fund for the children of Astor's nephew Joseph Astor.[127] Astor's holdings must have been £4,500.

From this fragmentary account of Astor's investments in State stocks during less than a score of years at the end of his life, it is evident that his holdings during most of this time must have amounted to over $2,000,000 — more than a million in Ohio stocks, about half a million in those of New York, a quarter-million in Pennsylvania stocks, and the rest in those of other States. The interest on these stocks at the lowest estimate must have amounted to $100,000 annually.

Astor invested comparatively small sums in the bonds of various cities. In 1836 he purchased $15,000 of bonds in the city of Rochester, "created for the purpose of erecting a Market there."[128] On this stock he received the semiannual interest of $525.[129] Astor also owned bonds of the city of Detroit, 6 per cent bonds on which he received a semiannual interest of $750 and 7 per cent which brought him $340.20. His total holdings were, then, about $35,000.[130] As might be expected, Astor invested heavily in the stock of his own city. In 1828, with Prime, Ward, King & Co., he offered 4½ per cent advance for $416,900 of 5 per cent New York City stocks, which offer was accepted. In June, 1834, his son stated, "Neither my father nor myself are desirous to sell the stock we hold of the Corporation of this City."[131] Among the assets mentioned in Astor's will were $100,000 in New York City 5 per cent bonds and $50,000 New Haven 5½ per cent bonds.[132]

From his extensive investments in railroad, canal, insurance, bank, United States, State, and city stocks, Astor naturally acquired an intimate knowledge of their values, which in turn caused a demand for his services as a broker. This, however, probably never took any other form than a private accommodation for a few old and intimate friends and business associates. Early in 1832 he wrote Thomas Wilson of London: "if you find convenient I would rather that you appoint some other friend to receive this dividend for you — it is not on account of the compensation but rather on my contemplated retirement."[133] However, till nearly the end of Astor's life he continued to collect dividends and make investments for such individuals and firms as his son-in-law, Vincent Rumpff, at Paris, Ellice, Kinnear & Co., of London, C. W. Lutteroth, at Paris, William H. Burnley, of Trinidad, and Robert Neilson, at Philadelphia, charging one per cent for collection and the same percentage for investment.[134] However, these transactions were probably more of a personal than of a business nature.

Looking back over these miscellaneous business activities, we can observe certain tendencies. In the early periods of Astor's investments in railroads, banks, and insurance companies, he took a direct part as a member of their boards of directors in working for the success of these enterprises, but about the time of his withdrawal from the fur trade and foreign commerce in 1834, a little before or after this time, he ceased to exert any personal influence on the companies in which his money was invested. His interest in hotels and railroads did not begin till about the time he withdrew from commerce carried on in his own vessels, which took place about 1825, and seems to have been intended to occupy that portion of his mind which had previously been concerned with his shipping interest. His personal attention to his theater and hotels, being connected with the major interest of his later years, Manhattan Island real estate, continued, slight though it was, until the end. During Astor's last years two other tendencies appeared. One was to buy largely of State stocks, a field of investment which seemed fairly safe and therefore required little personal attention and which usually paid substantial interest; another was to transfer large blocks of stock to his descendants, either directly or through trustees. During the last decade of Astor's life his business was largely transacted by his son. It is to the period before his complete retirement from commerce that our interest in Astor's miscellaneous business activities is largely drawn. It will be observed that most of his interests in this period — hotels, banking, insurance, even railroads — were linked with Astor's major interests, the fur trade, foreign commerce, and real estate. Astor, though interested in steam transportation, had little or no concern with other developments, such as manufacturing, his only connection therewith, which can be discovered, being a loan of $60,000 at 7 per cent to the Matteawan Company made in 1834 for the purpose of expanding its textile mills.[135] Yet even with this limitation, the variety of his miscellaneous business interests and the prominent part he played in connection with some of them is a tribute to the breadth and vigor of his mind even when he was at the age of three-score-and-ten.

NOTES

1. Parton, James, *Life of John Jacob Astor* (1865), p. 50.
2. Irving, Washington, *Astoria* (1836), chap. xi.
3. Ms. book, Hall of Records, N. Y., Liber Conveyances 72, p. 514.
4. Ms. book, Baker Library, Astor Papers, Letter Book i, 1813–15, p. 278, John Jacob Astor, N. Y., September 10, 1814, to John K. Beekman; p. 436, John Jacob Astor by F. W. Bentzon, January 19, 1815, to Thomas A. Cooper and Stephen Price.
5. *Minutes of the Common Council of the City of New York, 1784–1831,* vol. xi, p. 557, April 2, 30, 1821.
6. *Brevoort, Henry, Letters of, to Washington Irving,* George Hellman, ed., 2 vols. (1916), vol. i, pp. 134, 140.
7. Bonner, William Thompson, *New York: The World's Metropolis, 1623-4-1923-4* (1924), p. 472.
8. Ms. book, Office of the Astor Estate, N. Y., Untitled land book, about 1819, p. 55.
9. *Hone, Philip, The Diary of, 1828–1851,* Allan Nevins, ed., 2 vols. (1927), vol. i, p. 138. It has been said that Aaron Burr's house at Richmond Hill "was sold . . . to John Jacob Astor and was by him converted into the Richmond Hill Theater" which opened in 1831 (Wilson, James Grant, ed., *Memorial History of the City of New York, from its Settlement to 1892,* 4 vols. (1891–93), vol. iv, p. 483). This is an error. On November 23, 1836, Astor informed C. Du Bois, Treasurer of the Finance Committee of the House of Refuge, in reply to a letter from him dated the 21st, that "he is not and has not been the proprietor of the Richmond Hill Theatre" (ms. book, Baker Library, Astor Papers, Letter Book ii, 1831–38, p. 447. John Jacob Astor, N. Y., November 23, 1836, to C. Du Bois). It would be of interest to know what inspired Treasurer Du Bois's communication.
10. Ms. book, Office of the Astor Estate, N. Y., Untitled memorandum book.
11. *Ibid.,* Valuation of Houses & Lands, October, 1846.
12. *Hone, Philip, The Diary of, 1828–1851,* vol. ii, pp. 857, 860.
13. Williamson, Jefferson, *The American Hotel: An Anecdotal History* (1930), p. 31.
14. *New York Evening Post,* April 8, 1828, p. 2, col. 4; ms. book, Hall of Records, N. Y., Liber Conveyances 237, pp. 46, 48.
15. *New-York Gazette and General Advertiser,* June 9, 1817, p. 3.
16. *New York Commercial Advertiser,* April 25, 1833, p. 2, col. 4.
17. *Hone, Philip, The Diary of, 1828–1851,* vol. i, p. 91.
18. Ms. book, Hall of Records, N. Y., Liber Conveyances 391, p. 210.

19. Ms. book, Baker Library, Astor Papers, Letter Book iii, 1845-48, pp. 144, 145, 149, William B. Astor, N. Y., January 26, 26, February 2, 1847, to Nelson Sargent, Boston.

20. Ms. book, Office of the Astor Estate, N. Y., Untitled memorandum book; *ibid.*, Valuation of Houses & Lands, October, 1846.

21. Williamson, *op. cit.*, chap. i, note 23, quoting from the New York *Tribune*, March 30, 1848.

22. Irving, *op. cit.*, chap. ii.

23. Parton, *op. cit.*, p. 73.

24. Ms. book, Hall of Records, N. Y., Liber Conveyances 274, p. 60.

25. *Ibid.*, 308, p. 98; [Armstrong, William], *The Aristocracy of New York* (1848), p. 7; [Scoville, Joseph A.], *The Old Merchants of New York City*, 5 vols. (1889), vol. i, pp. 413-414; Parton, *op. cit.*, pp. 73-74.

26. *Hone, Philip, The Diary of, 1828-1851*, vol. i, p. 121.

27. *Ibid.*, pp. 121, 126, 127.

28. Ms. book, Baker Library, Astor Papers, Letter Book ii, 1831-38, p. 189, William B. Astor, N. Y., November 2, 1833, to John Dorr, Boston.

29. *Ibid.*, letters to Isaac Rogers, Boston.

30. *Ibid.*, letters to William W. Berwick, Newburgh, N. Y.

31. *Ibid.*, p. 195, W. B. Astor, N. Y., December 11, 1833, to W. W. Berwick, Newburgh, N. Y.

32. *Hone, Philip, The Diary of, 1828-1851*, vol. i, p. 133; *New York Evening Post*, July 8, 1834, p. 3, col. 1.

33. Ms. book, Baker Library, Astor Papers, Letter Book ii, 1831-38, letters to Philetus H. Woodruff and Peter J. Bogert.

34. *Ibid.*, p. 288, John Jacob Astor by William B. Astor, N. Y., March 13, 1835, to J. A. G. Otis, Boston (see below, vol. ii, pp. 1228-1229).

35. *Ibid.*, p. 344, John Jacob Astor by William B. Astor, November 2, 1833, to S. Boyden.

36. Bonner, *op. cit.*, p. 151.

37. Ms. book, Baker Library, Astor Papers, Letter Book ii, 1831-38, pp. 395-396, John Jacob Astor by William B. Astor, N. Y., April 13, 1836, to John Dorr, Boston.

38. Ms. book, Hall of Records, N. Y., Liber Conveyances 310, p. 484.

39. *Ibid.*, 356, p. 437.

40. *Ibid.*, 346, p. 54. Williamson says that "Boyden's lease was obtained at a compromise figure of $17,000 a year. Astor had wanted $20,000." (*Op. cit.*, chap. i, note 23.)

41. "Fitz-Greene Halleck, the poet, who was John Jacob Astor's secretary, used to say that Astor copied all the features of the Tremont, even locating his hotel in a block adjacent to a cemetery, so that guests might have prospects beyond the grave. The Astor was across the street from the St. Paul's churchyard on the Vesey Street side, while the Tremont

was adjacent to the Old Granary burying-ground." (Williamson, *op. cit.*, pp. 32–34.)

42. Those features of the Astor House which particularly impressed visitors as "astonishing" and even "incomprehensible" are described in great detail by Williamson (*op. cit.*, pp. 14, 22–23, 31–34, 63, 197, 207).

43. The story has been told that at a time when Stetson's lease was about to expire some Bostonians tried to hire the hotel over his head. "In a private interview with Mr. Astor, they wanted to know his terms. He replied, 'I will consult Mr. Stetson, and let you know. I always give my old tenants the preference.' To consult Mr. Stetson was to defeat the object they had in view, and they pressed it no farther." (Smith, Matthew Hale, *Sunshine and Shadow in New York* (1868), p. 71.)

44. Williamson, *op. cit.*, p. 141, and chap. i, note 23.

45. Ms. book, Office of the Astor Estate, N. Y., Valuation of Houses & Lands, October, 1846.

46. *New-York Gazette and General Advertiser*, July 19, 1826, p. 2, col. 2; July 22, 1830, p. 2, col. 1.

47. *Ibid.*, May 30, 1828, p. 2, col. 4; Stevens, Frank Walker, *The Beginnings of the New York Central Railroad* (1926), pp. 14, 15, 20, 23, 24, 398.

48. Ms., Syracuse University, Gerrit Smith Miller Collection, Letters, John Jacob Astor, N. Y., August 7, September 9, November 21, 1829, to Gerrit Smith, Peterboro.

49. *Ibid.* (copy), Gerrit Smith, Peterboro, December 3, 1829, to John Jacob Astor, N. Y.

50. *Ibid.*, John Jacob Astor, N. Y., December 21, 1829 (see below, vol. ii, pp. 1199–1200), February 22 (see below, vol. ii, pp. 1201–1202), March 6, 13, 1830, to Gerrit Smith, Peterboro.

51. Stevens, *op. cit.*, pp. 23, 30, 95, 108.

52. *The One Hundredth Anniversary (1826–April 17–1926) of The New York Central Railroad* (n. d.), p. 35.

53. Ms., Syracuse University, Gerrit Smith Miller Collection, Letters, John Jacob Astor, N. Y., March 5, 1831, to Gerrit Smith, Peterboro.

54. Stevens, *op. cit.*, p. 96.

55. *The New York Central Railroad, 1831–1915* (n. d.), p. 3.

56. *The One Hundredth Anniversary (1826–April 17–1926) of The New York Central Railroad*, p. 35.

57. Stevens, *op. cit.*, p. 24.

58. *The One Hundredth Anniversary (1826–April 17–1926) of The New York Central Railroad*, p. 3.

59. Stevens, *op. cit.*, p. 24.

60. Ms. book, Baker Library, Astor Papers, Letter Book ii, 1831–38, pp. 27–28, John Jacob Astor, N. Y., January 27, 1832, to Francis Granger, Albany (see below, vol. ii, pp. 1213–1214)

61. *Ibid.*; Stevens, *op. cit.*, p. 59.

62. Ms. book, Baker Library, Astor Papers, Letter Book ii, 1831–38, pp. 30–31, 35–36, John Jacob Astor, N. Y., February 4, March 5, 1832, to C. C. Cambreleng.

63. Stevens, *op. cit.*, p. 26.

64. Ms. book, Baker Library, Astor Papers, Letter Book ii, 1831–38, pp. 35–36, 38, John Jacob Astor, N. Y., March 5, 30, 1832, to C. C. Cambreleng, Philadelphia; pp. 39–40, John Jacob Astor, N. Y., April 2, 1832, to Gerrit Smith, Albany.

65. *Ibid.*, pp. 88–89, William B. Astor, N. Y., August 29, 1832, to George W. Erving, Washington; p. 374, William B. Astor, N. Y., February 12, 1836, to John Warren; p. 504, John Jacob Astor, N. Y., July 11, 1837, to Samuel Glover; p. 335, John Jacob Astor by William B. Astor, N. Y., October 5, 1835, to Gallatin Brothers.

66. Stevens, *op. cit.*, p. 398.

67. Wilson, William Bender, *History of the Pennsylvania Railroad Company*, 2 vols. (1899), vol. i, p. 218.

68. Ms. book, Baker Library, Astor Papers, Letter Book ii, 1831–38, p. 408, William B. Astor, N. Y., June 7, 1836, to John Naglee, President of the Philadelphia and Trenton Railroad Company; p. 404, John Jacob Astor by William B. Astor, N. Y., May 23, 1836, to John Naglee, Philadelphia.

69. Wilson, W. B., *op. cit.*, vol. i, pp. 219–223.

70. Ms. book, Baker Library, Astor Papers, Letter Book ii, 1831–38, p. 404, William B. Astor, N. Y., May 23, 1836, to John Naglee, Philadelphia.

71. *Ibid.*, pp. 480, 482, John Jacob Astor, N. Y., April 10, June 24, 1837, January 15, 1838, to Charles W. Lutteroth, Paris; p. 554, William B. Astor, N. Y., January 15, 1838, to Charles W. Lutteroth, Paris.

72. *Ibid.*, pp. 460, 556, 603, letters to John Naglee, Philadelphia; *ibid.*, Letter Book iii, 1845–48, pp. 3, 100, 142, 199, 260, letters to J. Morrell.

73. *Ibid.*, Letter Book ii, pp. 540–611, letters to Captain R. F. Stockton, December 4, 1837–August 28, 1838; p. 598, John Jacob Astor by William B. Astor, N. Y., July 10, 1838, to James Neilson, New Brunswick, N. J.

74. *Ibid.*, p. 262, John Jacob Astor, N. Y., October 13, 1834, to Joseph Vance, Urbana, Ohio.

75. Stevens, *op. cit.*, pp. 115–118.

76. Ms. book, Baker Library, Astor Papers, Letter Book ii, 1831–38, pp. 338, 376, 377, 384, 426, 428, 463, 510, 513, 563, 610, John Jacob Astor by William B. Astor, N. Y., October 16, 1835, February 23, March 14, August 23, 27, 1836, January 30, August 23, 29, 1837, February 15, August 20, 1838, to Erastus Corning, Albany; *ibid.*, Letter Book iii,

pp. 14, 40, 62, 81, 92, 93, 112, 113, 132, 160, 185, 186, 207, 245, John Jacob Astor by William B. Astor, N. Y., August 27, November 20, 1845, February 19, May 2, June 15, 20, August 31, September 3, November 28, 1846, February 26, May 29, June 2, August 18, December 7, 1847, to Erastus Corning, Albany; pp. 13, 39, 68, 114, 133, 161, 185, 187, 188, 208, 266, 269, 272, John Jacob Astor by William B. Astor, N. Y., August 22, November 20, 1845, March 13, September 4, November 30, 1846, March 6, May 29, June 7, 10, August 23, 1847, February 9, 19, 25, 1848, to Alonzo C. Paige, Schenectady.

77. *Ibid.*, Letter Book ii, 1831–38, pp. 342, 347, John Jacob Astor by William B. Astor, October 26, 30, November 12, 1835, to Gallatin Brothers.

78. Stevens, *op. cit.*, pp. 120–123.

79. Ms. book, Baker Library, Astor Papers, Letter Book ii, 1831–38, p. 381, William B. Astor, N. Y., March 5, 1836, to John Warren.

80. *Ibid.*, p. 512, John Jacob Astor by William B. Astor, N. Y., August 26, 1837, to Gallatin Brothers.

81. Stevens, *op. cit.*, p. 125.

82. Ms. book, Baker Library, Astor Papers, Letter Book iii, 1845–48, pp. 185, 186, John Jacob Astor by William B. Astor, N. Y., May 29, June 2, 1847, to Erastus Corning, Albany; p. 187, John Jacob Astor by William B. Astor, June 7, 1847, to A. C. Paige, Schenectady; p. 188, John Jacob Astor by William B. Astor, N. Y., June 10, 1847, to John V. L. Pruyn, Secretary, Utica and Schenectady Rail Road Company; p. 191, William B. Astor, N. Y., June 19, 1847, to Jacob Little & Co.

83. *Ibid.*, Letter Book ii, 1831–38, p. 432, John Jacob Astor, N. Y., September 15, 1836, to G. H. McWhorten, Oswego.

84. *Ibid.*, pp. 497–498, William B. Astor, N. Y., June 24, 1837, to C. W. Lutteroth, Paris.

85. Ms. book, Syracuse University, Gerrit Smith Miller Collection, Note Book, 1829–43, pp. 255–256, Gerrit Smith, Peterboro, August 18, 1841, to William B. Astor; *ibid.*, Letters, William B. Astor, August 26, 1841, to Gerrit Smith, Peterboro.

86. Ms. book, Baker Library, Astor Papers, Letter Book iii, 1845–48, pp. 154, 156, 158, 166, William B. Astor, N. Y., February 13, 22, 23, March 18, 1847, to G. S. Howland.

87. "The Astors Organize a Trust," *Detroit Journal*, February 12, 1898.

88. Ms. book, Baker Library, Astor Papers, Letter Book ii, 1831–38, pp. 36–37, John Jacob Astor, N. Y., March 23, 1832, to Gillespies, Moffat, Finlay & Co., London.

89. *Ibid.*, p. 44, John Jacob Astor, N. Y., April 9, 1832, to Vincent Rumpff, Paris (see below, vol. ii, pp. 1214-1215).

90. *Ibid.*, p. 241, John Jacob Astor, N. Y., August 7, 1834, to Gillespies, Moffat, Finlay & Co., London.

91. *Ibid.*, p. 386, John Jacob Astor, N. Y., March 22, 1836, to Hottinguer & Co., Paris.

92. *Ibid.*, Letter Book iii, 1845-48, pp. 152, 154, 266, John Jacob Astor by William B. Astor, N. Y., February 12, 17, 1847, February 9, 14, 1848, to Corcoran and Riggs, Washington.

93. *Ibid.*, pp. 188, 189, 203, John Jacob Astor by William B. Astor, N. Y., June 10, 14, July 29, 1847, to Corcoran and Riggs, Washington.

94. *Ibid.*, p. 217, John Jacob Astor by William B. Astor, N. Y., September 27, 1847, to Daniel Graham, Register of the Treasury, Washington.

95. *Ibid.*, pp. 275, 277, John Jacob Astor, Jr., March 11, 17, 1848, to Daniel Graham, Register of the Treasury, Washington.

96. *Ibid.*, pp. 203, 212, 217, 246, John Jacob Astor by William B. Astor, N. Y., September 10, 27, December 8, 1847, to Corcoran and Riggs, Washington.

97. *Ibid.*, pp. 179, 180, William B. Astor, N. Y., May 12, 17, 1847, to R. H. Gillet, Register of the Treasury, Washington.

98. *Ibid.*, pp. 254, 257, 267, William B. Astor, N. Y., January 3, 10, 12, February 14, 1848, to Daniel Graham, Register of the Treasury, Washington.

99. *Ibid.*, Letter Book ii, 1831-38, p. 59, John Jacob Astor, N. Y., June 11, 1832, to Silas Wright, Albany.

100. *Ibid.*, p. 59, John Jacob Astor, N. Y., June 11, 1832, to Dudley Selden.

101. *Ibid.*, p. 61, John Jacob Astor, N. Y., June 14, 1832, to Silas Wright, Comptroller, Albany.

102. *Ibid.*, pp. 67, 615, William B. Astor, N. Y., June 29, 1832, September 28, 1838, to Thomas W. Olcott, Mechanics and Farmers Bank, Albany; *ibid.*, Letter Book iii, 1845-48, John Jacob Astor, N. Y., January 17, 1846, to Thomas W. Olcott, Albany.

103. *Ibid.*, Letter Book ii, 1831-38, pp. 257, 258, John Jacob Astor, N. Y., September 15, 16, 1834, to Thomas Wilson, London.

104. *Ibid.*, pp. 257, 258, 266, John Jacob Astor, N. Y., September 15. 16, November 30, 1834, to Gillespies, Moffat, Finlay & Co., London.

105. *Ibid.*, pp. 266, 287, 306, 394, 487, John Jacob Astor, N. Y., November 30, 1834, March 7, June 18, 1835, April 8, 1836, May 1, 1837, to Thomas Wilson & Co., London.

106. *Ibid.*, pp. 490, 492, John Jacob Astor, N. Y., May 10, 23, 1837, to Gillespies, Moffatt & Co., London.

107. *Ibid.*, p. 484, John Jacob Astor by William B. Astor, N. Y., April 17, 1837, to John Warren.

108. Scoville, *op. cit.*, vol. i, pp. 391–393.

109. "Debts and Finances of the States of the Union — Ohio," *Hunt's Merchant Magazine*, vol. xxi (October, 1849), p. 402.

110. Ms. book, Baker Library, Astor Papers, Letter Book ii, 1831–38, pp. 20–21, 26, 36–37, 485, 488–489, 490, 503, 508, 514, 550, John Jacob Astor, N. Y., January 6, 21, March 23, 1832, April 24, May 8, 10, July 17, August 15, 31, December 30, 1837, to Gillespies, Moffatt, Finlay & Co., London.

111. *Ibid.*, Letter Book iii, 1845–48, p. 57, John Jacob Astor by William B. Astor, N. Y., February 6, 1846, to Ebbets Brothers.

112. *Ibid.*, p. 200, William B. Astor, N. Y., July 20, 1847, to John Ward & Co.

113. *Ibid.*, Letter Book ii, 1831–38, p. 423, John Jacob Astor by William B. Astor, N. Y., August 11, 1836, to Walter Mead, Cashier, Merchants Bank.

114. *Ibid.*, Letter Book iii, 1845–48, p. 56, William B. Astor, N. Y., January 31, 1846, to Robert Neilson, Philadelphia.

115. *Ibid.*, p. 57, John Jacob Astor by William B. Astor, N. Y., February 6, 1846, to John Ward & Co.

116. *Ibid.*, p. 149, William B. Astor, N. Y., February 3, 1847, to Robert Neilson, Philadelphia.

117. *Ibid.*, p. 174, William B. Astor, N. Y., April 23, 1847, to George Philler, Cashier, Bank of Pennsylvania, Philadelphia.

118. *Ibid.*, Letter Book ii, 1831–38, pp. 38, 49, 396, John Jacob Astor, N. Y., March 29, May 4, 1832, and William B. Astor, April 15, 1836, to Thomas Wilson & Co., London.

119. *Ibid.*, p. 224, John Jacob Astor by William B. Astor, N. Y., April 17, 1834, to Walter Mead, Cashier, Merchants Bank.

120. *Ibid.*, Letter Book iii, 1845–48, pp. 23, 70, 74, 120, 166, 171–172, 215, 220, 279, John Jacob Astor by William B. Astor, N. Y., September 22, 1845, March 24, April 7, September 21, 1846, March 24, April 13, September 21, October 6, 1847, March 21, 1848, to Josiah Quincy, Jr., Treasurer of Western Rail Road Co., Boston.

121. *Ibid.*, Letter Book ii, 1831–38, p. 251, John Jacob Astor, N. Y., August 8, 1834, to Prime, Ward & King.

122. *Ibid.*, Letter Book iii, 1845–48, p. 177, William B. Astor, N. Y., May 3, 1847, to Robert Neilson, Philadelphia.

123. *Ibid.*, Letter Book ii, 1831–38, p. 97, William B. Astor, N. Y., October 8, 1832, to P. Chouteau, Jr., St. Louis.

124. *Ibid.*, pp. 601–602, John Jacob Astor by William B. Astor, N. Y., July 14, 1838, to John Smith, President, Bank of Missouri.

125. *Ibid.*, Letter Book iii, 1845–48, pp. 123, 124, John Jacob Astor by William B. Astor, N. Y., October 19, 22, 1846, to John C. Edwards, Governor of Missouri.

126. *Ibid.*, p. 188, John Jacob Astor by William B. Astor, N. Y., June 10, 1847, to Corcoran & Riggs, Washington.

127. *Ibid.*, pp. 207, 220, 223, John Jacob Astor by William B. Astor, N. Y., August 17, October 5, 14, 1847, to John S. Gettings, Commissioner of Loans, Baltimore.

128. *Ibid.*, Letter Book ii, 1831–38, pp. 455–456, 501, John Jacob Astor by William B. Astor, January 3, July 5, 1837, to the Mayor of Rochester.

129. *Ibid.*, p. 456, John Jacob Astor by William B. Astor, N. Y., January 4, 1837, to E. D. Smith, Treasurer, Rochester.

130. *Ibid.*, Letter Book iii, 1845–48, pp. 27, 68, 73, 109, 119, 123, 162, 172–173, 173, 174, 184, John Jacob Astor by William B. Astor, N. Y., October 2, 1845, March 14, April 3, August 22, September 21, October 10, 1846, March 12, April 17, 23, May 22, 1847, to John R. Williams, Mayor of Detroit; pp. 211, 218, 273, John Jacob Astor by William B. Astor, N. Y., September 6, 28, 1847, March 3, 1848, to Theodore Williams, Deputy Treasurer, City of Detroit; ms., Detroit Public Library, Burton Historical Collection, J. R. Williams MSS., vol. xii, p. 329, John Jacob Astor by William B. Astor, N. Y., March 14, 1846, to J. R. Williams, Mayor of Detroit.

131. *Ibid.*, Letter Book ii, 1831–38, p. 241, William B. Astor, N. Y., June 25, 1834, to Hubert Van Wagenen; *Minutes of the Common Council of the City of New York, 1784–1831*, vol. xvii, p. 479.

132. Youngman, Anna, *The Economic Causes of Great Fortunes* (1909), chap. ii, pp. 7–54, drawn from "The Will of John Jacob Astor," which is to be found in Parton, *op. cit.*, pp. 90–121, and in ms., Baker Library, Astor Papers (see below, vol. ii, pp. 1260–1296).

133. Ms. book, Baker Library, Astor Papers, Letter Book ii, 1831–38, p. 22, John Jacob Astor, N. Y., January 6, 1832, to Thomas Wilson, London.

134. *Ibid.*, pp. 469, 473, John Jacob Astor by William B. Astor, N. Y., March 8, 23, 1837, to Ellice, Kinnear & Co., London; p. 608, William B. Astor, N. Y., July 31, 1838, to C. W. Lutteroth, Paris; *ibid.*, Letter Book iii, 1845–48, pp. 7, 60, 107, 153, 258, 268, John Jacob Astor by William B. Astor, N. Y., July 30, 1845, February 12, August 14, 1846, February 13, 1847, January 13, February 19, 1848, to Ellice, Kinnear & Co., London;

pp. 5, 53, 104, 148, 201, 262, John Jacob Astor by William B. Astor, N. Y., July 23, 1845, January 23, July 29, 1846, January 28, July 22, 1847, January 28, 1848, to C. W. Lutteroth, Paris; pp. 4–5, 54, 101–102, 155–156, 221, John Jacob Astor by William B. Astor, N. Y., July 23, 1845, January 27, July 23, 1846, February 19, October 6, 1847, to William H. Burnley, Trinidad; pp. 36, 82, 128, 177–178, 231, William B. Astor, N. Y., November 6, 1845, May 5, November 9, 1846, May 5, November 5, 1847, to Vincent Rumpff, Paris; pp. 242–243, William B. Astor, N. Y., November 27, 1847, to Robert Neilson, Philadelphia.

135. *Hone, Philip, The Diary of, 1828-1851,* vol. i, p. 130. Astor gave notice late in 1837 that he would within three months require payment of this bond, described as amounting to $40,000; in July, 1838, he acknowledged payment of $10,000 on account and extended the time of payment of the remainder for a year. (Ms. book, Baker Library, Astor Papers, Letter Book ii, 1831–38, pp. 548, 586–587, 599, John Jacob Astor by William B. Astor, N. Y., December 26, 1837, May 24, July 10, 1838, to Philip Hone, President of the Matteawan Co.)

CHAPTER XXIII

FAMILY, FRIENDS, AND CULTURAL INTERESTS

THERE is, as we have seen, considerable uncertainty as to Astor's ancestry and consequently great differences of opinion among the various genealogists who have studied the question. Astor's great-grandfather is believed to have been Johann Jacob Astor, born in 1664, who married Anna Margaretha Eberhard in 1692 and died in 1711, his wife surviving until 1723. This Johann Jacob Astor is sometimes said to have been a French Huguenot, whose name was originally Jean Jacques D'Astorg and who fled to Germany in 1685. However this may be, his descendants seem to have settled down in the Duchy of Baden, married daughters of the land, and become quite good Germans, indistinguishable from their neighbors. The only child of Johann Jacob Astor of whom we have any knowledge was Felix, who is said to have been born in Nussloch, Baden, in 1693. The date of his marriage is variously given as 1713 and 1719, and the name of his first wife as Eva Dorothea, daughter of Johann Martin, and as Eva Dorothea Freund. They had four children, the youngest of whom. Johann Jacob, born in 1724, became the father of the John Jacob in whom we are particularly interested. Felix Astor's wife died in 1725 and her husband promptly married again, Before his death at Waldorf in 1765 he became the father of sixteen more children,[1] half-brothers and half-sisters of John Jacob Astor's father, and uncles and aunts to John Jacob himself. The relatives of John Jacob Astor whom we have just mentioned do not appear in the drama of his life, though they doubtless influenced it indirectly. For example, it is not surprising that Astor's father, the eldest son in a family of twenty children, was unable to give his own children the advantages in education which would have kept them in Germany and probably doomed at least one of them to a life of comparative obscurity, though perhaps not necessarily of lesser happiness.

John Jacob Astor's father has been described on the one hand as a rather improvident butcher of convivial habits and on the other as the worthy bailiff of the village.[2] The first description seems to come most directly from those who had known him personally. From whatever side of the house John Jacob Astor inherited his financial ability, there is no doubt that it was from his father that he derived his longevity, for though Johann Jacob was born on July 7, 1724, his death did not take place until April 18, 1816.[3] Undoubtedly, for this boon alone, he deserved the pension he received from his son during the last years of his life.[4]

Astor's father married Maria Magdalena Vorfelder on July 8, 1750. After bearing him six children, the first of whom lived less than two years, she died in 1766, about three years after the birth of her youngest and most famous son, who could hardly have known his mother as more than the vaguest memory. Johann Jacob promptly married again, and by his second wife, Christina Barbara, had six children, of whom the first and last died in infancy.[5] Thus Astor was reared by his stepmother, and, according to a familiar tradition, left home at the age of sixteen, partly to avoid her ill treatment. Doubt is cast on this story, however, by the fact that "after Mr. Astor became established in New York, he commissioned an artist in Waldorf to paint his father and [step]mother as he remembered them — the father selling fish and game and the mother selling flowers [sic] in the market."[6] He would hardly have done this had his memories of his stepmother been altogether unpleasant.

Of Astor's brothers and sisters, the oldest was George Peter, who was born on April 28, 1752.[7] He was the first to leave

ASTOR'S STEPMOTHER

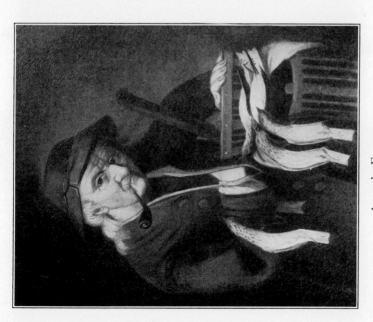

ASTOR'S FATHER

home, going to London, where he is said to have had an uncle connected in some capacity with the musical-instrument manufacturing firm of Shudi & Broadwood. This uncle was doubtless one of those six sons of Felix Astor's second wife, Susanah, who had lived to maturity. Quite likely it was George Peter, born in 1740,[8] who invited his namesake to come to London. John Jacob's brother later set up in the musical-instrument business for himself, married Elizabeth Wright, and was able in 1779 to invite his brother Johann Melchior to come to London, an invitation to which John Jacob responded in his brother's stead. George Peter gave his brother a home and employment and, after Astor had gone to New York, sold him goods for his musical-instrument store and acted as his London agent in various transactions.

George Peter Astor died in December, 1813, leaving his affairs in a rather involved condition.[9] His widow, contrary to John Jacob's advice, pluckily continued to carry on "the business of pianoforte making." [10] In Astor's will, dated July 4, 1836, Mrs. Elizabeth Astor was bequeathed "*two hundred pounds sterling,* yearly for her life," and this legacy was repeated in the codicil of January 19, 1838.[11] In 1834 and 1837 Astor sent his brother's widow bills on London amounting to £500 and £200 sterling,[12] respectively, apparently quite on his own initiative.

George Peter Astor left a family of four sons and four daughters. One son, George Astor, Jr., who has often been confused with his father, came to the United States shortly before the War of 1812 and was employed by his uncle in fur-trade transactions in Canada and the Great Lakes region in the years 1813–14.[13] After the war, he set up in the fur trade for himself.[14] He died in 1832,[15] leaving a son, George Peter Astor, Jr., to whom on July 4, 1836, Astor bequeathed $3,000, repeating the legacy in the codicil of January 19, 1838.[16] In 1838, Astor gave his grandnephew permission to draw on him for $150 and recommended that he should look out "for some employ-ment by which you can make a living for yourself." [17] George Peter Astor, Jr., died in 1846. "He left a wife but no children: he left no property and for sometime before his death received support from his friends." [18] During the last year of his life his great-uncle had occasionally, through William B. Astor, fur-nished him with small sums of money, which assistance was continued to his widow after his death.[19]

Another son of Astor's brother George Peter, Benjamin by name, also came to New York. It was probably this nephew (though described as the "son of a brother residing in Ger-many") who was said in 1848 to have come "to this city a few years since, was employed by his uncle in some menial occupa-tion, the only patronage he could succeed in obtaining from him, and was afterward employed as a porter in various parts of the city." [20] Benjamin died in 1834. According to Astor, he "left his Wife pennyless." [21] Another of George Peter's sons, William Henry, who seems to have been the heir of the musical ability of the family, became a music teacher in New York.[22] Astor, on July 4, 1836, bequeathed to him the sum of $10,000, which on January 19, 1838, he changed to "the *annual sum of five hundred dollars* during his life." [23] George Peter's fourth son, Joseph, seems never to have come to New York. In reward for this forbearance, Astor, whose fondness for his brother's sons seems to have varied directly with the distance they managed to stay from the United States, bequeathed him on July 4, 1836, $25,000, which on January 19, 1838, was in-creased to $50,000, with the provision that the executors might at their discretion retain this amount and apply it and the in-come therefrom to the support of Joseph and his family during their life and give any balance to his children or next of kin. On October 24, 1839, this bequest was again changed to an annuity of three hundred pounds sterling.[24]

On July 4, 1836, Astor bequeathed $20,000 to each of George

Peter's four daughters, one of whom married a Mr. Oxenham. It has been said that "a relative of Mr. Astor's named Miss Oxenham from London came over to this country and for many years kept house for Mr. and Mrs. Astor, and she was very much liked by all the relations." [25] This Miss Oxenham must have been a daughter of Astor's niece, Mrs. Sarah Oxenham, to whom in December, 1827, he sent a draft for £200 sterling.[26] On January 19, 1838, her legacy was raised to $30,000 and on March 3, 1841, was reduced to the former amount, $20,000.[27] In 1845, 1846, and 1847, Astor sent Mrs. Oxenham £250 sterling each year on account of the amount bequeathed to her in his will.[28] To another of George Peter's daughters, Mrs. Mary Reynell, Astor on December 7, 1837, sent a bill on London for £200 sterling, as he had to others of her brothers and sisters.[29] On March 3, 1841, Astor reduced her legacy from $20,000 to $15,000.[30] Another of George Peter's daughters married Thomas G. Holt and died in November, 1845. Astor, during the years 1845, 1846, and 1847, sent the bereaved husband a total of £350 sterling, probably on account of the sum he had bequeathed to his niece by his will.[31] On December 7, 1837, Astor sent his niece Catherine £100 sterling,[32] and in the years 1845, 1846, and 1847, after she had become Mrs. Epworth, he sent her annually £100 sterling on account of his legacy to her in his will.[33]

Astor's next brother, John Henry, born on January 4, 1754, had gone to New York on a British war vessel, deserted, and set up as a butcher. He is said to have invited John Jacob to leave London and come to the United States. When Astor did arrive, Henry assisted him to get his first job and at various times lent him money.[34] He it was who sold Astor his first piece of Manhattan Island real estate. Henry became a wealthy man, though his fortune was overshadowed by his younger brother's colossal riches. He married Dorothea Pessenger on March 14, 1784,[35] but they had no children. They consequently formed the "habit of selecting young girls, adopting, educating, and starting them in life when they married." [36] When Henry died in 1833 he left an estate of about a million dollars, the largest share of which went to William B. Astor,[37] to the very natural disappointment of certain of his other nephews and nieces whose prospects in life were not so promising.[38]

Astor's only full sister, Catherine, was born in 1757 or 1758, and married a distiller named Ehninger, whose Christian name has been variously given as George and John Christopher.[39] They came to America, where Ehninger was killed in "an accident caused while burning spirits." Catherine, like most of the Astor women, whether by birth or by marriage, possessed a strong will and an independent mind. She continued her husband's cordial distillery, "married Michael Miller, taught him the secrets of the business, and carried it on with him for years." [40] Astor remembered his sister in his will by the small legacy of $1,000, which he later revoked, perhaps because of her death.[41] By her first husband Catherine had a son, George, born in New York in 1792. George Ehninger went out to Astoria on the *Beaver* and thence to China, where he acted as assistant to Captain Sowle and Nicholas G. Ogden. He did not shine in this capacity, and his sins of omission drew from his uncle the sarcastic exclamation: "what a merchant you are!"[42] George Ehninger married Eliza Whetten, daughter of John Whetten, Astor's associate and China captain and his wife's nephew, but this did not prevent occasional friction between uncle and nephew,[43] which probably was the reason that George was not remembered in his uncle's will. Each of his children, however, was bequeathed $1,000;[44] one was John Whetten Ehninger, who became a well-known painter. In Astor's will he gave $5,000 to be equally divided among the children of Catherine's daughter, Maria Moore. This legacy was revoked in a later codicil by which $5,000 was left to the children of Catherine's daughter, Hannah Moore.[45] Perhaps there had been an error in the statement of her Christian name.

Astor's connection with his brother Johann Melchior, who had been born on October 30, 1759, was less close than that with either of his other two older brothers or with his older sister. Melchior, unlike the other children of Maria Magdalena Vorfelder, remained in Germany and, having no interest in trade, became the tenant of a farm at Neuwied.[46] Astor owed him somewhat of a debt of gratitude for having rejected George's invitation to come to London, thus giving John Jacob his opportunity. Astor is said to have visited Melchior in 1819, but nothing further is known of their relations. In Astor's will, however, he bequeathed $5,000 to his "niece Sophia Astor, of Nieuwid in Germany," and on January 9, 1839, he added to this legacy "an annuity of *three hundred dollars per annum*," another indication that Astor's fondness for his nephews and nieces seems to have varied in direct ratio to the distance at which they contrived to remain from New York.[47]

Little is known of the children of Astor's father by his second marriage. The first two, born in 1767 and 1768 — the older of whom died in the year after her birth — are both said to have been named Maria Magdalena, presumably in honor of their father's first wife. That the second wife consented is very creditable to her disposition and would seem to be a count against the story of her cruelty to John Jacob. Some of those who give credence to the tale of her traditional stepmotherly nature have tried to avoid this difficulty by making the two Maria Magdalenas children of the first wife, born after John Jacob.[48] However this may be, we know nothing of the subsequent history of the surviving Maria Magdalena. There also seems to be a difference of opinion as to the identity of the next child born to Johann Jacob and his wife Christina Barbara. According to one account their next child was Ann Eve, born in 1770 (or on January 29, 1771). She came to New York in

1795, and married Dr. Richard Corner, who died in 1799; in the next year she married Peter Cook, a cartman.[49] She died in 1859,[50] but was not remembered in Astor's will. Another daughter, Elizabeth, according to one account, was born in 1769; according to another, in 1773.[51] She, too, came to the United States and married, with her brother's approval, John Gottlieb Wendell, a porter in Astor's employ. Astor later set Wendell up in business as a fur dealer in Gold Street and, following in his brother-in-law's footsteps, by the purchase of land he became very wealthy.[52] Elizabeth probably died in the early 1830's.[53] Nothing is known of Sebastian, born in 1775, while Maria Barbara, born in 1778, died in infancy.

One of Astor's chief desires, as displayed in his will, was to prevent any of the descendants, then living, of his brothers and sisters, who required aid and who had not, in Astor's opinion, forfeited by their conduct their right to his consideration, from falling into want and distress. His care in some cases extended to his father's great-grandchildren.

On September 19, 1785, Astor married Sarah Todd, who had been born about 1762, the youngest daughter of Adam Todd and Sarah Cox, both of Scottish descent.[54] Her father had died when she was only a child. Sarah Todd brought to her husband a dowry of perhaps $300 and a connection, through her mother, with various influential New York families; but these advantages were insignificant compared to her industry and business ability and her willingness to utilize these qualities without stint in building up her husband's business. Her thrifty, pious personality has unfortunately been lost sight of in the shadow thrown by her husband's overpowering commercial genius. During the first few years of her married life, perhaps up to about 1792, her time was largely occupied in assisting in her husband's musical-instrument and fur store, and in taking care of her growing family, which by 1792 consisted of two sons and two daughters, born since 1788. But by the later date, if

MRS. ASTOR IN MIDDLE LIFE

not before, her husband had so prospered as to allow him to relieve his wife from other than family cares — which were weighty enough. From the few pieces of descriptive material which have come down to us, we see Mrs. Astor as a canny, religious, home-loving body; devoted to her Bible-reading and church-going; fond of entertaining her husband's friends and their families from out-of-town, particularly Peter Smith and his wife, formerly Elizabeth Livingston; on rare occasions getting her children together and going on a trip as far as Albany, but never, of course, accompanying her husband to Montreal, far less to Europe. Even when her children were all grown and most of them safely married, she never went with her husband on his European tours, and one gets the impression that she was not interested in travel, particularly in foreign lands. Her death took place on March 27, 1834,[55] in her seventy-third year,[56] about a week before her husband's return from his last voyage to Europe.[57] How he must have regretted the series of delays which kept him from her side during those last days!

The Astors' long married life of nearly half a century was evidently a happy one. There is no reason to doubt that the current of their affection was deep and strong, unbroken by the rocks of jealousies and misunderstandings. Neither Astor nor his wife was of an emotional or demonstrative nature, but the feeling they had for one another could not always be concealed. If John Jacob and Sarah ever had a serious disagreement, it was over Astor's Germanic indulgence to his grandchildren, against which his wife, reared in the Scottish tradition of strict discipline, sometimes felt her soul rebel. On one occasion she had just corrected a granddaughter — I suspect one of the little Langdons — when the child turned indignantly to Astor and exclaimed with flashing eyes: "Grandfather, *why* did you marry grandmother, anyhow?" The old man sat in silence for a moment, and then, with a whimsical smile and a courtly inclination of his head to his wife, replied gently: "Because she was so pretty, my dear." [58] None of his Huguenot ancestors, whether of the *noblesse* or no, could have improved upon that reply.

When Astor first entered business his main purpose, no doubt, was to secure a competency for himself; when this had been achieved, his next thought was to make all his children independent, and this idea dominated him till past the mid-point of his active business career. After this the joy of achievement for its own sake, which probably had been strong throughout his life, may — perhaps unconsciously — have taken precedence. Although Astor probably derived more satisfaction from his family than from any other factor in his life, it is also true that his children seem to have involved him in more than his fair share of difficulties.

Astor and his wife, from 1788 to 1802, became the parents of eight children, four sons and four daughters, of whom two sons and one daughter died in infancy. Their first child was Magdalen, born January 11, 1788, and named after Astor's mother. Magdalen occasionally accompanied her father on his trips to Montreal, as we have seen, and his prominence in the fur trade gave her the entrée to the best social circles of the Canadian metropolis. On September 14, 1807, she married Adrian Benjamin Bentzon, who had earlier in the year been ousted by the British from his position as governor of the Island of Santa Cruz in the Danish West Indies. They had two children: John Jacob, born in 1810, was named after his grandfather; the other, born about 1813, was given the name of Sarah, in honor of her grandmother, and died young. John Jacob Bentzon was drowned in February, 1818, in the Tyber at Washington, where he had gone with his grandfather, who was prostrated by the experience.[59] In the meantime, Bentzon, when Santa Cruz was returned to Denmark by the Treaty of Paris, had reassumed his position as governor-general and commander-in-chief of the Danish West Indies, leaving his family in New York.[60] In 1819 his wife secured a divorce from him in New York on the grounds of desertion and adultery, both of which he cheerfully admitted to Benjamin Clapp, the Astorian, who was acting as Astor's agent in Santa Cruz.[61]

On March 9, 1820, Magdalen married John Bristed,[62] who had been born in England in 1778, and, while still in his native country, had practised law and medicine and begun to write. In 1806 he came to New York, where he edited a magazine, practised law, lectured, and engaged in miscellaneous literary activities. His ideas upon social questions are said to have been rather radical for that day. It may have been partly his literary interests which gave him an entrée into the Astor household. However, the marriage did not prove to be a success and in the fall of the next year Bristed returned to England, finding it "impossible," as Henry Brevoort wrote, "to bear the matrimonial yoke any longer with that Lamb of Bellzebub, my well beloved Couzen the late Mrs. Bentzon. . . . She is certainly a maniac," Brevoort charitably concluded.[63] Bristed later returned to the United States, studied for the Episcopal ministry, and spent the rest of his life as rector of a church at Bristol, Rhode Island.

Magdalen died in 1832, leaving a son, Charles, who had been born on October 6, 1820. After his mother's death he was brought up under the care of his grandfather, who "often reproved his grandson . . . for taking butter that he did not eat," [64] and had him prepared for college by tutors so that he entered Yale at the age of fifteen, graduating in 1839 with a brilliant record. Astor also paid young Bristed's expenses at Trinity College, Cambridge, from which he was graduated in 1845. Charles Bristed, who assumed the middle name of "Astor" in 1844, on January 14, 1847, married Laura Brevoort, daughter of Henry Brevoort, Astor's nephew-by-marriage and former employee.[65] Like his father, he became a miscellaneous writer. Astor's fondness for this grandson was evidenced by his will, in which he bequeathed Bristed his own residence on Broadway, his country estate at Hell Gate, eighty-four lots of land in various parts of New York City, and, upon attaining the age of twenty-five years, the *"income and interest of one hundred and fifteen thousand dollars."* Bristed was also made a trustee of the Astor Library.[66]

Astor's second child, Sarah, named after her mother, was born in 1790, and died young. The great tragedy of his family life was in connection with his eldest son and namesake, John Jacob, who was born in 1791, and throughout a long life of seventy-six years was mentally incompetent. This condition is variously said to have been insanity or imbecility, and to have existed from birth or to have been caused at an early age by a fall and blow on the head. Another account makes his affliction a lack of muscular control, caused by softening of the brain. He is also said "to have had periods of restored mentality, when he wrote verses of some merit."[67] From the few contemporary descriptions of his case which we possess, it would seem that his condition was one of disordered rather than enfeebled mentality, but that, if insane, he was so only periodically; the statement that his incompetency was due to an accident seems the most reasonable. Whatever the character of his incapacity, or its cause, it is certain that his father never gave up hope that his son might some day be restored to a normal mental condition.

John Jacob Astor, Jr., accompanied by a nurse, spent the winter of 1820–21 in Paris with his father and his sister Eliza. "The former [John Jacob Astor, Jr.]," Washington Irving wrote in the spring of 1821, "is in very bad health, and seems in a state of mental stupor. His situation causes great anxiety & distress to his father & sister; and there appears but little prospect of his recovery."[68] Astor probably had his son brought to Paris in the hope that travel would stimulate his mind, or perhaps for the purpose of submitting his case to European specialists; but by July he was convinced that no good purpose would be served by his remaining longer, and on the 5th Astor paid for his namesake's passage to New York.[69]

Later, Astor had his son cared for in an institution at Cambridgeport, Massachusetts, conducted by a Mr. Chaplin and his wife Hannah, and by the latter's two sisters, at an expense of approximately $2,000 annually. Astor also employed a certain Dexter Fairbank as his son's companion. Early in 1832 Astor procured "a Report . . . made to our Legislature of last year, about Hospitals for the Insane," and was so impressed by it that he was "undecided whether it would not be advisable to place my son John at one of the publick institutions which of late have been so highly recommended, and have acquired by their successful operation more confidence than the private institutions." However, he finally decided to leave his son with the Chaplin family, under whose "kind and excellent treatment" his physical health had much improved. In the spring of 1838 Mrs. Chaplin died and Astor wrote "to Dexter Fairbank to come here with him, provided such visit can be made without disturbing his mind too much or proving injurious to him." After this visit, Astor "concluded . . . that as Dexter has been so long with him, and appears so well to understand the treatment of his case, now to put him under his charge." In the late summer Astor instructed Fairbank, who had returned with John Jacob, Jr., to Cambridgeport, to procure "a good horse and wagon for the use of yourself and my son." The son's visit to his father, however, inclined Astor "still more to the opinion that it will be more conducive to the welfare of my son that he should be near me" and he therefore requested Fairbank "to be prepared to make arrangements to come here with him should he desire you so to do." [70]

John Jacob, Jr., was later established in New York City, "at Chelsea . . . as the sole occupant of a large and commodious mansion. He was here under the care of Dr. O'Donnel, now of Brooklyn, who devoted his attention exclusively to him, and was liberally remunerated by Mr. Astor." [71] In Astor's will, his executors were directed "to provide for my unfortunate son . . . and to procure for him all the comforts which his condition doth or may admit," up to $5,000 annually, or up to $10,000 "in case he should be restored." In a codicil, signed January 9, 1839, Astor mentioned that "in order more comfortably to accommodate my unfortunate Son John," he had "provided for the erection of a dwelling-house on Fourteenth-Street" which he thereupon bequeathed to the said son. In this same codicil his son's income, under the will, was "enlarged to *ten thousand dollars* per annum." [72]

The second son of John Jacob Astor and his wife, born on September 19, 1792, helped to compensate them for the unhappiness caused by their eldest son's condition. William Backhouse,[73] named after a merchant, recently deceased, who had proved a friend to Astor in his early days in New York, became the center of his father's hopes. He received a careful preparatory education in the United States, and from 1808 to 1814 spent most of his time in Europe, in travel and study. He had intended, after the conclusion of the Napoleonic Wars, to study in France and Italy, but, as we have seen, was called home to enter his father's business. From 1818 to 1827 he was the junior member of the firm of John Jacob Astor & Son, and sometimes served as president of the American Fur Company. After his father's retirement from the American Fur Company and the China trade, William B. Astor took almost complete charge of at least the routine matters of his remaining business interests. In personality William B. Astor, "a rather shy and silent man" with "a love for letters," [74] is said to have resembled his mother rather than his father, his business operations being marked by quiet efficiency rather than by bold strokes of commercial genius.[75] At his father's death he inherited practically all his great wealth, save for a few legacies of a comparatively minor character, to relatives and for public purposes. During the latter part of Astor's life, after 1834, he had conveyed several valuable pieces of property to his son.[76]

In 1818 William B. Astor married Margaret Armstrong, daughter of John Armstrong, Madison's secretary of War. They had seven children. The oldest, Emily, born in 1819, married Samuel Ward, Jr., of Prime, Ward & King.[77] Emily soon died, and Ward, not long after her death, married again. Henry Brevoort, in the fall of 1843, referred to this episode in rather unfeeling tones.

> An ontoward event has just happened in his [Astor's] family, which has stirred his ire; a thing which always does him good. Master Sam W—— has married Miss Medora Grymes and settled upon her *his* house in Bond Street, which house had been purchased, & previously given or settled upon his first wife, but by our laws, became his, after her decease. — This affair sticks deep into the old gentleman's gizzard. He views it as a sort of impeachment of his accustomed sagacity; a sort of outwitting & overreaching in the art of bargaining. . . . the resentment of the A's, is, I think, carried beyond all just bounds.[78]

By 1846, however, William B. Astor was engaging in friendly enough correspondence with Ward in regard to his little daughter, Margaret Astor Ward, who was under the guardianship of her grandparents.[79]

William B. Astor's eldest son, John Jacob, usually known as John Jacob Astor II, was born on June 10, 1822, graduated from Columbia in 1839, studied at Göttingen, as his father had done before him, later studied law, and in 1847 married Charlotte Gibbes.[80] As his grandfather's namesake he received special consideration in his will, being granted a life interest in half Astor's lands "lying between Bloomingdale Road, Hudson River, Forty-second Street, and Fifty-first Street," the other half to be divided between his two brothers. He also received a lot on Lafayette Place, near the site of the projected Astor Library, and was made an executor of the will.[81]

William B. Astor had two other daughters, Alida and Laura E., to each of whom Astor bequeathed $200,000, to "be settled on them on their respectively attaining the age of twenty-one years, or their marriage" with the consent of their father or his wife. In a codicil dated December 22, 1843, these bequests were left to William B. Astor's discretion.[82] The only one of William B. Astor's daughters, other than Emily, to marry during Astor's lifetime was Laura, who became the wife of Franklin H. Delano, of the firm of Grinnell, Minturn & Co.[83] The tale is told that Astor gave one of his granddaughters a check for a quarter of a million dollars on her wedding day,[84] and if any such incident actually occurred — which is doubtful — the details of the story seem to fit in better with Laura's marriage than with any other.

William B. Astor's second son, William, was born on July 12, 1829. His grandfather willed him a life interest in one-fourth of the lands of which his elder brother, John Jacob, was to receive half. He also received a lot on Lafayette Place. A third son, Henry, was to receive a one-fourth interest in these lands.[85] All these legacies were contingent upon their father's good pleasure throughout his lifetime.[86] A daughter of William B. Astor, Sarah, was born in 1832 and died the same year.[87]

Dorothea, Astor's second daughter to reach maturity, was born on January 11, 1795, and named after the wife of his brother Henry.[88] In 1812 Albert Gallatin wrote to Astor inviting Dorothea to come to Washington for a visit. While there she met Colonel Walter Langdon, of Portsmouth, New Hampshire, a member of the governor's staff, a young man about five years older than herself, described as "very handsome and very fascinating," who had been "sent on a trip to visit the large cities and to see the world by going to Washington where he fell in with 'this fat German, Dolly Astor,'" as one of his relatives ungallantly described her. Langdon "made a very rapid courtship," and Gallatin, seeing how matters

stood, wrote to Astor that "he had better send for his daughter
to return home," since "Col. Langdon had every recommendation except wealth, being one of a large family." The young
couple thereupon "took matters in their own hands and
eloped." They were married on September 24, 1812 — perhaps war time and Langdon's uniform had something to do
with the rapidity of their romance — and settled in New York,
"but it was many years before Mr. Astor forgave them. They
had a large family of children. Some years later Mr. Astor
went to a children's party given at the house of some friends.
He noticed a very attractive looking little girl, and to his host-
ess's distress he spoke to her and asked her her name. She
replied, 'My name is Sarah Sherburne Langdon.' Then said
he, 'For your sake I shall have to forgive your father and
mother.'" The reconciliation was complete, and thereafter
Astor spared neither money nor effort in demonstrating his
affection for the Langdons.

Astor gave Mrs. Langdon "a house on the Northwest corner
of Astor Place and Lafayette Place," which he is said to have
built for himself "but . . . never lived in it as he had some
superstition about a corner house." [89] It is not explained why,
in that case, he should have built it in the first place or why he
should have then turned it over to a daughter. In his will
Astor left Dorothea all his household furniture, the house and
lot on Lafayette Place, and a life income from $100,000 of the
debt of the city of New York, 500 shares of the capital stock of
the Bank of America, 1,000 shares of the capital stock of the
Manhattan Company, and $25,000 deposited with the New
York Life Insurance and Trust Company. To this bequest he
later added the income of $100,000 deposited with the same
trust company; also two lots on Lafayette Place. In 1842
Astor provided that, should Dorothea predecease her husband,
he should be entitled to an annual income of $5,000. [90] Lang-
don, however, died in August, 1847. [91]

Sarah Langdon, the little girl who had been the unconscious agent of reconciliation between her grandfather and her parents, married, in Paris, Baron Robert Boreel, first secretary of the Dutch Legation. Her grandfather built for her a house, adjoining his own, which "was situated on Broadway between Prince and Spring streets." [92] In 1845 Astor sent her a present of 7,893.75 francs, probably only one of many such gifts.[93] In his will Astor left her a house and lot on Broadway and the City Hotel, for life.[94] Another of Dorothea's daughters, Louisa, followed the family tradition by eloping with De Lancey Kane of Albany, an action for which her father inconsistently refused to forgive her.[95] Astor, at various times during the years from 1846 to 1848, sent her gifts totalling nearly $6,000.[96] In his will he had left her a life interest in one-seventh of 100 lots in New York City, and in one-fourth of 4 lots on Broadway. She was also to receive a lot on Lafayette Place, a life interest in one-sixth share of 9 other lots, and 2 legacies of $25,000, at the age of 21 and 30, respectively, as well as a one-sixth share of $100,000 in the New York Water Loan. In 1841 Astor entirely revoked his bequests to Louisa save for one-half the land legacies. This was probably because of her runaway marriage. But he also gave her mother the right to will or deed to Louisa one-half the property taken from her by this codicil and given to others — her mother and sisters.[97] Moreover, he deeded her two Broadway lots, one with a dwelling-house, in 1844 and 1845.[98] The gifts to Louisa in Astor's last days may have been tokens of forgiveness, or perhaps were intended to keep her from making trouble over the will.

Another of Dorothea's daughters, Eliza, married Matthew Wilks. At least one of her children was born at Hell Gate.[99] Eliza received the same bequests in Astor's will as did her older sister Louisa, but no codicil deprived her of part of her legacy. During the years 1846 and 1847 Astor sent her gifts amounting to more than $5,000.[100] John Jacob Astor Langdon was bequeathed about the same amount of property as Eliza, but died in 1837. Walter Langdon, Jr., Woodbury Langdon, and Eugene Langdon received similar bequests, as did Cecilia, the youngest child in the family. Walter and Woodbury were both married in November, 1847.[101] Astor took a great interest in their weddings and, though within a few months of his end, once took occasion to reprove Woodbury's wife "because she would sit near the open fire when wearing her valuable furs." [102]

On December 26, 1797, Astor's third son was born and named after his uncle Henry,[103] but this "fine Little boy" died at the age of twenty-three months.[104] Astor's youngest daughter, Eliza, was born in 1801. Apparently of a gentler and less forceful spirit than her sisters, who seem to have drawn largely upon their father's energetic nature, she nevertheless inherited his interest in literature and is said to have herself indulged a taste for writing. She is described as "distinguished for her benevolence and piety." [105] Being the last of the family to marry, she became her father's companion on the trips to Europe which he began to take after his son had entered the firm. She spent the winter of 1820–21 in Paris with her father and unfortunate eldest brother, and Washington Irving, who met her there, spoke of her as "quite a clever, agreeable girl." [106] She seems to have returned to the United States with her father in the spring of 1822, and again accompanied him to Europe in the early summer of 1823.[107] While in Paris, either on this or on the earlier occasion, she met Count Vincent Rumpff, who was a Swiss, acting as minister of the Hanseatic Free Cities to France.[108] On December 10, 1825, they were married.

Eliza received a liberal marriage portion, as had Magdalen. In Astor's will she was also bequeathed the income, for life, of $50,000 of the public debt of Ohio, $50,000 of the debt of the city of New Haven, $50,000 deposited in the New York Life Insurance and Trust Company, 1,000 shares of the capital stock of the Merchants' Bank of New York, and 1,604 shares of the capital stock of the Mechanics' Bank of New York. If she took up her residence in the State of New York, she was also to receive a life interest in such of Astor's residuary real estate as she might select, up to $50,000. To Eliza and her husband was also granted a life estate in Astor's "lands and *estate in the Canton of Geneva,* in Switzerland." Eliza's "lamented death" late in 1838 caused the revocation of his legacy to her. Later, in view of "the advantages which Mr Vincent Rumpff has received from the marriage Settlement of my daughter," he also revoked Rumpff's life interest in the estate near Geneva.[109]

Arthur D. Howden Smith, in his recent biography of Astor, has sponsored the theory that Eliza's marriage with Rumpff was an unwilling one into which she was forced by her father. According to his account, in 1823 or 1824 she had fallen in love with a rising young dentist, Eleazar Parmly, and in 1824 had become engaged to him with the knowledge and consent of her mother, who assisted in keeping the matter secret until Astor announced that he wished his daughter to marry Rumpff. Eliza, supported by her mother, refused, and Astor was forced to compromise. Eliza was to go to Paris and see what she was giving up. After that, they would see. Accordingly, father, mother, and daughter sailed for Paris — where they were received by Count Rumpff. Thereupon the mother immediately wrote Parmly to come and "snatch his sweetheart away." Parmly accordingly sailed for Europe in the fall of 1825, but arrived after the marriage had taken place. Eliza, according to this story, preserved by the descendants of Parmly's friend, Solyman Brown, died eight years after her marriage, probably of a broken heart.[110]

Now it is, of course, at least a possibility that there was a love affair between Eliza Astor and Eleazar Parmly which was broken up by the former's father, but the story as told is so riddled with inconsistencies that its claim to authenticity is seriously weakened if not altogether extinguished. The two are supposed to have met "in 1823 or '24." Eliza, as we have seen, had joined her father in Paris, probably late in 1820, and seems to have returned with him to New York in the spring of 1822. Therefore she was well enough acquainted with Paris to know without any further illustration "what she was giving up" if she married Parmly. She again accompanied her father to Europe in the early summer of 1823. It is, however, not impossible that Eliza fell in love with her dentist during the latter half of 1822 or the first half of the succeeding year, although it is unlikely that she became engaged to him in 1824, since she was in Europe at the time. But on her return to Europe with her father she was not accompanied by her mother, who therefore could scarcely have written to the dentist to hasten to Europe and tear his beloved from the clutches of the titled villain of the romance. Even if the mother had been in a position to play the part assigned to her, Parmly was extraordinarily slow in responding, since Eliza had been in Europe well over two years before her betrothed arrived, "bloody with spurring, fiery red with speed" — but too late for the wedding. Even in the story as told by the descendants of Parmly's friend, Eleazar does not seem exactly suited to the Lochinvar rôle, for he is said in July, 1825, to have referred in a poem "to his imminent departure for 'far distant countries'" — and yet he could not manage to get to Paris in the four or five months between the date of this poem and Eliza's wedding! Certainly he did not long mourn his bereavement, since he himself married within a year and a half of Eliza's wedding. Moreover, it is not true that Eliza "only lived eight years after her marriage;" she did not die until 1838, or more than thirteen years after the event which is supposed to have been responsible for her early decease. But this point need not be stressed; if a heart is to be eight years in breaking, it may as well take an additional five.

I am inclined to think that the broken engagement — if it ever existed, which I have come regretfully to doubt — can be explained in a much simpler and less romantic, but more convincing, fashion. Eliza went to Paris, met Count Rumpff, and after a couple of years decided that the Parmly episode had been all a mistake. Parmly, however, who had claims to being a poet, found that the affair possessed possibilities which were quite too romantic to be overlooked and, therefore, for years continued to find in his exaggerated memories an inexhaustible supply of material for poems about aching hearts and broken flowers. When we consider the promptness with which Parmly's own marriage followed that of Eliza's, his cool assumption that her death, thirteen years later, was caused by sorrow over her loss becomes a deliciously absurd specimen of naïve egotism.

Astor's last child, "a fine Boy," born November 13, 1802,[111] probably died before he could be christened. Of Astor's eight children, only three — William B., the unfortunate John Jacob, Jr., and Dorothea — outlived him. He was, however, survived by fifteen grandchildren and at least three great-grandchildren.

The picture of Astor which has been preserved by the earlier generations of his descendants — a handsome, courtly old gentleman, with the long silver hair and the silver shoe-buckles of a former generation, striking in personality, affectionate in manner, fastidiously fond of music, never so happy as when surrounded by a group of grandchildren whom he had collected at his country estate for an evening of music — hardly seems to belong to the man who, as head of the American Fur Company, wrecked the government trading houses, which had for their purpose the furnishing of goods to the Indians at fair prices, in order that his organization might secure their furs at low rates, who paid low wages to his *voyageurs* and sold them necessary supplies at exorbitant rates, and who charged goods to his subordinate traders at such high prices that they were forced to mortgage their lands to the Company.

Yet there was another side to Astor's relations with his subordinates and associates which harmonizes more closely with the Astor whom his grandchildren knew. Many of Astor's clerks later became successful merchants on their own account, and their success was doubtless due in part to the training they received in his counting-house. We have already mentioned Cornelius Heyer and Cornelius Heeney. Nothing is known concerning the later life of William Sanders, who was Astor's clerk in 1804 and 1805, but his successor, John Meyer, who was employed by Astor in 1806 and 1807, may have been the John Meyer who, in the latter year, became the secretary of the Eagle Fire Insurance Company.[112] William Roberts, who had acted as Astor's bookkeeper during his employer's absence in Europe, later became an independent dealer in wines and brandies.[113] Another clerk, George Merle, a Swiss, became in 1823 a member of the firm of Dias & Merle, trading with Le Havre.[114]

Several of Astor's superior agents and captains — despite the "chronometer story" — assisted him for long terms of years, to their mutual satisfaction.[115] In 1836, Astor remarked of Crooks that he had "been more than 20 years more or less connected with me," [116] and the same could have been said of Astor's other early partner in the American Fur Company, Robert Stuart. John Ebbets had also been "more or less connected" with Astor as captain and agent in the China trade, particularly as carried on in relation to the North West Coast and the Hawaiian Islands, from 1809 to 1829. Any of the Astorians who returned to New York, such as Clapp, Farnham, Matthews, and Franchere, could be sure of a job with the American Fur Company. To his chief subordinates Astor paid liberal salaries, and agents employed for special services were given large fees. It is said that "to his agent, Mr. Smith, who had the full charge of all his real estate, he paid a salary of five thousand dollars, and gave him the use of an elegant house on Fourteenth Street, well furnished, and contracted to pay this sum during Mr. Smith's natural life." [117] Before Cogswell became his companion, a commission requiring only a week's time in Boston, which the former executed for Astor, was repaid by a check for $500.[118]

Even the families of his agents were regarded by Astor as having a claim on his consideration. Jacob B. Taylor, "a sort of chief business man for John Jacob Astor," otherwise described as his "rent collector," died in Astor's service. His son Moses engaged in the business of importing sugar from Cuba, and it was said that "old Mr Astor always backed up Moses when he needed aid." [119] John Jacob Astor Ebbets was probably the son of Astor's veteran captain, John Ebbets. Astor seems to have taken young Ebbets under his wing, paid his bills at Yale College (incidentally giving him good advice), and, on his graduation in 1832, offered him a position with the American Fur Company. Five years later Astor wrote to his namesake, at London, requesting him to return to New York and stay with him, and offering to pay him a good salary.[120] Thirty years after Richard Ebbets had acted as clerk and captain of Astor's brig *Forester*, Astor sent his widow a check for $300 "from regard for him." [121]

There is a close relationship between Astor's indulgence to his family and his comparative liberality to those of his agents with whom he was brought into the closest contact. Astor seems to have taken a patriarchal attitude toward those of his subordinates whom he knew personally, and regarded them as having some special claim to his consideration — as coming within a sort of extension of his own family circle. But Astor's imagination was too narrowly limited by the practices of his class and generation for him to feel the same sense of responsibility for the hundreds and thousands of men who had contributed to his wealth but whom he had never seen — the sailors on his China vessels, the sandalwood cutters of the Hawaiian Islands, the Indian hunters and trappers, the French-Canadian *voyageurs*, even the subordinate traders and their clerks. Had Astor ever come into contact with the misery among Indians and *engagés* in the fur country, and among the commoners of the Hawaiian Islands — for which he could not escape a measure of responsibility — it is not likely that he could have remained unmoved. But he never took the trouble to examine these conditions for himself; indeed, to do so probably never occurred to him, nor would it have occurred to any of his commercial rivals. Astor's establishment by his will of a school and asylum at his birthplace, Waldorf, was a kindly, if belated, act, and demonstrated his sympathy for and his interest in the people whom he had known as a boy and with whom he had renewed his acquaintanceship on his various trips to Europe. But it probably never occurred to him that it would have been even more appropriate to establish a home, perhaps at Detroit, for *voyageurs* who had spent the best of their lives in the service of his fur company.

Astor's imagination, great as it was within its sphere, was at its best when dealing with such tangibles as specie, furs, and tea. A good judge of character in most cases, although he fell down rather badly in some points in connection with the Astoria enterprise, his understanding of the men with whom he came into contact seems to have been limited. They were efficient or inefficient captains, supercargoes, or real-estate agents. Apparently he did not, through most of his life, see beyond these utilitarian aspects of character. It has been said that "one of his [Astor's] early protégés — [probably C. C. Cambreleng], since, a distinguished leader of the Democratic party, and subsequently, our representative at St. Petersburgh — [made] the remark that 'Mr. Astor was capable of commanding an army of 500,000 men!'" [122] To this judgment,

Parton, one of Astor's earliest biographers, replied: "That was an erroneous remark. He could have commanded an army of five hundred thousand tea-chests, with a heavy auxiliary force of otter skins and beaver skins." [123] This estimate is also somewhat unjust; Astor did command, through his headship of the American Fur Company, an army of at least a great many hundred men. It is true that Astor's attitude toward those men employed in his various enterprises, with whom he had not become personally acquainted, was similar to that which he had toward his bales of furs and his blocks of stock; but perhaps for this very reason Cambreleng's comparison of Astor with the commander-in-chief of an army may be regarded as valid.

It is not without significance that the largest bequest by Astor to an object of public benefit was for the establishment of a public library. This legacy was a monument to Astor's fondness for literature and his friendship with literary men, one of his greatest interests in life other than participation in successful financial or commercial operations and safeguarding the welfare of his family. An early example of his patronage of the arts was his appearance at the head of the list of subscribers to Samuel Low's poems, published in 1800.[124]

One of the literary men with whom Astor came into closest relations was the poet Fitz-Greene Halleck, who had formerly been employed by Jacob Barker, Astor's rival in the days of the war loans. In May, 1832, Astor, just before leaving for Europe, made to Halleck, who was then unoccupied, owing to the failure of his former employer, "a proposition . . . to take a charge in his business." [125] Halleck accepted and continued as Astor's confidential secretary until his employer's death. There is no doubt that, although Halleck's business ability was probably a prime requisite for his position, his social graces and literary standing were decisive qualifications. After his return from Europe in 1834 Astor invited Halleck to reside with him, and in the summer of 1835 Halleck was quartered at Astor's summer home, Hell Gate, on the East River.[126]

"With the acceptance of a position with Mr. Astor," it has been said, "Halleck's productiveness in poetry came virtually to an end." In literary circles the blame for his silence was, of course, ascribed to the "pressure of his official duties, together with a desire not to expose himself to the prejudice which business men of the day felt toward the literati." Astor was denounced for having "the hard assurance / To hold a Son of Song in durance," and a literary journal set up the battle cry: "Discharge Halleck, oh Astor." How being out of employment would have been of advantage to a poet who had no other source of income than his own exertions, or why being employed by Jacob Astor should be so much more harmful to the Muse than a similar but probably more arduous engagement to Jacob Barker, these complainants did not discuss. The true reason for Halleck's desertion of poetry is probably found in these lines from his most recent biography: "Halleck's last years in New York were ones of happiness. The recipient of a good salary from Astor, he was now left free to enjoy the social life which the city afforded." In other words, Halleck was merely less interested in creating poetry than he was in participating in New York society. Perhaps had Astor given Halleck a less generous compensation for his services (his salary is said to have been $5,000 per year) his poetic genius might not have perished from overmuch luxury; however, its decease certainly cannot be ascribed to any "prejudice . . . toward the literati" on Astor's part.[127]

The character of the relations which had endured between Astor and Halleck for sixteen years comes out in Astor's will. One codicil designated Halleck as a trustee of the Astor Library, but it was a section of an earlier codicil which aroused the most interest; it read: "I give to my friend Fitz Greene Halleck, *an annuity of two hundred dollars*, commencing at my decease, and payable half yearly for his life; to be secured by setting apart so much of my personal estate as may be necessary; which I intend as a mark of my regard for Mr. Halleck." When the meagerness of this bequest was made public, after Astor's death, it caused a miniature tornado of unfavorable comment in the press and among Halleck's friends. By one periodical it was termed "a shabby affair," and many of the poet's friends, it is said, "expressed the hope that he would reject it with indignation." Halleck, however, remained altogether unaffected by the protests of his indignant sympathizers. It is probable that he had a shrewd suspicion both as to the inspiration for this legacy and the reason for its rather small amount.

As a matter of fact, this bequest seems to have been the result of Astor's irrepressible prankishness, which cropped out in some of his most serious and successful business *coups*, and which could find pleasure in laying plans even for a practical joke which could not take effect till after his death. Apparently Halleck and Astor occasionally engaged in bouts of verbal fencing which would have seemed quite appropriate had the participants been a couple of young students instead of a multimillionaire who had completed his three-score-and-ten and a secretary who was twenty-seven years his employer's junior. On one occasion, the story goes, Halleck was rallying his employer on his zeal in accumulating wealth, despite his fondness for preaching contentment to his less prosperous friends.[128] "Mr. Astor," Halleck remarked, "of what use is all this money to you? I would be content to live upon a couple of hundreds a-year for the rest of my life, if I was only sure of it." Astor apparently had no answer ready at the time, but Halleck, when he heard the fifth section of the "Further Codicil" to Astor's will read out, must have smiled wryly as he realized that Astor had had the last word if not the last laugh. A story like this makes one wonder whether Astor did not derive more lasting satisfaction from the wrath mingled with unwilling amusement which greeted the *Beaver's* "mandarin voyage" than from the several hundred thousands of dollars which were the material rewards of the exploit.

Astor's intimacy with another leading literary figure of the period was one of the numerous by-products of the Astoria enterprise. Astor had been "always on terms of intimacy" with the Irving family, and was particularly friendly with Washington Irving. In 1834, shortly after his return from Europe, Astor applied to Irving to write a work concerning the Astoria settlement which would "secure to him the reputation of having originated the enterprise." He felt "the want of occupation and amusement" and thought that he might "find something of both in the progress of this work." Accordingly, Astor offered to furnish the necessary material for such a book and pay for having it put into a rough form, ready for Irving to work it over in his own literary style. Irving therefore wrote on September 15, 1834, to his nephew, Pierre M. Irving, offering him the opportunity to do the preliminary work on the material to be furnished by Astor, and informing him that Astor would pay him $3,000 for a year's work and would wish both Pierre and Halleck to reside with him while engaged on the task.

By June, 1835, Irving had begun work on *Astoria*, as the narrative was to be called, and in August he was quartered at Astor's country estate, a thirteen-acre farm at Hell Gate on the East River, in a rather plain but "spacious" and "well-built house" of colonial type, surrounded by trees, "with a lawn in front of it, and a garden in rear." The greensward swept down to the water's edge and in front of the house was "the little strait of Hellgate," which formed "a constantly moving picture." Here Astor kept bachelor hall with Halleck and with his grandson, Charles Astor Bristed, a boy of fourteen, whose later *flair* for literary pursuits may have owed something to his early association with these two writers, as well as to his father, John Bristed. By October 8 Irving had completed the first draft of the work, and on Christmas Irving and Pierre were still at Hell Gate with Astor, waiting the completion of the town house which was to take the place of the one torn down the previous year to make room for the new hotel. "Mr. Astor," Irving wrote, "does everything in his power to render our residence with him agreeable, and to detain us with him." Early in February, 1836, Irving was giving his "last handling to the Astor work." *Astoria* "was going through the press at the close of June, [and] was published in October." The work was well received by the critics and by the public. "Old Mr. Astor appears to be greatly gratified, which is very satisfactory to me," Irving wrote.

Astor might well have been pleased with *Astoria*, especially if he had at the time foreseen that it was largely to the pen of Irving that he would owe his immortality in the popular mind after his death. It was natural that Astor should wish to make Irving some special compensation for lending his literary gifts to the immortalizing of Astor's favorite project. The story went about that Astor had given Irving $5,000 "to take up his manuscripts." This, however, Irving denied. "He was too proverbially rich a man," he wrote some three years after Astor's death, "for me to permit the shadow of a pecuniary favor to rest on our intercourse." Irving, however, while *Astoria* was still in the process of composition, did join with Astor in the land speculation at Green Bay, which at the time gave every evidence of proving profitable, but insisted on paying for his share in cash, "though Mr. Astor wished the amount to stand on mortgage." When this enterprise proved to be a failure, Astor took back the share and returned Irving the original purchase price. Astor, however, was not to be thwarted in his desire to make Irving some monetary recompense for the immortality he had received from his pen, and consequently made Irving one of his executors. The amount Irving received from his commission as executor amounted to $10,592.66.

The publication of *Astoria* caused the friendship which had formerly existed between Astor and Irving to become of a much more intimate character. Their new relationship was inaugurated, the month after the book had appeared, by a visit from Astor to Irving's residence, "Sunnyside." In a letter written December 12, 1836, Irving said: "Old Mr. Astor most unexpectedly paid me a visit at the cottage about a month since. . . . He landed at Tarrytown and hired a vehicle, which brought him to the cottage door. He spent two days here, and promised to repeat his visit as soon as there shall be good sleighing." On January 10, 1838, Irving was visiting Astor and expected to remain two or three weeks. Early in 1848, the year of Astor's death, Irving was again visiting in Astor's New York home, and while there "often urged [him] . . . to commence his noble enterprise of the Astor Library and enjoy the reputation of it while living." [129] But Astor's physical powers were too nearly exhausted for even Irving's influence, added to that of Astor's companion, Joseph Green Cogswell, to cause him to take any decisive steps in the matter which he had inaugurated a decade before.

As we shall later see more fully, Astor's association with Joseph Green Cogswell was much more intimate than that with either Halleck or Irving. Cogswell resided in Astor's house for most of the time from 1842 until his friend's death six years later.[130] His position was a curious one and his duties seem to have combined those of a companion, secretary, nurse, spiritual adviser, and director of the prospective Astor Library. Philip Hone, in his diary, spoke of him as Astor's "train-bearer and prime minister." [131] In any case Cogswell's position must sometimes have been trying to his patience, especially as his employer's health steadily grew weaker, though doubtless there were compensations in conversing with a man of such wide experience in various business activities. Cogswell was also occasionally amused by the way in which the habits of economy which Astor had found necessary in his early business life still persisted under certain circumstances to an almost ludicrous degree. Astor and Cogswell frequently went for excursions into the country or up the Hudson, by carriage or boat. On one occasion "the two gentlemen took supper together at a hotel recently opened." There was a lull in the conversation, broken by Astor's suddenly remarking: "This man will never succeed." "Why not?" enquired Cogswell. "Don't you see," Astor replied with a triumphant gesture, "what large lumps of sugar he puts in the sugar bowl?" All things considered, it was probably fortunate that Astor never tried to run the Astor House on his own account. Upon another occasion they were "walking to a pilot-boat which the old gentleman had chartered for a trip down the harbor," at a pace proper to Astor's age and physical infirmity, when Cogswell, who must have been moved by a spirit of pure deviltry, remarked gravely: "Mr. Astor, I have just been calculating that this boat costs you twenty-five cents a minute." Astor immediately quickened his steps, reluctant to lose a moment of the time for which he was paying at so high a rate.[132]

Astor had also acquired, partly, perhaps, from his son, the pupil of Bunsen and correspondent of the Humboldts,[133] something of an interest in science. The agents of the American Fur Company were instructed to give every facility to scientists engaged in research within the area of its operations. The English naturalists John Bradbury and Thomas Nuthall accompanied Hunt's Astorian expedition up the Missouri in 1811. In 1832, George Catlin was a passenger on the American Fur Company's boat, the *Yellowstone*, the first steamboat to navigate the Missouri to the mouth of the river after which the vessel was named, and in the next spring Maximilian, Prince of Wied, went up the Missouri on the same boat.[134]

The only work which Astor personally bought for the projected Astor Library was Audubon's *Birds of America*, which began to appear in 1827 and the publication of which was completed in 1838. The subscription price of this work was $1,000, and upon Astor's patronage of the publication there hangs an amusing tale.

> During the progress of the work [the story goes], the prosecution of which was exceedingly expensive, M. Audubon, of course, called upon several of his subscribers for payments. It so happened that Mr. Astor (probably that he might not be troubled about small matters) was not applied to before the delivery of all the letterpress and plates. Then, however, Audubon asked for his thousand dollars; but he was put off with one excuse or another. "Ah, M. Audubon," would the owner of millions observe, "you come at a bad time; money is very scarce; I have nothing in bank; I have invested all my funds." At length, for the sixth time, Audubon called upon Astor for his thousand dollars. As he was ushered into the presence, he found William B. Astor, the son, conversing with his father. No sooner did the rich man see the man of art, than he began, "Ah, M. Audubon, so you have come again after your money. Hard times, M. Audubon — money scarce!" But just then catching an inquiring look from his son, he changed his tone: "However, M. Audubon, I suppose we must contrive to let you have some of your money, if possible. William," he added, calling to his son, who had walked into an adjoining parlour, "have we any money at all, in the bank?" — "Yes, father," replied the son, supposing that he was asked an earnest question, pertinent to what they had been talking about when the ornithologist came in, "we have two hundred and twenty thousand dollars in the Bank of New York, seventy thousand in the City Bank, ninety thousand in the Merchants', ninety-eight thousand four hundred in the Mechanics', eighty-three thousand —" "That'll do, that'll do," exclaimed John Jacob, interrupting him; "it seems that William can give you a check for your money."[135]

Of course it is unlikely that the details of this story — and particularly the figures — are correct, but it may have some basis in fact.

Astor's literary interests were narrowly restricted by the circumstances of his early life. He never learned to write the

English language without marvelous errors in grammar and spelling, though usually, except when under great mental stress, with considerable force and clarity, and occasionally with a certain happiness of expression. Consequently creative literary work was entirely outside his power. It was doubtless his consciousness of these early disadvantages which led him to fall in with the idea of establishing a public library in the city of his adoption. Cogswell, however, implies that, after his retirement from commerce, he found his principal enjoyment in reading, until his impaired eyesight no longer permitted this occupation. He is said to have been particularly fond of history, and as late in life as November 20, 1844, was, indeed, nominated for membership in the New York Historical Society.[136] It seems clear, nevertheless, that his chief contact with literature was through friendship with its creators.

There was another cultural interest, however, in which Astor was able to enjoy more direct personal participation. It was hardly an accident that Astor's older brother, George, had become a manufacturer of pianos, hand-organs, and flutes in London, and that Astor himself had worked in his brother's musical-instrument manufactory for three or four years; neither was it a mere matter of chance that Astor had come to America with the intention of peddling musical instruments, and, two years after his arrival, had set up in business as the proprietor of a well-appointed music store. One can hardly imagine a salesman of music and musical instruments who was not able by personal example to convince his customers of the superior tone of his flutes and to lend his own skill as a musician to the task of demonstrating the qualities of the latest airs from London. It may safely be assumed that the barrel organ was not the only musical instrument upon which Astor was a proficient performer.

In Astor's later years he frequently held musical evenings, for which he "engaged the services of a professional pianist."

Astor's memory for music was illustrated by a remark he made upon being "much pleased at recognizing, one evening, the strains of a brilliant waltz. . . . 'I heard it at a fair in Switzerland years ago. The Swiss women were whirling round in their red petticoats.'" He was especially fond of having his granddaughter, Emily Astor, who had married Samuel Ward, and her sister-in-law, Julia Ward, sing for him, either together or separately. On one occasion, as they stood together, the old gentleman gallantly remarked: "You are my singing birds." At another time as they were singing "the well-known song, 'Am Rhein,'" Astor, though "very stout and infirm of person, rose and stood beside the piano," joining lustily with the singers but in a version of his own. "'Am Rhein, am Rhein, da wachset süsses Leben,' he sang, instead of 'Da wachsen unsere Reben.'" [137]

Music and the theater were undoubtedly the two forms of recreation in which Astor took the greatest pleasure. We have little knowledge of his interest in such arts as painting and sculpture. His attitude toward them was probably the conventional one of a wealthy man. We are told: "His style of living was in keeping with his wealth; his house was furnished in the richest and most costly manner, and his rooms embellished with expensive works of art, among others, a Cupid, by Mignard, which was esteemed remarkably fine, was purchased at a munificent price." [138] Astor's principal interest in form and color is said to have found expression in his admiration for particularly fine pieces of fur. He used to hang the skin of an otter or a silver fox upon the wall of his counting-house, as another man might an oil painting, and draw the attention of all visitors to the softness and luster of the fur, his pleasure apparently being principally aesthetic, though he would usually remember to mention the price it would bring in Canton.[139]

Despite, or perhaps because of, the spirit of fierce political partisanship which dominated the days in which Astor lived, it is difficult to determine his own political affiliations. Astor was not of the type to be interested in politics for its own sake, as to a certain extent he was in business, and during his first score or so of years in this country he was too engrossed with laying the foundations of his fortune to spare much attention to the consideration of how governmental policies might affect his business. During this period, too, his position was not one of sufficient influence to make his intervention in political matters a factor of any great importance. At this time Astor was interested only in each particular governmental measure as it was brought to public attention, when he judged it on its own merits. Indeed, the party system was not sufficiently well developed to enable a person to decide upon the value of any proposed policy according to his affiliation with the group which acted as its sponsor.

Astor would at first undoubtedly have approved of almost any government which would give him peace and security and encourage commerce. He naturally welcomed the ratification of Jay's Treaty. As a former resident of England, who still had close ties of business and kinship with that country, he could not be expected to sympathize greatly with the enthusiasm which was shown for the tricolor by a large body of the American people. It is of interest to note that late in life, in 1832, he remarked sagely of the French: "You know they are not to be dependend on." [140] Here the traditional enmity of the Huguenot for the nation which had expelled his forebears may have been cropping up, as it did in the case of John Jay. Up to about 1800 Astor seems to have associated himself most closely with members of the Federalist party. William Laight, with whom he was concerned both in land investment and in the China trade, had been a loyalist during the Revolution. This, however, does not necessarily indicate that Astor, who was not the man to let politics interfere with business, was himself avowedly Federalist, and, indeed, it is not probable that at this time he would have found a congenial political home with the more aristocratic party.

It was more likely that, when Jefferson's followers coalesced into a party, Astor would associate himself to some extent with the political group which included such foreign-born citizens of his acquaintance as Stephen Girard and Albert Gallatin. Indeed, it seems evident that early in the nineteenth century Astor regarded himself as affiliated with the party founded by Jefferson, though this may have been due as much to the fact that it seemed destined to retain control of the machinery of government for some time as to his sympathy with its principles. Astor was on good terms with George and De Witt Clinton and other Republican politicians of New York, including Aaron Burr, carried on a friendly correspondence with Thomas Jefferson, and was intimate with James Madison,[141] James Monroe, and Albert Gallatin.

He opposed, as we have seen, the declaration of war against Great Britain in 1812, but was one of the leading financial supporters of the government during the conflict, though he was strongly in favor of ending the struggle by a conciliatory policy on the part of the United States. In the long and futile series of attempts to establish a national bank during the war he was a prominent supporter of the administration, as opposed to the Federalists, the strict constructionists, and Calhoun's group. That he was regarded as a Republican in 1816 was evidenced by his appointment with Stephen Girard, William Jones, Pierce Butler, and James A. Buchanan as one of the government directors of the second national bank.[142] In this position, however, it is evident that he, with Stephen Girard, acted much more as a business man than as a political partisan.

Astor was conspicuous among those who welcomed President Monroe on his visit to New York in June, 1817,[143] and later in the summer he was first on the Committee of Arrangements to call upon John Quincy Adams, newly-appointed secretary of State, at his hotel, and invite him to a public dinner at Tammany Hall, to which he later acted as Adams' escort.[144] In 1817 and 1818 Astor was giving Monroe advice on the dispensing of patronage in offices connected with the port of New York — in which Astor, as a large importer, was naturally personally interested — and requested that Wilson P. Hunt should be put in charge of a land office in Upper Louisiana.[145] There is not much doubt that Astor would have supported Monroe for re-election in 1820, but he was in Europe at the time, as he was also during the presidential year of 1824.

In 1822, when the campaign had already begun, he wrote from New York to Gallatin at Paris: "We have plenty candidates for President; Mr. Clay, Mr. Calhoun, and Crawford are the most prominent. Mr. Crawford, I think will get it."[146] In this opinion he expressed merely the popular judgment, which Crawford's illness later reversed. Yet Astor expressed no open preference for any one of the three. His friendship for Clay probably lay in the future, and his only direct contact with Calhoun had been in connection with the latter's bank bill during the war, of which he had strongly disapproved; moreover, Calhoun's attitude toward the American Fur Company as secretary of War had not been distinguished by a willingness to co-operate whole-heartedly with that organization. Astor's relations with Crawford, such as they were, seem to have been friendly,[147] and it may be that his expressed belief in the probability of the latter's election also represented a hope.

We do not know whether Astor approved or disapproved of the election of John Quincy Adams in 1824. If he was acquainted with Adams' character he must have realized that, so far as the president was concerned, the era of special privilege for the American Fur Company had come temporarily to an end. There may be some significance in the fact that during the four years of Adams' administration the Company seemed to find government officials somewhat less complaisant than they had been under Monroe.[148] Lewis Cass, the Company's most consistent friend, and Thomas Hart Benton, one of its attorneys, were both Jackson men, and it is unlikely that Astor would have set himself in strong opposition to any candidate, not definitely objectionable, who was favored by these allies and who had a fair chance of success.

Astor was in Europe again in 1832, as he had been in 1820 and 1824, and so had no opportunity to take any personal part in favor of either Jackson or Clay, even had he had the desire, which is not likely. Astor undoubtedly disapproved of Jackson's war on the Bank of the United States, but since he was at this time nearly withdrawn from business it did not noticeably arouse his ire.

Clay's defence of the Bank, however, may have first put Astor and Clay on that friendly footing which found expression in the statesman's becoming financially indebted to the rich man in 1833 and remaining so over a considerable period of years. In 1836 Astor was much more likely to have favored the election of Martin Van Buren, a New Yorker, whose principal lieutenant, C. C. Cambreleng, had been more or less associated with Astor for more than twenty years, than of a Virginia Whig like William Henry Harrison, and this would probably also be true in 1840. In 1838 Astor's intimate friend, Washington Irving, was regarded as a good enough Democrat to be offered the nomination for mayor of New York by Tammany Hall and the secretaryship of the Navy by Van Buren.[149]

It is not till 1844 that we find Astor, even according to a traditional account, coming out definitely for a presidential candidate by rather reluctantly making a large contribution to the campaign fund of Henry Clay.[150] In this, perhaps, can be detected the influence of Joseph Green Cogswell, whose opinions on the wickedness of the annexation of Texas were vigorous and unconcealed.

It is evident, from the fact that Astor's political affiliations at various times in his life are so largely conjectural, that his attitude toward politics had little of the partisan spirit. We know quite definitely what his attitude was on many public questions, we have a pretty good idea of his opinion of various public men, but we cannot imagine his attitude toward any question or person being modified by the opposition of a political party. We may guess with some confidence for what presidential candidates Astor cast his vote from 1808 to 1844, upon those occasions when he was in this country, but we should look in vain for any definite statement over Astor's signature, even in his familiar letters to Peter Smith, that he intended to support any particular candidate, although in a letter to James Monroe he rather broadly hinted that Monroe would be quite satisfactory to him, and on another occasion he spoke in rather contemptuous tones of Rufus King's qualifications. Nor do we find him expressing pleasure or regret over the results of an election save in a letter of April 30, 1814, to Monroe, in which he remarked: "you See the Ellection here as gone as it aught to." [151]

It is probably not altogether an accident that those of Astor's associates during his active business life whose political affiliations can be traced seem to have been predominantly — though by no means exclusively — Federalists before 1800, Jeffersonian Republicans till about 1824, and Jacksonian Democrats up to about the time of his retirement. In each of these periods they were drawn from the dominant party. He aroused no enmity among any group by conspicuous advocacy of the claims of some other, and so had little difficulty in securing favorable consideration from whatever party was in power. Only twice did he appear openly as a political partisan, in the Madison-Monroe period as a member of the administration party, then apparently irremovably in the saddle, and in 1844 as a Henry Clay supporter, when his stand could not in any way affect his business. His concept of the proper attitude of the business man to politics would seem to have been at the opposite pole from that of his contemporary and friend, that staunch Whig Philip Hone.

We have observed the vague and unsatisfactory character of our information concerning Astor's political affiliations, and the negative nature of the influence which such impulses toward political partisanship as he may have possessed seem to have exerted upon his business life. Our knowledge of Astor's formal religious connections is a good deal more exact, but evidences that religion played any considerable part in his business life are even less available than are indications that he was influenced by political considerations.

Astor was brought up in Waldorf as a Lutheran under the ministry of the Reverend John Philip Steiner, and in the village school was taught to repeat the catechism from memory and to sing church hymns, as well as to read, write, and cipher. At about the age of fourteen he was, according to custom, confirmed in the Lutheran Church.[152] He is quoted as saying that, during the years spent in London, he used to arise every morning at four in order to read the Bible and the Lutheran prayer book before going to work.[153] However, soon after going to America he left the Lutheran Church for the German Reformed. We do not know exactly when Astor severed his relations with Lutheranism, but it is significant that his marriage to Sarah Todd on September 19, 1785, took place in the German Reformed Church.

His shift in church membership may have been a result of his wife's influence. She was of Scottish descent and perhaps regarded the German Reformed Church as representing a happy medium between her own religion and that of her husband. Its Calvinism would agree with her theological principles and its language would appeal to John Jacob. Mrs. Astor is said to have been "a member in full communion of the

Grove Street Baptist Church" — though information concerning this church and her affiliations with it seems to be lacking — and her "house was always open to ministers of religion." [154] She is also said to have been "a good woman, very fond of reading books of a religious nature, her especial favorite being Doddridge's 'Rise and Progress,' next to her Bible, which she read daily." [155]

It is also possible that Astor was attracted to the German Reformed Church by the fact that a former resident of Waldorf, the Reverend John Gabriel Gebhard, had been its pastor up to 1776, when he had withdrawn to Claverack, on the Hudson, where Astor frequently stopped overnight while on his fur-trading expeditions. Quite likely Dominie Gebhard recommended the church to Astor as one in which the young German immigrant would find himself among congenial associates. It was not long until Astor became prominent in the affairs of the church. By the middle of the 'nineties he is said to have been occupying the position of a trustee, and the Consistory frequently met at his house; in 1803 it was still being recorded that "Consistory met with John Jacob Astor in his Broadway home." [156]

In 1804 Astor also became a pewholder in the French Huguenot Church, L'Église du Saint-Esprit, which, after financial difficulties, had conformed to the Episcopalian ritual and on March 27 had sold its pews to a number of persons, most of whom gave no evidence whatsoever by their names that they were of Gallic origin.[157] It is probable that Astor's purchase of a pew was merely an evidence of his interest in this church and of a desire to assist it financially, perhaps inspired by his traditional French ancestry, and it is doubtful whether he intended to, or did, occupy the pew to any great extent.

Although, as we have seen, Astor was prominent in the German Reformed Church early in the first decade of the nineteenth century, as his business interests increased his religious activities seem to have been crowded out. His interest in religion apparently came to the surface chiefly in the phrases of conventional piety with which he occasionally adorned his letters, and which consisted principally of expressions of gratitude to God and of confidence in Providence.[158] Most of these pious expressions are to be found in letters of consolation and counsel addressed to the ultra-religious Peter Smith, and after reading some of his more elaborate utterances we can in fancy see Astor thoughtfully brushing his chin with the plume of his pen as he searched for words which would have the proper effect upon a person of his friend's temperament. Reflections such as, "remember . . . how soon you may have to Leave this world & remember that Lick all men you will Seek for forgiveness. for give your children as you wish aur father in heaven to forgive you," when they appear in Astor's correspondence give an impression of having been composed with an eye single to the effect they would have upon the recipient. They lack the spontaneity of those good round oaths and sulphurous comparisons with which Astor, though not ordinarily a profane man, could on occasion spice his correspondence [159] — especially when he seemed in danger of losing some money.

There may have been another reason, in addition to the crowding in of the cares of the world, for Astor's interest in the church apparently declining rather early in the nineteenth century. About 1805 a struggle began in the congregation between two factions, one Calvinistic, the other agreeing theologically with their Lutheran brethren. Matthew Hale Smith, writing of Astor's religious affiliations after the beginning of the nineteenth century, says:

In religious belief Mr. Astor was a Lutheran. He was an elder in the church located on Nassau Street, near John [an error: the church referred to was German Reformed until the Lutherans captured it in 1834]. Here he worshipped till the house was sold [in 1822] and pulled down [an error: it was still standing in 1846, the congregation having withdrawn to Forsyth Street]. He seldom attended church after that, stating that he was sold out of house and home. Rev. Mr [Isaac] Labough [Labagh, who had been called in 1804] was his pastor [until his resignation in 1822]. Mr. Astor was afflicted with a complaint [anal fistula] that made it difficult for him to sit long at a time. To a clergyman he said, "Men think me a heathen. I cannot sit in church. I have a painful disorder that prevents me." [160]

It is quite probable that this dissension in the church, as well as the condition of his health, was partly responsible for Astor's loss of interest. His was not the type of mind to be concerned with controversy over abstract theological dogmas, and especially with a conflict between adherents of the religion of his childhood and supporters of the doctrines of the church he had joined on coming to the new land.

Astor, however, never definitely withdrew from the German Reformed Church, for in his will, signed July 4, 1836, he left "to the German Reformed Congregation, in the city of New York, of which I am a member . . . *two thousand dollars.*" A codicil of March 3, 1841, revoked this bequest.[161] The Lutheran faction in the church had gained the victory in 1834 and thereafter retained control save for a short period in 1838 and during the years from 1844 to 1846; therefore Astor's action in revoking his bequest can hardly be taken as indicating sympathy with either party in the struggle. It is more likely that he was disgusted with the whole affair and felt that a church in the throes of internecine conflict could hardly be expected to make the best use of even his small legacy.

During the last years of his life, with more time for meditation and abstract speculation, Astor developed somewhat more of an interest in theological problems. As might be expected, the question which perplexed him most was that of immortality. He had lived so long in this world that he found it hard to believe that his life would ever come to an end. New York, so far as he was concerned, had turned out to be a sort of Jerusalem the Golden, and he was willing to be convinced that death would prove to be comparable to another crossing of the

Atlantic in search of a land of promise. It was not that he was worried about the salvation of his soul; it never seems to have occurred to him that, if there was a future life, his success in it would prove to be less striking than it had been in his present existence. It was the very reality of a life to come on which he found himself undecided; no letters describing the advantages which the New Jerusalem possessed over New York had reached his hands, such as those which had come to Waldorf from America and set the sixteen-year-old John Jacob to making plans for the future.

"In the last years of his life," we are told, "he was afflicted with insomnia." On such occasions it became the duty of Dr. Cogswell to sit up with him for a great part of the night, and a favorite servant, William the coachman — who would probably have been quite willing to dispense with this mark of distinction — would also be called to make one of the party. "In these sleepless nights his [Astor's] mind appeared to be much exercised with regard to a future state. On one of these occasions, when Dr. Cogswell had done his best to expound the theme of immortality," Astor suddenly turned on his servant and said severely: "William, where do you expect to go when you die?" The sleepy William, to whom, just at that moment, bed would probably have seemed "Paradise enow," could only stammer out: "Why, sir, I always expected to go where the other people went." [162] William was evidently a better coachman than a diplomat; here was an opportunity for a graceful expression of personal loyalty which a well-trained French valet would hardly have allowed to pass unutilized. But it was probably just as well; even in his extreme old age Astor was not susceptible to flattery, save when it involved a jesting compliment to his financial ability.

Astor's nephew, Henry Brevoort, in a letter to his friend Washington Irving, written late in 1842, remarked that the "old gentleman [Astor] often engages him [Cogswell] upon serious topics & seems to derive hope from C's rational and pious views of things present & to come." But Astor's restless mind was not content merely to accept his friend's deliverances upon the subject, comforting as an unquestioning belief in their validity might have been. He refused to accept a mere statement as an adequate evidence of belief, and insisted upon examining the conduct of the professed believer to determine how it squared with his creed. To him there seemed something inconsistent between the conventionally enthusiastic proclamations of a faith in immortality and the universal reluctance to enter upon that happy condition. As Brevoort expressed it:

His [Astor's] skepticism & shrewdness often displays itself, & some times puzzles his friend to answer. A few days since, in speaking about the happiness which Christianity promises in the world to come, he remarked to C that it always appeared singular to his mind that these cheerful & confident anticipations were not oftner made the subject of ordinary conversations. Men were naturally fond of dwelling upon things which were expected to give them pleasure & yet the change which promised the highest state of happiness was rarely spoken of familiarly, until it was close at hand. — [163]

These discussions must have disquieted Cogswell more than a little. In a eulogistic article, published a few years after Astor's death, he remarked cautiously: "He was not wont to talk much on the subject of religion, or freely communicate his views in relation to the life beyond the grave; but it can not be doubted," he went on more cheerfully, "that such tranquillity as he exhibited in his near approach to it, must have been derived from that peace which the world can neither give nor take away." [164] Cogswell probably had more exact knowledge of Astor's religious beliefs than any other person, but he seemed to feel that his conscience would not permit him to make a stronger statement of his friend's faith than that contained in this rather noncommittal quotation.

The story is told that when Astor realized that his end was near he sent for a former clerk, whom he had once, many years before, refused to allow to work for him on the Sabbath, and who was "now an eminent minister of religion in the city. The party who had charge of the door did not know that the minister had been sent for by the dying merchant. Thinking the minister wanted money, he closed the door upon him, and would not allow him to enter. The dying wish of Mr. Astor was not gratified, and what he wished to breathe into the ear of the man of God was buried with him in his coffin." [165]

Baptized and confirmed in one church, a member throughout his mature life of a second, Astor was buried under the auspices of a third. "Though he expressly declares in his will that he was a member of the Reformed German Congregation, no clergyman of that Church took part in the services of his funeral." His son and principal heir, William B. Astor, was a member of the Protestant Episcopal Church — the institution from which John Jacob had secured so much of his Manhattan Island real estate — and, in consequence, "six Episcopal Doctors of Divinity assisted at the ceremony" and conducted the body to its resting place in the cemetery of St. Thomas' Church.[166]

It is evident that we can trace no definite connection between Astor's religion and his business life. How did this German-American Calvinist of Lutheran ancestry differ in this respect from the French-American freethinker, Stephen Girard, with his Catholic upbringing? Both were China merchants, a large element in the wealth of each was land, on Manhattan Island or in Philadelphia. It certainly cannot be said that Calvinism turned Astor to the fur trade, while freethinking made Girard a banker. The differences in their methods of conducting their respective businesses can hardly be ascribed to contrasting religious beliefs. Both were honest, at least within the restricted sense which that term implies in commerce.[167] They paid their debts and expected others to do the same; the goods they sold were of the quality and quantity they were represented to be. Astor was rather liberal in his dealings with those of his employees with whom he was brought into personal contact, his captains, supercargoes, and principal fur-trade or real-estate agents, was indulgent to his family and generous to himself, but was not conspicuously open-handed toward objects of a public nature; Girard, according to tradition, treated his employees in a miserly fashion, and was no kinder to himself, but was astonishingly lavish in his benefactions to public causes. One course of action may have been partly influenced by the orthodox idea that the great aim of human endeavor is individual salvation and consequently that individual well-being in this life is an achievement which is at least not to be despised. "If any provide not for his own, especially for those of his own house, he hath denied the faith, and is worse than an infidel," and "A good man leaveth an inheritance to his children's children"[168] — two texts which must have given Astor comfort and satisfaction upon occasion. On the other hand we have the more revolutionary concept of the deity of the people *en masse*, the elevation of whom must needs also uplift the individual members, but without which general amelioration it is futile to attempt the benefit of the scattered persons making up the community. Yet had Astor been childless and Girard the head of a large family, it is quite possible that their relative positions would have been greatly modified if not absolutely reversed. As it was, Astor's attitude was the normal and conventional one and requires no particular explanation; religion undoubtedly played a larger part in the life of the French free-thinker than it did in that of the orthodox member of the German Reformed Consistory. The names of Girard's ships — *Voltaire, Montesquieu, Helvetius* — as contrasted with Astor's *Beaver, Magdalen, William and John, Henry Astor*, and *Tamaahmaah*, reveal the difference in the bent of their minds.

It is hard for one who has read the correspondence, extending over more than forty years, which passed between Astor and Peter Smith, to avoid the conclusion that in that relationship, as well as in Astor's temperament and certain environmental conditions already mentioned, there lies some explana-

tion of the apparent decline of his interest in religion. Peter
Smith was probably the most deeply religious man whom
Astor ever knew, but his religion was of such a type that Astor
could not help feeling that it increased rather than lightened
the burden of those troubles which all men are forced to undergo. It was bad enough to have to confront difficulties in
your family, falling prices in the fur market, and restrictions
on the China trade, without the additional eternal problem of
your soul's salvation. Then, too, in Smith's case religion led
him into all sorts of curious freaks which could do no good to
the standing of a merchant, however innocuous they might be
in the case of a large landowner in backcountry New York.
Take, for example, his persistent distribution of tracts, his
naïve suggestion that Astor join with him in donating part of
their hard-won Mohawk Valley land to families of converted
Jews! [169] And his son Gerrit — a fine young man, Astor admitted — was as religious as his father, though in an even more
unconventional and inconvenient fashion. Religious tracts
and converted Jews were bad enough, but abolition literature
and runaway Negroes were several degrees worse. To Astor it
was quite clear that the Smith family was suffering from a
superfluity rather than a deficiency of religion. In his letters
of advice to Peter Smith, it was with reluctance and as rarely
as seemed judicious that Astor resorted to the religious appeal,
exhortations to have faith in God, etc., though upon occasion,
as we have seen, he found such language necessary. His philosophy, as expressed in these letters, was, on the whole,
definitely secular. "Make the best of things," was Astor's
motto for adversity. His own method of doing this was by
keeping his mind active with travel, plans for overcoming
competitors in the fur trade, or the collection of material for
Irving's *Astoria*.

Of course Astor was neither irreligious nor anti-religious.
In most respects he seemed, and doubtless was, a perfectly
orthodox if somewhat inactive churchman. The agents of the

American Fur Company assisted missionaries in the Indian country; Astor's captains and supercargoes headed every missionary subscription list in the Hawaiian Islands; Astor himself contributed to churches at Green Bay. All this, of course, was good business, but Astor stopped there. He did not trade on his religion even to the extent that he did on his politics. He did not claim that his China trade, with its opium-smuggling, had for its main purpose the conversion of the Chinese, or that his trade in liquor with the Indians and Hawaiian Islanders had as a principal end the Christianization of those backward peoples. He was no hypocrite, unless every religionist whose conduct does not conform to the loftiness of his tacit professions is to be so classified.

The attention Astor paid to religious problems during his last years demonstrates that his interest in such questions, though it would probably never have become dominant, was at least not entirely lacking. An unreligious man would not have bothered to discuss the question of immortality; he would either have felt no interest in the problem or would have accepted it unquestioningly without further thought. Astor took neither of these positions. His intellectual honesty would not allow him to accept any statement purely on authority, whether it was upon the validity of a future life or the value of an issue of railroad stock. One is inclined to wonder whether, in his conversations with Stephen Girard, the China trade and the national bank were the sole topics of discussion. After Peter Smith's religious hysteria, the cold stoical skepticism of Stephen Girard may have seemed somewhat refreshing to Astor's practical mind. Cogswell did not seem altogether sure of Astor's final decision upon the principal subject of their nocturnal discussions, but we can be confident that if he ever formed an opinion it was upon arguments tested and found valid by his own reason.

NOTES

1. Ms. book, Office of Vincent Astor, 23 W. 26th St., New York City, Gay, W. B., "Astor," dated November 7, 1912, 54 Dey St., N. Y., p. 2; Astor genealogy in the possession of Mrs. Richard Aldrich.

2. I am inclined to doubt the interesting tradition, preserved in one line of his descendants, that he was a farmer who acted on Sundays as a lay preacher in the Lutheran Church.

3. Ms. book, Office of Vincent Astor, 23 W. 26th St., New York City, Gay, W. B., "Astor," dated November 7, 1912, 54 Dey St., N. Y., p. 2.

4. Parton, James, *Life of John Jacob Astor* (1865), p. 26.

5. Astor genealogy in the possession of Mrs. Richard Aldrich.

6. Record of information given by Mrs. Byam K. Stevens, great-granddaughter of John Jacob Astor, in the possession of Mrs. Richard Aldrich. See above, vol. ii, facing p. 1026.

7. [Oertel, Philip] (W. D. Van Horn, pseud.), *Johann Jacob Astor* (Wiesbaden, 1855 [?]), pp. 17–18; Scrap Book, New York Historical Society, Notes on the Astor Family by William Kelby, p. 1.

8. Astor genealogy in the possession of Mrs. Richard Aldrich.

9. Ms. book, Baker Library, Astor Papers, Letter Book i, 1813–15, pp. 178–179, John Jacob Astor, N. Y., February 14, 1814, to John Wright (see above, vol. i, pp. 550–552).

10. *Ibid.*, p. 297, John Jacob Astor, N. Y., September 29, 1814, to George Astor.

11. Parton, *op. cit.*, pp. 96, 104; ms., Baker Library, Astor Papers, The Will of John Jacob Astor (see below, vol. ii, pp. 1267, 1276).

12. *Ibid.*, Letter Book ii, 1831–38, pp. 222, 541, William B. Astor, N. Y., April 7, 1834, December 7, 1837, to Mrs. Elizabeth Astor, London.

13. *Ibid.*, Letter Book i, 1813–15, letters from John Jacob Astor, N. Y., to George Astor, Jr., *passim*.

14. *Longworth's American Almanac, New-York Register, and City Directory* (1816–17), p. 109; *ibid.* (1817–18), p. 97. "Astor & Co. George, fur store 144 Water."

15. [Scoville, Joseph A.], *The Old Merchants of New York City*, 5 vols. (1889), vol. i, p. 421.

16. Parton, *op. cit.*, pp. 96, 104; ms., Baker Library, Astor Papers, The Will of John Jacob Astor (see below, vol. ii, pp. 1267, 1276).

17. *Ibid.*, Letter Book ii, 1831–38, p. 621, John Jacob Astor, N. Y., November 8, 1838, to George P. Astor, Mackinac.

18. *Ibid.*, Letter Book iii, 1845–48, p. 206, William B. Astor, N. Y., August 12, 1847, to George Reynell, 42 Chancery Lane, London.

19. *Ibid.*, letters from William B. Astor to George P. Astor and Mrs. George P. Astor, *passim*.

20. [Armstrong, William], *The Aristocracy of New York* (1848), p. 6.

21. Ms. book, Baker Library, Astor Papers, Letter Book iii, 1845–48, p. 212, William B. Astor, N. Y., February 20, 1834, to Benjamin Astor, 5th St. and Green St.; p. 260, John Jacob Astor, N. Y., October 3, 1834, to Mrs. Mary Reynell, London (see below, vol. ii, pp. 1227–1228).

22. *Longworth's American Almanac, New-York Register, and City Directory* (1835–36), "Astor, William H. music teacher Avenue 6th c. Thirteenth."

23. Parton, *op. cit.*, pp. 96, 104; ms., Baker Library, Astor Papers, The Will of John Jacob Astor (see below, vol. ii, pp. 1267, 1276).

24. *Ibid.*; Parton, *op. cit.*, pp. 96, 104, 113.

25. Record of information given by Mrs. Byam K. Stevens, in the possession of Mrs. Richard Aldrich. On October 18, 1843, Henry Brevoort wrote to Washington Irving: "Y^r. *favorite* Miss Oxenham is on furlough in England." (*Brevoort, Henry, Letters of, to Washington Irving*, George S. Hellman, ed., 2 vols. (1916), vol. ii, p. 128.)

26. Ms. book, Baker Library, Astor Papers, Letter Book ii, 1831–38, p. 541, William B. Astor, N. Y., December 7, 1837, to Mrs. Sarah Oxenham, Somerstown, England. On the other hand, Astor's housekeeper at one time may have been Mrs. Oxenham herself. Cogswell wrote in July, 1843, that "his [Astor's] niece . . . with her husband, had been staying with him." (*Cogswell, Joseph Green, Life of* (1874), p. 234.)

27. Parton, *op. cit.*, pp. 104, 117–118; ms., Baker Library, Astor Papers, The Will of John Jacob Astor (see below, vol. ii, pp. 1267, 1275, 1291).

28. *Ibid.*, Letter Book iii, 1845–48, pp. 45, 137, 253, William B. Astor, N. Y., December 12, 1845, December 31, 1846, December 31, 1847, to Mrs. Sarah Oxenham, London.

29. *Ibid.*, Letter Book ii, 1831–38, p. 541, William B. Astor, December 7, 1837, to George Reynell, London.

30. Parton, *op. cit.*, p. 117; ms., Baker Library, Astor Papers, The Will of John Jacob Astor (see below, vol. ii, p. 1291).

31. *Ibid.*, Letter Book iii, 1845–48, pp. 45, 137, 252, William B. Astor, N. Y., December 12, 1845, December 31, 1846, December 31, 1847, to Thomas G. Holt, London.

32. *Ibid.*, Letter Book ii, 1831–38, p. 541, William B. Astor, N. Y., December 7, 1837, to Mrs. Elizabeth Astor, London.

33. *Ibid.*, Letter Book iii, 1845–48, pp. 44, 137, 253, William B. Astor, N. Y., December 12, 1845, December 31, 1846, December 31, 1847, to Mrs. Catherine Epworth, London.

34. Astor sometimes reciprocated his brother's kindnesses by such actions as appearing before the commissioners of the almshouse and bridewell, in regard to a contract for furnishing beef to that institution, when Henry was out of town. Henry received the contract (ms. book, New York Public Library, Commissioners of the Alms House and Bridewell,

New York City, Minutes, 1791–1797, pp. 15, 17, 48, January 16, 23, 30, 1792).

35. Scrap Book, New York Historical Society, Notes on the Astor Family by William Kelby, p. 3.

36. Scoville, *op. cit.*, vol. i, p. 422.

37. [Beach, Moses Yale], *The Wealth and Biography of the Wealthy Citizens of the City of New York* (1846), p. 3; Armstrong, *op. cit.*, p. 8.

38. Ms. book, Baker Library, Astor Papers, Letter Book ii, 1831–38, p. 179, William B. Astor, N. Y., September 23, 1833, to Catherine Astor; p. 260, John Jacob Astor, N. Y., October 3, 1834, to Mrs. Mary Reynell, London (see below, vol. ii, pp. 1227–1228).

39. Scoville, *op. cit.*, vol. i, pp. 285, 326; *New York Genealogical and Biographical Record*, vol. xx (1889), p. 93.

40. Scoville, *op. cit.*, vol. i, pp. 325–326.

41. Parton, *op. cit.*, pp. 96, 104; ms., Baker Library, Astor Papers, The Will of John Jacob Astor (see below, vol. ii, pp. 1267, 1275).

42. *Ibid.*, Letter Book i, 1813–15, p. 100, John Jacob Astor, N. Y., November 10, 1813, to George Ehninger.

43. *Ibid.*, Letter Book ii, 1831–38, p. 492, John Jacob Astor, N. Y., May 22, 1837, to George Ehninger.

44. Parton, *op. cit.*, p. 104; ms., Baker Library, Astor Papers, The Will of John Jacob Astor (see below, vol. ii, p. 1276).

45. *Ibid.* (see below, vol. ii, pp. 1267, 1275, 1276); Parton, *op. cit.*, pp. 96, 104. A late account, which in many details is known to be inaccurate, states that Astor's sister Catherine "married Michael Miller, by whom she had a daughter, Hannah, and another, Maria, who married a Mr. Moore" ("The Descendants of John Jacob Astor," *New York Times — Illustrated Magazine*, March 6, 1898). This only makes the confusion worse.

46. Oertel, *op. cit.*, p. 18; Scrap Book, New York Historical Society, Notes on the Astor Family by William Kelby, p. 1.

47. Parton, *op. cit.*, pp. 96, 104; ms., Baker Library, Astor Papers, The Will of John Jacob Astor (see below, vol. ii, p. 1267, 1281–1282).

48. Astor genealogy in the possession of Mrs. Richard Aldrich; Scrap Book, New York Historical Society, Notes on the Astor Family by William Kelby, p. 1.

49. *Ibid.*

50. Personal information from Mrs. F. H. Potter, a descendant of Mrs. Cook. According to this account, however, she was only sixty-seven at the time of her death, which would put her birth at the impossible date of 1790. A late and inaccurate account says that one of Astor's three sisters "married William P. Woodcock" ("The Descendants of John Jacob Astor," *New York Times — Illustrated Magazine*, March 6, 1898).

51. Scrap Book, New York Historical Society, Notes on the Astor Family by William Kelby, p. 1; Astor genealogy in the possession of Mrs. Richard Aldrich.

52. Armstrong, *op. cit.*, p. 6; Scoville, *op. cit.*, vol. ii, p. 32.

53. Ms. book, Baker Library, Astor Papers, Letter Book ii, 1831–38, p. 229, John Jacob Astor, N. Y., May 4, 1834, to Wilson P. Hunt, St. Louis (see below, vol. ii, pp. 1224–1225).

54. Scrap Book, New York Historical Society, Notes on the Astor Family by William Kelby, p. 7. There is an unaccountable impression, which I have encountered in several places, that Astor was twice married. A scurrilous little tract, published some time after his death, says that his wife "was a Scotch woman named Furgerson, who kept an apple stand at the corner of Maiden Lane and Broadway." (*John Jacob Astor: The Richest Man in the United States*, Boston Public Library, 7689.9.) Smith refers to "the first Mrs. Astor, the mother of his children" (Smith, Matthew Hale, *Sunshine and Shadow in New York* (1868), p. 125). But since Astor was more than seventy when "the mother of his children" died, it is improbable that there was a second marriage. Strangest of all is a statement by one of Astor's descendants, Mrs. Byam K. Stevens: "Mr. Astor married twice, both times to girls from the Bowery. The first wife lived but a short time, and left no children. The second wife had a large family." Astor did not reach New York until April, 1784; he married Sarah Todd in September, 1785, and between those dates worked for a number of employers, peddled flutes and bought furs on his own account, in his spare time, and made a voyage to London. It does not seem consistent with what we know of Astor's character that he would also have found time to woo and marry two girls.

55. Scrap Book, New York Historical Society, Notes on the Astor Family by William Kelby, p. 7.

56. Greene, Richard H., "Astor American Ancestry," *New York Genealogical and Biographical Record*, vol. xxiii (1892), pp. 15–17.

57. *Hone, Philip, The Diary of, 1828–1851*, Allan Nevins, ed., 2 vols. (1927), vol. i, p. 121.

58. Anecdote preserved by Miss Katherine L. Wilks, a descendant of Dorothea Astor.

59. Scrap Book, New York Historical Society, Notes on the Astor Family by William Kelby, p. 7; ms. book, Office of Vincent Astor, 23 W. 26th St., New York City, Gay, W. B., "Astor," dated November 7, 1912, 54 Dey St., N. Y., p. 9; Greene, Richard Henry, *The Todd Genealogy* (1867), *passim; New-York Gazette and General Advertiser*, February 10, 1818, p. 2, col. 4; February 12, 1818, p. 2, col. 1.

60. On May 1, 1819, Astor deeded Magdalen a couple of lots in New York City (ms. book, Hall of Records, N. Y., Liber Conveyances 145, p. 420).

61. Scrap Book, New York Historical Society, Notes on the Astor Family by William Kelby, p. 22.

62. Ms. book, Office of Vincent Astor, 23 W. 26th St., New York City, Gay, W. B., "Astor," dated November 7, 1912, 54 Dey St., N. Y., p. 9.

63. *Brevoort, Henry, Letters of, to Washington Irving,* vol. i, pp. 150–151, October 9, 1821.

64. Record of information given by Mrs. Byam K. Stevens, great-granddaughter of John Jacob Astor, in the possession of Mrs. Richard Aldrich.

65. Greene, R. H., *The Todd Genealogy, passim.*

66. Parton, *op. cit.*, pp. 94–95, 119; ms., Baker Library, Astor Papers, The Will of John Jacob Astor (see below, vol. ii, pp. 1265–1266, 1293).

67. Beach, *op. cit.*, p. 3; Armstrong, *op. cit.*, p. 6; Smith, *op. cit.*, pp. 190–191; record of information given by Mrs. Byam K. Stevens; Spooner, Walter W., ed., *Historic Families of America* (N. Y., n. d.), p. 328; Gebhard, Elizabeth L., *The Life and Ventures of the Original John Jacob Astor* (1915), p. 248.

68. *Irving, Washington, The Letters of, to Henry Brevoort,* George S. Hellman, ed., 2 vols. (1915), vol. ii, pp. 162–163.

69. Ms. book, Office of the Astor Estate, N. Y., Untitled land book.

70. Ms. book, Baker Library, Astor Papers, Letter Book ii, 1831–38, p. 21, John Jacob Astor, N. Y., January 6, 1832, to Thomas W. Olcott, Albany (see below, vol. ii, p. 1212); pp. 9, 27, 48, 79, 103, 126, 153, 168, 187, 205, 226, 249, 263, 277, 297, 316, 341, 369, 399, 419, 441, 461, 486, 504, 533, 558, 582, 588, 591, 596, John Jacob Astor by William B. Astor, N. Y., November 12, 1831, January 27, April 30, July 27, October 27, 1832, January 24, May 1, July 23, October 28, 1833, January 24, April 25, July 24, October 25, 1834, January 24, April 25, July 23, October 23, 1835, January 23, April 26, July 23, October 25, 1836, January 23, April 24, July 26, October 25, 1837, January 25, April 23, May 31, June 16, 28, 1838, to W. J. Hubbard, Boston; pp. 63, 588, 596, 612, 615, John Jacob Astor, N. Y., June 18, 1832, by William B. Astor, May 31, June 28, August 28, September 20, 1838, to Dexter Fairbank, Cambridgeport.

71. Armstrong, *op. cit.*, p. 6; Smith, *op. cit.*, pp. 190–192.

72. Parton, *op. cit.*, pp. 96, 106–108; ms., Baker Library, Astor Papers, The Will of John Jacob Astor (see below, vol. ii, pp. 1267, 1278–1280).

73. Scrap Book, New York Historical Society, Notes on the Astor Family by William Kelby, p. 7; ms. book, Office of Vincent Astor, 23 W. 26th St., New York City, Gay, W. B., "Astor," dated November 7, 1912, 54 Dey St., N. Y., p. 14.

74. Howe, Julia Ward, *Reminiscences, 1819–1899* (1899), p. 73.

75. Smith, *op. cit.*, pp. 186–189; record of information from Mrs. Byam K. Stevens.

76. Ms. book, Hall of Records, N. Y., Liber Conveyances 310, pp. 483, 484; 402, p. 235; 423, p. 344; 483, p. 395; 490, p. 595.

77. Howe, *op. cit.*, pp. 65, 73.

78. *Brevoort, Henry, Letters of, to Washington Irving*, vol. ii, pp. 133–135.

79. Ms. book, Baker Library, Astor Papers, Letter Book iii, 1845–48, pp. 91, 109, 112, 187, William B. Astor, N. Y., June 6, August 20, 31, 1846, June 5, 1847, to Samuel Ward.

80. *Ibid.*, pp. 110–111, 177–178, William B. Astor, N. Y., August 28, 1846, May 5, 1847, to Vincent Rumpff.

81. Parton, *op. cit.*, pp. 95–96, 116, 118; ms., Baker Library, Astor Papers, The Will of John Jacob Astor (see below, vol. ii, pp. 1266–1267, 1290, 1291).

82. *Ibid.*; Parton, *op. cit.*, pp. 98, 105, 121.

83. Armstrong, *op. cit.*, p. 8; Scoville, *op. cit.*, vol. i, p. 100.

84. Smith, *op. cit.*, pp. 119–120.

85. Parton, *op. cit.*, pp. 95–96, 116; ms., Baker Library, Astor Papers, The Will of John Jacob Astor (see below, vol. ii, pp. 1266–1267, 1289).

86. Ms. book, Hall of Records, N. Y., Liber Conveyances 423, p. 342; 465, p. 457.

87. Greene, R. H., *The Todd Genealogy, passim.*

88. Scrap Book, New York Historical Society, Notes on the Astor Family by William Kelby, p. 7; ms. book, Office of Vincent Astor, 23 W. 26th St., New York City, Gay, W. B., "Astor," dated November 7, 1912, 54 Dey St., N. Y., p. 9.

89. Record of information given by Mrs. Byam K. Stevens; ms. book, Hall of Records, N. Y., Liber Conveyances 408, p. 628; 458, pp. 54, 563.

90. Parton, *op. cit.*, pp. 90–91, 108, 120; ms., Baker Library, Astor Papers, The Will of John Jacob Astor (see below, vol. ii, pp. 1260, 1272–1274, 1294–1295).

91. *Ibid.*, Letter Book iii, 1845–48, p. 210, William B. Astor, N. Y., August 27, 1847, to Vincent Rumpff.

92. Howe, *op. cit.*, pp. 73–76.

93. Ms. book, Baker Library, Astor Papers, Letter Book iii, 1845–48, pp. 45–46, William B. Astor, N. Y., December 13, 1845, to Mrs. Sarah Boreel, La Haye (see below, vol. ii, pp. 1249–1250).

94. Parton, *op. cit.*, p. 92; ms. book, Hall of Records, N. Y., Liber Conveyances 446, p. 354; 489, p. 325; ms., Baker Library, Astor Papers, The Will of John Jacob Astor (see below, vol. ii, pp. 1262, 1263).

95. Information given by Mrs. Byam K. Stevens.

96. Ms. book, Baker Library, Astor Papers, Letter Book iii, 1845–48, pp. 49, 79, 162, 185, 186, 260, William B. Astor, N. Y., January 6, April 25, 1846, March 12, May 29, June 1, 1847, January 21, 1848, to Mrs. Louisa Kane.

97. Parton, *op. cit.*, pp. 91, 92, 108, 109, 116, 118–119; ms., Baker Library, Astor Papers, The Will of John Jacob Astor (see below, vol. ii, pp. 1261–1263, 1280–1281, 1292–1293).

98. Ms. book, Hall of Records, N. Y., Liber Conveyances 439, p. 590; 459, p. 397.

99. Information given by Mrs. Byam K. Stevens.

100. Ms. book, Baker Library, Astor Papers, Letter Book iii, 1845–48, pp. 50, 79, 162, 225, William B. Astor, N. Y., January 6, April 7, 1846, March 12, October 23, 1847, to Mrs. Matthew Wilks.

101. *Ibid.*, p. 231, William B. Astor, N. Y., November 5, 1847, to Vincent Rumpff.

102. Information given by Mrs. Byam K. Stevens.

103. Scrap Book, New York Historical Society, Notes on the Astor Family by William Kelby, p. 7.

104. Ms., Syracuse University, Gerrit Smith Miller Collection, Letters, John Jacob Astor, N. Y., December 7, 1799, to Peter Smith, Old Fort Schuyler (see above, vol. i, pp. 387–389).

105. Armstrong, *op. cit.*, p. 6.

106. *Irving, Washington, The Letters of, to Henry Brevoort*, vol. ii, pp. 162–163.

107. *New-York Gazette and General Advertiser*, April 29, 1822, p. 2, col. 2; June 3, 1823, p. 2, col. 2.

108. Armstrong, *op. cit.*, p. 6.

109. Parton, *op. cit.*, pp. 93–94, 108, 119; ms., Baker Library, Astor Papers, The Will of John Jacob Astor (see below, vol. ii, pp. 1263–1265, 1274, 1280, 1295).

110. Smith, Arthur D. Howden, *John Jacob Astor* (1929), pp. 267–270; Brown, Lawrence Parmly, "The Greatest Dental Family," reprinted from the *Dental Cosmos* (March, April, May, 1923).

111. Ms., Syracuse University, Gerrit Smith Miller Collection, Letters, John Jacob Astor, N. Y., November 16, 1802, to Peter Smith, Utica.

112. *Ibid.*, John Meyer for John Jacob Astor, N. Y., October 7, 1806, January 24, 1807, to Peter Smith; Scoville, *op. cit.*, vol. ii, pp. 265–266, "the Eagle Fire Insurance Company was started in 1807 . . . John Meyer, Secretary, No. 59 Wall street."

113. *Ibid.*, vol. ii, pp. 50–51; ms., Syracuse University, Gerrit Smith Miller Collection, Letters, William Roberts for John Jacob Astor, N. Y., November 3, 1819, to Peter Smith; Scoville, *op. cit.*, vol. ii, pp. 50–51.

114. *Ibid.*, vol. iii, p. 128.

115. Apparently the only unforgivable sin in an Astor captain was to wreck his vessel. No Astor captain ever did so and, on returning to New York, was given the opportunity to wreck another. Throughout the more than a quarter of a century of Astor's career as a ship-owner, he lost only two vessels by wreck. The captains in command on both these occasions,

Samuel H. Northrop of the *Lark* and Vibberts of the *Fingal*, were making their first voyages as Astor captains.

116. Ms. book, Baker Library, Astor Papers, Letter Book ii, 1831–38, p. 451, John Jacob Astor, N. Y., December 7, 1836, to Joseph Ridgway, St. Croix.

117. Smith, M. H., *op. cit.*, p. 120.

118. *Cogswell, Joseph Green, Life of*, p. 214.

119. Scoville, *op. cit.*, vol. i, pp. 314–315; vol. ii, pp. 369–370.

120. Ms. book, Baker Library, Astor Papers, Letter Book ii, 1831–38, pp. 25, 74, 79, John Jacob Astor, N. Y., January 19, July 19, 27, 1832, to John Jacob Astor Ebbets, Yale College, New Haven; p. 483, John Jacob Astor, N. Y., April 17, 1837, to J. J. A. Ebbets, London.

121. *Ibid.*, Letter Book iii, 1845–48, p. 56, William B. Astor, N. Y., January 31, 1846, to Mrs. C. C. Canfield, late Mrs. Richard Ebbets, Morristown, N. J.

122. "John Jacob Astor," *Hunt's Merchants' Magazine*, vol. xi (1844), p. 158.

123. Parton, *op. cit.*, p. 56.

124. Stokes, Isaac Newton Phelps, *The Iconography* of *Manhattan Island*, 6 vols. (1915–28), vol. v, p. 1374.

125. Adkins, Nelson Frederick, *Fitz-Greene Halleck* (1930), pp. 253–254.

126. Irving, Pierre M., *The Life and Letters of Washington Irving*, 4 vols. (1862–64), vol. iii, pp. 64, 77.

127. Adkins, *op. cit.*, pp. 257, 285, 304, 311 note.

128. Astor's habit of gravely chanting the praises of contentment was one of his most amusing characteristics. The story is told that Philip Hone, at that time "one of the rich men of New York, and . . . not a little proud of his wealth," used to lean against the fence across the street from the "elegant mansion" he was building on the block above Astor's own residence, and, toying with his watch key, regard the progress of his fine house with a satisfaction too deep for words. One morning Astor observed him standing there, and, comparing Hone's wealth with his own, misinterpreted his neighbor's gaze as expressive of discontent; he thereupon approached him and in the innocence of his heart uttered these consoling words: "Mr. Hone, you are a successful merchant and a good citizen. You have a fine wife and some nice children. You have a snug little property, and are building a comfortable house. I don't see why you are not just as well off as if you were rich." It is probable that Hone had some difficulty in deciding whether he should be indignant or amused. (Smith, M. H., *op. cit.*, p. 117.)

129. Irving, *op. cit.*, vol. i, p. 59; vol. iii, pp. 60–64, 72–74, 77–79, 86–87, 88–89, 90, 92–94, 119–124; vol. iv, pp. 35, 38–39, 52–53.

130. *Cogswell, Joseph Green, Life of*, pp. 232–236, 238.

131. *Hone, Philip, The Diary of, 1828–1851,* vol. ii, pp. 595, 716.

132. Howe, *op. cit.,* pp. 73–76.

133. Aldrich, Mrs. Richard, "Notes of the Astors," *Washington Historical Quarterly,* vol. xviii (1927), pp. 21–27.

134. Chittenden, Hiram Martin, *The American Fur Trade of the Far West,* 3 vols. (1902), vol. i, pp. 184, 340, 357; vol. ii, pp. 637–638; Bradbury, John, *Travels in the Interior of America,* Reuben Gold Thwaites, ed. (1904); Maximilian, Prince of Wied, *Travels in the Interior of North America,* Reuben Gold Thwaites, ed. (1905).

135. "John Jacob Astor," *Hogg's Weekly Instructor,* vol. i (new series, 1848), pp. 235–237.

136. *Adams, John Quincy, Memoirs of,* Charles Francis Adams, ed., 12 vols. (1875), vol. xii, p. 108.

137. Howe, *op. cit.,* pp. 73–76.

138. Armstrong, *op. cit.,* p. 7; Beach, *op. cit.,* p. 3. There is also a record that in 1837 Astor sent Henry Brevoort "a check for $250 for a picture" (ms. book, Baker Library, Astor Papers, Letter Book ii, 1831–38, p. 500, William B. Astor, N. Y., July 3, 1837, to Henry Brevoort, Jr.).

139. Frothingham, W., "Astor and the Capitalists of New-York," *Continental Monthly,* vol. ii (August, 1862), pp. 207–217.

140. Ms. book, Baker Library, Astor Papers, Letter Book ii, 1831–38, p. 29, John Jacob Astor, N. Y., January 30, 1832, to George W. Erving.

141. His intimacy with the Madison family is particularly well brought out in a letter of September 19, 1812, to Mrs. Madison (Clark, Allen C., *Life and Letters of Dolly Madison* (1914), pp. 144–145).

142. Catterall, Ralph C. H., *The Second Bank of the United States* (1903), p. 22.

143. *New-York Gazette and General Advertiser,* June 20, 1817, p. 2, col. 1; ms., New York Public Library, Monroe Papers, John Jacob Astor, N. Y., June 16, 1817, to the Committee of Arrangements; Thomas R. Smith, N. Y., June 17, 1817, to John Jacob Astor, N. Y.; John Jacob Astor, N. Y., June 19, 1817, to James Monroe.

144. *Adams, John Quincy, Memoirs of,* vol. iv, p. 4; Adams, James Truslow, *The Adams Family* (1930), pp. 168–169.

145. Ms., New York Public Library, Monroe Papers, John Jacob Astor, N. Y., November 7, 1817, November 20, 1818, to James Monroe, President; ms., Thomas Addis Emmet Collection, no. 11, 645, recommendation of James C. Forbes to the secretary of the Treasury as appraiser of merchandise, N. Y., May, 1818, by John Jacob Astor and other merchants. In November, 1814, Astor asked Monroe for a post abroad for Dr. John Bullus, naval agent at the port of New York (Brock, H. I., "Sea Heroes Live Again in their Old Letters," *The New York Times,* October 7, 1928, sec. x, p. 24).

146. Adams, Henry, *The Life of Albert Gallatin* (1880), p. 584.

147. *Adams, John Quincy, Memoirs of*, vol. iv, p. 430.

148. Adams, of course, was sympathetic to the legitimate requests of Astor's company, as for a revenue cutter on Lake Superior to prevent smuggling (*ibid.*, vol. vii, p. 446).

149. Irving, *op. cit.*, vol. iii, p. 126.

150. Parton says definitely: "He [Astor] had little to say of politics, but he was a supporter of the old Whig party for many years, and had a great regard, personal and political, for its leader and ornament, Henry Clay. He was never better pleased than when he entertained Mr. Clay at his own house." (Parton, *op. cit.*, pp. 69–70.) I should not wish to deny this statement of Astor's political affiliations, but the only confirmatory evidence that he was a consistent Whig which I have been able to unearth is found in Parton's own pages. There is no reason to doubt, of course, that Astor was a Whig by 1844. Two years later, his son wrote: "The late election here and those recently held in other States show a great increase of the Whig party and its probable triumph; and this change in politics I ascribe in a great measure to the Sub-treasury scheme, the Mexican War, New Tariff and the annexation of Texas — all of which have contributed to produce the same result." (Ms. book, Baker Library, Astor Papers, Letter Book iii, 1845–48, p. 128, William B. Astor, N. Y., November 9, 1846, to Vincent Rumpff, Paris.) Astor derived a sentimental pleasure from the recognition of the claims of the United States to Oregon, but the cry of "54° 40' or Fight" found no sympathetic response in his breast.

151. Ms., Library of Congress, Monroe Papers, vol. xiv, Writings to Monroe, November, 1813–March 19, 1815, John Jacob Astor, N. Y., April 30, 1814, to James Monroe, Secretary of State (see above, vol. i, pp. 554–556).

152. Parton, *op. cit.*, pp. 20–22.

153. [Cogswell, Joseph Green], "The Astor Library and its Founder," *The United States Magazine*, vol. ii (1855), pp. 137–145.

154. Smith, M. H., *op. cit.*, p. 125. There is also a tradition, among some of her descendants, that she was of Quaker stock (Aldrich, *loc. cit.*).

155. Greene, Richard H., "Astor American Ancestry," *New York Genealogical and Biographical Record*, vol. xxiii (1892), pp. 15–17.

156. Gebhard, *op. cit.*, pp. 67–71, 85–86, 126. It is not unfair to point out that considerations of social advancement may have been an influence with Astor in selecting his church home. Among the members of the German Reformed Church in New York, for example, was Baron von Steuben. (Gebhard, *op. cit.*, p. 71.) Such considerations may have also influenced Astor in his becoming a member of the Masonic order. In 1790 he joined Holland Lodge no. 8, which had been established in 1787 with a charter which allowed the members to perform "their Labours in the Low Dutch Lenguage." Astor was admitted in the same year as such

distinguished men as De Witt Clinton, Cadwallader Colden, and Henry W. Livingston. Clinton was senior warden in 1793 and master in 1794, but the German immigrant was not much behind this member of one of the first families in the State, for in 1797 Astor became senior warden and the next year he was master. (*Holland Lodge No. 8, F. & A. M.* (1930), pp. 7, 40–41, 58, 61, 68.) In 1801 "Sir J. J. Astor" was treasurer of the Knights Templar order (*Longworth's American Almanac, New-York Register, and City Directory* (1801), p. 80), but after this there is no evidence that he continued to be interested in Freemasonry. He may have felt that his social and financial standing now required no artificial aids.

157. *Collections of the Huguenot Society of America*, vol. i (1886), p. lxxviii.

158. Ms., Syracuse University, Gerrit Smith Miller Collection, Letters, John Jacob Astor, N. Y., March 24, 1801, November 16, 1802, February 19, 1828, to Peter Smith, Utica and Peterboro; Irving, Washington, *Astoria* (1836), chaps. li, lv; ms. book, Baker Library, Astor Papers, Letter Book i, 1813–15, p. 27, John Jacob Astor, N. Y., July 19, 1813, to Ramsay Crooks.

159. Ms., Syracuse University, Gerrit Smith Miller Collection, Letters, John Jacob Astor, N. Y., March 11, Ballston Springs, August 13, 1798, N. Y., February 19, Albany, August 10, 1799, N. Y., December 1, 1800, March 22, 1811, to Peter Smith, Old Fort Schuyler, Utica, and Peterboro; ms. (copy), Detroit Public Library, Burton Historical Collection, and Missouri Historical Society, St. Louis, Letters of Ramsay Crooks, John Jacob Astor, and the American Fur Company, 1813–43, John Jacob Astor, N. Y., March 16, 1827, to Ramsay Crooks.

160. Smith, M. H., *op. cit.*, p. 125; Greenleaf, Jonathan, *History of the Churches of New-York* (1846), pp. 25–28.

161. Parton, *op. cit.*, pp. 97, 115; ms., Baker Library, Astor Papers, The Will of John Jacob Astor (see below, vol. ii, pp. 1268, 1288).

162. Howe, *op. cit.*, p. 76.

163. *Brevoort, Henry, Letters of, to Washington Irving*, vol. ii, p. 125.

164. Cogswell, *loc. cit.*

165. Smith, M. H., *op. cit.*, p. 126.

166. Parton, *op. cit.*, p. 81; Hone, Philip, *The Diary of*, 1828–1851, vol. ii, p. 848.

167. Among the anecdotes told concerning Astor's honesty in commercial matters is the following: "When John Jacob Astor was a leading merchant in New York, he was one of the few merchants who could buy goods by the cargo. A large dealer in teas knowing that few merchants could outbid him, or purchase a cargo, concluded to buy a whole shipload that had just arrived and was offered at auction. He had nobody to compete with, and he expected to have everything his own way. Just before the sale commenced, to his consternation he saw Mr. Astor walking

leisurely down the wharf. He went to meet him, and said, 'Mr. Astor, I am sorry to see you here this morning. If you will go to your counting-room, and stay till after the sale, I'll give you a thousand dollars.' Without thinking much about it, Mr. Astor consented, turned on his heel, and said, 'Send round the check.' He found that he had made one thousand dollars, and probably had lost ten thousand dollars. But he kept his word, and that is the way he did his business." (Smith, M. H., *op. cit.*, pp. 70–71.) If this incident ever actually happened, it was doubtless creditable to Astor's honesty, but it must have been a strange exception to his usual method of doing business — that is, if he had ever had any intention of bidding on that cargo of tea.

168. I Tim. v, 8; Prov. xiii, 22.

169. Ms., Syracuse University, Gerrit Smith Miller Collection, bundle labelled "Correspon. Messrs. Laights' & Sister — Also M^r. Astor—," E. W. Laight, N. Y., March 12, 1825, to Peter Smith, Peterboro.

CHAPTER XXIV

PHILANTHROPY, TRAVEL, HEALTH, AND OLD AGE

THERE are two questions which are sure to be asked soon after the death of any wealthy man and which will continue to be asked as long as his name is remembered. They are: "How did he make his money?" and "How much did he give away?" We have for some time been endeavoring to answer the first question; it seems only fair that we should devote some attention to the other. In the twenty years after Astor's death there sprang up two definite schools of opinion upon the extent of his participation in philanthropies during his lifetime.[1] Parton, writing in 1865, remarked cautiously: "We are told that he did, now and then, bestow small sums in charity, though we have failed to get trustworthy evidence of a single instance of his doing so."[2] Matthew Hale Smith, three years later, said positively: "His gifts . . . were munificent, and constant." Both authors, however, would doubtless agree that "for vagrants, street begging, and miscellaneous calls, Mr. Astor had no ear."[3] Parton said: "He held beggary of all descriptions in strong contempt, and seemed to think that, in this country, want and fault are synonymous."[4] In this he was probably like most self-made men, who find it hard to part with any of the wealth which they have personally accumulated.[5] One could place more credence in the author who is inclined to stress Astor's generosity, did he not go on to give a specific illustration. "Attached to his house on Broadway, above Prince," writes this Astor eulogist, "was a narrow alley leading to his kitchen. This kitchen was as large as that of a hotel. A supply of beef and bread was always kept on hand for the poor. Families known to be needy, who were cleanly in person, orderly in their behavior, who came and went quietly, were daily supplied with food. He kept a regular account of the disbursements in this matter, as much as if he were keeping a hotel." [6] It is difficult to believe that Astor would have expressed his interest in the welfare of the poor by turning his own home into a soup kitchen, and it is not much more plausible that he could have carried on such a charity without its becoming widely known. It is certain that during his lifetime Astor, justly or unjustly, had the reputation of being very close, to say the least, and this could hardly have been the case if it were known that he was feeding all the deserving poor in the city.

Nevertheless, Parton, if he had gone into the matter further, would have had no difficulty in discovering that Astor, during his lifetime, had made contributions to philanthropic purposes. True, the amounts thus expended were not conspicuously large. Astor had a pretty good knowledge of himself and would probably have been among the first to admit that reference to him as "highly and deservedly esteemed for his extraordinary philanthropy" [7] was a eulogy which he did not deserve. Julia Ward Howe, a friend and admirer of John Jacob Astor, whose granddaughter Emily married Samuel Ward, tells the story that "a clergyman . . . called upon him in the interest of some charity. The visitor congratulated Mr. Astor upon the increased ability to do good which his great fortune gave him. 'Ah!' said Mr. Astor, 'the disposition to do good does not always increase with the means.'" [8]

There is no doubt, however, that he did contribute, though few benefactions are mentioned in the letter books which have come down to us, doubtless in part because most applications were made to him personally. During the years 1831–38 only one letter accompanying a contribution appears. This was with a check for $100, apparently unsolicited, "in aid of the needy who have suffered by the tornado which visited New

Brunswick," New Jersey.[9] However, during these years are found no refusals of requests for contributions to charitable and philanthropic objects. These become a prominent feature in his letter book for 1845–48. Someone had "published in the papers," apparently those of Michigan, a statement to the effect that "Mr Astor proposed to assist indigent young men under certain conditions." Astor, as might be expected, was forced to inform several young men, answering to that description, that "the notice . . . is without foundation" and that he must decline to assist them under any conditions.[10] Requests for a loan, from the United German Lutheran Churches,[11] and for contributions, from the rector of the Church of the Epiphany, Washington, D. C.,[12] from a professor at Columbia College, to assist in establishing an observatory,[13] and from the president of Farmers College in Ohio,[14] met with no less unfavorable replies. During this same period, however, Astor did make two contributions, one of $500 and one of $200; both were to the Fire Department Fund.[15] It is probable, nevertheless, that these were but a fraction of the contributions made about this time for this purpose and for others equally worthy.

In January, 1829, Astor subscribed to stock in the Clinton Hall Association for the purpose of erecting a building to house the Mercantile Library.[16] The amount of his subscription was $1,000 — the same as that subscribed by Arthur Tappan & Co.,[17] the firm noted for the abolitionist tendencies of its members. On November 5, 1835, Philip Hone made the following entry in his diary:

My feelings as a friend to the good object which is to be its recipient have been excited, and my pride as a New Yorker gratified, by seeing in a little book which was just handed to me by the ladies who are begging for the "Society for the Relief of Aged Indigent Females" the noble donation of John Jacob Astor of $5,000 towards the erection of a building for the accommodation of the objects of the Society's bounty. This amount is subscribed on condition that the whole sum raised shall amount to $20,000, of which the ladies say there is very little doubt. . . . I have great pleasure in recording this munificent act of Mr. Astor's, because public opinion does not give him as much credit for liberality as I have thought him entitled to. I am inclined to think that he has become more disposed of late than formerly to give "of his abundance." He begins to grow old and has come to the wise conclusion that as he cannot take his money away with him the latter days of his life are not likely to pass less pleasantly for the reflection of his having sprinkled a little sweet into the bitter cup of the widow and fatherless.[18]

It is evident even from this friendly comment that Astor's generosity was of a cautious nature. His conduct upon one occasion, as described by the admiring Matthew Hale Smith, must, if it has any foundation in fact, have been a strange exception to his usual method of procedure. Smith says:

The day of his death he was the master of his business. . . . He kept an open fire of hickory wood, and laid in a large supply. The wood-sawyer charged him three and six-pence a cord, while the market price was three shillings. Mr. Astor refused to pay a penny above the regular price. While he was disputing with the sawyer, some ladies came in to solicit a donation for a charitable institution. He paused in the debate, heard the plea of the ladies, ordered Bruce, his confidential clerk, to draw up a check of five hundred dollars, signed it and handed it to the ladies, bowed them out, and then renewed the dispute with the laborer, by whom he did not choose to be cheated out of a single penny.[19]

Against this anecdote may be set one of a different character, in which Fitz-Greene Halleck, the poet, from 1832 to 1848 Astor's confidential man of business, plays the leading rôle. On a certain occasion, so the story runs, "Astor refused to subscribe to a charitable object, on the ground that at present he had no money. Halleck coolly remarked, 'Mr. Astor, if you're out of money I'll endorse your note for a few hundred dollars.'" [20] Tradition does not tell us what was Astor's response to this ingenious suggestion, but it would have been quite in accord with his character had he signed his name to a substantial check, accompanying the action with a series of hearty chuckles. Apparently the open sesame to Astor's treasury was a joke of some kind, coupled with a more or less graceful compliment, open or implied, to his financial success.

[A certain] Colonel Stone . . . engaged [in 1826] in securing subscriptions for the Greeks, called upon John Jacob Astor . . . for a considerable amount. To all his persuasions the old fur-merchant turned a deaf ear, finally alleging that he himself was really quite poor. "Yes, Mr. Astor," replied the Colonel, "every one is poor nowadays but you and me." Astor knew that the Colonel was, at this time, very much embarrassed, having lost nearly all his property by endorsing; and, upon this reply . . . he joined in the laugh, and handed the Colonel his check for considerably more than the sum asked for.[21]

A somewhat similar story is told about an incident which took place nearly twenty years later.

The last considerable sum he was ever known to give away was a contribution to aid the election to the Presidency of his old friend, Henry Clay [probably in 1844]. . . . When the committee were presented to him he began to excuse himself. . . .
"I am not now interested in these things," said he. "I haven't anything to do with commerce, and it makes no difference to me what the Government does. I don't make money any more, and haven't any concern in the matter."
One of the committee replied: "Why, Mr. Astor, you are like Alexander when he wept because there were no more worlds to conquer. You have made all the money, and now there is no money to make." The old eye twinkled at the blended compliment and jest.
"Ha, ha, ha! very good, that's very good. Well, well, I give you something."
Whereupon he drew his check for fifteen hundred dollars.[22]

However munificent Astor's philanthropies were during his lifetime, there is no doubt that a much larger amount was left to public purposes by his will. It is interesting to trace the development of his philanthropic intentions from the first version of the document through the succeeding codicils. In the will as signed on July 4, 1836, he left the German Society of New York City $30,000 to be invested in bonds and mortgages of lands, the income from which was to be used in maintaining an office where advice and information should be given gratuitously to German immigrants.[23] Another bequest was of $25,000 to Columbia College for the purpose of establishing a professorship of the German language and literature. Another bequest of $25,000 was to the Association for the Relief of Respectable Aged Indigent Females. He also left $2,000 to the German Reformed Congregation in New York City. On January 19, 1838, the first codicil made various changes in and additions to his bequests for philanthropic purposes. The legacy to the German Society was reduced to $25,000. He had in the meantime given $5,000 to the Association for the Relief of Respectable Aged Indigent Females — this, of course, in addition to his contribution of the same amount in 1835 — and this sum was consequently to be deducted from his legacy to that object. He also left $5,000 to the Institution for the Blind, $5,000 to the Society for the Relief of Half-Orphans and Destitute Children, and $2,000 to the New-York Lying-In Asylum. The third codicil, dated August 22, 1839, provided for the bequest of $400,000 for the establishment of a public library. This legacy will later be examined more in detail. The fourth codicil, dated October 24, 1839, unfortunately revoked the legacy of $25,000 to Columbia College, and the fifth, dated March 3, 1841, revoked the legacy of $2,000 "*to the German Reformed Congregation* in the City of New York, intending," so Astor said, "during my life, to apply that amount to the religious and moral welfare of Germans in some other mode." It does not appear just how Astor carried out this expressed intention. The fifth codicil also directed his executors "to apply *fifty thousand dollars* to the use of the *poor of Waldorf*, near Heidelberg, in the Grand Duchy of Baden, by the establishment of some provision for the sick or disabled, or the education and improvement of the young, who may be in a condition to need the aid of such fund." [24] This same codicil again reduced the legacy to the German Society by $5,000, leaving it at the sum of only $20,000, "of which," Astor went on, "I have already advanced them fifteen thousand six hundred and ninety seven dollars fifty cents, to be deducted, therefore, from the said last mentioned sum." [25]

Upon the legacy to the German Society and its various reductions there hangs a tale, told by the author who is most insistent upon Astor's extraordinary benevolence. Astor had belonged to the German Society since 1787,[26] but, according to Smith, he never attended any of its meetings. In 1837, however, he was elected president of the Society, probably in acknowledgment of the legacy mentioned in his will of the previous year, of which the Society had been notified. In 1839 he was still the president,[27] despite his reduction of the legacy early in 1838. At this time the German Society was much embarrassed financially.

They chose a committee to wait upon Mr. Astor, to see if he would not anticipate his death by giving them the twenty thousand dollars. Mr. Astor shook his head when the committee made the proposal. . . . "You'll get the money," the old man said. They pressed the matter, and finally Mr. Astor said, "I'll give you twenty thousand dollars in Pennsylvania five per cent bonds." These bonds were at a discount of twenty-five per cent. . . . The committee . . . represented to him the hardship of losing five thousand dollars, while it could make no difference to Mr. Astor. He ended the interview by quietly saying, "It is in the will, gentlemen, and I can easily strike it out." They closed with the proposal, Bruce was called for, the bonds were delivered, and with a face radiant with pleasure, leaning on his staff, he tottered into the back office, chuckling as he went, to tell William that he had made "five thousand dollars that morning." [28]

This story, inconsistent as it is with the other anecdotes told by the same author — which are themselves in contradiction to those recorded by other contemporary writers — may have some foundation in fact. The fifth codicil, dated March 3, 1841, reveals that Astor had advanced the German Society the sum of $15,697.50, which, being an uneven amount, it would seem had probably been given in stocks or bonds at a discount. On the other hand, it is clear that this advance was not to be considered as satisfying the entire legacy of $20,000, since it was specified that it was to be deducted from the latter sum. However, it is also true that the same codicil which mentioned this advance also reduced the legacy from $25,000 to $20,000.

It may be, then, that Astor consented to advance the Society bonds worth $20,000, par value, at a 25 per cent discount, on the condition that the Society would agree to the reduction of the legacy by $5,000. Thus Astor would combine business with philanthropy, furnishing the Society with a large sum of money at the time when it was most needed, and at the same time recouping himself — or his heirs — for the decline in the value of his bonds.

The Astor Library, Astor's greatest benefaction, was a monument to his chief interest outside of business and his family, his friendship for literary men, and for one in particular, Dr. Joseph Green Cogswell. Late in 1837, during a visit to New York, Cogswell met Astor and dined with him several times. "He is not," Cogswell said, "the mere accumulator of dollars, as I had supposed him; he talks well on many subjects and shows a great interest in the arts and literature." Cogswell seems to have made an equally favorable impression upon Astor, who began to make use of his legal services, giving him generous compensation. About the same time, Astor consulted Cogswell "about an appropriation of some three or four hundred thousand dollars, which he intended to leave for public purposes." Cogswell urged him to give it for a library, which Astor consented to do, but as soon as it became known, in the summer of 1838, that he intended to make "to the corporation of the city of New York, a donation amounting to $350,000 for the establishment of a Public Library" [29] he was "beset by innumerable applications for money, in all possible amounts, from five to five thousand dollars. . . . This his own penetrating mind had foreseen, and it had induced him to change his intended donation to a legacy." Astor offered Cogswell "a most liberal pecuniary compensation" for a portion of his time that winter, and Cogswell at first considered accepting the offer "in the hope of advancing the great project" of the library. However, Cogswell disliked to give up his independence and so declined, becoming instead the editor of the *New York Review*. Neither Astor nor Cogswell allowed the project of the library to be long absent from his mind, and in the spring of 1839 Cogswell, at his own suggestion, was given carte blanche to purchase suitable books whenever they came upon the market, and was also authorized to begin a catalogue of the necessary books and to obtain an estimate of the costs of the building. Late that year Cogswell went abroad to place William B. Astor's son in school, on condition that he should be allowed $60,000 for the purchase of books in Europe. Returning to New York the next spring, Cogswell agreed to spend five hours per day preparing a catalogue of 100,000 volumes for the library, at a salary of $1,500 per year; Astor was also to have the right to an hour or two of his society per day, as he might desire. In the summer of 1840, before this agreement went into effect, Cogswell was in hopes that work would soon begin on the library, as the plan had been agreed upon. However, "Upjohn, the architect . . . put a notion of a Gothic building into his head, and the moment an excuse was offered him for hesitation, he yielded to what has now become the weakness of his age, and shrunk from a decision."

Cogswell, nevertheless, according to the previous agreement, was installed in a house next to Astor's. Here he continued for some months, until early in 1842 he was offered the position of secretary of legation to his friend Washington Irving, who was going to Madrid as minister to Spain.

Mr. Astor [he wrote] is . . . very reluctant to have me leave him, but that I should have done at any rate, if he kept on as undecided as ever about his library. . . . I told him I would give up the Secretaryship if he would engage to begin at once upon the library, and that unless he did so I should certainly accept it. All the reply I got to the proposition was, "Say what consideration will induce you to stay with me, and leave the question of the library to my future decision," to which I had but one answer to make, "None whatever." . . . I have not a reproach to fear from my own conscience that I have abandoned the object too soon. Nothing short of a miracle will induce him to undertake it during his life.

A few days later, however, it seemed that the miracle had happened. "At the last moment," Cogswell wrote, "Mr. Astor agreed to all that I asked of him: to go on immediately with the library, to guarantee to me the librarianship with a salary of $2,500 a year, as soon as the building is finished, and, in the meanwhile $2,000, while engaged upon the catalogue, or otherwise employed." Despite this arrangement, however, "no advance was made toward the practical founding of the great library." On May 3, 1842, Cogswell wrote: "Immediately after the 1st of April I began with him [Mr. Astor] about the building, when he got together architects, masons, contractors, etc., and, just as all seemed to be going on rightly, he got into one of his nervous fits, and, as yet, I have not been able to bring him back to the work again." [30] It was not till Astor's death that anything further was done toward the establishment of the library. It is not surprising, in view of the indecision displayed by Astor in this matter, that his Green Bay land investment, which was in need of vigorous attention at the same time, also suffered from this weakness.

Astor's legacies to public objects, all told, amounted to $507,000. Under ordinary conditions his generosity would probably have been the chief topic of conversation in connection with the will, but two circumstances turned a section of the public mind into other channels. One of these was the death, in 1831, of Stephen Girard, who, having no children, had left virtually all of his large estate to various public purposes; the other was the fact that most of Astor's fortune came not directly from commerce but through the increase in value of his real estate on Manhattan Island. As a result of this first circumstance, Astor, the year after his death, was violently attacked by Horace Mann, who described him as

the most notorious, the most wealthy, and, considering his vast means, the most miserly of his class in this country. Nothing but absolute insanity can be pleaded in palliation of the conduct of a man who was worth nearly or quite twenty millions of dollars, but gave only some half million . . . of it for any public object. If men of such vast means will not benefit the world by their *example* while they live, we have a right to make reprisals for their neglect, by using them as a *warning* after they are dead. In the midst of so much poverty and suffering as the world experiences, it has become a high moral and religious duty to create an overwhelming public opinion against both the parsimonies and the squanderings of wealth.[31]

The second circumstance — the direct source of Astor's estate — caused James Gordon Bennett, owner and editor of the *New York Herald*, to remark, apropos of the publication of Astor's will:

If we had been an associate of John Jacob Astor . . . the first idea that we should have put into his head would have been that *one-half of his immense property — ten millions at least — belonged to the people of the city of New York*. . . . The farms and lots of ground which he bought forty, twenty and ten and five years ago, have all increased in value entirely by the industry of the citizens of New York. Of course, it is plain as that two and two make four, that the half of his immense estate, in its actual value, has accrued to him by the industry of the community.

Gustavus Myers, commenting upon this dictum, enquires: "If Astor was entitled to one-half of the value created by the collective industry of the community, why was he not entitled to all?"[32] Astor was not responsible for the social system which allowed him to levy on "the collective industry of the community;" he merely took advantage to the utmost of the opportunities which the system offered. In any apportionment of blame, this fact should be kept in mind. Astor's friend Gerrit Smith gave away large quantities of the land which his father had acquired from the Indians, but even Gerrit Smith's views on the iniquity of land monopoly might have experienced a rare sea-change had his real estate been on Manhattan Island rather than in the New York backcountry.

Although Astor's career belongs to American history, it must not be forgotten that by birth he was, and in many points of sympathy he remained throughout his life, a European. To the end he spoke — and wrote — with a broad German accent, and one of the qualifications which commended Cogswell to his attention was his ability to make fluent use of Astor's mother tongue. Of Astor's long life of more than eighty-four years, no less than one-third was spent in Europe. Twenty of these years, to be sure, belong to the period before his departure for America. It is noteworthy that, when Astor found leisure for travel, he sought out an environment which would be as little reminiscent as possible of the scenes of his commercial life. Astor never visited any of the Pacific ports with which he carried on an extensive commerce in his own vessels for a score of years or more. Indeed, he never seems to have had the slightest desire to gain a personal knowledge of these savage or exotic regions; the reports of his captains and supercargoes upon trade conditions sufficed.

Nor was Astor an extensive traveller within the bounds of the United States, even in the regions where his fur trade was carried on. He knew well the routes from New York north to Montreal and west to the Lakes, but his wanderings seldom carried him farther. He may have made a journey to Mackinac in one of his very early years in America, but it is unlikely that his visit was repeated more than a very few times, if at all. Once, in 1808, as we have seen, he considered visiting St. Louis, but soon abandoned the idea; this man who dominated the fur trade of the United States never saw the Mississippi, far less the Rockies. Washington — or perhaps Norfolk — to the south, Boston to the east, Montreal to the north, and possibly Michilimackinac to the west, with New York as a center, defined the limits of Astor's travels in North America, which during most of his life were kept within an even more restricted sphere.

When Astor wished to travel, he doubled back on the path he had taken at the age of twenty years and crossed the Atlantic to his native continent of Europe. His earliest voyages to Europe — to London in 1784,[33] to London and to "Gearmaney & francs" in 1795 [34] — were purely commercial in motive. In the fall of 1802 and the spring of 1803 Astor was considering going abroad with his daughter Magdalen, but the idea had been abandoned by July, 1803.[35]

He did not again plan on a visit to Europe until 1819, by which year both his China trade and the reorganized American Fur Company had been put on a stable footing and William B. Astor, recently admitted to partnership with his father, had gained enough experience to justify leaving in his care the affairs of the New York end of the firm of John Jacob Astor & Son. Consequently, Astor determined to make a belated grand tour of Europe. His health probably had more than a little to do with this decision, but in any case he felt that, since all his family, down to the last generation he was likely to live to see, were now more than adequately provided for, it would be proper for him to take a long vacation from ledgers, land conveyances, tea chests, and fur bales. Moreover, the death by drowning of his grandson, John Jacob Bentzon, in the previous year, had left him in low spirits, and he felt the need of some new occupation for his active mind, which he thought that travel would furnish. Then, too, while he was travelling through Europe, he could keep in touch with the state of the fur market. Astor still had an uneasy feeling that such a trip as he intended to make to Europe must, to be entirely justified, have some economic purpose.

Astor left New York on June 2, 1819, on the "elegant new ship Stephania, Captain Burke . . . for Havre," [36] where he arrived late in the month. In the next month he was at Paris, and in September at Geneva. In November he was at Rome, and the next month at Naples, where he spent the winter, and where he is said to have taken up the study of Italian. By March, 1820, he was back at Rome,[37] where on April 5 he wrote a familiar letter to President Monroe. It seemed to Astor "that all Europe is threanstend with Revolution" and "that thos in Powe[r] are trimbling." Astor had doubtless been led to this conclusion by such episodes as the Spanish revolt in January of that year and Thistlewood's conspiracy in London in the following month. His prophecy was promptly justified by the Neapolitan uprising of July and the Portuguese revolution of the following month. From Rome, at which place he still was in June,[38] Astor journeyed to Germany, visited the Black Forest, probably looked up his brother Melchior and family and cousins innumerable, and on September 5, 1820, was at Frankfort, from which place he again wrote to Monroe, re-emphasizing his belief "that a Revolution of extend is Soon to bee Lookd for." [39] Astor's manner of conveying this alarming judgment gives no hint as to whether he welcomed or deprecated the political convulsions which he so confidently anticipated. One does receive the impression that Astor was at least glad that, if these disturbances must take place, he would be on hand to watch the proceedings at close range. We know, too, that he had letters to men prominent in the opposition to Louis XVIII's government, and he is said to have contributed a few years later to the cause of Greek independence.[40] This time, however, Astor's prophecy of political upheavals was fulfilled only by a mutiny in St. Petersburg in October, Ypsilanti's invasion of Moldavia in March, 1821, and the revolt in the Morea of the following month.

Astor intended to spend the winter of 1820–21 in Paris. He had, it is asserted, acquired some knowledge of French while in New York, he had letters of introduction from President Monroe to "General La Fayatta" and "Comte Marbois" (perhaps François, marquis de Barbe-Marbois, or Jean Baptiste Antoine Marcelin, baron de Marbot), and his friend Albert Gallatin was United States minister to France. He was thus well prepared for a pleasant and profitable winter in the French capital. In November, 1820, Astor dined with Albert Gallatin and his family and horrified the fastidious James Gallatin by his table-

manners, which if reported correctly — and somehow I am inclined to suspect the young man of exaggeration — would have
been considered rather uncouth even in a butcher's family at
Waldorf.[41] Astor had been joined at Paris by his youngest
daughter, Eliza, and by his first-born son, John Jacob, Jr., who
had, as we have seen, been mentally incompetent from birth or
from a very early age. George Ehninger, Astor's nephew, was
also in Paris at this time.[42] Early in July Astor's son was sent
back to America.[43] While in Paris Astor also dabbled in the in-
trigues of Madame Patterson Bonaparte, who was trying to
arrange for her son a marriage which would be consonant with
his dignity as a prince of the House of Bonaparte. Astor, in
whom she is said to have had great confidence, "informed her
that she must not put any reliance in any members of the
Bonaparte family. Madame *mère* is the most sincere and the
Princess Pauline Borghesi is absolutely unreliable." [44] Apparently Astor had come into contact with the Bonapartes while
in Italy. He had become acquainted with Joseph Bonaparte in
America and is said to have made certain "propositions" to the
fallen monarch, the character of which it would be exceedingly
interesting to know. Gallatin acted as interpreter in these
negotiations, which apparently came to nothing.[45]

In the midst of his travels Astor had still found time to devote to the interests of the American Fur Company.[46] On
January 10, 1821, Astor wrote President Monroe from Paris,
urging that no measure be adopted by the government which
would injure private fur traders.[47] In the spring of the same
year Ramsay Crooks came to Paris and on March 27 renewed
for a period of five years his agreement with Astor for the
American Fur Company, which had expired earlier in the
month.[48]

Late in May, 1821, Astor was still in Paris, planning to return to New York in the fall,[49] but late in November Ramsay
Crooks was still writing on fur-trade matters to him in Eu-

rope.[50] Astor seems to have still been in Paris early in February, 1822.[51] Indeed, we do not positively know when he returned to the United States. A newspaper item of April 29, 1822, records that "the ship Cincinnatus, Champlin, 23 days from London. . . . April 13th, lat. 43, lon. 35, spoke the brig United States, 14 days from Norfolk for Liverpool. Passengers John Jacob Astor, Esq. Miss Astor, and servants." [52] This would imply that Astor had returned to America some time earlier in the year and was almost immediately sailing again for Europe; but, since we know that Astor was in New York at least as early as June 21,[53] it seems almost impossible that he would have crossed the Atlantic twice to so little purpose. There seems a strong probability that Astor was actually bound *from* Liverpool *to* Norfolk. This probability is strengthened by the fact that Crooks, who surely must have known his partner's whereabouts, on April 23 wrote a letter from New York to Astor at New York in regard to the establishment of the Western Department; [54] this important move was probably one of the reasons for Astor's return at this time.

Astor remained in the United States only long enough to see the Western Department well established. He learned that Gallatin was intending to leave France, and, realizing the advantage to him of having his friend in Paris as American minister, he, "with great courage," as Gallatin's son James, with whom Astor was no favorite, sarcastically expressed it, wrote to Gallatin "begging him to remain. Rather amusing," James continued, "as it is evidently for his own interests, as he is shortly coming to Paris." [55] W. H. Crawford on May 26, 1823, wrote to Gallatin, urging him to return, but remarking that "Mr. Astor thinks you will not, and that you ought not. He is probably governed in this opinion," Crawford further commented, "by his interests and wishes."[56] Gallatin carried out his purpose and sailed from Le Havre for New York, arriving on June 24. "John Jacob Astor, Esq. and servant, Miss Astor and servant," had left New York "in the line ship Paris, for Havre," on June 2.[57]

The Astor party had arrived at Le Havre by the last day of June and the next month were in Antwerp.[58] By February, 1824, they were at Geneva. It was probably at this time that Astor purchased for $50,000 a villa, named Genthod, on Lake Geneva.[59] At any rate Astor's headquarters throughout the years 1824 and 1825 seems to have been at Geneva, and from here, though not altogether in good health, he corresponded with his partners in New York, giving detailed instructions for the management of the fur trade.[60] Astor had intended to return to the United States in the fall of 1825, his health permitting, but the marriage, on December 10, of his daughter Eliza to Count Vincent Rumpff, a Swiss who was the minister of the Hanse towns to Paris, of course caused him to postpone his return until the spring of 1826. While in Paris during this sojourn he had, it is said, been presented at the court of Charles x, and had also met Guizot and Metternich, although these last experiences may have been enjoyed during his tour of 1819-22.[61] Astor sailed from Le Havre on March 10 on the brig *Danube*, arriving at New York on April 9.[62] The years from 1819 to 1826 had been spent chiefly in Europe, but he was not to see that continent again until more than six years had passed.

Astor had more than one reason for re-visiting Europe in 1832. William B. Astor was perfectly well qualified to take care of his interests in his absence. Indeed, it was not many months later that William B. Astor announced: "My father and myself have withdrawn from commercial business." [63] Moreover, the Morris land case, which had been dragging on for more than twenty years, had recently been settled in Astor's favor. Desire for a change of scene would in itself justify such a trip. The reason which Astor himself gave was that he was going "to leave here for France to see some of my family."[64] Both of his younger daughters, Dorothea, the wife of Walter Langdon, and Eliza, who had married Count Vincent Rumpff, were then in Europe. Another reason, which he did not himself give, was that he wished to consult French specialists in regard to an ailment which had been troubling him for some time.[65] An outbreak of the cholera, which had already run its course in Europe, was anticipated in New York in the summer of 1832, and a desire to escape the menace of this plague may have also influenced him.

For whatever reason or reasons, Astor, on June 20, 1832, sailed on the packet for Le Havre,[66] where he arrived "after a short passage of 19 days," as he announced in a letter giving and requesting information concerning the fur trade, written in August to his partners at St. Louis.[67] Although he may have intended either to return to New York in the early fall or to go on to Geneva,[68] the rest of the year was probably spent at Paris under the care of physicians, which had been made even more necessary by a fall which confined him to his bed and room till late in September and made him decide to postpone his return, at least till the spring of 1833.[69] Early in October he had recovered sufficiently to hire horses and a carriage, and two months later was apparently strong enough to resume his favorite exercise of horseback riding.[70] Indeed, notations in his memorandum book and correspondence entered in the letter book at New York reveal that while in Paris he was still keeping in touch with the fur trade and the commerce with China, though much less closely than he had during his sojourn of six years before.[71]

Astor's nephew and former employee, Henry Brevoort, was in Paris at this time, and on January 18, 1833, the latter wrote to their mutual friend, Washington Irving, in a tone of airy self-appreciation: "Old John Jacob Astor and I are again united in the bonds of intimacy. The old Gent finds me vastly entertaining, if one may judge from the frequency of his visits." [72] While in Paris Astor is said to have been presented to the "Citizen King," Louis Philippe.[73]

The spring and summer of 1833 were spent at Geneva, and Astor had planned to return home late in October, but the advanced state of the season and the condition of his health again caused him to postpone his departure.[74] On June 25 he had notified Bernard Pratte & Co., in a letter from Geneva, that he was withdrawing from his association with them in the Western Department of the American Fur Company "with the outfit of the present year."[75] Astor's original intention had been to return to the United States in the fall of 1832, or at least no later than March, 1833; his departure had then been delayed till the fall of that year, and he was not actually ready to leave Europe till the spring of 1834. He was naturally anxious that there should be no further delay, and so was much disappointed to find that all the staterooms on the *Utica*, the ship on which he wished to sail from Le Havre, had already been engaged. Fortunately, however, the *Utica's* commander, Frederick De Peyster,[76] who had once been an Astor captain, consented to give up his own stateroom to his old employer.

The captain later compensated himself for this act of renunciation by giving an account of his passenger's conduct during the voyage, which may be regarded as either humorous or pathetic, according to choice, but which at any rate is certainly significant. Bad weather made it difficult for the vessel to get out of the Channel, and Astor finally became so alarmed that he asked the captain to run in and set him ashore in England. The captain evaded the request, but Astor persisted and at last said: "I give you tousand dollars to put me aboard a pilot-boat." Finally, the captain, to escape his importunities, consented to yield to his request if they did not get out of the Channel before the next morning. A change of wind that afternoon sent the vessel into the open sea, but she was then driven for some days by a heavy gale along the coast of Ireland, and again Astor besieged the captain with entreaties to be put ashore, it made no difference where, this time raising his offer to $10,000. Again the captain declined, this time on the ground that to accede to Astor's request would result in forfeiting his insurance. "Insurance!" Astor exclaimed, "can't I insure your ship myself." Again the captain was forced at last to yield, on condition that the other passengers would consent and the weather permitted. The gale abated, Astor's shipmates took pity on his plight, and the multimillionaire disappeared into his cabin to write out a draft on his son for $10,000 in favor of the owners of the ship. Presently he emerged with a piece of paper which he handed to the captain, who viewed it with unconcealed astonishment. The paper was covered with writing which was totally illegible. "What is this?" he enquired. "A draft upon my son for $10,000." "But no one can read it." "Oh yes, my son will know what it is. My hand trembles so that I can't write any better." "But," the captain objected, "you can at least write your name. I am acting for the owners of the ship, and I can't risk their property for a piece of paper that no one can read. Let one of the gentlemen draw up a draft in proper form; you sign it; and I will put you ashore." There is no reason to believe that the draft, illegible though it was, would not have been honored in New York, but the captain was of course justified in his stipulations, to which Astor, however, probably through sheer obstinacy, refused to accede. A favorable wind now somewhat quieted Astor's fears, but when two-thirds of the way across, on the Banks of Newfoundland, the captain went upon the poop to speak a ship bound for Liverpool, Astor climbed up after him, clamoring: "Tell them I give tousand dollars if they take a passenger." [77]

After a voyage which must have been almost as nerve-racking for the captain as for Astor, the *Utica* finally reached New York on April 4, 1834.[78] Half a century before, within a few days, Astor had first reached America, after a voyage the incomparably greater severities of which he had met with a fortitude compounded of stolidity and whimsicality. But Astor was now an old man; his days of voyaging, whether in the North Atlantic or through the even stormier waters of active commercial life, were finally over.

The state of Astor's health played a great part in his career, particularly in his later years, and it should be of interest to examine in some detail its influence and trace its condition as near as possible to its origin. Astor seems to have come of a long-lived stock, if his father's age at death—ninety-two years—is of any significance. Astor has been described at the age of sixteen or seventeen as "a stout, strong lad . . . exceedingly well made, though slightly undersized." [79] In his early thirties, if we are to trust two portraits by Gilbert Stuart, made in 1794, he was a somewhat sparely built young man, with an ascetic, scholarly, rather handsome face, distinguished by a high, well-shaped forehead, deep-set, intent eyes, traditionally said to have been brown, a prominent, strongly arched nose, a straight, thin-lipped mouth, and a resolute chin.[80] He is said to have been of medium height, or perhaps somewhat above, broad-shouldered, and browned by the sun.[81] At this time he was not far from his forest-running days, and these exertions, coupled with the strain of fighting his way to such a position that he could afford to sit to Gilbert Stuart, had doubtless trained every ounce of superfluous flesh from his body.

The remaining years of the century were to be decisive for Astor's future. He was to emerge as the leading fur merchant of the United States with a fortune estimated at a quarter of a million, but in the meantime he was to experience such financial difficulties that "the bank directors in discounting his notes, always predicted his failure at an early day, and made their calculations accordingly." [82] The mental anxiety caused by being under this constant pressure for funds at last began to prey upon his physique. The long land litigation in which he, in association with Peter Smith and William Laight, was engaged from 1794 to 1802 took its toll. It is significant that the first signs of a break in Astor's health began to appear at a time when this land case was at its most discouraging point and his other business interests were most seriously involved. The hardships he had experienced as a tramping fur trader may have made the first crack in the armor of his naturally rugged constitution, or, on the other hand, the transition from an outdoor life of strenuous physical activity to a more sedentary existence of harassing mental struggles may have been partly responsible.

Whatever the underlying causes, we know that late in 1796 Astor was taken ill, so as to be unable to answer important business letters written by his friend Peter Smith. By May, 1797, he had recovered sufficiently to be able to continue his correspondence, but announced that "an account of my health I am obligd to the Springs" in June.[83] Apparently by "taking the waters" his health was temporarily restored, but again early in March, 1798, he "was very unwell," and in July wrote: "I am again obligd to go to Balltown Springs & exspect to Stay about 5 or 6 weeks."[84] No further evidences of indisposition appeared until a year later, when Astor informed Smith that he had been "very ill in Bed." He went on: "I am [in] Bade health & much trouble for money. . . . I expect to be at Balltown springs in 16 or 18 days – "[85] It seems evident that when a man of thirty odd is, at about the same time in three successive years, attacked by serious illness, necessitating a sojourn, after his partial recovery, at a watering place, he cannot be regarded as possessing robust health. However, by this time his illness seems to have run itself out; at least we hear no more complaints of his health for three or four years. It is quite possible that this may be accounted for by the near approach of a successful conclusion to his land litigation and by his generally improved financial condition.

In the fall of 1802, while "going to Canada," Astor "was taking Ill with a Slight Lake fever" and "was Detained 14 Days Langer than I expected," but this was a mere incident. However, late in April of the next year Astor described himself as having "ben unwell & at Same time mush engagd in Buisness" — conditions which seem to have endured for some weeks.[86] Late in May, 1805, Astor announced: "I have been unwell for Several weeks but am getting Better," and in consequence of that illness he was forced to resort to the springs late in the summer.[87]

With the end of Astor's land litigation, his personal correspondence with Peter Smith — almost our only source of information for many aspects of Astor's early life — largely languished and we are unable to trace the condition of his health for some time. It is probable that it remained at least reasonably strong, and it is noteworthy that in the many letters written during the trying days of the War of 1812, and especially while the fate of the Astoria enterprise hung in the balance, he never complains of ill-health. His freedom from illness was doubtless due in part to the regularity of his life. It is said that, despite the multiplicity of his interests and the personal attention he gave to their every detail, he "did not bestow at his counting-house more than half the time most merchants feel compelled to give their concerns."[88] He would come to his office early in the morning, transact the necessary business, and leave at two in the afternoon.[89] This was possible because of the efficiency he displayed in conserving time and energy. "He possessed marked executive ability. He was quick in his perceptions. He came rapidly to his conclusions. He made a trade or rejected it at once. . . . He made distinct contracts. These he adhered to with inflexible purpose." "In trade," it is said, he was "an autocrat in bearing," [90] yet withal "he is represented as being a pleasant man to do business with, seldom being ruffled in temper or intemperate in speech." [91]

The office both of John Jacob Astor & Son and of the American Fur Company was at 8 Vesey Street, and the building "extended back so that the rear wall was on a line with the north side of Mr. Astor's dwelling at 223 Broadway. . . . At 223 Broadway he could go from his yard into the store. There was an open piazza, supported by pillars and arches, where he frequently sat of an afternoon, after he had had his dinner, at three o'clock. He would play three games of checkers, and no more, and drink a glass of beer. He did not drink anything else, in his working days."[92] After an early dinner he would "mount his horse and ride about the island till it was time to go to the theatre"[93]—keeping a lookout for promising pieces of land which might be for sale.

Although easy living and comparative freedom from financial worries may have stabilized Astor's health, they apparently did not improve his appearance, if a portrait by Alonzo Chappel, which must have been made when Astor was in his fifties, can be regarded as a faithful likeness. Instead of the hard, clean lines, the thoughtful, aristocratic features, of the Stuart portraits, we see an unwieldy body, the protuberant abdomen straining at the waistcoat, thick, clumsy arms and legs, a broad face with pouches beneath the eyes, heavy cheeks, and a double chin.[94] In short — eliminating the background of ledgers, letter books, and legal papers — it is the likeness of a prosperous, self-satisfied butcher, rigged out in his Sunday best, and celebrating his retirement by having his portrait painted. A casual observer would at first be inclined to doubt that the portraits by Stuart and that of Chappel — even allowing for the twenty odd years of difference in the age of the subject — could be of the same man. But a closer examination would resolve this difficulty. There was the same high, broad forehead, the prominent, strongly arched nose, the straight, thin-lipped mouth; the jaw, beneath its loose folds of flesh, was still iron. The greatest change, a closer inspection would reveal, was in the eyes, which seemed smaller and more deeply set than before and from being distinguished by an expression of thoughtful melancholy had become characteristically shrewd and keen. It was a countenance perhaps more actively good-humored than the one of twenty years before, but at the same time harder, more aggressive, more inflexible, despite its superficial easy fleshiness. On the whole, the impression created by this portrait of Astor at the half-century mark is one of physical stagnation rather than degeneration, yet coupled with an intensity of mental activity which was at the same time marked by cool self-confidence.

It seems likely, as we have said, that there were reasons of health behind Astor's European tour of 1819–22, but these probably pertained to his mind rather than to his body, since he had been badly depressed by the accidental death of one of his grandchildren in 1818. We are told that he "was well at Paris on the 24th May," 1821,[95] and this is all we hear of his health for some time. He was not so fortunate during his European sojourn of 1823–26, and "suffered much from sickness during the . . . spring" of 1824,[96] having been taken "quite ill," probably in April. In the previous month, also, he had "ben mush unwell." [97] In June he "was again recovering his strength." [98] In this year Astor sat for a portrait which may reveal something of his general physical condition at this period.[99] It may be due to the consideration of the artist that this portrait is by far the most satisfactory likeness of Astor in existence; it is the Astor here portrayed who looks like the man who could fight his way up from nothing to the possession of the greatest fortune in America, build up a complicated system of trade with China, conceive the Astoria enterprise, organize the American Fur Company, and carry out his far-seeing if non-social program of investment in Manhattan Island real estate. The face, though in general bearing a marked resemblance to that of the Chappel portrait, has nothing of its flabbiness of the flesh, and evidences something of the refinement of the Stuart portraits; the expression is one of conscious power rather than of smug bourgeois self-satisfaction. The intent, piercing eyes are more thoughtful, less acquisitive, than those of the Chappel painting. Perhaps his sojourn in Europe, his physical remoteness from the New York counting-house, had done something to brace him physically and mellow him spiritually. This, one is convinced, is at least Astor as he should have looked.

Astor returned to New York in 1826 and plunged again into the varied interests of his business life. It was not his custom to speak of his health in business letters written to his agents; consequently there is more significance than appears on the surface in the almost involuntary remark which appears in a letter of late September, 1827, to Ramsay Crooks: "I wish much you could have been here as I am not at all well." [100] One gets the impression that, if there was a weakness in Astor's health at this time, it was a matter of his nervous system. Otherwise it is almost impossible to account for his astonishing flare of temper directed at Peter Smith, his friend of forty years' standing, because Smith had stated, in a letter containing some mild and unaccustomed attempted pleasantries, his understanding that he was to receive some compensation in land for his activities as agent for the Charlotte River and Byrnes Patent tracts over a period of more than thirty years.[101]

Deaths among his relatives in the next year led to further mental depression. His physical condition must have been deteriorating for some time before it became so serious that he was led to announce early in April, 1832: "I am about to retire from all mercantile or money transactions, my health being feeble." He had previously remarked: "The cold weather keeps me still confined." [102] The condition of his health was undoubtedly influential in causing him to make a voyage to Paris in the summer of 1832. Soon after his arrival he was "so unfortunate as to Receve a fall which," he said, "has obligd me to confine my Self to my Bed & Room. I am now well anough to go about." This was late in September. He continued: "I think now to Remain in Europe till Spring in Deed I am not able to go back & in winter I Do not wish to." [103] Early in October he had recovered sufficiently to hire a carriage and horses for a period of two months, and early in December he hired a riding horse.[104]

At some time during his stay in Paris, Astor "underwent . . . a painful fistula operation " [105] for the correction of a complaint from which he seems to have suffered for some time.[106] Vincent Nolte, who had known Astor personally, wrote of this:

He was compelled, by a physical infirmity, to repair to Paris, where he could avail himself of the skilful assistance of Baron Dupuytren. The latter thoroughly restored him, and advised him to ride out every day. He frequently took occasion himself to accompany his patient on these rides. One day — and this anecdote I have from the Baron's own mouth — when riding, he appeared by no means disposed to converse; not a word could be got out of him: and at length Dupuytren declared that he must be suffering from some secret pain or trouble, when he would not speak. He pressed him, and worried him, until finally, Astor loosed his tongue — "Look ye! Baron!" he said; "How frightful this is! I have here in the hands of my banker, at Paris, about 2,000,000 francs, and cannot manage, without great effort, to get more than 2½ per cent. per annum on it. Now, this very day I have received a letter from my son in New York, informing me that there the best acceptances are at from 1½ to 2 per cent. per month. Is it not enough to enrage a man?" [107]

On the first day of 1833 William B. Astor wrote to his brother-in-law, Vincent Rumpff, at Paris: "I am happy to receive from you so favorable an a/c of my father's health, which by moderate exercise will I trust continue to be good, particularly," he sagely added, "if he does not think too much about it." Astor's health continued to improve during the succeeding months through the summer, near the end of which season it was described as "good." [108] However, William B. Astor, writing of his father's condition as it was in late October, said:

"His health is good, but he complains much of the weakness of his nerves, and his spirits are not good." [109] Early in January, 1834, William B. Astor wrote to Rumpff: "I was much disappointed by my father's not returning to this Country in October — I hope he will however certainly return in the Spring. Occupation of mind which he will get here only is, I believe the only cure for his nervous affection." [110]

Astor's conduct on his return voyage to America, as described by the captain of the vessel, indicates the pitiful extent to which his nerves were shattered. He reached New York on April 4. On the 7th, Philip Hone set down in his diary: "I called to see Mr. Astor yesterday. He looks poorly and is much thinner than he was when he went to Europe. The hand of death has laid heavily upon his family during his absence, and his spirits are much depressed in witnessing the blanks which have been created." On the first day of the next month Hone added: "I am sorry to observe since Mr. Astor's return from Europe that his health is declining. He appears feeble and sickly, and I have some doubt if he will live to witness the completion of his splendid edifice [the Astor House]. [111]

Although about the middle of April William B. Astor was "happy in being able to say that my fathers health and spirits are improving," [112] a more exact picture of his condition, as well as an explanation of the reason behind it, probably appears in a letter written by Astor himself to his friend Wilson Price Hunt, formerly his agent at the Columbia River, now postmaster at St. Louis: "I past some time [in Europe], to the loss of much health. I am getting some better, but slowly. . . . while absent, I lost Wife Brother Daughter Sister, Grandchildren & many friends & I expect to follow very soon. I often wish you were *near me*, I should find much in your society which I am in need of. being no longer disposed to business, or rather not able to attend to it, you know that I gave up a good part, & am about to dispose of the rest." [113]

However, it was not like Astor to remain long in such a despondent mood. On the last day of the same month in which he had written so hopelessly to Wilson P. Hunt, he wrote to his son-in-law in Paris: "Myself I am getting well. . . . Tho' my health is much better, its painful for me to write," [114] and late in June his son wrote: "My father continues in excellent health, he is at present staying at Hell Gate," [115] his country home on the banks of the East River. Despite his own prediction of his early decease, backed up by the judgment of Philip Hone, Astor settled himself as doggedly to fight for health as he had ever done to crush a competing fur company or a rival in a lawsuit. He again took up horseback riding, and about the middle of July cheerfully wrote to Wilson P. Hunt: "Mine [my health] is good, but I suffer from a fall — my horse fell and I with him," he was careful to explain, "and [I] am much bruised." [116]

At other times Astor read, attended the theater, went on excursions by land and water,[117] enjoyed musical *soirées*, and visited friends and relatives about the city in his famous "yellow chariot," which was a particularly familiar sight on New Year's Day.[118] The accident he had experienced while horseback riding in 1835 did not disturb his newly restored nerves and he continued this exercise until 1837. Late in May, however, he "received a fall from his horse from which he suffered much pain" and which resulted in his being "confined to his bed" for some weeks. Late in June he was "gradually recovering," and early in the next month he had "almost entirely recovered from his fall" — at least sufficiently to be able to receive visits at Hell Gate from his relatives. However, late in July he was still incapacitated by his accident from writing. A month later his son was able to write: "My father's health is better . . . and he is now strong enough to ride to the City & even to travel in a steamboat." Astor gradually grew stronger and late in December his son could write: "My father . . . is at present suffering under the effect of an attack of rheumatism;

otherwise his health is good." [119] This accident, however, from which it had taken Astor the better part of a year to recover, finally convinced him that his horseback-riding days were over.

A portrait of Astor painted about this time reveals more of his physical condition than any words written by himself or his son.[120] His hair had turned white, but the massive brow, the strongly arched nose, the straight set mouth, and the resolute chin were the same. And yet the whole expression of the face had changed. The features expressed neither smug content nor conscious power; they had returned to the thoughtful, melancholy character of the Stuart portraits, made when he was younger by more than forty years. The eyes were no longer intent and piercing, but weary, reminiscent, and introspective. It was the face of a tired but dignified old man.

In July, 1838, Astor's son was able to write: "My father in particular enjoys excellent health – To day he is on an excursion in a pilot Boat for a few days in search of cooler & better air." [121] Yet it seems that from about this time, his seventy-fifth year, [122] can be approximately dated the almost imperceptible, yet inexorable, decline in Astor's health which was to be completed a decade later. Of this decline his accident was probably at once a symptom and a contributing cause.

In the fall of 1838 Astor was "very feeble," and in September, 1840, Cogswell referred to his "weakness." [123] In March, 1841, Astor mentioned "the feeble state of my health," though in December he described it as "tolerably good at present." [124] In April, 1842, Cogswell, who had earlier in that year become his companion, referred to "his nervous fits." [125] In June, however, Astor wrote: "My health . . . is somewhat better than it was during the past winter and spring." [126] Late in 1842 he experienced a serious illness. Henry Brevoort wrote to Irving on December 28: "Our old friend Mr. Astor has been confined to his room, and mostly to his bed, these three months past. I saw him yesterday. He was lying in his bed, in his parlor, looking feeble & emaciated, but much recovered. His appetite remains healthy & his mind as clear & as much occupied with old cares, as usual. His years are bearing him downward, & probably his next, the eightieth will be his last." [127] In this judgment Brevoort, like Philip Hone, made the error of considerably underestimating Astor's vitality.

Through all Astor's last years Cogswell was "his prop & comfort." Astor became so dependent upon his friend that his absence made him "dreadfully nervous." "Mr. Astor," Cogswell wrote, "has now no one but myself to amuse him, and I am chiefly occupied with doing that. . . . Every pleasant day we take a steamboat and while away some three or four hours in the inner or outer bay." [128] At this time, the summer of 1843, Astor was "unable . . . to give his attention to business," because of "his extreme debility." [129] It is significant of Astor's character that at the age of four-score he should have even considered devoting any of his time to such matters.

In October, 1843, however, Brevoort was able to write to Irving: "Old Mr. Astor stills [*sic*] holds out, & is better, body & mind, than he was before you left us [in the spring of 1842]. An untoward event has just happened in his family, which has stirred his ire; *a thing which always does him good.*" [130] The italics are mine. We have already mentioned the occurrence referred to by Brevoort, the remarriage of Samuel Ward, after the death of his first wife, William B. Astor's eldest daughter. This improvement, however, proved to be only temporary. Late in April, 1844, William B. Astor wrote: "My father's health . . . is pretty good, and will improve I trust on his being able to enjoy the open air more frequently and which the advancing season of the year now will permit him to do." But late in August the son wrote: "He is not so strong as he was last summer but I think he is more comfortable–He takes a drive at least once every fine day." In the next month he described his father as "in pretty good health considering his very advanced age." [131] However, when we recall Astor's "extreme debility" in the summer of 1843, it is evident that the further decline in strength, which, according to his son's account, occurred in the succeeding year, must have been a very serious matter.

Just how serious Astor's condition was is revealed by an entry in Hone's diary for October 9, 1844. On the 8th he had dined in a company which included Astor and Cogswell, and wrote:

> Mr. Astor . . . presented a painful example of the insufficiency of wealth to prolong the life of man. . . . His life has been spent in amassing money, and he loves it as much as ever. He sat at the dinner table with his head down upon his breast, saying very little, and in a voice almost unintelligible . . . a servant behind him to guide the victuals which he was eating, and to watch him as an infant is watched. His mind is good, his observation acute, and he seems to know everything that is going on. But the machinery is all broken up, and there are some people, no doubt, who think he has lived long enough.[132]

Against the background furnished by the description of this keen but detached observer, we can better evaluate the comparatively optimistic reports given by William B. Astor to enquiring relatives and friends. It is evident that Astor's nerves had been so shattered that he might be described as afflicted with a palsy. He was paying the penalty in his last years for the rapid pace he had maintained in his early business life. Worst of all, he had reverted to his despondent condition of a decade before, just after his return from Europe. Early in May, 1845, Cogswell wrote: "Mr. Astor is particularly feeble and helpless. He thinks he can never get out again." For two months he continued "very ill," so that Cogswell had for several weeks to sit up with him "a greater part of every night." [133] By early July, however, he was "considerably better," and by the middle of July, though still "quite feeble," he had "left his bed" and was "able to ride out for an hour a day." His health continued to improve through August, but he was still "very weak having lost both flesh and strength since the last Spring."

Late in September, Astor's health was "such as to permit him to take a drive occasionally on the 3^d Avenue and almost daily to be rolled over the garden walks at Hell Gate in his Bath Chair, and he is stronger, I think than he was a few weeks ago." Early in November Astor's health was "tolerably good," though he was "quite infirm," but in the next month William B. Astor was forced to write to Mrs. Sarah Boreel: "The cold weather and the city do not agree with your Grandfather as well as the warm weather at Hurl Gate; and he has lost somewhat both in flesh and strength since he moved in from the country. He is however able occasionally to take a short drive, and to walk out for a little while." [134]

Nevertheless, Astor came through the winter of 1845–46 remarkably well, "without much pain," having "escaped colds and illness." The spring found him, "altho' infirm," enjoying "tolerable health." Unfortunately, however, he "became very weak as the warm weather came on." "He removed to Hell Gate" about the middle of June, after which his health improved. Late in October, Astor "moved to town," where he felt "the want of the good air and the exercise he got, while at Hell Gate." Still, his health remained good, though he continued, as he had for years, to be "quite feeble." [135] Thomas L. McKenney summed up Astor's condition in this year in a letter written on July 4 to Mrs. Madison: "Your old friend M^r. Astor is very feeble. He is at hurl-gate, and may linger on awhile longer, but can have no pleasure in life. I am told by those who best know him that his relish for wealth is as keen as ever; That gone, he is gone." [136]

Astor came through the winter of 1846–47 even better than he had the one before, but his "strength . . . failed rapidly" during 1847. Early in May his son wrote: "My Fathers health, I am grieved to say, has been alarming of late so that we were apprehensive of a fatal termination of his illness. He is now better than he has been, and I trust out of danger for the present." From this time on the decline of Astor's health was fairly rapid. Increasingly feeble as he had been for years, his strength now became less and less; in addition he was afflicted with insomnia.[137] In an interview with Gerrit Smith, he said: "I am broken up. It is time for me to be out of the way." [138] Yet he fought on for the little life that might remain to him with the same grim determination which, many times a millionaire, he had shown in striving to avoid the loss of a few hundreds of dollars. He could no longer walk save with the aid of attendants,[139] and his health was weakened by the warm weather, but in August, 1847, he was still "able to move about in his Carriage & Bath Chair" when the weather was fine "and to take a short airing for an hour or so." [140] At the back of his country home, "steps led down to a summer house where . . . Astor loved to sit and watch the Boston night boat go through Hell Gate to the Sound . . . he would refuse to go in to his dinner until it passed, no matter how cold and dark it was." [141] Perhaps he was thinking of the days when his ships wove a web of commerce over all the seas from New York to London, Hamburg, Le Havre, Smyrna, Gibraltar, Calcutta, Canton, Kamchatka, the islands of the Pacific and the western coast of both the Americas, and of the American Fur Company's steamboat *Yellowstone*, pushing her way up the Missouri to the mouth of the river from which she took her name.

Early in November, 1847, he left Hell Gate for his town house in New York City for the last time. He "bore the drive . . . very well," but deprived of the fresh air and exercise of Hell Gate his strength and appetite both rapidly failed. It was said during his last few months "that he cannot *converse* . . . neither listen nor reply" and that "he now lives on the milk of a wet nurse" and was "daily tossed in a blanket for exercise," yet it is also asserted that "he still retained a strong interest in the care and increase of his property," [142] and he was able to enjoy a visit from Washington Irving. Late in February, 1848, his son wrote: "he has for some weeks past suffered from an attack of cold which has reduced his strength much and made him quite thin and altho' now much recovered from the cold he is so debilitated that he can leave his bed but for a few hours at a time." [143] Late in March, 1848, Astor took to his bed and it was evident that the end was near. Though for forty-eight hours he was "unable to speak," he still held out. At the end of that period, at nine o'clock, March 29, 1848, "he breathed his last . . . without a struggle, and apparently without pain." [144] His death was due to simple old age and not to the effects of any disease. [145] To himself, as well as to others, it was doubtless a merciful release.

Obituary comments varied. The reformer Gerrit Smith lamented the death of his "fast friend," [146] while the scarcely less liberal Horace Mann compared him unfavorably with Girard, in language of extraordinary severity. [147] Philip Hone spoke of the "liberality" which Astor had always displayed in his business relations with the Hone auction firm, [148] but T. A. Ward referred to him as "the man whose word by his own acknowledgment should never be taken, nor his promise considered binding, unless in writing." [149] The *New York Herald* dismissed him as "a self-invented money-making machine." [150] The main implication of this last judgment cannot be doubted or denied, despite the uncomplimentary phraseology. To cast doubt upon Napoleon's military genius would be no more futile than to deny that Astor was a great business man — indeed, the German, unlike the Corsican, never met his Waterloo. In each case there is a definite standard of achievement: in the one, the winning of battles against forces equal or superior in numbers, equipment, and position; in the other, the amassing of property by means not contrary to law nor regarded as improper in the best business circles, and without other advantages than those given by one's own industry and ingenuity.

There can be little doubt that Astor need not have feared to be judged by this criterion. Perhaps he was a "money-making machine," but, even so, the rest of the phrase was equally pertinent: he was a machine of his own invention. Starting life with absolutely nothing, financially speaking, he possessed, when he began his career in America, not the slightest external advantage of influence or position. He took advantage to the utmost of the opportunities offered him by the New World and died as the wealthiest citizen of his adopted country. Astor's progress has been described as steady but unspectacular. "The only hard step in building up my fortune," he would say, "was making the first thousand dollars. After that it was easy." [151] But doubtless this was the situation as it appeared through the rosy mists of half a century of affluence. "He used to relate, with a chuckle, that he was worth a million before any one suspected it. . . . He had a strong aversion to illegitimate speculation, and particularly to gambling in stocks. . . . It was his pride and boast that he gained his own fortune by legitimate commerce, and by the legitimate investment of his profits." [152]

According to the standards of the time his pride was justified. It may fairly be asserted that his commerce with China was carried on in accordance with the best business traditions of the day. His organization of the fur trade contained potentialities of great public benefit, which would doubtless have been fulfilled in a greater measure had his project for a virtual monopoly been more nearly achieved. The methods of the Astor fur company, questionable or positively anti-social though some of them were, certainly tended to no greater public detriment, though they were probably more successful, than those of its competitors. If we are to accept big business and metropolitan economy as great gains made by modern society, then we must allot to Astor a high place in the field of social achievement. In the growth of New York City, first as a commercial and later as a financial center, Astor played a part as vital as it was early. It may prove to be a valid judgment that he did more than any other single man in the early days to prepare the way for New York's material hegemony.

Although Astor fully recognized the pre-eminent position held by his Manhattan Island real-estate investments as a factor in the building up of his fortune, and though his daring and foresight found one of their most characteristic expressions in the increasing of his holdings in and near New York City, nevertheless his heart was not in the processes of real-estate development to the extent that it was in the intricacies of mercantile transactions. Consequently, the social services which developed from his real-estate activities were less conspicuous than were those arising from his commercial career. Nevertheless, a by no means uncritical biographer, writing less than a score of years after Astor's death, spoke of the concentration of New York real estate in his hands as resulting in an unmixed good to the city in which he was for so long one of the most prominent business men.[153] It is probably true that part of the profits which Astor reaped for himself from the increase in value of Manhattan Island real estate sprang from the benefits which he had planted for New York City in foreign and domestic trade.

There is, as we have said, no doubt that Napoleon was a great general and Astor a great business man, but opinions may differ as to whether either was a great man. There were certain qualities of Astor's character, partly, perhaps, inherent, largely, no doubt, due to his environment, which an *advocatus diaboli* might present as counts against any claims to greatness in an unrestricted sense. The poverty of his early surroundings probably caused him to lay upon the acquisition of wealth an emphasis which was too extreme to make for the highest happiness to himself and the greatest good to society. Energy and ability which might have been expended more beneficially in other channels were concentrated too exclusively upon the sterile task of piling up property, largely for the mere joy of accumulation.

Astor did not lack imagination — indeed in some respects he possessed it in a unique degree; but he had harnessed its powers so long and so closely to the service of his business enterprises that it was difficult to turn it into other channels. Throughout his career Astor worked within the limits of the business life of his time, content to be the greatest within the area which he had originally marked out for himself, but never considering that it might be possible to transcend — even to transform — the business *mores* which he had inherited, to take, perhaps, less profits and accept partial compensation in the consciousness of having performed a social benefit possible to no other. What could not a man of keener social vision have done, for example, with Astor's real-estate holdings on Manhattan Island? This is not to say, of course, that Astor was less backward in recognizing his social responsibilities than other men of his time and class. The contrary is more likely true. It is only in contrast with his extraordinarily far-seeing qualities on the economic horizon that his range of social vision seems limited. In his later years, especially, there is evidence that as his physical eyesight dimmed he began to see his own relation to society more clearly. The most disappointing aspect of the situation is that no adequate influence was earlier brought to bear upon Astor's mind, turning it to such matters, inasmuch as he seems to have been held back from their consideration by no temperamental lack of interest or capacity. No man who could be simultaneously the friend of Philip Hone, Whig aristocrat and staunch supporter of the *status quo*, and of Gerrit Smith, enthusiastic abolitionist and radical reformer extraordinary, could justly be accused of essential narrowmindedness.

But this consideration of whether Astor might or might not

have been a greater man, had he been more disinterested and consequently less successful purely as a merchant, is largely aside from the main subject of the investigation and may be decided by each person according to his own standards. Astor regarded himself as a business man and it has been my purpose to show what, as such, he accomplished. What he might have achieved in other fields can be no more than a matter of conjecture. Considered in the aspect of a business man, and in that aspect alone, it seems clear that Astor was pre-eminent in his period. Indeed it is doubtful whether in the art of buying and selling he has ever been approached, much less surpassed.

NOTES

1. During Astor's lifetime a book intended for the guidance of immigrants to the United States published a glowing tribute to Astor, stating that his "early life was passed in the country, where he was known as *the honest boy*," and concluding: "Mr. Astor is still living in the city of New-York, without a stain upon his character; and though unobtrusive in his charities, giving with a liberal hand to the poor, and to all objects of public importance. There are few such specimens in any country, of the bold and enterprising merchant, the honest man, the unassuming gentleman, as John Jacob Astor." (*Wiley & Putnam's Emigrant's Guide* (London, 1845), pp. 46–48.) Another account, published in the year of Astor's death but before that event took place, remarked more conservatively: "Although sufficiently close and parsimonious, he is at the same time occasionally liberal and forbearing" ([Armstrong, William], *The Aristocracy of New York* (1848), p. 7).

2. Parton, James, *Life of John Jacob Astor* (1865), p. 72.

3. Smith, Matthew Hale, *Sunshine and Shadow in New York* (1868), p. 121.

4. Parton, *loc. cit.*

5. As far as the available records show, William B. Astor was probably more consistently philanthropic, even during the elder Astor's lifetime, than was his father (ms. book, Baker Library, Astor Papers, Letter Book iii, 1845–48, pp. 53, 149, 195, William B. Astor, N. Y., January 26, 1846, February 1, 1847, to Robert B. Minturn, July 9, 1847, to Rev. G. T. Bedell). The contributions that he made were chiefly to the "Association for the improvement of the condition of the poor." John Jacob, however, would have been entitled to remark: "But then William has a rich father."

6. Smith, *op. cit.*, p. 120.

7. Menzel, Wolfgang, *The History of Germany*, 3 vols. (London, 1849; translated by Mrs. George Hornocks), vol. iii, p. 447, note.

8. Howe, Julia Ward, *Reminiscences, 1819–1899* (1899), p. 76.

9. Ms. book, Baker Library, Astor Papers, Letter Book ii, 1831–38, p. 308, John Jacob Astor by William B. Astor, N. Y., June 27, 1835, to J. J. Janeway, New Brunswick, N. J. (see below, vol. ii, p. 1229).

10. *Ibid.*, Letter Book iii, 1845–48, pp. 176, 204, letters to L. H. Bailie, Erie, Monroe County, Michigan, May 3, 1847, and to Charles M. Gregg, Adrian, Michigan, August 9, 1847.

11. *Ibid.*, p. 26, John Jacob Astor by William B. Astor, N. Y., September 27, 1845, to C. G. Gunther, C. H. Hoyer, and Henry Ludwig.

12. *Ibid.*, p. 73, Letter to the Reverend J. W. French, Rector of the Church of the Epiphany, Washington, D. C., April 4, 1846.

13. *Ibid.*, p. 163, William B. Astor, N. Y., March 17, 1847, to Professor Heckley, Columbia College, N. Y.

14. *Ibid.*, p. 230, Letter to F. G. Cary, President of Farmers College, Hamilton County, Ohio, November 3, 1847.

15. *Ibid.*, pp. 72, 136, letters to John S. Giles, Treasurer of the Fire Department Fund, April 2, December 30, 1846.

16. *Hone, Philip, The Diary of, 1828–1851*, Allan Nevins, ed., 2 vols. (1927), vol. i, p. xiv. Astor's interest in libraries comes out in a letter to James Wadsworth, to whom he writes: "I am glad to see the mission of M^r. [John Orville] Taylor has been crowned with success, which must be particularly gratifying to you who are the founder of this noble work" (ms. book, Baker Library, Astor Papers, Letter Book ii, 1831–38, p. 412, John Jacob Astor, N. Y., June 25, 1836, to James Wadsworth, Geneseo). The "noble work" to which Astor referred was probably the campaign for the establishment of school libraries in New York State which was being carried on by Wadsworth and Taylor.

17. *New-York Gazette and General Advertiser*, January 30, 1829, p. 2, col. 3.

18. *Hone, Philip, The Diary of, 1828–1851*, vol. i, pp. 182–183. It is probably to the proviso attached to Astor's subscription that the *New York Herald* referred in its obituary notice: "If Mr. Astor was industrious in the accumulation of riches, he was likewise very penurious and niggardly in money matters. . . . He would, however, never object to subscribing for charitable objects when solicited to do so; but would almost invariably insist upon having others subscribe first." (*New York Herald*, March 31, 1848, p. 2, col. 4.)

19. Smith, *op. cit.*, p. 118.

20. Brigham, Johnson, *The Banker in Literature* (1910), pp. 89–90.

21. Stone, William L., *History of New York City* (1872), p. 413, note.

22. Parton, *op. cit.*, p. 80.

23. It will be remembered that Astor had some lands at Green Bay, Wisconsin, to which he was anxious to attract settlers. It may be that his willingness to advance a large part of his legacy to the German Society was partly owing to the thought that, through the information office to be established and maintained by means of this bequest, German immigrants might be directed to the vicinity of Green Bay. We know that in 1845 Astor, in a letter to one of his associates in the Green Bay Lands, promised: "I shall endeavour, as far as I can, to get the German Emigrants to take the route to Astor" (ms. book, Baker Library, Astor Papers, Letter Book iii, 1845–48, pp. 18–19, John Jacob Astor by William B. Astor, N. Y., September 9, 1845, to Robert Stuart, see below, vol. ii, pp. 1246–1248). Two years later Astor wrote to the agency of the German Society, introducing his friend and agent, Professor Mersch, who had just returned from a visit to Green Bay and who had, Astor said, valuable information

in regard to settlement in that vicinity (ms. book, Baker Library, Astor Papers, Letter Book iii, 1845–48, p. 212, John Jacob Astor per William B. Astor, September 9, 1847, to John E. Allstadt, Agency of the German Society). It is unlikely that the information imparted by Astor's friend and agent would be of a nature to turn German settlers away from the Green Bay district. In 1839 Astor contributed $500 to the building fund of the Congregational Church at Green Bay, and also made the congregation the gift of a bell, worth $300 (Durrie, Daniel S., *The Early Out-Posts of Wisconsin. Green Bay for Two Hundred Years, 1639–1839* (1872), p. 12). In this case, certainly, Astor was fully as much influenced by the business consideration of building up the town in which he was a large owner as he was by the philanthropic purpose of advancing religion on the Wisconsin frontier.

24. This bequest, partly intended for the education in the industrial arts of the youth of Waldorf, is especially interesting from the fact that had such an institution been in existence when Astor was a boy in that village it is quite probable that he would never have left Germany. It is creditable to Astor's good sense that he did not assume, as is so often done, that what he had done others could likewise accomplish with no additional advantages.

A tradition concerning this legacy is preserved among Astor's descendants. One version runs as follows: "The old gentleman was much plagued by begging letters, most of which began with the plea that the writer was a relative. Finally the following formula was used in replying:

"'My Dear Sir: You ask me to support you on the ground that your father was my cousin and playmate. I remember my cousins and playmates very distinctly. I do not find your father among them; but if he was I refer you to the Home for the Destitute Old which I have built and endowed at Waldorf. I know of no reason why it should not be occupied by my own relations.'" (Aldrich, Mrs. Richard, "Notes of the Astors," *Washington Historical Quarterly*, vol. xviii (1927), pp. 21–27.)

It is quite probable that Astor did have many relatives in Germany. His grandfather, Felix Astor, in addition to four children by his first wife, one of whom was Astor's father, between 1725 and 1750, as we have seen, had sixteen children by a second marriage (Astor genealogy in the possession of Mrs. Richard Aldrich). However, the story of Astor's reply to these requests from children of his alleged cousins must be fictitious, for the institution founded by Astor at Waldorf was not opened until six years after his death (Parton, *op. cit.*, pp. 83–84).

25. Parton, *op. cit.*, pp. 96–97, 105, 110–113, 115, 116, 117; ms., Baker Library, Astor Papers, The Will of John Jacob Astor (see below, vol. ii, pp. 1267–1268, 1276–1277, 1288, 1291).

26. [Scoville, Joseph A.], *The Old Merchants of New York*, 5 vols. (1889), vol. v, p. 109.

27. Ms. book, Baker Library, Astor Papers, Letter Book ii, 1831–38, p. 468, John Jacob Astor, N. Y., March 4, 1837, to F. A. A. Melly, Secretary p. t., German Society; *New York As It Is In 1837* (1837), p. 107; *New York As It Is In 1839* (1839), p. 107.

28. Smith, *op. cit.*, pp. 118–119.

29. *Evening Post* (N. Y.), July 28, 1838, p. 2, col. 1, quoting from the Boston *Daily Advertiser*.

30. *Cogswell, Joseph Green, Life of* (1874), pp. 213, 214, 216, 217, 219, 220, 221, 222, 225, 226, 229, 230, 231, 232, 233; *Hone, Philip, The Diary of, 1828–1851*, vol. ii, p. 595; Howe, *op. cit.*, pp. 73–76. One of Astor's obituaries preserves an anecdote which, though it may not be correct in detail, nevertheless probably is true in spirit. It gives one of the reasons for Astor's repeated postponements of beginning work on the library, despite his promises to Cogswell. "The specifications [for the library] . . . seemed to please Mr. Astor very much. After looking at them for a while, he enquired what the outlay for the first year would be, and was informed that it would be probably sixty-five thousand dollars. 'That will do,' said Mr. Astor, rising from his chair, and placing the specifications in a large trunk, where they have remained from that day to the present." (*New York Herald*, March 31, 1848, p. 2, col. 4.)

Henry Brevoort, Astor's nephew, in a letter written to Washington Irving on October 18, 1843, also tells an amusing story which helps to explain Astor's hesitation to go on with his plans for the library. "Dr. Williams . . ." Brevoort wrote, "told me a good story about the old boy [Astor]. . . . He consulted the Dr. as to what items of property he might conscientiously conceal from assessment. The Dr. thought the Library legacy was a fair one for exemption — Oh! said Money-bags, I had tought of dat & so he continued to every proposition of the Doctor's. At this rate the Legacy, if the old man holds out long enough will turn out a profitable speculation! — " (*Brevoort, Henry, Letters of, to Washington Irving*, George S. Hellman, ed., 2 vols. (1916), vol. ii, p. 138.)

31. Mann, Horace, *A Few Thoughts for a Young Man* (1853), pp. 64–65. Astor's grandson Charles Astor Bristed, son of Astor's daughter Magdalen, came to the defence of his grandfather by declaring that he had possessed political insight and enjoyed the society of literary men, and by denying that his fortune exceeded $8,000,000 (Bristed, Charles Astor, *A Letter to the Hon. Horace Mann* (1850), pp. 14–18.

32. Myers, Gustavus, *History of the Great American Fortunes*, 3 vols, (1909), vol. i, pp. 199–200, quoting from the *New York Herald*, April 5, 1848.

33. Irving, Washington, *Astoria* (1836), chap. ii.

34. Ms., Syracuse University, Gerrit Smith Miller Collection, Letters, John Jacob Astor, N. Y., November 10, 1794 (see above, vol. i, pp. 375–

377), London, February 19, 1795, N. Y., August 26, 1795, to Peter Smith, Old Fort Schuyler.

35. *Ibid.*, John Jacob Astor, N. Y., November 16, 1802, April 26, July 5, 1803, to Peter Smith, Utica.

36. *New-York Gazette and General Advertiser*, June 3, 1819, p. 2, col. 1.

37. Ms. book, Office of the Astor Estate, N. Y., Untitled land book; Astor, William Waldorf, "John Jacob Astor," *Pall Mall Magazine*, vol. xviii (June 1899), p. 179.

38. *Adams, John Quincy, Memoirs of*, Charles Francis Adams, ed., 12 vols. (1875), vol. v, pp. 152–153.

39. Ms., New York Public Library, Monroe Papers, John Jacob Astor, Rome, April 5, 1820, Frankfort, September 5, 1820, to James Monroe, President.

40. Some years later William B. Astor followed the fashion by demonstrating at least a verbal sympathy for the Polish revolutionists. "We look always for interesting news from France & England who we hope will yet interpose in favor of the Gallant Poles," he wrote on one occasion. (Ms. book, Baker Library, Astor Papers, Letter Book ii, 1831–38, p. 1, William B. Astor, N. Y., September 30, 1831, to Vincent Rumpff.) His feelings had not changed fifteen years later, when he again wrote. "The Polish insurrection it appears has been put down, and what a sad affair for the poor Poles! The result of it must strengthen conservatism in Europe." (Ms. book, Baker Library, Astor Papers, Letter Book iii, 1845–48, p. 82, William B. Astor, N. Y., May 5, 1846, to Vincent Rumpff, Paris.)

41. Gallatin, Count, ed., *A Great Peace Maker: The Diary of James Gallatin, Secretary to Albert Gallatin* (1914), pp. 167–168.

42. *Irving, Washington, The Letters of, to Henry Brevoort*, George S. Hellman, ed., 2 vols. (1915), vol. ii, pp. 162–163.

43. Ms. book, Office of the Astor Estate, N. Y., Untitled land book.

44. Gallatin, *op. cit.*, p. 179.

45. Ms., Library of Congress, Monroe Papers, vol. xv, Writings to Monroe, March 19, 1815–October 21, 1816, George W. Erving, N. Y., March 18, 1816, to James Monroe. Erving apparently had such dark and vague suspicions of Gallatin and Astor that the mere fact of the two men having dined together seemed to him to justify dispatching a letter to Monroe, inscribed with some variant of "Quite private & confidential" (*ibid.*, George W. Erving, N. Y., January 13, February 24, 1816, to James Monroe). Just what nefarious deed he thought Astor and Gallatin were planning does not seem at all clear. By 1832, however, Astor and Erving seem to have come to be on quite good terms (ms. book, Baker Library, Astor Papers, Letter Book ii, 1831–38, p. 29, John Jacob Astor, N. Y., January 30, 1832, to George W. Erving).

46. Ms. book (copy), Detroit Public Library, Burton Historical Collection, and Missouri Historical Society, St. Louis, Letters of Ramsay Crooks, John Jacob Astor, and the American Fur Company, 1813–43, Ramsay Crooks, N. Y., December 4, 1819, to John Jacob Astor, Europe; ms. (photostat), Wisconsin Historical Society, Madison, Wisconsin, Ramsay Crooks' Letter Book, Mackinac, etc., 1816–20, Ramsay Crooks, N. Y., May 30, 1820, to John Jacob Astor.

47. Ms., New York Public Library, Monroe Papers, John Jacob Astor, Paris, January 10, 1821, to James Monroe, President (see below, vol. ii, pp. 1169–1170).

48. Ms. book (copy), Detroit Public Library, Burton Historical Collection, and Missouri Historical Society, St. Louis, Letters of Ramsay Crooks, John Jacob Astor, and the American Fur Company, 1813–43, John Jacob Astor, Paris, March 27, 1821, to Ramsay Crooks, Present; ms. (photostat), Wisconsin Historical Society, Madison, Wisconsin, Ramsay Crooks' and Robert Stuart's Letter Book, Mackinac, Detroit, N. Y., etc., 1820–25, pp. 83–84, Ramsay Crooks, Liverpool, April 18, 1821, to John Jacob Astor, Paris.

49. Ms., Syracuse University, Gerrit Smith Miller Collection, Letters, John Jacob Astor & Son, July 16, 1821, to Peter Smith.

50. Ms. (photostat), Wisconsin Historical Society, Madison, Wisconsin, Ramsay Crooks' and Robert Stuart's Letter Book, Mackinac, Detroit, N. Y., etc., 1820–25, Ramsay Crooks, Mackinac, July 11, N. Y., November 30, 1821, to John Jacob Astor, Europe.

51. Gallatin, *op. cit.*, p. 201.

52. *New-York Gazette and General Advertiser*, April 29, 1822, p. 2, col. 2.

53. Ms., Syracuse University, Gerrit Smith Miller Collection, Letters, John Jacob Astor, N. Y., July 16, 1822, to Peter Smith, Peterboro (see below, vol. ii, pp. 1170–1171).

54. Ms. (photostat), Wisconsin Historical Society, Madison, Wisconsin, Ramsay Crooks' and Robert Stuart's Letter Book, Mackinac, Detroit, N. Y., etc., 1820–25, pp. 261–265, Ramsay Crooks, N. Y., April 23, 1822, to John Jacob Astor, N. Y.

55. Gallatin, *op. cit.*, p. 229, January 5, 1823. Astor, however, thought enough of James Gallatin to make him an executor of his will (Parton, *op. cit.*, p. 99; ms., Baker Library, Astor Papers, The Will of John Jacob Astor, see below, vol. ii, p. 1271).

56. *Gallatin, Albert, The Writings of*, Henry Adams, ed., 3 vols. (1879), vol. ii, pp. 269–270, W. H. Crawford, Washington, May 26, 1823, to Albert Gallatin.

57. *New-York Gazette and General Advertiser*, June 3, 1823, p. 2, col. 2.

58. Ms. book, Office of the Astor Estate, N. Y., Untitled land book.

59. *Ibid.*, Untitled memorandum book.

60. Ms. book (copy), Detroit Public Library, Burton Historical Collection, and Missouri Historical Society, St. Louis, Letters of Ramsay Crooks, John Jacob Astor, and the American Fur Company, 1813–43, John Jacob Astor, Geneva, February 16 (see below, vol. ii, pp. 1173–1175), March 13, 19, 19, 1824, to Ramsay Crooks, N. Y., March 24, 1824, to W. B. Clapp, N. Y., April 17, September 21, November 10, December 4, 1824, January 10 (see below, vol. ii, pp. 1176, 1178), March 11, May 20, Schentznach, July 5, Geneva, August 20 (see below, vol. ii, pp. 1179–1180), 1825, to Ramsay Crooks, N. Y.; William B. Astor, N. Y., June 28, July 2, 1824, to Ramsay Crooks, St. Louis; ms., Syracuse University, Gerrit Smith Miller Collection, Letters, William B. Astor, June 14, 1824, to Peter Smith.

61. Astor, *op. cit.*, p. 179.

62. *New-York Gazette and General Advertiser*, April 10, 1826, p. 2, col. 3.

63. Ms. book, Baker Library, Astor Papers, Letter Book ii, 1831–38, pp. 166–167, William B. Astor, N. Y., July 16, 1833, to Alexander Hammett, Naples.

64. *Ibid.*, p. 64, John Jacob Astor, N. Y., June 19, 1832, to B. Pratte & Co., St. Louis.

65. Nolte, Vincent, *Fifty Years in Both Hemispheres* (1854), pp. 140–143.

66. Ms. book, Baker Library, Astor Papers, Letter Book ii, 1831–38, p. 65, William B. Astor, N. Y., June 23, 1832, to Benjamin F. Butler, Albany.

67. Ms., Missouri Historical Society, St. Louis, P. Chouteau Collection, Pierre Chouteau Papers, John Jacob Astor, Paris, August, 1832, to P. Chouteau, Jr.

68. Ms. book, Baker Library, Astor Papers, Letter Book ii, 1831–38, pp. 95–96, William B. Astor, N. Y., September 29, 1832, to Vincent Rumpff, Paris.

69. Ms., Missouri Historical Society, St. Louis, P. Chouteau Collection, Pierre Chouteau Papers, John Jacob Astor, Bellevue, September 28, 1832, to P. Chouteau, Jr.

70. Ms. book, Baker Library, Astor Papers, personal memorandum book of John Jacob Astor in Europe, August 11, 1832–January 31, 1834.

71. *Ibid.*, Letter Book ii, 1831–38, p. 117, John Jacob Astor, Paris, November 9, 1832, to James P. Sturgis & Co., Canton, and to Charles N. Talbot, N. Y.

72. *Brevoort, Henry, Letters of, to Washington Irving*, vol. i, p. 105.

73. Astor, *op. cit.*, p. 179. The sole authority for the statement that, during his travels in Europe, Astor was presented to such men as Charles x, Louis Philippe, Metternich, and Guizot is William Waldorf Astor's article, cited above. That he did meet these celebrities is not at all improbable; we know that he had letters of introduction to such men as

Lafayette. However, internal evidence indicates that the above-mentioned article, which is almost our only source for many details of John Jacob Astor's activities and movements during his European sojourns, was written largely from memory and the imagination. The dates it gives for Astor's stays in Europe are 1820–22 and 1829–34, instead of the correct periods of 1819–22, 1823–26, and 1832–34. The statement has been made that Astor witnessed at Naples the accession of Ferdinand II, but this is impossible since that event took place in 1829, when Astor was in New York; we have no evidence that Astor so much as visited Naples at any time during King Bomba's reign. I am inclined to think that the author first recalled incorrectly the years of his ancestor's last European sojourn and then assumed without further proof that he was a witness of almost any event occurring during that period which would be of a character to arouse Astor's interest.

74. Ms. book, Baker Library, Astor Papers, Letter Book ii, 1831–38, pp. 195–196, 198–199, 202, William B. Astor, N. Y., December 6, 1833, to Wilson P. Hunt, St. Louis, December 31, 1833, January 7, 1834, to Vincent Rumpff, Paris. Parton (*op. cit.*, p. 77) says that Astor "remained abroad till 1835" and then "hurried home in consequence of . . . General Jackson's war upon the Bank of the United States." The error in the date of his return refutes the reason given for it. Arthur D. Howden Smith speaks of Astor's lingering in Europe till the death of his daughter Eliza in 1833 (Smith, Arthur D. Howden, *John Jacob Astor* (1929), p. 271). As a matter of fact, Eliza did not die until late in 1838 (*Hone, Philip, The Diary of, 1828–1851*, vol. i, p. 374). Arthur D. Howden Smith was doubtless deceived by Richard Henry Greene's *The Todd Genealogy*, which so far as dates are concerned is pretty hopeless.

75. Ms., Missouri Historical Society, St. Louis, P. Chouteau Collection, Pierre Chouteau Papers, John Jacob Astor, Geneva, June 25, 1833, to Bernard Pratte & Co., St. Louis (see below, vol. ii, p. 1224).

76. Ms. book, New York Custom House, New York Register, no. 281, August 31, 1833; no. 303, August 31, 1835.

77. Parton, *op. cit.*, pp. 76–78. It is quite evident that Frederick De Peyster was the authority for Astor's astonishing conduct on board the *Utica* on his final return to New York. It seems quite likely that the other stories preserved by Parton, having to do with Astor's relations with his captains, came from the same source. This is particularly probable in the cases of the anecdotes about the "chronometer voyage," the death of Astor's Canton agent, the quick-witted but unrewarded captain, etc. We have already shown De Peyster's probable connection with some of these tales. If they do come from a single source, this fact may assist the reader in estimating the extent of their authenticity.

78. *Hone, Philip, The Diary of, 1828–1851*, vol. i, p. 121.

79. Parton, *op. cit.*, p. 24.

80. See above, vol. i, facing p. 86 and p. 112.

81. He is described loosely as "about five feet eight or ten inches high" "when in his prime" (Armstrong, *op. cit.*, p. 7); "Astor war von mittleren Grösse, breitschulterig und von der Sonne gebräunt" (Stocker, C. W. F. L., *Chronik von Walldorf* (Bruchsal, 1888), p. 14).

82. *New York Herald*, March 31, 1848, p. 2, col. 4.

83. Ms., Syracuse University, Gerrit Smith Miller Collection, Letters, John Jacob Astor, N. Y., January 14, May 8, 26, 1797, to Peter Smith, Old Fort Schuyler.

84. *Ibid.*, John Jacob Astor, N. Y., March 3, July 13, 1798, to Peter Smith, Old Fort Schuyler.

85. *Ibid.*, John Jacob Astor, N. Y., July 13, 29, Albany, August 10, 1799, to Peter Smith, Old Fort Schuyler.

86. *Ibid.*, John Jacob Astor, N. Y., November 16, 1802, April 26, 1803, to Peter Smith, Utica.

87. *Ibid.*, John Jacob Astor, N. Y., May 27, 1805, William Sanders for John Jacob Astor, August 27, 1805, to Peter Smith.

88. [Beach, Moses Yale], *The Wealth and Biography of the Wealthy Citizens of the City of New York* (1846), p. 3.

89. "John Jacob Astor," *Hunt's Merchants' Magazine*, vol. xi (1844), pp. 153-159.

90. Smith, M. H., *op. cit.*, pp. 115, 127.

91. Armstrong, *op. cit.*, p. 7.

92. Scoville, *op. cit.*, vol. i, pp. 415-416.

93. Parton, *op. cit.*, p. 51.

94. See above, vol. ii, facing p. 598.

95. Ms., Syracuse University, Gerrit Smith Miller Collection, Letters, John Jacob Astor & Son, July 16, 1821, to Peter Smith.

96. Ms. (photostat), Wisconsin Historical Society, Madison, Ramsay Crooks' and Robert Stuart's Letter Book, Mackinac, Detroit, N. Y., etc., 1820-25, pp. 122-125, Robert Stuart, Mackinac, October 15, 1824, to John Jacob Astor, Europe.

97. Letter in possession of Katherine L. Wilks, Cruickston Park, Galt, Ontario, John Jacob Astor, Geneva, March 19, 1824, to Mrs. Dorothea Langdon (see below, vol. ii, pp. 1175-1176).

98. Ms., Syracuse University, Gerrit Smith Miller Collection, Letters, William B. Astor, N. Y., June 14, 1824, to Peter Smith; ms. book (copy), Detroit Public Library, Burton Historical Collection, and Missouri Historical Society, St. Louis, Letters of Ramsay Crooks, John Jacob Astor, and the American Fur Company, 1813-43, William B. Astor, N. Y., June 28, July 2, 1824, to Ramsay Crooks, St. Louis.

99. See above, vol. i, frontispiece.

100. Ms. book (copy), Detroit Public Library, Burton Historical Collection and Missouri Historical Society, St. Louis, Letters of Ramsay

Crooks, John Jacob Astor, and the American Fur Company, 1813–43, John Jacob Astor, N. Y., September 26, 1827, to Ramsay Crooks, St. Louis.

101. Ms. (draft), Syracuse University, Gerrit Smith Miller Collection, Letters, Peter Smith, Schenectady, February 16, 1828, to John Jacob Astor; John Jacob Astor, N. Y., February 19, 1828, to Peter Smith, Schenectady.

102. Ms. book, Baker Library, Astor Papers, Letter Book ii, 1831–38, p. 40, John Jacob Astor, N. Y., April 3, 1832, to Benjamin Mooers, Plattsburgh; p. 37, John Jacob Astor, N. Y., March 23, 1832, to Thomas W. Olcott, Albany.

103. Ms., Missouri Historical Society, St. Louis, P. Chouteau Collection, Pierre Chouteau Papers, John Jacob Astor, Bellevue, September 28, 1832, to P. Chouteau, Jr.

104. Ms. book, Baker Library, Astor Papers, personal memorandum book of John Jacob Astor in Europe, August 11, 1832–January 31, 1834.

105. "Im Jahre 1833 und 34 verweilte der hochbetagte Greis im Paris und hielt dort sogar eine schmerzhaste Fisteloperation aus" (Stocker, *op. cit.*, p. 14).

106. Smith, M. H., *op. cit.*, p. 125.

107. Nolte, *op. cit.*, p. 143.

108. Ms. book, Baker Library, Astor Papers, Letter Book ii, 1831–38, pp. 118–119, 163, 181–182, William B. Astor, N. Y., January 1, June 27, September 26, 1833, to Vincent Rumpff, Paris.

109. *Ibid.*, p. 194, William B. Astor, N. Y., December 6, 1833, to Wilson P. Hunt, St. Louis.

110. *Ibid.*, p. 202, William B. Astor, N. Y., January 7, 1834, to Vincent Rumpff, Paris.

111. *Hone, Philip, The Diary of, 1828–1851*, vol. i, pp. 121, 125–126.

112. Ms. book, Baker Library, Astor Papers, Letter Book ii, 1831–38, p. 223, William B. Astor, N. Y., April 15, 1834, to Vincent Rumpff.

113. *Ibid.*, p. 229, John Jacob Astor, N. Y., May 4, 1834, to Wilson Price Hunt, St. Louis (see below, vol. ii, pp. 1224–1225).

114. *Ibid.*, p. 232, John Jacob Astor, N. Y., May 31, 1834, to Vincent Rumpff, Paris.

115. *Ibid.*, p. 240, William B. Astor, N. Y., June 23, 1834, to Vincent Rumpff, Paris.

116. *Ibid.*, p. 311, John Jacob Astor, Hell Gate, July 15, 1835, to Wilson P. Hunt, St. Louis.

117. Astor, *op. cit.*, p. 180.

118. Howe, *op. cit.*, p. 32.

119. Ms. book, Baker Library, Astor Papers, Letter Book ii, 1831–38, pp. 497, 497, 500, 505, 512, 521, 549, William B. Astor, N. Y., June 20, 1837, to Wilson P. Hunt, St. Louis, June 24, 1837, to C. W. Lutteroth,

Paris, July 3, 1837, to Henry Brevoort, Jr., July 29, 1837, to C. W. Lutteroth, Paris, August 25, 1837, to Robert Neilson, September 23, 1837, to Vincent Rumpff, Paris, December 28, 1837, to George Reynell, London.

120. See above, vol. ii, frontispiece.

121. Ms. book, Baker Library, Astor Papers, Letter Book ii, 1831–38, pp. 598, 608, William B. Astor, N. Y., July 7, 1838, to Vincent Rumpff, Paris, July 21, 1838, to C. W. Lutteroth, Paris.

122. Astor, *op. cit.*, p. 182.

123. *Cogswell, Joseph Green, Life of*, pp. 217, 226.

124. Ms., Syracuse University, Gerrit Smith Miller Collection, Letters, John Jacob Astor, N. Y., March 15, December 13 (see below, vol. ii, pp. 1241–1242), 1841, to Gerrit Smith, Peterboro.

125. *Cogswell, Joseph Green, Life of*, p. 233.

126. Ms., Syracuse University, Gerrit Smith Miller Collection, Letters, John Jacob Astor per William B. Astor, N. Y., June 22, 1842, to Gerrit Smith.

127. *Ibid.*, John Jacob Astor per William B. Astor, N. Y., December 30, 1842, to Gerrit Smith; *Brevoort, Henry, Letters of, to Washington Irving*, vol. ii, p. 125.

128. *Cogswell, Joseph Green, Life of*, p. 234.

129. Ms., Syracuse University, Gerrit Smith Miller Collection, Letters, Joseph Green Cogswell, Hellgate, June 9, 1843, to Gerrit Smith, Peterboro (see below, vol. ii, pp. ooo–ooo); William B. Astor, N. Y., June 29, 1843, to Gerrit Smith, Peterboro.

130. *Brevoort, Henry, Letters of, to Washington Irving*, vol. ii, p. 133.

131. Ms., Syracuse University, Gerrit Smith Miller Collection, Letters, William B. Astor, N. Y., April 29, August 30, September 20, 1844, to Gerrit Smith, Peterboro.

132. *Hone, Philip, The Diary of, 1828–1851*, vol. ii, p. 716.

133. *Cogswell, Joseph Green, Life of*, pp. 235–236.

134. Ms., Syracuse University, Gerrit Smith Miller Collection, Letters, William B. Astor, N. Y., June 21, 1845, to Gerrit Smith; ms. book, Baker Library, Astor Papers, Letter Book iii, 1845–48, pp. 2, 4, 14, 24, 36, 45–46, William B. Astor, N. Y., July 16, 23, 1845, to Robert Neilson, Philadelphia, August 28, 1845, to Vincent Rumpff, Paris, September 24, 1845, to Robert Boreel, Beverwych, November 7, 1845, to Gerrit Smith, Peterboro, December 13, 1845, to Mrs. Sarah Boreel (see below, vol. ii, pp. 1249–1250).

135. *Ibid.*, pp. 47, 53, 63, 70, 82, 95, 128, 136, William B. Astor, N. Y., December 29, 1845, to Robert Boreel, La Haye, Holland, January 23, 1846, to C. W. Lutteroth, Paris, February 24, 1846, to Vincent Rumpff, Paris, March 27, 1846, to Robert Boreel, La Haye, Holland, May 5, 1846, to Vincent Rumpff, Paris, June 24, 1846, to Robert Boreel, La Haye,

Holland, November 9, 1846, to Vincent Rumpff, Paris, December 29, 1846, to Robert Boreel, La Haye.

136. Clark, Allen C., *Life and Letters of Dolly Madison* (1914), p. 384, quoted in Minnigerode, Meade, *Certain Rich Men* (1927), p. 33.

137. Ms. book, Baker Library, Astor Papers, Letter Book iii, 1845–48, pp. 159, 177–178, 202, William B. Astor, N. Y., February 26, May 5, 1847, to Vincent Rumpff, Paris, July 26, 1847, to Robert Boreel, New Port, R. I.

138. Ms. book, Syracuse University, Gerrit Smith Miller Collection, Letter Book, 1843–55, p. 317, Gerrit Smith, Peterboro, April 6, 1848, to William B. Astor (see below, vol. ii, p. 1259).

139. Armstrong, *op. cit.*, p. 7; information from Mrs. Byam K. Stevens.

140. Ms. book, Baker Library, Astor Papers, Letter Book iii, 1845–48, pp. 204, 206, 210, William B. Astor, N. Y., August 11, 1847, to Vincent Rumpff, Paris, August 12, 1847, to George Reynell, London, August 27, 1847, to Vincent Rumpff, Paris.

141. Information from Mrs. Byam K. Stevens.

142. Parton, *op. cit.*, p. 80; Clark, *op. cit.*, pp. 398–399, Mrs. Madison, September 24, 1847, to her son.

143. Ms. book, Baker Library, Astor Papers, Letter Book iii, 1845–48, pp. 231, 271, William B. Astor, N. Y., November 5, 1847, February 24, 1848, to Vincent Rumpff, Paris.

144. *Cogswell, Joseph Green, Life of*, p. 238.

145. Ms. book, Baker Library, Astor Papers, Letter Book iii, 1845–48, pp. 280, 281, William B. Astor, N. Y., April 3, 1848, to Gillespies, Moffatt & Co., London, April 4, 1848, to C. W. Lutteroth, Paris.

146. Ms. book, Syracuse University, Gerrit Smith Miller Collection, Letter Book, 1843–55, p. 317, Gerrit Smith, Peterboro, April 6, 1848, to William B. Astor (see below, vol. ii, p. 1259).

147. Mann, *op. cit.*, pp. 64–65.

148. *Hone, Philip, The Diary of, 1828–1851*, vol. ii, p. 848.

149. Ms., Public Archives of Canada, Ottawa, Baring Papers, T. A. Ward, Boston, April 7, 24, 1848, to Joshua Bates, London.

150. Quoted in the *Dictionary of American Biography*, vol. i, "John Jacob Astor."

151. Smith, M. H., *op. cit.*, p. 115.

152. Parton, *op. cit.*, pp. 50, 51.

153. *Ibid.*, pp. 87–89.

DOCUMENTS
1816–1848

DOCUMENTS

97. Mortgage from Edmond Charles Genêt to Astor, April 1, 1816, on Land in New York City.

Edmond Charles (Citizen) Genêt had been French minister to the United States, and on being recalled had, instead of returning to France, married a daughter of Governor George Clinton and become an American citizen.

Registered [1] for and at the request of John Jacob Astor this 2nd. day of April 1816 — at 1/2 past 5 oclock P.M.
Memorandum that on this first day of April in the year of our Lord One thousand eight hundred and sixteen Edmond Charles Genet, of Greenbush in the County of Rensselaer, in the State of New York Esquire, and Martha B. his wife Did Mortgage to John Jacob Astor, of the City of New York, in the State of New York, Merchant, All that certain lot piece or parcel of ground situate lying and being in the Eigth Ward of the City of New York Bounded on the rear or Easterly side by lands belonging to David Sherwood, on the South Side by lands belonging to the said John Jacob Astor, on the North side by Spring Street, and on the front or Westerly line by Broadway Being in breadth in front and rear twenty five feet be the same more [or] less and in depth one hundred feet. Being the lot of ground heretofore leased by the said John Jacob Astor to Moses Dodd and Richard Kidney of the City of New York Builders, by a certain Indenture of lease, bearing date the first day of August in the year of our Lord One thousand eight hundred and twelve, Together with all and singular &c. —

[1] Ms. book, Hall of Records, N. Y., Liber Mortgages 34, p. 467.

Provided always that if the said parties of the first part, their heirs executors or administrators, shall well and truly pay, or cause to be paid unto the said party of the Second part, his executors, administrators, or assigns the Just and full sum of Four thousand five hundred dollars lawful money of the United States of America, with lawful interest by Instalments as follows to wit: One thousand dollars on or before the first day of April next, and the remaining sum of three thousand five hundred dollars on or before the first day of April, in the year of our Lord One thousand eight hundred and nineteen interest payable half yearly, according to the condition of a certain bond in the said Mortgage recited, then the said Mortgage to be void Which Mortgage was acknowledged by the said Edmond Charles Genet and Patty B. Genet his wife before John A. Graham Master in Chancery, this second day of April 1816 which said Mortgage also contains a certain power or clause of sale in the words following to wit: And it is hereby mutually covenanted and agreed, by and between the parties of these presents, that if default shall be made in the payment of the Said Sums of money mentioned in the condition of the said bond or obligation, and the interest which shall accrue thereon, or of any part thereof, at the times specified for the payment thereof, according to the tenor and effect of the said condition of the said bond or obligation, that then, and from thence forth, it shall be lawful for the said party of the second part his heirs, executors, administrators, and assigns, to enter into and upon all and singular the premises hereby granted, or intended, so to be and to grant bargain, sell, and dispose of the same, and all benefit and equity of Redemption of the said parties of the first part their heirs, executors, administrators, or assigns therein, at public auction, according to the act of the legislature in such cases made and provided, And as the Attorney of the said party of the first part, for that purpose by these premises duly constituted and appointed to make, seal, execute and deliver to the purchaser and purchasers thereof, a good and sufficient deed or deeds of Conveyance in the law for the same, in fee simple, and out of the monies arising from such sale, to retain the principal and interest which shall then be due on the said bond or obligation, according to the Condition thereof. Together with all the Costs and charges of advertisement and sale of the same rendering the overplus of the purchase monies, (if any there shall be) unto the said Edmond Charles Genet — party of the first part, his heirs, executors, administrators, or assigns, — which sale so to be made shall forever be a perpetual bar, both in Law and Equity, against the said parties of the first part their heirs and assigns, and all other persons claiming or to claim the premises or any part thereof, by from or under them, or any of them.

98. LETTER FROM ASTOR TO CHARLES GRATIOT, MAY 26, 1816, IN REGARD TO AN ARRANGEMENT WITH ST. LOUIS FUR TRADERS.

Robert Stuart and Ramsay Crooks had both gone out to Astoria, the first on the *Tonquin*, the second with the overland party. They had returned together overland and reached New York in 1813, after which they were employed by Astor in the fur trade. Crooks, before joining the Pacific Fur Company, had been engaged in the fur trade of the Missouri. Both were to become, in 1817, Astor's partners and agents in the reorganized American Fur Company, and were to continue in this relationship till his retirement in 1834. John P. Cabanné, a leading St. Louis fur trader, was later a member of the American Fur Company's Western Department.

New york 26 May 1816 [1]

Dear Sir

I wrot to you Some Days ago & now Improve the oppertunity by Mr Robert Stuart with whom I belive you are allready acquainted and who I Recomend to your friendly care

[1] Ms. (photostat), Missouri Historical Society, St. Louis, Bernard P. Bogy Collection.

& attention Mr Stuart & Mr Crooks engagd me Last Year to Import Some goods for tham for the purpose of trading with Indians & & in your quater of the Cauntry Mr Cabbanne wrot to me Some time after that if I would not Suply anny others with goods to trade in the part of this Cauntry Where he Dos he would preferr it & would take a muish Larger quantity of goods than what he had orderd — I have Reflected a good Deal on the proposal & I can not but think it best for Mr. Cabbanee to have these goods as therby prevent anny Interferencs in the trade I have therefor advised Mr Stuart to go on With the goods & to make Some arrangement with Mr Cabbanne it is natural to Supose that Mr Crooks & Stuart must have Some Compensation for time Lost & perhaps giving up the object of which they might make Some money and under this cansideration I have Encouragd Mr Stuart to belive that Mr C. will give him a Liberal Profit you being the frind of Mr C. and well compatend to judge of the advantages now offerd to him I begg you to aid in the accomplishment of this object I have no Doubt but Mr S. will be reasonable the Goods are of best quality — I have tought a good Deal on the proposition made me Some time Since by your frinds to make Some genral arrangement for the Indian Trade & if our Government Do exclude Canada traders from aur Cauntry as I belive thy will the trade will becom an object & I would Licke to cam to the arrangement of which I will thank you to Inform tham

I am Dear sir
Most Resptfully your
Hul Servet
John · Jacob · Astor

[Addressed]   Charls Gratiote Eqr, St Louis

99. LETTER FROM ASTOR TO JAMES MONROE, MAY 27, 1816, REQUESTING FUR-TRADE LICENSES FOR CANADIAN EMPLOYEES.

The act referred to was passed April 29, 1816; the "provisional Agreement," which had been reached in the fall of 1815, was for the continuance of the South West Fur Company.

New York May 27. 1816 [1]

Sir,

I am informed that Congress have at about the close of the Session passed an Act for the regulation of the trade with the Indians within the territory of the United States, and that by this act none but Citizens of the United States are permitted to come among our Indians unless by special permission of the President

I am glad that this Law has passed, it ought to have been so some years ago, and in that case the trade would have been in proper hands ere this. It is however to be feared that unless some few Canadian traders are permitted to go in this year we will not find a sufficient number of Men acquainted with the trade to supply the Indians and especially those who reside far in the interior. I made last year a provisional Agreement with the People in Canada to carry on a trade for joint Account with them unless Congress passed some act and regulation which should render such connection incompatible, and this act I understand will render it Completely so and of course the agreement becomes void. The result will be that the trade will now fall more to my lot and I propose to prosecute it extensively. There is however a difficulty for the moment in getting proper and trusty men who are acquainted with the trade and we want from 6 to 9 more good traders. I wish therefore that the President would please to give six to nine Licenses, they might be sent in blank & filled at Michilimackinac to such persons as

---

[1] Ms., New York Public Library, Monroe Papers.

the Collector or Commanding officer shall judge best — The
Goods which I have sent to that place last fall and this spring
amount to at least $150M, and unless we can get some of the
Canadian traders we shall not find the means to dispose of
them, and there will be great distress among the Indians next
year we shall have no need for foreigners.— I have written to
Mr. Crawford on this subject. As the measure is very urgent
on account of the season, I am from necessity induced to write
to you and to beg you would have the goodness to speak to the
President. [Only below this in Astor's hand.]

The Honbl   I have the Hannour
James Monroe   To be most Respctfully
Secretarry of State   Sir your most obdt Sert
    &c &c &c   John · Jacob · Astor

100. BILL OF SALE OF THE SHIP *Albatross* BY NATHAN WIN-
SHIP TO ASTOR AND JOHN EBBETS, SEPTEMBER 21, 1816, AND
BY EBBETS TO TAMAAHMAAH, OCTOBER 16, 1816.

The *Albatross* had previously been one of the most conspicuous
of the vessels engaged in the maritime fur trade of the North West
Coast and in the sandalwood trade of the Hawaiian Islands. She
had entered the Columbia River in 1810, where her captain had
unsuccessfully endeavored to establish a trading post. It was on this
vessel that Wilson Price Hunt had come from the Hawaiian Islands
to Astoria in 1813. Since sandalwood was at this time worth about
$10 per picul in Canton, it is evident that the sale to Tamaahmaah
resulted in a substantial profit. It may be that the sale was not
made by Winship directly because of a controversy he had had with
the king over a sandalwood contract. John Ebbets, it will be remembered, had been the captain of Astor's first North West Coast
vessel. Some of those signing these documents as witnesses are
worthy of comment. Richard Ebbets, probably John Ebbets'
brother, had been clerk and later captain of Astor's brig *Forester*.
Francisco de Paula Marin, usually known as Manini, was a Spaniard, of great influence in the kingdom, and acted as Tamaahmaah's

secretary. William Bush seems to have been a protégé of Astor; he had been wrecked in the *Lark* in 1813 and apparently found the atmosphere of the Islands so congenial that he did not take advantage of the opportunities offered him to return home. He died at Honolulu in September, 1818, after a ten months' illness. Henry Gyzelaar was a well-known Pacific trader. I am unable to identify the other witnesses.

(Copy)

KNOW [1] ALL MEN BY THESE PRESENTS that I Nathan Winship for and in consideration of the sum of Two thousand dollars in Specie to me in hand paid by John Jacob Astor and John Ebbets the receipt whereof I hereby acknowledge, have and by these presents do grant, bargain, sell, transfer, and set over unto the said John Jacob Astor and John Ebbets, the Ship called the Albatross now at anchor in the harbour of Honarooru, Island of Woahoo, Sandwich Islands, together with all her masts, yards, sails, rigging, anchors, cables, boats, tackle and appurtenances. Which said vessel is registered in the Port of Boston and Charleston in the words following, to Wit.

Permanent

No. 153 One hundred fifty three

In pursuance of an Act of the Congress of the United States of America entitled "An Act concerning the registering and recording of Ships or Vessels" Abiel Winship of Boston in the State of Massachusetts having taken or subscribed the oath required by the said act and having sworn that he with Benjamin P Homer of Boston aforesaid, — Jonathan Winship Jun. & Nathan Winship of Brighton State aforesaid only owners of the Ship or Vessel called the Albatross of Boston whereof Nathan Winship is at present Master and is a Citizen of the United States

---

[1] Ms., Archives of Hawaii, Honolulu, F. O. & Ex.

as he hath sworn and that the said Ship or Vessel was built at Weymouth State aforesaid in the year 1803 as appears by Register No. 290 issued at this Office November 26th. 1806 now cancelled property transferred: Said Vessel altered from a Brig to a Ship. And Thomas Melville, surveyor for this District having certified that the said Ship or Vessel has two decks and two Masts and that her length is seventy seven feet eight inches, her breadth Twenty two feet one inch, her depth Eleven feet one half inch and that she measures One hundred and sixty five tons & $\frac{31}{95}$ that she is a square sterned Ship has no Galleries and no figure head. And the said Abiel Winship having agreed to the description and admeasurement above specified and sufficient security having been given according to the said Act the said Ship has been duly registered at the Port of Boston & Charlestown.— Given under our hands and Seal at the Port of Boston and Charlestown this twenty fifth day of May in the year One thousand eight hundred and nine.— [In margin: Joseph Nouye Register (L.S) H. Dearborn Collector James Lovell Nav^l. Off^r.]

To have and to hold the said Ship Albatross unto the said John Jacob Astor and John Ebbets their Executors, and assigns forever. And I the said Nathan Winship for my heirs, executors and administrators do hereby covenant and agree to and with the said John Jacob Astor and John Ebbets their executors, assigns and administrators that at the execution of these presents, that Abiel Winship, Benjn. P. Homer, Jonathan Winship Jun. and myself named in the above Register were the true and lawful owners of the said Ship Albatross and appurtenances, and that I have power and authority to sell and dispose of the same, free from and cleared of all demands, claims and incumbrances whatsoever. —

In Witness whereof I the said Nathan Winship have hereunto set my hand and seal at the Island of Woahoo this twenty
first day of September in the Year of our Lord One thousand
eight hundred and sixteen.

Signed, sealed and delivered
in presence of us. —
R^d. Ebbets
Fran^{co}. de Paula Marin   (Signed) Nathan Winship (L.S)
Wm. Bush Jr.
Daniel W Frost
Henry Gyzelaar

KNOW ALL MEN BY THESE PRESENTS that I John Ebbets
for and in consideration of Four hundred Piculs Sandal Wood
to me in hand paid by His Owhyhean Majesty Tamaahmaah,
the receipt of which I hereby acknowledge, have and by these
presents do grant bargain, sell, assign transfer and set over
unto the said Tamaahmaah the Ship called the Albatross, now
at anchor in the harbour of Hanarooru Island of Woahoo together with all her masts, yards, sails, riggings, anchors, cables,
boats, tackle, apparel and appurtenances. —

Which said vessel is registered in the Port of Boston and
Charlestown as per the annexed bill of Sale. —

To have and to hold the said Ship Albatross, unto the said
Tamaahmaah, his executors and assigns forever, and I the
said John Ebbets for my heirs, executors and administrators
do hereby covenant and agree to and with the said Tamaahmaah, his executors, assigns and administrators, that at the
execution of these presents I am the true and lawful owner of
the said Ship Albatross and appurtenances as per annexed bill
of Sale and that I have power and authority in virtue of the
same to dispose of said Ship and appurtenances, free from and
cleared of all claims, incumbrances or demands whatsoever.

In Witness whereof I the said John Ebbets have hereunto set my hand & seal at the Island of Woahoo this Sixteenth day of October in the year of our Lord One thousand eight hundred & Sixteen. —

Sign'd in presence of
Fran^{co}. de Paula Marin
George Beckley   John Ebbets
Wm. Bush Jr.

We the undersigned certify that the preceeding bill of Sale subscribed by Nathan Winship is a true copy of the original by us duly compared and that the latter is a transfer of the Ship Albatross and appurtenances executed by John Ebbets in favour of his Owhyhean Majesty Tamaahmaah therein mentioned. —

In testimony whereof we have hereunto set our hands at the Island of Woahoo this Sixteenth day of October in the year of our Lord one thousand eight hundred & Sixteen

> Fran^{co}. de Paula Marin
> George Beckley
> Wm. Bush Jr.

101. INVOICE OF THE CARGO OF THE SHIP *Beaver*, JUNE 30, 1817, INTENDED FOR SOUTH AMERICA.

The character of the commodities included in this cargo makes it quite clear that the vessel's captain did not intend to trade on the North West Coast or in the Hawaiian Islands or at Canton, as he claimed after his capture by the Spaniards.

J. J. Astor, Invoice [1]

26 cases Men's hats	2103.50	
3 " Boys "	211.50	
7 " Fline [?] "	1400.00	
2 " — "	400.00	4,115.
4 Bales Cloths	3541.63	
1 Bale "	778.25	
1 Bale "	693.08	
3 " "	67.28	5,880.24
1 " Cassimeres		2,662.66
21 Cases German Linens	4,284.33	
5 " " "	2,459.—	
6 " " "	3,400 —	
1 " " " ⎫		
8 " " " ⎬	4,350.85	
2 " " " ⎭		
3 " " "	710.	20,204.16
12 " Irish " ⎫		7,545.04
2 " " " ⎭		
1 " Long Lawns		406.16
3 " French goods – Silks etc.	1955.39	
3 " " " " "	4359.67	6,315.06
12 Bales India goods		
7 " " "		
2 " " "		
2 " " "	5564.13	
.	270.—	
3 " " " ⎫		
13 " " " ⎪		
2 " " " ⎬		
1 " " " ⎪		
7 " " " ⎭	5615.52	
3 " " "	1990.62	
2 " " " ⎫		
1 " " " ⎭	566.66	14,006.93

[1] Ms., Department of State, Washington, D. C., Claims on Spain, Convention, 1819, vol. xiii, Schr. Beaver, Ship Beaver, Schr. Boston, Schr. Baltimore, Invoice of the Beaver.

2 casks German Tapes		930.26
2 cases Pins		340.50
24 dozen Fancy Chairs & 2 Settees		1,085.—
7 cases French Furniture	540 —	
2 cases Mahogany "	240 —	780 —
		64,271.01

1721 Bars ⎫		
1999 " ⎬ Iron. Tons 55.16.1.7		3,100.29
649 Bolts ⎭		
42 Boxes of Tin Plates		546.—
7 Pipes Flayal [?] Wine		621.02
10 Hhds Tobacco		1,033.85
40 Boxes Pint & Half Pint Tumblers		1,311.—
2 Bales ⎫		
5 Bales ⎬ Blue Nankeens	1407.—	
32 Bundles ⎭		
5 Bales Long Yellow Nankeens (Mammee)	900 —	
28 B'nd'les " " " (Companys)	896 —	
9 Bales " White "	1088 —	
15 Bales ⎫		
25 B'nd'les ⎬ Short Yellow "	1720 —	6011 —
2 Cases Black Silk Handkfs		500
10 Boxes Table China	500 —	
10 Boxes China Cups & Saucers	400 —	
5 Boxes China Plates	166.67	1066.67
1 Case Fans		205 —
70 Cases Cassia		2632.14
35 Crates ⎫		
1 Hhd ⎬ Earthenware		1347.11
5 Tierces ⎬		
4 Crates ⎭		
22 Casks ⎫		
6 Boxes ⎬ Hardware		7393.55
12 B'nd'les ⎭		
39 cases British Cotton Goods	13,751.60	
29 " " " "	11,234.44	24986.04
2 " Cotton Hose	427.77	
2 " " "	517.96	
1 Trunk ⎫ " "		
1 Box ⎬ " "	772.78	
One Trunk	4.00	1722.51

2 Cases Sewing Cotton	490.90
2 " Madras Handkfs	350.00
2 Cases {Lace Shawls, veils, Thread Lace, Needles}	
Gloves, Umbrellas, Linen Combs, Lace Hhfs etc	1229.00
2 Cases Table Linen, Towells, Napkins	5063.25
5 Chests ea contg 25 Muskets & Bayonets – 125 @ $7 ea.	875.—
132 Boxes German Steel average wt. 200 lbs. ea.	

26400
Tare of boxes 1056   25344 lbs wt @ 12c   3041.28

---

1 Chest Cloths, Cassimeres, Cotton goods & Sundries	967.62	
off 10 pc. discount on $883.92	88.39	879.23
		128675.85

1 Can containing

29 Baize Shirts @ 11/.	$33.			
18 Monkey Jackets 26.	58.50	91.50		
12 Woolen Caps 2/6	3.75			
18 Pair Trowsers 16/.	36.—	39.75		
36 Yarn Stockings 5/.	22.50			
Box Cartage	1.56	24.06	155.31	
24 Pair Coarse Shoes 8/6			25.50	
Salve etc }				
1 Case Pocket Books, Snuff Boxes }			513.24	
1 do Paint boxes & Lead Pencils			117.90	
2 do Glass Lamps, Goblets & Decanters			155.72	
1 do Glass Animals, Coffee Dishes Shells etc }			74.75	
5 do Glass Tumblers			383.60	
5 do Ribbons (China Satin)			3552. a	
2 do Glass Lusters etc			97. a	
30 Barrels Tar @ $2 pr. bbl. Boat hire $1.80			61.80	
70 di }				
8 dbl di } Powder wg. 8.600 lbs @ $20.			1720. a	

Dollars $135532.67

Errors Excepted
New York 30th June
1817

102. LETTER FROM ASTOR TO J. B. PREVOST, CAPTAIN BID-
DLE, OR JEREMY ROBINSON, NOVEMBER 11, 1817, GIVING AN
ACCOUNT OF THE LOSS OF ASTORIA.

The gentlemen to whom this letter was addressed had gone out
to the Columbia River in the sloop *Ontario* to reclaim, according to
the terms of the Treaty of Ghent, Astor's establishment, which had
been taken possession of during the war by the British sloop *Raccoon*. The notes following Astor's signature were evidently added
by one of those to whom the letter was addressed. "Paul Denaut
Jereny [Jeremie]," from whom most of this information and mis-
information was evidently derived, had gone out to Astoria on the
Tonquin and, according to Franchere, had — instead of being
taken "a prisoner to Eng^d." — voluntarily shipped himself on the
Raccoon as an underclerk. His statements that "300 men started
from St Louis and went across" and that there were at the Columbia
River "abt million Chenooks, Clatsops," indicate the care with
which his information should be tested before being accepted.

New York 11th Novr. 1817 [1]

Dear Sir

I will be most happy if this meets you well & as I hope in
perfect health — I repeat my request your sudden departure,
The Presidents did expect it, for 4 or 5 days after you sailed I
received a Letter referring me to I wrote that you sailed 24
hours after receipt of your Instructions — The American
Establishment was made only in 171 [*sic*] as before stated and
it was taken possesion of by the British in 1714 [*sic*] it was first
obtained by the Northwest Company in consequence of the
absence of my agents Mr Hunt they prevailed on the sub agent
[interlineated: to sell our property &] to leave the place contrary to all my expectations or Instructions — Soon after this
shameful transaction took place the British Sloop Racoon of
War Captn Black arr^d. and took possession in the name of his
B M — it is at present in the possession of the N West and

---

[1] Ms., Library of Congress, Miscellaneous Personal Collections.

under the Charge of Mr Daniel [sic] McKensie who was first employed by me and is one of those who aided in the Intrigue by which I lost the post it may be well to aprize you of his Character he is a dis cgainy [?] Man and no confidence to be placed in him you must be on your guard against him there are few few [sic] his Coleagues who [wish — stricken through] make matter of conscence to encourage the Indians to murder — and I w^d not trust one of them — it is stated that a British ship of war has been lately sent to that part of the World — give my respects to your worthy Captn. & do request him to be carefull on going & coming out of the River, he must not Confide in any information which the people there may give him — you know that one of our Country men did attempt to settle there in about 181[o — stricken through]7 [sic] or 1808 but not thinking it safe on Account of the Indians he Came away — news I have none to give to yo Mr Tompkins wishes to be Collector of this Port, gen^l. Surveyor Whether eather of them will succeed I do not know — M Monroes friends are ferm and increase a/c from England state that [afficers — stricken through] many officers are going to South America & it is reported here that our Govt. are in treaty with Spain fo the Floridas how that is I do not know, I must pray you to be so good & deliver the inclosed if you meet the Beaver Believe me Dr Sir most respectfully yours

(s^d)   John Jacob Astor

J B Prevost Esqr &c &c or Captain Biddle or J Robinson Esqr.

[None of the above in Astor's hand; the following added in pencil.] Ports on the west coast nearest the Columbia where supplies can be had viz San Frances Drake 600— Sant-Monterey–about 120 miles from S. F. Drake — San Pedro about 180 miles from Monterey – St John – San Blas on the south side of the gulf of Calafornia Lat 25 North.— from the Columbia 600 leagues to the [Mississippi River — stricken through] fork or confluency of the Missouri River from there to nochilvehes 300 leagues

2000 Sea Otter Skins – at 16 doll[s] worth 60 doll in Canton

80000 Beaver Skins " 4 [pr — stricken through] each
worth in Canton 40 dolls pr lb.

These were sold in the absence of Hunt were sold by McDougle to John Mc'Tavish — as the ostensible person. M[c]Dougll rec'd one eighth of the am[t]. viz 6000 —

McDouglle remitted to Mr J. J. Astor — 42000 dollars

The establishment was sold for — *48000 dollars*

The skins and establishment at that was worth at least *100000 dollars*. Two lots containing about 9 acres were then cleared — a sloop of 52 tons — 14 canoes timber for an other sloop vessell of 42 tons with two suits of sails cables anchors &c. The furs by Mc'Dougles fears and bad management all the furs in the interior fell into the hands of the enemy. Also a quantity of goods were sold and 300 stand of muskets. cutlasses pistols and about 50 barrels of powder. 2 long six pounder field pices. 8 iron 2 pounder swivels– 6 four pounder field pieces of brass 30 blunderbuses. twenty goats 50 hogs 6 horses implements of husbandry shovels hoes plows iron rakes – bars – locks – and 900 steel edged axes— This sale was clandestine without witness or attestation Mr Hunt was then at the Sandwich Islands: 7 clerks: who drew one fith [sic] afterfive years service. This transfer or sale was made in November 1814. The clerks served four years without emolument. This statement is made by Paul Denaut Jereny at Lima November 8th 1818. The Raccoon Captain Black to this person Jereny a prisoner to Eng[d]. as he was the only one and because he resisted. In Plymouth Eng[d]. he was summoned to give evidence before Admiral Duckworth. At the Columbia he says there is no snow in winter but that it rains the whole time. The establishment is situated on the south side of the River 18 miles from Cape disappointment. The current is rapid when the tide is on ebb 7 knots or when running down. 3 at other times There is a small island or shoal between Cape disappontment & point adams, visible at low water. The bar is very bad. 3 fathoms or $3\frac{1}{2}$ at low water. breaks very high The Channel at the bar is generally narrow and shifting. The climate is fine dry and hot in summer. The soil is good. corn pototas borley gorden vegitabls. wheat &c – The timber is of Pine chesnut Hemlock chery trees. Above the settlement in the interior is ash ceder oak wallnut — Clover and a species of high wild berry is in abundance. There are generally about 300 white people belong to the establishment — 20 remain at the Fort. the others are employed in hunting dressing skins and protecting the furs— also in making boats houses &c.— a trade is carried on with the neighboring Indians — probably 10000 in number: In four years but one vessel went there Viz^t the Beaver which left about 3000 dollars worth of goods.

The face of the country near the settlement is very hilly— and well watered with creeks and springs suitable for mills— The interior is more level. Mr Hunt agent for M^r A thought he discovered a lead mine. country sandy dry but [three words illegible] water no wood cow dung used for fuel or grass

300 men started from St Louis and went across — these were from Vermont N. Hamp and Macinac — clerks employ chiefly

Articles of trade — blankets, coarse blue cloth arms of inferior quality knives scissors white gurrahs molasses calico beads powder tobacco. Manufactured ornaments of iron and brass for bracelets. rings buttons abt million Chenooks, Clatsop.— Comcomly is the chief of both. a shrude one eyed old man and a great warrior. these are the nearest natives. he posesses arms and has a warlike son.–

[Marginal note in pencil: for the benefit of the North west company [?]]

103. LETTER FROM ASTOR TO W. W. MATTHEWS, DECEMBER 20, 1817, WITH INSTRUCTIONS FOR HIS CONDUCT OF THE AMERICAN FUR COMPANY'S BUSINESS AT MONTREAL.

William W. Matthews, of New York, was one of the clerks who went out on the *Tonquin*. After his return he, like several of his associates, was employed by the American Fur Company and acted as Montreal agent for several years.

New York 20 Dec. 1817.[1]

Dear Sir:–

I have to pay to the Agents of the North West Company, Messrs. McTavish McGillvery & Co. on the 1/4 [?] of January nst $16929 27/100 which you will pay to them for this purpose.

I give you sundry bills on London as on the other side which please to sell as soon as you can obtain a fair offer in case after your arrival there.

As I wish by all means to pay them the money on the day, say first of January, and not later than the 3 of that month.

I understand that exchange on London is at 4 per cent above par, and I hope you will obtain at least 3 to 3-1/2 for those which I send by you. When the bills are sold, I presume you will have from 1000 to 1300$ over for which I would like you to buy me some red fox skins for those that are large and good Canada, I would have you give as high as 2$ [?].

You will however know that the skins of lower Canada are better than those of upper Canada, and those below Montreal, and at about Quebec, better than those above, perhaps it will be well to buy some as also some Fishers skins at about 1/4 to ½$ per skin for good.

I would also recommend you to contract for all the Fox you can, both in and out of Canada. I would not give more

---

[1] Ms. book (copy), Detroit Public Library, Burton Historical Collection, and Missouri Historical Society, St. Louis, Letters of Ramsay Crooks, John Jacob Astor, and the American Fur Company, 1813–43.

than 14/ to be delivered here by the 1 of May, and you may take a turn to upper Canada for the purpose of buying Fox and Fishers skins, also some good otter at 5$[?] per skin or 5–1/4$[?]

You will engage with some person who can be relied on for 6000 Ear *boobs* Round for the Indian Trade, these I want to have as early as possible, you will have a pretty large order as soon as Mr Crooks arrives here for Silver works – I will write to you by mail, and I presume you will stay at least in the 1 instant 8 days in Montreal, when you will recieve my further instructions in the sale of the bills you will be careful to get the money so as to comply with my engagement, and you will write to me and let me know the rate of exchange. I will thank you to look after our canoes etc. at Montreal.

I am Respectfully yours,

John Jacob Astor.

Enclosed – Huntington on Lester Taylor & Co.

Commy Genlrs. Bill on Treasury		£340
My draft on McTavish Fraser Co.		700
Do	Do	600
I Ogden on Bolton and Ogden		700
Do	Do	600
Do	Do	500
Do	Do	400

£3840
Sterling

Mr. W. W. Mathews

[Endorsed] J. J. Astor 20th Dec. 1817 Instructions answered to myself in N. York.

104. LETTER FROM ASTOR TO PETER SMITH, MARCH 16, 1819, WITH REFLECTIONS ON THE WAY TO ENDURE MISFORTUNES.

Astor's low spirits were the result of the death by drowning, in the previous year at Washington, of his seven-year-old grandson, John Jacob Bentzon, who had accompanied him to that city, and who was the son of his eldest daughter, Magdalen, and of A. B. Bentzon, who had returned to Santa Cruz, and from whom in the year of this letter she secured a divorce in New York on the grounds of adultery and desertion. The latter part of the letter refers to lands owned by Astor in various parts of New York State.

New york 16th [interlineated: March] 1819 [1]

My Dear Sir

It is Lang Since I had the pleasure of Receiving a Letter from you — the Last you wrote to me I was Sorry to See you ware in bade or Low Spirits, this indeed has been my case for these 13 Months past and tho' I can not Recover mine I would willingly Recameed my friends to endevour to Recover theirs the best is to travel about & to attend to bussiess — to keep body and mind engaged & not reflect too much on our Afflections which we all must have at Some Period or other these will came & when they Do we must Suport aurselfs as well as we can — I hope you are mush better than you ware Some time ago. where is your Son Peter I hope he will Soon get through his mis fortunes he was I think Cruelly treated & Decived–

How cames an aur Lands in Charlote & Buyns — I hope your attention is Still to tham— I belive by a Late Law— I aught to have my Deed for the Lot in Virgil Recorded in the town I enclose it to you for that purpose will thank you to have it Done – you ware So good as to promise me Some Information Relative to the value & Situation of this Late when your time will permit be so good as to write to me & tell me

---

[1] Ms., Syracuse University, Gerrit Smith Miller Collection.

what I best Do about it   Let me know how you are &c &c &c
Da¹. Henry has made no progress in the Sale of my lands & I
feare I must Change agent

I am most truly
Dear Sir your friend &c

Peter Smith Eqʳ   John·Jacob·Astor
[Sealed with black wax.]
[Addressed]   Mr. Peter Smith, Peterboro', Madison County,
N Y
[Postmarked]   New-York, Mar 17   Postpaid, Paid 55 [cents
postage]

105. LETTER FROM ASTOR TO PETER SMITH, APRIL 13, 1819,
WITH ADVICE ON FAMILY LIFE.

Smith's "other Son g." — Gerrit — later distinguished himself
as an abolitionist and as a leader in other radical reform movements.

New york 13 Apil 1819 ¹

Dear Sir
   I have Rid your letter of 25 & 26 [Ist — stricken through]
ulto with Chick for ane thousand Dollars 1/2 of which I pay to
Mʳ. Laight & the other half gos to your Cridet on account of
our Land concern — I thank you for your attention to my Lot
in Virgil & will be glad to have particulars of the Same & &c
   I regret very mush yaur Distresd Situation yet I Can not
but think that it is greatly in your awen power to elivat it &
to mak yaurself & those of your famely more happy you had
the misfortune to Loose an affectiond wife but you have yet
Several fine Children who would be glad to mak you happey
Whey Do you nat think properly for yourself & for tham your
happeyness I Should think must more or Less Depend on
theres and theres an yaurs why Do you nat endevuer to make

¹ Ms., Syracuse University, Gerrit Smith Miller Collection.

thire Situation more Comfordable you have the means & thy are in need Relive your Son Peter make your other Son g. who is a very fine man Independend & recancile yourSelf to your unfortunate Daughter remember my Dear frind haw Soon you may have to Leave this world & remember that Lick all men you will Seeke for forgiveness for give your Children as you wish aur fathr in heven to forgive you Let tham Come to you & Suport tham & thy will Suport you thire thankes for all your wealth will Do you no good in your Grave Devid Some of it with tham See tham happy & Comfordable & you will bee So your Self Donte tell me that it is easey to give advise — I Say to you that I Do Devid with my Children Lick you I workd for tham & I wish tham to have all the Good of it the more they enjoy it the more happy am I — forgive me for writing to you So freely I Do it as your frind & I Know I am right in the Priniple it is your Comford as well as that of your famely that Intrests me take my advise & you will never bee Sorry for it belive me to be allways

Your faithfull frind

Peter Smith Eq^r   John · Jacob · Astor

[Addressed]   Peter Smith Esq^u, Peterboro, Madison County, state of Newyork

[Postmarked]   New-York, 13 Apr   p[aid]

106. LETTER FROM ASTOR TO PETER SMITH, MAY 13, 1819, GIVING THE SUM OF HIS PHILOSOPHY.

New York 13 May 1819 [1]

My DearSir

I have your Letter of the 28 ulto & thank you for the trouble you had in the getting my Lot in Virgil Survayd — I find it to bemore valuble than I calculated — if you ware Disposd to

---

[1] Ms., Syracuse University, Gerrit Smith Miller Collection.

buy it I would take 2000$ for it payeble with Interest, to bepaid the Precipble [principal] at 5 or 10 years if you do not wish to buy perhaps you can find a purchaser for me — what you remark on Matters of more Importancs is very Right to get our mind reconscild to that which will truly premate our Real happyness here or hereafter is one great requisite but it is Chiefly in our owen power & wants nothing but our owen Consent & Som Resolution on our part my Dear frind you have So mush property it gives you too mush trouble why not make yourself Easy — [who — stricken through interlineated: how] many things must not you & me Leave undone & what of it have we not Done anough allready for others now let us act for our Selves. Let us prepare for a better world & endeaver to be Tranquil & Happy here this is what I am Daily endevoring to Do & I trust you are not Doing less — with great good Wishes I am DearSir

yours

The Honble Peter Smith   John · Jacob · Astor

[Addressed] Peter Smith Esqr, Peterboro (Madison County, New York)
[Postmarked] New York, May 13   18 1/2 [cents postage]
[Endorsed] J. J. Astor Esq., Lot 40 Virgil

107. MEMORANDUM FROM ASTOR TO WILLIAM B. ASTOR, 1819, WITH INSTRUCTIONS FOR THE CONDUCT OF THE AMERICAN FUR COMPANY AND THE CHINA TRADE DURING ASTOR'S ABSENCE IN EUROPE.

William Roberts was one of Astor's most trusted clerks and had evidently been acting as one of the Company's dummy directors. The details of "the Agreement with Stone [Bostwick] & Co," the Company's most dangerous rival, are not known; in 1820 this firm was forced to agree to abandon the Michilimackinac trade for five years. "M^r. Dausman" was probably Hercules Dousman, who managed the Company store at Prairie du Chien; Michael Dousman was a prominent figure in the Wisconsin fur trade. "M^r. Mathewes" was, of course, W. W. Matthews. "Young M^r. fawler of Albany" was probably the son of William Fowler, with whom Astor had been trading in furs as early as 1802. The whole document gives considerable insight into Astor's detailed knowledge of his two closely related commercial interests, the fur trade and the commerce with Canton.

My Dear William [1]

I would recomend you acatinally to Looke aver the notes which will here follow as I propose to note Some points which may otherwise be for gotten —

J J A

I have Some considerable anexiaty about the Buisniss of the American furr Compay haveng Considerable Intrest there in and as I think nat a persan who is capopable to Derrit or manage the whole So as to prevent a Loss or to make the most of it— the Charter or Requirs that there be 3 Dercitors to be Citzons of the u.s. at the next Ellection We must have an other Dercitor & M^r. Roberts must be left aut

attention must be paid that the Elliction is anually held according to the Charter— the next will be to Retrensh the buisness as mush as posible and to bring it with in the amaunt Stipulated by the Agreement with Stone & Co Say 300m$ & never to exced it— M^r. Crooks I thinke aught to Reside in this City — greate Care to be taking in given Instructians to the agents — all orders for Goods from Europe are to be Send to me & an estimate of the Proveble cast of tham with the order— So all goods Shipd are to go consignd to me—

Stone & Co are to pay 7 pct Int for the money advanesd to the Company an thire proportion an which thy are to a Low 2 1/2 pC cammision for the advanes & to pay up on the 15 Nav^r. next thy [are — stricken through] Stone Bostwicke

[1] Ms. book, Office of the Astor Estate, N. Y., Untitled memorandum book.

& Co are not to Revce their Stacke till it is paid for by tham—
M^r. Dausman is to have 20 of my shares an paying for tham
with the Intrest on the amount for which the stacke has ben
paid up— or an such part as has ben paid— as pr his agreement — M^r. Mathewes is to be Intrested to amaunt of ten
shares— but he can not Recie the Stacke unless he pays for
it —

I would recomend you to Looke actinally at the agreement
with Stone & Co

What otter & Red fox Skins the American furr Company may
have aught to bee shipd to Canton as also Some of the Lake
Superior Beaver — Such as Does not vigh [weigh] ave [over?]
ane pound pr skin

the Commen Beaver Racown & Musrat Skins to be sold at
publick Sale by the 1 of ac^r. next than will be a good tim to
Sell the Russia Hare Skins I sold by can tract 1000 Boffolo
Ropes to young M^r. fawler of Albany at 4$ to be Delivrd to
him. . . .

Capt. Ebbetts

accaunt with him for the first voyage of Enterprize *is Settld*
that of the Secand I am willng to have Settld agreable to the
agreement which is in the Letter Book Say in Letter of Instruction and I am unwillng to Settle otherwise— it is to be
observed that no fright is Chargd an the goods – if any of the
Disbursments are to be Deducted than I Supose frght ought
to be alowd

Ship Enterprize

I thinke proveble we may Recie Some more Quicksilver from
Cadiz if 100 m pounds is rcid unless it can be sold here to agood
profit I would Send her with it to Canton & take the Skins of
American furr Compay Say the atters to bee recid this Years
Return and Send Some 20 or 30m$ with tham to by A Cargo
of tea Cassia & Same Say 20 or 30,000 Short Nankeens to go to
Europe take Some Sugor.   500 Casses Cassia

10,000 Bundels   Do
200 Chets Gunpowder
200 Imperial
600 Singlo tea
600 Skin
600 young Hyson
800 Hyson
go to Europe Derict
Stop at Cowes for orders [?]

108. POLICY OF INSURANCE FROM THE BOSTON MARINE INSUR-
ANCE COMPANY TO JOHN JACOB ASTOR & SON, DECEMBER 1,
1820, ON THE SHIP *Henry Astor* FOR A VOYAGE TO CANTON.

This is a typical insurance policy for a China voyage carried out
under normal conditions in the period after the War of 1812.

N°. (6259) —

BY THE BOSTON MARINE INSURANCE COMPANY.[1]

This Policy of Assurance witnesseth, [in margin: Sum insured $25000+] That the President and Directors of the BOS-
TON MARINE INSURANCE COMPANY do by these PRESENTS
cause (John Jacob Astor & Son) to be assured, lost or not lost,
(twenty five thousand dollars on Ship Henry Astor & Cargo at
& from Newyork to Canton & at & from thence to her port of
discharge in Europe or the United States with liberty to stop
at Gibraltar for orders or to discharge in whole or in part — &
at the usual places for refreshments. If the Ship returns direct
to the United States, from Canton, the risk is to terminate
there. one eighth on Vessel. seven eights on Cargo.) whereof
is Master for this present voyage, — (Clark) — or whosoever
else shall be Master in the said vessel, or by whatsoever other
name or names the said vessel, or Master thereof, [in margin:

[1] Ms. book, Massachusetts Historical Society, Boston, Boston Marine Insurance Company Records, vol. Aa, no. 6259, December 1, 1820.

Vessel valued at $(28500) — Premium (included)]] is or shall
be named or called: Beginning the adventure upon the said
(Vessel & Cargo) as aforesaid, and to continue and endure
during the voyage, on the Vessel, until she shall be arrived and
moored at anchor twenty-four hours in safety, and on the
Cargo until landed. And it shall and may be lawful for the
said vessel in her voyage, to proceed and sail to, touch and
stay at, any ports or places, if thereunto obliged by stress of
weather, or other unavoidable accidents, without prejudice to
this Assurance.

Touching the adventures and perils which the said INSUR-
ANCE COMPANY are contented to bear, and take upon them in
this voyage, they are, of the (Seas, Men of War, Fire, Enemies,
Pirates, Rovers, assailing Thieves, Jettisons, Letters of Mart
and Counter Mart, Surprisals, Takings at Sea, Arrests, Re-
straints and Detainments of all Kings, Princes, or People, of
what nation, condition, or quality soever, Barratry of the Master) unless the assured be owner of the vessel (or Mariners),
and all other perils, losses, and misfortunes, which have, or
shall come to the hurt, detriment, or damage of the said (Vessel
& Cargo) or any part thereof. And in case of any loss or misfortune, it shall be lawful, to and for the assured, (their) factors, servants, and assigns, to sue, labour, and travel for, in
and about the defence, safeguard, and recovery of the said
(Vessel & Cargo) [in margin: Premium $(1000 NB. Four
Cases of merchandize, being part of the property to which this
policy, with others of the same date, relates, having been left
out of the Henry Astor, & afterwards shipped on board Ship
Huntress; it is agreed that they [interlineated: are] insured
outward to Canton in the same manner as if on board the Henry
Astor. May 28, 1821.—) or any part thereof, without prejudice to this Assurance, to the charges whereof, the said INSUR-
ANCE COMPANY will contribute, in proportion as the sum
assured is to the whole sum at risque. And so the PRESIDENT

and DIRECTORS aforesaid, are contented, and do hereby bind
the capital stock and other common property of the said IN-
SURANCE COMPANY to the assured, (their) executors, administrators, and assigns, for the true performance of the premises,
confessing themselves paid the consideration due unto them for
this Assurance, by the assured, at and after the rate of (Four
per cent — should she stop at Gibraltar & proceed thence to
the United States) [& — stricken through interlineated: (an)]
(addition of half a per cent is to be paid. And if she proceed for
any port in Europe north of Havre, & do not arrive safe before
the 1st. November 1821 or after the 1st. March 1822 an additional premium of one per cent is to be paid.)

And it is hereby agreed, that if the assured shall have made
any other assurance upon the (Vessel & Cargo) aforesaid, prior
in date to this Policy, then the said INSURANCE COMPANY shall
be answerable only, for so much as the amount of such prior
assurance may be deficient towards fully covering the property
at risque; and the said INSURANCE COMPANY shall return the
premium excepting half per cent. upon so much of the sum by
them assured, as they shall be exonerated from by such prior
assurance. And in case of any assurance upon the said (Vessel
& Cargo) subsequent in date to this Policy, the said INSURANCE
COMPANY shall nevertheless be answerable, to the full extent
of the sum by them herein assured, without right to claim contribution from such subsequent Assurers; and shall accordingly
be entitled to retain the premium by them received, in the
same manner, as if no such subsequent assurance had been
made. And in case of loss, the assured is to abate one per
centum; and such loss shall be paid in sixty days after proof
and adjustment thereof, the amount of the note given for the
premium, if unpaid, being first deducted. And it is also agreed
between the parties, that the Assurers are not liable for any
partial loss on *Sugar*, *Flax Seed*, *Bread*, *Tobacco*, and *Rice*, unless the loss amount to five per cent– but the assured shall

recover on a general average. And it is further agreed between the parties, that the Assurers are not liable for any partial loss on *Salt, Grain, Hemp, Fish, Fruit, Hides, Skins,* or other goods that are esteemed perishable in their own nature, but the owners of such goods shall recover on a general average, and on a particular average when the damage happens by stranding; provided such damage amount to seven per cent. And it is further agreed, that if any dispute shall arise, relating to a loss on this Policy, it shall be submitted to the judgment and determination of arbitrators mutually chosen, whose award in writing shall be conclusive and binding on all parties.

IN WITNESS whereof, the PRESIDENT of the said BOSTON MARINE INSURANCE COMPANY hath hereunto subscribed his name, and caused the same to be countersigned by their SECRETARY, at their Office in Boston, this (first—) of (Decem^r.) One thousand eight hundred and twenty —

[The above is a printed form. Words in parentheses are filled in by hand.]

109. LETTER FROM ASTOR TO PRESIDENT MONROE, JANU-ARY 10, 1821, URGING THAT CONGRESS REFRAIN FROM INTER-FERENCE WITH THE FUR TRADE.

Although on a tour of Europe, Astor kept closely in touch with conditions in the fur trade.

Paris 10 Jany 1821 [1]

Sir

I observed in your Excellent Measuage of the 14 Na^r. you recomend congress to Dercit there attention to the trade with aur Indians If any Change is contemplated I hope it will not be to opràte against Citzons who are at present engagd in that trade under the System which governent adopted Some years ago. I may confidently asert that the trade has been muesh

---

[1] Ms., New York Public Library, Monroe Papers.

extented & Chiefly So by the american furr Compay of whom I am principle relyng on that we shall be permiteted to trade under that Syestem we have made many and extensive engagements Some of which will not expire for Some years to cam in fact aur men for the canducting of that trade are genrally engagd for 4 to 5 years & whether the trade is good or bade thy must bee paid & must be fead at a great expence aur property too becams So engagd that it taks years to retire I have at present not Less than than [*sic*] 400000 Say faur hundred thousand Dollars Engagd in this particular trade no fav^r. iss askd but I trust that no [interlineated: new] measure will be adopted by government to the Injury of us or other Privert traders & that if congress who perhaps may not bee fully Informd as to the nature of the trade pass any act thy will Leave it to the Discression of the excutive to Carry the Same in to efect as the good of aur Cauntry may Require

Your friends here all will Speeck of you with muish cordiality & good feeling

I have the Hanner
to bee most Respctfully

James Manrae Eq^r   Sir your H Sert
    President   John·Jacob·Astor

---

110. LETTER FROM ASTOR TO PETER SMITH, JULY 16, 1822, WITH MORE GOOD ADVICE.

General Obadiah German became Astor's agent for the management of his lands in Chenango County, township no. 11.

New york 16 July 1822[1]

Dear Sir

Senic my return from Europe I have reid 3 Letters from you the first on the 21. ulto the Day I Left home for Boston the other two yesterday on my Return from Boston one of these

---

[1] Ms., Syracuse University, Gerrit Smith Miller Collection.

contain a Chick for one thousand Dollars one half of which I pay to Mesr Laightet the other on aur land concern— I was Sorry to See by your first Letter that the Da^r. whom you had recomented to me as agent had turnd aut Bade I presume he has Done me not mush harm & no good — pray would Mr German be a good hand for me to Employ for that purpose of attenting to my lands — I regret to See by y[our] first Letter that you are not very happey — I presume its your owen fault if not quite So Certainly to a Degree to be compleatly happy is what you ought not to exspect but as you have the means to be at Least as happy as any *other man* you aught not to complain but be thankfull advise is all I can give you the rest is with your self & you best use it to your own advantage all will Soon be over with you & with me

I am truly yours

John · Jacob · Astor

P. S. about the grind Stone it is as you Say 4 are to be accounted for but what has becom of tham I know not will endevour to Assertain—
P Smith Eq^r.

[Addressed] Peter Smith Esqr., Peterborough, Oneida County
[Postmarked] New-York, Jul 16   18 [and] 2 [cents postage]

III. LETTER FROM ASTOR TO RAMSAY CROOKS, JANUARY 27, 1823, GIVING TERMS FOR THE EXTENSION OF THEIR ASSOCIATION IN THE FUR TRADE.

Stone, Bostwick & Co., which had in 1820 been forced into an agreement to withdraw from the Michilimackinac trade for five years, was now to enter into partnership with the American Fur Company for the trade of the Western Department, which had been established in 1822.

Mr R. Crooks,[1]

D. W. R. [?] Street,

Dear Sir: — You have seen the agreement proposed to be entered into between the American Fur Company and Stone Bostwick and Co and others, as also between me and them, that they are to become interested in and trade with the American Fur Company and that their concern is to join with the American Fur Company for a term of three and a half years from the first of April next which term being sometime longer than the term of our agreement, it becomes desireable that this later be extended to the first day of Oct. Eighteen hundred and Twenty-six — it being understood that your interest as to profit and loss is to remain as before, say one fifth of my interest.

Meantime I have no objections to increase your interest as to profit and loss if you desire it, so that you shall have one-fifth of the whole of the American Fur Companys business, provided however that you give it to me by the first of May next.

Security for the payment of any loss which may accrue on such additional interest, otherwise your proportions of interest is to remain as it now is say one-fifth of my interest or the profits and loss thereon say on the business conducted under the firm of the firm of [sic] the American Fur Company.

This intention is to include Mr Stewart as well as yourself as to the length of the term.

I am Respectfully Yours,

J. J. Astor.

New York 27 Jany. 1823   for the American Fur Co.

[1] Ms. book (copy), Detroit Public Library, Burton Historical Collection, and Missouri Historical Society, St. Louis, Letters of Ramsay Crooks, John Jacob Astor, and the American Fur Company, 1813-43.

112. LETTER FROM ASTOR TO RAMSAY CROOKS, FEBRUARY 16, 1824, SURVEYING THE FUR TRADE OF THE PAST YEAR.

During Astor's sojourn at Geneva, he gave close attention to the details of the fur trade. Joseph Jacques Porlier was a fur trader of Green Bay.

Geneva 16, Feby. 24.[1]

Dear Sir: –

I have already acknowledged receipt of your letters to 7 Ulto. In looking over the accounts which you have sent me, I am sorry to see so great a loss to be sustained by the concern of 1817 which I fear will prove still more when the sales of furs are recieved.

I do not recollect whether the debts due to this concern have been transferred to that of the succeeding one or not.

In the outfit of 1817 only one debt is stated that by Parlier $4032.84 why only this one. There are I presume others for I see in the amount of the succeeding concern, the company has credits by debts due at Mackinac 54,129$ valued at 40,080$. You will be so good as to tell me why the debt of Parlier was not transferred as well as all the rest of them.

In the statement of furs and property of the American Fur Company N/A the company takes credit for 3 Packs of Beaver send Na[es]. [Nov. ?] 22 to Phila. also 199 1/2 ⚹ Beaver sent in August 1823, this last I know nothing of, but the 3 Packs I think have been long ago sold or sent back to New York.

I think you or Mr G. Astor mentioned that the furs bought of Sampson were to be for my account there, I see are in the skedule or account here attested to see shipment & etc. Sporten [Spartan?] to Marcelles [sic]. I care not whether these are for my account or not. I mentioned it now only to correct any mistake if there be one.

[1] Ms. book (copy), Detroit Public Library, Burton Historical Collection, and Missouri Historical Society, St. Louis, Letters of Ramsay Crooks, John Jacob Astor, and the American Fur Company, 1813–43.

What strikes me very forceable in the account is the large amount of which the company is in debt at Mackinac, Detroit and St. Louis, if not too much trouble please tell me what there [*sic*] are for or for what object the Company became so much in debt.

In the statement of the new concern that is the present Company it shows property at St. Louis on hand 37818.88/100$ and at Mackinac 59603.85/100$ which sums appear very large, and unless there were prospects of making sales in course of the winter which I should not suppose.

I should think this to be a burden to the Company, I consider it of the utmost importance that no more goods be bought or imported than can well be sold this season so imported as we not only loose much interest, the goods become no better and perhaps fall in price and presently you are induced in order to get rid of them to see people who never pay for looking at our accounts the losses by bad debts, are very great.

In the valuation of the furs on hand – you put 1$ for each Deer skin, this is more than what they will sell for and it will make some difference as to the profits besides, which will be great deductions from the value of the payment.

Racoons were invoiced at 80 cents and sold in London at about 45 cents etc.

I am sorry to say, the prospect for this article is bad, and we have all of last years on hand as well as many of 22.

Beaver I mentioned before, I thought a safe article, and that the Company should buy at St. Louis. Of deer, I wish those of Stone & Co. had not yet came to Europe, as I am in negotiation for all ours and this *parcil* if arrived will checke the negotiation so I fear a few days more I hope will decide.

I am Dear Sir

Yours

Mr Crooks.   John Jacob Astor.

[Addressed] Mr. Ramsy Crooks, New York
[Endorsed] Geneva 16 Feby. 1824 John Jacob Astor Recieved 26 April [1824] Answered 26 June [1824] From Frederick, Maryland.

113. LETTER FROM ASTOR TO MRS. DOROTHEA LANGDON, MARCH 19, 1824, ON PERSONAL AND FAMILY MATTERS.

Dorothea, Astor's second daughter, had in 1812 married Walter Langdon without her father's permission. By this time, however, the breach was completely healed. Eliza, Astor's youngest daughter, was his companion on his European trips at this period. Late in the next year she was to marry Count Vincent Rumpff. The "Likeness" to which Astor refers is probably the one which is in the possession of Miss Wilks, one of Dorothea's descendants. "Saraha" was Dorothea's daughter, Sarah Sherburne, one of Astor's favorites among his grandchildren, who later married Baron Robert Boreel, first secretary of the Dutch Legation at Paris. Like a good German, Astor never took his wife on his European trips, and it is rather amusing to read his request to his daughter Dorothea to "give my love to your mother."

Geneve 19 March 1824 [1]

My Dear Dolly

It is Long Since I Recid any letter from You nor have I of lat wrot to you because I have ben mush unwell & had also mush to Do—William tells me you will remain in the House in Broadway I hope it will turn for the best of your family. I must Say I like the neighbourhood better than R. Hill—at Same time I hope you have followed your awen Inclination or at least thought best for your Children in Doing what you have Desited I would rather have you take a 3 Storry house in the neighbourhood where you are than go to R hill—where you would be mush out of the way—Eliza is very well & very

---

[1] Ms., letter in possession of Katherine L. Wilks, Cruickston Park, Galt, Ontario.

happy I never knew her So mush So — Some time ago She was very Cross with me but I belive it arose from Indisposition which she feels ocatinally

I Donte know whether I mantiond it to you but I have ben Setting a number of times to get a Likeness to present to you I hope it will please you — tell Saraha that presantly I will writ to her Give my love to your mother & my Respts to M^r. Langdan & belive me Dear Dolly your

affactiond father
J. J. Astor

[Addressed]   M^rs. Langdan, New york

---

114. ACCOUNT OF PROFIT AND LOSS OF AMERICAN FUR COMPANY OUTFITS MADE UP AT MACKINAC IN THE SUMMER OF 1823, OCTOBER 15, 1824.

The sketch on the opposite page shows the three principal types of outfits to which the Company furnished goods.   The large profit made by the retail store at Mackinac is of particular interest.

---

115. LETTER FROM ASTOR TO RAMSAY CROOKS, JANUARY 10, 1825, OUTLINING PLANS FOR THE NEXT YEAR'S FUR TRADE.

It will be observed that already Astor was at least considering selling out his interest in the Company.

Geneva 10. Jany 1825 [1]

My Dear Sir: –

I hope soon to recieve some information from you relative to our old concerns – You see by my letter of this date to the President that I as Chief agent of the Company consider it my duty to act for them as shall appear to me for the interest of the

[1] Ms. book (copy), Detroit Public Library, Burton Historical Collection, and Missouri Historical Society, St. Louis, Letters of Ramsay Crooks, John Jacob Astor, and the American Fur Company, 1813–43.

	amt. of goods	our half Gain	
v Fond du Lac	$14,800	" propt^n. "	$2047
v Lac du Flambeau	" 3,000	" half "	1046
v Grand River	" 7,000	" half "	401
v Chicago Outfit (from us)	" 10,000	" share "	1100
v Upper Mississippi	" 37,500	" half "	3351
x Folleavoine, Lake Superior	" 2,583	" net "	914
x Ance Quiwinan	" 3,300	" " "	594
x St. Joseph, Lake Michigan	" 2,780	" " "	368
x Retail Store, Mackinac	" 8,300	" " "	7200
			$17021
x Upper Wabash	" 3,800	Loss $367	1523
x Lower do	" 3,100	" 1156	
	$96,163		$15498
		say 16% net gain	

	amt. of goods
⊕ Amt. Goods sold Lyman Warren	2575
" " " W^m. Aitkin	4500
" " " J. Bt. Corbin	700
" " " Michel Cadotte	900
" " " E & W. Mitchell	2300
" " " E. Biddle	2900
" " " Joseph Bailly	850
" " " Green Bay C^o.	12200
" " " J. B. Beaubien	5100
" " " Alexandre Laurent	800 — $32.825

N. B.   The Outfits marked thus v are on shares, and the goods put in at Cost, charges (including Interest) & 5% Commission — The Inventories of 1822, the same, adding transportation &c — Those marked x thus were on our own a/c, and charged as above, the whole shewing a gain of about 16%, exclusive of our 5 prct: Commission, and making in all about 21% on our Goods — Those marked thus ⊕ were on account of the individuals named, and the Goods charged at the usual advance, say 33⅓ prct. net gain — R. S —

[1] Ms. (photostat), Wisconsin Historical Society, Madison, Robert Stuart's Letter Book, Mackinac, 1823–30, p. 124.

Company till the termination of the agreement and consequently I will order goods for 1826, for be the agreement extended or not, the trade will be carried on by some one, and be it who it may they must have goods – what will be prudent if not necessary to make no engagement which will extend beyond Oct. 1826, if it can be avoided of which you and the other Agents can judge better than me.

I will be glad to have your undivided and private opinion on this, and all that concerns the Company — it appears to me that our new friend will prefer to sell out, and excepting Stone, I should as leave be without them, though I may also wish to sell out, but whether I do or not, it will be of great satisfaction to me to see the Companys affairs in a good state at the exporation of the [illegible — agreement?] or winding up of the concern.

Should there be an improvement in the price of Racoon and Deer of which there is no great prospect, I shall hope that the trade will pay well next year, but you and all the gentlemen agents must be prudent, but not too sanguine.

Don't give out goods too freely, and pay not too high for skins.

I shall be glad to learn that all our Muskrats have been sold at about 40 Cents. As I am not judge of the consumption I cannot so well judge of the prospect of there keeping so high, but no doubt they will support about 37 1/2 —

I am glad to see our friend Stuart has done so well, some of our Bear skins sold pretty well in London.

I am Respectfully yours,

John Jacob Astor.

[Addressed]   Mr Ramsay Crooks, New York.
[Endorsed]   John Jacob Astor, Geneva 10 Jany. 1825   Recieved 7 April [1825]   Answered 14 [April 1825]

116. Letter from Astor to Ramsay Crooks, August 20, 1825, expressing Uncertainty as to his Continuance in the Fur Trade.

In this letter the possibility of Astor's retirement becomes still stronger. The principal reason for his attitude comes out in the mention of his precarious condition of health.

Geneva 20 Aug. 1825.[1]

My Dear Sir:–

I think I have already replied to your letter of the first July, that it is my intention to come home this coming Autumn, providing my health will permit the same, as traveling by land is not without inconvenience.

If not attended with danger for my health be that as it may, I shall set out from this very soon.

With regard as to whether I continue in the trade I really cannot now tell. Much will depend on situation of matters when I get home, but whether I do or not I never had any other thought than that I did retire, I would like you and Mr Stuart to be fully satisfied.

I must say that I never intended to make any arrangement contrary to your interest. Quite otherwise, nor did I contemplate that you or Mr Stuart would ever separate from the concern while I continued.

I hope that both of you on reflection have come in the late agreement.

You tell me indeed that you will at all events go on as if you had come into it.

Prospects for furs for Europe Market, say Racoon, Deer and Bear as also Fishers skins are bad, and we shall realize much less for what we have now in Europe than the invoice cost, so

[1] Ms. book (copy), Detroit Public Library, Burton Historical Collection, and Missouri Historical Society, St. Louis, Letters of Ramsay Crooks, John Jacob Astor, and the American Fur Company, 1813-43.

that our former concerns, will I fear, leave a balance on the wrong side.

I was sorry to see Mrs Crooks had been unwell. I hope that you and her are enjoying good health.

Believe me Dear Sir to be Yours

Mr Crooks.   John Jacob Astor.

117. Conveyance by Astor to Christopher Delano, October 5, 1825, of a Forty-year Lease to a Lot in New York City.

This lease is typical of those made by Astor for comparatively long terms and on the payment of a lump sum. Astor himself was in Europe at the time this conveyance was made. The conditions under which the lessee might remove buildings erected by him on the property will be noted. See document 120.

This [1] Indenture made this fifth day of October in the year of our Lord One thousand eight hundred & twenty five Between John Jacob Astor of the City of New York Merchant of the first part and Christopher Delano of the same place Grocer of the other part Witnesseth that the said party of the first part for and in consideration of the sum of Seven hundred and fifty Dollars lawful money of the United States of America to him in hand paid or secured to be paid by the said party of the second part the receipt whereof is hereby acknowledged and also in consideration of the covenants hereinafter contained on the part and behalf of the said party of the second part to be kept and performed hath granted bargained leased demised and set over and by these presents doth grant bargain lease demise and set over unto the said party of the second part his executors administrators or assigns All that certain lot or piece of Ground part and parcel of the farm or piece of land in the Eigth

[1] Ms. book, Hall of Records, N. Y., Liber Conveyances 281, p. 610.

late Seventh Ward of the City of New York which on the first
day of May One thousand Seven hundred and ninety Seven
was granted and demised by the Corporation of Trinity
Church in the said City unto Aaron Burr and his assigns and
by the said Aaron Burr afterwards sold assigned and conveyed
to the said party of the first part his Executors Administrators
and assigns and known and distinguished in and by a map of
the said farm made by Stephen Ludlam one of the sworn Surveyors of the said farm made by Stephen Ludlam one of the
sworn Surveyors of the said City of New York by number 140
One hundred and forty Bounded northerly in front by Charlton
Street Southerly in the rear by lot number 135 One hundred
and thirty five Easterly on one side by Varick Street and
Westerly on the other side by lot number 136 One hundred and
thirty six the said lot number One hundred and forty containing in width in front and rear twenty five feet and in length on
each side Seventy five feet together with all and singular the
rights members hereditaments and appurtenances thereunto
belonging To Have and to Hold the said lot or piece of ground
with the appurtenances unto the said party of the Second part
his Executors administrators and assigns from and after the
first day of May in the year of our Lord One thousand eight
hundred and twenty five for and during and until the full end
and term of forty years from thence next ensuing and fully to
be complete and ended and the said party of the second part
his Executors Administrators or assigns doth hereby covenant
and agree to and with the said party of the second part his
Executors Administrators or assigns doth hereby covenant and
agree to and with the said party of the first part his Executors
Administrators and assigns that he the said party of the Second
part his Executors Administrators or assigns shall and will at
his own proper cost and expenses bear pay and discharge all
such lawful duties taxes and assessments as shall during the
said term of forty years be laid rated assessed and imposed by

the authority of the United States the Legislature of the State of New York or by the Corporation of the City of New York upon the said premises demised or any part thereof excepting only the Ground rent of said premises payable to the said Corporation of Trinity Church which the said party of the first part hereby covenants to pay and to save harmless the said party of the second party his Executors Administrators and Assigns therefrom and from all trouble and molestation on account thereof and it is hereby mutually declared and agreed that in case default shall be made in the payment of the said duties taxes and assessments or any part thereof that then and from thenceforth it shall be lawful for the said party of the first part his Executors Administrators or assigns into the said demised premises lot or piece of ground or any part thereof in the name of the whole to reenter and the said lot or piece of ground and premises to repossess and have again as if this present Indenture had never been made and it is further covenanted and agreed that the said party of the second part his Executors Administrators or assigns shall have liberty to remove and carry away any building or buildings erected on the said lot provided the same is done within ten days after the expiration of the said Lease and not thereafter and that on the last day of said term or other sooner determination of the estate hereby granted the said party of the second part his Executors administrators or assigns shall and will peacably and quietly leave surrender and yield up unto the said party of the first part his heirs or assigns all and singular the said demised premises and the said party of the first part for himself his heirs Executors and Administrators doth covenant and grant to and with the said party of the second part his Executors Administrators and assigns by these presents that the said party of the second part his Executors Administrators and assigns performing the covenants and agreements aforesaid on his and their part shall and may at all times during the

said term hereby granted peaceably and quietly have hold and
enjoy the said demised premises without any manner of let
suit trouble or hindrance of or from the said party of the first
part his heirs or assigns or any person or persons whomsoever
In witness whereof the said parties to these presents have hereunto affixed their hands and seals the day and year first above
mentioned John Jacob Astor by Wm. B. Astor his Atty (LS)
In presence of Dv^d. Hardenbrook City and County of New
York on the 7th. day of October 1825 personally came and appeared before me William B. Astor known to me to be the same
person who executed the foregoing Indenture and also known
to me to be the authorized agent for John Jacob Astor who is
described therein and acknowledged that he had executed the
same and that it was his free act and deed I do allow it to be
recorded.   M. Cunningham Commissioner
        Recorded the preceding at the request of C. Graham
        the 24th. of february 1832 at 3 min past 3 P M
                              Gilbert Coutant Register

118. Letter from Albert Gallatin to James Barbour,
June 30, 1826, interceding for the Release of Goods
belonging to the American Fur Company.

The goods mentioned were seized by the Indian agent at Fort
Wayne because liquor was found among them. Gallatin, by this
time, seems to have discarded the suspicion he manifested toward
Astor upon the occasion of the *Beaver's* "mandarin voyage" in
1808.

                                    New York 30th June 1826 [1]
Sir
    I beg leave to apply once more to you in behalf of my friend
Mr Astor, as President of the Fur Company of New York.
There has been a seizure some time since of goods belonging to

----

[1] Ms., Department of the Interior, Washington, D. C., Indian Office Records,
Miscellaneous.

the Company. The trial respecting these is still pending. And as they will be utterly destroyed, if not taken care of, he wishes an order to be sent to the Indian Agent at Fort Wayne; in whose hands they are, to have them appraised and given up to the Company on bond and security to pay the amount, if finally condemned. The security of the Company being amply sufficient, the arrangement is in fact as advantageous to the public as to them; and I therefore feel no hesitation in recommending the application to your attention.

It is very possible that amongst the numerous agents & persons necessarily employed by a Company who has a capital of 700,000 dollars in that trade, there may have been some evasions of the law, and they must abide the consequence. But it is a business which should be rather countenanced than discouraged by Government, and which, so far from giving large profits as generally supposed; has hardly paid interest on the capital employed for the last ten years. Of the great merits of Mr Astor there can be no doubt. The United States are indebted exclusively to him for the settlement of Astoria, which constitutes our only right *of possession* to the Columbia territory. He did this without the least public assistance and lost near 100,000 dollars by it. I think therefore that he is at least entitled to a liberal treatment, so far as is consistent with law and with the ultimate security of the United States.

I have the honour to be with great respect and regard
Sir
Your most obedient Servant
Albert Gallatin

[Addressed] The hon ble James Barbour, Secretary of War, City of Washington

[Postmarked] New-York, Jul 3   Free

119. ACCOUNT OF THE CHARLOTTE RIVER AND BYRNES PATENT TRACTS, JANUARY 1, 1827, TWENTY-FIVE YEARS AFTER THEY HAD FINALLY COME INTO THE UNDISPUTED POSSESSION OF ASTOR AND HIS ASSOCIATES.

It is interesting to observe how Astor's early interest in undeveloped New York backcountry land was still continuing, side by side with his much more important activities in the American Fur Company and Manhattan Island real estate.

Recapitulation [1]

Lands in both Tracts Unsold (tho' a few it may [be] noted are under contract, not probable to be fulfill'd) including those still under Lease, likewise noted,

Charlotte River Patent, A. A. fo L.		$13.900\frac{2}{10}$ acres	
Bryne's	" B. B. " U.	9.924	
		23.824 2/10 a.	

These Lands with the various improvements, in the situation & under the circumstances they now are, I must deem an average value six dollars per acre

$142.945\frac{20}{100}$

let us however deduct *say* 25 p^r. ct.   35.736.30

$107.208\frac{90}{100}$

due us upon items not included in the above [due on contracts of sale] $10,515.00

$117.723\frac{90}{100}$

This will prob. be realized in a few years with Int.

There is due us originating out of those Patents, for Rents not cancelled (nor absconded debtors) and for Lumber Grindstones, Mer-

---

[1] Ms. book, Syracuse University, Gerrit Smith Miller Collection, Duplicate/ Vide Book B. fo. 117–118. Exhibit State of the Unsold Lands in Charlotte River and Byrne's Patents, January 1st., 1827, pp. V and W.

chandize, Grain, Hay, Cattle, farming Utensils, &c. &c. various small sums; And still on
hand,

amt. up　　　$117.723.90

Turnpike stock, Lumber, Grindstones, Grain,
Hay, Cattle, farming Utensils &c. &c. [inter-
lineated: altogether] say $5000. Now after
deducting for Bad, for depreceation, & for
small demands against us, on acct. of this Concern, leave *say*　　　　　　　　　　　2,000.00

$119,723$\frac{90}{100}$

N. B. will be perceived no charge, for my own personal services
& time in the premises, yet brought into the account.

I must add

Errors Excepted,

To arrange this exhibit has been a great Jobb, not very well
myself, much of the time intensely cold! I hope however it
may prove to be correct, & Satisfactory, made up to, & intended as of 1st. January 1827. —

To Mess. Astor & Laight.　p. Smith of Peterboro

120. CONVEYANCE BY ASTOR TO CORNELIUS DEGROOT,
FEBRUARY 1, 1827, OF A TWENTY-YEAR LEASE TO A LOT IN
NEW YORK CITY.

This lease is typical of those made by Astor for comparatively
short terms, on the basis of an annual rental. The provisions for the
erection of a building by the lessee and the granting to him of a new
lease will be noted.　See document 117.

Recorded [1] for and at the request of Richd. Legerafty this 16th.
of July 1828 at 43 minutes past 1 P M
This indenture made the first day of February in the year of
our Lord one thousand eight hundred and twenty seven Be-

---

[1] Ms. book, Hall of Records, N. Y., Liber Conveyances 239, p. 143.

tween John Jacob Astor of the City of New York merchant of
the one part and Cornelius De Groot of the same place Stone
Cutter of the other part Witnesseth that the said John Jacob
Astor in consideration of the rents and covenants hereinafter
contained on the part of the said Cornelius De Groot be paid
kept and performed hath granted bargained leased demised
and set over and by these presents doth grant bargain lease
demise and set over unto the said Cornelius De Groot his executors administrators or assigns All that lot or piece of ground
part and parcel of the farm or piece of land in the eight (late
Seventh) Ward of the City of New York which on the first day
of May one thousand seven hundred and ninety seven was
granted and demised by the Corporation of Trinity Church in
the said City unto Aaron Burr afterwards sold assigned and
conveyed to said John Jacob Astor his executors administrators
and assigns and known and distinguished in and by a Map of
the said farm lately made by Stephen Ludlam one of the sworn
surveyors of the said City of New York by number one hundred and thirty one bounded northerly in front by Charlton
Street Westerly by lot number one hundred and twenty nine
Easterly by lot number one hundred and thirty three and
southerly in the rear by lot number one hundred and thirty the
said lot number one hundred and thirty one being in breadth
front and rear twenty five feet and in depth one hundred feet
with the appurtenances To have and To hold the said lot or
piece of ground with the appurtenances unto the said Cornelius
De Groot his executors administrators and assigns from the
day of the date hereof for the full end and term of twenty one
years yielding and paying therefor yearly and every year during the said term of twenty one years unto the said John Jacob
Astor his executors administrators or assigns the rent or sum of
seventy dollars lawful money of the United States of America
free and clear from all abatements and deductions whatsoever
in quarterly payments the first whereof to commence and be

paid on the first day of May next ensuing the date hereof and so to continue to be paid quarterly during the said term of twenty one years hereby demised Provided Always that if the said rent or sum of Seventy dollars or any part thereof so to be paid as aforesaid shall be behind and unpaid for the space of thirty days next after any of the quarterly days of payment whereon the same ought to be paid that then it shall be lawful for the said John Jacob Astor his executors administrators or assigns into the said demised lot or piece of ground and premises or any part thereof in the name of the whole to reenter and the said lot or piece of ground and premises to repossess and have again as if this present Indenture had never been made and the said Cornelius De Groot his executors administrators and assigns doth hereby covenant and agree to and with the said John Jacob Astor his executors administrators and assigns that the said Cornelius De Groot his executors administrators or assigns shall and will during the said term pay to the said John Jacob Astor his executors administrators or assigns the said yearly rent quarterly in manner aforesaid and also shall and will pay and discharge all such lawful duties taxes and assessments as shall during the said term of twenty one years be laid rated assessed and imposed by the authority of the United States the Legislature of the State of New York or by the Corporation of the City of New York upon the said premises demised or any part thereof excepting only the ground rent of the said premises payable to the said Corporation of Trinity Church which said ground rent the said John Jacob Astor hereby covenants to pay to and to Save harmless the said Cornelius De Groot his executors administrators and assigns therefrom and from all trouble and molestation on account thereof And the said Cornelius De Groot doth also covenant and agree that he will within two years from the date of these presents build and erect or cause to be built and erected on the said lot a good and substantial dwelling house at least two stories high the front whereof to be built of brick and it is hereby further covenanted and agreed by and between the said parties that at the expiration of the said term of twenty one years a fair and reasonable valuation shall be made of such dwelling house which the said Cornelius De Groot his executors administrators or assigns shall have erected on the said lot hereby demised by two indifferent persons one to be chosen by each of the said parties and who shall have power in case of disagreement to choose another person as an umpire and if the said John Jacob Astor his executors administrators or assigns shall not within thirty days after such valuation made and notice thereof pay to the said Cornelius De Groot his executors or administrators the amount of such valuation then the said John Jacob Astor shall make and execute a new lease of the said premises to the said Cornelius De Groot his executors administrators or assigns for the further term of Thirteen years at the yearly ground rent of five per cent interest per annum on the fee simple value of the said lot to be made and determined by two indifferent persons one to be chosen by each of the said parties and who shall have power in case of disagreement to choose another person as an umpire the rent aforesaid payable quarterly In witness whereof the parties to these presents have hereunto set their hands and seals the day and year first above written   John Jacob Astor (L S) Corn^s. De Groot (L S) In presence of "Charles Loss" on the first page stricken out and "Stephen Ludlam" interlined Dv^d. Hardenbrook State of New York City & County of New York SS. on this Sixteenth day of July A. D. one Thousand eight hundred and twenty eight before me personally appeared David Hardenbrook the subscribing witness to the above Indenture to me Known who being by me duly sworn deposed and said that he knows John Jacob Astor and Cornelius De Groot and that he saw them respectively sign seal and deliver the said Indenture as their respective act and deed And that he subscribed his name as a witness thereto at the time of the execution thereof all which is satisfactory evidence of the due execution of the said Indenture the alterations being noted I allow the same to be recorded Henry S. Richards Commissioner &c.

121. LETTER FROM ASTOR TO RAMSAY CROOKS, APRIL 12, 1827, DESCRIBING THE SITUATION IN THE NEW YORK FUR MARKET.

Munson, Bostwick, and Stone had been associated with the American Fur Company in the Western Department. Pierre Menard was a Missouri fur trader, procuring his goods through Astor's company, who was later forced to become one of the Company's subordinate traders. B. Berthold was a Missouri fur trader associated with Bernard Pratte & Co. The Astorian W. W. Matthews, the Company's Montreal agent, has already been several times mentioned.

New York, 12 April, 1827.[1]

Dear Sir: –

I recieved yesterday your letter of 21st Ulto. and was rejoiced to see your health was better (take care of it) We had a sale 4 Int. and sold about 80 M. Muskrats at 35 1/8 Cents; besides those I sold about 100 M at a private sale at 35 Cents, so that here we have about 120,000 to sell and I expect not to get less than 35 for them.

Beaver sold very low. Rocky Mountain 4 1/2 Missouri 3 1/2 to 375 [sic] – Lake Superior 5 to 5 1/2 Mackinacs 4 to 4 1/4 – About 5000 good Hatters. Racoon at 15 to 16 Cents.

Sampson had a large sale of Beaver 2 days before ours – The Beaver bought of Ashley is not good and if I had it I could not get 4$ for it. —

[1] Ms. book (copy), Detroit Public Library, Burton Historical Collection, and Missouri Historical Society, St. Louis, Letters of Ramsay Crooks, John Jacob Astor, and the American Fur Company, 1813–43.

I have no doubt Muskrats good will be 36 to 37 next Autumn, Beaver I think will keep about as it is.

We have no good accounts from Europe not for any one single article.

Mr Munson is here, and I have bought him and Mr Stone out. Mr Bastwick is interested, but some of the others not yet decided, no doubt they will come in.

Valle is here and tells me he wants no more good than the triffling order they gave us, so I suppose gets them by other means. he has here some few good deer skins, but says he wants to sell all they get together & I will not buy without seeing them nor would I recommend you to meddle with them except it be for good heavy skins, only I think they will not rise in Europe as we have still more than 300 Bales there unsold and have just now nearly as many going

Deer goods not yet arrived but we expect them next week, they come still pretty high, but not so high as last year. Otter skins sold well in Canton, we had none there. I recommend your attention to them.

I think you may take Berthold & Co.'s Bear at 3$ and the Rocky Mountain at 3 1/2 or thereabouts as the quantity may be.

About Buffalo, I think they will do if you can get the whole and not otherwise, when I speak of the whole I mean something like it, at least 5/6 of them, so as to have the command of the market.

Deer skins I think we can buy them better here unless you meet some good heavy skins.

Mathews has his men and will be in time.

I am Dear Sir Respectfully

Your ob. Servt.

R. Crooks Esq.   John Jacob Astor, Prest.

Agent Am. Fur Co.   Am. Fur Co.

P. S. – Touch not Racoon, get all the Muskrats you can as also the other.

Please present my compliments to Mrs. Crooks and tell her that her fine bird is very well and I hope her little girl is the same —

J. J. A.

[Addressed] Ramsay Crooks, Agent American Ins. [Fur?] Co., St. Louis, Mo.

[Postmarked] New York, Apr. 12

[Endorsed] John Jacob Astor, New York 12, April 1827 Recieved 23 May 1827 Answered 24 [May 1827]

122. ENGAGEMENT OF JEAN BAPTISTE GIBEAU TO THE AMERICAN FUR COMPANY, FEBRUARY 9, 1828, TO ACT AS A *Voyageur* FOR THE TERM OF THREE YEARS.

This is a typical engagement for a common *voyageur*. Wages, and sometimes other conditions, vary when a baker, guide, or other superior *engagé* is hired, but the printed form remains the same, words being stricken out or added. Gabriel Franchere, a native of Montreal, had gone out to the Columbia River on the *Tonquin* and was the author of the earliest published account of the Astoria enterprise, which was written in French and appeared at Montreal in 1820. In the later years of his life he published, in 1854, an English version under the title, *Narrative of a Voyage to the Northwest Coast of America*. He became the Montreal agent of the American Fur Company, probably succeeding W. W. Matthews, and later entered the fur business in New York City. He died in 1863 at the age of seventy-seven, perhaps the last survivor of the Astoria expedition. His portrait is in the Château de Ramezay at Montreal.

PARDEVANT[1] LES NOTAIRES de la Province du Bas-Canada, résidans à (Montreal sous-signé)

FUT PRESENT, (Jean Baptiste Gibeau, macon residant en la paroisse de Laprairié) LEQUEL S'EST VOLONTAIREMENT

[1] Ms., Palais de Justice, Montreal, Notarial Records of P. Lukin, 1439.

ENGAGÉ et s'engage par ces présentes à MR. GABRIEL FRAN-
CHERE fils, de la ville de Montréal, Marchand, agissant pour
et au nom de la Compagnie connue sous le nom de AMERICAN
FUR COMPANY, duement autorisé par la dite Compagnie à
l'effet des présentes, a ce présent et acceptant pour à première
requisition partir de la dite ville de Montréal en qualité de
(Milieu) [et — stricken through] Voyageur, dans un de ses
canots ou bateaux, tant pour faire le voyage que pour hiverner
dans les limites ou les dépendances des Etats-Unis, dans le
Haut-Canada, et à la Rivière Missourie, et leurs dépendances,
pendant TROIS années consécutives qui expireront dans le
mois d'Août de l'année mil huit cent (trente un) le dit Sr.
Franchère se réservant le droit de décharger le dit engagé à
Makinac, et dans ce cas de lui charger et faire payer cent livres
ancien cours, pour sa descente à Montréal, et pendant les
dites trois années le dit Sieur Franchère, agissant comme ci-
dessus, promet nourrir le dit engagé au blé-d'Inde ou autres
aliments obtenus dans les pays sauvages — Et le dit engagé
promet avoir bien et duement soin pendant les routes, et étant
aux dits lieux, des marchandises, vivres, pelleteries, ustensiles
et de tout autre chose nécessaire pour le voyage et l'hyverne-
ment — — Servir, obéir et exécuter fidèlement tout ce que le
dit Bourgeois ou tout autre représentant sa personne, auquel
le dit Sieur Bourgeois est autorisé par ces présentes de trans-
porter le présent engagement, lui commandera de licite et
honnête; faire son profit, éviter son dommage, l'en avertir s'il
vient à sa connaissance, travailler dans les postes, villes, vil-
lages et campagnes qui ne sont pas considérés comme pays
sauvages, s'il en est requis et généralement faire tout ce qu'un
bon (& fidele —) et voyageur doit et est obligé de faire, sans
pouvoir faire aucune traite ou commerce pour son particulier
soit avec les blancs ou les sauvages, s'absenter, ni quitter le dit
service, sous les peines portées par les lois et ordonnances, et de
perdre ses gages.

CET engagement ainsi fait, pour et moyennant la somme de (cinq cents Livres —) ancien cours par année, égale à (quartre vingt trois piastres et un tiers —) argent des Etats-Unis, que le dit Sieur Franchère, agissant comme ci-dessus, promet et s'oblige de faire bailler et payer au dit (Jean Bte Gibeau) un mois après son tems échu.

LE dit (Jean Baptiste Gibeau —) reconnait avoir reçu à compte de ses dits gages la somme de (six piastres —) et le dit Bourgeois lui payera de plus en partant (quatre piastres —) aussi à compte de ses gages.

EN même tems est comparu pardevant les mêmes Notaires (Joseph Bourdeau Cultivateur residant en la dite paroisse de [Mon — stricken through] Laprairie —) Lequel s'est volontairement rendu Caution envers le dit Bourgeois, solidairement avec le dit (Jean Baptiste Gibeau) pour le vrai accomplissement des présentes de la part du dit engagé, et pour les sommes d'argent ainsi avancées et à être avancées en vertu des présentes.

CAR AINSI, &c. Fait et passé à (Montreal etude de M. Lukin) l'an mil huit cent (vingt huit) le (neuvieme —) jour du mois de (fevrier avant) midi (le Sr Franchere a signé avec les Notaires les autres —) ayant déclaré ne le savoir faire de cet enqui (sont) fait (leur) marque ordinaire — après lecture faite

(Marque

Jean   X   Bte Gibeau

Marque de

Joseph   X   Bourdeau

Gabriel Franchere

A. T. Kimber N. p.   P Lukin N P)

[The above is a printed form. Words in parentheses are filled in by hand.]

[Endorsed] No 1439 9^r fev^r. 1828 Engagement de J. B^{te} Gibeau à Gabriel Franchere fils agent de l'A. F. Company Expé

123. LETTER FROM JOHN EBBETS TO CAPTAIN WILLIAM B.
FINCH, OCTOBER 26, 1829, IN REGARD TO THE SALE OF A BRIG
TO THE KING OF THE HAWAIIAN ISLANDS, WITH COPY OF THE
BILL OF SALE, FEBRUARY 19, 1828.

John Ebbets and John Meek were the most prominent of the
Astor captains engaged in the Pacific trade.

William B. Finch Esqr.[1]

Sir –

Understanding you intend takeing your departure from
these Islands in the course of a few days. I take the liberty of
thus early laying the case of the late American Brig Tameah-
meah before you. this vessel of which I was the Owner, was
built in New York, year 1824, by Henry Eckford, expressly for
the present King Kauikeaouli on Her arrival at these Islands,
the Chiefs declined purchaseing Her. according to our contract– notwithstanding I had been at great expense in having
her built. & she was consider'd to be a Vessel of the finest class,
as to workmanship, model &c in New York. She continued to
be employ'd in the freighting business untill February 1828
when I commenc'd lodeing her for Manilla– the King and Boki
requested Capt. Meek, Her Commander to stop lodeing, as
they were desireous of purchaseing. tho they observ'd they had
not the Wood. to pay for Her at the present moment– but if I
would wait six months I should positively be paid, on these
conditions the Brig was sold the King. Feby 19th 1828 for
Three thousand four hundred piculs of Sandal Wood. to be of
the finest merchantable quality– and if not paid for in six
months, the obligation to bear Interest– at the rate of Five pr
ct. annum of the amount due. I have receiv'd One thousand,
one hundred and sixty one piculs of wood, and four hundred
dollars in Specie– the remaining wood, say Two thousand One
hundred sixty five piculs with Interest remains due– a true

[1] Ms., Department of the Navy, Washington, D. C., Archives, Capt. Finch's
Cruise in the U. S. S. *Vincennes*.

copy of the sale I enclose you. I have been thus particular. as I expect to leave the Islands in a short time for America, it would be a satisfaction situated as I am to have the justness of the debt acknowledged to be correct. before the Chiefs – I have no doubt Sir you will endeavour to assist. not only Myself, but also all the Citizens of the U. S. who may have just claims on this Government – time appears not to be an object of moment with these people – they cannot accuse us of not waiting patiently for debts, long since justly due. I have no dout Sir, your laying our claims, before the Chiefs will have great weight.

Accept Sir my wishes for your restoration to Health and continued prosperity

With sentiments of Esteem

I am

Respectfully

Yours &c

Jno. Ebbets

Oahu Octr 26th
1829.

— It is hereby agreed between John Meek – Master of the Brig Tamaahmaah on the one part, and Kaukiaoli King of the Sandwich Islands on the other part – that the said Jno. Meek, doth hereby sell the said Brig to the King of the Sandwich Islands – for Three thousand-four hundred piculs of good fair Merchantable Sandal Wood. One half to be paid in Sixty days & the other half in Six months – from the date hereof – All the wood paid at this Island to be receiv'd at Honolulu – All the Wood paid at Hawaii to be receiv'd at Kailua – all Wood paid at Maui to be receiv'd at Lahaina – all Wood paid at Kauai, to be receiv'd at Waimea – and the said Kaukioli, King of the Sandwich Islands, doth hereby agree to purchase said Brig and to have and receive Her, as conditioned by Bill of Sale – for the aforesaid Amt of Three thousand four hundred piculs of good. fair merchantable Sandal Wood – at the times & places above specified – and if the said Sandal Wood. shall not be paid. at the end of Six months, from date hereof, all remaining unpaid. shall bear interest at the rate of five per ct pr annum untill paid.

In Witness Whereof the parties have hereunto set their hands and seals – this Nineteenth day of February – One thousand eight hundred and twenty eight

Witness	(Signed)	King Kauikeaouli	(L.S.)
J. C. Carter	(Signed)	Jno Meek–	(L.S.)
J. Mitchner	(Signed)	Boki	(L.S.)

True Copy

124. Acknowledgment of Indebtedness by the King, Regent, and Chiefs of the Hawaiian Islands to John Ebbets, November 2, 1829.

Among the witnesses to this document may be noted William B. Finch, commander of the U. S. S. *Vincennes*, and Hiram Bingham, the missionary. When Astor's brig *Forester* was sold to Kamehameha I, it was given the name of his favorite wife, Kaahumanu, one of the signers of this document.

We,[1] the King, Regent, and Chiefs of the Sandwich Islands, acknowledge to owe John Ebbets, the sum of Two Thousand one hundred and sixty-five Piculs of good merchantable Sandal Wood, with interest as provided for in a Bill of Sale entered into with John Meek, on the 19th of February, 1828, for the Brig Tameameah; and we confirm the terms of said Bill of Sale, and promise to liquidate it finally, in nine months time from this date.

Witness—
Wm. B. Finch,
Thos. Dornin,
Saml. B. Malone
H. Bingham.

(Signed) Kauikeaouli,
Boki,
J. Adams,
Hoapile,
Naihe,
Kaahumanu.

Honolulu, 2d November, 1829.

[1] Ms., Department of the Navy, Washington, D. C., Archives, Capt. Finch's Cruise in the U. S. S. *Vincennes*.

125. LETTER FROM WILLIAM B. ASTOR TO JAMES KEITH, DECEMBER 15, 1829, OFFERING TO CO-OPERATE WITH THE HUDSON'S BAY COMPANY IN EXCLUDING LIQUOR FROM THE CANADIAN–AMERICAN BORDER.

New York 15th.Dec.ʳ. 1829.[1]

James Keith Esqʳ.
Agᵗ. Honble.Hudson Bay Cº.
Sir

Having been lately informed that the Honbleᵉ. The Hudson Bay Company, were from humane motives desirous of stopping the introduction of spirituous Liquors among the Indians inhabiting the region bordering on the line of demarcation between Great Britain & the United States, (from Lake Superior, to the Lake of the Woods,), where their Traders come in contact with those of the American Fur Company; I hasten to notify you, that it is also my wish; and I hereby agree that the people of the American Fur Cº. shall not in future, either directly or indirectly, carry in, or in any way give ardent spirits to the Indians of that region, or vicinity; provided the Honbleᵉ. The Hudon Bay Cº. pledge themselves to the same effect– will you have the goodness to ascertain this fact, and notify me as early as convenient– The United States Indian Agent at the Sault de Sᵗᵉ.Marie, has promised that if the two Companies agree on this subject, he will not permit any individual Traders to take Liquor into the country under any pretence whatever.

I am respectfully
Sir
Your Ob: Sᵗ.
(Sgd.) Wᵐ. B. Astor
Presᵈᵗ. Amⁿ. Fur Co.

---

[1] Ms., Hudson's Bay House, London.

126. LETTER FROM ASTOR TO GERRIT SMITH, DECEMBER 21, 1829, IN REGARD TO THE MOHAWK AND HUDSON RAILROAD.

When Astor withdrew from the China trade, conducted in his own vessels, he looked around for other interests; among those on which he fixed his attention, railroads were prominent. Astor was a director and a large stockholder in the Mohawk and Hudson Railroad, the first railroad in New York State and the earliest constituent of the New York Central. Gerrit Smith, Peter Smith's son, about this time took his father's place in the correspondence which had gone on for about forty years between the two families. George William Featherstonhaugh, "the originator and sole promoter" of the Mohawk and Hudson, had, owing to family and personal misfortunes, become discouraged, resigned as director, and turned in his stock, earlier in the year. John J. De Graff, a Schenectady merchant, although he did not become the company's commissioner, took an active part in the construction of the road. The Welland Canal, in which Astor declined to concern himself, connected Lake Erie and Lake Ontario and was completed by the Canadian government in 1833.

Newyork 21 Dc^r. 1829 [1]

Dear Sir

I Recd your Letter of 3 It & ought to have Lang Since Reply^d to the Same but I put off writing to you in the hope to have Somethig pasitive Relating to aur progress to comunicate in which I have ben Disapointed & I wih not to Delay any Longer to Say that I amglad that you have agreed to tak the Intrest as propasd Say 250 Shares which are engag^d for you of the parit which belongd to M^r. Featherston hough thy are not yet Transferrd which is of no Ineowery to you the Sctch of agreement which you have Send is in the main if not in all Respcuts Right & when I Recie the Stock I Will Send you one to Sign— you Speck about Mismanagement So fare its Bade a nough but I Do belive there will now be an end to it thy Spend 8 or 9000$ not much for it — altho this is considerabl its not muh Matter because I Do thnk that 10 or 20.000$ ane Way or

---

[1] Ms., Syracuse University, Gerrit Smith Miller Collection.

other So as we com Right at Last is of no consequence the objict will bare it. I am quit of opinion with you that the Stack will be the best in the State & I exspect next Sprig we Shall get Seriously about it —

In confidene I ask you will M^r. Degroff be aproper persan to be the campainys agent or commissnor he has been askd & I belive will tak it nothing is however Done about he has mearly benn Sounded — what would you think if aproud Should be the Compensation we are in treaty with M^r. White for engineer – all the Stack is takng up unless M^r. Degraff may have Some not Dispasd off more could be sold here but I would Rather have Sam Resputobl pepol in the country. Interested we want more men of Practicabl Knowladge in the Derection we are now muh better than we ware I Know it would bee pleaseng to the Board to have you with tham as Deritor if you cauld cam to meet twise ayear or perhops anly ones may Do

Will you permit meto prapose you at apropertime —

the wealland Cannal buisness Dos not Suit me & I mantiand it to one of the Parties here I am

DearSir very Resptfully
yours

Gerrit Smith Eq^r John · Jacob · Astor
[Sealed with black wax.]

[Addressed] Gerrit Smith Esqr., Petersbraw, Madison Caunty State New york

[Postmarked] New-York, Dec 23   18 [and] 2 [cents postage]

127. LETTER FROM ASTOR TO GERRIT SMITH, FEBRUARY 22, 1830, IN REGARD TO THE MOHAWK AND HUDSON RAILROAD.

John I. De Graff, James Renwick, a professor of natural and experimental philosophy and chemistry in Columbia College, and Churchill C. Cambreleng had been "appointed a committee to examine and report a proper location for the railroad." Proceedings upon their report had, at the meeting of September 25, 1829, on Astor's motion, been suspended until a future meeting. On May 22, 1830, Cambreleng, Astor's friend and former agent, was appointed the commissioner at an annual salary of $2,000, or considerably more than that which Astor thought too high in De Graff's case. The agreement between Astor and Smith, to which the former referred, concerned the purchase of stock by Smith from Astor.

Newyork 22 feb^y 1830 [1]

Dear Sir

I have your letters of 29 Decr. and 20 Jany what you mantion to me in confidence Shall & will allways Remain So — nothig has ben Done of late about the Rail Road we Did not get M^r. White for while we Reflected he came to Say that he was engagd to the South — we have Sence than had Several offers of the Servis of gentlemen but none with whom we are certainly Satisfied Several are under consideration & I Supose an allection will take place in the cours of 2 or 3 weeks

M^r. Degroff M^r. Renwick & Cambrelig ware a Commitee on Some buississ of the Road in Sepr. last & So continu the 2 latter gentlemen Left finally the Motter to M^r. Degroff *who in my opinion Did not* give it the attention Requisit & I think he Showd him self the off handed man which you Describd — he is not nor is any one else apointed as agent his pric is 1500$ I thik it too mush — we want very mush agood engineer all the Rest we caught tho I have and allways have had Some fears about getting the Proper quantety of land at the Dermination of the Road at Albany M^r. D G had a Chance to Secure it but

[1] Ms., Syracuse University, Gerrit Smith Miller Collection.

he put it off and now the owner gel Van Ransselear is gone South & we must wait his Return thus you See nothig or little has ben Done M^r. DG made Some Bargain at or near Schenectady good or Bade I know not also a very Loose one at Albany *I writ to you in confidenc & for yourSelf only* —

with all this I have agood opinion of the undertaking & have no Doubt but it will all com Right

On Reflection it is found that the agreement which you Send me Sctch off will not So well answer & I Send you ane which in the Result is the Same as to yours if you aprouve you will Sign if not State your objectians — a Bond & Mortage given by you to M^r. Bonner has ben offerd for Sale here & I have agreed to take it its for 12000$ I presume all is Right & that you have no objectians to my holding it —

the 250 Shares of Rail Road Stock which I Sold to you are of what I Subscribed for as I have not ben able to get the 250 which I originaly ment for you & tho I engagd tham it is not Certain that I will get tham at present there is none to be had as I Know of & I thick that So Soon as we get a going the Stock will Rise cansiderably — I am Dear Sir

Respectfully yours

John · Jacob · Astor

P S. I presume in the Cause of 2 or 3 weeks we Shall have an Engineer & proseed in the *work*
Girrit Smith Eq^r.

Peterboro Madison County St Nyk
[Sealed with black wax.]
[Addressed] Gerrit Smith Esq., Petersbro, Madison County, State Newyork
[Postmarked] New-York, Feb 22

128. LETTER FROM THE HUDSON'S BAY COMPANY TO WILLIAM
B. ASTOR, MARCH 3, 1830, THROWING THE BURDEN OF INITIA-
TING THE ABANDONMENT OF THE LIQUOR TRADE ALONG THE
BORDER UPON THE AMERICAN FUR COMPANY.

See document 125.

Hudsons Bay House [1]
London the 3ᵈ. March 1830

William B. Astor Esqʳ.
    Newyork

Sir
    I am directed by the Governor and Committee of the Hud-
sons Bay Company to acknowledge receipt of your letter dated
15th Decbʳ. last addressed to James Keith Esqʳ. a chief Factor
in the Companys Service, stating that you had been informed
the Company were desirous of stopping the introduction of
spirituous Liquors among the Indians on the line of demarcation between Great Britain and the United States and proposing to pledge yourself that the People of the American Fur
Company shall not in future carry in, or in any way give ardent
Spirits to the Indians of that Region or vicinity, provided the
Hudsons Bay Compʸ pledge themselves to the same effect, and
that the United States Indian Agent at Sault St. Marie has
promised, that if the two Companies agree on the subject, he
will not permit any Individual trader to take any Liquor into
the Country – and I have to inform you that the Governor
and Committee are most anxious to see such a measure carried
into effect, having already accomplished this most desirable
object in a large portion of the Interior with the most beneficial
results to the Indians and to the Trade. The Governor and
Committee have this Season confirmed and repeated the orders
given last year by Govʳ Simpson, that in the event of the
American Traders discontinuing the practice, those in the Serv-

---

[1] Ms., Hudsons' Bay House, London.

ice of the Company should so the same; But the Governor and Committee do not feel justified in leaving their trading Posts on the Frontier totally deprived of Spirits, at the same time I am directed to assure you, that the Governor and Committee have the means of strictly enforcing the instructions given to their Traders; the discontinuance of the Practice will therefore entirely depend on the conduct of the American traders, to which I am to call your attention; and am

Sir

Your m. o. h. St.

WS Sec^y.

129. LETTER FROM ASTOR TO RAMSAY CROOKS, JUNE, 1830, GIVING INSTRUCTIONS FOR A VISIT TO MACKINAC AND DETROIT IN THE INTERESTS OF THE AMERICAN FUR COMPANY.

This letter is of particular interest because it is almost the last written by Astor concerning the affairs of the Northern Department. The instructions are less detailed than usual, indicating Astor's confidence in Crooks. Astor again reverts to his wish to sell out at Detroit — a move steadily resisted by Crooks and Robert Stuart. David Stone, as a member of Stone, Bostwick & Co., had been one of Astor's partners in the Western Department of the American Fur Company.

New York June 1830.[1]

Dear Sir: —

You are so well informed of the object of the contemplated trip which which [*sic*] you are about to make that I need say no more than that you will act at Mackinac & Detroit as shall seem best for the Company. A fair and liberal conduct towards our friends and connections will best become us, and such you,

[1] Ms. book (copy), Detroit Public Library, Burton Historical Collection, and Missouri Historical Society, St. Louis, Letters of Ramsay Crooks, John Jacob Astor, and the American Fur Company, 1813–43.

I know will pursue, particularly with people who have been and are still with us, and who may be interested in our good wishes — this much in general terms — In the purchase of furs it is our business to give them a fair price taking care however not to expose us to any heavy loss, there may however be a case when it may be necessary to extend, and even give more than the goods are worth; the more so when they are of articles in demand and of good quality.

The chief business, however, is the making the new arrangement with the people, and here its the same with the skins for good men.

We cannot pay too dear, and indifferent ones *are at any price too dear.*

You will please note that the engagements are always with the Company and condition that the Company shall long continue.

At the Detroit, you will do the best you can to sell out, would be most agreeable provided it can be done to safe people.

You will probably see Stone, if so, I would like very well that you buy his furs and you may give the price as per note or I would ship them for him charging the same commission as the last and to sell them with and the same as the Company's furs.

If you can, buy Brewster's furs. His Racoons last year were very good, and we might give 55 to 57 1/2 Cents for them, Round Supposing that none have been taken out.

I hand you note of prices etc. and hope you will soon return in good health, let me recommend you not to expose it on any account.

Believe me Dear Sir to be

Yours

J. J. Astor,

R. Crooks Esq.   Pres. Am. Fur Co.

130. LETTER FROM GEORGE BOYD TO JAMES B. GARDINER, AUGUST 18, 1830, DESCRIBING THE PRACTICES OF THE AMERICAN FUR COMPANY.

George Boyd was the brother-in-law of John Quincy Adams and had become Indian agent at Mackinac as the successor to W. H. Puthuff, removed through the influence of the American Fur Company, and soon after his accession he was induced to issue a statement praising the conduct of the Company which now, a decade later, had become in his mind a "great monied Aristocracy." This whole document is valuable for the picture it gives of the workings of the American Fur Company, by one located at the headquarters of its Northern Department and brought into daily contact with its agents and employees, and with the Indians among whom its trade was carried on.

Confidential   Mackinac 18. August 1830 [1]
    Dear Sir,
        Your communication of yesterdays date has been duly received, and I hasten to reply to it.

In answer to query 1st. From official documents it appears, that the sum of $67,408.07 was forwarded to the Indian Country within the year 1826: including the trade on the Upper & Lower Misisippi, Lake Superior & Lakes Huron & Michigan – & this I believe to be a fair average of the Amount Employed in the trade for the preceding four or five years: since 1826 by orders from the War Dept. the usual Agents have been directed to grant Licences only within the limits of their respective Agencies consequently the Amount of capital Employed within the last five years can only be correctly stated by the U. S. Agents at the Sault St Marys & at Prairie du Chiens [sic]

2^{d} Query. The Amount of furs & peltries brought yearly to this Island, are supposed to be worth from 250 to 300,000 dollars — nineteen twentieths of the same being for and on account of the American Fur Co. —

[1] Ms., Wisconsin Historical Society, Madison, Wisconsin MSS., 3 D 122.

3^{d} Query. It is believed to be the policy of the Company [to] control the Indian trade within the limits of the U. States– Either by purchasing out any opposition which may at any time arise contrary to its interest — or by the mere power of money to Crush the individual trader. —

4th. Query. The Traders for the Company generally receive their goods at an advance of 75 per Cent on the Sterling cost— Some on an annual Allowance, & others for a certain [proportion] of the gain on the Outfit — With a full understanding that the Company shall have the refusal of the Returns.

5th It is not within my knowledge that exchanges of any kind have been made between the American Fur C^{o}. & the Hudson's Bay fur C^{o}. within their respective Wintering grounds.

[The answers to the sixth, seventh, and eighth queries deal with attempts of the British to influence the Indians. They contain nothing concerning Astor or the American Fur Company.]

9th query. From the circumstance of more individual capital being about to be Employed in the N^{o}. West fur trade for the present year than formerly, we are induced to believe that the trade is increasing — altho it has been nearly stationary for some years.

10th Query– The amount of Capital Employed by the Company must be very considerable – not so much on account of the goods actually taken into the Indian Country, & sold as the great number of men Employed to carry on the trade. The number of men thus Employed, I should suppose to be from 4 to 500. In 1826, They occupied 50 trading posts.

11th query The principal trading posts are Anna Quiwinnon, Yellow River, Lac Coutoreille, Falls of St Croix, Sandy Lake, Leech Lake, Fond du lac, Red Lake, Grand Portage, Leaf Lake, Vermillion Lake, Lac La Plauie, Capina Lake, Crow Wing River, &^{a}. Lake Superior. — Riveur des Roches, Red

Cedar River, Traverse des Scieux, White Wood River, Lac Traverse, Riveur des Chayennes, Old Mines, Montagne qui parle, Black River, Riveur des Moines, Riveur aux Embaras, & Upper & Lower Mispipippi — Grand River, Beau Clerk Lake, little Kallimink, Kinkikee & Muskegon, Grand Traverse, Lake Michigan — Sandy River, Presquile, Lake Huron.

12 query. The posts [on — stricken through interlineated: at the Red] Cedar Lake & Leech Lake, are contiguous to the Hudsons Bay C°. Posts. — This information however can be more readily obtained from the agent within whose limits the above posts are situated. —

13 query Beaver $3.50 per H Otter $450 per lb Martin $125 pr Skin, Muskrat 20 cts. Bear $4. — Deer Skins 28 pr lb. Foxes $125. Raccoon 45 cts & I should suppose that $5000 dollars would be about the Amount of furs & peltries sold by the Company on the Island annually.

14. query & 15. you you [*sic*] are respectfully referred for answer to those queries, to those agents, who grant Licinces to the American Fur Co. — viz M^r. Schoolcraft, Mr. Stambrough & General Stuart — — I have very little to do with the Comp^y.

16th query. I am well acquainted with Samuel Abbott Esquire of this place— He is a man of honor – faithiful & inteligent & patriotic – in the Employ of the Am. Fur C°. as a clerk I believe at $1000. per annum: and independant in point of property —

17 query – Whisky is allowed in small quantities to each Outfit for the use of the Engagés or men Employed in the laborious part of the Trade, with an explicit assurance that no part of the same be given under any pretences to Indians. —

18th. – Suffer the Indians, in particular ([*sic*] cases as in Robbery or Murder) to give testimony in our courts, and it will go far to do away many of the Evils they at present suffer from our violence & our avarice — and at the same time give the poor Canadians, hirelings for a term of years to hard task-masters, an assurance that there is a power vested somewhere in the Government, to Call this great monied Aristocracy to account, not only for aggressions practised on the red man, but for any maltreatment of any free man trading by their permission within these limits, and under the sanction of their laws, and you will at once divest them of a great portion of that power, which is but too often used to grind down & oppress all within the Circle of their influence:

To effect this let a Board of Comptrol, or of accounts, be established, under the authority the War Dept., composed; say of the principal Agent of the American Fur Co., the Ind. Agent, & the Commanding officer of the post; whose duty it shall be, to see that justice is rendered to all &c Every Canadian, Employed by the Company, & receiving his discharge — With hopes that your labors may be Crowned with success & that they may be honorable to yourself & useful to our Government   I Remain

With great Respect & consideration
to James B. Gardiner Esqr.   Your M^o. Ob^t. Servt. —
    Mackinac.   G[eorge] B[oyd]

131. LETTER FROM ASTOR TO D. W. C. OLYPHANT, APRIL 8, 1831, WITH TERMS OF AN AGREEMENT FOR THE SHIPMENT OF QUICKSILVER TO CANTON.

After 1827 Astor ceased to carry on commerce with China in vessels owned or chartered by himself, but his connection with the trade in furs, the best market for the finer qualities of which was offered by Canton, kept him from withdrawing entirely from the China trade, though now his goods had to be sent and their proceeds returned, as freight. Quicksilver, from the Spanish Peninsula, was one of the staple commodities in the China trade. Charles Talbot and D. W. C. Olyphant were members of Talbot, Olyphant & Co., the Canton branch of which, Olyphant & Co., is said to have been the only American firm at Canton which refused to participate in the illegal trade in opium. Olyphant, the founder of the Canton house, was a Quaker.

(Duplicate)   New-York 8th. April 1831 [1]
Sir,

The eight hundred flasks of Quicksilver shipped on board the Nile, it is understood are for joint account of M^r. Talbot, yourself and me, each one third. The proceeds are to be vested in Teas and Silks in quantity and kind in pro rata with your and M^r. Talbot's own shipment on board the same Ship, and to be consigned to order– Bills of Lading and Invoice to be forwarded to me in duplicate– The said Goods are to pay thirty dollars per ton freight, to be paid here sixty days after arrival – no commission to be charged here or in Canton for doing the business – you are to insure the Goods out and home payable to me – seven per cent interest is to be charged for advancing money for the Quicksilver here.

The proceeds of the fifteen thousand Pounds Sterling, which M^r. Talbot has authority to draw on me for, are to be vested in like manner and terms on board the Ship Nile as that of the Quicksilver. Two and a half per cent commission is to [interlineated: be] allowed to me on the amount and one per cent for Banker's commission in London. You guaranty the faithful performance of this agreement on the part of M^r. Talbot. [Only below this in Astor's hand.]

I am Respectfully Dear Sir your
Mr Olyphant   Humble Servant
                                                         John·Jacob·Astor

[Endorsed] New York April 11. 1831 I hereby confirm the within   Da. W. C. Olyphant   (Duplicate) Letter to Olyphant 8th April 1832 [sic]

---

[1] Ms., Baker Library, Astor Papers.

132. Agreement by Bryant & Sturgis to Purchase Teas from Astor, July 11, 1831.

Bryant & Sturgis was a leading Boston firm engaged in the China trade.

Bryant [1] & Sturgis have purchased of [Messrs. — stricken through] John Jacob Astor [& Son — stricken through] all the Young Hyson Tea imported by them in the Ship Sultan from Canton, Excepting the Canisters– They are to receive the Tea from the Ship; One pound to be added to the black mark on the whole chests; half chests to be taken at actual tare, & boxes at Inv°. weight–

The Purchasers are to pay for Said Teas by their Note at eight months for fifty Cents p^r. pound, & to give Security, Satisfactory to the Sellers, for the Amount of duty whenever the Teas shall be taken out of bond– The Teas are to be wholly at the risk of the purchasers from the time they are landed, & in case of injury, or destruction, by fire, or otherwise, while under charge of Custom House officers, Bryant & Sturgis engage to hold [Messrs. — stricken through] J. J. Astor [& Son — stricken through] harmless for the amount of duties, which they are to pay whenever they become due to the United States—

New York July 11th 1831   Bryant & Sturgis

Witness Geo: n Sewell

[Endorsed] Agreement with Bryant & Sturgis for Young Hyson Tea p^r Sultan

[1] Ms., Baker Library, Astor Papers.

133. LETTER FROM ASTOR TO THOMAS W. OLCOTT, JANU-
ARY 6, 1832, REQUESTING THE RECOMMENDATION OF SOME
GOOD BANK STOCK.

Thomas W. Olcott was the cashier of the Mechanics and Farmers
Bank at Albany. This letter reveals the policy guiding Astor in his
investments in banks in the New York backcountry. Astor doubtless had his unfortunate son, John Jacob, Jr., in mind in penning the
second paragraph. At this time Astor was considering withdrawing
from business.

Tho⁸. W. Olcott Esq.   New-York 6 January 1832 [1]
   Albany, Dear Sir,
        I will have to receive in the course of this month from 20
to 30m dollars, which I would like to invest as a permanent
investment in some safe stock — no objections to large dividends, but whether that be a little more or less is not so much
a matter, as to have it perfectly safe. Can you recommend me
something. I don't care about putting more than 5000 or
10m in any one Bank, not less than $5000, some of the money
is now in Bank, and all can be had at 5 or 6 days notice.

I see in the excellent message of the Governor, he mention
a Report having been made to our Legislature of last year,
about Hospitals for the Insane, could you obtain me a copy of
that Report and send it to me, I would be much obliged to you
for it.

Money is in demand here and good notes are offered at 9
per cent per ann: I suppose matters will remain so a few
months longer– I don't like to discount paper or make temporary loans, wishing to close my Books – Believe me to be
                                Respectfully your's
                                (signed) John Jacob Astor

P.S. Did not know that I wrote on a half sheet till it was done,
you will excuse it.

[1] Ms. book, Baker Library, Astor Papers, Letter Book ii, 1831–38, p. 21.

134. Letter from Astor to Francis Granger, January 27, 1832, describing the Difficulties attending the Construction of the Mohawk and Hudson Railroad.

Francis Granger was evidently a member of the New York assembly, before which, at this time, was an act authorizing the construction of a branch road and the issuance of an additional $100,000 of capital stock, to be subscribed by the stockholders of the Albany and Schenectady Turnpike Company, with which the Mohawk and Hudson had come into competition. This act was passed April 2.

Francis Granger Esq.   New-York 27th. January 1832 [1]
    Albany, Dear Sir,
         On receipt of a request from The Honorable the House of Assembly, to answer several inquiries, in accordance with the resolution by you introduced; immediate attention was of course given thereto, and I presume the statement requested will go forward by the mail which carries this.

Permit me, for your information, to make a few remarks, which may in some degee account for the heavy expense attending the construction of the Rail Road, as I now understand and believe to be true. It was several years before the Stock was subscribed for, and after that, many of the Stockholders became discouraged and proposed rather to forfeit the payment made, than to pay more until some change in the Direction took place. This so much shortened the time allowed by the charter to finish the Rail Road, that it became necessary to use and employ all means to get the work done with the utmost possible expedition, which has put the Company to an expense of perhaps $40m more than if there had been more time to do the work in. Next it was resolved to construct the Rail Road in the most solid and best manner possible, to make it useful and durable, so as to answer the purpose contemplated by the Honorable the Legislature and the Public. The

---

[1] Ms. book, Baker Library, Astor Papers, Letter Book ii, 1831–38, pp. 27–28.

Company were also in some cases obliged to pay more for the land, than was contemplated – The Engines & Machinery in expense exceeded our calculation, so that you will see by the statement sent that the Company have expended about $480m, and that about 70 to 75$m more will be required to pay engagements and to finish and complete the work – The Branch Rail Road we do not know what it will cost, but suppose $100m.

Although this work cost greatly more than was first contemplated, I am still of the opinion that it will pay. No doubt a Rail Road can be built at a less price, but I doubt the policy of it, saving the extra expense we have been put to. I was a large subscriber to the stock, but I am not so much interested, having given most of it to different persons at par.

If you wish for any other information it will be given with pleasure – The winter having set in early with extreme severity has operated much against us – You will readily perceive that this [interlineated: being the] first undertaking of the kind in our State we laboured under many disadvantages

> I am Respectfully, Sir,
> Your Ob^t. Servant
> (signed) John Jacob Astor

135. Letter from Astor to Vincent Rumpff, April 9, 1832, in regard to the Morris Case and Miscellaneous Matters.

Viscount Vincent Rumpff, a Swiss and minister from the German Free Cities to France, had married Astor's youngest daughter, Eliza, on December 10, 1825. Astor took care of his investments in America, some of which were doubtless derived from the marriage portion brought him by his wife. Astor's second daughter, Dorothea, who had married Walter Langdon in 1812, was visiting in Europe at this time. The payment made to Astor by the State legislature was for the purpose of extinguishing his claim to lands in Putnam County, to which he had purchased the rights of the

Morris family, from whose parents, who possessed only a life interest in the property, it had been confiscated during the Revolution. It will be observed how casually Astor speaks of investing in a quarter million of stock.

Vincent Rumpff Esq New-York 9 April 1832 [1]
    Paris, Dear Vincent,
        I received your kind letter of 1st March and trust you will have received one I wrote to you by last packet. since then I bought for you some shares in the Union Bank as you will see per Account herewith, they stand in the name of William, in trust for you, the interest they pay is uncertain, but is generally from 5 to 6 per cent per annum.

You will find enclosed Bill for Balance of your Account. I remit this to you because I have no other directions how to apply it – if hereafter you wish it to be vested, then please write to William to that effect. Please say to Eliza that I will write to her by next packet and to inform M[rs]. Langdon that we are all well.

You will be glad to learn that our State Legislature have passed a law to pay me $560.000, which they say is ready in 5 per cent stock which they will pay perhaps in 60 or 90 days – $40.000 of this belongs to other people and the rest $520.000 to me, I had much trouble and little profit by this transaction, though people think I made a fortune by it– The 3 per cent stock will be paid in October– I made arrangement for that of our dear Eliza to put it at 5 per cent for 10 or 15 years interest half yearly – before I leave here, I will see this carried into effect, I think it safe, it is at least as much so as any local Stock we have– I take myself $250.000 of it – my love to dear Eliza, with great regard I am Dear Vincent
                        Your's most truly
                      (signed) J. J. Astor
[Endorsed] 1st. per Sully   10 Apr
    2" " Francois 1.20 "

[1] Ms. book, Baker Library, Astor Papers, Letter Book ii, 1831–38, p. 44.

136. LETTER FROM ASTOR TO F. & N. G. CARNES, JUNE 5, 1832, AGREEING TO SEND GOODS ON FREIGHT FROM CANTON TO NEW YORK IN ONE OF THEIR SHIPS.

F. & N. G. Carnes was not one of the old and well-established firms in the China trade and had till recently been engaged in trade with France. Shortly after this the firm gained notoriety by having French goods copied in China at ridiculously low prices. The provision in this agreement that Astor should have some cargo space from New York to Canton, free, will be noted. Furs, the outward cargo, were, of course, more valuable in proportion to their weight than was the return cargo of tea.

F. & N. G. Carnes   N York June 5 1832.[1]
Gentlemen.

I agree to take One Hundred Tons freight in the ship Howard from Canton to New York and to pay at the rate of Thirty Dollars pr ton, payable in sixty days after the goods are delivered here and I am to have Twenty Tons freight out say from this to Canton freight free. The goods home will be Tea, & out furs.

                                    Signed   J. J. Astor

137. LETTER FROM W. B. ASTOR TO JOHN K. BEEKMAN, AUGUST 4, 1832, IN REGARD TO THE UNPAID RENT OF THE PARK THEATRE.

The Park Theatre, the leading New York playhouse of its time, was owned jointly by Astor and Beekman and leased by Edmund Simpson. The cholera epidemic which occurred in the summer of 1832 naturally caused the suspension of all theatrical performances. J. G. Coster's lot was one of those occupying the block on which Astor planned to erect a hotel.

[1] Ms. book, Baker Library, Astor Papers, Letter Book ii, 1831–38, p. 57.

John K. Beekman Esqr.   New York 4th. Augst. 1832.[1]
Saratoga Springs
  Dear Sir
      I have received your favor of the 30th. Ulto: And will
take an early opportunity to get the alteration in the policies of
the Theatre made – Since I wrote you M^r. Simpson's check for
rent has been returned as unpaid and we have also a second
check from him which is unpaid, but which he says he will
make good in a day or two: To day we shall receive another
check so that unless he makes good the checks we already have
in the conn [course?] of this day we shall have three unpaid.
I presume you are willing under the present distressed state of
the city to indulge him. Indeed to urge him at present would
be I am sure of no avail. I deposit to day the $1000 to your
credit in the Bank of New York. My father has bought
Coster's lot.

I am very respectfully
Your Obed^t Servt.
(Signed) W. B. Astor.

138. INVOICE OF GOODS DELIVERED TO THE IROQUOIS OUTFIT,
SEPTEMBER 1, 1832.

The territory occupied by each department of the American Fur
Company was divided into a number of areas, each of which was
assigned to a particular outfit, at the head of which was a trader, to
whom the goods delivered to the outfit were charged and who presided over the clerks who managed the various trading posts located
at strategic points throughout the outfit's region. This is a fairly
typical small outfit; the ordinary annual invoice, however, would
be somewhat larger. The "high wines," mentioned in this invoice,
was a trade term for practically pure alcohol, much favored by Indian traders because a quantity occupying only a little space could
be greatly increased by the addition of water.

[1] Ms. book, Baker Library, Astor Papers, Letter Book ii, 1831–38, p. 82.

Invoice of Sundry Goods delivered Noel Vasseur for and on a/- of Iroquois Outfit. 1832[1]

Quantity & Description	No.	yds.	Price	£	s	d
1 pair 3½ pt Blue Blankets			22/9	1	2	8
1 " 3 " Green "			18/8		18	8
40 " 3 " White "			17/7	35	3	4
35 " 2½ " "			13/-	22	15	
6 " 2 " "			8/11		13	6
6 " 1½ " "			6/9			6
6 " " "			6/2		17	
2 ps Com: Blue Strouds B. C.			62/4	6	4	8
1 " Savid List Blue Cloth No	549—	18 yds.	2/10	2	11	
1 " " " "	5—	19 "	2/9	2	12	
1 " " " "	9—	19¼ "	2/9½	2	13	
1 " Grey " "	155—	18¾ "	2/10	2	13	
1 " " " "	659—	18¼ "	3/11	2	16	
4 " " " "	39—	20 "				
" " " "	49—	20 "				
" " " "	19—	19¼ "				
" " " "	18—	19¾ "				
" " Scarlet Cloth	78—	78¾ "	5/9	22	12	10
1 " " "	127—	20¾ "	2.37½	49	2	8
1 " Sattinett		18 "	3/1	2	15	6
1 " White Molton		13¾ "	56	7	7	0
			43/4	2	3	4

[1] Ms. book, Public Archives of Canada, Ottawa, Invoices Outward C, American Fur Company, Northern, September, 1829–May, 1834, pp. 288–290.

3	ps Domestic Stripe	$141\frac{1}{2}$ yds.	11^c				15	57
5	" " "	186 "	$12\frac{1}{2}^c$				23	25
4	" " Plaid	147 "	$10\frac{1}{2}^c$				15	44
3	" " "	$91\frac{1}{4}$ "	$10\frac{3}{4}^c$				9	80
4	" " $\frac{3}{4}$ Brown Cotton	$117\frac{1}{4}$ "	7^c				8	21
4	" " $\frac{4}{4}$ " "	$138\frac{1}{2}$ "	$7\frac{1}{2}^c$				10	39
1	" Printed "	30 "	$15\frac{1}{2}^c$				4	65
4	" $\frac{3}{4}$ Bleached "	$119\frac{1}{4}$ "	$10\frac{1}{4}^c$				12	22
2	" Printed Cotton	57 "	16^c				9	12
1	" " "	29 "	$16\frac{1}{2}^c$				4	79
1	" " "	28 "	17^c				4	76
5	" " "	$138\frac{3}{4}$ "	18				24	97
3	" Navy Blue "	$86\frac{3}{4}$ "	$18\frac{1}{4}$				9	98
2	" " " "	56 "	$12\frac{1}{2}$				7	00
3	" " " "	92 "	15^c				13	80
12	" " " "	$345\frac{1}{4}$ "	$16\frac{1}{4}^c$				56	18
1	" $\frac{4}{4}$ Printed Shawls	$1\frac{2}{12}$ doz	7/10		9	2		
1	" $\frac{5}{4}$ " "	1 "	13/5		13	5		
1	" $\frac{6}{4}$ " "	11/12 "	15/4		14	1		
1	" $\frac{8}{4}$ " "	$1\frac{6}{12}$ "	31/6	1	1			
1	" Blue Cotton Hdkf:	$\frac{8}{12}$ "	2.19				3	29
1	" " Flag "	$1\frac{1}{12}$ "	$1.87\frac{1}{2}$				2	03
1	" Black Silk "		7.50				7	50
2	prs Fine Sattinett Pantaloons		3.00				6	00
6	" " " "		2.25				13	50
2	doz Country Socks		3.00				6	00
26	Rolls Taffeta Ribbon		$62\frac{1}{2}$				16	25

Item	Price			Amount
4 Gro: Scarlet & Striped Gartering	9/8	1	18 8	7 84
8 Pierced Broaches No 2	98ᶜ			8 20
10 " " " 3	82			
20 " " " 4	62ᶜ			12 40
20 " " " 5	36			7 20
100 " " " 6	30ᶜ			30 00
200 Large Com: "	3.00			6 00
200 Small	2.00			4 00
632 Pairs Large Round Ear Bobs	8ᶜ			50 56
400 " Small "	7ᶜ			28 00
1 doz Am: Playing Cards	1.50			1 50
4 lbs All Col: Thread No 22	2/4		9 4	
1 " White " 60	3/5		3 5	
1 " " 80	4/4		4 4	
6 Gro:Stone Finger Rings	3/6	1	1	
1 " Brass Thimbles	2/4		2 4	
6 doz Cartouch Knives	3/3		19 6	
6 " Scalping "	3/5	1	" 6	
1¼ " Brass Inlaid "	6/–		7 6	
2 Cards plated Spurs	1.87½			3 75
2 doz Horn Combs	44			88
1 " "	.37½ᶜ			38
1 " 2½ In Ivory "	87½ᶜ			88
1 " 3 "	106¼ᶜ	1		1 06
4 Papers Hawk Bells	37½			1 50
1 M Rifle Flints	87	8	"	
⅓ doz 18th: Cod Lines	22/10	7	8	

Description	Rate		
1 doz Snaffle Bridles	4.75	4 75	
1 " Curb "	5.25	5 25	
½ " Plated "	24.00	12 00	
1 " Leather Surcingles	7.00	7 00	
2 " Waist Belts	3.75	7 50	
6 prs Ox Hide Shoes	80ᶜ		4 80
5 " Mens " 2ᵈ	87½ᶜ	4 38	
5 " " "	85ᶜ	4 25	
1 doz Pint Tin Cups	87½	4 88	
10 Bunches Mock Garnets	40ᵒ	4 00	
1⅓ lbs Black Beads	30ᵒ	1 43	
1⅓ " Vermillion	1.10ᵒ	1 47	
2 Gro: Pipes	2/3	4 6	
6 American Rifles	9.50	57 "	
6 North West Guns 3 feet	5.56	33 36	
1 Nest Brass Kettles 46 lbs	48ᶜ	22 08	
2 " Tin " 14 "	13.50	27 00	
2 Boxes Balls 160 "	11ᶜ		17 60
1 " Shot B 75 "	7ᶜ	5 25	
24 Half Axes	60ᶜ		14 40
24 Tomahawks	40ᵒ		9 60
1 Box Soap 28 "	7½		2 10
1 Barrel Shrub 34 Gals	103	35 02	
10 " High Wines 339½ "	48		162 96
1 " Sup: Fine Flour	535		5 35
2 " Biscuit 150 lbs	7ᵒ		10 50
1 " Pork	8.56		8 56
1 Keg Tobacco 110 "	10ᵒ		11 00

4 Kegs Powder	9.25		37 00	
108 lbs Maple Sugar	6¼ᶜ		6 75	
4 English Bale Cloths	1.50ᶜ			6 00
8 " "	75ᶜ			6 00
1 N. Y. Trunk	2.25			2 25
1 Box for Guns	1.25			1 25
2 Boxes	75ᶜ			1 50
6 " for Shot &c	40ᶜ			2 40
1 Keg " Tobacco	37½ᶜ			38
1 Cask for Shrub	125			1 25
2 " " Biscuit	50ᶜ			1 00
	123 16 11		775 45	275 65
	100 6 3		100 81	876 26
Advance on Stg: 81 per Cent & on N. York	224 3 2 Equal to		996 26	
13 p Cent Entered September 1. 1832				
				2148 17
5 per Cent Commission				107 41
				$2225 55 [sic]

[In margin: Overcharge of 40 Gallons H. Wines on Beads

        "   on Beads

19 20	
38	
$19 58	
98	
$20 56]	

5 p Cent

139. LETTER FROM ASTOR TO OLYPHANT & CO., MAY 3, 1833, IN REGARD TO THE CHINA TRADE.

Although Astor was in Europe at this time, he kept closely in touch with his interests in the fur trade and the commerce with Canton. This letter, written in his name by his son, might as well have been written by Astor himself. Part of the goods which Astor had his correspondents in Canton ship to him at New York might be paid for from the proceeds of furs and quicksilver he himself shipped to Canton. For the rest, his Canton correspondents would draw on his London agents from funds which Astor had placed in their hands, sometimes from the sales of furs or of stocks in Europe.

Messrs. Olyphant & Co New-York 3^d May 1833 [1]
   Canton,
      Gentlemen,
         Since my respects of the 13th. March of which the above is copy, I am favored with your esteemed letters of 8 and 30 Novr. 12. 13. 14. 20 and 29 Decr. last with a/c Sales of the 9 casks Otter Skins per Howard which did very well, nett proceeds \$16702^{01}.

I observe that you had drawn for £5000 and £3000 on London to be employed in filling for my account in the Morrison, and that you had also drawn on Messrs. Gillespies Moffatt, Finlay & Co. for the £15000 say fifteen thousand pounds sterling being the credit given M^r. Olyphant in favor of M^r. Talbot in June last. I am sorry to see the very low rate of exchange with you on London & the more as the prices of teas in Canton are so high that there is not much prospect of making a saving trade this season. We are daily expecting the Howard and the Morrison – In the Autumn I propose to ship you a considerable parcel of fine furs

                I am very respectfully
                Gentleman Your Ob^t. Servt.
                   John Jacob Astor
                   (signed) Wm B. Astor

[Endorsed] 1st. per Superior sailed May
      2^d " Clematis   "   "

140. LETTER FROM ASTOR TO BERNARD PRATTE & CO.,
JUNE 25, 1833, ANNOUNCING HIS INTENTION OF DISSOLVING
THEIR CONNECTION IN THE FUR TRADE.

Ill-health had caused Astor to decide to withdraw entirely from
commerce. One step in this process was to terminate the partnership with Bernard Pratte & Co. in the Western Department of the
American Fur Company.

Geneva 25th. June 1833– [1]

Gentlemen

Wishing to retire from the Concern in which I am engaged
with your House, you will please to take this as notice thereof,
& that the agreement entered into on the 7th. May 1830– between your House & me on the part of the American Fur Company will expire with the outfit of the present year on the terms
expressed in said agreement

I am Gentlemen your humble Serv[t].

Mess[rs]. Bernard, Pratt & Co.   John · Jacob · Astor
       St. Louis   For Self & AmfurCo

141. LETTER FROM ASTOR TO WILSON P. HUNT, MAY 4, 1834,
ON PERSONAL MATTERS AND MISSOURI LAND.

Hunt had been a member of the Pacific Fur Company and Astor's personal representative at the Columbia River. Astor had
assisted him to obtain the postmastership at St. Louis. Benjamin
Clapp, formerly a clerk of the Pacific Fur Company, had more
recently been engaged in the fur trade both as an employee of the
American Fur Company and on his own account. This letter reveals the weakness of Astor's nerves shortly after his return from
Europe and also mentions one of the reasons for his condition. Yet
despite his feebleness he could still think of business. He was in

[1] Ms., Missouri Historical Society, St. Louis, P. Chouteau Collection, Pierre
Chouteau Papers.

the process of withdrawing from the American Fur Company, and Hunt, residing at the headquarters of its Western Department, had been applied to for assistance. Astor had loaned money to Hunt in order to enable him to purchase and develop lands near St. Louis, taking security in the form of a mortgage; the investment had proved to be unprofitable.

Wilson P. Hunt Esq: New York. 4th May 1834 [1]
  Postmaster

S^t. Louis. Dear Sir, I rec^d. your letter 21st. March 1833. in Europe, where I past some time, to the loss of much health. I am getting some better, but slowly. I hope my dear Sir you are well. Poor Clapp lost his Wife after 24 hours indisposition. As to me, while absent, I lost Wife Brother Daughter Sister, Grandchildren & many friends & I expect to follow very soon. I often wish you were *near me*, I should find much in your society which I am in need of. being no longer disposed to business, or rather not able to attend to it, you know that I gave up a good part, & am about to dispose of the rest. I believe you have been written to for assistances which I hope you will give. About our own matter I was sorry to see that some claim is made on part of the Land: how much of it, you did not mention. Whether it will be best to take a conveyance from you now, or wait I cannot say, perhaps you can judge best, and I would like to have your opinion. I should like to have it closed if you deem best. Of this you will please write to me, and also say if you please what may be the supposed value of it. M^r. Pratte seemed to think 2 years ago, that it would rise much Believe me, Dear Sir, to be ever,

Respectfully Yours
(Signed) John Jacob Astor

[1] Ms. book, Baker Library, Astor Papers, Letter Book ii, 1831–38, p. 229.

142. LETTER FROM ASTOR TO ROBERT STUART, JUNE 4, 1834,
IN REGARD TO THE FUR TRADE AFTER ASTOR'S RETIREMENT
FROM THE AMERICAN FUR COMPANY.

When Astor withdrew from the American Fur Company he sold
his interest in the Northern Department to a group headed by Ramsay Crooks, and disposed of his interest in the Western Department
to the St. Louis traders who had been his partners since 1826 in the
fur trade of the Missouri. Astor did not, however, at one stroke
sever all connection with the fur trade. It is evident from this letter
that he still possessed an interest in the returns of some of the Company traders in the Northern Department ("our own people"),
though most of "the property, debts &c" had doubtless been sold.
"Mr. Hoghland" apparently sometimes acted as the Company's
agent in making fur purchases. He may have been identical with
J. C. Hoghland, of Steubenville, Ohio, a fur trader with whom Astor
had some correspondence about this time. The "Indian treaty"
was that recently made at Chicago. The Company intended to lay
claim to part of the funds received by the Indians thereunder, on the
ground that the Indians were indebted to Company traders.

Robert Stuart Esq   New York 4 June 1834 [1]
    Dear Sir,
        We are at last agreed about the agreement. The form is
different from the one you have seen, but the terms and spirit
is the same. After you receive this it will *not* be consistent to
buy furs but from our own people and you will inform M[r].
Hoghland not to purchase any for our account, nor can we be
concerned in any purchase with any one – on the other hand
the new concern are not to buy of our people – I think you will
do well to close as much as you can of all our interest in the
Northern and Detroit departments. You will of course deliver agreeably to agreement & make over to them the property, debts &c sold to them. Of Furs I see no great prospect of
high price except Marten and Deer Skins, these will be higher

---

[1] Ms. book, Baker Library, Astor Papers, Letter Book ii, 1831–38, pp. 232–
233.

than last year. Buffalo Robes will be $4 – fishers and Lynx — wild cats will also do well — fine Beaver will do to ship at 4½ to $5 per pound. Muskrats very low say good 16 to 18 cents, of these we have too many & no sale as yet – should not be surprized if they were to fall to 15 cents – you best sell all you can at Mackinac – good Otters are wanting. I am told that the Indian treaty is all arranged

Respectfully your's
(signed) John Jacob Astor

143. LETTER FROM ASTOR TO MRS. MARY REYNELL, OCTO-BER 3, 1834, IN REGARD TO A CHARGE TO HER OF INTEREST ON MONEY ADVANCED.

Mrs. Mary Reynell was one of the daughters of Astor's brother George Peter. This correspondence was in regard to an advance which had been made to her by Astor on account of a bequest by Henry Astor, on which advance some clerk had probably charged her interest. There was some friction between Astor and his nephews and nieces, which was not ameliorated by the action of Henry Astor in willing most of his large fortune of one-half a million to William B. Astor instead of to his less prosperous relatives. Astor occasionally replied to appeals for assistance from some of his relatives by sending them sums of money and advising them to look for work.

New York 3ᵈ Octʳ. 1834.[1]

Dear Mary, (Mʳˢ. Mary Reynell, London)

I have received your letter of the 14ᵗʰ August in which you express your surprise at being Charged Interest on money advanced you. Permit me to state to you that the charge of Interest is not only Correct but strictly just. I was not here when it was made. If I had been it is very probable that it would not have been made, at least for the time that I advanced the money. As to the rest it is matter of the Executors

---

[1] Ms. book, Baker Library, Astor Papers, Letter Book ii, 1831–38, p. 260.

of whom there are four. On looking at the account, I find the whole amount of Interest Charged to you is about £19. and not £50. as you suppose or are pleased to state. The difference is in the Exchange between this and London which was then about 8 p^r Cent against you. There was no intention on my part nor that of my Son to make a profit out of you and I think your remark is not well applied. As to the division of my Brothers estate not being to the satisfaction of all, it is no fault of mine. As it Certainly was not my intention to charge you interest, I remit you herewith a Bill for the Amount. — I suppose you have been informed of the death of your brother Benjamin. He left his Wife pennyless.

I am dear Mary Yours
Sig^d. J. J. Astor

Drt. enclosed on Gillespies Moffat Finlay & C°. sight for £19. st^g

[Endorsed] 1st. per Geo: Washington to Liv^l.

      2"   "   Montreal   Lon. 16 Oct.

144. LETTER FROM ASTOR TO J. A. G. OTIS, MARCH 13, 1835, IN REGARD TO THE TERMS OF LETTING ASTOR'S HOTEL.

Astor evidently intended to take no risk of loss from having the hotel operated on his own account.

J. A. G. Otis Esq   New York 13th March 1835 [1]
    Boston

    Sir, I have received your letter of the 9th inst: I have not let the Hotel I am building on Broadway, nor do I intend it for any particular person.

    In regard to furnishing the Hotel, I should expect the tenant to provide a large proportion of the furniture required, if not the whole of it. I observe your remarks as to the course pur-

---

[1] Ms. book, Baker Library, Astor Papers, Letter Book ii, 1831–38, p. 288.

sued in regard to the Tremont Hotel, and its having been managed for the three first years for account of the proprietors, in order to determine the probable income of the establishment, and also what would be a fair rent for the 10 ensuing years. I have no wish to have the Park Hotel managed for my own account – nor do I think such course would be the least desirable in order to ascertain what a fair rent might be. I should be willing to let the Hotel at a fixed rent to be agreed upon and to extend the term of lease on reasonable terms

I am respectfully

Your Ob^t Servant

John Jacob Astor

(signed) W^m. B. Astor

145. Letter from Astor to J. J. Janeway, June 27, 1835, enclosing a Contribution for Tornado Sufferers.

Astor's contemporaries did not regard him as greatly given to charity. This letter is interesting as fixing one occasion upon which he did contribute, apparently unsolicited.

J. J. Janeway Esq   New York 27 June 1835 [1]
  New Brunswick, N. J.
    Sir,
        I enclose you a check for $100 which please receive in aid of the needy who have suffered by the tornado which visited New Brunswick

I am respectfully

Your's

John Jacob Astor

(signed) W^m. B. Astor

[1] Ms. book, Baker Library, Astor Papers, Letter Book ii, 1831–38, p. 308.

146. LETTER FROM ASTOR TO JAMES DUANE DOTY, JULY 16, 1835, IN REGARD TO THE ESTABLISHMENT OF A TOWN AT GREEN BAY.

Among the assets of the American Fur Company, which came to an end in 1834 with Astor's retirement, were lands at Green Bay which had been mortgaged by some of the fur traders who had been forced to take goods at high prices from the Company and had thus fallen into debt. These lands, through foreclosure of the mortgages, now became the property of Astor and his partners, Crooks and Stuart, who associated with themselves, as local agent, the Wisconsin speculator and politician, J. D. Doty, and decided to take advantage of the land boom then going on to lay out a town on their property at Green Bay. Daniel Lord was Astor's attorney in a case arising out of the claims to part of this land, advanced by the children of one of the original owners and an Indian woman. Daniel Whitney was the promoter of Navarino, another town being established at Green Bay for speculative purposes. John Lawe was a leading fur trader at Green Bay, one of those on part of whose land the town of Astor was to be laid out. "Arnat" is probably an error for John P. Arndt, a prominent early citizen of Green Bay.

Judge J. D. Doty   New York July 16th. 1835 [1]
    Green Bay, Dear Sir,
        Since I wrote to you with Mr. Lord's opinion which I hope you have received, I have been called on by the Agent of Mr. Whitney, offering $25.000, which of course was refused, as I do not want to sell other than as I wrote to you, say some lots to people who will build, and reside there. I have now your favor of 16th. June, with a plan or map which I have looked over, and have also submitted to a friend. The plan is thought a good one provided it be suitable to the surface of the ground, which I suppose is the case. There is no objection to any part of it, and you may sign my name, and I suppose Mr. Crooks and Mr. Stuart will have no objection. They are absent, and I

---

[1] Ms. book, Baker Library, Astor Papers, Letter Book ii, 1831–38, p. 312.

think you may sign for all of us. With respect to the name to be given to the town, I can have no objection to mine being used, if it be agreeable to you and the people of the County, I consider it a compliment paid me. I quite agree with you as to the public squares. They will ornament the place and we shall lose nothing by giving them. If there are any trees on any of them, some should be preserved. I fully approve of your plan to be liberal with M^r. Lawe and I regret if his feelings have been hurt. I see you have named some of the streets – Should we not have also a Madison and Monroe Street or Square? And your own name to a street or square, which ever be most agreeable to yourself? I have no doubt, but that, acting on a liberal plan, and with your good management, we shall make something handsome both as to profits and a handsome town. I think $100 for a lot is very cheap, but it may be useful to sell some at that rate. I have no doubt but that useful exchanges can be made with Arnat &c

Yours very respectfully
(signed) John Jacob Astor

P. S. A gentleman by the name of Dawson has just called to purchase. I think he would give 35m, if not 40m dollars, but I will not sell. I return the map herewith

[Endorsed] Copy of this letter sent with map on the 12 Aug^t

147. LETTER FROM ASTOR TO PHILETUS H. WOODRUFF AND PETER J. BOGERT, OCTOBER 30, 1835, CALLING ATTENTION TO THEIR FAILURE TO CONFORM TO SPECIFICATIONS IN BUILDING THE ASTOR HOUSE.

Woodruff and Bogert were the contractors for building the Park Hotel (the Astor House); Isaiah Rogers was the architect. See document 144.

Philetus H. Woodruff $\Big\}$ Esq^{rs}.   New York 30 October 1835 [1]
Peter J. Bogert

Gentlemen,

Some days since M^r. I. Rogers called your attention to certain things at the Hotel, which had not been done agreeably to the contract for building the same, and requested you to make conform to the contract. As you have not yet done so, I give you herewith a memo: of them and desire that they may be made to conform to the contract.

The Walls at the Hotel are 8 inches from the Second floor; they ought to be 12. to the Roof and go only to the attic ceiling in place of going to the roof.

The principal Rafters. There are 3 principal rafters less in the whole roof than the specification requires

The Jack Rafters are 2 feet 6 inches from centres instead of 2 feet from centres.

Iron. The Ironwork required for the principal by specification, not furnished at the Hotel

Braces. There are no braces in the roof altho' they are required by the specification.

Uprights or Struts. No struts under the principals altho' they are required by the specification

Quantity of Timber. There are 4832 feet of Timber less in the roof than is required by the specification

I am respectfully yours
John Jacob Astor
(signed) W^m B Astor

[Endorsed] Deliv^d to M^r. Woodruff same day at his office Mercer S^t.   W. W. B

[1] Ms. book, Baker Library, Astor Papers, Letter Book ii, 1831–38, p. 343.

148. LETTER FROM ASTOR TO S. & F. BOYDEN, MARCH 19, 1836, IN REGARD TO FITTING OUT THE KITCHEN OF THE ASTOR HOUSE.

The Boyden brothers were to manage the Astor House for their own account as leaseholders. James Y. Watkins, Sr., is said to have furnished the kitchenware for the Astor House. John Jacob Astor Ebbets, probably the son of the veteran Astor captain John Ebbets, seems to have been one of Astor's protégés. See documents 144 and 147.

New York 19th. March 1836 [1]

Messrs S & F. Boyden
    Gentlemen

I mentioned to Mr Rogers that I would pay One thousand Dollars towards fitting up the Kitchen &c &c of the Hotel, provided that you should procure and pay for the articles mentioned in a note left with me, as wanted from Messrs Nott & Comp^y. viz Two steam boilers for heating water for the

Bathing Apartments, for washing, cooking, and stewing, that will cost	$1500
A Steam Engine	750
For the Stew table, Ironing table, and fixtures for the drying room,	250
That among articles wanted in the kitchen a boiler to cost	150
	$2,650

All which are to remain as belonging to the Hotel at the expiration of your lease

Respectfully your Obt Sert
(Signed) John Jacob Astor

[Endorsed] Delivered by J. J. A. Ebbets to S. Boyden in person J. J. A. E–

---

[1] Ms. book, Baker Library, Astor Papers, Letter Book ii, 1831–38, pp. 385–386.

149. LETTER FROM ASTOR TO GOVERNOR MARCY, MAY 11, 1837, DISAPPROVING OF THE SUSPENSION OF SPECIE PAYMENTS.

The Panic of 1837 was the climax of a process which had been under way for several years. In the spring of 1834 William B. Astor mentioned "dreadful times" and many failures in New York. On April 15, 1837, he had written: "The failures thus far are confined to heavy land speculators, sufferers by the fire of 35 and such as have imported too largely from Europe." On May 15, 1837, Astor wrote: "Our Banks, it is calculated, will resume specie payments within the year." Had he written "within a twelve month," he would have been correct almost to a day; specie payments were resumed on May 12, 1838.

His Excellency   New York 11 May 1837 [1]
   Governor Marcy,   Dear Sir,
                        If you are told that I had been in favor of the suspension of specie payment, I beg leave to assure you that the contrary was the case. I consider it a great misfortune to our country. 3 or 4 days more would have carried us safe. The mischief is done and we must now make the best of it – if an act is passed (as I suppose there will be) in favor of the Banks; I hope the Banks will be well restricted in their new discounts, by which means they may soon resume specie payment say within 12 months–

                    I am Dear Sir
                        very respectfully
                        your Ob[t] Servant
                        (signed) John Jacob Astor

150. LETTER FROM ASTOR TO GERRIT SMITH, AUGUST 5, 1837, AGREEING TO LOAN SMITH MONEY ON THE SECURITY OF REAL ESTATE AND BANK STOCK.

Astor loaned this money to Smith during the Panic of 1837 because the latter was "land poor," his father having just died and

[1] Ms. book, Baker Library, Astor Papers, Letter Book ii, 1831–38, p. 491.

left him about 1,000,000 acres of land, of great potential value but of little immediate productivity.

Gerrit Smith Esq,   New York 5 Augt. 1837 [1]
    Peterboro', Dear Sir,
        I have your favor of the 3^d. inst: and note all you say. I will loan to you as you desire $200.000 as you propose to pay 2 bonds which I hold, it will be the more easy to make up this sum. You will please to draw on me for $25.000 at sight, as I have that sum in Bank and do not wish to lose interest – I expect to charge you interest after the 12th inst: on this sum, but you may draw on receipt of this — the money is at your order. My son is absent – on his return will write to you more fully – The Loan will be for 3 years for the whole amount, and after that to be paid by seven instalments – the security you will make satisfactory– The Oswego property I expect will do, if not, you will please add some Bank Stock as you mentioned in your letter

               I am Dear Sir
               Respectfully Your Ob^t S^t.
               (Signed) John Jacob Astor

P. S. The Bond (of course) you will send to me hereafter, and I will let you know from time to time when to draw on me.

151. LETTER FROM ASTOR TO J. D. DOTY, MAY 31, 1838, IN REGARD TO THE GREEN BAY LANDS.

Astor found it difficult to realize that in developing lands in Wisconsin other methods must be employed than those which proved effective on Manhattan Island. To lease lots rent-free, for example, was something which it was hard for him to approve. See document 146.

----

[1] Ms. book, Baker Library, Astor Papers, Letter Book ii, 1831–38, p. 507

J. D. Doty Esq   New York. 31 May 1838 [1]

   Astor, Green Bay,

      Dear Sir,   I have your favour of the 1st. inst: and note you have leased some lots, for which we get no rent, how the proprietors will approve I know not. I see you had also some additions made to the Hotel, you do not say what, if any additional rent Mr Rogers is to pay. I observe, your State contemplates making a loan. At present stocks are low – I do no business of that or any kind, it will however give me pleasure if I can to be of use. Should Congress give a grant for some lands, it will facilitate the negotiation

                    Your's respectfully
                    (signed) John Jacob Astor

152. LETTER FROM ASTOR TO GERRIT SMITH, DECEMBER 5, 1839, IN REGARD TO OVERDUE INTEREST ON SMITH'S BOND.

Smith sometimes found it hard to meet his interest payments promptly. In such cases Astor required additional security. See document 150.

Gerrit Smith Esqu

Peterboro   New York 5th. Decr 1839 [2]

   Dear Sir

      I am favored with your letter of the 2nd inst. enclosing three Certificates 2 of Rochester City Bank, and one of Utica Banks with assignments –

   I regret that I cannot grant the request you make, to let you draw on me for $4000, on or after the 1st. proxo., retaining the Stock and Assignments as security for your repayment of that amount, and, for the payment of the $7000 interest on your

---

[1] Ms. book, Baker Library, Astor Papers, Letter Book ii, 1831–38, p. 589.

[2] Ms., Syracuse University, Gerrit Smith Miller Collection.

bond, until it shall be convenient for you to pay those amounts. — I am sorry that you should be obliged to make sacrifices. Having many engagements to comply with myself and meeting with various disappointments in the Collection of monies, I must make sacrifices in order to fulfil them — If you cannot pay me the Amount of interest on your bond, Shall I sell as much of the Stock you have sent me Certificates for, at the price it will bring, as will pay it. — There are two modes here of selling Stock, one by Publick Sale or Auction and the other at the Brokers Exchange Board. Please say which of these two, in case of a Sale, you prefer; and also whether you wish any more of the Stock Sold, than may be sufficient to pay your Interest — if you do I would comply with the wishes you might express on that Subject, by having the Stock Sold and remintting you the proceeds or letting you draw on me for them when I have received them.

I am, Dear Sir,
with great regard
Your friend
John Jacob Astor
P^r W^m. B Astor

Dr Sir,

My father begs me after hearing the preceding letter read to express to you his deep regret in not being able to accede to your wishes in regard to the accomodation you ask —

I am with
great regard
your friend & Servt.
W^m. B Astor
New York   5 Decr. 1839

[Addressed] Gerrit Smith Esq., Peterboro (New York)
[Postmarked] New York, Dec 5   18 [and] 2 [cents postage]

153. LETTER FROM ASTOR TO GERRIT SMITH, JUNE 11, 1840, IN REGARD TO PAYMENT OF INTEREST ON INTEREST.

Astor's scrupulous desire not to accept anything more than he believed to be due to him in a transaction of this kind comes out in this letter. See documents 150 and 152.

My Dear Sir,[1]

I am favored with your letter of the 8th. inst. enclosing your Check for $140 say One Hundred & forty dollars for interest on the interest of your bond & also an allowance for having paid the interest in several Sums and because money has been worth more than 7 percent. — We make the amount of interest on interest $120.65 taking one day less than you do— The difference between 2[d]. amount of $120.65 & $140. the amount of your check say $19.35/100 I do not think you ought to pay, or should be charged with, and I shall credit you with that amount, and let it go against interest to become due hereafter on your bond —

I am Dear Sir,
with great regard
Your Friend
John Jacob Astor

Gerrit Smith Esquire   P[er]. W[m]. B Astor
    Peterboro'   New York   11th June 1840

154. LETTER FROM ASTOR TO GERRIT SMITH, MARCH 24, 1841, OFFERING TO SELL STOCK IN THE COMMERCIAL BANK OF OSWEGO AT A DISCOUNT.

Gerrit Smith Esq[r]   New York 24th March 1841 [2]
    Peterboro   Dear Sir!

I wrote you on the 15th. inst a letter of which a copy is herewith, & have note been favored with a reply —

[1] Ms., Syracuse University, Gerrit Smith Miller Collection.
[2] *Ibid.*

This afternoon M^r. L. Beardsley, the Pres^t. of the Bank of Oswego, called upon me & stated the loss and inconvenience that a suspension of that institution would occasion to the surrounding neighborhood & the very injurious effect it would have on the Value of Real Estate & urged me to make the required advance — as it does not suit me to do so, and being very desirous to avert the anticipated evils he speaks of, I am willing to [part with — stricken through interlineated: sele] my stock at a very heavy sacrifice, say at Thirty three & One third Pr Cent on its par Value

If it suits you to take it at that rate, 33 1/3rd P Cent — you can pay for it at any period, within a reasonable time, that it suits you allowing me Interest from the date of the Sale — I have no doubt I could do better with it here but as I do not wish to injure the institution, or those interested in – its wele doing, I shall take no farther steps until I hear from you, which I beg may be as speedily as possible –

I enclose you a Statement handed to me of the affairs of the Bank which contains ale the information I am in possession of

I am Dear Sir

The amount of Stock I own is Yours Respectfully
$16500 at Par. J. J. Astor
[J. J. A's seal in black wax.]

[Addressed] Gerrit Smith Esq., Peterboro, Madison County, N. Y.
[Postmarked] New York, Mar 25 Paid 3 1/2 [cents postage]

155. LETTER FROM ASTOR TO GERRIT SMITH, APRIL 5, 1841, EXPRESSING HIS BELIEF IN THE FUTURE OF THE COMMERCIAL BANK OF OSWEGO.

Fitz-Greene Halleck, the poet, Astor's amanuensis in this letter, was employed as his secretary from 1832 to his death. See document 154.

New York 5th April 1841 [1]

Gerrit Smith Esq.

Dear Sir,

I have received your favor of the 1st. inst: in which you were so good as to propose the terms upon which you will take my bank stock, which I regret to say I cannot accept. Since I wrote to you I have been informed by persons upon whom I have some reason to [believe — stricken through interlineated: rely] that the assets of the Bank are worth from 50 to 60 per cent. The real estate I am told, is very valuable and will be more so. I believe the Bank is in good hands and if sustained will do well, I trust therefore that on reflection you will conclude to take the stock at the price which I have offered it to you. As respects the payment we will arrange that, tho' at present money is scarce here and very valuable

I am respectfully

Your Ob^t. Servant

John Jacob Astor

P^r. F. G. Halleck

[Endorsed]   J. J. Astor, Ap^l 5th 1841 —

156. LETTER FROM WILLIAM B. ASTOR TO GERRIT SMITH, APRIL 26, 1841, ACCEPTING, ON BEHALF OF HIS FATHER, SMITH'S OFFER FOR THE OSWEGO BANK STOCK.

See documents 154 and 155.

New York 26th April 1841 [2]

Gerrit Smith Esqr

Peterboro,

My Dear Sir,

My father desires me to acknowledge for him the receipt of your letter of the 9th. inst: and to say that he accepts the offer

---

[1] Ms., Syracuse University, Gerrit Smith Miller Collection.
[2] *Ibid.*

you have made of 27 per c^t. for his stock in the Bank of Oswego, and on the terms also mentioned in your letter to him of the 1st. inst. He would prefer, as you suggest he probably would to make the loan for less than $9500 and he therefore understanding that the whole amount for which you are to give your bond be but $1200 or $1300; he would prefer the former amount — My father has received this morning a letter from Mr Beardsley in which he says that you were expecting an answer from my father in regard to the offer you had made him for his stock.

I am my Dear Sir,

with great regard,

Your friend

W^m. B Astor

157. LETTER FROM ASTOR TO GERRIT SMITH, DECEMBER 13, 1841, ACKNOWLEDGING WORD OF THE OSWEGO BANK'S FAILURE.

The check was in payment of the interest on Smith's bonds to Astor. Evidently Astor's optimistic opinion of the bank's future had not been justified. See documents 154, 155, and 156.

Gerrit Smith Esqr New York 13th dec^r 1841 [1]
Peterboro!

My Dear Sir

I am favored with your letter of the 9th inst: and have received from the N Y R State Bank a check for $3920 say three thousand and nine hundred & twenty dollars as advised by you.

I am very sorry to hear of the failure of the Commercial Bank of Oswego — My health is tolerably good at present – I need not say that I should be most happy to see you should

---

[1] Ms., Syracuse University, Gerrit Smith Miller Collection.

you visit our City— The Writer begs to offer his very Cordial
regards to you — I am, Dear Sir, very truly

Your friend

John Jacob Astor

P^r. W^m. B Astor

[Endorsed]   Decr. 13 1841

158. Letter from Astor to Gerrit Smith, May 31, 1843,
requesting Further Security for Smith's Bond.

This letter well illustrates Astor's mingled forbearance and insistence that his interests should be carefully safeguarded in the matter of his large loan to Smith. See documents 150, 152, and 153.

Hellgate near New York May 31. 1843[1]

My dear Sir

Your favour of the 26th inst. addressed to my son, who is
now absent, with the inclosure, has been duly received & its
contents [interlineated: noted] – in reply, I may state, that in
asking additional security for my loan to you, I ask no more
than you offered, at the time the loan was made, as you will
see by referring to your letter of Aug. 1837, and as the security
then given has lessened in value, I trust you will not think it
unreasoneble, that I now ask to have it made good. Your
objections to giving me the additional security do not strike
me as being as well founded as they seem to you to be — in
answer to the first — that it would be unjust to your other
creditors & render them uneasy, it is sufficient to observe, that
they are now well securd — that your original debts to them
have been in every instance more or less diminished, by the
partial payments you have made, & that they ar small compared with that to me — the second objection — that it would
put obstacles in the way of selling the property pledged as

[1] Ms., Syracuse University, Gerrit Smith Miller Collection.

security, should it be for your interest so to do, is removd by an assurance on my part, that I would at any time give up my lien upon such portions as you might wish to sell, upon receiving a just consideration for the amount released — the last objection, that it would impair your credit & trammel your business operations would be an in convenience, to which I should be very unwilling to subject you, but I am persuaded the measur I propos to you would not have that effect, as the security I ask for would still leave a very large amount of unincumberd property in your hands – I do not wish to press the payment of your debt to me, abundant time shall be afforded you for effecting it, provided I have good security, I therefor hope you will give me a mortgage upon the 2500 acres of land, described in your last letter to my son & on assignment of 87 shares in the Oswego Canal Company & I trust you will not consider this an unreasonable requisition.

Should your present debt to me be satisfactorily securd, it would give me great satisfaction to afford you the accommodation of a farther loan. for the purposes specified in yours of the 26th. inst if the security you offerd for it should be found sufficient. . it would not however be convenient to furnish the money, as early as the first of next July.

I have just receivd the cashier's check on the Merchant's bank for $3917.70/100. which will be passed to your credet

very respectfully

J. J. Astor

[Addressed] Gerrit Smith Esquir, Peterboro', New York
[Postmarked] New-York, Jun 2   18 [and] 2 [cents postage]

159. LETTER FROM JOSEPH GREEN COGSWELL TO GERRIT SMITH, JUNE 9, 1843, DECLINING ON ASTOR'S BEHALF TO MAKE A LOAN.

Cogswell had become Astor's companion in the previous year. The weakness of Astor's nerves and his resultant indecision come out clearly in this letter. See documents 150, 152, 153, and 158.

Hellgate June 9th. 1843 [1]

Gerrit Smith Esq.
    Dr Sir

Your favor of the 6th. inst to Mr Astor has just been received by him, which from its contents he finds requires immediate attention, but being enfeebled by the great heat of the weather, he is unable to attend to it himself & has requested me in the absence of his son, to answer it for him— In what he said in his respects of the 31. ult. respecting the proposed loan of $75000, he did not mean to be understood as absolutely binding himself to make it, but as expressing the pleasure it would give him to afford you that accommodation, if the security should be perfectly satisfactory, & he regrets that you should have taken any steps in the business, before this important question was decided. — property in the country has lessened so very much in value within a few years that he would not be willing to take any former estimate of it as the basis of its present value, but he would have as entire confidence in your representation as in that of any man.

Mr Astor is unable at present from his extreme debility, to state in what way this business could be arranged to his satisfaction, he can only say that he cannot proceed with it, in the manner you propose

With very high respect
Your obn sr
Jos. G Cogswell—

[Endorsed] J. G. Cogswell in behalf of John Jacob Astor, June 9 1843 –

[1] Ms., Syracuse University, Gerrit Smith Miller Collection.

160. LETTER FROM WILLIAM B. ASTOR TO GERRIT SMITH,
JULY 11, 1843, GIVING TERMS FOR A LOAN.

Smith declined to furnish the required security and the loan consequently fell through. William B. Astor was of the opinion that
the matter could have been arranged had Smith paid a visit to New
York; he also informed Smith that his father would allow him to
postpone the interest payment, due on the first of the following year,
until the next spring. Evidently Astor wished to assist the son of his
old friend, but could not square the loan with his ideas of how business should be conducted. See documents 150, 152, 153, and 158.

New York 11 July 1843 [1]
My Dear Sir,
    Your favor of the 1ˢᵗ inst: I had the pleasure to receive on
my return after a few days absence from the city. — I have
communicated the contents of your letter to my father, who
requests me to say, as you desire much to borrow the $26000,
that altho' it is not convenient for him to make the loan; still
in order to accede to your wishes, he will lend you that sum; it
being understood that in addition to the mortgage for the 2500
acres in Madison County, and the property in Schenectady
& Oswego, and the Certificate for the Oswego Canal Stock;
you give him mortgages satisfactory to him to the extent of
$26000 and also an assignment of the mortgage held by Mʳ
D. S. Jones: these mortgages & the Oswego Canal Stock to
held by him as security until the payment also of your bond &
mortgage for $200,000. — Should this be acceptable to you,
he would desire you to send an extract of the boundaries &c of
the mortgages & particulars of the bonds you propose to give
that he may form some opinion of the security—

I remain, My Dear Sir
                        with much regard & esteem
Gerrit Smith Esquire   Your friend & Oᵇᵗ Servᵗ.
    Peterboro'   Wᵐ. B Astor
[Endorsed]   W B Astor, July 11, 1843

[1] Ms., Syracuse University, Gerrit Smith Miller Collection.

161. LETTER FROM ASTOR TO ROBERT STUART, SEPTEMBER
9, 1845, IN REGARD TO THE LANDS AT GREEN BAY.

The Panic of 1837 checked the Wisconsin land boom, and consequently wrecked the hopes of Astor and his associates that they
might make large profits from laying out a town at Green Bay to be
sold by building-lots. Their aim henceforth was to salvage what
they could from the wreckage. The great lack of the community at
Green Bay was transportation facilities connecting it with the East.
It will be observed that James Duane Doty, formerly the agent for
the town of Astor, at the time of this letter Governor of Wisconsin
Territory, had tried to keep up land values by mentioning a larger
sum in the deeds he gave to land than was actually paid. Among
those mentioned in this letter whose names are comparatively un-
familiar are Henry S. Baird, a pioneer of Green Bay, formerly president of the territorial council; Daniel Whitney, proprietor of the
town of Navarino at Green Bay; Nathan Goodell, agent of Astor
and his associates; and Morgan L. Martin, who had been elected
territorial delegate to Congress in 1844. It is hard to tell how much
this letter owes to Astor and how much to his son. It is probably
true that in a general way, at least, it expresses Astor's opinions.
See documents 146 and 151.

Robert Stuart Esq.   New York 9 Sep^t. 1845 [1]
        Detroit, Dear Sir. I have the pleasure to own receipt
of your Several letters, say of 5th. July, 28th. ulto: & 3^d. inst:
Messrs Baird, Whitney and Goodell arrived here on the 3^d.
inst: and brought your letter of the 28th. ulto: and Mr Newberry's proposal for a Boat to be built. The objection to accepting Mr. Newberry's offer was that the Steam Boat could
not be made a good security to me for the amount proposed of
$15.000 to be loaned on her, either by taking a bond on the
boat, or in any way we could devise. The security would be
little if any thing more than personal security – Mr Walker,
however, reached here since, and I expect that an arrangement
will be made, and this day consummated with him, to run the

[1] Ms. book, Baker Library, Astor Papers, Letter Book iii, 1845–48, pp. 18–19.

Columbus, or some other boat of equal size and capacity, from Buffalo to Astor, every 14 days for and during the seasons of navigation of the years 1846, 1847 & 1848, commencing upon the opening of the navigation and remaining to the close of it, for which he is to receive $1000 the first year, $500 the second year and $500 the third year. For your more particular information, I send you enclosed a copy of the agreement. Your high recommendation of Cap[t]. Walker was a strong inducement for making an arrangement with him, and the strong reasons urged by you for establishing a steam boat communication to Astor seemed to render an arrangement for that purpose necessary for the prosperity of the Town of Astor, and our interests there. I hope that you will, as I am sure must be the case, approve of this arrangement and signify your approval of it at your early convenience. Mr Walker says that he will probably put the Great Western on this route this Autumn. I shall endeavour, as far as I can, to get the German Emigrants to take the route to Astor, and I understand from Cap[t]. Walker that he will take measures here to get as many passengers as possible. Mr Goodell has given us all the information he has brought with him relative to the lots &c, at Astor, but it is very probable that we shall have to ask both you and him for further information before we see matters clearly, and we shall not fail to send you a list of any discrepancies that we may find as you suggest. I note what you say in relation to instructing Mr Goodell where verbal sales and leases have been neither complied with nor realized to purchase the tax title, but Mr Baird informs me that doing so would not accomplish our object of getting a good title to them. I shall as I have not ceased to do desire Mr Goodell to induce Mr Martin to release the lots he bought for sale of taxes. We have examined the new map Mr Goodell brought down with him which we believe is correct, and may be recorded, excepting such part of the Town as has been vacated, and we have by advice of Mr Baird, inserted a few lines on the map stating that the part vacated is not to go on record. I regret that Govr. Doty appeared hurt, thinking a suspicion was entertained by me from the circumstance that a larger sum was named in the deeds he gave than the sum received. I think he did wrong to name in the deeds any other than the actual consideration. I hope your explanation has been satisfactory to him I note you recommendation to sell now some 50 or 100 lots cheap, but if the opening of a Steam Boat communication with Astor is to be of any avail, it seems to me that it would be better to let the benefit of it be felt before making any sales. Respecting the sale of the Wisconsin Bank lots I shall direct Mr Goodell to interpose, if on further reflection it shall seem for our interest, but we have since he has been here been so much occupied, that on that and some other matters I must write to him a few days hence. I have informed him that I shall soon let him know respecting the purchase he wishes to make of the 3 lots, as also respecting the exchange with the Presbyterian Church, and the Astor Warehouse. Your dft for $603 $\frac{35}{100}$ has not yet appeared, but will be duly honored. I observe that you have received the appointment of superintending the concerns of the Illinois & Michigan Canal C^o. which I am happy to hear is very acceptable to you, and I shall avail myself of your kind offer of your services while at Chicago.   I remain My Dear Sir

Very respectfully & truly your's

John Jacob Astor

(signed) W^m B Astor

P. S. The agreement with Capt. Walker has been completed that is to say executed as before your's &c J. J. A per W. B. A

162. LETTER FROM WILLIAM B. ASTOR TO MRS. SARAH
BOREEL, DECEMBER 13, 1845, ON FAMILY MATTERS.

Mrs. Sarah Boreel was the wife of Baron Robert Boreel, first
secretary of the Dutch legation to France. She was the daughter of
Astor's daughter Dorothea, the wife of Walter Langdon, and was a
favorite with her grandfather. Eliza (Mrs. Matthew Wilks) was
also one of Dorothea's daughters. Christopher Hughes had been
chargé d'affaires at the Hague and Sweden. Charles Bristed was the
son of Astor's daughter Magdalen and John Bristed; he had been
studying at Cambridge University at his grandfather's expense.
John Jacob Astor II, the oldest son of William B. Astor, had also
been studying in Europe at Göttingen. William B. Astor had married Margaret Livingston. The continued feebleness of Astor's
health and his interest in his descendants are both well brought out
in this informal letter from his son.

Mrs Sarah Boreel   New York 13 Dec: 1845 [1]

My Dear Sarah. Your Grandfather desires to send you
his love with the enclosed bill of Prime, Ward & King at 60 d/s
on Hottinguer & Co for frs: 7893. 75/100 a present. The cold
weather and the city do not agree with your Grandfather as
well as the warm weather at Hurl Gate; and he has lost somewhat both in flesh and strength since he moved in from the
country. He is however able occasionally to take a short drive,
and to walk out for a little while. Three weeks ago, I received
a letter from Robt and which refers to a letter he had written
to Mr Cogswell who had not yet answered it. Mr Cogswell on
my referring to him, he said he had omitted to answer the
letter, but it was because he was not able to comply with
Robert's request of introducing the gentleman who brought
the letter to any of our commercial Houses as he (Mr C,) had
no acquaintance with any of them. I presume your mother
and Eliza keep you advised of our city news so far as it may be

[1] Ms. book, Baker Library, Astor Papers, Letter Book iii, 1845–48,
pp. 45–46.

likely to interest you, and therefore I say nothing on those matters. Your mother's house is very magnificent and is greatly admired: it is certainly far superior to any thing we have on this side the water. And your father and mother are quite well satisfied with it. C. Hughes and his daughter are settled at Baltimore which I believe they do not find so agreeable a place of residence as the Hague. We expect Chas. Bristed and John back in the Spring; so that your Grandfather will then have all his grandsons here, which gratification I fervently hope he will have. Your Aunt Margaret unites with me in affectionate remembrance to you and Robert and all your children, and I remain very truly

Your affectionate uncle
(signed) W^m. B. Astor

To save you trouble the bill is drawn in favor of Robert who will have to endorse it.

[Endorsed] 1st. Steamer Cambria from Boston 16 Dec.
2^d. Per Zurich to Havre   16 "

163. LETTER FROM ASTOR TO NATHAN GOODELL, FEBRUARY 5, 1846, IN REGARD TO THE CARE OF THE PROPERTY OF ASTOR AND ASSOCIATES AT GREEN BAY.

The stagnation which had overtaken the town of Astor at Green Bay is clearly revealed in this letter. It is impossible to tell how much of this letter expresses Astor's own ideas and how much those of his son, but the passages about the "deed from the Presbyterian Church" and the silver spoons at the hotel are quite characteristic of Astor. See documents 146, 151, and 161.

Nathan Goodell Esq,   New York 5 Feb: 1846 [1]
    Green Bay, Wisconsin T.
    My Dear Sir. Since writing you on the 30th. ulto: I have your's of the 17th ulto: with receipt for the taxes, also

[1] Ms. book, Baker Library, Astor Papers, Letter Book iii, 1845–48, p. 58.

your account current and advise your draft of the 9th ult: for $300 and of also your draft on the 16[th] ulto: for 552\frac{41}{100}$ both of which have appeared and been accepted. Your acct: has been examined and with the following exceptions is I believe correct. You charge in your a/c 87 cents for recording deed from the Presbyterian Church, of lots 7 and 8 in block 27 which the Church ought to pay: please collect it. In block N°. 8 you have paid taxes for 1845 on lots N[os]. 3. 10 & 11. In your statement of September last you say that N°. 3 was leased to a German who paid taxes and that N[os]. 10 and 11 are leased to Arndt for taxes. In block N°. 19 you have paid taxes on lots N[os]. 14. 15 & 16 Mr Mitchell paid taxes on these last year, and according to your statement was by agreement to continue to pay taxes on them. In block N°. 75 there are 16 lots: you have omitted to pay taxes on two of them say N[os] 12 and 13 please explain the above discrepancies. Please also procure and forward me the statement of the Board of Supervisors as to the valuation of the property taxed for 1845 similar to the one you rendered me in Feb'y 1845. In the receipt of taxes it is mentioned that the amount received is in full of taxes for 1846 instead of 1845. In place of the blank deed which you sent me for execution, I send you one executed such as it is our practice to give. Standing in the light of trustee I do not warrant for title which I mentioned to you in my letter of the 28th. June 1843. I observe that you have sold several articles of furniture belonging to the Hotel. You will please not sell the one dozen silver table spoons and one dozen silver tea spoons: they are not of a perishable character nor likely to sustain damage by keeping, and I would therefore not sell them. A time will I hope arrive when they will be wanted for the Hotel and you will therefore please see that good care is taken of them, and also of the other articles of furniture, which please have examined from time to time. The taxes are very heavy this year, about double what I expected they would be. I hoped that some consideration in laying them would be had of the circumstance that the property produces nothing, and that a similar rate of taxation continued will ere long amount to more than the value of the property. Please inform me whether you hear of any arrangements being made or being about to be made by Capt. Walker to run his steamboat according to agreement to Astor &c. this year

> I am Dear Sir
> Very truly, Your friend &c
> John Jacob Astor
> (signed) W^m. B. Astor

164. LETTER FROM WILLIAM ROBERTS TO DANIEL LORD, MARCH 19, 1847, IN REGARD TO THE SUIT OF SAMUEL G. OGDEN *vs.* JOHN JACOB ASTOR & SON.

Samuel G. Ogden, the brother and heir of Nicholas G. Ogden, Astor's partner and Canton agent from 1817 until his death in 1823, sued the Astor firm, alleging that when a foreign shipment brought a loss it was charged to the partnership but when it resulted in a profit it was credited to the Astor firm. In this letter, William Roberts, the bookkeeper of the Astor firm during Ogden's Canton agency, writing to Astor's attorney, Daniel Lord, describes the case from the standpoint of the Astors. It gives an interesting picture of the state of the China trade at the time of the Astor-Ogden partnership.

Daniel Lord Esq   New York 19 Mch 1847 [1]

Dear Sir. "We regret to say we have not been able to make up the a/c sales of any one voyage in which you are interested. This is owing to our having shipped off the property to different places, the West Indies, N. Orleans &c, &c. To

---

[1] Ms. book, Baker Library, Astor Papers, Letter Book iii, 1845–47, pp. 167–169.

avoid this in future we propose that when we ship any thing again to ship it on our own a/c & to give credit at the price and on the terms we sell to others: We ship as some times it relieves the market somewhat and occasionally gives us some dollars."

The above extracts from John Jacob Astor & Son's letters to Nic: G. Ogden, dated the 2^d Mch 1819 is the only announcement on which I conceive Saml G. Ogden can found his pretensions to "modify" the co-partnership agreement between the Messrs. Astors and his brother as I find nothing else relating to the subject in any of their letters to him after a most careful examination. The receipt of this letter in Canton is acknowledged by Nic: G. Ogden under date of Canton 3 Augt. 1819 in the following terms. "I am favored with your esteemed letters of 6th. 7th. and 8th. Jany & 2^d Mch and take note of their contents to which shall pay every attention." In none of his many subsequent letters does he ever revert to it although at times of leisure he often wrote what he calls a long desultory letter "touching upon every thing that he considered of interest either to them or himself in regard to their joint business. In none of his letters does he express the least wish to have a/c sales furnished to him or make the slightest complaint of any part of the conduct of the House here in their manner of transacting the business but acquiescing in what he seems to consider as their better judgment and discretion. I can perfectly remember & can bear testimony to the difficulty that existed in the years 1819 & 1820 in the sale of Canton goods of all descriptions arising from the enormous importations, the general poverty of the country, and wretched state of commerce in all parts of the world. The consumption of this country was of the most limited description, and the influx of importation increasing and to an extent treble what was required for the home demand. To force sales was to sacrifice the goods at ruinous prices and at a great risk of not realizing the price at which you made sales from the insolvency of the buyers. The only mode of realizing the goods at the smallest probable loss was by watching the foreign markets, and supplying them as openings seemed to offer, according to Mr J. J. Astor's advice who was then in Europe, and to the best information we could obtain from the West Indies and the distant cities of this country. Of this state of things and the course adopted by the house here Mr N. G. Ogden was regularly and constantly advised by the letters of J. J. Astor & Son & his letters in reply constantly reverted to his knowledge, from them, and private sources of information of the miserable state of things in Europe, and to the exuberant exports from Canton. In none of these letters does he express the slightest dissatisfaction with any thing that had been done, & in a letter written to me, (who then conducted the correspondence of this house here) he acknowledges his approbation of the ample advices that were given to him. It is self evident that he did not consider those shipments to be for the sale a/c of J. J. Astor & Son, or why need he have entertained and expressed such gloomy apprehension of the result of operations to Europe if he had not believed himself interested therein. He ought to have rejoiced that the house here were Quixotic enough to take the thorn out of his foot to run it into their own. He would naturally have said, "by your letters of the 3^d Mch 1819, you propose to take all future shipments to your own a/c at N. York prices & terms" and though I did not in direct terms accept your proposal yet as I did not dissent from it I shall consider *you* bound by it tho' I am not. How far this would have been equitable in the eye of the law is not for me to say but surely he having made a waver of his right then his representatives cannot come nearly 30 years afterwards and set up pretensions which he when living did not see fit to put forth. As to what was the price the goods would have brought if sales had been forced here instead of their being exported it is now almost impossible to say except by reference to the auction prices of such as were sold in that way, but I am certain that the small slow sales that were made privately were at prices 20 or 25 per cent higher than could have been obtained by pressing them on the market. I distinctly remember one large sale was made to a German House at the nominal N. Y. prices after considerable hesitation, and the result was that they only paid 50 cents on the dollar, and if we had pressed sales in that way, I am confident the result would have been the same in other instances if even not worse. There was a general & well founded distrust of the solvency of export buyers rendering it better to take the risk of shipping ourselves than to sell to those who would have purchased them for export. All this Mr N. G. Ogden was fully advised of at the time and it is evident that his expectation of profit from his share of the operations with J. J. Astor & Son were of a very limited description as will more fully appear by the extracts from his letters which accompany this. Certainly if he had supposed he was to have received the prices in N. York, low as they were, for all his interest in the different cargoes he would have estimated his profits very differently. It is evident from his letters he contemplated not a large part of the cargo's must seek foreign markets and in some instances he even recommends that course to be adopted. I trust this letter will place the business in a plain light, but if any further explanation or remark is necessary, I shall be happy to supply it and remain

With great respect, Dear Sir
Your Ob^t. Ser^t.
(signed) Wm Roberts

165. Letter from Joseph Green Cogswell to Robert Stuart, May 20, 1847, in regard to Steamboat Communication between Buffalo and Green Bay.

This letter is of interest as being one of the last which we can be sure expresses Astor's own thoughts upon a business subject. His questions in general reveal the clarity of his mind at this time, while the last query by its indecision evidences the weakness of his nerves. Of the "persons named in the charter" several are already familiar to us. Samuel Abbott had represented the American Fur Company at Prairie du Chien, St. Louis, Detroit, and Mackinac, and Hercules L. Dousman had been in charge of the Company's trading post at Prairie du Chien. Concerning the others I know no more than did Astor himself. David Stuart, Robert Stuart's son, acted for Astor in selling a lot at Mackinac. See documents 146, 151, 161, and 163.

Robert Stuart Esq.   New York May 20. 1847 [1]
    Lockport, Illinois, Dear Sir,
        I have not had the pleasure of hearing from you for a long while and I now write to ask your opinion on several matters connected with our Green Bay interests. Captain Walker, who contracted, you know, to run a steamboat from Buffalo to Green Bay, disappointed us, and failed to fulfil his contract – but the experiment imperfectly as it was tried shows the importance of having a line of boats between the Green Bay Settlement and Buffalo; and a company has since been started for accomplishing this object – this company has been chartered by the assembly of Wisconsin, by the name of the Mississippi and Lake Erie Navigation Company, for transporting freight and passengers to & from the Mississippi and Buffalo – the capital is $100.000 divided into 5000 shares of $20 each, with power to increase it to $200.000 should it be deemed expedient by the stockholders – Mr W. B. Astor and R. Crooks are two

----

[1] Ms. book, Baker Library, Astor Papers, Letter Book iii, 1845–48, pp. 181–182.

of the persons named in the charter – the others are Samuel
Abbott, Daniel Whitney, Morgan L. Martin, T. F. Meade,
Daniel Butler, H. E. Eastman, H. Conklin L. M. Miller, G. F.
Wright, Loyall H. Jones and H. L. Dousman. Please give me
your opinion of these gentlemen or such of them, as you personally know and also as to the plan generally – what is the
probability that the business will be well and prudently managed by such a company — how many boats will be required
— what is the usual cost of a boat proper for the service – information on these and on such other points as you may deem
important, will be very acceptable. From all I learn, I do not
think any great reliance is to be placed on our present agent at
Green Bay, we need a man of more energy, and one who will
devote himself more closely to our interests – please bear this
in mind and write me word if you hear of or see the right man.
How is it with our lands at Praire du Chien, are they worth
any thing? Would our interest suffer, if the proposed steam
boat communication should be delayed a year or two? The
above was written from Mr J. J. Astor's dictation.

Respectfully
(signed) Jo^s. G. Cogswell

Robert Stuart Esq.   New York 20th May 1847
        Lockport Ill: Dear Sir. Your favor of the 17th. Oct:
has been duly received: the power therein referred to has been
received. Can you inform me whether your son has done any
thing in regard to disposing of the lot at Mackinac – Please
let me know what has been done in the matter

I am, My Dear Sir,
very truly your's
John Jacob Astor

(signed) W^m. B. Astor

166. Letter from W. B. Astor to Gerrit Smith, January 4, 1848, declining on behalf of his Father to Return Bank Stock given as Security for Smith's Bond.

To the last Astor was interested in the details of his business, as is revealed by his insistence on retaining adequate security for Smith's bond. See documents 150, 152, 153, 158, and 160.

Gerrit Smith Esq. New York Jany. 4 1848 [1]
Peterboro' Madison C^o. N York
My dear Sir, I have your favor of the 27th Ult^o. and observe that you request the Cashier of the New York State Bank to pay my father $25600. on your account. On receiving that amount you desire me to satisfy the mortgage for $50000 on Lands in Madison C^o. which will be done accordingly. In regard to the Bank Stocks, he would, as he understood them to be given as security for the payments of your large Bond, prefer to transfer them after a further reduction of it, to correspond with the amount of the security you desire. My fathers health remains as it was when we had last the pleasure to see you here, excepting that he is rather weaker. He is much obliged for your kind remembrance and unites with me in best wishes for the welfare & happiness of yourself & all your family.

I am My dear Sir
with great regard your friend
W. B Astor.

[1] Ms. book, Baker Library, Astor Papers, Letter Book iii, 1845–48, p. 254.

167. LETTER FROM GERRIT SMITH TO WILLIAM B. ASTOR, APRIL 6, 1848, WITH CONDOLENCES ON THE DEATH OF JOHN JACOB ASTOR.

One of Astor's most attractive characteristics was his ability to make himself interesting to and to find interest in men of all varieties of opinion. His long friendship with the radical reformer Gerrit Smith is striking testimony to this capacity.

Peterboro April 6. 1848 [1]

William B. Astor Esquire

   My dear Sir

Todays mail brings me your letter of 3ᵈ. inst. For this very kind remembrance of me, I beg you to accept my warmest thanks.

You have lost an affectionate father. I have lost a fast friend — a friend, too, – who had the ability, as well as the disposition to render me very important Services –

Your beloved fathers death recalls to my mind the Striking words, which he used in my last interview with him. I remember having repeated them to Mrs Astor. "I am broken up. It is time for me to be out of the way."

Brief, indeed, is the longest human life! Our fathers whose close attachment to each other began in their youth, are dead. We are fatherless — and how soon our Children will be fatherless! May God graciously enable us to improve all our admonitions to prepare for our departure from this world & our entrance into a better.

Mrs. Smith joins me in affectionate regards for Mrs. Astor yourself & children

very truly your friend

Gerrit Smith

[1] Ms. book, Syracuse University, Gerrit Smith Miller Collection, Letter Book, 1843–55, p. 317.

168. THE WILL OF JOHN JACOB ASTOR.

Astor's will reveals two dominant intentions on the part of its framer: one was to "provide amply and safely for his children, grandchildren, nephews, and nieces," with special attention to the welfare of his own descendants; the other was to keep the great bulk of his estate in the hands of his eldest mentally competent son. Something over half a million dollars was bequeathed to public objects. The sole legacy to an employee, or to any person not connected with Astor by blood, was the small annuity to Fitz-Greene Halleck. The eight codicils, made between January 19, 1838, and December 22, 1843, were intended to amend and adjust his legacies to relatives and public objects. It is therefore incorrect to state, as was done by Matthew Hale Smith in *Sunshine and Shadow in New York*, p. 123, that "during the last few years of his life he added, from the accumulations of his property, five hundred thousand dollars every six months in codicils to his will." Since William B. Astor was the residuary legatee, this procedure would have been quite unnecessary.

In [1] the name of God, Amen.

I, John Jacob Astor, of the City of New-York, desiring to dispose of all the real and personal Estate to which I may be entitled at the time of my decease, [interlineated: in the manner hereinafter expressed] do make this my last Will and Testament.

First. To my daughter Dorothea, wife of Walter Landgon Esquire, I give and bequeath all *my household furniture*, also the use, during her life of all *my silver plate*, my new service of plate excepted. Also, I give and bequeath to her for her life, the *income* of the following stocks, debt and money, that is to say: *One hundred thousand dollars* of the *debt of the City of New York*, bearing five per cent interest; *five hundred shares* of the capital stock *of the Bank of America; one thousand shares* of the capital stock of the *Manhattan Company; twenty five thousand Dollars deposited with the New York Life Insurance and Trust Company*, (for which I hold certificates;) all which income I

---

[1] Ms., Baker Library, Astor Papers.

devote expressly to her sole and separate use to be at her own disposal when received by her, and not otherwise, and to be free from all claim interest or interference of her husband. And to enable her to receive the said income, I order my executors (in whose names the funds aforesaid are to stand during the life of my said daughter) from time to time, as she may request, to execute such revocable letters of attorney as may be requisite to enable her to receive the said income.

Also, I devise to her the *house and lot* on *Lafayette Place*, in the City of New York, being twenty seven feet feet [*sic*] six inches wide, and one hundred and thirty seven feet six inches deep, now occupied by her; to have and to hold the same during her natural life, free from and exclusive of, any interest or interference of her husband, and to her sole and separate use.

And on her death, I give the said plate (except as above) sums of debt and deposit, and stocks, to her then surviving issue, and their executors and administrators.

And I devise the said house and lot to her then surviving issue, and their heirs and assigns forever; intending that if any of her children shall have died before her, leaving issue, such issue are together to take what their parent would have taken if surviving.

Second. To John Jacob Astor Langdon [see codicil], Eliza Astor Langdon, Louisa Langdon, Walter Langdon Jr. Woodbury Langdon, Cecilia Langdon and Eugene Langdon, children of my daughter Dorothea, or to such of them as shall survive me, I devise *all my lots* on the *Easterly side of Lafayette Place*, in the City of New York, and fronting thereon. Also *my lots* in *the rear* of my lots on the said *easterly side of Lafayette Place*, extending to the Bowery, and fronting thereon. Also, my *lands* in the said City, between *Charlton-Street, Morton-Street, Greenwich-Street, and Hudson's River*, being one hundred and — lots; to have and to hold the same to them, my said grand-children, in equal shares, for and during their lives respectively. And on the death of each of them, my grand-children, I give the share which he or she shall have enjoyed for life, to their surviving issue in fee simple to be divided according to the number of their children; and in case of death without issue then surviving, I devise the share of such deceased to my said other grandchildren above named, then surviving, in fee simple.

Third. To my said grandchildren, John J. A. Langdon, Walter Langdon Junr., Woodbury Langdon and Eugene Langdon [see codicil], or to such of them as shall survive me, I devise the eight lots of land belonging to me, with the improvements thereon, fronting *on the Easterly side of Broadway*, in the City of New York, between Broome Street and Spring-Street; to have and to hold the same in equal shares, during their lives respectively. And on the death of each, I devise the share to which he had been entitled, to his issue him surviving, in equal shares, according to the number of his children, and to their heirs and assigns forever. And in case of deaths without such issue, I devise such share to his then surviving brothers, and their heirs and assigns forever.

To my said grandchildren Sarah Astor, wife of Robert Boreel Esq., Eliza Astor, Louisa and Cecilia, or to such of them as may survive me, I devise the *four houses and lots* fronting on the *Westerly side of Broadway*, between Prince-Street and Houston Street, now known as *numbers* 579, 581, 583 and 587, extending in the rear to Mercer Street; to have and to hold the same to them respectively, in equal shares, during their lives; and on the death of each I devise her share to her issue then surviving, to be divided according to the number of her children, and to their heirs and assigns forever: and in case of death without issue then surviving, I devise such share to her then surviving sisters, and their heirs and assigns forever.

To each of my said grandsons, John J. A. Langdon, Walter Langdon Jr. Woodbury Langdon, and Eugene Langdon, and to each of my said granddaughters, Eliza, Louisa [codicil modifies] and Cecilia, on their respectively attaining the age of twenty four years, I give *twenty five thousand dollars*, and on their respectively attaining the age of thirty years, *the further sum of twenty five thousand dollars*.

To my granddaughter Sarah, wife of Robert Boreel, I give the lands and building now known as *the City Hotel* in in [*sic*] the City of New York, bounded by Broadway, Thames-Street, Temple-Street, and Cedar-Street; to have and to hold the same to her for life: on her death, I devise the same to her then surviving issue, (according to the number of her children) and to their heirs and assigns forever; and in case of her death without such issue, then I devise the same to her then surviving brothers and sisters, and their heirs and assigns forever. And I authorize her, with the approbation of my executors, in case the building shall be burnt down or otherwise destroyed, to sell the said lands, in fee simple, or to mortgage the same to raise money for rebuilding on the said lands; in which case, the proceeds and money shall be received by my executors, and invested by them, and the income shall be paid to the said Sarah Boreel for her life, provided she shall reside within the State of New York; but in case she shall not reside therein, then ten thousand dollars per annum of such income shall be paid to her, and the residue to her mother, or in case of her death, to the brothers and sisters of the said Sarah. And on the death of the said Sarah, the capital shall be disposed of as is herein directed as to the land itself, of which it is the proceeds.

Fourth. [Revoked by codicil.] To my daughter Eliza, Wife of Vincent Rumpff, Esquire, I give the income for her life, of the following funds: *Fifty thousand Dollars* of the *Public debt of Ohio*, bearing six per cent interest; *fifty thousand dollars* of the *Debt* of the *City of New Haven*, bearing five and a half per cent interest; *fifty thousand Dollars deposited in the New York Life Insurance and Trust Company*, (of which I have certificates;)

one thousand shares of the capital Stock of the Merchants' Bank, in the City of New York, and *Sixteen hundred and four shares of the Capital Stock of the Mechanics Bank,* in the City of New York: Also, if she shall come to the State of New York, and there take up her residence, then I give to her *such part of my residuary real estate* as she shall select, not exceeding in value *fifty thousand dollars,* according to a just valuation thereof by my executors; which estate so selected shall be set apart to her by deed, to be executed by her and my executors; to have and to hold the same to her during her life, if she shall not discontinue her residence in New York: and on her death, I give the capital of the said funds, and the said real estate so selected, to her then surviving issue, their heirs, executors and administrators respectively, to be divided according to the number of her children; but in case of her death without such issue, I authorize her to dispose of the said funds and lands by appointment in the nature of a will in such manner and in such shares, and for such estates, as she may think fit, to and amongst all or any of her relations by consanguinity, who might by possibility take lands from her by descent, according to the law of the State of New York, as it shall be at the date of such appointment; and in case of her death without such issue, and not leaving any such valid appointment, then I give the said funds and lands, one fourth to the children of my son William B. Astor; one half to the children of my daughter Dorothea, and one fourth to my grandson Charles Bristed, and their heirs executors and administrators respectively.

Also, I give *to my said daughter Eliza,* and to *her husband Vincent Rumpff,* my lands and *estate in the Canton of Geneva,* in Switzerland; to have and to hold the same to them during their lives, and the life of the survivor of them; And on the death of the Survivor, I give the same to her issue surviving her at her death, and to their heirs, executors, administrators and assigns forever, to be equally divided, according to the number of her children; and I hereby give her power to appoint the said Genevese estates, in case of her death without such issue, to and amongst my grandchildren, or to such one or more of them, and in such shares, for such estates, and on such conditions as she may direct by *instrument* instrument [*sic*] in the nature of a Will; and in case of her death without issue as aforesaid, and without leaving any valid appointment, then I devise the said Genevese estates to my grandchildren as follows: one third to the children of William B. Astor; one third to the children of my daughter Dorothea, and one third to my grandson Charles Bristed, and to their heirs, executors and administrators, respectively, forever.

Fifth. To my grandson Charles Bristed, I devise all that *lot of land* belonging to me fronting on the *Westerly side* of Lafayette Place, adjoining my house, now occupied by my daughter Dorothea, and being twenty seven feet six inches wide, by one hundred and thirty seven feet six inches deep. Also the *lot* and house now occupied by me on the *Westerly* side of Broadway, Known as *number* 585, being about twenty nine feet in the front on Broadway and twenty five feet on Mercer-Street, to which it extends. Also *a lot* of land belonging to me on the Westerly [easterly — see codicil] side of Broadway between Spring-Street and Prince Street; also *nine lots* of land *on the Eighth Avenue* and Twenty Sixth Street seven of which lie on the westerly side of the avenue including the two corner lots of twenty Sixth Street, and two lie on the northerly side of Twenty Sixth Street, near the avenue. Also, *forty three lots* of land fronting on Seventh Avenue, Bloomingdale-road, *Thirty seventh Street* and *Fortieth Street;* Also *eight lots* of land *on Avenue A, between Sixth and Seventh Streets;* also *my country seat*, at Hellgate, and my lands there, containing about thirteen acres; also the *twenty two lots* owned by me *in the Block formed by* Hammersley-Street, Varick-Street, Bedford-Street and Downing-Street; — to have and to hold all and singular the said lots of land and premises for and during his natural life. Also, I give to him, on his attaining the age of twenty five years, the *income and interest of one hundred and fifteen thousand dollars*, to be set apart by my executors, out of my good bonds and mortgages, to have and enjoy such income during his life. And as to the income of the real estate above devised to him for life, I devise the same to my executors in trust to receive the same, and to apply it, or so much and such part thereof as they may think fit, to the use of the said Charles Bristed until he shall attain the age of twenty five years; and upon the death of the said Charles Bristed I give the said lands and capital of one hundred and fifteen thousand Dollars, to his then surviving issue (to be divided according to the number of his children) and to their heirs, executors, administrators and assigns, respectively forever. And in case of his death without such issue, then I give the said lands and money, one half to the children of my son William B. Astor, and one half to the children of my daughter Dorothea Langdon, and to their heirs, executors and administrators respectively forever.

Sixth. To my grandsons, John Jacob Astor, William Astor and Henry Astor, sons of William B. Astor, or to such of them as may survive me, I devise all *my lands* lying between Blooming-dale-road, Hudson River, Forty-second-Street, and Fifty-first-Street, to be divided in the proportion of two shares to John and one share each to William and Henry; to have and to hold the same to them during their lives respectively: Provided however that if my son William B. Astor should consider either of them to have become unworthy of this devise, he may convey the share of such one or more of them to the others or other, by appointment under his hand and seal; and on their respective deaths I devise the share devised to each for life, to his then surviving issue, and their heirs and assigns forever, to be divided according, to the number of his children. And in case of death without such issue, then I devise the same to his surviving brothers and their heirs and assigns forever: or in case they should not survive, to William B. Astor and his heirs forever.

Seventh. Seventh. [*sic*] [Codicil modifies the whole.] I direct my executors to provide for my unfortunate son John Jacob Astor, and to procure for him all the comforts which his condition doth or may admit, and to bear the expense thereof, *not exeeding five thousand dollars a year.* And in case he should be restored then I direct them to apply to his use *ten thousand dollars a year* during his life. And if he shall leave lawful issue surviving him, then I direct my executors to pay to such issue the sum of five thousand dollars per annum to each child for life. And my executors are directed to set apart from my estate such funds as in their judgment shall be sufficient to defray these annuities: and also all other annuities bequeathed in my will: which annuities shall stand secured on such funds exclusively of any of my lands.

Eighth. [Revoked by codicil.] To each of the *four daughters* of my deceased brother, George Astor, I give twenty thousand Dollars; to his son Joseph, I give *twenty five thousand dollars;* to his son William H. Astor, I give *ten thousand dollars;* to George Astor, Jr., I give *three thousand dollars;* to the widow of my said brother George, I give *two hundred pounds sterling*, yearly for her life, commencing the first payment one year after my death, the same to be estimated here at the current rate of exchange. To my niece Sophia Astor, of Nieuwid in Germany, I give *five thousand dollars.* To my Sister Catherine wife of Michael Miller, I give *one thousand dollars;* to the *children of her daughter*, Maria Moore, I give five thousand dollars, to be equally divided among them and to be paid to their mother for their use.

Ninth. To the German Society of the City of New York [modified by codicils], I give *thirty thousand dollars*, upon condition that they do, as soon as conveniently may be done after payment of the money, invest and keep the same invested, in security of bond and mortgage of lands, and apply the interest and income thereof to establish and maintain an office in some suitable place in the City of New York, and proper persons attending, who shall speak the German language, and be otherwise qualified for their duty, who shall attend daily in such office during the usual [business — stricken through] hours of business in this City, for the purpose of giving advice and information, without charge, to all emigrants arriving here, touching their establishment here, and their course of life; and for the purpose of protecting them against impositions to which strangers without knowledge of the country or its language, may be exposed.

To the Trustees of Columbia College [revoked by codicil] in the City of New York I give *twenty five thousand dollars*, upon condition that they do, within a reasonable and convenient time, establish a professorship of the German language and literature, and do appoint and continue a professor therein of competent learning, who shall give proper lectures and instruction in the said language and literature.

To The Association For The Relief of Respectable Aged Indigent Females in the City of New York, I give twenty five thousand dollars, on condition that they cause the same to be put out and kept at interest on bonds and mortgage of real estate, and apply the interest to the objects of their association. And in case of a breach of any of the said conditions, or from any legal or other impediment, any of the three last legacies shall fail to take effect, then I give the same to my executors, confiding in their honor alone to make such disposition of such sums as they shall deem most analogous to the aforesaid purposes.

To the German Reformed Congregation [revoked by codicil], in the City of New York, of which I am a member, I give *two thousand Dollars*.

Tenth. All the rest, residue, and remainder of my real and personal estate [changed by codicil], I give and devise to my son William B. Astor; to have and to hold the said real estate to him him [*sic*] for his life. And I authorize him to appoint the same after his death, to and amongst his children and their issue in such shares and for such estates, and on such conditions as he may think fit, by deed or by will: and in case he shall leave no such valid appointment, I devise the same to his children and their heirs and assigns forever, including as well those now born as subsequently born children. And I hereby charge upon the said residuary estate thus devised, portions of two hundred thousand dollars [changed by codicil], to be settled upon each of his daughters and her issue, in such manner as he may think fit, subject to the condition of their marrying with the consent of himself or his wife, or such persons as he may nominate in his will: which portions are to be set apart out of the real estate devised to him as above, and which, when set apart are not to form any incumbrance upon the residue. And in case of his leaving no appointment as aforesaid, these portions are to be considered as part of his daughters' shares on the division of the estate now devised among his children. And as to the personal estate bequeathed to him, it is my will that he employ the same in the improvement of the real estate to him herein above devised, in such manner as he may think fit.

My *service of plate*, above mentioned, I give to be used by my son William B. Astor, for life; and after his death, to such of his sons as he may appoint.

Eleventh. And considering that the uncertainty of life estates may embarrass the advantageous enjoyment of lands thus situated, and considering also other matters of convenience, I do hereby authorize *each and every person who shall take an estate under this will, which may terminate with his or her life, to make any lease* of the premises to them devised, and of any and every part thereof, *for any term or terms of years not exceeding twenty one years from the date thereof*, with covenants therein for allowing to the lessee or his assigns the actual value at the termination of the lease of the buildings then standing on the demised premises and useful as a dwelling house, or for any mercantile or mechanical business; which covenant shall bind the remainder man in respect to such lands, if he shall enter thereupon: *Provided* that such leases be made with the assent of one of my executors uniting in the same for this purpose, and that the fair yearly value of the premises be reserved as rent payable annually, without any anticipation by way of premium, and be made payable to the tenant for life, and to the persons in remainder successively, according to the nature of their several estates.

Also, I do *authorize any such tenant for life*, with the assent of one my executors uniting in the deed to manifest the same, *to sell and convey in fee simple, to the extent of one half in value of the lands* devised to such life tenant, in order to raise money for the improvement of the residue; for which application of the money so to be raised, such executor shall make provision before giving such assent; and his uniting in the deed shall make the same an effectual conveyance to the parties accepting the same, who shall thereby be freed from seeing to the application of the purchasemoneys.

In case any of the stocks or funds herein specifically bequeathed, should not be in my hands at my decease, the several bequests shall be made up by purchases, at the expense of my estate, of stocks or funds, of the same or a similar kind and to the same amount, at their par values. *And in case any of the said Stocks or funds should be paid off, or become, in the judgment of my executors, insecure*, then it shall be lawful for them to sell and dispose of the same, at the request, or with the assent of the person entitled to the income thereof; and to invest the proceeds in such other safe securities as my executors shall think expedient, and so on from time to time. But no change of the form of investment shall change the right or interest of any person in the income and proceeds of such property.

I appoint William B. Astor, James G. King, Washington Irving, James Gallatin —— to be executors of this my Will, and *give to such of them as shall act* herein, and the *survivors and survivor of them,* the several powers, authority and discretion herein granted. And whenever, *and as often as their number shall be reduced to two,* my acting executors shall appoint such proper persons as they may select to be united with them in the execution of the objects of this Will; and upon such appointment being accepted and acknowledged, and recorded as a deed, the persons so appointed shall be invested with the same interest, right, discretion and control as if appointed by name in this Will. And so, from time to time, until all the purposes of the Will shall be accomplished or completed. And I expressly declare that those who shall act in the executorship of this Will, *shall not be answerable for the losses* which shall occur through the acts of the others of their number, or of any agents by them employed, nor otherwise than from their own fraudulent misconduct; and they shall be in all respects indemnified out of my estate, and *may employ such agents* and servants as they may deem necessary; and *may make* any *arrangement for the settlement of any difficulties* which may arise in relation to any of my estate, by composition or arbitration, as they shall think fit. *I authorize my executors,* at the request of any person or persons to whom lands are herein devised in common, *to set apart their shares in severalty;* and thenceforth the limitations of future estates applicable to the shares before separation, shall apply to the separate share, and they may charge the lands with sums for equality of partition.

Lastly. I revoke all other Wills by me made prior to this date; and publish and declare this to be my last Will and Testament. In Witness whereof, I have signed and sealed these presents, this forth day of July in the year of our Lord one thousand eight hundred and thirty six.

John Jacob Astor [L. S.]

Published in the presence of us before whom the testator declared these presents to be his last Will and testament, and requested us to sign our names as witnesses which we do in his presence, and in presence of each other. Dated 1836 July 4th W^m. W. Bruce Prince Street New York. Hanah Norman, Hellgate New York. December 30. 1836 Geo. B. Smith 640 B^d. way New York; Edwin Smith 71 Bleecker Street New York. Declared by Mr. J. J. Astor to be his last Will and Testament by him subscribed as such before us signing as witnesses at his request. 1845 January 11. Joseph G. Cogswell 585 Broadway N. Y. Charles J. McIlvaine, 44 Great Jones St. Daniel D. Lord Nineteenth St. Wm W. Bruce 481 Houston St. N. York.

A Codicil
to the Will of John Jacob Astor.
[January 19, 1838]

In order to render some provisions of my Will more plain, to make some alterations therein, and to consolidate sundry codicils thereto, (which codicils I hereby revoke,) I make this codicil to my will bearing date the fourth day of July Eighteen hundred and thirty six; and do declare the said Will and this codicil to contain my last Will.

First. I give to my daughter, Dorothea Langdon, the lot on the west side of Lafayette Place, in the City of New York [revoked in codicil 3 March, 1841]; twenty seven feet wide and one hundred and fifty five feet deep, on the north side of the house and lot, in my will given to her for life; to have and to hold the same to her for life, free of any interference of her husband, and to her sole and separate use, being the same lot given in my will to Charles Bristed, and which I confirm to him after Mrs. Langdon's life; and *in relation to the income given to my daughter,*

Mrs. Langdon, and to the house and lots devised to her for
life, in order the better to secure the same to her, I devise and
direct, that in case her husband, present or future, or any one
claiming under his act or default, shall attempt to interfere
with, dispose of or incumber the said legacy of income or devises of land, or any part thereof, then, in that case, I do from
that time give the said income and lots of land on Lafayette
Place to my executors, during her life, in trust, to receive the
income and the rents and profits of the land, and to apply the
same to the use of my said daughter and her children, in such
manner and proportions as she may request; and should there
be any surplus of such income beyond what may be so applied,
I give the same to her her [sic] children from time to time as it
shall accrue.

Second. Inasmuch as my grandson, John J. A. Langdon, has
departed this life, whereby two legacies of twenty five thousand dollars each have become lapsed; I therefore *add to the
lands* devised in the *second item* of my will to him and his
brothers and sisters in that item named, or to such of them as
may survive me, *three lots* of land lying *on the westerly side of
Lafayette place* [modified in codicil March 3, 1841], next north
of a lot which in my will is given for life to Charles Bristed, and
is above given for her life to my daughter; each of which three
lots is twenty seven feet in width, and one hundred and fifty
five feet in depth, subject to and with the benefit of a gangway
running from Art-Street across the rear of the said lots, parallel
with Lafayette Place, and twenty feet wide, and lying at a distance of one hundred and ten feet therefrom; which three lots
of land I give to my said grandchildren; to have and to hold in
equal shares as tenants in common for their lives respectively;
and on the death of each, I give his or her share to his or her
surviving issue in fee simple, and in case of death without surviving issue, I give such share to his or her other brothers and
sisters, in the same item named, surviving, in fee simple.

Third. In relation to the above lots on Lafayette Place, and to the house and lot given in my will to Mrs. Langdon and to Charles Bristed for life; and in relation to my other lots on the West side of Lafayette Place, I have laid out the same so as to include a gangway [revoked March 3, 1341[?]] twenty feet wide, as above mentioned, and a piece of land twenty five feet deep in the rear thereof, for a stable lot; which gangway is to be used as a carriage-way by the residents on the said lots appertaining thereto; and is to be regulated and kept in order with a gate, by such residents, each lot bearing an equal share of the expense. And I direct and devise, that the said lots so given to Mrs. Langdon and Charles Bristed, shall be extended so as to include each one hundred and fifty five feet deep from Lafayette place, with the privilege of such gangway, and subject thereto.

Fourth. If the yearly income (of stocks and funds) *given to my daughters, Mrs. Langdon and Mrs. Rumpff,* respectively, shall in any year, fall short of fifteen thousand Dollars, then the deficiency shall be made up from my residuary personal estate remaining in the hands of my executors; but if such deficiency shall arise from any temporary suspension of dividends or income, not occasioned by actual losses in the stocks or funds, then such advances shall be refunded from the excess of income over fifteen thousand dollars per annum afterwards accruing on such stocks or funds. Also in relation to the real estate of Mrs. Rumpff, in case she should come to this State to reside, as provided in item fourth of my will, I direct that the selection be made by my executors as soon as may be after my decease, and that upon the event contemplated in the said item of my will, she shall take the estate therein given in such selected land.

Fifth. I give to Charles Bristed *the lot* of land belonging to me, lying *on the easterly side of Broadway*, between Prince and Spring Streets, which is the lot I intend in the fifth item of my will, wherein the same is erroneously described as lying on the

Westerly side of Broadway; and the lot now correctly described is hereby given as the other lands in that item mentioned.

Sixth. As to *all my lands at Green Bay*, and in its vicinity, in the territory of Wisconsin, (in which there are others connected with me) and also as to all my lands not within within [*sic*] the City and County of New York, I authorize and fully empower my executors or any two of them, or of the survivors of them to seal and deliver all deeds of conveyance in fee simple, or for partition if needed, and to execute all other instruments of every kind needful, or in their judgment proper, in relation to the lands, and every part thereof; and also to appoint such agents from time to time, subject to their control and direction, as they may think fit, with the like powers; the proceeds of all such sales to be disposed of as part of my personal estate. And for the purpose of such sales, and for the protection of the lands in the mean time, I give the same to my executors as joint tenants, and not as tenants in common, in fee simple, in trust for such purposes.

Seventh. The service of plate excepted from the gift to Mrs. Langdon in my will, and therein mentioned as my new service of plate, and given for the use of William B. Astor for life, I describe more particularly as my service of French plate, at this time in his possession. And in case he shall not leave any appointment of it among his children, I give the same, on his death, to his eldest surviving son.

Eighth. I revoke and annul the eighth item of my said Will and the legacies therein given, and in lieu thereof, I give as follows: To Mrs. Sarah Oxenham [modified in codicil of March 3, 1841], daughter of my late brother, George Astor, I give *thirty thousand dollars;* to his son, Joseph Astor [modified Oct. 24, 1839], I give *fifty thousand Dollars;* provided however, that my executors if they think fit, may retain the same in whole or in part, and apply the same, and the income thereof, to his use, and the maintenance of him and his family during his life; and any balance is to be given to his children, or next of kin. *To each of the other daughters* [modified as to Mrs. Reynell, March 3, 1841] *of my said brother George,* surviving me, I give *twenty thousand dollars.* To William Henry Astor; son of my said brother George, I give the *annual sum of five hundred dollars* during his life, commencing the first payment six months after my decease; but if he shall attempt to assign or incumber the same, or it shall be claimed by any of his creditors under any legal proceedings or claim in the law, then I direct my executors to cease paying it to him, and require them to apply the same in their discretion to his use, maintenance and support. To George Astor, Junior, I give *three thousand dollars.* To the widow of my brother George I give *two hundred pounds sterling yearly* for her life, to be estimated at the current rate of exchange at the time of payment, the first payment of two hundred pounds to be made six months after my decease, and then yearly afterward. To my niece, Sophia Astor of Nieuwid in Germany, I give *five thousand Dollars.* To the children of Hannah Moore, daughter of my sister Catharine, who may survive me, I give *five thousand dollars,* to be equally divided between them. To each of the children of George Ehninger, who may survive me, I give *one thousand dollars.* These legacies of which the time of payment is not above declared, are to be paid, one half in six months, the balance in twelve months from my decease. And my executors are to set apart funds, from my personal estate, to discharge the annuities which are to be allowed up to the death of the annuitants.

Ninth. I reduce the legacy to the German Society of New York, from *thirty thousand dollars to twenty five thousand dollars. I I* [*sic*] *have given* to the Association for the Relief of Respectable Aged Indigent Females, in the City of New York, *five thousand dollars,* which is to be deducted from the legacy of twenty five thousand dollars given in my will. To the Institution for the Blind, in the City of New York, I give *five thousand Dollars*. To To [*sic*] the Society for the relief of Half Orphans and Destitute Children in the City of New York, I give *Five thousand dollars*. To the New York Lying-In Asylum I give *Two Thousand Dollars*. And in case of any of these three legacies failing to go into effect, I give the same to my executors, confiding in their honor alone to make such dispositions of such sums as they shall deem most analogous to the objects of the said charities.

Tenth. I direct that the portions of *two hundred thousand dollars* [see codicil, Dec. 22, 1843], for each of *the daughters* of my son, William B. Astor, shall be settled on them on their respectively attaining the age of twenty one years, or their marriage. I give *to my son William B Astor one half of my residuary personal estate* absolutely: and also *the income of the other half*, until he shall think fit to expend such other half in the improvement of my residuary real estate; and the balance thereof unexpended at his death, I give to his children, or to such of them and in such manner and proportions as he may appoint by Will.

Eleventh. In case any devises, bequests or legacies, trusts, powers, conditions, limitations or other dispositions or clauses *in my said will or in this codicil, or in any subsequent codicil should for any reason be deemed invalid* (having intended, however in all things to make them conformable to the law) then it is my will, that in all events the said Will and codicils shall stand valid as to all other parts and provisions; and that no failure of any clause of my will, or the codicils thereto, shall defeat or render void any other parts thereof; and in case of the invalidity of any devises or legacy, or other provision, I direct that the property or subject of such invalid disposition, shall be given to the persons for whose benefit the same appears by the expressions of such defeated clause; as to which property or subject I authorize my executors to appoint the same to said person or persons, in such estates, manner and proportions as they shall judge conformable to my will, and as shall be lawful. And inasmuch as I make advancements or beneficial provisions for persons or purposes provided for in my will and codicils, it is my direction that such advancements, if charged in my books of account, shall be deemed so much on account of the provision in my will or codicils in favor of such person or purposes.

Lastly. I appoint Daniel Lord, Jr. *to be an executor* of my will with the other executors thereof, in the same manner as if he had been named therein, and I give him all such estate, interest, authority, trust and power as is given to my other executors. I publish this codicil and my said will as hereby modified, as together containing my last Will and testament; and I have signed and sealed the same in the presence of the subscribing witnesses hereto, this nineteenth day of January in the year of our Lord one thousand eight hundred and thirty eight.

John Jacob Astor [L. S.]

Published with the Will this 19th day of January A.D. 1838, by Mr. John J Astor as a codicil and will in presence of us signing at his request, and in presence of him and of each other. Geo. B. Smith 640 Broadway, Edwin Smith 71 Bleecker Street, W^m. W. Bruce 471 Houston Street. Declared by J. J. Astor to be a codicil to his last will and testament by him subscribed as such before us signing as witnesses at his request 1845 Jan 11. Jos. G. Cogswell 585 Broadway N. Y. Charles J. McIlvaine 44 Great Jones St. Daniel D. Lord, Nineteenth St—

[Second Codicil, January 9, 1839]

I, John Jacob Astor, do make this further codicil to my will, bearing date July 4th 1836:

First. In order more comfortably to accommodate my unfortunate Son John, I have provided for the erection of a dwelling-house on Fourteenth-Street, in the City of New York, upon a certain piece of land which I attach thereto, bounded as follows: Beginning on the Northerly side of Fourteenth-Street, one hundred and twenty five feet, westerly from its intersection with the westerly side of the Ninth Avenue, running thence northerly parallel with the said Avenue, to the south side of Fifteenth-Street, then Westerly along the same one hundred feet, then Southerly parallel to the line of the said Ninth Avenue to Fourteenth Street, then along the same easterly one hundred feet to the place of beginning, which house I intend to furnish and provide for his convenience and that of the persons who from time to time shall take charge of his personal comfort. Now therefore, *I do hereby give to my son John*, the said house and land, with the furniture appropriated thereto; to have and to hold so long during his life as the same shall be used and kept for his personal accommodation and convenience, *with remainder* to my daughter Dorothea, to be held by her so long during her life as she shall use the same, or the income thereof, for her own use, free from all control or interference of her husband, and so long as she or her husband shall not attempt to dispose of her interest therein, and shall not permit the same to be incumbered or taken under any incumbrance, but not longer. And in case during her life, she or her husband, or any claiming under or against them shall attempt to incumber or divert the same from her actual use, then I give the same to my executors in trust, during her life, to receive the rents and profits thereof, and to apply the same to her use for which her receipts shall be a full voucher to my executors. *After her death I give and devise the said lands and furniture*, one equal *half* part thereof, to the then surviving *children and issue of my* [*son William* — stricken through] *daughter* Dorothea, Dorothea [*sic*], the other *half* to the then *surviving children and issue* of my son William, taking in fee simple, and the issue representing its parent deceased.

Provided, however, *and I hereby authorize my executors*, in case they shall think that the comfort of my son will be more promoted by a change of his residence, or any other appropriation of the property for his benefit, *to lease* the said premises for any lawful term of years, or *to sell* the land and execute the proper deeds to convey the same in fee simple, *and to invest the proceeds*, from a sale in other lands, for his personal use and accommodation during his life, or in bonds secured by mortgage of real estate or public stocks, and so on from time to time; in which case of investment, I give the income to be applied by my executors to the use of my son John for his life; after his death, I give the said income to my daughter Dorothea, and my executors as above expressed, in relation to the land; and the capital on her death, I give to the then surviving children of my said daughter and my son William, as above expressed. *Item.* The sum which my executors are authorized under the seventh item of my will to expend for my son John, is hereby enlarged to *ten thousand dollars* per annum.

Item. In consequence of the lamented death of my daughter Eliza, the provisions of the fourth item of my will are defeated, and I revoke the said item. And I give the use of my estate near Geneva, to Mr. Vincent Rumpff, for his life, and after him I give the said estate to my *granddaughter Cecilia Langdon*, and her heirs forever. *I give to my daughter Dorothea, the income of one hundred thousand dollars, deposited* in the New York Life Insurance and Trust Company, bearing interest at five per cent per annum, to take and receive the income thereof, so long during her life as she or her husband, present or future, or any one claiming under them, shall not attempt to incumber, charge or assign the same, in whole or in part; and in case of any such attempt, then I give the said income to my executors, in trust, during her life, to apply the same to her use, for which her own receipt shall be a voucher; and *upon her death, I give the* [interlineated: *said*] *capital sum* to her daughters [see codicil of June 3, 1841], Eliza, Louisa, and Cecilia, and to her sons

Walter, Woodbury and Eugene, and to such of these six children as may survive me, to be equally divided among them, and to be accumulated as to the share of each one under the age of twenty one years, for his or her benefit; and on their attaining that age respectively, to be paid to them by my executors; and if any of them shall die before that age, without surviving issue, his or her share shall be given to the survivors.

Also, I give to the said six children, of my daughter Dorothea, or to such of them as may survive me, *one hundred thousand dollars of the public debt of the City of New York,* bearing five per cent interest, usually called the Water Loan; to be paid to each on attaining their age of twenty one years; and the interest of the shares of those under that age, to be accumulated for their benefit until that period; and in case any of them shall die before that age, without surviving issue, then his or her shares shall go to the survivors.

Item. I give to my said grandchildren, Eliza, Louisa [see codicil of 3d June, 1841], Cecilia, Walter, Woodbury and Eugene, and to such of them as may survive me, *five lots of land* fronting on the *South side of Grand Street,* between Ludlow and Orchard Streets; and *also four lots of land, fronting the southerly side of* Grand-Street, between Norfolk and Essex Streets, in the City of New York, with their improvements respectively; to have and to hold the same to my said grandchildren in equal shares, for their lives respectively. And on the death of each, I give the share enjoyed by such deceased to his or her issue, then surviving in fee simple, to be divided according to the number of his or her children, and if such deceased shall leave no surviving issue, then I give the share of such deceased to the survivors of of [sic] the said six, and to their heirs or assigns forever. As to which lots I direct and order that the eleventh article of my will shall apply in all respects in the same manner as if this devise had been contained in the body of said Will.

Item. I give to my niece Sophia Astor, of Nieuwid in Germany, in addition to her legacy, an annuity of *three hundred dollars per annum*, to commence from my decease, and paid up to the time of her death, payable yearly.

And this codicil with my said Will and the other codicils thereto, I publish and declare to contain my last Will and testament.

In Witness whereof I have hereunto subscribed my name, and set my seal, in the presence of the witnesses subscribing with me, the ninth day of January, in the year of our Lord one thousand eight hundred and thirty nine.

John Jacob Astor. [L. S.]

Published and declared by Mr. John Jacob Astor, to be a codicil to his will, this ninth day of January A.D. 1839 in presence of us signing at his request and in the presence of him and of each other. Geo. N. Sewell, Wm W. Bruce. Declared by J. J. Astor to be a codicil to his last Will and testament by him subscribed as such before us signing as witnesses at his request 1845 Jan. 11. Jos. G. Cogswell 585 Broadway N. Y. Charles J. McIlvaine 44 Great Jones St. Daniel D. Lord Nineteenth St.

[Third Codicil, August 22, 1839]

I, John Jacob Astor, do make this additional codicil to my last Will, bearing date the fourth day of July in the year of our Lord Eighteen hundred and thirty six.

Desiring to render a public benefit to the City of New York, and to contribute to the advancement of useful knowledge and the general good of society, I do by this codicil, appropriate *four hundred thousand dollars* out of my residuary estate to the establishment of a *Public Library* in the City of New York.

For this purpose, *I give to my executors four hundred thousand dollars*, to be taken from my personal estate, or raised by a sale of parts of my real estate to be made by my executors, with the assent of my son William B. Astor, upon condition, and to the intent, that the said amount be settled, applied and disposed of as follows, namely:

First. In the erecting of a suitable building for a Public Library.

Second. In furnishing and supplying the same from time to time with books, maps, charts, models, drawings, paintings, engravings, casts statues, furniture and other things appertaining to a library for general use upon the most ample scale and liberal character.

Third. In maintaining and upholding the buildings and other property, and in defraying the necessary expenses of taking care of the property, and of the accommodation of persons consulting the library.

The Said sum shall be payable, one third in the year after my decease, one third in the year following, and the residue in equal sums, in the fourth and fifth years after my decease.

The Said library is to be accessible, at all reasonable hours and times, for general use, free of expense to persons resorting thereto, subject only to such control and regulations as the trustees may from time to time exercise and establish for general convenience.

The affairs of the institution shall be conducted and directed by eleven Trustees, to be from time selected from the different liberal professions and employments in life, and the classes of educated men. The Mayor of the City of New York, during his continuance in Office, and the Chancellor of the State of New York, during his continuance in office, shall always be trustees. The vacancies in the number of trustees, occurring by death, resignation, incapacity, or removal from the State, shall be filled by persons appointed by the remaining trustees; the acts of a majority of the trustees, at a meeting reasonably notified, shall be valid.

All the property and effects of the institution shall be vested in the said trustees. They shall have power to direct the expenditure of the funds, the investment, safekeeping and management thereof, and of the property and effects of the institution; also to make such ordinances and regulations from time to time, as they may think proper, for the good order and convenience of those who may resort to the library or use the same; also to appoint, direct, control and remove the superintendent of the library, and all librarians and others employed about the institution; and also they shall have and use all powers and authority for promoting the expressed objects of this institution, not contrary to what is herein expressed. They shall not receive any compensation for their services, except that if any one of their number shall at any time be appointed superintendent, he may receive compensation as such.

The trustees shall be subject to the visitation of the proper courts of Justice, for the purpose of preventing and redressing all mismanagement, waste or breach of trust.

And I direct that the said public library be established on my land, at the corner of Lafayette Place and Art-Street, on the Westerly side of Lafayette Place, in the City of New York, beginning on the Westerly line of Lafayette Place, eighty one feet northerly from the corner of the house in which my daughter, Dorothea Langdon, now resides, and running thence perpendicular to Lafayette Place, one hundred and thirty seven feet six inches to the alley way in the rear; thence along the alley way to Art-Street; thence along Art-Street to Lafayette Place, and thence to the place of beginning, with the right and benefit of way in the alley; which land I direct my executors to convey to the said trustees in fee simple by such proper assurances as shall secure the land for the purpose of the library, and on condition to be applied and used therefor. And inasmuch as one of the lots so to be conveyed is devised to the children of Mrs. Langdon, I order that twelve thousand five hundred dollars be paid to the said devisees as a compensation for the lot. And I direct, that all the said land, hereby appropriated, be valued at forty thousand dollars, and form a part of the said four hundred thousand dollars.

I further direct, that a sum not exceeding ——— thousand dollars may be expended in the erection of the building for the library. One hundred and twenty thousand Dollars may be expended in the purchase of Books and other objects for the establishing of the library, and the residue shall be invested as a fund for the maintaining and gradually increasing of the library.

All investments of the funds of the institution shall be made in the public debt of the United States of America, or of the States of the Union, or of the City of New York, as long as such subjects of investment may be had, giving a preference according to the order in which they are named. And in case the income of the fund shall at any time exceed the amounts which the trustees may find useful to expend for the purposes above named, and particularized, they may expend such surplus in procuring public lectures to be delivered in connection with the library, upon useful subjects of literature, philosophy, science, history and the fine arts, or in promoting in any other mode, the objects of the Institution as above expressed. I direct my executors to cause and procure the necessary legal assurances to be made for establishing and securing the application of the funds and property hereby appropriated, for the purposes of these presents, and in the mode herein pointed out. And it is my request that the Trustees would apply to the legislature of this State, for such acts as may fully secure, establish and perpetuate this institution, and render its management easy, convenient and safe, both to themselves and the public. And as this property is devoted wholly to public purposes, I trust that the legislature will so far favor the institution as to exempt its property from taxation. And as a mark of my respect to the following gentlemen, I name them to be the first trustees, that is to say, The Mayor of the City of New York, and The Chancellor of the State, for the time being, in respect to their offices; Washington Irving, William B. Astor, Daniel Lord Junior, James G. King, Joseph G. Cogswell, Fitz Greene Halleck, Henry Brevoort Junior, Samuel B. Ruggles and Samuel Ward Junior. In witness whereof, I have set my hand and seal to this codicil, and publish the same as a codicil to my will this twenty second day of August, in the year of our Lord, one thousand eight hundred and thirty nine.

John Jacob Astor [L. S.]

On this day John Jacob Astor declared this to be a codicil to his [last — stricken through] Will and requested us to sign the same as witnesses which we have done in his presence, and in presence of each other. Dated 22ⁿᵈ August 1839. Geo. N. Sewell, Lucy Sewell, Hinrich Siefko Declared by Mr. J. J. Astor to be a codicil to his last Will & testament by him subscribed as such before us signing as witnesses at his request 1845 Jan 11. Jos. G. Cogswill [*sic*] 585 Broadway N. Y. Charles J. McIlvaine 44 Great Jones St. N. Y. Daniel D. Lord Nineteenth St.

[Fourth Codicil, October 24, 1839]

A further codicil to the will of John Jacob Astor, bearing date the fourth day of July A.D. 1836.

First. I *revoke* and annul *the legacy* of fifty thousand dollars given *to Joseph Astor* and his children, or next of kin, contained in the eighth item of the codicil to my Will, which codicil bears date the nineteenth day of January A.D. 1838; and *I give* to the said Joseph Astor for his life, an annuity of *three hundred pounds sterling* per annum, to commence from my decease, and to be paid half yearly, and up to his decease, provided that my executors, if they think fit, may retain the same, or any payment thereof, and apply the same to the use of him or his family, as they may judge most beneficial to him.

Second. I *revoke* and annul the legacy of *Twenty five Thousand Dollars* given in my will to *the Trustees of Columbia College,* in the City of New York.

Third. I direct that the commissions chargeable by my executors be divided among such of them as shall act in the executorship, exclusively of William B. Astor, who receives the benefit of the general residuary gifts of my will.

In witness whereof, I have subscribed this codicil, and do publish the same as an additional codicil to my last will and testament, this twenty fourth day of October in the year of our Lord one thousand eight hundred and thirty nine.

J. J. Astor

Signed and declared by John Jacob Astor as a codicil to his will, this 24th day of October A.D. 1839 in the presence of us signing at his request and in his presence as witnesses. Lucy Sewell, New York Hurlgate. Geo. N. Sewell do. Declared by Mr. J. J. Astor to be a codicil to his last Will and Testament by him subscribed as such before us signing as witnesses at his request. 1845 Jan 11. Jos. G. Cogswell 585 Broadway N. Y. Charles J. McIlvaine 44 Great Jones Street, Daniel D. Lord Nineteenth St.

[Fifth Codicil, March 3, 1841]

A further codicil to the Will of John Jacob Astor, bearing date the fourth day of July in the year of our Lord eighteen hundred and thirty six.

Having before me the said will and the four several codicils thereto, bearing date January 19. 1838, January 9 August 22 and October 24 1839, I do make this additional codicil, that is to say:

First. I *revoke* so much of the codicil dated in January eighteen hundred and thirty eight, *as gives to my daughter, Mrs. Langdon, for her life, the lot on Lafayette Place, given in my will to Charles Bristed, for life;* so that the estate of Charles Bristed in the said lot shall not be subject to any estate of my daughter therein. And in relation to the plan of the lots on the West side of Lafayette Place, by which a gangway is established as is mentioned in the second item of the said codicil, I hereby *revoke* so much of the said codicil as relates to the establishment or enjoyment of the *gangway* therein mentioned; and I abolish and annul the said gangway, and impose it as a condition on my daughter and grandchildren holding lands adjacent to it that such gangway be wholly abandoned.

Second. I *revoke the legacy* of two thousand dollars given in my will *to the German Reformed Congregation* in the City of New York, intending during my life, to apply that amount to the religious and moral welfare of Germans in some other mode.

Third. In relation to the *Library* provided for in my codicil, bearing date the twenty second day of August, eighteen hundred and thirty nine, I have concluded to change the site thereof; and I therefore direct that the land in that codicil appropriated for this purpose be discharged therefrom; and so much of the said codicil as appropriates the site for the said library and the compensation to be paid for it, is hereby revoked; And instead thereof, *I allow the building for the said library to be erected on the Southerly side of Astor Place* (formerly Art-Street) between Lafayette Place and Broadway, on the land described as follows: Beginning on the Southerly line of Astor Place, at a point distant one hundred and fifty one feet westerly from the Westerly corner of Astor Place and Lafayette Place; thence running westerly along Astor Place, sixty five feet; thence in a line perpendicular to Astor Place [sixty of — stricken through], one hundred and twenty five feet nine inches to the northerly side of a lot given to my daughter, Mrs. Langdon; thence along the same, northerly and easterly, in a line perpendicular to the Westerly side of Lafayette Place, fifty seven feet; thence along the rear of the lot given to Charles Bristed and in that direction parallel with the Westerly side of

Lafayette Place, thirty one feet one inch; thence in a line perpendicular to the Southerly side of Astor Place, one hundred and twenty five feet to the place of beginning; which site I direct my executors to convey to the trustees of the said library instead of the site in the said codicil expressed; and I estimate the site now above described at thirty five thousand [interlineated: dollars]; *but if the trustees* of the said library shall, before commencing the building, *think a site on the easterly side of Lafayette Place preferable,* I authorize my executors, instead of the site aforesaid, to convey to the trustees of the library, as a site therefor, so much land on the easterly side of Lafayette Place as shall be sixty five feet in front and one hundred and twenty feet deep, to be located out of my lands there, by the said trustees; and direct that the site so selected be fairly and justly valued by my executors, and the amount of such valuation to be apportioned among the devises of the lands, out of which the selection shall be made, to be held and disposed of as the land was, both as to capital and income.

I direct that *the sum* to be appropriated for erecting *the library building* shall not exceed *seventy five thousand dollars.*

And I also allow, that the funds of the said library may, in the discretion of the trustees, be invested in bonds secured by mortgage of improved real estate as well as in the stocks enumerated in the codicil establishing such library.

Fourth. I give *unto my grandchildren* herein next named, the following *lots of land on Lafayette Place,* of which I have caused a map to be made, and the lots to be numbered from one to seven, each lot being twenty seven feet in width on Lafayette Place, and to be bounded by lines perpendicular thereto, and extending to the above described site for the Library; and if that shall be located on the easterly side of Lafayette Place, then extending to the rear of my lands there, namely: to my grandson, William Astor, I give *the Southernmost lot* next to that of Charles Bristed which lot now given is number two: to

John Jacob Astor, I give the *next lot north*, being number three; to Louisa D. Langdon [see codicil, June, 1841], the *lot next north*, being number four: to Eliza Langdon, *the lot next north*, being number five: and to my daughter Mrs. Langdon, I give the *two lots six and seven;* the latter being a corner lot, forty feet front, and narrowing to the rear; to have and to hold to them respectively, and to their heirs and assigns forever: *Provided* however, and on condition that no buildings be erected on the said lots (including also the lot of Charles Bristed) but dwelling-houses at least three stories high, and covering the full front of the lots, and the necessary offices on the rears of the lots.

Provided, also that it shall be lawful for my executors, at any time during the life of the devisee, to make and execute a settlement of the lots given to the said ladies, securing the enjoyment to them as a separate estate of the said lots during life, and a power of giving the same as they please among their issue, brothers and sisters, and their issue, such power to be discretionary with my executors; *with a power to the said ladies respectively* of leasing for terms of years, allowed by law. And I authorize my executors, at the request of any of the said grandchildren (including Charles Bristed and his lot) to lay out any part of the personal estate given to them, or to their use respectively, in the erection of a suitable dwellinghouse and its appurtenances, on the lot so given, fronting on Lafayette Place.

Fifth. I give to my friend Fitz Greene Halleck, *an annuity of two hundred dollars*, commencing at my decease, and payable half yearly for his life; to be secured by setting apart so much of my personal estate as may be necessary; which I intend as a mark of my regard for Mr. Halleck.

Sixth. I direct my executors to apply *fifty thousand dollars* to the use of the *poor of Waldorf*, near Heidelberg, in the Grand Duchy of Baden, by the establishment of some provision for the sick or disabled, or the education and improvement of the young, who may be in a condition to need the aid of such fund; requesting my executors to consult on this subject my esteemed friend, Mr. Vincent Rumpff, and to procure the appointment or establishment of such trust or legal body, from the authorities and government of the place, as may be requisite or deemed useful by my executors.

Seventh. I *reduce* the legacy bequeathed to the German Society of New York, from *twenty five thousand dollars* to *twenty thousand dollars*, of which I have already advanced them fifteen thousand [dollars — stricken through] six hundred and ninety seven dollars [and — stricken through] fifty cents, to be deducted, therefore, from the said last mentioned sum. Also I *reduce* the legacy which my niece, Mrs. Mary Reynell, wife of George Reynell, would have taken, under the first codicil to my will, to *fifteen thousand dollars.* I *reduce the legacy* of my niece, Sarah Oxenham, given in the said codicil, from thirty thousand to *twenty thousand dollars.*

Eighth. I appoint my grandson, John Jacob Astor to be an executor of my Will, with the other executors thereof, in the same manner as if he had been named therein; and I give him all such estate, interest, authority, trust. and power as is given to my other executors. And I apply the provisions of the eleventh item of my Will to all my codicils, so far as the same can be applied to the subjects thereof.

Last. I recognize and publish anew the said Will and several codicils, as together with this codicil, forming my last Will and testament.

In Witness whereof I have hereunto set my hand and seal this third day of March, in the year of our Lord one thousand eight hundred and forty one, in presence of the witnesses subscribing with me.

J. J. Astor [L. S.]

Signed & declared by John J. Astor as a codicil to his Will before us Subscribing with him at his request and in his presence our names and places of abode. Lucy Sewell Broadway New York, W^m. W. Bruce Fulton St. N. York declared by Mr. J. J. Astor to be a codicil to his last Will and testament by him subscribed as such before us signing as witnesses at his request. 1845 Jany 11. Jos. G. Cogswill [*sic*] 585 Broadway N. Y. Charles J McIlvaine 44 Great Jones St. Daniel D. Lord Nineteenth St.

[Sixth Codicil, June 3, 1841]

A further Codicil to the Will of John Jacob Astor, dated July 4. 1836.

First. As to all such shares, estate and interest in land, (except the lot on the West side of Lafayette place, mentioned beneath) as are in my will, or in any codicil thereto, given on my decease to Louisa, daughter of Mrs. Dorothea Langdon, or to the issue of the said Louisa, I give one half thereof to the other children of my daughter Dorothea, to be taken and held as an increase of the shares or sums given to them and their issue in the same property; the other half I give to my executors in trust, to receive the rents, issues and profits thereof for the life of the said Louisa, and to apply the same to her use, clear of any control, debts or right of her husband thereto; and after her death I give the same to her surviving children, or if she leaves none, to her surviving brothers and sisters or their issue.

Second. As to all the estates, rights and interests in lands, stocks, personal effects or money to which the said Louisa or her issue would have been entitled, under my will, or any codicil thereto, after the death of her mother, brothers or sisters, I give the same to her brothers and sisters and their issue, as an increase of their respective shares or interests in the same property.

Third. As to the two legacies of twenty five thousand dollars each, and the share of water-stock, to which the said Louisa would have been entitled under my will and a codicil thereto, I revoke the two legacies entirely; I give the income of her share of stock to my daughter Dorothea for life, and on her death I give the capital to her other children, and their issue, in case of their decease.

Fourth. As to the lot on the Westerly side of Lafayette Place, given to the said Louisa in a codicil to my will, I give the same to Cecilia Langdon, to be had and holden as if her name had been written in the devise thereof, instead of Louisa, with every advantage, power and benefit, and subject to every condition power and limitation therein contained.

Fifth. I expressly authorize my daughter, Dorothea Langdon by deed or will, to appoint and give to the said Louisa and her issue, or to her or their use, any part not exceeding in value one half of the real or personal estate by this codicil taken from Louisa and given to others.

Sixth. I direct and devise that Charles Bristed be one of the Trustees of the devise and legacy for a public library, provided for in former codicils to my will, and I give him the same estate, interest and power, as if he were originally named in such devise and legacy.

Seventh. Considering the advantages which Mr Vincent Rumpff has received from the marriage Settlement of my daughter, I revoke the devise to him for his life of my estate near Geneva. But if an accounting shall take place between us, touching the property in the said settlement, after this date, and within two years, and the balance of that account shall be paid, then I renew such devise to him for life, of the estate near Geneva.

In relation to the same estate which I give to the said Cecilia, subject to the said life estate to Mr. Rumpff, I furthermore devise, that if she shall depart this life before attaining the age of twenty one years, then I give the said estate to her issue surviving her; and if she shall leave none surviving, then I give the same to her surviving brothers and sisters, and their heirs and assigns forever.

Last. I publish this as a codicil to my will, and as altering and revoking the same, and the codicils thereto, so far as a different disposition is made by the present codicil.

In Witness whereof, I have hereunto set my hand and seal this third day of June, in the year of our Lord one thousand eight hundred and forty one.

J J Astor [L. S.]

Signed & published as a codicil to his Will, by John Jacob Astor this third day of June A.D. 1841 in presence of us attesting it at his request, and in his presence. Geo. B. Smith Resides in 23ᵈ Street City of New York. Geo. N. Sewell 585 Broadway. Declared by Mr. J. J. Astor to be a codicil to his last will & Testament by him subscribed as such before us signing as witnesses at his request 1845 Jan. 11 Jos. G. Cogswell 585 Bway N. Y. Charles J. McIlvaine 44 G Jones St. N. Y. Daniel D Lord Nineteenth St.

[Seventh Codicil, December 15, 1842]

I, John Jacob Astor, of the City of New York, do make this additional codicil to my last Will, bearing date July 4th 1836.

In order to make a provision for Mr. Walter Langdon, after the decease of my daughter, his wife, in case he should survive her, I do hereby direct that an annual sum of *five thousand* dollars be appropriated to his use, from the rents and income of my lands in the City of New York, bounded by Hudson River, Charlton, Morton and Greenwich Streets, such annual provision to commence from the death of my daughter, to be paid quarterly and to continue during the life of the said Walter

Langdon. And I authorize empower and direct my executors to select from the said lands, such as will in their judgment suffice to secure the said annual sum, and to settle the same by such conveyance in trust, or otherwise, as will secure the same to the use of the said Walter Langdon.

In Witness whereof, I have hereunto set my hand, this fifteenth day of December in the year of our Lord one thousand eight hundred and forty two.

J. J. Astor.

Published and signed by J. J. Astor as a codicil to his will in our presence signing with him as witnesses at his request, December 15 A D 1842 Jos. G. Cogswell, Lucy Sewall. Declared by Mr. J. J. Astor to be a codicil to his last Will and testament by him subscribed as such before us signing as witnesses at his request. 1845 Jan. 11 Jos. G. Cogswell 585 Broadway N. Y. Charles J. M°Ilvaine 44 G Jones St. Daniel D. Lord Nineteenth St.

[Eighth Codicil, December 22, 1843]

A further codicil to the Will of John Jacob Astor, bearing date July 4. 1836.

Whereas in my will I charged upon the residuary estate devised to my son, William B. Astor, in the tenth item of my Will, portions of two hundred thousand dollars, to be settled upon each of his daughters and her issue in such manner, as he might think fit, subject to the conditions therein expressed, which portions were to be set apart out of the real estate devised to him, and which when set apart, were not to form any incumbrance upon the residue; and in case of his leaving no appointment, the said portions were to be considered as part of his daughter's shares on the division of the estate thereby devised among his children; and whereas in the tenth item of a codicil to my said will (such codicil bearing date January 19,

1838,) I directed that such portions should be settled on them, on their respectively attaining the age of twenty one years, or their marriage; now, thinking it best for my said grand daughters, and for other reasons expedient, I do hereby declare, direct and will, that the said Will and codicil so far as relates to the said portions of two hundred thousand dollars, be modified and so far revoked that it shall be wholly discretionary with my said son, William B Astor, to give or appoint [the Same — stricken through] such portions or not; and if he shall choose to appoint the Same, it shall be discretionary with him to appoint the Same in such manner and in such trusts and conditions as he may think fit; and unless he shall choose to appoint such portions to his daughters and their issue, they shall not be charges on my estate, or on the estate devised to my son in any manner whatever; and I revoke so much of my said will, and of any codicil thereto, as is contrary or repugnant to this present codicil.

In Witness whereof, I have hereunto set my hand and seal, and have published this as a codicil to my will, this twenty second day of December, in the year of our Lord one thousand eight hundred and forty three, in presence of Joseph G. Cogswell, Lucy Sewell and William W. Bruce, witnesses subscribing with me.   J. J. Astor [L. S.]

Signed, published and declared by J. J. Astor as a codicil to his will, in our presence subscribing with him at his request in his presence, our names and abode. Jos. G. Cogswill [sic] 585 Broadway N. Y. Lucy Sewell 585 Broadway N. York W^m. W. Bruce 160 Grand St. N. Y. Declared by Mr. John J Astor to be a codicil to his last will and testament by him subscribed as such before us signing as witnesses at his request, 1845 Jan 11 Jos. G. Cogswell 585 Broadway N. Y. Charles J. M^c. Ilvaine 44 Great Jones St[reet — stricken through] N. Y. Daniel D. Lord, Nineteenth St.

BIBLIOGRAPHICAL NOTE

BIBLIOGRAPHICAL NOTE

ORDINARILY, in writing the biography of a merchant, we should expect to depend chiefly upon his own private archives and the records of his business. For the business life of John Jacob Astor such sources are not extensive, owing to the wholesale destruction of Astor's personal and commercial papers, a generation or so after his death. In the early 1870's — probably between 1873 and 1875 — James Armstrong, a nephew of Mrs. William B. Astor, who was then acting as his uncle's companion or secretary, took, under William B. Astor's orders, a leading rôle in the destruction of fifteen large packing cases, containing "the miscellaneous records & papers left behind by John Jacob Astor." A similar holocaust took place in the next decade, when the office of the Astor estate was moved from Prince Street, where it had been during John Jacob's later years, to its present location on Twenty-sixth Street. At this time, "to save a few dollars' truck hire," as a veteran clerk in the office, who witnessed this affair, expressed it, nearly all the remaining books and manuscripts, save those which were immediately pertinent to the real-estate holdings of the Astor estate on Manhattan Island and in Wisconsin, were burned.

A few letter books and bundles of papers were marked for preservation, probably as souvenirs, and apparently almost at random. One bundle of papers consisted of letters, invoices, and accounts relating to the Astoria enterprise, and a couple of others had to do with litigation against the Astor estate by former partners of Astor in the fur trade or the commerce with China, or by their heirs. A few journals and small account books of the Pacific Fur Company were saved, but the most important material to escape destruction was three letter books for the years 1813–15, 1831–38, and 1845–48. Even these volumes are decidedly unrepresentative in character, for the first lies within the period of the War of 1812, the second begins at a time when Astor was withdrawing from commerce, and all the letters in the third are signed by William B. Astor, either for his father or entirely for himself. When we consider that three letter books were required for correspondence covering parts of only fifteen years, during eight of which Astor considered himself as retired, it can easily be imagined how many letter books, to say nothing of account books, there must have once existed for Astor's life of more than three-score years in New York City, during nearly half a century of which he was actively engaged in commerce. It is also easy to see, from the scattered and fragmentary character of the material remaining in the possession of the Astor estate, that much of the information concerning the commercial side of Astor's business life must be derived from such general sources as newspapers, and from the papers of his correspondents, associates, and business rivals.

Doubtless there are compensations in this situation, aside from the obvious one of exemption from winnowing such a mass of material as would have been presented had all Astor's business papers over a period of sixty years been preserved. To write a biography from the subject's own papers exclusively — and the temptation to do so would have been great, had the available documents been sufficient — would almost inevitably result in a one-sided picture. The opinions which a business man's rivals and associates have of his character and commercial policies are usually of more significance than his own. But, all compensations considered, it is a matter for lasting regret that there are so many points in Astor's career which will remain forever obscure, because of our lack of information which could be found only in his own papers.

Something should be said at this point concerning earlier biographies of Astor. Setting aside such brief narratives as magazine articles, biographical notes, and accounts in biographical collections, some of which appeared in Astor's own last years, we find that four separate volumes dealing with his life have been published. The first of these, Philip Oertel's *Johann Jacob Astor* (1855?), written in German, is chiefly valuable for the information it gives concerning Astor's life in Germany, supposedly derived from the reminiscences of some of his boyhood companions. Another biography, James Parton's *Life of John Jacob Astor* (1865), is based principally on Oertel's biography, Irving's *Astoria*, and Scoville's *The Old Merchants of New York*. Its value lies in the fact that it also preserves anecdotes concerning Astor which were floating about New York, from ten to twenty years after his death, among men who had known him in his prime. Both of these biographies, however, are very brief and can make no pretension to completeness. Elizabeth L. Gebhard's *The Life and Ventures of the Original John Jacob Astor* (1915) was quite the most ambitious Astor biography to appear up to that time and does purport to give a complete account of his life. A great mass of material was brought together in this book and presented with pleasing enthusiasm, but a glance at the bibliography, which consists almost entirely of printed matter and contains but few pieces of source material, being, indeed, largely magazine articles, will reveal the great weakness of the work, which is, moreover, quite uncritical and put together in a rather heterogeneous fashion. Nevertheless it is both suggestive and of value in preserving certain of the author's family traditions concerning Astor's early life in Germany and the United States. Arthur D. Howden Smith's *John Jacob Astor* (1929) uses much the same material as does Miss Gebhard, but in a manner at once more critical and more imaginative. His estimate of Astor's character is illuminating, and it is hard to see how he could have written a more authentic biography, considering the material employed, or a more entertaining one under any circumstances. However, I believe it is fair to say that no attempt has hitherto been made to write a complete biography of Astor with authenticity as the chief consideration, utilizing for that purpose only the prime sources whenever possible, and giving a definite authority or authorities for every significant statement. The present work is an attempt to conform to these conditions.

Inasmuch as the narrative chapters in this work are of a topical nature and the notes following each chapter are given with considerable exactness, it has been thought best to dispense with a formal bibliography and substitute for it bibliographical notes on certain particular topics.

Our information concerning Astor's early activities in Montreal is drawn principally from the notarial records of the Palais de Justice, Montreal, which are a mine of material for the social and economic history of Canada. For his relations with backcountry New York, particularly in the fur trade and land investment, almost the only source is the Gerrit Smith Miller Collection at Syracuse University, consisting of the papers of Peter Smith and his son Gerrit, which furnish invaluable information on the social and economic history of the New York backcountry.

For the vessels employed by Astor in the trade with the Orient the only complete and authoritative source is the New York Registers in the New York Custom House. Unfortunately they are stored in an unventilated, unlighted, unfurnished room just under the roof of the building, and even the courtesy of the officials of the Marine Division, in whose charge they are and who bitterly deplore the fashion in which the previous orderly arrangement of these important records has been disrupted, can hardly compensate for their practical inaccessibility. The earlier registers stored in the Treasury Building at Washington are not much more accessible. For the Canton side of Astor's China trade the only available source is the records of the East India Company at the East India Office, Whitehall, London. For the New York side of the trade, dates of clearance and arrival, and goods offered for sale at New York, the advertisements and the marine news of the New York newspapers are the principal source. There is a general impression that all the New York customs records for this period have been destroyed. This is not the case. A good many of them are in the Library of Congress; they are in no sort of order, but even at that will repay inspection. For re-exportation of China goods from New York they are virtually the only source, though there is a list of such shipments for a few years in the Astor Papers at Baker Library, Soldiers Field, Boston. For the question of insurance, see the records of the Boston Marine Insurance Company at the Massachusetts Historical Society, Boston. There is material on the last years of Astor's China trade in Letter Book ii, 1831–38, Astor Papers, Baker Library.

For Astor's fur trade during the War of 1812, and for the American Fur Company under his leadership, the main sources are the following:

Letter Book i, 1813–15, Astor Papers, Baker Library, Astor's general letter book kept during those years; Charles Gratiot's Letter Book, 1798–1816, in the Gratiot Collection, Missouri Historical Society, St. Louis; and letters from John Jacob Astor to Charles Gratiot, 1810–16, in Bernard P. Bogy's private collection at St. Louis, some of which letters have been photostated for the Missouri Historical Society. The Peter Sailly Palmer Papers in the New York State Library at Albany give a good picture of conditions on the border between New York and Canada, smuggling, and so forth, during the War of 1812.

Another principal source is Letters of Ramsay Crooks, John Jacob Astor, and the American Fur Company, 1813–43, copies of which collection of letters are to be found in the Burton Historical Collection, Detroit Public Library, and in the Missouri Historical Society; the originals, which I have not been privileged to see, are in the possession of Mrs. Joseph R. Ramee, of New York City, a descendant of Ramsay Crooks. These letters are partly from Crooks to Astor and partly from Astor to Crooks. The latter are almost the only letters we possess dealing with the American Fur Company from Astor's own point of view. Another important source is the three letter books of the American Fur Company: Ramsay Crooks' Letter Book, Mackinac, etc., December 18, 1816–August 1, 1820; Ramsay Crooks' and Robert Stuart's Letter Book, Mackinac, Detroit, New York, etc., June 21, 1820–July 29, 1825; and Robert Stuart's Letter Book, Mackinac, June 28, 1823–June 24, 1830. Several of the more important historical societies of the Midwest possess photostats of these books; I used the ones belonging to the Wisconsin Historical Society at Madison. The originals were formerly at Mackinac Island, but some of them seem to have become somewhat scattered in recent years. The latest letter book was recently in the possession of Mr. P. W. A. Fitzsimmons, of the Michigan Mutual Liability Company, Detroit. He also has four minor account books, kept at Michilimackinac, which have not been referred to in the notes. I am informed, moreover, in a letter from Mrs. Rosa Webb, president of the Community House at Mackinac Island, transmitted to me through the kindness of Mr. Milton Tootle, of St. Joseph, Missouri, that four or five account books and letter books of the American Fur Company are still deposited with that institution.

Another valuable source is the Indian Office records in the Department of the Interior, Washington, D. C. It is very hard to locate anything in these records, and there are no adequate facilities for research, which makes the publication of documents from the Indian Office archives of particular value. Some have been published by Reuben Gold Thwaites in "The Fur-Trade in Wisconsin, 1815–1817," *Wisconsin Historical Collections*, vol. xix (1910), pp. 375–488, and "The Fur-Trade in Wisconsin, 1812–1825," *Wisconsin Historical Collections*, vol. xx (1911), pp. 1–395. Not all the documents in these publications are taken from the Indian Office records; some are from manuscripts in the Wisconsin Historical Society and in the Burton Historical Collection at the Detroit Public Library, both of which repositories are valuable for our purpose. The Burton Historical Collection, for example, has about a dozen miscellaneous account books of the American Fur Company, none of which have been referred to in the notes, and which might be of value to one wishing information concerning particular Company outfits or traders and their activities in the Indian country.

There are six important account books of the American Fur Company, Northern Department, 1817–35, in the Public Archives of Canada. They consist of two ledgers, two journals, an invoice book, and a blotter. Of these I found the most valuable to be the ledgers, which told of the various outfits, sometimes gave the names of the traders in charge, and showed the profit and loss of each outfit for the year's business, and the invoice book, which showed the kinds and quantities of goods delivered to the various outfits, with the advances charged on the cost price in London or New York.

There is some information about the last days of Astor's connection with the American Fur Company in Letter Book ii, 1831–38, Astor Papers, Baker Library. For information on the American Fur Company's Western Department I have leaned heavily on Hiram Martin Chittenden's *The American Fur Trade of the Far West*. Anyone wishing to go more deeply into the minutiae of the Western Department's business dealings might consult the account books in the P. Chouteau Maffitt Collection at the Missouri Historical Society, St. Louis. These are nearly twenty in number and consist of ledgers, journals, invoices, cash books, and so forth, extending from 1822 to 1835. Mr. Willoughby M. Babcock, of the Minnesota Historical Society, tells me that there is some information on the Western Department of the American Fur Company in the William Clark Collection belonging to the Kansas State Historical Society at Topeka, which collection consists of twenty-six volumes of the record books of the Indian superintendency at St. Louis, covering the period from 1813 to 1855, with many serious gaps.

Anyone interested in the history of the American Fur Company after Astor's retirement should consult Dr. Grace Lee Nute's "The Papers of the American Fur Company: A Brief Estimate of Their Significance," *The American Historical Review*, vol. xxxii, no. 3 (1927), pp. 519–538, which has to do chiefly with the American Fur Company papers, covering the period from 1834 to 1847, at the New York Historical Society, but which also mentions papers in other collections.

The principal source for Astor's interest in western real estate is the Astor Papers at Baker Library, both Letter Books ii, 1831–38, and iii, 1845–48, which deal with land investments among other matters, and the books and papers relating specifically to Green Bay and Prairie du Chien. The letters to Astor from his land agents in Wisconsin contain a great deal of information concerning social and economic conditions. For general information concerning Astor's money-lending policies, and for his miscellaneous business interests, the two letter books mentioned immediately above are of the greatest importance.

For information concerning New York business men whose names appear in connection with Astor, Joseph A. Scoville's *The Old Merchants of New York* has been invaluable, though it must be used with caution. The files of New York newspapers, particularly the *New-York Gazette and General Advertiser*, have been used constantly and for some chapters have been absolutely indispensable. For Astor's commercial activities the consular letters from the various ports with which he traded, in the Department of State, Washington, D. C., sometimes contain material of unique value.

Contemporary journals and letters which assist us in catching the spirit of the times in which Astor lived are Pierre M. Irving's *The Life and Letters of Washington Irving; Letters of Washington Irving to Henry Brevoort; Letters of Henry Brevoort to Washington Irving* — Henry Brevoort was one of Astor's clerks and a nephew of his wife; *A Great Peace Maker: The Diary of James Gallatin, Secretary to Albert Gallatin* — especially valuable for the European background; Julia Ward Howe's *Reminiscences, 1819–1899* — Julia Ward's brother Samuel married William B. Astor's daughter Emily; and *The Diary of Philip Hone, 1828–1851*, probably the most valuable of all. Unfortunately all these mention Astor only as a well-established merchant. In 1811, for example, Irving referred to him as the "Great Mandarian" and compared him to Croesus. We get no casual picture of him during his early struggles as an unconsidered young immigrant shop-keeper.

INDEX

INDEX